# The Credibility Of Dowsing

*Prof. W. F. Barrett*

# The Credibility Of Dowsing

## *Scientific Proof Of Water Dowsing*

Originally published as
*'On The So-Called Divining Rod: Or Virgula Divina'*
Presented in 1897

and

*'A Psycho-physical Research on a Peculiar Faculty Alleged to Exist in Certain Persons Locally Known as Dowsers'*
Presented in 1899
By Professor William Barrett

Edited and with an introduction by
Nigel Percy

Introduction and additional footnotes
Copyright © 2013 - 2017 Nigel Percy and Sixth Sense Solutions

ISBN: 978-0-9978816-3-9

The original materials comprising this publication can be seen in:

Proceedings of the Society For Psychical Research

Volumes XIII and XV (published 1898 and 1901)

*Prof. W. F. Barrett*

# Introduction

The content of this book, consisting of two reports compiled over a period of six years, is the single, most detailed examination of the dowsing phenomenon ever undertaken.

The sheer size and depth of the reports (here presented together for the first time) is an indication that it was not undertaken as a way of endorsing dowsing, specifically dowsing to find water, but as a means of either dismissing it as practiced by charlatans intent on duping the public at large or inquiring into what might actually be happening if the intent to dupe was not the motivating factor.

The fact that this impressive body of research has been overlooked for so long is hard to comprehend. It is one of the very few examples of reporting careful research into dowsing by someone eminently well-versed in the scientific method.

The research was carried out by Professor William Fletcher Barrett. He was Professor of Experimental Physics at the Royal College of Science for Ireland in Dublin. Later he became a Fellow of the Royal Society, the oldest and most respected scientific society in the kingdom, as well as a Fellow of the Royal Society of Edinburgh and the Royal Dublin Society, and was knighted in 1912, 13 years before his death.

His interest in the divining rod, particularly the use of it to find water, was the result of an earlier interest in the paranormal.

He believed that thought transference was behind the idea of mesmerism (hypnotism) and published a paper to that effect in the respected journal, Nature. This caused a deal of controversy and it, in turn, caused him to found a society of like-minded individuals who would help further his research in this area. This was the origin of the Society of Psychical Research (SPR).

After his paranormal research tailed off, he founded the American Society of Psychical Research, although he continued to submit papers to the original Society, becoming its President in 1904.

Before looking more closely at the work itself, it will be useful to attempt to put it into some sort of social setting, the better to understand how it reflected the times.

The Society for Psychical Research (SPR) was not the place where a few 'crackpots' hung out swapping crazy theories. The previous decades had seen a sudden and impressive growth in interest in such things as séances, hypnotism, automatic writing and so forth. These were areas which seemed to suggest another aspect of reality, another level of communication.

To anyone with an enquiring mind, such instances seemed to offer great opportunities for careful study. Sir Arthur Conan Doyle, of Sherlock Holmes fame, was an ardent supporter of, and perhaps the most well-known figure of the time to show an interest in, séances and 'contact' with the 'other side'.

But he was not a lone, eccentric voice. There were plenty of people able and willing to give careful consideration to the possibilities which such 'psychic' events seemed to offer up. In fact, to the rear of the Journal of the Society's Proceedings, the list of members included many luminaries from a variety of fields. The vice presidents included the future British Prime Minister, as well as other MP's, three Fellows of the Royal Society, two American Professors (including William James, the philosopher and eminent psychologist), as well as one of the chief Bishops of England.

The list of overseas members included learned men from Europe, Russia, North and South America as well as Australia and New Zealand. This was not a society of idle dabblers.

Started by a Professor, other eminent scholars were attracted by investigating new and intriguing problems in the company of fellow intellects. Hypnotism, fire-walking, psychology, speaking in tongues, nothing was beyond examination. Reviews of books and articles by people such as Freud and Jung, together with detailed reports of séances and automatic writing, all given the critical eye of academics, were the regular fare of the Society.

## *The Credibility Of Dowsing*

The major concern of the Society, and the thread which ran through all of its works was that there was a need to establish a methodology, a framework, within which such events as clairvoyant visions, precognitive dreams, apparitions, contacting the dead and so on, could be more closely examined to see if there was any validity in such claims. It should be stated clearly that the Society was not interested in a biased approach. Its work was exhaustive, wide ranging and, above all, intent on opening up debate about these areas which the science of the time seemed not to be able to account for.

Hence, it was necessary to apply as stringent scientific methods as could be used in such situations to examine the varieties of psychic phenomena which presented themselves. For example, the society undertook a Census of Hallucinations; an investigation of public encounters with paranormal apparitions. 17,000 people were canvassed. A publication, 'Phantasms of the living', researched reports of communications from people dying or in life-threatening situations using telepathy – a term coined by one of the leading researchers. In this instance, over 700 cases were carefully analyzed.

These were careful, committed people undertaking painstaking research.

These researches were happening in a time of intellectual ferment. Uncertainty in the nature of the world as it had always been accepted was rife, at least amongst intellectuals. Experiments and new research were revealing un-thought of complexities, ideas and insights at an alarming rate..

Darwin's ideas of evolution were challenging long-held concepts and beliefs. Industry was expanding, and changing society with it as railways spread, internal combustion engines became more common, as the telegraph joined countries, and was swiftly followed by the telephone. The use and application of electricity was a new influence acting upon all levels of society.

Society itself was changing, creating a new middle class of industrialists and professionals. The growth of cities led to the growth of social sciences, where scientific methods were applied to the study of the inhabitants in ways previously un-thought of. Sigmund Freud's work made it possible to examine human actions and interactions in new ways through psychoanalysis (Freud's own term). Louis Pasteur's germ theory, together with the use of antiseptics revolutionized medical treatment.

The periodic table of elements was being constructed as chemists began measuring the atomic weight of elements and were tentatively working towards a new theory of matter.

In other words, there was huge progress in virtually every aspect of society, from intellectual pursuits, such as changing the way history was studied (placing the emphasis on primary sources with proven authenticity instead of narrative and folklore), to practical results of technology appearing in peoples' homes. And the challenge of Marx and Darwin to the established ideas of society had the same explosive potential as Nobel's new dynamite.

New styles of art (such as seen in the works of Cezanne, Renoir, Monet, etc.) and music (such as that which Beethoven, Mahler, Wagner, Debussy, Satie and others composed) were themselves reflections of this chaotic and stimulating period. Photography, the swift capture of life itself, by anyone, was making huge technical advances.

In such a whirlwind of change and potential, it would have been strange if an area would have been thought of as being outside the possibility of examination and discovery. The sudden rapid growth of Spiritualism could be seen as a reaction against the material advances of civilization by focusing on the immaterial, the apparently non-measurable possibilities of being human. Arising in the 1840's in America, it soon gained massive interest in Europe. Its popularity was no doubt accounted for by its belief in the possibility that death was not the end, that contact with the departed was not only possible but routine. Such a belief made traditional views of religion open to question in ways previously unthinkable.

This view of life beyond life, of the world somehow reflecting something more than plain natural understanding as gained through the five senses, allied to such things as telekinesis, faith healing, and, as in this report, water divining, were all fair game for academic research.

## Prof. W. F. Barrett

At one end of the scale then, there was a growing investigation and control over the physical world. At the other was a belief that this life was only a part of the journey and that the soul continued on.

In the middle sat the SPR attempting to discover what truth there might be in the latter by using the techniques of the former.

This report is an excellent example of the way the SPR worked.

The two reports Professor Barrett submitted on the divining rod, and which are presented hereafter, were highly labor-intensive, as he himself ruefully acknowledged. In our present age of immediate correspondence, of making public any writing an easy task, it should be remembered how different things were at the turn of the last century. He did have the luxury of a typewriter, but was still limited by the speed of the postal service.

As he says, *"…not far short of 6,000 letters had to be written for the purposes of the previous report (the first of the two reports). Upwards of 200 cases of water-finding by dowsers in recent years have been investigated; in each case the independent evidence of disinterested persons who had witnessed the experiments was sought."*

He may well have written over 6,000 letters (for just the first half of the work!), but he received many times that number in return, not to mention the innumerable press-cuttings as well as journal extracts and books. This was truly a Herculean task he had given himself.

He tried to steer his own way through the vast amount of data he uncovered.

He was as contemptuous of charlatans as he was of those who denounced the subject merely through bias and not through careful examination. For example, when speaking of the methods he would use in his report, he says (of the movement of the rod),

> *"It is, in fact, almost impossible to imitate its characteristic movement by any voluntary effort. Hence nothing but sheer ignorance leads any one to assert, as does an English geologist in a letter now before me, that "the whole thing is a fraud, and the motion of the forked twig a bit of clever legerdemain." Nor is any evidence, however conclusive it may appear to others, likely to affect those who approach the study of a novel subject with such a determined parti-pris. [bias]"*

He readily admits his own bias when he began the research.

> *"…it was with great reluctance, and even repugnance, that, some six years ago…I began an investigation of the matter; hoping, however, in my ignorance, that a few weeks' work would enable me to relegate it 'Into a limbo large and broad, since called the Paradise of fools'."*

This is from part of the introduction to the first book of the report. In the second, he continues thus:

> *"…those who may have had the patience to read the mass of evidence given in my former paper will probably have come to the same conclusion as that to which I have been led,—in spite of very different preconceived ideas,—namely, that the whole subject is one eminently worthy of careful investigation; not only as a question of folk lore and of historical interest, but also because several problems of considerable psychological and also physiological interest appear to be involved."*

In other words, the careful examination he made of the subject convinced him that, although there were charlatans at work, there was something else going on which demanded exploration and not dismissal. Barrett was intellectually and practically averse to simple dismissal of any phenomenon without an attempt to understand it, or to expose it as fraud after careful investigation. Thus, in Part 2, he remarks that the 'superficial and easy dismissal of the whole subject' is something he has seen happening in various countries in the preceding two centuries.

Sweeping conclusions which reveal bias, not facts, are always treated with disdain throughout this whole report.

The report as a whole, and Professor Barrett's exploration of the matter is, as always, a reflection of the times he lived in.

# The Credibility Of Dowsing

You will notice the formal method in answering letters and you will undoubtedly notice how the levels of society, the classes, becomes obvious. Professor Barrett refers, often, to the dowsers as being uneducated men. This, despite the fact that most of them run their own small businesses. 'Uneducated', however, does not here mean illiterate. It simply means that such men did not have the benefit of a classical education and book learning and, therefore, were unable, in Barrett's view, to be sufficiently well-versed in ideas essential for them to be able to present themselves as intellectual equals. Their ideas about their subject lacked the necessary acquaintance with the new scientific theories.

Barrett refers, for example, to the fact that some of those who wrote to him were unimpeachable merely because they held a title, were magistrates or held a similar socially important position. The truth of their testimony is, he believes, beyond question simply because of that status. (It is interesting to compare this to the modern skepticism which is rife and which pervades virtually every facet of public life. Nowadays, no-one is beyond suspicion. Indeed, the higher a person rides in society the greater the degree of cynicism is applied to their every utterance. Is one approach to truth necessarily better than the other?)

You will also notice the use of numerous quotations in foreign languages, assuming his readers' ease with such things. Where the meaning is not obvious from the context, I have added translations. I do not necessarily say that they are the best translations, but I can say that they give enough of the meaning to understand why Barrett inserted them.

Why, then, given the antiquated nature of the report itself, should it be considered as having value in our day and age? It would have been possible to have tidied up the letters, replacing the old, formal style with something more modern, more abrupt. It would have been possible to have abbreviated the geological reports. Indeed, it would have been very easy to have cut the length of this down by more than half. Perhaps, by not doing so, there is the risk that it will be unread or lie dormant on bookshelves, because we are accustomed to brevity nowadays. We cherish the sound-bite, the snippet, the tweet. Yet here is a report of great length.

And therein lies the answer to the question of the value of it all.

To assume that a complex subject can be summarized accurately and a judgment made without revealing the basis for that judgment is overly optimistic. And as Professor Barrett shows, water divining is far more complex than it might appear.

In addition to the in-depth examination of water-dowsing, this report provides the single, most investigative analysis of the term 'dowse' that I have ever come across. If you are interested in why it is called dowsing and where that word might have come from, I can do no better than refer you to Part 1, Appendix A where Barrett takes you through all the possible explanations and derivations to come to some sort of conclusion. (Note: there is no definitive answer to the origin of the words 'dowse' and 'dowser', but you get treated to a range of fascinating possibilities along the way.)

I urge you, whatever your own opinions might be about dowsing, to read through this report, skimming the letters, scanning the geology, looking at the failures and the successes, and come to the same conclusion which Barrett expressed:

> "The a priori improbability of any alleged phenomena, or the difficulty of finding any immediate explanation, are grounds for demanding ample and trustworthy evidence, but are not reasons for rejecting such evidence, or science would not have accepted the aid to surgery given by the Rontgen rays [X rays -Ed.]—among other instances that might be cited. On the contrary, it is the received dictum of scientific investigation, as long ago pointed out by Sir John Herschel, that "The observer ... in any department of science ... will have his eyes, as it were, opened, that they may be struck at once with any occurrence which, according to received theories, ought not to happen; for these are the facts which serve as clues to new discoveries,"—a sentence that might well form the motto of our Society."

He spent six years amassing the information and arranging it for anyone who might be interested. He knew that many people would disregard whatever he wrote simply because of the nature of the subject itself: a view he regarded as completely unscientific. Throughout, he is dismissive of those who wish to deny the existence of any real ability just as he is of those who wish to promote it as a universal truth or a secret ability. Anything which present science cannot explain after examining the evidence is something worthy of further investigation.

> *"...the spirit of the true philosopher...should not deny any phenomena merely because in the actual state of our knowledge they are inexplicable."*

And,

> *"...the usual rough and ready explanations, given by the scoffer on the one hand and the believer on the other, are wholly inadequate from any rational point of view. Problems of considerable scientific interest appear to be involved."*

To put it simply, Professor Barrett's labors were an attempt

> *"to bring these elusive and perplexing phenomena out of the 'disorderly mystery of ignorance', in which they have lain neglected for so long, into the 'orderly mystery of science,'"*... and to do so, *"...by a careful collection of trustworthy evidence, supplemented by experimental investigation wherever it is possible, and then by the fearless suggestion of some working hypothesis which will enable future investigators to direct their inquiries to definite issue, and thus overthrow or establish the provisional explanation that has been suggested. This is obviously the method by which the whole edifice of modern science has been reared; it is nothing more than the application of the inductive philosophy to psychical research."*

To repeat, this is a wonderfully detailed and well-researched investigation. In his conclusion, he acknowledges that although he began by investigating an apparently simple matter, the ramifications of the inquiry lead, inevitably, in his opinion, elsewhere.

> *"Thus we have been led from the study of such a matter-of-fact and practical question as the discovery of underground water by the dowser to the very centre and mystery of our complex personality."*

He had no doubt that the investigation of the phenomena of dowsing for water would, eventually, reveal something larger and grander than the finding of water.

It would, he said, reveal another aspect of what it is to be human.

This, perhaps, is the most important result of all the work involved; that there is something beyond our natural, physical world which is accessible in one way or another to most people, and that dowsing or divining for water is merely one manifestation of that aspect.

Even today, over one hundred years after this work, there is still no agreement as to how dowsing might work, yet it does.

That there has been no significant progress made in the study of this area is not, perhaps, too surprising. In the century since Professor Barrett published his results, there has been no comparable investigation by any competent authorities. His work remains as the most thorough and comprehensive study of one aspect of dowsing.

There is a rich field of study waiting for the individual sufficiently intrigued by anomalous results not to dismiss them summarily, as so often happens. But it will require a considerable amount of time and effort, together with a sufficiently un-biased approach, if such a study is to rank alongside Professor Barrett's exhaustive report.

> [Editor's Note: Please be aware that the original (British English) spelling has been retained throughout. All drawings and diagrams have been reproduced as faithfully as possible, but the state of the originals is, in most cases, the reason for any problems in legibility. Terms familiar to his readers but requiring explanation today have been briefly explained in footnotes, where applicable. Any such note appears in square brackets as per this example.]

*Taken from The Proceedings of the Society for Psychical Research Volume 13 1897-8*

# BOOK I

## PART I

*Introductory* — 2

*The Rod an Indicator of Sub-conscious Impressions* — 5

*Nomenclature* — 6

*Autoscopes* — 7

## PART II

*Brief Historical Statement* — 9

*Modern Literature on the Divining Rod* — 9

## PART III

*The Rod as used in the Search for Underground Water* — 16

    Group I Amateur Dowsers Nos. 1-20 — 17

    Group II Miscellaneous Cases Nos. 21-41 — 32

  Professional Dowsers — 50

    Group III (a) W. S. Lawrence Nos. 42-50 — 50

    Group III (b) W. Mereweather No. 51 — 55

    Group IV (a) J. Mullins Nos. 52-75 — 57

    Group IV (b) H.W. Mullins Nos. 76 – 84 — 75

    Group V W. Stone Nos. 85 – 98 — 100

    Group VI B. Tompkins Nos. 99 – 111 — 119

    Group VII J. Stears Nos. 112 -119 — 134

    Group VIII L. Gataker Nos. 120 – 129 — 145

    Group IX (a) H. Bacon Nos. 130, 131 — 161

| Group IX (b) H. Chesterman | 165 |
| Group IX (c) F. Rodwell No. 132 | 165 |
| Group X (a) Thos. Heighway No. 133 | 169 |
| Group X (b) R. Rothwell Nos. 134, 135 | 172 |
| Group X (c) R. W. Robertson Nos. 136, 137 | 176 |
|     Cyrus Fuller nos. 138 - 140 | 177 |

## DETAILED REPORTS

| *The Waterford Experiments—J. Mullins* | 83 |
| *The Horsham Experiments—J. Mullins* | 94 |
| *The Kingstown Experiments—J. Stears* | 143 |
| *The Richmond Experiments—H. W. Mullins and L. Gataker* | 155 |
| *The Wimbledon Experiments— F. Rodwell* | 167 |

## PART IV

*Geological Opinions—*

| Professor Sollas, F.R.S | 182 |
| Mr. T. V. Holmes, F.G.S | 183 |
| Mr. J. H. Blake, F.G.S | 190 |
| Mr. C. E. De Rance, F.G.S | 192 |

## PART V

| *Brief Survey of the Evidence* | 195 |

## PART VI

| *Theoretical Conclusions* | 199 |

## APPENDICES

*A. The Words "Dowse" and "Dowser"*   207

*B. Geological Views of the Distribution of Underground Water*   213

*C. How the Rod is Held;*   214

*D. Sensations said to be Experienced in Dowsing*   220

*E. Note on the Horsham Experiments*   225

*Prof. W. F. Barrett*

# ON THE SO-CALLED DIVINING ROD, OR VIRGULA DIVINA:

*A SCIENTIFIC AND HISTORICAL RESEARCH AS TO THE EXISTENCE AND PRACTICAL VALUE OF A PECULIAR HUMAN FACULTY, UNRECOGNISED BY SCIENCE, LOCALLY KNOWN AS DOWSING;*

By *W. F. Barrett, Professor of Experimental Physics in the Royal College of Science for Ireland.*

"There are two ways of investigating the facts or fancies about the divining rod. One is to examine it in its actual operation—a task of considerable labour, which will doubtless be undertaken by the Society for Psychical Research; the other, and easier way, is to study the appearances of the divining wand in history."—

A. Lang. *Custom and Myth* p.181.

# *The Credibility Of Dowsing*

# Part I

## *INTRODUCTORY*

At first sight few subjects appear to be so unworthy of serious notice and so utterly beneath scientific investigation as that of the divining rod. To most men of science the reported achievements of the "diviner" are on a par with the rogueries of Sir Walter Scott's *Dousterswivel*. That any one with the smallest scientific training should think it worth his while to devote a considerable amount of time and labour to an enquiry into the alleged evidence on behalf of the rod, will appear to my scientific friends about as sensible as if he spent his time investigating fortune-telling or any other relic of superstitious folly. Nor was my own prejudice against this subject any less than that of others. For I confess that it was with great reluctance, and even repugnance, that, some six years ago, yielding to the earnest request of the Council of the S.P.R., I began an investigation of the matter; hoping, however, in my ignorance, that a few weeks' work would enable me to relegate it

> *"Into a limbo large and broad, since called*
> *The Paradise of fools."*

Moreover, geologists might well make an objection *in limine* to any such investigation.[1] For it is a matter of common geological knowledge that the mode of distribution of underground water is very different from that imagined by the professional "diviner" or "dowser".[2] The latter with the utmost assurance locates a spring on a particular spot, and gives its exact depth from a foot to 100 feet, and its yield of water, and then probably will tell you there is another spring a few feet further off, perhaps at a very different depth, but that between no water will be found. Or, putting his interpretation on other indications of the rod, he will confidently assert that under his feet an underground river exists, yielding so many gallons per hour. By the same means he will profess to ascertain the direction in which the imaginary river is running, and give you its depth below the surface. Hard by he will trace other invisible streams, and follow them to their source, maintaining that a perfectly dry rock or sub-soil separates underground waters. Most of this is ridiculous to the practical geologist.[3] Here, for example, is an extract from a letter I lately received from the Rev. Osmond Fisher, M.A., (author of *Physics of the Earth's Crust*), which gives the geological statement of the case with admirable clearness and brevity:—

Harlton Rectory, Cambridge, *February 4th,* 1896.

> It appears to me that the assumption which underlies the belief in the divining rod is erroneous. It is only under exceptional circumstances, as among crystalline rocks, or where the strata are much disturbed, that underground water runs in channels like water in a pipe, so that a person can say, "I am now standing over a spring," whereas a few paces off he was not over one. What is called a spring, such as is readied in a well, is usually a widely extended water-saturated stratum. Ordinarily where water can be reached by a well, there are few spots [in the neighbourhood] where a well would not find it.

---

[1] Here is an extract from a recent letter from a well-known geologist:— "It is sad to find you troubling about that wretched divining rod! . . . Why is it that of late years this 'pestilent heresy' has cropped up so? And why are educated people bitten by it? Squires, M.P.'s, doctors, and alas, parsons!" As an instance of the general treatment of the subject by scientific men, I may refer to a recent letter from Mr. C. Tomlinson, F.R.S., in *Notes and Queries* for April 25th, 1896; p. 336. The writer quotes as fact a series of statements about the "rod," which a very brief investigation of the subject would have shown him to be entirely unfounded. Nevertheless, he says to those who give credit to the water-finders, and who point out that facts are stubborn things; "My answer is, *verification* of facts is still more stubborn," a sentiment which we all agree with, and wish all who write on this subject would attend to.

[2] The derivation of this word is obscure; the subject is discussed in Appendix A.

[3] I have ventured to give in Appendix B a brief outline—based on the authority of eminent geologists—of the chief points at present known concerning the production and circulation of underground waters. The unscientific reader may thus be better able to appreciate, or to question, the orthodox geological view regarding the divining rod. References are there given to some standard works on underground water.

## Prof. W. F. Barrett

The question which is really worthy of investigation in this and similar cases seems to be how such an idea ever originated, and to what it owes its vitality.

Furthermore, if instances of the successful use of the divining rod be quoted, the geologist would doubtless reply that these are either shrewd guesses of the "diviner," or else purely cases of chance coincidence; the few successes being recorded, whilst the numerous failures are overlooked. This, indeed, is a common fallacy, for "the mind is arrested by the affirmative instances, whereas the numberless instances in which there is no correspondence between the one set of facts and the other, altogether escaped our notice." [1]

Hence, from the geologist's point of view, the rod of the diviner is no more a mystery than the wand of a conjurer. So far as its use in finding water or mineral veins is concerned, the geologist argues that precisely the same degree of success would be obtained by tossing a coin, or throwing dice, and then sinking wells on the spots indicated by one's greatest luck in guessing.

Nevertheless it is impossible to read the voluminous evidence, collected with such painstaking care by Mr. Vaughan Jenkins of Oxford, which is given in Mr. Pease's S.P.R. report of thirteen years ago, without coming to the same conclusion as that arrived at by Mr. Pease, namely that:—" The evidence for the success of 'dowsing' as a practical art is very strong—and there seems to be an unexplained residuum when all possible deductions have been made."[2] Forty years ago, Dr. Mayo, F.R.S., arrived at a similar conclusion after experimental trials made with the rod both in England and abroad, and he published a paper on this subject in his entertaining little book *On the Truths contained in Popular Superstitions*. Prior to this, in 1814, Dr. C. Hutton, F.R.S., after examining the then accessible evidence on behalf of the divining rod and witnessing Lady Milbanke's success with the rod, published a statement of his own belief in the practical value of the divining rod, though unable to explain its behaviour.[3] And recently, in 1883, Dr. R. Raymond read a paper before the American Institute of Mining Engineers in which, after considerable investigation, the conclusion is arrived at:—"That there is a residuum of scientific value, after making all necessary deductions for exaggeration, self-deception, and fraud," in the use of the divining rod for finding springs and deposits of ore.[4] This testimony gains additional weight from the fact that Dr. Raymond is the distinguished secretary of that important Institute.

In like manner, it is impossible to study this subject *historically* without being impressed by the number of those who have accepted as indisputable the practical value of the rod, during the four centuries it has been in use. And these believers in its efficacy were not a set of silly, superstitious men, easily duped by cunning rogues,—credulous fools, capable of believing any nonsense;—on the contrary, among them were some of the most learned writers and the most painstaking investigators of their day, together with an array of practical miners and well-sinkers; men who ought to have known what they were talking about. The popular off-hand view about the rod—that it is merely another instance of the perennial superstition, or roguery, of mankind—seems therefore somewhat inadequate. For the curious problem that meets one in the examination of the subject is, not only the long survival and wide extent of the belief in the rod, but the singular and unselfish enthusiasm of its advocates, together with the general probity and intelligence of the "dowsers" themselves. Quakers, farmers, ladies, children, poor-law guardians, clergymen,

---

[1] Fowler's *Inductive Logic*, p. 239

[2] *Proceedings* S.P.R., Vol. II., p. 89. An abstract of the evidence collected by Mr. Vaughan Jenkins up to the date of Mr. Pease's report (January, 1884), is given in the *Proceedings* .S.P.R., Vol. II., pp. 90-107.

[3] See Montucla's edition of Ozanam's *Mathematical Recreations*, translated and enlarged by C. Hutton, LL.D., F.R.S., Vol. 4, 2nd edition, Longmans, 1814. In the first edition of this translation, belief in the use of the "rod" is treated as absurd. When this view was challenged, Hutton made enquiries for himself, with the result stated above. He had the courage to publish his conviction in later editions of the book, pp. 210—231. See also on this Dr. Ashburner's edition of Reichenbach's researches, p. 91, and the *Quarterly Review* for 1822, p. 373, *et seq.* The writer in the *Quarterly* says, "The fact of the discovery of water being effected by the divining rod, when held in the hands of certain persons, seems indubitable. . . . The faculty, so inherent in certain persons, is evidently the same with that of the Spanish Zahories, though the latter do not employ the hazel twig." This is much the same view as that taken by the editor of the *Spectator i*n an article in that journal for October 14th, 1882. The Zahories, as will be seen in the sequel, I have traced back to a writer in the 16th century.

[4] Mr. Pease in his S.P.R. report refers to Raymond's paper, which I find was read a second time at the U.S. International Electrical Exhibition in 1884, and is again published in the Journal of the Franklin Institute for 1885. I shall return to this paper later on.

# The Credibility Of Dowsing

magistrates, etc., are among the English dowsers of to-day, and these are not the class of people one would expect to find hoodwinking a gullible public. They may, of course, be the victims of self-deception; if so, does this also apply to the professional dowsers (in England alone I know of nearly twenty who make a living by their practice), whom numerous agents of estates and owners of land find it to their interest repeatedly to employ?[1]

Furthermore, it is to be noted that at the present day, as in the past, those who have had the opportunity of examining most closely the practical use of the "dowser's art" are not to be found among the scoffers. The opinion expressed to me by many well-informed and critical observers who live in that region of the South West of England where the "rod" has been longest in use, and is still extensively employed, is by no means contemptuous or even unfavourable. Here, for example, is an extract from the *West Somerset Word Book*, by Mr. F. T. Elworthy (author of *The Evil Eye and Kindred Superstitions*), an able and impartial authority.

DOWSE [daew'z], *v*. To use the divining-rod for the purpose of finding springs of water.

> The faculty possessed by some individuals is truly marvellous, and is not to be explained by the ordinary method, of ascribing the action to chicanery, as the evidence to unbiased minds is beyond cavil. Moreover, the power is not hereditary nor communicable. Nascitur non fit ('born not made'). The power of the Dowser to discover water is not merely a surviving superstition, but is believed in by hard-headed, practical men of the world, who still habitually pay their money for the advice of these men, and who have proved by repeated trials that it is always correct, and worth paying for.
>
> Quite recently a Sanatorium was to be built upon a high and apparently very dry spot, where of course the first necessity was water. Three professional Dowsers were sent for separately, and unknown to each other. Each came on a different day from the others, and under the impression that he alone was being employed, with the result that all three pointed to the same spot, where a well was dug and abundant water found.
>
> Inasmuch as one of my own daughters has the power to some extent, I am able to testify that trickery plays no part in the performance, and she herself is quite unconscious of anything by which the rod is acted on.
>
> The rod or twig I have seen used is a fork of about a foot long, cut off just below the bifurcation, and in size each limb is about as large as a thick straw. The wood, it is said, must be either "halse" or white thorn, and may be used either green or dry. The operator holds an end of the twig firmly between the fingers and thumb of each hand, and with the elbows pressed rigidly against the sides; consequently the two ends of the twig are pulled asunder, with the centre, or juncture of the fork pointing downwards. He then moves very slowly forward, and when over a spring the twig turns outwards, and twists upon itself into an upright position. This movement may be repeated any number of times—the rod twisting over and over again upon reaching the same spot, and with equal freedom when both rod and fingers are held by sceptical witnesses. The position in which the twig is held seems to make it impossible that it can be turned by any conscious muscular action. Indeed both

---

[1] I am glad to be able to bear testimony to the fact that several of these professional dowsers, notably those who have been most successful, are simple unassuming men, who do not disguise their ignorance, nor occasional failures, and are ready to impart, all they know. On the other hand, as might naturally be expected, the possession of any peculiar "faculty" tends to inordinate self-conceit and vanity, especially among the illiterate class from whom the professional dowser is usually drawn. This is traceable from the 17th century dowser down to the present day. Among such men a great mystery is made of their "art"; an apprenticeship must be served, and initiation to its mysteries could, in former times, only be gained by a knowledge of the magic rites and ceremonies with which the practice was surrounded. At the present day these magic rites are swallowed up by the more magic dollar. For example, the son of an English rector having accidentally found he had the faculty of dowsing, the father tells me he applied for information to a young professional dowser—who certainly understands the art of self-advertisement,—and received the reply that "Mr.___ declines to take less than one hundred guineas for giving the youth three months' training"! I hope the present paper may make such premiums a little more difficult to catch.

my daughter and the professional Dowser I have seen, assert that they cannot twist the rod by any conscious effort.

In some parts of the county the operation is called Jowsing and the operator a jowser.

Even the President of the Royal Geological Society of Cornwall, Mr. J. D. Enys, F.G.S., is not a scoffer; on the contrary he himself is an amateur dowser, and in a recent letter, writing from Penryn, Cornwall, Mr. Enys states, "I have tried it [dowsing for water] often. On one occasion I cut a small slight rod and held it till I came to the place [where underground water existed], when it always acted by turning. On this occasion I was able to hold the rod, but it broke short off in front of my hands, and did so a second time in the same place. ... I always feel the effects afterwards if I go on too long using the rod." This is another instance of the testimony afforded by a scientific man living in a locality where the rod has been in use for centuries. It is always ignorance, and not knowledge, that blindly denies what is unfamiliar.

Here then we find a widespread belief existing at the present day, and extending backwards for centuries; though it seem contemptible, how are we to account for the origin and survival of this belief, and for its appearance and persistence in regions remote from each other? As Dr. Lauder Brunton, F.R.S., has remarked *a propos* of this very subject ——"when we find certain things implicitly believed in by some people, whilst they are laughed at as ridiculous and absurd by others, it is worth while to enquire whether there may not be an element of truth as well as of falsehood in both belief and ridicule. Ignorance is the parent both of blind belief and of scoffing scepticism, and leads not only to implicit belief in untruth, but also to a rash denial of what is true." One main object of our Society is to endeavour to dispel such ignorance by carefully examining, in the clearer light of the present day, the evidence that exists on behalf of phenomena rejected as trivial or valueless by orthodox science.

## *The Rod Merely An Indicator Of Subconscious Impressions*

It may, however, be asked in what way does the subject of the divining rod come within the scope of a Society for *Psychical* Research? This I think will be evident in the sequel of this paper; here it is only necessary to point out that the rod, or forked twig, is not a chemical or physical re-agent indicating the object sought by some specific action of that object on the material of the rod. The rod must be regarded simply as the *indicator* of some action taking place upon or within the living mechanism of the individual who holds the rod; just as a "planchette" or a tilting table is used to indicate muscular impressions made by, or through, the so called "medium." In fact, the rod is not always used by the "dowser"; a piece of wire or watch-spring, or merely the out-stretched hands, are used by some of the most successful "diviners". Hence there can, I think, be little doubt that the subject we are discussing is a special case of that large group of phenomena belonging to our subliminal consciousness which Mr. F. W. H. Myers has done so much to elucidate: the movement of the rod being due to involuntary reflex action.

Some such view, I find, has been held by nearly all who have in recent years carefully considered the subject. Thus Dr. Lauder Brunton, F.R.S., says:—

> "I am inclined to think that the success of the divining rod, in some hands, for finding water or even for tracing criminals, is due to its causing involuntary muscular action, and thus enabling the person using it to consciously recognise that impressions have been made upon him which would otherwise never have arisen above the state of sub-consciousness." Dr. Brunton goes on to say: "When we hear that a man is able to discover water at a considerable distance below the ground on which he stands, we are at first apt to scout the idea as ridiculous, while if we were told that a caravan was crossing a desert, and that all at once the thirsty camels started off quickly, and at a distance of a mile or more water was found, we look upon the occurrence as natural. In the same way we regard as very remarkable the story of a man tracing criminals with a divining rod, but it becomes quite ordinary if we put a bloodhound in the man's place." In conclusion, Dr. Brunton remarks concerning the

divining rod and the allied popular beliefs: "The whole subject is a deeply interesting one, and its thorough investigation is much to be desired."[1]

The discovery of water or a mineral lode by a hazel twig, therefore, no longer becomes so absurdly improbable if it is the individual who is in some way the discoverer, and the rod merely the indicator of some impression made upon him, an impression too slight and too subtle to rise to the level of consciousness. After all, it is not the improbability of the quest that should deter us, it is simply a question of what amount of trustworthy evidence exists upon the subject to make the quest worth pursuing.

## *Nomenclature*

The term *divining rod* is unfortunate, and has probably led to a good deal of the opprobrium under which the subject rests, as it is frequently confounded with the ancient superstitious practice of divination by a rod, or Rhabdomancy, one of the oldest methods of augury (Hosea iv., 12, or by arrows as in Ezekiel xxi., 21). The considerable literature of Rhabdomancy is a distinct question, and it need hardly be said, of no value to physical science.[2]

A rod or wand was not only used for divination, it was and is, the symbol of power; as in Exodus iv., 17, 20; Psalm xxiii, 4, etc., as in the *lituus* of the Roman augur, in the pastoral staff of a bishop, in a monarch's sceptre or in the special constable's staff of to-day.[3] The Arch-Druid's wand is another instance of this, and the conjurer's wand is a survival of the same thing; even the native Irish name for the latter is *Slaitin Draoidheachta*, Druid's wand, or *virgula divinationis*. On this subject Mr. Lang has given us the benefit of his scholarship in a passage I have quoted in the foot-note below.[4]

---

[1] Dr. Lauder Brunton on "Truth and Delusion." in the *Universal Review*, January, 1889. The *Quarterly Review* for July, 1895, p. 206, says "Dowsing . . . is either conscious imposture, or it is an act prompted by the sub-conscious element in the personality of the 'dowser.' ... It is only a question of steady scientific examination, as in the study of any other condition of human faculty."

[2] The most learned and exhaustive work on ancient divination is that by M. Bouché-Leclercq, entitled *Histoire de la Divination dans l'Antiquité*, 4 vols., Paris, 1880. Lenormant in his *Chaldean Magic* refers to the use of rhabdomancy among the Chaldeans. (Eng. trans., p. 237). See also article *Divination* in Smith's *Dictionary of the Bible*, and Mr. Myers' brilliant essay on *Greek Oracles*. Brand's *Popular Antiquities* contains a lengthy and erudite article on rhabdomancy, in which reference is made to the divining rod (Vol. II., p. 622.) The most concise and excellent article on Divination which I have met with is that in *Chambers' Encyclopedia*. Even among the Mongol tribes, inhabiting the eastern portion of the plateau of central Asia, divination is rife, as that able and devoted missionary, the Rev. J. Gilmour, M.A., shows in his remarkable work, Among the Mongols. Mr. Gilmour says (p. 188 ) that the Mongols expected him to divine for them where to sink their wells so as to get a good water supply, or where to find any lost cattle, etc., and when he confessed his inability to do so, their amazement and incredulity were profound.

[3] There are, I find, some 130 references to a "rod" or "staff" as a symbol of authority or power in the Old Testament alone. There has recently been added to the South Kensington Museum "a sceptre of blue glazed ware made for Amenhotop II of the 18th Dynasty, from the temple of Nubt." This sceptre is some 7 feet high, thicker than the girth of one's arm and shaped like a huge shepherd's crook or pastoral staff. The symbolical, sacred, or magical power of a rod or crook is therefore as ancient as it is widely diffused. What gave rise to this is an interesting question.

[4] "In all countries rods or wands, the Latin v*irga,* have a magical power. Virgil obtained his medieval repute as a wizard because his name was erroneously connected with *virgula,* the magic wand. But we do not actually know that the ancient wand of the enchantress Circe, in Homer, or the wand of Hermes, was used, like the divining rod, to indicate the whereabouts of hidden wealth or water. In the Homeric hymn to Hermes (line 529), Apollo thus describes the *caduceus* or wand of Hermes: 'Thereafter will I give thee a lovely wand of wealth and riches, a golden wand with three leaves, which shall keep thee ever unharmed.' In later art, this wand or *caduceus* is usually entwined with serpents; but on one vase, at least, the wand of Hermes is simply the forked twig of our rustic miners and water-finders. The same form is found on an engraved Etruscan mirror."Now, was a wand of this form used in classical times to discover hidden objects of value? That wands were used by Scythians and Germans in various methods of casting lots is certain; but that is not the same thing as the working of the twig. Cicero speaks of a fabled wand by which wealth can be procured; but he says nothing of the method of its use, and possibly was only thinking of the rod of Hermes, as described in the Homeric hymn already quoted. There was a *satura,* written by Varro, called the *Virgula Divina;* fragments remain, but throw no light on the subject. A passage usually quoted from Seneca has no more to do with the divining rod than with the telephone. Pliny is a writer extremely fond of marvels; yet when he describes the various modes of finding wells of water, he says nothing about the divining wand. The isolated texts from Scripture which are usually referred to clearly indicate wands of a different sort."—*Custom and Myth,* p. 182.

Instead, therefore, of the word "divining rod," I would suggest the use of the provincial word *dowsing-rod*, or of the term *winchel-rod*: the former is common enough and the latter has been, and still is, used in certain parts; it was, I believe, first employed by a writer in a book translated from the German, called the *Laboratory*, published in 1740. The word probably arose from the German name for divining rod, *Wünschel-ruthe*, the pronunciation being similar. One writer, however, attributes the word, less probably, to the English *winch*, as the rod turns over hidden springs.[1]

## *Autoscopes*

As the divining rod is only one of many instrumental means, whereby imperceptible, involuntary, and unconscious muscular movements are revealed by the visible motion of an external object, it is desirable to group these various appliances under a generic name. I would suggest for this purpose the term AUTOSCOPE.[2] Other autoscopes besides (1) the divining or dowsing rod, are, (2) a little ring or ball suspended by a thread, the *pendule explorateur* of French writers, the use of which goes back at least to the fourth century;[3] similar to this is (3) a poised index, or a simple pointer, traversing the letters of the alphabet, (4) a pencil lightly and passively held so that it can write on note-paper, (5) planchette, (6) a small table, or other object such as a chair,[4] easily tilted or rotated (table-turning, etc.), (7) a passive living person lightly touched by another, as in the "willing game," where a hidden object is found, or a secret command obeyed by the quasi thought-reader, or living autoscope.

Doubtless other autoscopes exist, or will be invented, but, however different in detail, there are, broadly speaking, only two distinct kinds, (a) those wherein the indicator is in *stable* or neutral equilibrium, as the pendule or planchette, and where a succession of ideas may be conveyed by a series of uninterrupted movements, (b) those wherein the indicator, or the muscular system of the person using the indicator, is in a "sensitive" state, *i.e.,* one of balanced strain or *unstable* equilibrium.[5] Here a slight impulse, or nervous stimulus, may produce a profound effect, the displacement not being in the least proportional to the force that initiated it. Autoscopes of this class, which convey only a single idea, require to be restored to their initial condition by an independent operation, before a second displacement can occur or a second idea be conveyed. I shall show later on that, if rightly held, the forked dowsing or divining rod belongs to this class. It is in this class we should expect to find that any sense perceptions, which are too faint to excite consciousness, would probably reveal themselves.

Here permit a brief digression. Our conscious personality speaks through various *voluntary* muscular movements, ideas chiefly expressing themselves in articulate language. The large unconscious background of our personality always speaks through *involuntary* muscular movements, to which ordinarily we give no heed, though these movements are ever going on within us, and if external are generally imperceptible. Now if reasoning, as we know it, cannot exist without language, which need not be speech but some form of expression, then autoscopes furnish a means

---

[1] Other terms used in old time for the divining rod were Aaron's rod, Moses' rod, and Jacob's rod. A work on the divining rod was published in Lyons in 1693, and an English translation called *Jacob's Rod* has been made by a Mr. Welton. The fact that the divining rod was in old times often called "Moses' rod" doubtless arose from the description given in the book of Exodus of Moses obtaining water in the wilderness by means of his rod, irreverent persons concluding he had learnt the use of the divining rod whilst in Egypt.

[2] In physical science the termination "scope" (Gr. Σκοπεῖν - to view) is restricted to instruments which reveal or detect a hidden object or force, and do not measure the amount of the force, *e.g.,* magnetoscope, electroscope, etc. The word *Cryptoscope*— instrument for showing hidden things,—is for some reasons preferable to autoscope, but it has already been adopted by some French writers for the fluorescent screen used with the X-rays.

[3] For a modern illustration of the use of the *pendule,* see the *Reminscences* of the late Mrs. De Morgan, p. 214.

[4] *Juanita* was the name given to a *chair* in Guadaloupe in 1853, which composed prose and poetry after the manner of planchette. "Les oeuvres littéraires de la chaise," are set forth in a brochure published at the Government printing office in Guadaloupe, in 1853.

[5] In the region of physics, an inverted cone, a Rupert's Drop or a sensitive flame are familiar examples of bodies either in unstable or *poised* equilibrium..

[RUPERT'S DROPS OR Dutch tears are created by dripping molten glass into cold water, cooling the glass into a tadpole shape with a long, thin tail. The slower cooling in the bulbous head gives it unusual properties. The bulbous end may be hit with a hammer without breaking, but if the tail end is even slightly damaged, the whole drop will disintegrate explosively. - Ed]

## The Credibility Of Dowsing

whereby the hidden part of our personality, the dumb partner of our life, can reason and outwardly express itself; a means whereby an intelligence not under our conscious control can reveal itself by some physical manifestation.

It is just because these manifestations appear to be so novel, and detached from ourselves, that they are apt to be so misleading to some and so mischievous to others. Interpreted on the one hand as the play of a wonderful occult force, science has refused to have anything to do with phenomena which seem to obey no physical laws, but are capricious and self-determined. Interpreted on the other, truly enough, as the exhibition of a free and intelligent agent, some infernal or discarnate spirit has been fixed upon as the cause, and a fictitious authority for which there is no warrant has been given to their indications. Whether in any case these intelligent automatic movements exhibit information outside the memory, either active or *latent*, of the individual who uses the autoscope; or a knowledge beyond that which may have been unconsciously derived from those present by sign-reading or thought-transference, is a problem which can only be solved so as to gain general acceptance by long and patient enquiry, of which our *Proceedings* are an earnest, and to which this monograph may afford a small contribution.

# Part II

The literature of the divining rod is extensive, and several modern writers have given historical outlines of this subject. But upon comparing these accounts it soon became evident that they were all, more or less, drawn from some earlier historian. I therefore devoted part of two summer vacations to a thorough historical examination of this subject, and thanks to the valuable libraries to which I have had access in London, Liverpool, and Dublin, I venture to hope that the historical survey appended to this paper is somewhat more complete and exact than its predecessors. In connection with this part of my task, most grateful acknowledgements are due to my friends, the Rev. Maxwell Close, M.A., and Mr. E. Westlake, F.G.S., for their kind and valuable co-operation; the latter devoting many weeks to this work at the British Museum Library.[1]

The historical evidence adduced in the sequel—some of which has hitherto escaped observation—renders the following facts, in my opinion, practically certain: (1) The birthplace of the modern divining or dowsing rod is the mining districts of Germany, probably the Hartz mountains. Germany is the home of mining, and the most approved processes were in use there prior to elsewhere. (2) The first record of the use of the dowsing rod was for mining purposes and dates from late in the 15th or early in the 16th century, though it must have been in use for at least a generation before this. Its introduction was coincident with, and perhaps a symptom of, that great movement of thought in Germany when tradition began to give way to reason, and superstition to the observation of nature. (3) The use of the dowsing rod for finding mineral veins was introduced into England, by German miners, at the latter part of the 16th century, and early in the 17th century its use in Cornwall for mining is noticed by some English writers. (4) The employment of a rod for finding underground water possibly began in Germany, but at least a century later than its use in mining. At the present time the dowsing rod is far more in use for the former purpose (water-finding) than for the latter. (5) The use of the rod in the "moral world," for detecting criminals, etc., was a phase which arose towards the end of the 17th century and quickly passed away; its use for this purpose (but this *only*) being condemned by a decree of the Inquisition in 1701. (6) To A. Kircher and G. Schott, about 1660, we owe the theory of unconscious muscular action as the explanation of the *pendule explorateur*, which they connect (but obscurely) with the motion of the divining rod. By Malebranche and Lebrun in 1692 the importance of the prior *intention* of the diviner as to the object of search was first pointed out.

Postponing to the conclusion a detailed account of the early history of this subject, it will be convenient, before entering upon an examination of the evidence on behalf of a dowsing faculty and how far it is of practical value, to give an outline of what has been written on the subject in comparatively modern times, that is, since, the first scientific investigation of the question by Dr. Thouvenel a century ago.

## Modern Literature On This Subject

The standard treatise on the subject is usually considered to be a work by M. Chevreul, entitled *La Baguette Divinatoire*, Paris, 1854.[2] The immediate cause of Chevreul's treatise was a paper presented to the French Academy of Sciences, in March, 1853, by a M. Riondet, entitled *Sur la baguette divinatoire employée à la recherche des eaux souterraines*. As usual in such cases, the Academy ordered a report on this paper to be made, and nominated for this purpose three eminent scientific members of its body, MM. Chevreul, Boussingault, and Babinet. M. Chevreul was requested by his colleagues to draw up the report, which led to the publication of his book on the subject. The author states he found it impossible to dissociate the movement of the *baguette* from that of the *pendule explorateur* and table-turning; these subjects therefore occupy a considerable part of his work. (Meanwhile M. Riondet's paper seems to have been forgotten, for it is not discussed by Chevreul and no publication nor summary of it, nor of a subsequent paper

---

[1] My hearty thanks are also due to the various able and courteous Librarians, more especially to those in Dublin. The library in Trinity College, and Archbishop Marsh's library, Dublin, are particularly rich in 16th and 17th century literature; the latter has some works which apparently are not in the British Museum library. I am also indebted to the National Library of Ireland and to the scientific libraries at the Royal Irish Academy, the Royal Dublin Society, and the Royal College of Science for Ireland, and to the valuable Picton Library in Liverpool, etc.

[2] Chevreul, as is well known, was a distinguished French chemist, the author of numerous scientific papers on colour and the artistic and industrial applications of chemistry. He died in 1889 at the age of 103 years, retaining his faculties and industry almost to the last.

# *The Credibility Of Dowsing*

which M. Riondet sent in,—was made in the *Comptes Rendus* of the Academy). Chevreul's book was certainly useful in drawing attention to, and examining, a wide-spread belief which hitherto had not been seriously discussed by any writer of recognised scientific position. But its importance has, I think, been largely over-rated; it was believed to be the first attempt to give a rational explanation of the movement of the rod; but this is an erroneous belief; as Kircher, I find, anticipated Chevreul by two centuries. Chevreul is content with the popular view that the indications afforded by the rod are always fallacious; hence he gives no modern evidence of its success or failure, and makes no experimental examination for himself. The historical portion of his book up to the year 1700 is also largely derived from a remarkably learned but little known work by Father Pierre Lebrun, S.J., entitled *Histoire Critique des Pratiques Superstitieuses,* etc., Paris, 1702, a work I shall have occasion to refer to later on. Lebrun was evidently a man of great intellectual power and wide reading, and I do not wonder at Chevreul dedicating his treatise to the memory of this erudite Jesuit.[1]

Subsequent writers (with one or two rare exceptions, such as Mr. A. Lang), have been content with copying Chevreul, often at second or third hand. The Rev. S. Baring-Gould, for example— whose interesting and lengthy article on the divining rod in *Curious Myths of the Middle Ages,* London, 1868, is probably the best known essay on the subject to English readers,—appears entirely indebted to a recent popular and excellent French author, M. Louis Figuier,[2] though he does not acknowledge the source of his information. M. Figuier's work is called *Histoire du Merveilleux dans les temps modernes,* Paris, 1860, and half of the second volume is devoted to the divining rod. Though Figuier relies on De Vallemont for most of his historical data and on Chevreul for his theory of the rod, yet his work is *by far the best* memoir on our subject that has yet appeared; he makes, however, no attempt to collect or discuss evidence of the practical value, or otherwise, of the rod.

Perhaps the most extraordinary medley ever put together on the divining rod is an article by Professor Fiske, of Harvard, called the "Descent of Fire," in his interesting volume, *Myths and Myth-makers,* the 18th edition of which is dated 1893. Having once met a "water finder" whom he promptly proved to be a rogue by showing that the rod would not move when he (Professor Fiske) used it, and having read that "learned author," Mr. Baring-Gould, Professor Fiske feels himself qualified to clear up the subject. Accordingly he tells us that as the divining rod "has been used in Europe from time immemorial," and as "the one thing essential about it is that it shall be *forked,"* it is obvious that its origin, "hopeless as the problem may at first sight seem," is "nevertheless solved:"—it is, he says, unquestionably the wooden incarnation of forked lightning! There was, however, he finds subsequently, *"one* exception to this rule of a forked rod, and if any further evidence be needed to convince the most sceptical that the divining rod is nothing but a symbol of the lightning, that exception will furnish such evidence."[3]! So much for "myths and myth-makers."

Mr. A. Lang has a capital though brief essay on the rod in his *Custom and Myth,* London, 2nd edition, 1885 (a reprint of an article which appeared in the Cornhill Magazine for January, 1883). I am glad to find that the view already expressed as to the irrelevancy of discussing rhabdomancy in connection with our present subject has the support of Mr. Lang; every other writer follows the lead given by Father Lebrun, and mixes up these two entirely distinct questions. I have already quoted from Dr. Mayo's excellent essay on the rod contained in his book on *Popular Superstitions;* this essay originally appeared in *Blackwood's Magazine* for February, 1847, under the *nom de plume* of "Mac Davies," and was copied into Littell's *Living Age* of April the same year.

One of the latest scientific essays on our subject is the paper by Dr. Rossiter Raymond of New York, read before the American Institute of Mining Engineers, and already mentioned on p. 3. This is a serious and thoughtful attempt

---

[1] Some ten years prior to the publication of Lebrun's *Histoire,* etc., the Abbé de Vallemont published a work called *La Physique Occulte, ou traité de la Baguette Divinatoire;* the latter part of this work contains an even fuller historical review of the subject than that given by Lebrun, who, in his turn, had doubtless borrowed largely from De Vallemont. I shall return to De Vallemont's work in the historical review at the end of this paper.

[2] Not primarily to Chevreul, as Mr. Lang suggests in his *Custom and Myth,* page 188. Why does Mr. Lang always write "Chevreuil"?

[3] It need hardly be said that Professor Fiske's alleged facts are as mythical as the origin he claims for the rod, which is based on Dr. Kuhn's work, *Die Herabkunst des Feuers.*

to investigate the subject; contemporary evidence, though not adduced, has been considered by the author, and his conclusion has already been stated. The bulk of his paper is historical, and this part, as Dr. Raymond frankly says, is derived from Chevreul and Figuier. The same parentage is traceable in other writers, to whom I need not refer. An exception to this rule is the excellent, though brief, article on the divining rod in the *Penny,* now the *English, Cyclopedia;* the only English encyclopedia I can find that contains anything of value on this subject. One or two historical references to the rod occur at the end of the article *Hazel* in the *Encyclopedia Britannica.*

De Quincey has several references to dowsers and dowsing, or jowsing, as he terms it, in his writings. Thus, in *Modern Superstitions,* he writes:—

> There are in England (especially in Somersetshire) a class of men who practise the Pagan rhabdomancy in a limited sense. They carry a rod or rhabdos (ῥάβδος) of willow: this they hold horizontally; and by the handing of the rod towards the ground, they discover the favourable places for sinking wells; a matter of considerable importance in a province so ill-watered as the northern district of Somersetshire. These people are called jowsers [dowsers]. The experimental evidences of a real practical skill in these men, and the enlarged compass of speculation in these days, have led many enlightened people to a stoic εποχή, or suspension of judgment, on the reality of this somewhat mysterious art.

In a foot-note to this passage De Quincey says:—

> For twenty miles round Wrington, in Somersetshire, the birth-place of Locke, nobody sinks for wells without their [the dowsers'] advice. I myself knew an amiable Scottish family, who, at an estate called Belmaduthie, in memory of a similar property in Ross-shire, built a house in Somersetshire, and resolved to find water without the help of the "jowser." But after sinking to a greater depth than ever had been known before, and spending a large sum of money, they were finally obliged to consult the jowser, who found water at once.

Again, in his *Confessions of an Opium Eater,* page 84, De Quincey speaks of the value of "jowsing" to the inhabitants of Somersetshire, and remarks:—

> I have myself not only seen the process tried with success, but have witnessed the enormous trouble, delay, and expense accruing to those of the opposite faction who refused to benefit by this art. To pursue the tentative plan (i.e., the plan of boring for water at haphazard) ended, so far as I was aware, in multiplied vexation. In reality, these poor men are, after all, more philosophic than those who scornfully reject their services. For the artists obey unconsciously the logic of Lord Bacon: they build upon a long chain of induction, upon the uniform results of their life-long experience. But the counter-faction do not deny this experience; all they have to allege is that, agreeably to any laws known to themselves, a priori, there ought not to be any such experience. Now, a sufficient course of facts overthrows all antecedent plausibilities. Whatever science or scepticism may say, most of the tea-kettles in the Vale of Wrington are filled by rhabdomancy.

Among English scientific works the only one I can find that gives an account of the dowsing rod is the great treatise on *British Mining,* published in 1884, by the late Robert Hunt, F.R.S., keeper of the Mining Records. The author treats the indications of the rod as illusory, but devotes considerable space to quotations showing the use of the rod, taken from Agricola's work on mining of the 16th century, and Pryce's well-known folio on Cornish mining of the 18th century; these works are fully noticed in the Historical Survey appended to this research.

## *The Credibility Of Dowsing*

The English scientific societies have as a rule given the subject a wide berth.[1] Nevertheless, a few stray papers on the divining rod are to be found in their *Proceedings*. Thus, to go back to 1814, the *Transactions of the Geological Society*, Vol. II., contain illustrations of the practical use of the rod in a paper by Mr. W. Phillips, who had also previously contributed an interesting article on the subject to *Tilloch's Philosophical Magazine* for 1801, Vol. XIII. The *Quarterly Mining Review* for 1830 has also a lengthy article on the dowsing rod, several instances being given of its successful use in the discovery of mineral lodes, the same spot being indicated even when the dowser was blindfolded. In the *Proceedings of the British Association* for 1875, Miss A. W. Buckland alludes to the divining rod in a paper on Rhabdomancy, but is evidently mistaken in the origin to which she traces the rod; in a letter Miss Buckland contributes to the *Standard* newspaper for January 3rd, 1889, she gives a striking instance of the practical value of the rod in finding water, the spot indicated by the dowsing rod yielding a good water supply on a well being sunk, whereas close by a well sunk to a greater depth was quite dry. The numerous other similar cases I shall be able to cite render it less probable that this is a case of mere chance coincidence. In the *Proceedings of the Bristol Naturalist's Society* for 1874, Messrs. Tawney and Pass relate experiments with a dowser finding hidden coins, and they attempt to explain away the considerable degree of success attained, but the result was probably due to unconscious indications given by the spectators, or to true thought-transference; when both of these are excluded the failure of such experiments is invariable and complete, as will be shown in the course of this paper. Experiments of this kind are misleading, as they have really nothing to do with whatever peculiar faculty the dowser may possess for detecting underground springs or veins of ore. In the *Proceedings* of the same Society for 1884 is a paper by a distinguished geologist, Prof. Sollas, F.R.S., on the result of the experiments he made at the request of the S.P.R. to test a dowser at Locking, Somerset. The substance of this paper appeared in Vol. II. of our own *Proceedings*. Prof. Sollas arrives at a conclusion adverse to the dowser, but, with all deference, I venture to submit that a more inconclusive paper has rarely been published by a scientific authority. In the *Proceedings of the Bath Natural History Society and Field Club* for 1889, Vol. VI., is a lengthy paper on the dowsing rod by Mr. Forder Plowman; several cases of more or less evidential value are quoted by the author, who is a warm believer in the indications afforded by the rod. At the Folk Lore Congress in 1891, Miss M. R. Cox read a paper on dowsing, which is published in their *Proceedings,* and in the *Wiltshire Notes and Queries* for 1893. The paper deals with a dowser, W. Stokes, and relates some remarkable successes which had attended his practice. A good picture is given showing the method of holding the rod employed by Stokes in dowsing.

In 1853 a Mr. F. Phippen published a brochure entitled, *Narrative of practical experiments proving to demonstration the discovery of water, coal, and minerals in the earth by means of the dowsing fork or divining rod*. Mr. Phippen being on a visit to Somersetshire heard and saw so much of the practical use of dowsing that he wrote a full report of his enquiries in the *Morning Chronicle* and *Morning Advertiser* of November 10th, 1844. He gives many facts that came under his own observation, and quotes some cases of evidential value that I have included in the subsequent record of experiments. An excellent frontispiece, by A. Crowquill, shows a "dowser" at work, the flexed arms being held tightly to the sides of the body, and the prongs of the fork (which is of larger size than those now generally used) passing between the index and the next finger of each hand. This is not the method of holding used by Stokes, pictured by Miss Cox; in fact at the present day the method of holding the rod varies with the individual dowser.

Another method of holding the forked twig is described in a little book on the divining rod, written by two amateur dowsers, Messrs. Young and Robertson, of Llanelly, South Wales, and recently published. This brochure is not in any sense a critical or scientific production, but it is of interest as presenting the experience of two men who are enthusiastic believers in the practical value of the rod, and have at considerable self-sacrifice freely given their neighbours the benefit of the peculiar faculty which they, in common with other successful dowsers, appear

---

[1] In the *Philosophical Transactions* of the Royal Society for 1606 (Vol. I., p. 333) will be found a question by the Hon. Robert Boyle as to whether the *virgula divina* is of use in finding mineral veins. This famous philosopher devotes some space to the divining rod in his *Philosophical Essays,* as will be seen in the concluding part

to possess. A straight rod, as well as a forked twig, and even a tiny (waistcoat pocket) fork of aluminium, are used indifferently by Messrs. Young and Robertson.[1]

*Notes and Queries* contain frequent references to the divining rod. By far the most useful are two papers by Mr. W. Bates of Birmingham (*Notes and Queries,* Vol. X., 1854, pp. 449 and 467). Mr. Bates gives some valuable bibliographical memoranda which I have not found in any other writer and to which I refer those who are interested.[2]

The subject of the divining rod was discussed and several well-authenticated cases quoted in the *Standard* newspaper during the last week of 1888, and the first of 1889. A still longer discussion took place in the *Mining Journal* for 1875, to which reference will again be made. From time to time ephemeral articles on the divining rod are to be found in magazines, etc., to which it is needless to refer; a list of these will be found in Poole's *Index to Periodical Literature.*

In the United States the *American Journal of Science* (Silliman's Journal), the leading and authoritative American scientific journal, contains a capital paper on the rod by (the Rev.) Ralph Emerson, in 1821,[3] and a long and able discussion of the subject in 1826. I shall return to these. There are also papers on the rod and its use in finding oil springs, as well as water and mineral veins, in other American magazines of more recent date; notably a lengthy article in the *Democratic Review* for 1850, which refers to the use of a new type of divining rod, or ball, similar to the *pendule explorateur.*

In 1876, Mr. Chas. Latimer, an American Civil Engineer, published an essay on the divining rod which contains an interesting record of his own experience. Having accidentally discovered that the rod moved in his own hands, he was led to try whether its indications were of any practical use, and the experiments which he narrates, convinced him that it was. The involuntary movement of the forked twig enabled him to discover underground springs in places where his conscious experience and judgment would not have led him to locate them. He also arrived at a method of estimating their depth below the surface. I will quote the evidence of an eye-witness to Mr. Latimer's powers later on. I have before me numerous cuttings from American newspapers which illustrate the fact that "water-witching," as they call it, is in considerable vogue in certain parts of the United States.

On the Continent the old province of Dauphiny corresponds to our Somersetshire as regards the esteem in which the divining rod is held and the number of "diviners" for which it has been remarkable; they were known by the name of *tourneurs,* or more frequently *sourciers.* It was in Dauphiny that the charity boy Bleton was born, and at the age of seven years found he could successfully discover underground springs and streams by means of the divining rod. In the year 1780 a distinguished physician, Dr. Thouvenel, having heard of Bleton, sent for him, and was so struck with the simplicity of the lad and his frank demeanour, that he determined to see what truth there was in his alleged powers. The result was a prolonged investigation, which satisfied Thouvenel that the lad had the power imputed to him, and he published a short treatise on the subject, entitled *Mémoirs Physique et Médicinal, montrant des rapports évidens entre les phénomènes de la Baguette divinatoire, du Magnétisme et de I' Electricité, etc.,* Paris, 1781. Three years later, M. Thouvenel, whose adherence to *Bletonisme,* as it was called, had drawn on him a host of antagonists, published a *Second Mémoire Physique,* etc., Paris, 1784, giving affidavits regarding Bleton's discoveries, and a narrative of his experiments with Bleton and another Dauphiny youth, named Pennet, whom he found similarly endowed.[4] Thouvenel was the first to submit the alleged claims of the divining rod to systematic scientific investigation, and

---

[1] I have had a long correspondence with Mr. Young, who has given me many instances of his success in dowsing for water. I may add that, though self-taught, and with few opportunities, Mr. Young has devised and carried out some extremely interesting and novel experiments in electricity.

[2] Every series of *Notes and Queries,* except the third, contains much useful information on the divining rod. Having examined all the references, it may save trouble to others if I name only the more important notes. Notes and Queries.—1st Series (1853), Vol VIII., 400, 479, 623; Vol. X. (1854), 18, 155, 449, 467. 4th Series (1873), Vol. XII., 412. 5th Series, Vol. V. (1876), 507; Vol. VI , 19, 33,150, 210; Vol. X. (1878); 295, 316, 355. 6th Series, Vol. VI. (1882), 325. 7th Series, Vol. VIII. (1889), 186; Vol. IX. (1890), 214, 338; 8th Series, Vol. III. (1893), 107; Vol. IX. (1896), 266, 335.

[3] This is not Ralph Waldo Emerson, but an able contemporary of his, who entered the ministry a little earlier than his more famous namesake.

[4] The author of these works was well known to be Dr. Thouvenel, although on the title page of both is only put "par M. T\*\*\*D. M. M." Both these *Mémoires* are in the British Museum Library (where I have read them), but they are difficult to find in the catalogue.

though his work is to some extent vitiated by the erroneous theory which pervades it, still it is fair and scientific in tone, and animated by the spirit of the true philosopher, who, as Laplace has well said, "should not deny any phenomena merely because in the actual state of our knowledge they are inexplicable." The best summary of Thouvenel's treatise will be found in the *Monthly Review* for 1781 *et seq.*, appendix to Vols. 65, 67, and 71; a briefer account is given by Dr. Ashburner in his English edition of *Reichenbach's Researches*, p. 96 *et* seq., and by Mr. Bates in *Notes and Queries*, 1854, p. 449, and by Baring-Gould and Chevreul.

Some of Thouvenel's experiments with Bleton I will quote later on. The interesting point in the case of Bleton is that, like some "diviners" of the present day, he cared little for the rod, which in his case was merely a bit of stick lying horizontally upon the fore-fingers of the two hands, and served simply as a visible *index* of an internal "commotion," the access of which he could neither account for nor control. In addition to some 600 experiments with Bleton, Thouvenel sent circulars to all he could find who had employed the lad to discover water, etc., and obtained a multitude of testimonies of his success—often when all other means had failed—from learned and critical persons as well as others. Two *savants*, M. Jadelot, Professor of Medicine at Nancy, and M. Sigaud de Lafond, then took up the matter, and after numerous experiments joined Thouvenel in ardent support of Bleton's mysterious powers.

Thouvenel, having moved his residence to Italy, invited several distinguished *savants* of that country to test his new *sourcier* Pennet, whom he brought with him. Amongst those that responded was Spallanzani, who, whilst astonished at what he saw, did not consider the experiments conclusive, and finally decided against the reality of the indications of the rod, as a new form of "hydroscope." In the *Mémoires* by Fortis, 1802, quoted by Chevreul, the discussion is continued, and several other "sensitives" are named by the author who could find underground water by the peculiar sensations they experienced.

Few more instructive instances of the effect of prejudice on scientific judgment could be found than in this famous discussion a century ago. Thus the astronomer Lalande, in a letter to the *Journal des Savants*, for August, 1782, denies Bleton's power, and asserts that the baguette turns merely by the adroitness with which Bleton handles it. He then proceeds to demonstrate the roguery of Bleton by showing that an almost imperceptible muscular effort can cause a curved twig (such as Bleton generally used) to rotate when resting on the fingers. Other scientific men took the same line, and when a mannikin was made which, by mechanism, could turn the baguette like Bleton did, the proof appeared complete; after this believers like Thouvenel could only be fools or knaves! Others again demonstrated Thouvenel's electrical theory of the rotation of the baguette to be baseless, and hence concluded that the facts themselves had no foundation. All these *savants*, starting with the *a priori* conclusion that the alleged facts were impossible, did not consider it necessary to examine the evidence as to the facts, and, moreover, they appeared to forget that Bleton often used no baguette at all, and always regarded it merely as a visible index to some internal spasm that seized him in the vicinity of underground springs.[1] This strange physiological effect, of the genuineness of which Dr. Thouvenel satisfied himself, was still more marked ten years earlier in the case of Parangue, a little girl who from infancy was thrown into convulsions when brought over running water or underground springs; hence she was constantly used as a "hydroscope," the Abbés Sauri and de la Roquette testifying to the facts and giving minute descriptions of the effects produced on the child.

In Fortis' *Mémoires pour servir a l'histoire naturelle, etc.*, several Italian hydroscopes or dowsers are referred to, one a child, 10 years old, named Anfossi; another more notable was Campetti, who was taken to Munich, in 1806, to have his water-finding powers tested. Amoretti, who relates the facts in an essay on Rhabdomancy, states that several of his own relatives had the gift of using the rod and finding water by its means.

The next conspicuous French work on this subject is by the Count de Tristan, entitled *Recherches sur quelques effleuves terrestres*, Paris, 1826. Count Tristan states that he was led to undertake the investigation of the divining rod by

---

[1] In spite of the weight of scientific authority arrayed against Bleton, a few savants carefully tested the youth, and had the courage to publish a statement of the successful results they obtained. I will refer to this when dealing with the evidence on behalf of Bleton later on; there can be no doubt that he was one of the most remarkable "dowsers" of whom we have any record.

witnessing the remarkable performance of the rod in the hands of a personal friend. Upon experimenting with different people he found, in spite of his incredulity, five others had the same faculty, and to his astonishment discovered that he himself possessed it. For some years he had no leisure to investigate the matter, but ultimately in 1822 he commenced a long series of experiments, from 1,500 to 1,800 in number, and which occupied him nearly 15 months; "The results," M. Tristan states, "of 1,200 experiments were written down at the time of their performance." Dr. Mayo, F.R.S., in his *Truths Contained in Popular Superstitions*, p. 7 *et seq.*, gives a summary of Tristan's work, and so does Chevreul. I have not myself seen Tristan's book, but there is no doubt he was an enthusiastic believer in the rod. Unfortunately his experiments are of little value, except as illustrations of the effect of sub-conscious suggestion on the rod, an effect due to the dominance of a theory which he endeavoured to establish. This theory was that electric effluvia were given off by various substances; the bodies of certain persons conducted this effluvia, which thereby passing down their arms caused a turning of the forked divining rod—this he names the *furcelle* (from *furcilla*),—or a rotation of the straight rod, which he calls the *bacillogire* (from *bacillum* and *gyrus*). It is a pity so much industry was wasted from the want of an elementary knowledge of physics.

In 1849 a M. Mortillet published a little book called *Histoire de l'hydroscopie et de la baguette divinatoire*, in which he reviews the experiments of Thouvenel and others, and claims that he himself was an expert with the baguette. He became, in fact, a professional "dowser," but owns that he was not always successful, and ultimately abandoned this calling, studied art, and was appointed sub-director of the museum at St. Germain

In 1863 was published a quarto volume written by the Abbé Carrié, called *Hydroscopographie et Metalloscopographie, ou l'art de découvrir les eaux souterraines et les gisements metalliferes*. This is an ambitious attempt to convert the divining rod into a scientific instrument and to explain its motion by an application of Ampere's well-known laws of electro-dynamics. The Abbé was himself an expert water-finder or *hydroscopist*, and the introduction to his book contains abundant testimonies to his success in finding water springs; but his explanation of the motion of the rod is hopelessly wrong, as was the very similar attempt to explain it given by Dr. Thouvenel a century ago; electricity is still believed to be the cause of the motion of the rod by the majority of dowsers and others ignorant of physics at the present day. The Abbé Paramelle was another famous *Hydroscopist* in 1830, and so was the Abbé Jacquet a little later (see Carrie's book, and the *Journal d'Agriculture Pratique* for April, 1845); but both Paramelle and Jacquet claimed to be and were *hydro-geologists* and rejected the use of the rod; a 4th and revised edition of Paramelle's *L' Art de découvrir les Sources* was issued in 1896 (see Appendix B).

Several French encyclopaedias refer fully to this subject. Under the heading *Baguette*, is a lengthy article in Larousse's *Dictionnaire Universel du XIXe siecle*. Under the same heading in the *Dictionnaire des Merveilles de la Nature* the writer gives some illustrations of the successful use of the rod he himself had observed, and states that two persons who tried could not stop the rod when it turned. Under the word *Abaris* there is an article, chiefly on J. Aymar and the rod, in Bayle's *Dictionnaire;* but this is not modern, for the first edition of this dictionary goes back to 1710. All these are useful historical essays, but throw no fresh light on the subject. There are also various essays on the divining rod in French periodical literature. I have read many of these going back to 1740, when an excellent, though brief, discussion of the subject, with some striking evidence, appeared in a little work called *Caprices de l'Imagination*.

Modern German, Spanish and Italian literature I have not yet been able to examine.

# Part III

## THE DIVINING ROD AS USED IN THE SEARCH FOR UNDERGROUND WATER

Let us now examine what evidence exists on behalf of *dowsing; i.e.,* of a special faculty, peculiar to certain individuals, by which they believe they are enabled to locate the position of mineral lodes or underground springs. Though the search for metallic veins by dowsing is the older, yet the dowser is now mainly in request as a "waterfinder," and as the evidence now obtainable is much more abundant for this latter use of the rod, I will take this part of my subject first, and, so far as possible, subsequently deal with the use of the rod in finding metallic ores.

An attempt to arrive at some *general laws* which will furnish an adequate explanation of the varied phenomena presented by the divining rod both in ancient and modern times, will be made after the first and larger portion of the evidence has been presented. Meanwhile it will be obvious from the evidence cited in Group I that—

> The movement of the rod is not due to trickery, nor any conscious voluntary effort, but is a more or less violent automatic action that occurs under certain conditions in certain individuals.

Those who have ever seen a successful dowser at work will not need to be convinced of this statement. So vigorous is the motion of the twig that one of its limbs is frequently twisted off in the effort to restrain it, and yet there is often little or no sign of muscular exertion on the dowser's part. Sometimes a violent tremor convulses the arms and even the whole body of the dowser when he comes over an underground spring, or what he believes to be such. A striking instance of this is to be seen in the case of Mr. Lawrence, cited in Group III., and also in the case of Mr. Young, senr., mentioned later. The cause of this muscular storm, and the physiological aspect of dowsing in general, are worthy of attention, but are matters with which the trained physiologist must deal. In no case is the dowser conscious of having exerted any muscular action in turning the rod, and thereupon naturally ascribes its motion to some influence external to himself. It is, in fact, almost impossible to imitate its characteristic movement by any voluntary effort. Hence nothing but sheer ignorance leads any one to assert, as does an English geologist in a letter now before me, that "the whole thing is a fraud, and the motion of the forked twig a bit of clever legerdemain."[1] Nor is any evidence, however conclusive it may appear to others, likely to affect those who approach the study of a novel subject with such a determined parti-pris. [bias - Ed]

---

[1] There are, no doubt, counterfeit dowsers, as there are counterfeit sovereigns, but it is needless to waste any time over them.

## *Prof. W. F. Barrett*

# Group I — Amateur Dowsers

The first group of evidence I will cite is obtained from those who cannot be suspected of making use of the "rod" for the purpose of gain or trickery. This evidence also shows that success has attended the practical use of the rod in finding water springs, but in several of the cases given below, data are wanting to show how far the success in these cases exceeds that due to chance.

To arrive at some estimate whether underground water might or might not be found by chance sinking at any spot in the places named, I consulted a high geological authority,—my colleague, Professor Cole, F.G.S., etc.—who kindly went into this question for several of these localities, chosen at random; as far as his personal knowledge and the geological maps would allow. Professor Cole sent me his report before seeing any of the letters here given, so that it was an entirely independent opinion, based on geological grounds. In some of the cases, Professor Cole reports that spring water might be found anywhere and near the surface:[1] in some, only by sinking to a considerable depth; but in others, Professor Cole reports the chances of finding a spring (not surface water) were extremely small unless a very deep well was sunk. As I do not rely on this group of cases for any *conclusive* evidence as to the existence, or not, of a dowsing faculty, it is hardly necessary to discuss the question of chance success farther at this point.

It is worthy of note that, in many of these cases, wells *had* been sunk fruitlessly before the advent of the "dowser," who was in every case an amateur, that is one who had no professional object to serve in making the experiment. It will also be noticed that a "dowsing faculty," if such there be, is not confined to any particular age, sex or class in life. Thus in case No. 1, the dowser was a clergyman; in No. 2, a judge; in No. 3, a local manufacturer; in Nos. 4, 13, 14, 18, and 19, a lady; in Nos. 5 and 9, a gardener; in No. 6, a deputy lieutenant; in No. 8, a respected member of the Society of Friends; in No. 12, a miller; in No. 10, a little girl; in Nos. 11 and 15, a boy; in No. 20, a French Count, etc.

No. 1.—The following case was sent by Miss Grantham:—

100, Eaton-square, London, S.W., *February 1st,* 1893.

> My father (Judge Grantham) was going to dig a well on one of his farms. The Rev. J. Blunt was then residing in our parish, and as he had previously told us he was able to discover the presence of water underground by means of a twig, we asked him to go with us one day to see if he could find water. Mr. B. began by cutting a twig out of the hedge, of hazel or blackthorn, V shaped, each side about 8 inches long, then taking hold of one end in each hand between the thumb and first finger, and pointing the angle to the ground, he walked about the field in which my father proposed digging a well, and at two spots the point of the twig turned right up exactly reversing its previous position; in fact so strong was its impulse to point upwards, that we found that unless Mr. B. relaxed his hold the twig broke off near his fingers. We put small sticks in these spots, and then took a boy about 12 years old who was in Mr. B.'s employment, and who had since quite a child shown that he possessed this power, over the same ground; he had not seen the spots at which Mr. B.'s twig found water, neither did we point them out to him, but at these places his twig behaved in the same way as Mr. B.'s. My father, mother, and four or five others then cut similar twigs out of the hedge, but with none of us would they divine water. My father then took Mr. B. over some ground where he knew of the existence of an underground stream; he did not tell Mr. B. this, but directly Mr. B. passed over the places the twig again turned upwards as it had done before. A well has since been dug at one of the spots in the first field where the twig indicated water, and it was found at the depth of 15 feet. Mr. B. and the boy both said that they did not feel any abnormal influence whatever when the twig divined water.
>
> Emma L Grantham

---

[1] Such, for example, as No. 10, though even here it will be seen that the Vicar of Lugwardine states that two wells were sunk *before* the dowser's visit, and *no water found.*

# The Credibility Of Dowsing

The following I subsequently received from the Rev. Jno. R. Blunt, of Bugbrooke, Weedon, Northamptonshire:—

*July 8th*, 1893.

> In answer to your inquiries, I fear I cannot add to what has already been told you. I have often tried the divining rod, to interest or amuse my friends, here the matter has ended; no trial for water has ever been made, except in the case at Barcombe (Sussex), when Sir W. Grantham sunk a well at the spot indicated by the rod, and found a good supply of water near the surface; this was of interest to me, as wells there are often sunk at great depth. I have found the rod move in scores of places, but have not seen it tested before. I mean, so far as my own experiments go. I know of several places where water has been found in this county after the rod has been used by Mr. Mullins.
>
> As to whether it moves, as you consider, owing to "some unconscious muscular action," I know not. Why it should move in my hands and not in the hands of every one who tries it, I know not.
>
> I have never tried it near to any pool or river, nor by the sea. I have only tried it for underground water.
>
> I was using the rod one evening for the amusement of some young men, in a garden last summer, but could not get it to move (to their great glee !), until at last close to the boundary wall it was agitated; of course they declared I moved it, etc., etc., but a few days after I was at a friend's house whose garden was on the other side of the wall, and there, to my delight, was a well! I stopped short and said, "Is this well of any use?" My friend at once said, "It is a splendid well of water and never fails." ... I have found the rod work equally well when wearing thick overshoes of rubber.

No. 2. —His Honour Judge Spink, of British Columbia, writes as follows to Mr. F. W. H. Myers:—

Vernon, Okanagan, B.C., *February 27th*, 1893.

> I see that your Society take some interest in the divining rod. We made some careful tests on this matter last year. The rod works in my hands. I was rather sceptical, and thought that my own mind might work in some unknown manner on the rod and cause it to turn down where I fancied there ought to be water. I was blindfolded and led about with the wand, for about an hour at least, until I could not hold the wand upright without great pain. Each time the wand dipped, a peg was driven into the ground to mark the spot. I was walked in all directions, and passed over the same ground again and again, but in no instance did the rod fail to dip when it came to a peg. I have sunk two wells on the credit of the wand, and in both instances have found water, in both these instances contrary to the advice of the well-sinking experts. The power appears to increase rapidly with use. When experimenting with the rod over a water hose, I had the water turned on and off several times, and could distinctly feel the jar that one hears in such cases.
>
> Wm. Ward Spink

In a subsequent letter Judge Spink writes:—

Vernon, Okanagan, B.C., *November 4th*, 1893.

> The divining rod has succeeded in finding me water for the third time. First well, at the foot of a rock bluff, 20 feet. Second well, half way down a steep slope, about 8 feet fall in 40 feet, at 25 feet from surface. Third well, at the summit of slope, 100 feet at least above second well, at 85 feet from surface. Those experiments are not very convincing, as water seems to be easily found round here. One peculiar fact, however, may interest you. I selected the three spots for the wells before the foundations were dug for my house. Around the foundations the wand would not act. After the wells

were begun, and the foundations dry, Mr. Attwood, who has had a great mining experience, went over the ground with me. He told me that the formation of the ground would lead him to expect water where the wells were being dug, but that it would be useless to dig for water where the foundations were, as the ground there was drift. The foundations are 100 feet from well No. 2, and immediately, or only a few feet from being immediately between wells 2 and 3.

No. 3.—The following is from the *Westminster Gazette,* of May 5th, 1894:—

A remarkable instance of the successful use of the hazel twig, generally termed the "divining rod," has just occurred at Cressing, near Braintree, Essex. Many fruitless attempts have been made in the parish to find water, the boring in several instances extending to great depths. Mr. E. Sach, of Jeffrey's farm, wanted a well provided for some cottages, they being without a water supply, and he invited Mr. H. W. Golding, of the firm of Messrs. Ashley, Adkins and Co., mat manufacturers, Booking, who has acquired some skill with the "rod," to look over the place. He did so, and near the cottages the twig turned up, and although every effort was made to keep it down it could not be done. Mr. Golding felt certain that water could be found there, and men were at once set to work boring, with the result that an abundant supply of water was found 22 feet below the surface.

In replies to my enquiries, Mr. Golding writes:—

Docking, Essex, *September 16th,* 1896.

I can fully confirm the Westminster Gazette report you sent me, in reference to finding water at Cressing by the divining rod. I may add that until this experiment was made, and the well sunk, it was the general opinion of those who knew the locality, that no water was obtainable.

H. W. Golding.

In a later letter Mr. Golding says:—

*September 21st.*

In answer to your questions, I had tested the rod with my eyes blindfolded, and also with my arms held by four men, two holding each hand and arms, leaving only freedom for the rod to move. Being thus held as tightly as possible, the rod would still go round, and if prevented it would break with the force.

H. W. Golding

Mr. Golding has also sent me particulars of several other cases, where he has been enabled to give his neighbours an abundant supply of water for which they had previously searched in vain. I will only cite one case of special interest.

No. 3a.—The following is from the *Daily News* of May 22nd, 1894:—

The divining rod has again been used in Essex with success, this time on the estate of General Thompson of Wethersfield-place near Braintree. Some years ago General Thompson had a field surveyed by an eminent engineer who, after testing the ground with boring apparatus, expressed an opinion that no water was obtainable there. Hearing, however, of the success of the divining rod in the immediate neighbourhood, the General invited Mr. H. W. Golding, of Booking, to walk over the field, with the result that at two places which Mr. Golding marked water was found at less than 10 feet from the surface.

## *The Credibility Of Dowsing*

The *Daily Telegraph* of the same date, the *Essex Herald,* and other newspapers also report this case. I wrote to General Thompson for particulars, but learnt with regret that he had died since the above experiments were made. His widow informs me that the newspaper report is correct and that "Mr. Golding, who was quite an amateur, indicated by the rod two places where springs of water would be found on the estate, and on digging at these places water was found." I have had an interview with Mr. J. Wycliffe Thompson (son of General Thompson,) who was present during the search for water at Wethersfield-place, and who gives me the interesting information that his father made the experiment *on purpose to test* in a systematic manner the value or otherwise of the indications afforded by the divining rod. Accordingly, in the first instance a boring was made to find water by advice without the use of the rod. Mr. Thompson tells me the boring was made to a considerable depth, but he does not know the exact depth. No signs of water were found. Then Mr. Golding was invited over, and, cutting a forked twig, traversed the ground. Presently the twig turned vigorously and, following its indications, he professed to trace an underground spring running not far from the experimental boring to a point some 50 yards away. The course indicated was staked out, and, after Mr. Golding left, a well was sunk in two places, chosen at random *on the course so marked*. The result was that water was found in both places at a depth of some 10 feet. Mr. Thompson is certain the first boring was "far deeper than this," and he tells me no doubt whatever was left in the mind of General Thompson and others present of the reality and practical value of some peculiar faculty for discovering underground water afforded by the movement of the rod.

No. 4.—In the next case, which reaches me through Mr. Myers, a lady, Miss Douglas P., found to her surprise the rod moved in as marked a manner in her hands as when it was used by a professional diviner. A series of experiments were made at a country house, both out of doors and indoors. Amongst those who witnessed the experiments indoors were Mr. Scott Gatty and Miss Egerton. The former writes:—

71, Warwick road, Earl's Court, S.W., *March 7th,* 1893.

> The great difficulty we found was to find a place where the rod would not work; it was forever turning round. At last two places were found, one in front of the fireplace in the entrance hall, and another about halfway up the stairs. While Miss D. P. went off with the rest of the party down some of the passages leading out of the hall, I secreted some sovereigns under the rug in front of the fireplace, and then joined the rest of the party. By degrees we worked our way back into the hall, and I asked Miss P. to test the hearth again, so as to make sure that the rod would not work there, when—lo and behold—it went round vigorously, and I then disclosed my hidden treasure. When that was removed, the rod refused to work again.
>
> I think there was nothing else very remarkable or worthy of note. The cause of the rod working so much in the house is that almost a river runs under it. ... In the drawing-room we hid money in the seats of chairs, and made Miss P. sit upon them, but if I remember rightly, she was not always successful.
>
> Scott Gatty.

The foregoing letter was sent to Miss Egerton, who replies:—

Whitwell Park, York, *March 12th,* 1893.

> Unfortunately the descriptions of the experiments made in the evening do not coincide with my impression of the same, which is that they were uniformly successful. I being one of the sceptical ones in the party (or shall we rather use the word agnostic ?) held one side of the forked stick, whilst Miss D. P. held the other, and as we moved over the chairs where the sovereigns were hidden, the effect was most marked, the motion coming evidently from the stick and not from Miss D. P.'s pressure. I tried to stop it, and it at once broke off at the fork. As Mr. Scott Gatty says, we were not thinking at the time of making any scientific investigations; we only wished to prove the fact that the

action of the stick was not a fraud on the part of Miss D. P. In this we were perfectly successful—it invariably turned over the chairs where the sovereigns were hidden, and she most certainly did not know where they were.

Mary L. Egerton.

In this case the involuntary movement of the rod over the hidden coins was possibly due to unconscious indications given by Mr. Scott Gatty, or others present, who knew where the coins had been hidden.[1]

No. 5.—I am indebted to Colonel Waring, D.L., (M.P. for North Down) for the following. Colonel Waring's trial of the professional diviner Mullins is given on a subsequent page.

Waringstown, co. Down, July 11th, 1893.

I have sunk a well 50 ft. deep on a spot indicated by my own gardener, who turned out to be possessed of the power of working the rod, and found water, though it did not come at once; in fact the well was abandoned as a failure and covered over with an old slipa, (i.e., a rough Irish sledge), and some months afterwards was discovered to be full within a few feet of the surface.

Thos. Waring.

In answer to enquiries as to the exact site, etc., Colonel Waring writes:—

Waringstown, September 21st, 1896.

My gardener tried his hand at a farm I have on the shore of Lough Neagh called Armadroughall (the only point at which the County Down touches the lake). We sunk a couple of years ago where he fixed and at 50 feet had got no water and gave up, harvest operations taking us off. We covered the well, thought no more of it till about Christmas when we found it nearly full and it has had a constant supply ever since.

It is impossible to disbelieve the fact that at certain places and under certain circumstances the hazel fork turns vigorously.

I tried our gardener with finding gold one day and he quite failed to detect a sovereign hid in the gravel of the walk, but a friend who was by said " My spectacles are pure gold, let us see what they will do," and he held them under the rod, which at once twisted violently. The gardener is entirely incapable of deception and I am unable to form any theory on the subject. If the operator is placed on a platform isolated by glass, say four inverted tumblers, he is powerless.[2]

Thos Waring

No. 6.—Through the kindness of one of our members, the Hon. Kathleen Ward, Colonel Aldworth, D.L., writes to me as follows:—

Newmarket, Co. Cork, June 19th, 1896.

It is quite true that I have the power of using the divining rod. I have done so for some years, but have not as yet opened any well; but as I want to conduct water into my garden, I hope to be able to do so in a few months' time from a source a couple of fields beyond it. I can hardly quote any facts to you at present that would be interesting, more than to say I found a source of water in a friend's grounds not many miles from this. He afterwards employed a man who is a professional water finder,

---

[1] Assuming thought-transference as a vera causa, the important part it probably plays in this class of experiment will be discussed later on.

[2] I shall return to this idea later. See also foot-note to No. 21.

## The Credibility Of Dowsing

and he found the water in the same place, and gave the depth below the surface as 26 feet, which I was not able to do, not having practised gauging the depth below the surface, but I understand this is merely a matter of practice, and depends on the force with which the rod rises in the hands.

R. W. Aldworth.

In reply to my enquiries, Colonel Aldworth writes:—

Newmarket, Co. Cork, *July 20th,* 1896.

In reply to your letter of June 21st, I beg to say I have tried the divining rod both with my eyes shut and open and it acts just the same in both cases. I know of a young fellow who possesses the power and who had a farm but a few miles from this. He was anxious to find water on his ground and he, by means of the rod, came upon water, digged for it and found it about 7 feet down, a fine spring. I have often tried the rod with my eyes shut, and the young man got his sister to bind his eyes in the case I mention and the rod indicated it in the same spot where he dug for it. I cannot in any way account for action of the rod; it certainly acts with some people and not with others.

R. W. Aldworth

Numerous cases from Somersetshire are given in the course of this paper; here are two or three. The following is an instructive case.

No. 7.—My friend Mr. F. J. Clark, F.L.S., writes to me as follows:—

Netherleigh, Street, Somerset, *September,* 1896.

Some twenty years ago an opportunity presented itself to me of testing the value of the indications given by the divining rod. The then manager of our local gas works, Mr. Stears, found he had the power of using the rod[1]; others in our neighbourhood also tried, and an old workman I knew well, Simon Seymour by name, was equally successful. I got Mr. Stears to go over my ground, and the rod indicated water at the spot A on the rough plan (Fig. 1).

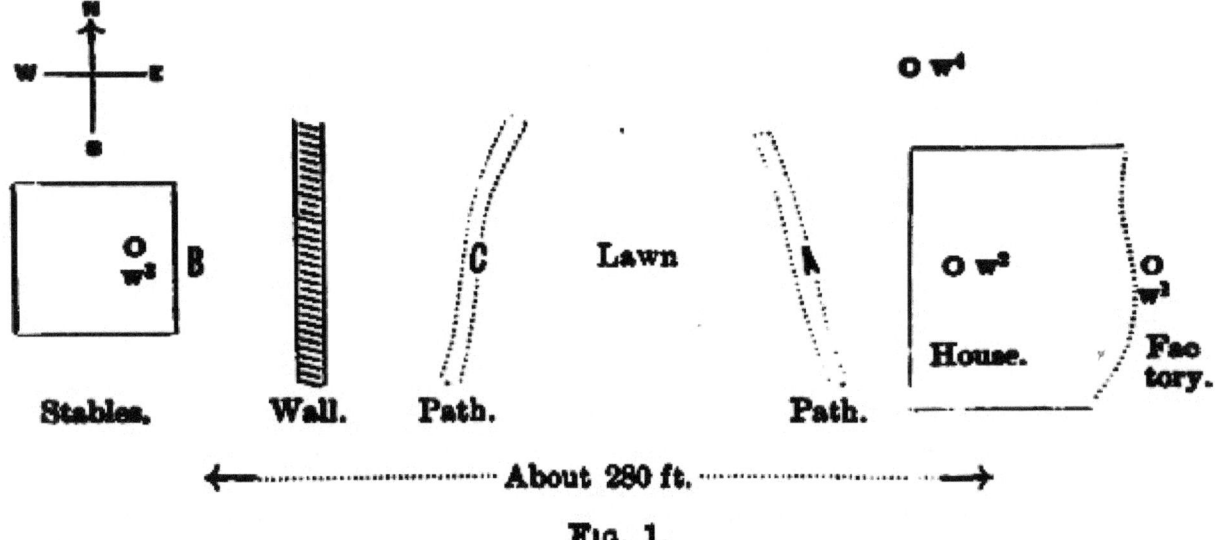

Fig. 1.

---

[1] Mr. Stears is now living in Yorkshire, and has recently devoted himself entirely to "dowsing" (see Group VII.).—W.F.B.

Some little time after I tried Seymour, who knew nothing of Mr. Stears' experiment. Seymour found the rod indicated water at B. Curiously enough a neighbour and member of our body (Society of Friends), Walter Wyburn, a poor-law guardian, found he also could use the rod. I invited Wyburn to my place, and asked him to try where he could find water. He did so, and the rod indicated water at C; he had no knowledge of what the others had done. Now it happens that a well had been sunk for our factory at $W^1$, and a good supply of water obtained at about 40 feet depth. Another well, in the cellar of my house, at $W^2$, gave us a supply of water at about 35 feet, and a third well at $W^3$, on higher ground, and about 280 feet distance, supplied the stable yard; this well was only about 27 feet deep. We had also since sunk a well at $W^4$, some 60 feet North of $W^2$, but had got little or no water from it even at a depth of 50 feet. We tunnelled about 20 feet in the direction of $W^2$, and found rather more water coming in. It seems, therefore, that a fault or fissure running East and West existed in the strata of the Blue Lias, and along this fissure water could be obtained. This conclusion is rendered very probable from the fact that, if we pump a large supply of water from the factory well, $W^1$, it completely drains $W^2$, and perceptibly affects $W^3$. Now it was just when the three dowsers crossed this line the rods indicated water beneath. Their trials, as I have said, were made independently, and they had no knowledge of the position, or (so far as I know) the existence of the wells on my place. I may also mention that the late rector of the parish found he too was an expert with the "rod," and on trying my grounds with it he also hit upon the same line of underground water, but I am not sure whether he knew of the other trials I have related.

F. J. Clark.

No. 8.—Mr. F. J. Clark also writes to me as follows:—

Netherleigh, Street, Somerset, *September,* 1896.

A few years ago I was appointed along with Walter Wyburn and the late A. R. Grace, of Bristol, a sub-committee of a Charitable Trust Committee belonging to our religious body [the Society of Friends]. One object of this committee was to get water for a farmhouse belonging to the Trust at Chelbro', in Dorset, about 25 miles south-west of Yeovil. We spent several days in a fruitless search for water, or for any likely place to sink a well. However, we made an attempt in the most probable spot, according to our local geological knowledge, and sunk a well 20 feet. Alas! no water was reached. At length Walter Wyburn suggested trying the divining rod, as he found to his surprise he could use it with some success. We agreed; he had cut a forked twig and tried over all the ground. After a good deal of perambulation the rod indicated a strong spring in a neighbouring wood. Accordingly we had a well dug at this spot, and to our delight found a capital spring; pipes were put down, and a constant supply for the house has been given ever since.

Francis J. Clark.

No. 9.—Another case [from Somersetshire] is given in the *Western Gazette* of February 10th, 1893. Evercreech is at the foot of the Mendips.

A well has recently been sunk on the premises of Messrs. W. Roles and Son, of Evercreech Junction, on the site of the proposed milk factory. Mr. Henry Smart, head gardener at Pennard House, was successful with the divining twig (or rod), and a well was sunk to a depth of 60 feet, when a spring was found which yielded no less than 15,000 gallons of water in ten hours. Water came at such a rate that a powerful pump had to be erected temporarily by Messrs. Hill and Son, of Bruton, and was kept working day and night in order to keep the water down for the purpose of walling [the well]. At the present time there is 50 feet of water in the well, the supply increasing daily.

## *The Credibility Of Dowsing*

I wrote to Messrs. Holes to know if a well had been sunk previously, and if the above statement was correct. They reply that the account is quite correct, and add, "We had previously sunk a well without the use of the rod, to nearly the same depth, but it was *unsuccessful*. Six yards from this useless well the diviner found the spring which now yields enough to supply a small village if required."

No. 10.—The next case, that of Miss Wood, is quoted from a letter addressed to the *Abingdon Herald* by our fellow-worker, Mr. Vaughan Jenkins:—

> Some time ago there appeared in a contemporary a short paragraph, which only recently came under my notice, giving the information that "Miss Wood, a daughter of Mr. George Wood, of the Vallets, and agent for the Whitfield estates, near Hereford, had again been successful in finding water at Lugwardine by means of the (so-called) divining rod." Being desirous of obtaining full and authentic particulars of this young lady's experimental operations, I addressed several specific enquiries, with special reference as to how and when Miss Wood discovered that she possessed the dowsing, or "so-called divining" faculty, to her father, who very kindly sent me the following interesting details:—
>
> Whitfield Estate Office, *February 4th*, 1890.
>
> "In reply to your letter of the 15th ult., I beg to say that in January last (1889) Mrs. Greathed of Whitfield, who is sister of the late owner of the estate — C. M. B. Clive, Esq., — wrote to Mullins, the well-known waterfinder by the use of the divining rod, asking him to come to Whitfield for the purpose of making some trials there. Mrs. Greathed requested me to conduct Mullins to various elevated places on the estate, which I did in company with several persons, including Mrs. Greathed herself, Mr. Percy Clive, the future owner of the estate, etc. I took Mullins to several places where I knew there was water running through the earth, but not the slightest trace of it on the surface. I did not tell him that I knew there was water anywhere. I merely took him to the gates of the different fields and asked him to try in each case. He quickly spotted each place to a great nicety, without the slightest hesitation.
>
> "The next thing was for each of the company to try with the rod, but not one of us had the 'faculty' excepting my little daughter May. Subsequently the rod indicated water in several places, both in the hands of May and Mullins — May finding it first sometimes and at other times Mullins.
>
> "I suggested that we should not make a trial by sinking wells until the autumn, when springs here are generally very low. Well, we made a trial in November last at a spot where Mullins said the water would possibly be found at a depth of 40 or 50 feet. We came on water at 40 feet. I may mention that previous to sinking this well the rod in my daughter's hand indicated the presence of an underground spring there. May is now thirteen years of age. She has proved successful in numerous cases; four wells have been sunk where she said there was water, and each one was a success, viz., one at Ledbury, one at Lugwardine, and two at Whitfield. Hitherto, all her predictions have proved invariably true. Two wells had been unsuccessfully sunk at Lugwardine previous to my daughter's visit there, the deepest of which was 16 feet. The place where May indicated water is distant 42 feet from this abandoned well, and at 11 feet deep a superabundance of water was found, and pipes are now laid to convey the water to the Vicarage, which is, I believe, several hundred yards away. As regards her modus operandi, she holds the forked hazel twig downwards when in search of water, and when she comes on a spring the twig quivers and rises upwards, sometimes from her body and sometimes towards it, until it comes to a perpendicular position. She practises the rod as you suppose, viz., as an amateur only, being only too happy to use her powers for the benefit of friends and neighbours."
>
> G. Wood

In confirmation of the foregoing statements, the following letters may be quoted: The Rev. Francis Curtis, rector of Coddington, near Ledbury, writes: — "The spring has been found at the Stonehouse 57ft. below the surface, exactly at the spot indicated by Miss Wood. She said she thought the depth would be as much as 50ft. So the event proves her judgment to have been very correct. We are very glad that we availed ourselves of her gifts." The Rev. A. C. Lee, of Lugwardine Vicarage, Hereford, writes: "The well sinker came to me an hour ago with the welcome intelligence that he had come upon a strong spring of water, at the depth of 11ft., on the spot Miss Wood ' found' on Monday, and which, you will remember, I marked with two sticks, and which was thought to have the strongest indications. Previous to Miss Wood's visit two wells had been sunk, but no water found." In my letter of thanks to Mr. Wood I expressed a wish to be informed of the results of any future experiments that his daughter may make, and on the 23rd February, 1890, I received from him the following communication: —"I have had occasion to sink a well for the use of four cottages and a public-house. I took my daughter, May, to the place, and she spotted a place where she said there was water. I had it tried, and we found water at 6ft. deep. I instructed the men to sink 6ft. further down, for the purpose of holding a supply, and the water rose 6ft. deep in the well in one night."

I wrote to Mr. Wood, sending him the above report and asking him to correct any inaccuracies, and also enquiring whether his daughter had had any further experiences with the "rod." In reply he writes:—

Whitfield Estate Office, Hereford, *May 9th*, 1896.

The report enclosed is quite accurate. My daughter May has been requested to go to very many places to find water since the report you send was written, and has always been successful. I have often been glad of her services myself.

G. Wood.

In answer to my enquiries, Mr. Percy Clive writes as follows:—

Tower of London, *April 24th*, 1897.

I can vouch for the accuracy of the statement made above by Mr. G. Wood, who is my estate agent at Whitfield. I saw Mullins "find" water in several places, where his findings were afterwards proved to be correct. I, as well as others, tried to find water in the same way, but had not the power. But when Mullins held my wrists, and I held the twig over running water, it turned round in my hands with such force that when I held it tight it broke. Miss May Wood has been very successful in finding water; and seems also able to make a pretty accurate guess at the depth at which it will be found.

Percy A. Clive.

No. 11.—A still more youthful diviner was found by Mr. Vaughan Jenkins in Cornwall, and is referred to in Mr. Pease's report. The case is given at length by Mr. V. Jenkins in the *Proceedings* S.P.R., Vol. II., p. 106. Since then Mr. V. Jenkins has sent me voluminous additional particulars, which I have incorporated in the following summary of the case:—

Mr. V. Jenkins having purchased some land for building purposes in Christchurch-road, Newport, Monmouth, the absence of a water supply necessitated his sinking a well. Guided by the best advice, a site was carefully chosen and a well commenced. When the well-sinkers had reached 51 feet, and no water found, it was decided from the nature of the ground, a hard, compact marl, it would be useless to proceed further. A consultation of local experts was held, and the conclusion arrived at that there was no chance of obtaining water in that neighbourhood. Thereupon the foreman of the masons (a Cornishman) suggested using the divining rod. He said it was in common and successful use for the purpose of finding water in his county, and his own son, eleven years old, had the power of using the rod in a remarkable degree. Mr. Jenkins, though at that time very incredulous, consented. The lad was sent for, and with a hazel rod he crossed and re-crossed the ground several times. At one spot the rod began to revolve, and continued to do so with such force that the lad was obliged to let it go, when the rod flew to some distance. Whereupon the father of the lad, George Lockyer, said, "I will stake my life we shall find a good spring of water under this spot. I will undertake to sink the shaft myself, and no water, no pay." Accordingly, a well was begun the next day on the spot indicated by the "rod." At the depth of 48 feet, so strong a spring was struck that the men employed had to beat a hasty retreat, the water rising to a depth of 10 feet in the well, and subsequently to 15 feet, and remains at that depth at the present time, constantly yielding an abundant supply. The lad neither asked nor expected any payment. The father stated that he himself also had the power of using the "rod" when he was a boy, but he lost it when about 16 years old.

The discovery of this water supply led to the old site for the house being abandoned, and a new site fixed on close to the abundant supply of pure spring water that was obtained. The relative position of the two wells, marked O O, is shown in the annexed plan, Fig. 2, drawn to scale..

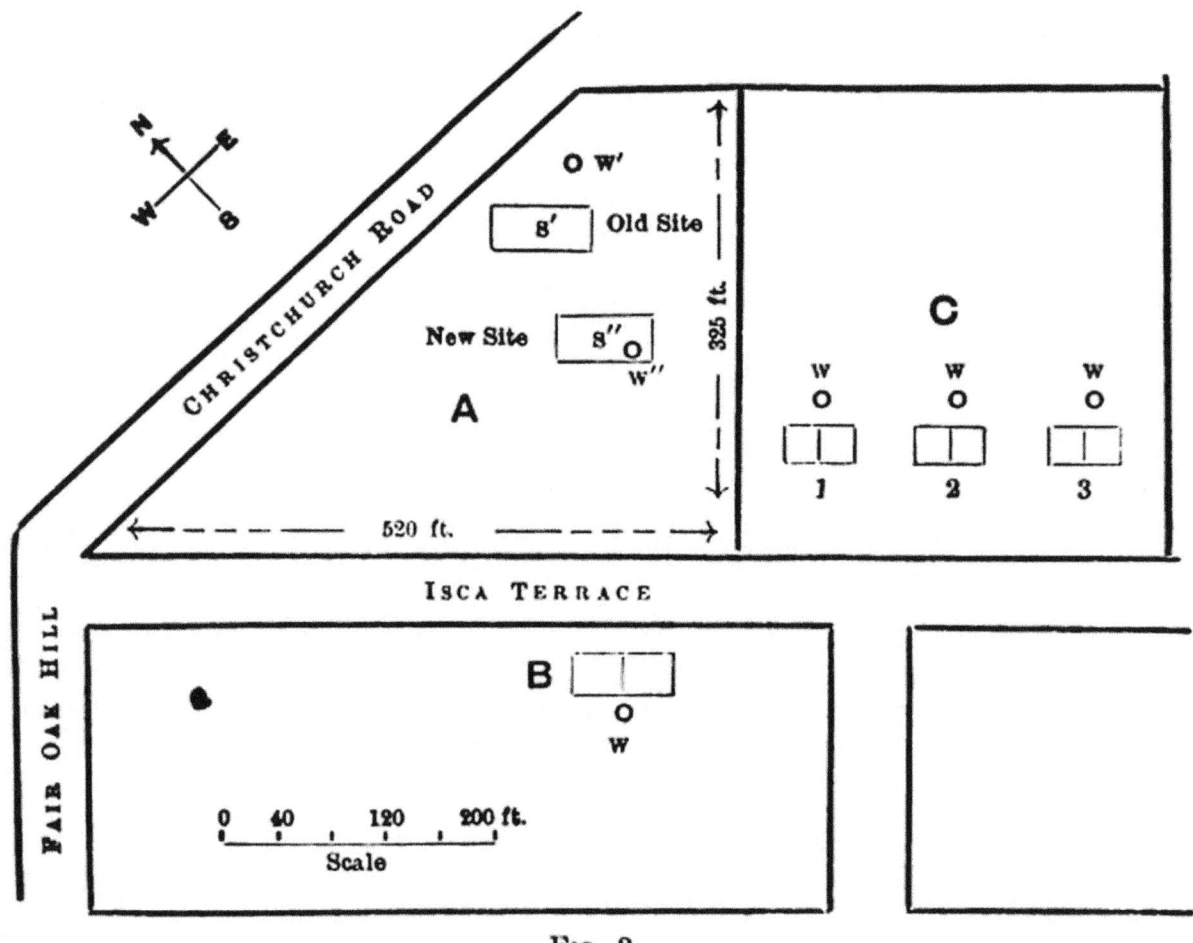

Fig. 2.

The old site is marked S', and the abandoned well shaft W, the new site is S", and the new well W" adjoins it. The plot A belongs to Mr. V. Jenkins. The owner of the adjacent plot B, which slopes somewhat steeply to the S.W., shortly after began to build two villas at B, and to sink the well W adjoining. He declined, indeed ridiculed, the use of the divining rod, and informed Mr. Jenkins that he was confident of getting water at 20 feet depth, but feared, as the land was so much lower, it would drain off the supply from Mr. V. J.'s new well.[1] Accordingly at B a shaft was sunk, but no water was met with at 25 nor even 50 feet. Eventually the well sinkers went down to 100 feet, and still no water was found. A boring was then made 25 feet deeper, and at 125 feet water was struck, but though the boring was continued still deeper, the water never rose beyond 18 to 24 inches in the well; a fair supply was, however, obtained. The water at Mr. J.'s well at S" was, and still is, entirely unaffected by the well at B. The soil at B was the same as that in the abandoned well shaft at S' in the plot A, viz., a "hard, compact marl." Three pairs of villas were subsequently erected on the plot C, and three wells sunk as shown at W, W, W. Water was obtained at 50 feet depth, but the supply "was poor, and is not sufficient to keep the wells from running dry in a very dry summer." These wells were therefore a comparative failure.[2]

The date of this experience is, I find, 1853, but full notes appear to have been kept. The plan, Fig. 2, I made from the estate drawing. It would be interesting to have a geological examination of this land, and a report on the foregoing case.

No. 12.—The Rev. Martin R. Knapp, M.A., vicar of Holy Trinity, Dalston, writes to me as follows:—

*72, Forest-road, Dalston, N.E., November 14th,* 1896.

In the summer of 1892 I entered on the vicarage of North Wootton, in North Somerset, and had reason at once to look for water. I was advised to try a "water-finder," and did so. The dowser was a retired miller, and came provided with a number of forked twigs. Holding one he traversed the place, and at certain points the twig oscillated violently in his hands, and there, he professed, he should find water.

There was an interesting side-light in the matter that I will tell you of. My builder, who came from Bath, was very sceptical about the whole thing. Three or four of us who were on the spot tried to see if the twigs would "play up" with us.

We were unsuccessful till this man tried his hand, scoffing the while. But directly that he came to the spots the dowser had found, the twig showed vigorous signs of animation. When his hand was being twisted in his efforts to keep the twig steady, I cried to him to hold fast, with the result that the twig twisted itself into two pieces.

At Wells, close by, a coachman, who was reported to have the power to find, not only water, but minerals. He carries neither rod nor twig, and told me, when I enquired, that his sensations are undoubted and extraordinary whenever he is directly above either water or minerals.

Martin R. Knapp.

---

[1] Upon getting this information, Mr. Jenkins asked the youthful "dowser" to go over the ground again and see if he could trace the direction of the underground water. This the lad did, and asserted, on the evidence of the rod, that water would be found on the West side of the new well W", but that little would be found on the South or East side of it; the North side had already been tried and abandoned. The father of the lad thereupon assured Mr. V. J. he had no cause for anxiety from the proposed well at B., which turned out to be correct.

[2] It was the success of the rod in this case, and its personal value to Mr. Vaughan Jenkins, that led him to devote much of his time for the past 40 years in collecting evidence bearing on the subject of the divining rod.

## *The Credibility Of Dowsing*

In answer to enquiries Mr. Knapp tells me the builder was a stranger to the locality, and the spots where the rod moved were unlikely to suggest water below. The twig in the builder's hand, Mr. Knapp says, in every case corroborated the dowser's indications, and hence he (the builder) was unmercifully chaffed, as he had treated the whole thing with such contempt. Mr. Knapp says it is possible that the places indicated by the dowser might have been perceived by the builder, but it was the spontaneous and vigorous movement of the twig, evidently contrary to the holder's intention and against his will, that excited their astonishment.

Unfortunately Mr. Knapp was unable to sink a well; one of the places indicated was unsuitable, and at another he began to dig, but at the time had no means of going deeper than a few feet, and afterwards moved his residence.

No. 13.—Another instance of a successful amateur diviner is the daughter of a clergyman in Buckinghamshire. Her father, the Rev. Seymour Ashwell, M.A., writes to me as follows:—

Finmere Rectory, *September 7th*, 1896.

> As regards my daughter's ability to find water, all I can say is that it has been a most useful gift. She has found springs all over the country, and wells have been dug at the spot indicated with the best results, and villages and private houses that had been badly supplied for years have now plenty. I might mention a curious feature of it is if she walks backward the stick does not move.[1] Also she can tell when she is getting near water quite twenty yards or more before she gets to the spot where the spring is. She is also equally successful in finding gold, as she proved at Lord North's, where they had buried some quartz containing gold for her to find. It would of course be much more satisfactory if you would come and see for yourself what she can do. I might mention she finds hazel the best wood to use, though some others will do, as also copper wire, but that acts best when well twisted in the middle.
>
> Seymour Ashwell.

In a subsequent letter the Rev. Seymour Ashwell writes from

Balnakilly, Blairgowrie, N.B., *September 11th*, 1896.

> I may add I this day had a letter from Worcestershire to say that two wells had been dug at spots pointed out by my daughter last July. The one is 13 feet deep and has 8 feet of water in it, the other 30 feet deep and has 17 feet in it. I should not think that the most sceptical need better proof as to the power of finding water. In what the power consists I don't pretend to explain.
>
> Seymour Ashwell.

No. 14.—In Mr. Pease's report is given an account of the successful use of the divining rod by another lady, Mrs. Bengough, of Bristol. See *Proceedings*, S.P.R., Vol. II., p. 104.

No. 15.—Having heard from the Rev. C. Bicknell, M.A., of Bordighera, Italy, of the remarkable dowsing faculty possessed by the young son of a friend of his, who was formerly rector of Uggeshall in Suffolk, I wrote for further particulars. Mr. Bicknell replies:—

Bordighera, Italy, *December 24th*, 1896.

> Oddly enough, Mr. Edgell, the father of the boy whom I mentioned, arrived here this evening. He tells me that his son (1) when at Uggeshall found the spring and well which supplied his pump; the whereabouts of which was not known to the present rector nor to the Edgells, the former occupants

---

[1] This is only the effect of a "fixed idea," as will be seen later on, and corresponds to a similar phenomena exhibited by Bleton in 1780, and by many other dowsers. In fact, in a later letter, Mr. Ashwell writes: "If my daughter holds the forked twig with the point *upwards*, and walks backwards, then the stick turns *down;* though if the point be held downwards it does not move when she walks backwards."—W.F.B.

of the rectory; and (2) that he also found water in his own garden at Teddington, the existence of which was not known to the boy or the father, but only to the old gardener, who had said, when Mr. E. told him about his boy's gift, "Well, sir, I know where there is a spring in the garden, and if he finds it I shall believe there is something in dowsing."

Mr. Hanbury (who lives near here) told me that many years ago while he was away a diviner indicated water in his garden, but, for some reason or other, they did nothing. Some years after, however, in digging, water was found on the spot that had been previously indicated.

Clarence Bicknell.

No. 16.—Sir Charles Isham, Bart., of Lamport Hall, Northampton, writes to me on

*March 19th*, 1890.

We found water at Lamport by means of the "divining rod" three years ago. My carpenter found he had slight power in doing the same; he could feel the stick move, but it was not visibly active.

Later on, Sir Charles writes:—

Lamport Hall, Northampton, *September 22nd*, 1896.

Three weeks since we discovered that my carpenter found water by the divining rod at a farmhouse we are building. He tells me he went over the ground, with his eyes shut, several times, and always came to within a yard of the place he had fixed on; accordingly a well was sunk there and a good supply of water was found.

No. 17.—This list of amateur English dowsers would be very incomplete without some notice of Messrs. Young and Robertson of Llanelly who, together with several of their children, possess remarkable dowsing powers, judging from the correspondence that is before me. Mr. Vaughan Jenkins, of Oxford, writes to me as follows:—

Among the most successful diviners are Mr. Young and Mr. Robertson, of Llanelly, South Wales, who have not only not received any fee or reward for their services, but have spent much time in the endeavour to ascertain the cause of the rod's movements. No two men could be found who would more readily co-operate with an honest and unbiassed scientific investigation of the matter.

Here the faculty seems hereditary, for Mr. Young's father was able to discover underground water, the effect on him, as on his son, creating a very unpleasant physiological disturbance. Mr. Young sends me the following illustration of his father's gift:—

My father, who is living in Dorsetshire, is now 87. Two years ago he pointed out a spot to a neighbour who was about to build two villas if water could be found. A well was sunk, and an abundant supply of beautiful water, at about 40 feet, was struck. Prior to the sinking, the owner of the land got three other local diviners to look for water in this field; the last he took blindfolded to the spot. They each and all pointed out the very spot my father did, and each one was perfectly ignorant that any one had previously tried. Now comes the curious part. The village doctor was building a villa about 80 yards away, (on the same level), and said he could find water anywhere in that locality without the rod. He tried, sank a well, (a built well,) to 50 feet, and never had a drop, and the well was closed. This was about two years ago. About three months ago the doctor decided to sink another well in a spot close by his first, where three members of my family and myself pointed out as being a likely spot. The well was sunk, and is now in daily use delivering, with a pump, a

# The Credibility Of Dowsing

plentiful supply at a less depth than the barren well a few yards away. He had been paying £12 per year for water carted for daily use.

Amid the letters which Mr. Young has written to me on this subject there are several instances of successful "dowsing" by himself and by his friend and neighbour, Mr. Robertson; nothing, however, of any particular evidential value is to be found, except possibly in two cases. In one of these, both he and Mr. Robertson independently fixed on an underground spring near the house of Mr. Meredith (son of the novelist), and subsequently a strong spring burst forth from the very spot, though no signs of it existed before. I wrote for corroboration, but Mr. Meredith had left Llanelly, and Mr. Young sends me a letter from a gentleman whose house was near, which in general terms confirms Mr. Young's statements. The other case was where Mr. Young and Mr. Robertson independently determined the position of a leak in the town reservoir and also fixed on the depth below the embankment of the culvert or out-flow from the reservoir. Neither of them knew this depth, both fixed on the same amount,—30 feet,—and subsequent inquiry proved they were exactly right. But in both these experiments other explanations than a dowsing faculty (such as unconscious indications, latent memory, or thought-transference), might account for the facts. Mr. Young tells me that by the sensations he experiences, when his mind is "set" on dowsing, he can discover an underground spring even when quickly driving in a vehicle. He adds that not only his father but all his sisters are able to use the divining rod with more or less success; the same seems to be true of Mr. Robertson's family, judging from the large family group represented as dowsing in the little book they have published.

Other cases have reached me of amateur dowsers, but what has now been made sufficiently clear is that the movement of the rod is not due to any voluntary conscious act on the part of the dowser.[1] I will therefore only add the evidence given by a few amateur dowsers of older date, as these are of some historical interest. The list might be largely extended.

No. 18.—The case of Lady Milbanke, the mother-in-law of Lady Byron, is a well-known example of an amateur diviner. In a letter to Dr. C. Hutton, F.R.S., dated February, 1805, Lady Milbanke describes how she was led to try the rod from witnessing its use by a peasant in Provence, who had successfully found water springs by means of the rod, so that the man got the appellation of *L'Homme à la Baguette*. Lady Milbanke says a large party assembled to watch the gyrations of the rod, which, in spite of the man's hands being stationary, twisted round so energetically when he stood over a spring that the rod was broken. Lady Milbanke continues:—

> After seeing him do this repeatedly, the whole party tried the baguette (a forked hazel twig) in succession, but without effect. I chanced to be the last; no sooner did I hold the twig as directed than it begun to move as with him, which startled me so much that I dropped it and felt considerably agitated. I was, however, induced to resume the experiment, and found the effect perfect. On my return to England, two years afterwards, being on a visit to a nobleman's house, Kimbolton, Huntingdonshire, and his lady lamenting that she was disappointed of building a dairy-house in a spot she particularly wished because there was no water to be found—a supply she looked on as essential—I told her I would endeavour to find a spring. I accordingly procured some hazel twigs, and in the presence of herself and husband, walked over the ground proposed till the twig turned with considerable force. A stake was immediately driven into the ground to mark the spot, which was not very distant from where they had before sunk. They then took me to another and distant building in the park, and desired me to try there. I found the baguette turn very strongly, so that it soon twisted and broke; the gentleman persisted that there was no water there, unless at a great depth, the foundation being very deep (a considerable stone-cellar), and that no water appeared when they dug for it. I replied that I knew no more than from the twig turning; that I had too little experience of its powers or certainty to answer for the truth of its indication.

---

[1] I am assuming that the dowser is not a rogue; one might no doubt by practice accomplish the twisting of the rod, with apparently no muscular effort, like any other piece of legerdemain.

He then acknowledged that when the building was erected they were obliged to drive piles for the whole foundation, as they met with nothing but a quicksand. This induced him to dig in the spot I first directed. They met with a very fluent spring. The dairy was built, and it is at this time supplied by it.[1]

No. 18a.—Dr. Hutton, F.R.S., the distinguished mathematician—to whom the Royal Society entrusted the gigantic labour of making an abridgement of the whole of the transactions of the Royal Society from its foundation in 1666 to the beginning of this century,—gives the following account of his experiments with the divining rod as used by Lady Milbanke.

At the time appointed, [11 a.m., May 30th, 1806,] the lady, with all her family, arrived at my house on Woolwich Common, where, after preparing the rods, etc., they walked to the grounds, accompanied by the individuals of my own family and some friends, when Lady Milbanke showed the experiment several times in different places, holding the rod in the manner described elsewhere. In the places where I had good reason to know that no water was to be found the rod was always quiescent, but in other places, where I knew there was water below the surface, the rods turned slowly and regularly in the manner above described, till the twigs twisted themselves off below the fingers, which were considerably indented by so forcibly holding the rod between them.[2]

All the company stood close to Lady M. with all eyes intensely fixed on her hands and the rods to watch if any particular motion might be made by the fingers, but in vain; nothing of the kind was perceived, and all the company could observe no cause or reason why the rods should move in the manner they were seen to do.

After the experiments were ended, every one of the company tried the rods in the same manner as they saw Lady M. had done, but without the least motion from any of them. And in my family, among ourselves, we have since then, several times, tried if we could possibly cause the rod to turn by means of any trick, or twisting of the fingers, held in the manner Lady M. did; but in vain, we had no power to accomplish it.

No. 19.—Dr. Mayo, F.R.S., in his book on Popular Superstitions, quotes the case of a Mrs. R., sister of Sir G. R., then living at Southampton, who, in 1806, observing the successful use of the divining rod by the wife of a Colonel Beaumont, tried it herself, and found she had the power in a remarkable degree. The rod, Dr. Mayo remarks, continued to move, even when Mrs. R.'s hands were grasped so firmly that muscular action by her wrists or fingers seemed to be prevented. V-shaped rods of iron or copper wire were as effective as a hazel rod, but no motion ever occurred when the two handles of the *rod* were covered with sealing wax. If, however, the uncoated parts were touched, the rod immediately revolved.[3]

No. 20.—The Comte de Tristan, whose book on the divining rod has already been mentioned, published in 1829 a record of his own experience with the rod, extending over 1,800 experiments, 1,200 of which were carefully noted. He mentions five or six friends of his who he found could also use the rod. Count de Tristan found the rod would only move when he passed over what he calls "exciting tracts" of ground, and that its motion was arrested when the hands were covered with thick silk. See foot-note to No. 19, also No. 5.

---

[1] See also a description by an eye-witness given in the *Quarterly Review*, Vol XXII., (1820) foot-note pp. 373-4. - W.F.B.

[2] Dr. Hutton does not say *how he* knew that water was, or was not, below the surface. He was not, however, one likely to make loose and random statements. According to a footnote in the *Quarterly Review,* Vol. XXII., p. 374. it appears that the ground chosen for the experiment was a field Dr. Hutton had bought, adjoining the new College at Woolwich then building.

[3] That "electricity has something to do" with the motion of the rod, is a widespread belief. This will be discussed later on; here I will only say that, in spite of the foregoing experiments, and others to be related, the electrical hypothesis is not one that any physicist could entertain.

# *The Credibility Of Dowsing*

## Group II — Miscellaneous Cases

The following cases of water finding by various dowsers, some amateurs and some not, illustrate the use of the divining rod in *various countries*, and also its employment at different periods during the last hundred years. The most remarkable of the foreign cases is unquestionably that of the French youth, Bleton, described by Dr. Thouvenel in 1781. This I have reserved for separate treatment in the list of special cases that are too long to be included in the varied collection of evidence which it is my object to present in the first instance.

No. 21.—In the American *Journal of Science*[1] for 1821, Vol. III., p. 102, the Rev. Ralph Emerson suggests the publication in that journal of "a sufficient number of well authenticated facts on the use of '*mining rods'* in discovering fountains of water underground, to put their utility beyond a doubt. For myself," he adds, "I was totally sceptical of their efficacy till convinced by my own senses." He then relates how the divining rod moved in the hands of his friend the Rev. Mr. Steele, and how he made a crucial experiment to test the value of its indications. Taking Mr. Steele to a place where a perennial underground stream existed, of which Mr. Steele was unaware, the rod instantly dipped down when he came over the stream,-and when asked to trace its course he did so for 50 rods until he arrived at its mouth "which was so situated as to prevent his discovering it" till close by it. "The mode of his tracing it resembled that of a dog on his master's track, crossing back and forth, and he proceeded with as little hesitation."

Here, however, it is possible that some unconscious indications given by Mr. Emerson might be assumed as exciting, sub-consciously, the suggestion which moved the rod in Mr. Steele's hands. But this explanation will not hold good of the next case quoted by Mr. Emerson, which is as follows:—

No. 22.—

> On a journey to the south-east part of New Hampshire, I found a practical use has been made of these rods in that region, for a year or two past, in fixing on the best places for wells. A man in that vicinity could not only designate the best spot, but could tell how many feet it would be needful to dig to find water, and had frequently been employed for this purpose without having failed in a single instance. I will recite one case out of a number. A man who had dug in vain for a good well near his house, requested his [the dowser's] advice. On trial with the rod, the best place was found to be directly under a favourite tree in front of the house; and there the proprietor was assured he would find abundance of water at a moderate depth. But on reflection, he was loth to sacrifice the tree, and concluded it would answer as well to dig pretty near it. He dug; and after sinking the shaft much deeper than had been directed, abandoned it in despair. He soon complained of his disappointment. "Did you then dig in the precise spot I told you?" "I dug as near it as I could without injuring the tree." "Go home and dig up that tree, and if you do not find water at the specific depth, I will defray the expense." He did so; and obtained an excellent well at the given depth.
>
> As to the depth, it occurred to me when seeing the operation of the rods in the hands of Mr. Steele, that it might be easily ascertained, by taking the angle they made at a few feet from the spot where they became directly vertical.
>
> Ralph Emerson.[2]

Mr. Emerson does not say whether he obtained the information at first or second-hand; this case, therefore, rests upon weak evidence.

In the next case the importance of sinking at the exact spot indicated by the dowser will also be seen.

---

[1] This monthly journal corresponds to our *Philosophical Magazine,* as a leading authoritative scientific organ.
[2] As I have already said this is not, as I at first thought, Ralph Waldo Emerson, but apparently a contemporary of his, who was ordained as a Congregational minister a little before Waldo Emerson entered the Unitarian ministry.

## *Prof. W. F. Barrett*

No. 23.—I am indebted to Mr. F. T. Elworthy of Foxdown, Wellington, Somerset, (from whose well-known *Somerset Word-book* I have already quoted) for several interesting cases of the reality and practical value of the faculty possessed by dowsers. Mr. Elworthy also sends me the following communication he received from Mr. E. Neville Rolfe, H.M. Consul at Naples, whose brother, a resident in Australia, wrote to him that the gift of "dowsing" was well known and its value recognised in Australia. Mr. Rolfe continues:—

> On the Queensland Central Railway and next to the cattle station I live on (say 400 miles west of Rockhampton) is a station named Coreena. Near the head station the manager had sunk a well, but the water proved salt. A diviner happened to pass; the manager showed him his well, and expressed his regret that he had been so unfortunate as to get salt water. Testing the ground, the diviner indicated the place where the manager ought to have sunk. The manager considered the matter and determined on a fresh trial, but thinking "there or thereabouts" was near enough, sunk, say 50 yards, from the spot indicated, and to his disgust again struck salt water. The diviner passed by a few months later and was upbraided by the manager for the waste of money he had caused him to make. "Let us see in the morning," said the diviner; "I don't understand this at all." In the morning, on seeing the new well, he said, "This is not where I told you to sink; here (indicating the exact spot) is where I told you." "I grant it," said the manager, "but I thought those few yards made no difference." "You try," replied the other, and again departed. The manager, after much deliberation, determined to sink a third well, and was rewarded by an abundant supply of fresh water. The three wells are there at this moment as evidence of the truth of this story—a truth I can vouch for myself, on what I consider the best evidence short of my being a principal in the transaction. No doubt corroborative evidence could be easily supplied. If it were required, I am sure an application to C. W. Little, Esq., Manager Union Mortgage and Agency Co., Rockhampton, Queensland, would meet with a prompt reply. Mr. Little is one of the owners of Coreena.

I wrote to Mr. Little's address, in Queensland, who kindly replied as follows:—

Box 237, G.P.O., Sydney, *January 27th*, 1897.

> Your letter addressed to Rockhampton reached me a day or two ago. Your information is quite correct with regard to the well you mention at Lochnagar, but I am sorry to say the other spots on other parts of the run pointed out by Mr. Sewell[1] did not fulfil expectations. Mr. E. H. King, Eton Vale, Toowoomba, Queensland, was at that time managing the station. I have sent a copy of your letter to him asking him to answer your questions. He has also had experience of the use of divining rods on the Darling Downs.
>
> I have also sent a copy of your letter to Mr. Vincent Dowling, of Lue, Rylstone, N.S.W., who has, I believe, had some experience, and may be able to give you some interesting information.

C. W. Little.

Sydney, *February 8th*, 1897.

> I am enclosing copies of letters from Mr. Dowling and Mr. King. With regard to the latter, I may say that when Mr. Sewell—who used the rod— was at Coreena, an artesian flow of water had just been obtained by the railway department on the run at 180 feet, and Mr. Sewell endeavoured to select sites where we should be equally successful, but entirely failed; had he confined his attention to opening up springs, or sinking for supplies at about 30 feet, he could probably have been more successful.

C. W. Little.

---

[1] This is the name of the amateur dowser referred to in No. 23.—W.F.B.

## *The Credibility Of Dowsing*

The following is Mr. Bowling's letter to Mr. Little:—

"Lue Homestead," Lue, *February 2nd,* 1897.

Yours of the 27th ult., enclosing copy of Professor Barrett's letter, received.

For the Professor's information, I might state that for years I scoffed at the "divining rod "; no one could have been more sceptical than myself. I have, however, changed my views during the last few years, as I have had many instances placing beyond all possibility of a doubt the fact that there is something in the art, or gift, or electric power, whatever you like to call it.

I have discovered three wells by the agency of the rod, two of them are deep, one about 100 feet, another about 130 feet, and another about 40 feet. The first I do not use, though there is plenty of water, but it is deep, and I have another well near; the second was used in the 1888 drought, but never since; the third is in constant use, and waters about 6,000 sheep and 700 head of cattle. I have an aermotor mill with an open top lift pump, pumping into a tank holding about 23,000 gallons water; the water is abundant, and the tank often full, running water back into the well.

I know of several wells near my Gummin station, discovered by the agency of the rod. The eldest son of my overseer at Gummin, a man now about 35 years of age, can and does use the rod, and another man (Hitchins) living near Gummin also possesses the gift. To give you an instance of the use of this gift, the following is a fact. In the drought of 1888 the Ryder Bros., of Calga, were very badly off for water, in fact were losing stock heavily. They wrote and asked me if I would lend them young Passworth, the overseer's son, to see if he could find them water. I lent them the man, and he found them three sites for wells, following light streams of water until they joined and formed a large body. The Ryder Bros, were not satisfied altogether, so without letting the other man — Hitchins — Passworth, or myself know anything, they paid Hitchins to go over and see if he could find water; the site of Passworth's wells was not marked except to the initiated, the Ryders themselves. Hitchins followed the same streams and marked the same sites within a few yards or feet. The Ryders then put down three shafts, and obtained abundance of fresh water in two; the third was never finished, as the rain came. However, they struck the water before the rain fell, but did not go on. These wells saved thousands of sheep for Calga.

To give you another example, I once got Passworth (overseer's son) to follow the stream from the "Swamp Well" (the well I have mentioned as watering so many sheep and cattle), as I wished to see whether the same stream supplied other old wells I have some miles distant, but in the same fall. The stream was not the same; we followed it for some distance and it suddenly turned into the main Mambelong Creek, and I said no doubt this is the same stream; but when we got into the bed of the creek, which was perfectly dry at the time, the rod stood erect when we faced down the stream, but bent when kept on its back; it crossed the creek, and I followed with him over a mile, the rod working well on a strong course of water, which eventually led us to the site of an old spring which I knew of, but the man knew nothing about, the spring having been trampled in and destroyed by cattle years before: it used to be a strong spring. This satisfied me there was virtue in the rod. It is extraordinary to see the rod working on a long course, directly the man gets off the stream, up comes the rod, more to the right or left, as the case may be, and down it comes when you get over the course.

Vincent Dowling.

The next is Mr. King's letter to Mr. Little:—

Elton Vale, Cambooya, *February 1st*, 1897.

> Sewell's experiments were interesting so far as they went, but were of no real practical value, I fear. You will remember we tried two of his sites in Emu Hills Park, both of which proved to be brackish or salt water, and small supplies at that, when big ones were promised; at the Jersey Bore we were to get a big flow at 300 feet, but nothing came of this; at head of Back Creek only a small stream found, and a big supply promised; his only success was at Locknagaar, where I believe he showed Conway where there was a supply of fresh water close to a spring that was known to be salt; and on opening it up it proved correct.
>
> E. H. King.

No. 24. — Mr. Phippen, in his little work published on the rod in 1853, gives several cases of abundant and perennial water supply found by the dowsers, Mapstone and Adams of Somersetshire; and relates experiments he himself made with Adams which made him an enthusiastic believer in the value of the rod. Like others, he and a friend could not hold the rod still when it was over a subterranean spring.

The Rev. Mr. Foster, of Sodbury, Gloucestershire, had sunk a well 60 feet deep without finding water. Adams was sent for, and by the dowsing rod fixed on a spot 6 feet from the dry well, where he said was a good spring about 20 feet deep; a tunnel was accordingly driven at this depth from the old well to the spot indicated, "when an abundant supply of excellent water was obtained which speedily filled the old well up to 40 feet," *i.e.,* to the level of the spring.

No. 25.—Mr. J. G. Marshall, of Leeds, a well-known manufacturer, seeing the account in the newspapers of that day, wrote to Adams, who lived at Rowberrow, near Shipham, in Somersetshire, to come to Leeds, as he needed a good supply of water. Adams came, and Mr. Marshall gives the following report in a letter he wrote, which I summarise:—

Monk Coniston, *October 24th*, 1846.

> I watched Adams closely: he appears a perfectly, simple, honest, straightforward man. At the spot he indicated, and about the depth he specified, a good spring of water was found. An old well sunk near the place but not so deep had no water, and other wells near, of the same depth, had much less water. I tested Adams by taking him over our factory where he had no possible guide from anything he could see; he pointed out remarkably nearly the position of the springs found by deep bore-holes. The same result was found at another factory where he could not have got any information, nor was there any guide from what was said.
>
> I then completely blindfolded him, and after walking him about in various directions I asked him to fix the spot where he had located a spring; in the first attempt he failed, but afterwards succeeded; he said he was not used to being blindfolded and was much confused by it.
>
> He thinks it is some sort of vapour comes from the water or mineral vein, which affects his nervous system, "giving him," as he describes it, "a sort of turn,"
>
> Adams failed to detect coins placed under hats, and yet the rod turned, which was the most suspicious circumstance I saw.
>
> I and several others repeatedly tried to detect some motion of Adams' fingers when the rod turned, but could find none whatever.
>
> J. G. Marshall.

## *The Credibility Of Dowsing*

Mr. Phippen says he has in his possession nearly 100 certificates from gentlemen in Somersetshire, testifying to the success of Adams in finding water by his "dowsing rod," and quotes the following as one instance:—

> Mr. M. Teek, of Hill House, near Wells, certifies that he had lived 40 years in that house, had sunk two wells to a depth of 50 feet each but found no water in either case, and consequently water had to be carried a considerable distance. Adams was at last sent for, and the dowser found an excellent spring of water close to the house.

Mr. Phippen thinks one in every seven or eight persons have the "gift" of using the rod if they tried, and concludes by giving directions as to holding the rod, which is quoted in Appendix C.

No. 26.—Mr. Young, of Llanelly, sent me some details of the finding of water for the Shepton Mallet gaol long ago by the dowser Kingston, who used to live at Evercreech; previously to the dowser's visit a fruitless well had been sunk. I asked Mr. Young to get me the exact particulars, and he sends me the following letter from Mr. W. Stone, an old man who was formerly employed at the gaol.

Shepton Mallet, *December 19th*, 1896.

> It is between 40 and 50 years ago the trial with the divining rod took place at the gaol. All I remember is that shortly after the enlargement of the gaol we wanted more water and a deep well was sunk, but no water was found. The magistrates then consulted and determined to call in a man named Kingston who used the divining rod. When he came, after trying various places he came to a spot in the front yard, and here he said "you will find water." A well was sunk, but I cannot remember the depth, it was not deep, when water rushed in and has continued to do so.
>
> W. Stone.

Mr. Young adds the gaol authorities used the water supply thus found for over forty years till a town supply was laid on. Shepton Mallet and Evercreech are at the foot of the Mendip Hills.

No. 27.—The following is a more remarkable case, and an important one from an *evidential* point of view; it is also from Shepton Mallet. I have not heard whether the "diviner" in this case was an amateur or not: he is now dead, I am informed. The *Bristol Times and Mirror*, of June 16th, 1891, states: —

> The Anglo-Bavarian Brewery at Shepton Mallet needed a large water supply; accordingly excavations had been made to find water, but without success. About two years since, during an exceptionally dry season, it became absolutely necessary to obtain a further supply of brewing water; hence several boring experiments were made on the property. At the suggestion of a gentleman in the locality, the services of a "diviner" were obtained, and although the principal members of the firm professed to have no faith in his "art," yet he was allowed to try the fields on the company's property, and those on the neighbouring estate, and discovered the well now used by the brewery. . . . The soothsayer, who carried the divining rod, a hazel branch, was Mr. Charles Sims, a local farmer, and a notable discoverer of wells in the district. Operations were immediately commenced, and, after excavating and dynamiting through the rock, to the depth of 50 feet, a magnificent spring was discovered in a fault of the rock, which proved to be of exceptionally fine water, and of even a finer quality than the town's supply.

I wrote to the Secretary of the brewery to make enquiries and he replies:—

## *Prof. W. F. Barrett*

Shepton Mallet, Somersetshire, *September 12th*, 1896.

Replying to your letter in regard to a local diviner, we had one of the name of Sims, from Pilton, who successfully denoted a spot on our ground where we have had an abundant supply of water since. This was some eight years ago.

The writer of this letter also has had some considerable experience with Mr. Lawrence of Bristol, who was one of the most noted divining rod men in the West of England. He also was successful in denoting a supply for a Bristol brewery with which the writer was connected; and in numerous other instances in the neighbourhood. Mr. Lawrence bore a very high reputation. We believe he died a few months ago at a ripe old age.

The Anglo-Bavarian Brewery, Limited,<br>J. Clifford, *Manager*.

Having written to ask if a previous boring had been made, and if so, to what depth, and with what result, the following reply was received:—

Shepton Mallet, Somersetshire, *September 18th*, 1896.

Replying to yours of the 14th, a boring was carried out to the extent of some 140 feet without success on another portion of our premises, before it was successfully done at the spot indicated by the water-finder; here a well was sunk and abundant water obtained at a depth of 40 feet.

The Anglo-Bavarian Brewery, Limited,<br>J. Clifford, *Manager*.

No. 28.—The next two cases also occurred in Somersetshire. Mr. W. G. Hellier, of Wick St. Lawrence, near Weston-super-Mare, Bailiff of the Merchant Venturers of Bristol, states:—

*January 7th*, 1897.

I should as soon think of planting a tree with its root upwards, as I should of digging a well for water without employing a "dowser." I never knew the rod to fail in the hands of Thomas Hares or John Blake, but I have heard of many failures in the hands of supposed dowsers. Thomas Hares used to find both water and minerals by the rod, but he told me that a watch spring would not do in his hands for finding water, though it was all right for minerals.

The following facts are within my own knowledge.

Within 200 yards or so of Rectory Farm house, at Locking, near Weston-super-Mare, four wells have been sunk, the position of which is marked on the enclosed rough tracing from the parish map. For No. 1 well, the spring was found by Thomas Hares. After walking over the field in different directions, with the rod in his hand, he crossed the fence, and, whilst on the top of it, the rod kept turning. He marked the spot of the spring, and on that spot I removed the fence and sank the well where the fence had stood. There has been a constant supply of water in it, even all through last summer, when there was a general drought.

For No. 2 well, the spring was found by John Blake, on the lawn of the Vicarage, opposite the drawing room window, a most unsuitable position. I sank the well and there is a plentiful supply of water, with no lack last summer.

No. 3 well was sunk without a dowser. It is 10 feet deeper than No. 1. There was no water in it all last summer, and I should not think it has 6 feet of water in it now.

No. 4 well was also sunk without a dowser, because the place was thought likely for water. It is nearly as deep as No. 1. There is water in it for about 9 months of the year, but last summer it was quite dry.

POSITION OF THE FOUR WELLS TAKEN FROM THE MAP OF LOCKING PARISH.

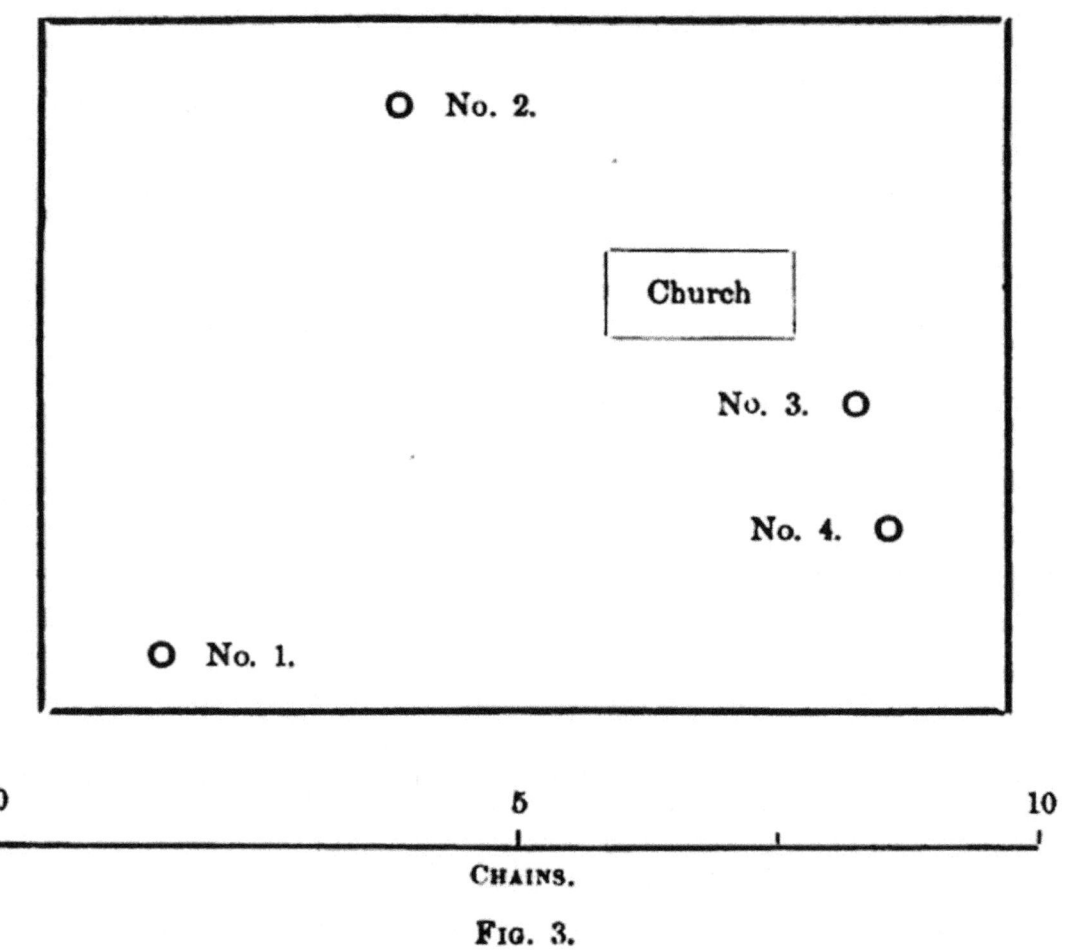

FIG. 3.

[1 chain ==66 feet or 22 yards - Ed.]

Water was wanted at Edbrook Cottage, in Fiddington, near Bridgwater. There was a good spring in a field 200 yards away, and the dowser traced it over field, fence and roadway, and marked the spot for a well just opposite the door of the cottage. I sank the well there, and the tenants have never had to go elsewhere for water since.

Whilst the dowser was tracing this spring, walking backwards and forwards across the line of its course, I hid my pocket compass in the long grass in his track, and, when he came to it, the rod turned over, and he said "There is summat here." I am certain that he did not see the compass until afterwards, when I showed it to him hidden.

The most striking case I know of is on Sandford Green, in the parish of Winscombe, Somerset, where Thomas Hares offered to sink his well for nothing, if he did not come to the spring. There was already a well on the green, but it had scarcely any water during the summer months. The well sunk by the dowser was so near it that the sinkers threw the dirt as they dug it out from the new well into the old one. The water rose to within 6 feet of the top of the new well. This was some 30 years ago. The spring was the talk of the neighbourhood at the time, and it is still a noted one.

I could go on telling yarns about dowsers, but all that I have written has come under my own observation, and I can vouch for the truth of it.

W. G. Hellier.

Mr. George H. Pope, Treasurer of the Merchant Venturers of Bristol, sent me the above account, with the following letter in reply to mine:—

Merchants' Hall, Bristol, *January 8th*, 1897.

I asked my bailiff, Mr. Hellier, for information, and digested what he told me into the above memorandum, which he says is quite correct and has signed.

The "dowsers" mentioned in it, Hares and Blake, died three or four years ago.

George H. Pope.

Mr. Pope kindly made enquiries for me as to the exact depth of the above wells and writes:—

Bristol, *February 1st*, 1897.

No. 1 well, Church Farm, is 20 feet deep.

No. 2 well, Vicarage Lawn, is 31 feet deep.

No. 3 well is dry, and is 33 feet deep.

No. 4 well, Garden well, about 12 feet deep.

Regarding the wells on Sandford Green, the one sunk at the spot indicated by the dowser, is 33 feet deep, and has at present 19 feet of water in it. Unfortunately the old well has been filled up.

George H. Pope.

No. 29. —In the *Proceedings of the Bath Natural History and Field Club* for 1894 (Vol. VIII., p. 61), Colonel Long gives the following account of the discovery of "a perennial water supply by the aid of two noted dowsers, Thomas Young and Thomas Day." Omitting a few details, the following is Colonel Long's statement:—

Woodlands, Congresbury, Somerset.

For many years I have been dependent on rain for my water supply, and those who do the same well know how unreliable this is. ... In 1885 I moved to Clevedon expecting to let this place easily, but the want of spring water prevented my getting a tenant. In 1888 I returned and determined to get water if possible. ... I sent for Thomas Young who lived at Rowberrow, and was noted as a successful dowser. ... I asked Young to dowse over a field called Taylor Hill. Almost immediately he struck on a stream and on the side of the Hill (exactly 300 yards from my house and several feet above it), the stick twisted considerably. Here a well was sunk 22 feet deep. This filled in the winter, but soon became dry in the summer, and in September, 1889 (Thomas Young had died), Thomas Day, another noted dowser who also lived at Rowberrow, descended the well with me. The twigs were much agitated, and, one after the other, if not allowed to twist, snapped off.

Day said, "There is a lot of water under here." He undertook the sinking and sunk 30 feet more, when the water came in so fast he had to leave, and ever since, even during this dry summer (1893) I have had plenty. Of dowsing I can offer no explanation. I am contented with the result.

In reference to the above, the Rev. H. H. Winwood, M.A., F.G.S., adds the following note:—

The well in question was sunk through the New Red Marl which here rests on the carboniferous limestone, and apparently the water was found before the limestone had been reached. It seemed an unlikely place to meet with a spring.

No. 30.—In the *Proceedings* S.P.R., Vol. II., P.105, is given a striking instance of water finding by the diviner, W. Stokes, an aged man, living in Newbury, Berks, where he has for many years been employed as a wheelwright. That Stokes really was an excellent dowser Miss Cox has shown in her paper before the Folk Lore Congress, already mentioned; space will not permit my quoting the evidence cited by Miss Cox. Stokes, however, professed to be able to discover which is spring water and which rain water. Some elaborate trials were made with him for this purpose at Donnington, near Newbury, in 1886, and the careful tests adopted showed that the result was no more than mere chance coincidence would have given. The full report is given in the *Newbury Weekly News* for July 29th, 1886, and signed by Dr. Palmer, H. I. Reid, F.S.A., and the three other members of the investigating committee.

Subsequently Mr. Reid wrote to Mr. Edmund Gurney as follows:—

Donnington, Nowbury, Berks., *August 2nd,* 1886.

A week last Saturday the old man came here again for another trial, but I could not be worried to go through all the test again, so we simply drew lots for five vessels, and placed the tickets under each bucket as drawn. He tried all five and was in each case wrong, three spring he called surface, two rain he called spring. The buckets were again emptied and refilled again by lot, he tried all five, and I then again told him before lifting the bucket, to try a second time to be certain. This he did, and the fifth bucket he had declared to be spring he then saw was rain, so that that bucket was discarded, for in one case he must of course have been right. The other four were then again lifted and the cards beneath showed he was in each instance wrong. A more complete failure cannot be imagined. He seemed very downcast and again requested another trial. This I am at present disinclined to trouble about, the more so as I am leaving here for town in a few days. It seems as if he wanted to be tested until he had achieved a success!

Herbert I. Reid.

This well illustrates the absurdity of many of the beliefs held about the divining rod. Probably Stokes had found he was sometimes successful in these experiments and so had been led to entertain the belief he expressed. But, as I shall show in the case of hidden coins, such success is due to chance coincidence or unconscious indications given by those present.

No. 31. —The accompanying letters refer to a dowser, Rufus A'Barrow, of Sturt Farm, Stalbridge, Dorset, who has since died. The first letter is from Mr. Dendy to the late Edmund Gurney:—

## Prof. W. F. Barrett

University College, Oxford, *November*, 1887.

You asked me to write you a short account of the search for water which I witnessed last July. The operator was one Rufus A'Barrow, of Stalbridge, Dorset. The locus in quo was chiefly slightly rising ground behind my father's house—Lattiford House, Wincanton, Somerset. The operator took a flexible forked twig between his forefingers and thumbs and carrying it, point downwards, quartered the ground. After a short search the forked stick sprung upwards; the two twigs of the fork bending and the man's thumbs remaining in their previous direction, that is, pointing downwards. The stick retained this position as long as he stood upon the spot of ground, where he was supposed to have discovered water, and returned to its downward direction as soon as he stepped off it. He then proceeded to trace the flow of the water and followed it some eighty yards to a small lawn behind the house when he recommended the digging of the well. He afterwards experimented for our amusement in other places with the same results. In all cases but one when the stick indicated water, he was able to follow its course. In that case he could find no flow away from the spot. Some of us tried to operate with the twig. It showed no movement in the hands of any but one lady, my brother's wife. When she held it over the course, which A. Barrow had indicated, it rose very slightly and slowly as I showed you when here, but still quite distinctly.

My father writes to me this morning. "Rufus A'Barrow has been most successful in these parts, not one failure. Bradney has twenty-five feet of water in his well." I have written to Bradney, a neighbour of ours, and have asked him to write an account to you of the discovery of his well.

A. Dendy.

Accordingly the following letter was received from Mr. Bradney:—

Bayford Lodge, Wincanton, *November 10th*, 1887.

Some time ago I was anxious to find a spring on my property, so sent for a farmer, by name Mr. Rufus A'Barrow, who was renowned for this kind of work with the divining rod. He duly came over, and the first thing he did was to cut a Y shaped twig out of the hedge he then held the two ends of the fork at A and B between the forefinger and thumb of his right and left hand, the point being straight-a-head of him; he then commenced his walk and in a very short time the twig pointed straight upwards thus:— here he said was the spring, which he traced for some distance and eventually pointed out to me where he thought was the best place for me to sink a well. He seemed to be able to trace to the eighth of an inch the course of the spring, as the moment he went to the right or the left of it or in any way got off its course, down went the twig immediately. As far as I could see, the twig pointed upwards quite of its own accord, but the best proof of the matter is that I sunk for water where he told me, and at the depth of some fifty feet came to a beautiful spring, and I have now twenty-six feet or more of water in the well. If there should be any more facts that you would like to ask about, I shall be most happy if in my power to give them.

John Bradney.

In answer to enquiries, Mr. Bradney writes:—

# *The Credibility Of Dowsing*

*December 4th*, 1887.

As to whether there might be water 10, 20, 30, or 100 yards on either side of my well, of course I can't say. I only can say that where he said there was water I sunk and found a good supply.

No. 32.—The same dowser is referred to in a letter I lately received from Major Goff, of Hale Park, Salisbury, who writes:—

Hale Park, Salisbury, *November 1st,* 1896.

Some years ago I had a water-finder, A'Barrow, of Stalbridge, to try and find water for the Home Farm. No one had any notion as to where any was to be found except from the existing wells, which wore some 30 to 50 feet deep. On the man's arrival he was taken to ground rising above the steading and at once found traces of water, which he said must be near the surface and sprung about 50 yards from the farm stables. A well was accordingly commenced and water was come to at 13 feet, to every one's astonishment. The farm and neighbouring people looked upon the proceeding as uncanny, and declared that the water found was only surface; however, the well has never given out, even in the driest summer, which rather does away with the surface idea.

I had the man over again a year or so after to try for water on one of our down farms in the chalk; he found traces, but said the water was very deep, so I did not dig on account of the expense, knowing that the existing wells were over 100 feet deep.

C. Goff

In reply to mine, Major Goff writes:—

*November 3rd,* 1896.

The astonishment of the local people was due to the water being found where it was not expected, and at a lesser depth than the other wells, which were within 100 yards and had a habit in a dry summer of giving out.

C. Goff.

P.S.—A'Barrow would take no fee if water was not found where he said it was.

No. 33.—The Rev. C. H. Mayo, M.A., of Long Burton Vicarage, Sherborne, Dorset, Editor of the *Somerset and Dorset Notes and Queries,* kindly sends me a lengthy account of another instance of Rufus A'Barrow's use of the rod, which Mr. Mayo witnessed in August, 1890. The place where the operations were conducted was a farm at Holnest, Dorset, and on sinking at the spot indicated by the dowser, water was found. A'Barrow stated that it was through watching a dowser named Kingston at Ditcheat, Somerset, 40 years previously, that he discovered he also had the power of using the rod; though at first he was disposed to think the indications it gave were worthless, he had found they were not so. Kingston was the dowser mentioned in No. 26.

I am also indebted to the Rev. C. H. Mayo for kindly obtaining full particulars of another case of dowsing for water in his neighbourhood, which turned out a complete failure; this will be given on a subsequent page.

No. 34.—The following details of a case of successful water-finding by means of the divining rod at Meredith, near Gloucester, were kindly written for our Society by Sir W. Wedderburn, Bart., M.P. It is an interesting and useful report from the careful description given. Note the straight rod used by the dowser:—

## *Prof. W. F. Barrett*

Meredith, Gloucester, *January 1st,* 1888.

Up to the present year the water supply at Meredith has depended mainly upon a well near the house. This well is 54 feet deep, and at the most favourable times is about half full of water; but after dry seasons, and when there is a large demand upon it, the level becomes much lower, and in 1885 there were only about five feet of water. Previous to the summer of 1887 the seasons had been exceptionally dry, so that the water supply began to cause considerable anxiety, and in May and June last the reduced amount coming into the well hardly met the day's consumption.

Under these circumstances I determined to sink a new well, and the time seemed opportune, because any spring running in so dry a season was not likely to fail at any other time. Also Mr. Price, of Tibberton's Court, had recently employed a water-finder, or "dowser," who had succeeded in finding a strong spring on Mr. Langford's farm, at Rudford; and I was inclined to try the same experiment, both because the water-finder, Mr. Thomas Willis, of Gloucester, was reported to be very successful, and because I was curious to see the working of the "divining rod," which is generally believed in in this part of the country. Accordingly, Mr. Willis came by appointment on the morning of Monday, 4th July...

I believe a forked rod is generally used, but this is not the case with Mr. Willis, who uses a simple wand, of hazel or honeysuckle for preference, some 18 inches in length, and as slender as it can be cut. He also uses sometimes a steel wire, such as can be taken out of the framework of an umbrella, and during his operations we found that he sometimes tried one kind of wand and sometimes another. He had brought a steel wire with him, and began by cutting a few wands from a hedge of filbert bushes and from a honeysuckle, and he then enquired whereabouts I wanted to find water. I pointed out to him, as the desired site, an orchard near the garden and stables; and also showed him where the old well is. Mr. Willis is a cabinet-maker by trade, and is a quiet young man, apparently about 25 years of age, and seems to be of a sensitive temperament.... After a few minutes he summoned us to where he was and said that he had found a spring. He pointed out the exact spot, where we drove in a peg; and he then showed us how the rod worked when held over the spot. What we saw was that the muscles of his arms appeared to work and twitch as if he was holding the handles of a mild galvanic battery, and the wand or wire, from being straight between his hands bent into a sort of bow and worked round like a crank, rotating upwards when passing the holder's body. As far as the observers could see, Mr. Willis was using all his force to keep the rod in its horizontal position, and the result of the tight hold he kept of the ends of the rod was that, as it rotated, the bark was crushed and twisted at the place where he held it, until he finally let go. When we came to consider the spot thus indicated, we found that it was 40 or 50 paces due south from the old well, and as the strata are believed to slope from south to north, there appeared reason to think that we had struck upon the spring which supplies the old well. We, therefore, decided to look for another spring further east in the same orchard, and after a little time Mr. Willis found one, some 30 yards to the east of the first peg. Another peg was driven in to show the centre of the new well to be dug. He was of opinion that the spring last found was a strong one. He does not profess to be able to say at what depth the water will be found, but ordinarily he is not able to detect it at a greater depth than 40 or 50 feet. He thought we should have to go some 25 or 30 feet in the present case. Later on we took him to another field at Rimless Hill, about half a mile off, where I wanted to find water. Here he tried for some time, but although he found indications of water, he did not think there was a sufficient quantity to justify digging. He also tried in a field below Meredith, to the north, and we marked places where he found water.

# The Credibility Of Dowsing

A few days later the new well was commenced on the spot indicated, the peg No. 2 being taken as the centre. For 30 feet we went down through red marl, with occasional veins of a somewhat harder rock, but no signs of water. We then came to a stratum, some 4 or 5 inches thick, of hard, tea-green stone, and from that time a little water began to come in, trickling in small quantities from the sides of the well. This continued till the well was about 47 feet deep, when water began to come in so fast as to impede the working. The men had to send up three buckets of water for one of marl, and by the time they had completed three feet more the water came in so quickly that they had to stop working. Subsequently experiments were made to ascertain whether there was any connection between the two wells. On the 10th of August there were about six feet of water in each well, and by levelling we ascertained that the bottom of the new well was some two feet above the surface of the water in the old well. It was, therefore, not possible that the water in the new well could come from the old well. Also at different times we pumped the water out of the two wells, and found that pumping one well did not affect the level of the water in the other. We, therefore, concluded that there was no connection between the two wells, and that Mr. Willis had discovered a new spring. We also ascertained that whereas the old well was replenished at the rate of about a gallon in ten minutes, the new well filled at the rate of a gallon a minute, being about ten times the supply of the old one. The water in the two wells was analysed by the public analyst for Gloucester, with the result that the water in the new well was found to be different from and superior to the water in the old well.

As regards the nature of the phenomena we witnessed, I may note that we were all satisfied of the bona fides of Mr. Willis. It may be added that, though almost always successful, he does not follow the occupation of a water finder professionally, and only accepts a moderate fee after the water has been dug for and found.

I can only add two facts mentioned to me by Mr. Willis. One is that he can only detect a spring or running water, the rod not being in any way affected when he stood over a large subterranean reservoir.

W. Wedderburn.

In reply to recent enquiries, Sir W. Wedderburn writes:—

19, Beaufort Gardens, S.W., *February 19th*, 1897.

I have little to add to the account of our water finding, except that the well continues to give a good supply of water. A few years ago, during a very dry season, I took the opportunity to deepen it a few feet, but ordinarily the water stands at the original level.

I do not remember whether in my former communication I mentioned that Mr. Willis told me that a friend of his polarised the steel wire he hail been using to find water, and from that time it would not act. This seems to show that electricity has something to do with the phenomenon, and this is confirmed by the fact that only moving water (which is accompanied by friction) seems to affect the " divining rod."

W. Wedderburn.

The effect of polarising (magnetising) the steel wire is another of the many illustrations, which this enquiry has brought to light, of the profound influence exercised by a preconceived idea upon the motion of the rod. Sir W. Wedderburn would find the inhibitory effect take place equally well if Mr. Willis had been *told* the wire was magnetised, and yet nothing at all done to it. In Germany, 200 years ago, not only hazel and willow and whalebone, but snuffers, tongs, and even a long bent German sausage were used as divining rods according to the idea of the particular dowser.

No. 35. — Mr. Barber, the principal of a firm of surveyors in London, writes to me as follows:—

22, Buckingham Street, Adelphi, W.C., *June 25th,* 1896.

I did a large mansion at Ross, in Herefordshire, and there we engaged a man who found water by the "divining rod," and plenty of it; but I can hear nothing of him, although I have written to two or three people, but I fancy he came from Wales. In this instance I spent a morning with him going over the Estate, and suddenly he broke out into a fearful perspiration, and, after tapping about the earth for some time, declared there was water beneath. We sank a well, and there was. I may add that water is very scarce in that neighbourhood, and at the time the man was considered very clever, and my client was delighted.

Walter W. Barber.

Mr. Barber is unable to remember the name of the dowser, but it was probably Mr. Heighway; see Group IX. This letter is only quoted as an instance of the remarkable, and, I believe, perfectly genuine and uncontrollable, physiological effect which seems, in many cases, to accompany the dowser's discovery of an underground spring.

No. 36.—In his little book on the divining rod, published at Cleveland, U.S.A., in 1876, Mr. Chas. Latimer, a civil engineer of repute in Ohio, gives several instances of his success as a dowser, especially in discovering the exact *depth* at which water would be found. This he arrives at by noting the position when the forked twig turns to 45 deg. as at A, then walking on till it points vertically downwards as at B; he concludes from this that the depth of the

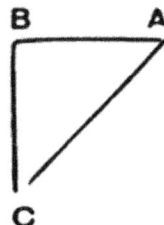

water from the surface B C is equal to the distance traversed, A B; BAC and BCA being equal angles: he states he has verified this repeatedly. This would be very satisfactory if it could be established, but Mr. Latimer furnishes no conclusive evidence of his theory, and the effect he has observed may be due to his own unconscious suggestion on the motion of the rod

In the Cleveland *Leader* (September, 1893) Mr. Whitelaw, the engineer to the township waterworks, states that the severe tests to which he has submitted Mr. Latimer have completely destroyed the profound scepticism he previously entertained as to the value of the indications afforded by the divining rod. Mr. Whitelaw narrates several of these tests; amongst others he took Mr. L. to a particular square where he (Mr. W.) knew, but the public did not know, that there was a certain water main running diagonally across the square. Casually remarking (apparently to mislead Mr. Latimer): "You know there are no mains in the square," they proceeded to cross it. At a certain spot the rod in Mr. Latimer's hand turned downwards, and Mr. L. remarked, "there *is* certainly something here." This was correct. Mr. Whitelaw adds: "When we came directly over the main the butt of the rod pointed down to it, and he (Mr. Latimer) told me the depth as well as I knew it myself." This experiment was repeated with equal success at other parts of the town, so that Mr. Whitelaw asserts Mr. Latimer found the different water mains and their depths as accurately as if he had gained beforehand a minute knowledge of their location. Of Mr. Latimer's good faith and high position the report furnishes evidence.

I add the following cases reported in newspapers, for which I have not been able to obtain any confirmation; partly because they are of some interest when taken together with the others, partly because I may possibly receive confirmation of some of them from readers of this paper.

# The Credibility Of Dowsing

No. 37.—*The Isle of Wight Express, for* March 18th, 1893, contains an interesting report of the success of two amateur dowsers at Shanklin. It seems that the Local Board were in straits for want of a good water supply Eventually they employed Mullins, whose remarkable career as a dowser will be evident later; Mullins came and fixed on two spots where, he said, water would be found. The Local Board employed a well sinker, Mr. Parsons, and then the majority thought they knew better than Mullins, and made a boring in a different place. The report goes on:—

> The Board paid a gentleman to tell them where the water was; but in their wisdom they decided to try a spot of their own choosing, with the result that Mr. Parsons has gone to a considerable depth, and broken his tools, without discovering the precious liquid. The divining abilities of Mr. Mullins were looked at very sceptically by some, because there seemed to be no reason why the hazel twig should rise when Mr. Mullins passed over a spring; but this divining quality dwells in others besides Mr. Mullins.
>
> Two members of the Local Board, Messrs. J. Bailey and J. Milman Brown, have found themselves possessed with the unknown power, and in consequence have been making experiments in the Great Woods, with the result that they have proved, to their own satisfaction, at least, that strong springs exist in the places indicated by Mr. Mullins, but stronger ones in other parts higher up the hill. The Board at their last meeting granted £10 to these two gentlemen to experiment with, and they have thought it best to try the strongest spot marked by Mr. Mullins first. This they have done, and after going down 22 feet, water was found and has risen 9 feet 10 inches. This is very gratifying.
>
> Our Shanklin correspondent accompanied Messrs. Brown and Bailey on one of their divining expeditions and witnessed the marvellous phenomenon; and while no explanation can he given, it is a fact beyond dispute that the twig turns over with an irresistible impulse when the operator is in the vicinity of a spring and cannot be kept back even by force. The experimenters are delighted with their success.
>
> A Mr. Watson, a carter in the employ of Mr. Moorman, has the divining quality even more strongly developed than Messrs. Brown and Bailey, and has amused himself and his friends by being blindfolded after indicating a spring and again finding the same spot.

No. 38.—The Dublin *Daily Express* for January 10th, 1889, states that:—

> A farmer named Griffen, living at Knocknaboley, near Tinahely, having seen the divining rod used for finding water in America, whence he had lately returned, discovered that he also could use it. Accordingly, finding on his return that his family were carrying water from a great distance, he tried the rod, which, contrary to the local belief, as the house was on a hill, indicated an underground spring close to the house. A well was therefore dug at this spot, and at a depth of only six feet, a splendid spring was struck, which has since given a copious supply.

I should be glad of any confirmation of the above statement from those living in the neighbourhood: Tinahely is a town in co. Wicklow.

No. 39.—The next account is taken from the *Western Mercury* of March 1st, 1890.

> The divining rod, as a means of finding a good supply of water, stood a very successful trial last week at Oundle, Northamptonshire. Mr. W. Todd, a landowner, requiring a well on a portion of his property, sent for a diviner, a man named Pearson. There has lately been some considerable difficulty in obtaining water in this town, and the Commissioners have spent £83 in trial borings. Although these trials were conducted by a professional man, they proved futile. In the presence of a number of spectators drawn together by the novelty of the experiment, Mr. Pearson walked over the estate with

the usual V-shaped hazel twig. The rod was visibly agitated in several places, but the diviner kept on until it almost bent itself double in his hands. At this spot he indicated with confidence that a good supply of water would be found. A well was accordingly sunk with the result that at 17 feet deep, water was found in such abundance that it rapidly rose to three feet of the surface, at which height it has since remained.

I wrote to Mr. Todd, but have had no reply, and should therefore be glad of any further information from the Oundle Commissioners or from my geological friends.

No. 40.—I had not before heard of the "dowser" named in the accompanying paragraph, which is taken from the *Wisbech Standard* of October 24th, 1890:—

> Mr. F. Read, of Wisbech Market, experienced great difficulty in getting a proper supply of water in a green field occupied by him at World's End. The result was that the aid of Mr. William Upcroft Hill was called in, and, by means of the divining rod, a spot was indicated and fixed upon, and well-sinking begun at once, the result being that at a depth of eleven feet a plentiful and continuous supply of water was obtained. In this case, at least, the use of the "divining rod" has been attended with success.

I wrote to Mr. Read for further particulars, but my letter was returned with the intimation that he had left the neighbourhood.

No. 41.—The *Blackburn Standard* of June 2nd, 1894, has a lengthy letter from an architect, Mr. T. C. M. Crook, giving an account of some successful dowsing operations in the neighbourhood of Blackburn by a dowser named Mr. Blanchard, of Wisbech, of whom I had not before heard. The first experiment was at Stanley Grange, Samlesbury, where a spot was fixed on by the dowser, and the spring said by him to be about 40 feet from the surface. A six-inch bore hole was made, and at forty feet water rose in the tube to within sixteen feet of the surface. The owner determined to go deeper to see if he could get a larger supply, and bored down 232 feet, finally breaking his tools in the rook, but he was disappointed, the greater depth was useless. He then sunk a well six feet in diameter and 36 feet deep on the same spot, and found an abundant supply; the dowser having remarked that the small bore-hole might not cover the whole of the water veins he had indicated. In two other places in the neighbourhood of Bridge Hall and Samlesbury paper mills, the dowser fixed on sites where water would be found, and in both cases a plentiful supply was found at these sites and at the depth stated by the dowser. It would seem however that the depth was approximately the same (40 feet) in all cases, so that probably at that depth a water bearing stratum was reached, yielding water anywhere it was tapped. Mr. Crook, on the other hand, states that at 20 feet from the surface a very hard rock, mostly of red sandstone, was reached and continued to a great depth. If the facts are correctly given, the interesting point is that a stranger, from a distant part of England, who probably knew nothing of, and cared still less for, geology, hits upon the exact depth where water is actually found. It may be a chance coincidence, but it is of frequent occurrence in other cases; or it may be the dowser had secretly made inquiries in the neighbourhood as to the usual depth of wells; but this is not their practice, as they seem to have a supreme contempt for everything but their own infallibility.

Through the kindness of one of our American members, Mr. Albree, of Allegheny, U.S.A., I received particulars of a remarkable case of successful dowsing which appeared in the *Pittsburg Leader* for January 14th, 1897; but when Mr. Albree, at my request, made private enquiries into the facts, he was unable to obtain any confirmation of them. The narrative is therefore omitted. It was, however, interesting to note the names by which a dowser is known in parts of America, viz, "water-witch" and "water-smeller."

After the miscellaneous cases in this Group had been printed, I received a collection of interesting cases relative to an amateur American dowser, Mr. Cyrus Fuller, which had been in Mr. Hodgson's possession for some time. This additional evidence, which might fitly have come in here, has been placed later, (see Group X.), partly to avoid alterations in the numbering of the cases already printed, and partly because it forms a small group by itself.

# *The Credibility Of Dowsing*

At the close of each group I will add *the failures* in that group that I have been able to discover, *i.e.,* where the dowser has been wrong; a boring having been made or a well sunk at the spot indicated by the rod, and no water found at or beyond the depth he predicted. These cases will be lettered F 1, F 2, etc. It has been much more difficult to obtain first-hand evidence of these failures than of successes; the prejudice against dowsing amongst the educated classes readily lends itself to rumours of failure, and I have found it a most laborious matter to trace such rumours to their source, often with the result that the failure was only in the actual depth or volume of water obtained not corresponding with the figures predicted by the dowser. At the same time there are unquestionably several cases of absolute and complete failure. The number of these it is very difficult to ascertain with any approach to accuracy; all that can be said is that the number varies with the particular dowser employed; some men (a) who claim to possess the faculty of water-finding being evidently charlatans or self-deluded, whatever success they have had being doubtless due to pure chance. On the other hand (b) some of the most remarkable water-finders, such as the late J. Mullins, occasionally fail in their prediction, as might be expected. Here are the only two failures I have met with in the group of miscellaneous cases; both appear to belong to the former class (a).

F 1.—I am indebted to the Rev. C. H Mayo, M. A., for the following instance of failure. Mr. Mayo says, after giving me instances of the successful use of the rod:—

Long Burton Vicarage, Sherborne, *January 21st*, 1897.

> Two other wells have been sunk at farms in Holnest, Dorsetshire, on the divination of other water-finders; one at Dyer's Farm,—which has been successful,—the other at Rye-water Farm, which has proved a lamentable failure. In the latter case, attempted early in 1895. a boring has been carried through dense clay to the depth of 269 feet, with no result beyond a useless expenditure of money, and the work has ceased. Holnest is situated on a thick bed of Oxford clay, capped with gravel here and there.

I wrote at once to ascertain further particulars and the name of the dowser. But Mr. Mayo could give me no more information, and two or three letters I addressed with the same object to the occupier of Rye-water Farm met with no response.

Subsequently Mr. Mayo most kindly ascertained for me the facts; these are given in his letter which follows : —

Long Burton Vicarage, Sherborne, Dorset, *February 19th*, 1897.

> I have been endeavouring to collect some further particulars relating to the case of Rye-water Farm, and have spoken to Mr. S. Thorne, the agent of the property, on the subject.
>
> It seems that two water-finders visited this farm—viz., W. J. Mitchell, of Cerne Abbas, Dorset (see enclosed memorandum), and shortly after, A. Russell, of Sturminster, Newton Common, Dorset. Both traced (it is affirmed) the spring along the same course. A well was begun, and then abandoned, and another begun close by, which was dug for 30 feet (4 feet diameter), and then bored for 269 feet more through clay. No water was found, and at this depth the head of the borer was broken oft., and I believe still remains at the bottom of the hole.
>
> I am told that Mitchell also claimed to discover gold by means of the rod, and met with a sovereign which had been concealed under a stone. Also, when using the rod, he trembled "and became as pale as death."
>
> Since writing the above, I have interviewed the wife of the tenant who was at the farm when the boring took place. Apparently, one well was sunk for 30 feet, and then bored for 90 feet, following the prognostications of Mitchell, and proved a failure. It was then filled up, and another waterfinder, Russell, consulted, whereupon the second well was dug for 30 feet deep, very near the former, and as

before stated, bored for 269 feet in addition, without result, till the breaking of the head of the borer stopped the work. These operations account for the time between the visit of Mitchell on March 23rd, 1893, and the boring which I witnessed in the spring of 1895. I have in my diary a memorandum written in May, 1895:— "This spring a well has been bored at Holnest (Rye-water Farm) for 269 feet without meeting water. The spot was indicated by Mitchell, of Cerne, and Russell, of Sturminster Common, with divining rods."

I hope these particulars will supply what you require. I shall be happy to help further if you still have any other point to clear up.

C. H. Mayo.

P.S.—I am informed that the second water-finder, Russell, was called in when the former of the two wells had been sunk with no effect. - C.H.M.

*Memorandum.*

Mr. W. J. Mitchell, of Cerne, attended at Rye-water Farm on Thursday, March 23rd, 1893. I cannot find I have an entry of Mr. Russell's coming, but he did shortly after Mr. Mitchell, and found the same spot as marked by Mitchell.

S. Thorne.

I know nothing beyond the above of the two dowsers named, Messrs. Mitchell and Russell, no record of any successes on their part having reached me.

F. 2.—The next case of failure illustrates the fact of a would-be dowser having evidently mistaken his vocation.

Mr. W. H. Barber, the head of a firm of surveyors in Buckingham Street, Adelphi (see case No. 35), sent me a memorandum he had received from Mr. Pullen, a friend of his in Guernsey, giving a list of wells sunk in Guernsey through the indications afforded by the divining rod. The dowser in this case was a Guernsey resident, a Mr. Mellish, who apparently wrote the memorandum himself. In subsequent correspondence I received from Mr. Mellish particulars of numerous cases where, according to his statement, attempts to find water by sinking wells or boring had been made unsuccessfully in various places in Guernsey before his visit, and how in each case he had, through the indications afforded by the divining rod, been able to find water close by and at a less depth than the useless wells. I wrote to each of the addresses given and received replies from the majority of the persons named. In no single instance was Mr. Mellish's statement confirmed. Mr. Mellish's claim to possess the "dowsing faculty," if such there be, is therefore so far entirely uncorroborated. This is the only instance I have met with of what looks like a deliberate attempt to mislead in the course of this prolonged investigation. I communicated the foregoing facts to Mr. Barber, who replies that he was greatly surprised, for "both Mr. Pullen and a friend of his have seen Mellish at work with the rod, and also found water as the result."

## Evidence Of Professional Dowsers

Let us now examine some of the evidence afforded by contemporary professional dowsers—that is to say, by those who make a livelihood, often a very handsome livelihood, out of the use of the divining rod. It will already have been noticed that the majority of dowsers a generation ago came from Somersetshire; from the esteem in which the "gift" is still held in that county this might be expected, just as the majority of French dowsers used to come (and perhaps still come) from Dauphiny. Thus about two-thirds of the English professional dowsers, whose names have been given in the miscellaneous cases, lived in Somersetshire, and others hard by, in Gloucestershire, Dorset, and Wiltshire.

Besides the foregoing, I know of nearly a score of contemporary professional dowsers in England and Wales, and there are doubtless others of whom I have not heard. With the following I have been in correspondence and with some have had interviews and experimental trials:—Messrs. W. S. Lawrence, J. Mullins, senr. (both of these famous dowsers have died since the beginning of this inquiry), H. W. Mullins, W. Mereweather, W. Stone, B. Tompkins, J. Stears, L. Gataker, T. Heighway, H. Chesterman, H. Bacon, F. Rodwell, W. Rothwell and R. W. Robertson.

I will begin with a few cases from Mr. W. Lawrence, who was one of the most remarkable and successful dowsers of this century. I much regret that Mr. Lawrence's death renders the evidence here presented of his powers so very meagre; his family would render a service to science if they would collect a trustworthy record of their father's experiences in water-finding.

### *Group III —(a) Mr. W. S. Lawrence*

The oldest of the professional dowsers is *Mr. W. Scott Laurence,* who resides at Bishopston, Bristol, where he is much respected.[1] His local standing is seen from the fact that he has been a Poor Law Guardian, was Chairman of the Highway Board, and for 21 years successively was elected vicar's churchwarden. He is a retired stone merchant, and is a hale and fine-looking old gentleman in his 86th year, the father of no less than 17 children! One of his sons, Dr. Lawrence, is a distinguished West of England physician, and is consulting physician to the Bristol General Hospital; another, a clergyman in the Church of England, appears to have inherited his father's peculiar "gift," and in reply to enquiry stated that he could not control the motion of the rod, which appeared to be even more violently affected with him than with his father. For 60 years Mr. W. S. Lawrence has been in repute as a "water finder," and judging from the lengthy list of testimonials he has received, his career in this direction has been singularly successful.[2]

Several instances of Mr. Lawrence's success are quoted in the previous S.P.R. report, and I had hoped in the appendix to this paper to have given a summary of Mr. Lawrence's experiences since that report. Mr. Lawrence

---

[1] Since the above was in type, the death of this remarkable octogenarian diviner has occurred, as already mentioned; Mr. Lawrence died in June, 1896.

[2] In the following letter (which was addressed to Mr. C. E. De Rance, F.G.S.), Mr. W. S. Lawrence describes how he happened to discover that he possessed the dowsing faculty. Bishopston, *October 5th,* 1893.[Many years ago] my father was the contractor for building a new Rectory House at Winterbourne, Gloucestershire. In the contract he was to find a supply of spring water, and had to sink a well for such; he had done this to about 40 ft. deep without success, when an old working man, a gardener, who passed the spot every day, stated it was quite useless to go on sinking it, being in the wrong spot. On being asked to mark the right spot, he went to the hedge of a field and cut a hazel forked stick, and on arriving at the well, marked a spot about 15 ft. away from the well, and desired us to sink there, which we accordingly did, and at about 15 ft. deep obtained a valuable spring of water. I then was about 20 years of age, and asked him to allow me to try and see if the forked twig would act same with me, but he said it would [probably] be quite useless; but if I would call on him next day at his cottage he would test me. I did so, and he placed in my hands a small steel watch spring, and desired me to walk about the kitchen with such, and to his great surprise it acted with me similar to what it did in his own hands. This was to prove and ascertain if I had the power, as he knew there was a capital spring of water under the floor of the cottage; he then stated his great surprise, he said as many as 100 persons had been there previously, and never one [had the rod] acted with previous. From which time I have made use both of steel spring and hazel rod. I do not believe I have any power without the rod or spring to discover such.. You may make any use whatever of these remarks. I have just returned from a visit to Aboynes and Drum Castle, Aberdeen, where I was sent for to go over a large quantity of land, farms, etc., and I marked about 30 or 40 places for sinking. I shall be most happy to give you any further information. W. S. Lawrence P.S.—I am now in my 84th year, and write this without the aid of glasses.

was, however, too ill to give me the necessary information or references when I applied to him in the spring of 1896. Mr. Lawrence had previously furnished me with references to about 100 different people, for whom he has successfully found water by the 'rod.' The list includes such well-known names as the Duke of Grafton, Lord Spencer, Lord Heytesbury, Lord Justice Fry, Sir H. W. Peak, Sir H. Selwyn Ibbetson, Lord Arthur Cecil, etc.

No. 42.—The following is from Mr. George H. Pope, the Treasurer of the Merchant Venturers' Society of Bristol, whose kindness I have already acknowledged in sending me other evidence.

*The Manor House, Clifton, Bristol, December 30th, 1896.*

> On the estates which I look after we always employ a "dowser," and I do not recollect any instance of failure to find water; we never sink a well before using the rod.
>
> My friend, Mr. R. W. Butterworth, (now of Percy House, Kensington, Bath) can tell you, I believe, that he sunk a deep well on his property at Henbury, near Bristol, without getting any water; that he then consulted a dowser (Mr. Lawrence) who asserted the presence of a spring a few feet off; that he drove a horizontal shaft from his own dry well in the direction indicated, and struck a copious spring, as predicted —but I should like him to tell you his own story.
>
> I once allowed an experiment to be made on one of our farms by Professor Sollas, and an account of it is given in Vol. II., pp. 73-78 of the Proceedings of the S.P.R., but in my opinion the experiment proved little or nothing.[1]

George H. Pope

I wrote to Mr. Butterworth as suggested by Mr. Pope. In reply, Mr. Butterworth states he cannot now recall the exact particulars, as the experiment was made so long ago. Happily, however, I found Mr. Crisp, of Bristol, the architect of Mr. Butterworth's house, had already put the facts on record, and they were printed in the appendix to Mr. Pease's S.P.R. report. Here is Mr. Crisp's letter:—

*Bristol, March 24th, 1883.*

> Prior to sinking the well, we consulted a geologist as to the probability of finding water, and at what depth. He informed us that it was not likely water would be found until we had sunk through the bed of the mountain limestone existing there, and which was about 150ft. deep, when we should come on a bed of clay and find an abundant supply of water. This applied to the district where this stone exists, and therefore the well could be sunk in any part with the same chances of finding water. We accordingly sunk a shaft to a depth of 150ft. through the rock, and then bored 10ft., but found no water. This may perhaps be accounted for to some extent, as by ill luck we came in contact with some faults (or saddle-backs as they are sometimes termed) in the rock. We then called in Mr. Lawrence with his rod; he held it over the mouth of the well and it was motionless, and Mr. Lawrence stated it was no use sinking any deeper there; he then walked in a spiral line round the well, and when at a distance of about 20ft., the rod moved vigorously, but nowhere else near the well. With his advice we drove a level heading from the shaft at a depth of about 100ft. from the surface, towards the spot indicated by the rod, and after proceeding about 30ft. the water suddenly flowed in at the end of the heading, and the men had to leave the heading at once and get to the surface. Since this there has been a good and regular supply of water.[2]

H. J. Crisp

---

[1] With this I quite agree, judging from the report Professor Sollas has published.—W. F. B

[2] In the previous S.P.R. report, Vol. II., p. 105, a note is added stating Mr. Crisp's account was "confirmed by Mr. Butterworth, the owner of the house, Mr. Lawrence and others. There is some slight discrepancy in the measurements, which, however, does not materially affect the case."

# The Credibility Of Dowsing

Mr. Mereweather, the contractor who sank the well, also gave a similar account in a letter he wrote long ago to Mr. Vaughan Jenkins, which the latter has sent me. Mr. Mereweather says the water was struck when the heading reached 24 feet from the shaft of the well; here they came upon a fissure in the rock which yielded so large a supply that the pumps were fixed at 80 feet from the surface.

No. 43.—Very similar testimony is borne by another architect, Mr. Henry Shaw, of New Broad Street, London. Here also a deep well was bored and no water found. Mr. Lawrence's aid was sought. The rod indicated water only a few yards from the old boring. A well was sunk, and 14 yards from the surface an abundant supply of water was obtained. The contractors, and the foreman who sunk the well, also send letters about this case, which will be found in *Proceedings* S.P.R., Vol. II., pp. 103 and 104. The foreman says that when Mr. Lawrence came to a certain spot the twig jumped violently up and down. A steel spring was then tried by the dowser with the same result. The position of the underground spring was then marked. The foreman also says that, owing to a drain being in the way, he had to dig a little on one side of the spot marked by Lawrence as the centre. On sinking to 40 feet "the spring burst out, as large as a hammer handle, beneath the *very spot* he [the dowser] had marked for the centre of the well."

No. 44.—The next case is an illustration of the implicit faith in his dowsing power which Mr. Lawrence appears to have inspired in those who had employed him. The letter, which is too long to quote in full, is from the before-mentioned well-sinker and contractor, Mr. Mereweather, who subsequently found he also could use the rod, and has had some success as a dowser. The following summary gives the chief facts:—

> The late Dr. Fox, of Brislington, directed Mr. Mereweather to sink a well to supply the Lunatic Asylum at that place. Instead of sinking at the spot suggested by the contractor, Dr. Fox took him to the Park and after searching found an iron peg driven in the ground, where he told the contractor to sink the well. Dr. Fox gave as his reason that Mr. Lawrence had been over the ground with his divining rod and fixed on that place. The well was sunk 90 feet through Pennant stone and no water found. Dr. Fox insisted that the work should go on, as he had absolute confidence that water would be found, but as the contractor's experience was dead against finding water there, he (Dr. Fox) at last consented to a four inch bore hole being driven; this was done and after 35 feet had been bored (125 feet from the surface) a large body of water was struck, which has supplied the Asylum ever since, has never failed, and could not be pumped dry.

No. 45.—The following letter gives a graphic account by an eyewitness of the muscular spasm which seems to lay hold of some dowsers (especially Mr. Lawrence) when they are over, or have reason to believe they are over, an underground spring. The letter was sent to me by my friend, Mr. H. W. Whitaker, the well-known geologist. I ought perhaps to add, to prevent misconception, that Mr. Whitaker is an utter disbeliever in the dowsing rod, or in any practical good resulting from its use.

*April,* 1890.

> We went yesterday and saw the divining rod used, and a stranger performance I never saw. The diviner, named Lawrence, an old white-haired, benevolent-faced man, walked about the place for some time, it appeared fruitlessly, holding between each finger and thumb a piece of flat steel wire bent round into a sort of horseshoe shape. This, he told us, would detect minerals as well as water, so that when it presently began to agitate as it did, scriggling, and wriggling, and twisting, and turning in his fingers, he could not say definitely that it was water he had come upon, until he took in his hand a strong forked hazel twig, holding an end of each fork in each hand, and keeping his elbows tightly down to his side. I can only describe the antics of that twig as a pitched battle between itself and him! It twisted, it knocked about, it contracted and contorted the muscles of his hands and arms, it wriggled, and fought, and kicked, until it snapped in two —and then—what made it painful to watch until you got used to it, the old man reeled, and clutched hold of any one nearest to him for a few moments. It evidently exhausts him very much, though afterwards I asked him what effect it had on

> him, and he said it only made his heart beat most violently for a short time. Certainly it has not shortened his life! Having found that spring, (I must tell you- the wire and twig will not act over stagnant water), the farmer asked him to try if there was a spring nearer home. He did not find one until, having gone into the garden, he suddenly came upon one close to the hall door. After that, he went further afield, and found two some distance from the house. He can also tell the direction the water takes underground and the probable depth they will have to bore for it. Mr. C.'s lawyer was there "to watch the case"; he was most sceptical, but was obliged to own that if they find the spring he must believe! He went behind Lawrence, and held his wrists with all his strength, to try and keep him quiet while the twig moved, but he could not.
>
> I asked Lawrence how he found out he possessed the power, and he told us that 60 years ago he saw a cottager do it, so he tried himself, and found he possessed the same property. We tried, Lady D. and I, but needless to say, we could do nothing. Lawrence makes no mystery of it, though he cannot explain it; he says it is a gift. He was asked if he could mesmerise, and he said, no. He held the wire over Lady D.'s watch, and it wriggled just as it had done over the water.
>
> We are going to see the water when it has been found, to see the conclusion of the matter.

In a later letter, dated May 1890, the same lady relates that, the farmer having expressed doubts as to the genuineness of the proceedings, Lawrence was taken again to the farm and *blindfolded*. The rod performed in exactly the same manner, on reaching the spot where it had indicated the water before. They then dug, and found the spring at 15 feet depth.

No. 46.—Lady Dorothy Nevill sent to the *Pall Mall Gazette*, of February 13th, 1897, an account of the successful dowsing for water at a convent at Mayfield, in Sussex; a place which was once the palace of Sir Thomas Gresham. There being a need of water, the aid of an amateur dowser was sought. He traversed the grounds, and fixed on a certain spot where he said water would be found. Before digging a well a second dowser was called in some time after; he selected the same spot as the previous one had done. Accordingly a well was dug, and at 30 feet deep water was found. Subsequently they wanted a well nearer the house, and sunk at another spot which both the amateur and expert dowsers had also fixed upon. Again water was found, and boring to a greater depth they have had an inexhaustible supply.

I have also had accounts of this case sent to me by personal friends; it is interesting, and whilst the fixing upon similar spots by independent dowsers is important, yet we are not told what precautions were taken to prevent any knowledge of the spots chosen by the first dowser reaching the second.

Lady D. Nevill, at my request, kindly forwarded to the Superioress of the Convent a letter I wrote asking for further particulars. In reply, I was informed that they had little additional information to impart; but, in answer to my questions, stated the expert was Mr. W. S. Lawrence, and the date of the experiment, June, 1893. The place was Mayfield, in Sussex, and the depth of the well sunk was 270 feet. They did not know what precautions were taken at Lawrence's visit, and so far as they knew no previous attempt to sink a well had been made. The name of the amateur dowser they were not at liberty to give. Lady Dorothy Nevill says the expert used a watch spring as his divining rod, which was Lawrence's custom, and that "he went into a species of convulsions, shook and trembled at the spots he considered to be over the water."

No. 47.—The next case is taken from the *Bristol Times and Mirror* of May 17th, 1890:—

> Mr. Lawrence marked two spots on the farm of Mr. Prout, Frampton-on-Severn, where he stated springs of water would be found, and in each case, after boring 10 feet, water was struck, and rose to within 6 feet of the surface; but as many persons said that water might be found in any other part of the field which Mr. Lawrence had passed over, the tenant, to test this matter, directed the men to bore in another part to the same depth, and the result proved the subsoil to be perfectly dry. Both the

## The Credibility Of Dowsing

steward and tenant consider the trial to be most satisfactory, and that Mr. Lawrence possesses, in a most remarkable degree, the power of finding water by aid of his divining rod. The following letters on the subject, have been received by Mr. Lawrence:—

"Dursley, *May 10th*, 1899.

"I have seen the two places at Mr. Front's farm where they bored at the spots indicated by you with the divining rod, and in both places there appears to be a good supply of water. Mr. Prout told me that he had also bored at a place between the other two, and which you had passed over without indicating water, and found the subsoil perfectly dry. This is a very satisfactory proof that you possess an extraordinary power of indicating where water is t» be found.

Trewren Vizard.

"The Park Farm, Frampton-on-Severn.

"Dear Mr. Lawrence,—We thought you would be pleased to hear that, after a few hours' work, on Friday the men came upon a spring of water about ten feet down, the spot being just outside the garden gate, on a line with the place in the garden. We have since bored at the place where you first declared there was a spring, and likewise found, at just about the same depth, and the water rises to within nearly six feet of the surface of the ground. Because some people were suggesting that perhaps water might be found anywhere in the same ground, we have made the men bore to the same depth midway between the places where water has been found in springs, and none has been found there; so I should now think that every one must be convinced and satisfied that you can find a spring of water.

Kate Prout."

No. 48.—I will conclude this group by quoting two or three letters. addressed to Mr. Lawrence, out of many similar testimonials that I have read. The first is a letter from Samuel Lang, Esq., Bristol.

After vain endeavours to obtain a supply of water for my kennels, and sinking 130 feet deep, I was advised to send for you, who, by aid of your divining rod, in my presence, indicated the spot within 20 feet of the spot where I had sunk, and directed me to drive there, which I did, and obtained at 30 feet deep most plentiful supply. I have the greatest belief in your powers with the divining rod.

Samuel Lang

No. 49.—The next (from the Ely Paper Works, Cardiff), is quoted in answer to an objection sometimes made that no *large* supply of underground water has ever been found by a dowser.

*May,* 1888.

At your request we have much pleasure in stating the result of your visit to our works. We sunk two wells in spots marked by you; in the first one we have a supply of over 20,000 gallons per hour at a depth of 31 feet; and in the other, about 300 yards away from the first, a supply of 12,000 to 14,000 gallons per hour of spring water.

Evans And Owen.

## Prof. W. F. Barrett

Again, we have the following addressed to Mr. Lawrence:—

No. 50.—From the Bristol Municipal Charity Trustees.

*February 26th*, 1892.

In reply to yours of yesterday's date, I am directed by the Trustees of the Bristol Municipal Charities to state that they have much pleasure in recording the fact that you were most successful with your divining rod in discovering water at the spot on their estate at Burnett, on which they afterwards bored, though the surface certainly afforded no evidence of the presence of water there.

Fred. W. Newton, Secretary

### *(b) Mr. W. Mereweather*

The name of *Mr. Mereweather* has occurred in connection with some of the preceding cases. It will be convenient if I give here the account Mr. Mereweather has kindly sent me of his own use of the dowsing rod, for he found it was so successful in his hands that he constantly uses it now when consulted about the best site to sink a well, his business being that of a well-sinker and contractor at Bedminster, near Bristol. Those who regard a professional dowser as a professional rogue will be surprised to hear that Mr. Mereweather, like the late Mr. Lawrence, is highly respected in his own neighbourhood. He is a Poor Law Guardian and Vice-Chairman of the Board. He was also for three years on the Bristol Town Council. In reply to my enquiries, Mr. Mereweather gave the following account of his powers:—

South View House, West-street, Bedminster, Bristol, *May 1st*, 1893.

For the last 45 years I have been more or less engaged as a contractor for water works, and in a great many cases I have executed the work for Mr. Wm. Scott Lawrence, who is noted for his power to find water. Finding what Mr. Lawrence said to come true, although I did not believe in the divining rod, I made an engagement to meet him, and after he had used the twig or steel spring, and pointed out where the water was, I asked him to let me try, and to my great astonishment, I could not keep it down, the tighter I held it the greater the indentation it made in my fingers, until I was obliged to let it go. It is about 16 years ago since I first tried it.

I do not know whether this power is hereditary, but I find that my youngest son can use it as well as myself. I do not notice any particular sensation in using the spring, but upon coming over underground water it suddenly seems to stiffen in my hands, raises itself up and turns towards the body. I notice there is a quicker motion wherever I find, on boring, the water is near the surface, or if there is a plentiful supply deeper down.

In the year 1880 I was consulted respecting the water supply at the residence of the late Captain Quayle, Backwell House. The house is situated nine miles from Bristol and stands 700 feet above the level of the sea. The hill is of mountain limestone. Hitherto the house had only been supplied with rain-water. At about 200 yards from the house there was a well, which had been sunk to the depth of 110 feet, but no supply of water could be obtained. I tried the steel spring round the well, but no action was produced upon it. After trying in different parts some time I came across a spot some 70 yards from the house where the spring turned vigorously. I traced the water some little distance across the lawn to a spot where it was decided to bore a three inch hole. This was done and at 60 feet deep we struck a good supply of water, which rose 10 feet in the bore hole.

In the year 1884 I found water by using the steel spring, at Messrs. James and Co.'s brewery, Midsomer Norton; the depth from the surface to the water was 12 feet; the stratification was conglomerate stone.

## *The Credibility Of Dowsing*

In 1886, the water supply of the workhouse at Bourton (Bedminster Union) was very deficient. I pointed out a spot where water could be found, a well was sunk through the new red sandstone formation to the depth of about 40 feet, a good and abundant spring of water was struck, the supply kept up, and the water is being used to-day. About two years ago a supplementary supply was laid on from the Bristol Water Works Co. main, chiefly because of the improved sanitary arrangements in the house.

In 1890, new oil tanks and stores were erected at Avonmouth. We were consulted respecting the water supply for the engine, boilers, etc. I found them water, and sunk a bore hole to the depth of 68 feet; the water rose to within 12 feet of the surface, and was pumped direct from bore hole, but after some time was given up, because the water was brackish, the hole being close to the tidal river.

In October, 1890, the Rev. C. O. Miles consulted me respecting a water supply for some 20 cottages and a cottage hospital that has since been built at Almondsbury; after some time searching I found water, and sunk a well to the depth of about 30 feet in the blue lias formation. The water rises to within 8 feet of the surface; it is pumped to a brick reservoir on the hill, and from this reservoir flows by gravitation to the stand-pipe and houses in the locality, and I believe the supply is sufficient for all their requirements.

In 1891 we found water and sank a well at a new house belonging to Miss Lippingcote in the parish of Over, adjoining Almondsbury; the well was 44ft. deep, the bore hole 50ft., a very good household supply was obtained, and I have no heard it has ever failed. The stratification was an uplifted coal shale.

In 1891 we opened a new brick-and-tile works at Parson-street, in the parish of Bedminster; the extent of our land is about 6 acres. Knowing that for this class of works and for steam purposes a great quantity of water would be required, which would be a very heavy item of cost if purchased from the Water Works Co., we decided if water could be found to sink a well. I tried the spring over a large portion of the land without any success and was on the point of giving it up, when within 6 ft. of our boundary the spring turned up, and I knew we were over the water. We sank the well 30 ft. through red marl, and bored 30 ft. through new red sandstone, when we struck the water at a depth of 60 ft. It rose to within 12 ft. of the surface. The whole of the water that has, and is still being used, for the whole of the works, which we approximate at about 5,000 gallons per day, is being drawn from this well, but at the very driest time the water in the well is within 16 ft. of the surface.

W. Mereweather

Mr. Mereweather, in reply to my enquiries, states that in all the above cases, and in many other trials (some of which he sent me subsequently), he employed a forked twig or steel spring to indicate where to sink; he does not pretend to explain *why* the spring moves, but he has great faith in it.

No. 51.—The Rev. C. O. Miles, Vicar of Almondsbury, in reply to enquiries writes as follows:—

Vicarage, Almondsbury, *May 21st,* 1893.

Colonel Master wished to supply water here to many of his cottages, and the finding of a supply close at hand was a very important matter. Watching, myself, the rod being used, I saw it rise up again and again when crossing veins of water known to me, but unknown to the operator. When the watch-spring used for the purpose was discarded, and strong forked rods cut from a hedge were used, these broke off short when crossing the veins of water. They were held in such a position, downwards, as to prove that the force that impelled them upwards was not naturally exerted by the operator; and when I add that the operator was Mr. Mereweather, of Bedminster, I have written enough to prove that no fraud on the part of the operator is even conceivable. I should add that Mr. Mereweather is quite unacquainted with this parish.

C. O. Miles, Vicar of Almondsbury.

## Group IV —(c) Mr. John Mullins

One of the most remarkable of the records of successful dowsing that I have obtained is the next series, where the dowser is the late *Mr. John Mullins*, of Colerne, Chippenham, Wilts, who for 30 years was professionally engaged all over Great Britain and Ireland in finding water springs by the divining rod. In business he was a well-sinker, and,

THE LATE MR. J. MULLINS.

if allowed to follow the indication of his rod, agreed I understand, to receive no payment for sinking a well if a good supply of water were not obtained. When one remembers the heavy outlay involved in making a well, often through solid rock to a depth of 70 to 100 feet or more, this agreement is a forcible illustration of the faith Mullins had in his divining rod; a faith that appears justified by its works, for Mullins had probably sunk more wells than any other man. Mr. John Mullins, whose portrait is here given, was only 56 when he died in May, 1894; he was quite an

## The Credibility Of Dowsing

uneducated man. His sons carry on their father's business. One of them, Mr. H. W. Mullins, seems to have developed the faculty of water finding, as several successful cases of his are quoted at the end of this group.

Some striking instances of Mullins' success were given in Vol. II. of the S.P.R. *Proceedings*. The volume of testimonials which Mr. Mullins has published is a remarkable collection of evidence on behalf of the practical usefulness of dowsing, and also contains an account of the manner in which Mullins was found to possess the faculty of dowsing. In the lengthy list of those who have employed him to find water, and have been led by actual experience to have faith in the dowsing rod, will be found nearly a score of distinguished noblemen, more than a dozen owners of breweries and distilleries, or of paper and cloth mills and print works; town commissioners, and clergymen; and landlords and their agents by the dozen. To many of these I have written and obtained corresponding statements to those printed by Mullins.

It is impossible to quote more than a few of these cases, and I shall therefore confine myself, as far as possible, to those which are of evidential value, that is, where unsuccessful attempts to find water by boring had been made in the neighbourhood prior to the dowser's visit.

No. 52.—The first case I will quote is a remarkable one, and I have to thank Mr. and Mrs. Christie-Miller for the trouble they have taken in obtaining for me the particulars here given. Mr. ChristieMiller writes:—

Britwell Court, Maidenhead, *December 5th,* 1891.

> Mr. Mullins came to us at Broomfield, Chelmsford, in June this year, and marked a number of springs. Two wells have been dug with great success. The depth in the first was exactly that indicated (40 feet), the direction of the spring also coincided. In the second case, the depth foretold was 50 to 60 feet; water was reached about 40 feet, the spring being very strong.
>
> Mr. Mullins' next visit was at Kircassock, Lurgan, Ireland. Out of 17 springs marked we have so far tested two. The first well coincided in depth and quantity with his expectations. The second yielded about 50 gallons per hour at 40 feet, and is now being bored to 60 feet, the depth foretold.

W. Christie-Miller.

In a subsequent letter Mrs. Christie-Miller tells me that the first well at Kircassock was 15 feet deep, the depth predicted, and supplies cottages; the second well supplies the house, garden, and stable-yard.

In reply to my enquiries Mrs. Christie-Miller writes:—

Britwell Court, Maidenhead, *December 31st,* 1896.

> As my husband is just leaving home, I write in reply to your enquiries. Our experience of the divining rod extends over nearly seven years. We were first persuaded to experiment in a place where we had bored some 1,000 feet without success. After Mullins left we again sunk on the spot indicated by him, which was only a few yards off, and at between 80 and 90 feet in depth, came on a spring which has proved excellent; yielding over 50 gallons per minute. Since then we have successfully sunk both in Essex and on our Irish estate, Kircassock (near Col. Waring's), so far without a failure.
>
> We are unable to quote an instance of failure with the divining rod, and can therefore speak most confidently in favour of water finding by the twig. We have seven wells sunk after marking by Mullins with his rod.

M. E. Christie-Miller.

In reply to my further enquiries Mrs. Christie-Miller writes:—

## Prof. W. F. Barrett

Britwell Court, Maidenhead, *January 4th*, 1897.

Mullins first worked for us in 1889, at Waterford. He was not aware of the attempt to find water by the Diamond Boring Co. who guaranteed to find it. When the boring failed at 1,000 feet, we were most reluctantly induced to have Mullins. The man marked several places, but said at one spot the several springs met, and we should succeed at between 80 and 90 feet. The same company were set to work and found a splendid spring at the spot marked by Mullins, at, I believe, about 84 feet. The supply has never varied or failed. In each instance Mullins' estimate of the yield per hour and depth were marvellously accurate. Mullins, after marking the site of well at Waterford, was taken to the abandoned boring, and said even at 2,000 feet we should fail. One of our Essex neighbours who had sunk in vain repeatedly had Mullins with marked success, after he had been with us.

M. E. Christie-Miller.

Mrs. Christie-Miller kindly writes again in reply to my wish for *exact* measurements:—

*January 8th*, 1897.

As regards the Essex well, the measurement of 40 feet 6 inches I know to be exact.

In reply to my enquiries I received the enclosed answers to my questions about the wells at Waterford; they are written by a gentleman on the spot who was a strong disbeliever in the divining rod, and opposed Mullins being brought. He walked with him over the ground and had the man guarded so that no one should give him a hint of the existing bore.

These figures you can use, and depend on their accuracy. I do not think you can find a stronger case.

M. E. Christie-Miller.

Enclosure.

Exact depth bored by Diamond Boring Company without finding water?

Answer: 1,011 feet.

Distance from this boring to place marked by Mullins?

Answer: 53 feet. This is the shortest distance: Mullins said we would find water anywhere in line between the two places where he made his marks. One mark, M', is in Hodges' field; another, M", is where the pump is. This latter is 296 feet away from the deep bore hole, O.

Exact depth of boring in Mullins' well? Answer: 79 feet.

Yield of water from this well? Answer: 3,000 gallons an hour have been tested.

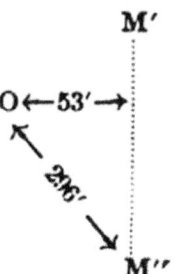

This case is rendered more important, as I have since learnt that the best geological advice was sought prior to Mullins' visit, but the boring made under that advice yielded no water. It seemed advisable, therefore, in this case to make a careful study of all the facts: this was done, and the details are given on a subsequent page, under the heading of "The Waterford Experiments."

No. 53.—Through the kindness of my friend, the Rev. Maxwell Close, M.A., of Dublin, I received the following account from Colonel Waring, M.P., of some of Mullins' operations in Ireland:—

# The Credibility Of Dowsing

Waringstown, co. Down, *November 5th*, 1891.

Mullins was employed by my neighbour, Mr. Christie-Miller, at Kircassock, and I was asked to see him at work there. He then volunteered to come to Waringstown, and did so the next day. He first walked across the gravel on the garden side of the house, and detected the source of the cellar well, at once saying it was a small and shallow spring, which is so. He then went into the yard and tried for a deep well there, and told us that it was sunk 12 feet to the eastward of the proper line, and that an abundant supply would be got by boring a tunnel from the bottom of our present well horizontally that distance. He then went over the fields and marked several places where water was to be found, some of which were known to me as such (but not to him or to any one else present). He found a covered-up well in an adjoining tenant's farm; the tenant, however, a young man, said the well was situated 12 or 15 yards from where Mullins said it was. But when the "oldest inhabitant" was summoned, Mullins proved to be right and the tenant wrong.

The gold-finding was not done by him here, but at Mr. James Bruce's. Mrs. Bruce hid half-a-sovereign in the gravel of a walk and sent Mullins to find it. She said to her husband: "He has passed the place"; a few steps further Mullins stopped and the gold was there, and not where Mrs. Bruce had fancied she put it.

Harwood, my gardener, can turn the twig for water nearly as well as Mullins... There is no trick; firstly, I watched Mullins closely; secondly, Harwood is incapable of deceit, and, lastly the twig turned in my own hands when Mullins grasped me by the wrists. Mullins cannot do it if placed on a stand insulated by four inverted tumblers or glass bottles; his feet must touch the ground.

Mr. Christie-Miller has sunk wells here, at Waterford, and in Essex, at Mullins' direction and never failed to find water at the depth and in the volume promised.

Thos. Waring.

In a subsequent letter Colonel Waring writes:—

Waringstown, co. Down, *November 11th*, 1891.

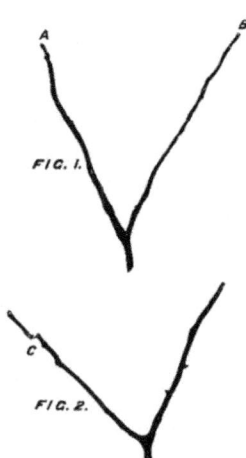

I send you herewith two of the "Dowsing" or divining rods, for discovering water or minerals; a fresh cut one (Fig. 1) and one after being used by Mullins (Fig. 2).[1] The portion nearly twisted off the end of it (C, Fig. 2), will show the action; it was done while I was looking on, and no movement of the hand was made to occasion the twisting. In fact, if you hold the rod, or rather fork, as directed, such action, whether voluntary or the reverse, on the part of the operator is impossible. You pass the ends of the fork between the second and third fingers of the hand, palm upwards, and close the thumb and first and second fingers tightly on the points of the fork (A and B, Fig. 1) and hold it, apex downwards, out before you; when you come on the spring the apex of the fork bends forward and upward, and if one end be held tight and the other allowed to revolve it will twist itself nearly (or quite) off, as in the specimen (Fig. 2.) The violence of the action, Mullins says, depends on the volume and proximity of the running water.

Thos. Waring.

---

[1] The cuts are drawn from photographs of the twigs sent me by Col. Waring. In Fig. 2 (the one actually used by Mullins), the end was nearly twisted off, only a shred of bark remaining at C. The twigs are of pliable green wood, about 15 inches in extreme length, three-sixteenths of an inch diameter at A and B, and a quarter of an inch diameter (not quite as thick as a cedar pencil) at the junction.

## Prof. W. F. Barrett

I enquired from my colleague, Prof. Cole, F.G.S., what chance there was, (geologically speaking) of finding water at Col. Waring's; Prof. Cole replies:—

*Waringstown, 3 m. S.E. of Lurgan, Co. Down.*

> Depends entirely on exact spot of boring. In town and West, Ordovician rocks, and no chance. Immediately East of town, admirable chances, through Triassic Sandstone,—the farther E. for a mile or so, the better.

Whereupon I wrote to Col. Waring to know the exact position that Mullins had fixed on. Col. Waring replies:—

> All the places at which Mullins said water would be found are West of the village, as it is on that side my demesne is situated, but I have not as yet sunk for water.

I trust, therefore, Col. Waring will, from the scientific interest of the question, if for no other reason, make the horizontal tunnel, 12 feet long, recommended by Mullins, and note the result.

With regard to the insulation on glass tumblers stopping the motion of the twig, the same result was found by Col. Waring's gardener (see No. 5). It seemed desirable, therefore, to make a decisive experiment to test this electrical belief held by nearly every dowser. Through Col. Waring's kindness I was enabled to do so, and paid a visit to his beautiful estate for this purpose. The result I have given in the theoretical discussion towards the end of this paper; suffice it to say that, as might be expected, the inhibitory effect is *not* due to insulation, but entirely to the preconceived idea on the part of the dowser.

No. 54.—In *Notes and Queries* for October 24th, 1896 (8th series, Vol. X., p. 345), occurs the following evidence from Mr. Leeson Prince, F.R.A.S.

*The Observatory, Crowborough Hill, Sussex.*

> The Divining Rod.—I must confess that I have been converted to belief in the power of the divining rod, and for the following reasons. Some eight or nine years since a stranger called upon me respecting a contemplated local improvement, and upon leaving me he said that he was a person who made use of the divining rod to find water. I took him into my garden and asked him to point out where water would be found. After wandering about over nearly an acre of ground, he came to a spot which he said would be successful. He then left me, and I thought no more of it. About three years since, a lady bought this property of me, and, having a large establishment, she was rather apprehensive of not finding a sufficient water supply. I pointed out to her the spot where it had been stated to me that water would be found. She did not, however, pay much attention to this, and dug for water in another part of the property; but she was not successful. Without having any further conversation with me, she sent for a "diviner," who, after walking about in various directions (and without her having mentioned to him what the other person had said), told her that she would find abundance of water if she dug down at a certain place which was within a yard of the same spot which the former person had pointed out. She accordingly acted upon his information, and at a depth of rather less than twenty feet she found an ample supply. When the lady saw the twig point downwards in the man's hand, she expressed a wish to try if it would act in the same way in her hand; which, of course, it did not. He then told her that if he put his hand upon hers it would, which it accordingly did. I may say that I report this case from personal information of the facts. Only a few weeks since I heard of another successful case, in an adjoining parish, precisely similar to the above in every particular.
>
> C. Leeson Prince.

I wrote to Mr. Prince for further information and he replies as follows:—

# *The Credibility Of Dowsing*

The Observatory, Crowborough Hill, Sussex,<br>
*October 26th*, 1896.

The lady I mentioned is Mrs. Gresson, and her property lies between my observatory and Dr. Roberts', F.R.S. The dowser who came to her was J. Mullins, from Colerne, who, I believe, is now dead.

C. Leeson Prince.

No. 55.—The following is taken from *The Garden* of April 11th, 1885. The writer is Mr. Crump, of Madresfield Court, Malvern:—

> Many successes in finding water on Earl Beauchamp's estates could be named; in fact, not a single failure is known. Amongst the most recent consultations with Mullins was one concerning a well that had been sunk 110 feet without finding water. Mullins selected a spot a few yards distant, where, at a depth of 50 feet, an inexhaustible supply was found by him. He again selected a spot, naming water at 30 feet deep, and it was found at 27 feet. Many other instances could be mentioned, and so certain is he of his power that he offers to dig the wells without charge if proved wrong in his judgment.
>
> Mullins was engaged to find some water on an estate at Madresfield last week, and on the day before his visit we prepared for him a series of severe tests. No. 1 was to send him into a field which he had never seen before, in which a six-inch socket glazed pipe drain conveyed a stream of water to supply the moat. On the surface there was not the slightest trace of this drain, the depth of which was about three feet. All being in readiness. Mullins commenced to cast about with his twig, when, to every one's astonishment, the moment he came upon, or over the water, up went the twig to the perpendicular. He further proved the exact subterranean position of the drain again and again. No. 2 test was similar to the last, but the pipes in this case were of iron rather deeper. Nevertheless the result was equally satisfactory; of course every member of the party tried to use the rod, but amongst them only one young lady had any influence over it.

Madresfield Court is the property of Earl Beauchamp, and Mr Crump is the head gardener. In reply to my enquiries, Mr. Crump writes as follows:—

The Gardens, Madresfield Court, Malvern, *February 22nd*, 1897.

> The enclosed [i.e., the above] account is strictly accurate, and could be corroborated by the Rev. G. S. Munn, of this parish, and by several others. Our tests were deeply planned, but Mullins was always correct. He has been employed here on many occasions since. I became a convert against my will, and so did others. Some of us held the hind part of the twig when in Mullins' hands, and we could feel the strong power of the twig to rise erect

W. Crump.

In a subsequent letter Mr. Crump writes to me as follows:—

The Gardens, Madresfield Court, Malvern, *February 27th*, 1897.

> Mullins must be seen at actual work before scepticism can be entirely overcome.
>
> The Rev. Mr. Munn and myself prepared the test, unknown to Mullins, who, in fact, was unaware he was being tested. The first test was to send him across a part of the pleasure grounds, where we knew lay six inch glazed earthenware pipes, conveying [running] water. As these pipes did not lie in the direction that a person would expect, judging from the surface, the test was a fairly "dodgey" one; but

the moment Mullins' twig reached the point where the pipes lay, up went the twig, and Mullins there and then said what was quite true, and pointed out, with the help of the little twig (previously cut from the nearest bush), the exact course of the water. He also was tried over other (iron and lead) pipes, very deep in the ground, all with the same result. He told us also of springs of water in various parts of the fields that he tried for us, but we couldn't prove this.

Mullins was such an unassuming man, and was most willing and communicative to all. He showed us how glass insulated him…[1]

W. Crump.

I wrote to the Rev. G. S. Munn, and he kindly replied as follows:—

Madresfield Rectory, Malvern, *February 24th*, 1897.

In reply to queries respecting Mullins and water-finding, I may say that I was told off to test Mullins on his first visit to Madresfield. Snow was on the ground two or three inches deep, entirely obliterating all external indications of water. Knowing the locality well, I took him alone in a line across two places beneath which water ran. One of these had been laid down so many years before that I believe it was known only to myself. In both cases the rod turned up exactly on the spot. I won't trouble [you] with other instances where, as in the above, all collusion and deception was quite impossible, except to say that on one of Lord Beauchamp's farms, which had been very short of water for many years, after much searching, he indicated a spot where water would be found at, so far as I remember, from 20 to 30 feet below the surface. A well was sunk through the rock; the water was found, and I believe there has been an ample supply since.

On the last occasion Mullins was here, a considerable number of persons came to see his performances; many tried to see if they had the power. When all had failed, I persuaded one of my daughters to take the rod, and to my great surprise, it acted in her hands as well as in Mullins'. She has used her power on some few occasions to find water for friends, and also to convince those who have doubted the possibility—as I did, entirely, before I was convinced.

If you saw the rod act when in the hands of those who have the power, you would see at once that no possible action of the hands could produce the results. I shall be happy to answer any further questions; or, if you should be in these parts, you can see for yourself.

George S. Munn.

P.S.—Since writing the enclosed, I have been talking to my daughter, and she thinks that her power, from some cause or other, has considerably decreased.

No. 56.—I am indebted to my friend Mr. W. R. Bruce (one of the Masters in the Queen's Bench Division of the High Court of Justice in Ireland), for a record of a similar experiment he also tried with Mullins. Master Bruce writes to me as follows:—

Rockford, Blackrock, Co. Dublin, *May 6th*, 1897.

I engaged Mullins to come here for a day on his way back from my brother's, where I had seen him try for water. To test his powers I took him into my yard, across which a small pipe ran underground, supplying the house with water from the main. Before doing this I turned the cock and stopped the

---

[1] Mr. Crump then describes how the twig would not move when Mullins was insulated, which, as already explained, is merely due, in all probability, to the influence of a preconceived idea.—W. F. B.

## The Credibility Of Dowsing

flow of water. Mullins passed the pipe and the rod gave no sign. While he and the persons about him were engaged in this, I went into the house unobserved, and having turned on the cock suggested his again making a circuit of the yard. He did so, and when he crossed the pipe, the rod turned up, the water then not being stagnant, but flowing through the pipe. There were certainly no signs in the yard to show that a pipe had been laid under the ground, and I am convinced there was no audible sound of running water, and nothing in my action to give Mullins any hint on the subject.

I put him to another test; he said that gold had the same effect as water. While he was in the house getting his dinner, I went out and hid half-a-sovereign in the ground on the marked line of a tennis ground. I am certain no one saw me do this. I then took him out and told him to try and find the coin, which was some place under the line. He did find the coin. I am certain that nothing in my face or manner gave him any indication of where it was, and it was absolutely impossible for any one to have discovered it by eyesight. In fact, I had some difficulty in finding the exact spot myself. I should add that in going round the tennis ground the divining rod turned up two or three times before Mullins arrived at the spot over the coin. This he accounted for by saying there was water there, which is quite comprehensible.

Wm. R. Bruce.

No. 57. — Master Bruce having told me his brother, who lived in Gloucestershire, had found difficulty in obtaining a water supply until he employed Mullins, I wrote for particulars, and obtained the following interesting evidence:—

Norton Hall, Campden, Glo'stershire, *April 23rd*, 1897.

With reference to Mullins, it is about 12 years since he came here. I believe he had never been here or in the neighbourhood before. We sunk at three places pointed out by him, and got water at each of them. The sub-soil here is blue lias clay, and goes down a great depth. A friend of mine, who bored near here five or six years ago got down over 1,200 feet before he got through the clay; this clay is quite impervious to water, the neighbouring hills are oolite brash.

This house is built on a levelled or terraced slope. When Mullins first got to work at the hall door, before he had gone 10 yards he stopped and said there was water there, but it was not a convenient place to sink, so we went on. It was some time before he got to another place, which was in the stable yard; there he said we would find water at about 30 feet. When we came to sink, we got to water at about the depth he said, which rose at the rate of about 6 feet a day (that is, 24 hours) till we had about 20 feet in the well of about 3 feet diameter. We then tried another place he pointed out, with a similar result. Then the men who were sinking for me, local men, said that any one would know how to find water there, that there was water anywhere along the bank, meaning the slope on which the house stands. I told them to go and pick a place and try. After some discussion, they sank close to my lodge; when they had got 30 feet down they had not got water, and they said there was no use going further, as they were then down into the blue clay; at the end of a week there were not 6 inches of water in that well.

We then tried another place that Mullins had marked close to the house, and about 20 yards from the place where he first stopped by the hall door. Mullins had told us we would find a very strong spring here, about 20 feet down. When we got about 12 feet down, we got signs of water, and when we got 17 feet the water came so fast the men could not sink any further; it was a case of getting out three buckets of water to one of clay.

The men that were sinking had up to now rather scoffed at Mullins' theories, but now the head man said, "This man must know something more than we do after all, for this water is coming through a vein of gravel not bigger than my hat, and if we had been three feet one side or other of it we would not have got a drop;" these men were well sinkers by trade. This well did not hold out when we got a long spell of dry weather, and I always think that there is an underground connection between it and the well in the stable yard, and also with another one in the house yard, and this well being the shallowest of the three gives out; probably the vein of gravel runs on and connects with the others. Once, in a very dry time,—1887, I think,—it was the well in the stable yard failed, and we had a lot of water from a pond filled into it; we found that the well in the house yard rose as we filled into the one in the stable yard, and the water was dirty like pond water. I don't think I can give you any more information on the matter.

Mullins also found a half-sovereign that I had buried in a walk we were then making. I would have lost the half-sovereign if it had not been for him, as I was so careful not to put any mark lest he might notice that I was not able to find the place myself, and when he stopped and said it was under his foot, I thought he was wrong, but there it was!

S. Bruce.

In reply to my enquiries Mr. Bruce writes:—

Norton Hall, Campden, Glo'stershire, *April 29th,* 1897.

Yes, certainly, this neighbourhood is very badly watered, and springs few and far between, at least those that are known to exist. As I mentioned, we are on the blue lias clay, and in one case this was found to go to a depth of over 1,200 feet. I have not the exact figures of the boring, but I think it was 1,250 feet of clay, and then they went on over 100 feet more and got no water that they could utilise.

S. Bruce.

The finding of the half-sovereign in both these cases, as elsewhere, must be considered in connection with the specific experiments made in this direction, to be related later on. Though the foregoing are certainly striking successes, I see no reason to doubt the explanation already given, which is discussed more fully on a subsequent page.

No. 58.—The next case is quite as remarkable as Mr. Christie-Miller's experience. Here also the best advice was obtained and some £1,000 spent fruitlessly searching for an underground spring prior to the dowser's visit. The first notice of this case appeared in a local newspaper, the *West Sussex Times and Sussex Standard,* from which the following letter is reprinted:—

Warnham Lodge, Horsham, *January 3rd,* 1893.

Having had very great difficulty in the supply of water to this house, I sent for John Mullins, of Colerne, near Chippenham, who, by the aid of a twig of hazel, pointed out several places where water could be found. I have sunk wells in four of the places, and in each case have been moat successful.

It may be said that water can be found anywhere—this is not my experience. I have had the best engineering advice and have spent many hundreds of pounds, and hitherto have not obtained sufficient water for my requirements, but now I have an abundant supply.

I certainly should not think of sinking another well without previously consulting John Mullins.

Henry Harben

Further details of this case are given, later under the head of **The Horsham Experiments.**

# *The Credibility Of Dowsing*

No. 59.—Having heard from Mr. Harben that a neighbour of his at Horsham had sunk two wells with very poor results, but that an abundant supply had been obtained at a spot indicated by Mullins, I wrote for particulars, and received the following letter from the owner of the estate in question:—

Hedgecocks, near Horsham, Sussex, *May 3rd,* 1897.

> There were two wells previously, but only land springs, about 27 feet deep, and apt to get dry. I then employed Mullins, and sank a well at a place where he said I should find water. The result was I found a good supply at about 26 feet. The water was found within 6 incites of where Mullins divined it.
>
> I have employed him since with equal success with three wells.
>
> William Renton.

No. 60.—The following is from Mr. F. Bastable, 14, Foskelt Road, Fulham, and appeared in the *Carpenter and Builder,* of September 30th, 1892. The contractor of the Somerset and Dorset Railway, Mr. T. A. Walker, here employed Mullins under the following circumstances:—

> At the Shepton Mallet Station, on that line, it was decided to sink a well close to the rails to supply water for the locomotives. We had sunk a depth of 250 feet entirely through blue lias rock as dense and hard as possible, and as dry as a bone, and began to look upon it as a forlorn hope, when Mr. Mullins was mentioned as a man likely to help us in the matter. After much hesitation and fear lest it should turn out to be a hoax—we were very incredulous—it was decided to ask the advice of Mr. Mullins, who came at once, and with very little trouble discovered for us close at hand that for which we had sought so long. . . . The most favourable spot was found to be about 50 feet from our well. Mr. Mullins, from his observations of the action of the forked twig, advised us to commence and drive a heading about 50 feet down the well, and under [where the twig turned] we should have abundance. This was done, and when at that spot our miners had to rush out and up for their lives, leaving behind them their steel drills, hammers, clothes, etc. The well soon filled up, and when we left in 1879 the water was within 12 feet of the surface.
>
> We procured two pairs of smith's tongs to see if the twigs did actually twist, and held them in a tight grip, with one pair securing the tips and the other the fork, but the contortions still went on between the points held. What the power consists of I am still at a loss to conceive; but this I know, not one of us present at the operation had any doubts afterwards as to his ability in discovering water in the earth.

In a letter to the *Daily Graphic* for March 30th, 1892, Mr. T. J. Hickes, of Truro, describes this same case. He writes from a personal knowledge of the facts, but both he and Mr. Bastable appear to write from memory, and it is, therefore, not surprising that the figures they give do not quite correspond. Mr. Hickes remarks that the water was found exactly at the spot Mullins predicted and came with such force that the well sinkers had to fly and leave everything. Mr. Hickes adds, "I have used the divining rod on many occasions myself to find and trace springs and thus been able to be of benefit to others."

Mr. F. J. Clark, F.L.S., who lives in Somerset, and kindly sent me one or two cases in Group 1, writes to say he is well acquainted with the foregoing facts, which came to his knowledge at the time they occurred, his father being then a director of the line. Mr. Clark adds:—

## Prof. W. F. Barrett

I went to see my father on receipt of your letter, and he tells me that the account you have printed [as above] is correct, though his impression is that the well was not quite so deep.[1] My father proposed their having a dowser from the first, but the contractor laughed at the idea; however, afterwards he was very sorry he had not taken my father's advice at the beginning.

No. 61.—I have to thank Mr. Clifford Gibbons for the following interesting case:—

Great Walstead, Lindfield, Haywards Heath, *January 7th*, 1897.

In reply to your letter, I have much pleasure in giving you particulars of the success of Mr. Mullins in finding water on my estate.

Three old wells, 20 feet apart, sunk without the dowsing rod, are 50 feet deep and communicate with each other by means of a tunnel. About 150 yards to the west of these, and at the spot indicated by Mr. Mullins, a large supply of water was found at a depth of 30 feet, and with much difficulty the well was sunk another 15 feet. There are two wells both about 50 feet from the above, one being to the north- and the other to the south-east; the latter is a very old farm well. When these two wells are dry, as they were last season, Mr. Mullins' well stood at 12 feet of water, and at least 1,000 gallons a day were pumped out. The three wells first mentioned were pumped once or twice a week, but gave only a little water.

The most remarkable thing to me is, that when Mr. Mullins was surveying the ground with his rod, I tried it myself without any result, but on going over it again with my wrists held by him the twig rose in my hands in the same manner as it had done in his.

The thing is altogether a mystery to me, but certainly if I were to sink another well, I should get Mr. Mullins to select the spot, as I have spent very large sums of money almost fruitlessly before I knew him.

Any further particulars you may desire, I shall be pleased to give you.

S. Clifford Gibbons.

Writing again to Mr. Clifford Gibbons, I asked him to give me the exact depth, distance apart, and relative level and position of the wells. Mr. Gibbons replied as follows:—

Great Walstead, Lindfield, January *20th*, 1897.

The accompanying rough sketch plan shows the relative position of the six wells on my estate at Lindfield.

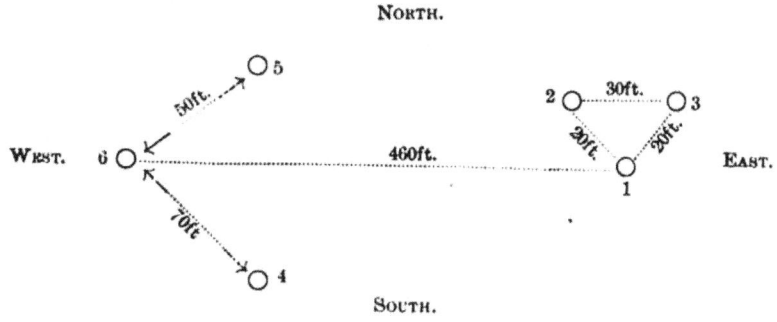

---

[1] On further enquiry, Mr. Clark informs me the depth was 100 feet.

## *The Credibility Of Dowsing*

Nos. 1, 2, 3, are the old wells about 50 feet deep. Nos. 4 and 5 wells are about 28 feet deep, the surface level of these west wells being about one foot higher than those at the east. No. 6 well is the one made by Mullins. It was commenced in October, 1893; abundant water was found at 30 feet deep, but it was sunk to 45 feet.

Nos. 1, 2, 3, 4, and 5, were almost dry in September and October last, but No. 6 well stood with about 12 to 16 feet of water in it, and supplied all the water that was required.

S. Clifford Gibbons.

This remarkable case would be still more instructive if Mr. Clifford Gibbons would sink either No. 4 or 5 well two or three feet lower, and see if the supply found in No. 6 would be reached. I wrote to ask Mr. Gibbons if this could be done as a matter of scientific interest, but he replies it is impossible at present, "as it might disturb all the pumping arrangements I have, which are most satisfactory, and the supply of water excellent from Mullins' well."

No. 62:— The next is from Mr. E. G. Allen.

Highfield, Metheringham, Lincoln, *March 25th*, 1893.

Having frequently availed myself of Mr. John Mullins' services during the last 20 years, I can say I have never known him to fail. I have sunk six wells, two on a heath farm about 30 feet deep (surrounding wells measuring about 70 feet) in limestone rock, thus saving a great expense in sinking. I took him one morning to a farm which was at that time farmed by the owner, the Right Hon. H. Chaplin, M.P. The well in the yard (nearly always dry) was about 30 feet deep, and water had to be led some distance from the Carr Dyke. In a few minutes, Mullins, carrying in his hand his twig, found a good spring a very short distance from the old well. A new well was sunk, and at 10 feet a splendid supply of water was found. It has never failed, and has supplied the yards, etc., with water ever since.

Being in want of water for a large grass field, called "Catley Abbey Field," I went with Mullins, who placed down a peg to denote a spring. We sank a well, and bored 70 feet, obtaining a good supply of water. Being struck with a peculiarity in the taste, it was submitted to Professor Attfield, Ph.D., who pronounced it to be the only natural seltzer spring in the kingdom.

E. G. Allen.

No. 63.—There is an interesting sequel to this case. The *Lincolnshire Chronicle* of June 8th, 1895, contains a long report of a visit of Mr. H. W. Mullins, the son of John Mullins, to Catley Abbey. The newspaper report, which I have abridged, is as follows:—

The object of the Catley Abbey Company in sending for Mr. Mullins was to secure a well of pure water for bottle washing. A well on the adjoining farm of Mr. Allen had run dry, and recently the seltzer water had been used for the purpose of bottle washing. Eight years ago Mr. J. Mullins, the father of the family, located the spot at Catley, where now stands the only natural seltzer spring in Britain, and the Company had ample evidence of the success which had attended the diviner in other directions. Proceeding to the site of the dried up well, Mullins took out a V shaped twig, the forks of which were each about a foot long, and walked slowly along the ground a short distance from the well. Suddenly the twig revolved, having the apex at the top, and Mullins confidently asserted that he was standing over a subterranean water-course. Proceeding to the other side of the well he traced, or professed to trace, the course of the hidden stream, and marked a spot contiguous to the buildings, where he asserted a good spring would be tapped at a depth of from 120 to 130 feet, and he advised that a well should be sunk there.

> It was told to Mullins that his father asserted the seltzer spring flowed under a hedge on the other side of the field, in which we were then standing, and he was asked to indicate the place. Starting at one end of the field he walked close by the hedge side. He had gone about 100 yards when the twig began to play, and digging his heel in the ground, he thus marked the spot. Mr. Allen, who was present when Mullins, senr., also located the spring, sent a man for a spade, and a stake was dug up, which eight years ago was driven in by Mr. Allen to mark the place. Mullins, junr., had touched the spot exactly.

The same newspaper of August 23rd, 1895, announces the result of digging in the spot indicated as follows:—

> Our readers will remember that a few weeks ago our columns contained an article relative to the finding of water at Catley Abbey by means of hazel twigs in the hands of Mr. Mullins, the eminent "dowser." We are now able to state that a well having been sunk in the position indicated by Mr. Mullins, a valuable supply of water has been obtained, and that at a depth of about five feet less than mentioned by him.

I sent Mr. Allen the foregoing account, and asked if it were correct, he replies that "it is perfectly accurate, the facts being most interesting, and occurred as stated in the letter and newspaper report."

No. 64.—The *Bath Chronicle* (date missing) gives the following account:—

> Captain A. K. Barlow, who recently purchased an estate near Braintree, Essex, had made several borings for water, but without the desired result, and he had reluctantly made up his mind to sell the property and leave the neighbourhood; but, being strongly urged to try the divining rod, he, without having much faith in the efficacy of the powers of the hazel twig, resolved to send for Mr. Mullins. Mullins came, and next morning walked up and down a portion of the estate with his hazel twig before him, and eventually marked a spot about 250 yards from an empty well. Mullins remarked that this spot was the very best place to sink a well, and if it was bored 50 feet a capital supply of water would be found. Captain Barlow set men on to dig a well at the place marked, and they have, at a distance of 34 feet from the surface, dug right into a fine body of water in a gravelly soil.

I wrote to Captain Barlow for confirmation of the above statements, which I enclosed, and he replies:—

Wivenhoe Hall, Essex, *February 24th*, 1897.

> I can only say that the report, as printed, is perfectly true and accurate. I have since sold Lynden Wood. The supply of water there is unfailing and constant. Lynden Wood also stands on the top of one of the highest points of land in this county. I remember noticing that Mullins had hard callosities on his hands just where the hazel twigs fitted between his fingers, and seemed to be in a very highly nervous state when operating with the twigs.

Alexander Barlow.

No. 65.—The following letter from Mr. W. D. Little, estate agent to the Earl of Jersey, is addressed to Mr. J. Mullins:—

Estate Office, Middleton Park, Bicester, Oxon, *August 20th*, 1890.

> In reply to your letter of inquiry, I have much pleasure in informing you that since August, 1884, I have had upwards of 25 wells dug on sites where you had found springs by means of the dowsing rod, and in every instance an abundant and unfailing supply of water has been obtained. These wells have been sunk on the estates of the Earl of Jersey in the counties of Oxfordshire, Warwickshire, and

# The Credibility Of Dowsing

Middlesex, and on the Charterhouse Estate in Wiltshire. I send you a copy of a letter which appeared in *Farm and Home* in 1885.

W. D. Little.

The following is the letter Mr. Little addressed to the journal he names:—

As it may, perhaps, interest some of the readers of Farm and Home, I venture to send a statement of the practical results of seven wells sunk during the autumn of 1884 on the Earl of Jersey's estate at Middleton Park, near Bicester, Oxon, on sites located by John Mullins, of Colerne, Chippenham, Wilts, by means of the dowsing rod. I may preface the following statement by saying that the unprecedented drought of last year was most severely felt in Oxfordshire, and water had to be carted a considerable distance at great expense for several months, for all descriptions of stock. Mullins' search for water was made during the last week in August, 1884, and the sinking of the wells was proceeded with as soon after as possible.

No. 1 was sunk 22 yards from a well sunk in 1879, which had proved to be useless even for supplying two cottages only. At a depth of 18 feet an abundant supply of water was obtained on the spot selected by Mullins. No. 2 was also sunk to substitute a well made in 1879, which, although in a position likely to yield plenty of water, had turned out useless. At a distance of 60 yards from the old well, the new well, sunk on a site selected by Mullins at a depth of 12 feet 0 inches, yielded more water than two ordinary portable pumps would keep down, the continued drought not seeming to affect it in any way. No. 3 was a well that had gone dry, and was deepened on the strength of Mullins' recommendation with a satisfactory result. No. 4, a well sunk to supply the mansion with drinking water; it is 49 feet deep, and has an excellent spring with the water standing about 25 feet deep in the well, the diameter of which is of large size. It is proposed to further increase the inflow of water by boring at some later period. No. 5 sunk to supply two cottages. Although situate in a district proverbially dry and badly off for water, a good supply was found at a depth of 30 feet. No. 6—this is perhaps the most remarkable well of the seven alluded to in this notice. At a depth of 13 feet 6 inches a spring (whose existence was not even suspected) was found that has been proved, after being tested by steam pumps for several days, to yield between 20,000 and 30,000 gallons of water per diem; and this after an abnormally low rainfall during the year. No. 7—at a depth of 18 feet an abundant supply has been found, and, like the wells Nos. 1 and 2, has been sunk to substitute a well that cannot be relied upon.

W. D. Little.

No. 66.—Among Mr. Edmund Gurney's papers were found several communications on dowsing. Here are two which relate to Mullins. The first is from Mr. Henley of Oxford.

Waterperry House, Oxford, *January 2nd*, 1887.

Having heard from Lord Jersey that Mullins had been successful in finding water on his estate in the previous year, and that his wells (eight in number) had stood the test of the late exceptional summer, I requested Mullins to come here for one day only to search for water on two farms that had been without any water for months, with the exception of one pond fed by a gravel spring.

(I) Mullins commenced at Park farm, situated on the clay, with gravel one field distant; he marked two spots where his stick indicated water: 1, near the house (clay), 2, near the pond before mentioned; result, water found near the pond at No. 2, but no water in bore of 30 feet at No. 1. The house is vacant, and having found water in one place I did not persevere at No. 1.

(II) Baker's farm—no water all summer, two places marked; water in both at bore hole about the depth indicated, well thereupon sunk; result, excellent supply. (III) Baker's house in village—present well in clay, no spring : place marked by Mullins near the existing well, bored between 30 and 40 feet without success, but I did not persevere as the other wells in the village are well supplied. (IV) Entrance Lodge—well sunk at place indicated—ample supply.

About fifty people, men, women, and children, tried the rod without success, with the exception of a young lady who was on that day and subsequently able to deflect the rod in the same manner as Mullins, though it appeared to have an injurious effect upon her nerves and this, I am told, is commonly the case.

Mullins has lately been employed by Messrs. Franklin Bros., the well-known land agents, to find water at Charndon, Bucks, on the estate of Mr. Wykeham Musgrave, and has been there eminently successful. You ask me to mention failures and I am only in a position to quote one in this neighbourhood, i.e., at Colonel Miller's on the top of Shotover Hill, where they are said to have gone to considerable expense without finding water, but it is only fair to Mullins to suggest that the depth of search was insufficient.

I was a disbeliever before seeing the experiment on my estate, but the evidence of my own eyes convinced me of its practical utility.

I tested Mullins by taking him over springs of which I alone was aware, and to other spots where I knew no springs existed, and he was in both instances correct.

J. J. Henley.

No. 67.—The next letter is from Mrs. Burton, of Shrewsbury:—

Longner Hall, Shrewsbury, *January 31st,* 1888.

On December 22nd, 1887, we sent for Mr. Mullins, the water-finder. He was driven from the railway station to the Weir Hill farm, where water has been scarce (and sometimes altogether absent) from time immemorial; and the consulting engineer thought it useless to make any further search.

Mr. Mullins having cut a number of twigs from nut trees, hold one by the two prongs and proceeded to walk over a field;—it sprung up suddenly and broke; he said, "there is water at a depth of 60 feet." He then followed the spring up a ploughed field and marked the spot where we were to dig. He said we should find a strong spring from 35 to 45 feet down, but if we failed at that depth we were to go on; he then took his fee and departed. We sunk to a depth of 45 feet and began to despair and doubt Mr. Mullins' powers extremely. However, we went on through a seam of coal, when suddenly, at 48 feet, the water rushed in and is now 29 feet in depth

C. I. Burton.

Mr. Gurney thereupon wrote to Mrs. Burton the following letter, which I quote as an illustration of the vast amount of letter writing that he undertook, and the admirable way he seized the main issue of an investigation.

26, Montpelier Square, S. W., *February 5th,* 1888.

Dear Madam,—Very many thanks for your account of the water-finding. But one would need to know one thing. Had there been ever digging to as great a depth as 48 feet before? If not, we cannot be sure that water might not have been found at numbers of other places, had the digging been continued to that depth; and so the evidential value of the case is left doubtful. Would you kindly let me know this? and believe me, yours very truly,

Edmund Gurney.

Mrs. Burton replies:—

Yes, we had dug before deeper than 48 feet, about 200 yards nearer the farmhouse 50 years ago and some water unfit for use was found. Last year we sank a very deep well also near the house; blasting through the rock we came to what is called a "pocket" of water and all the water disappeared and the well remained dry, the foul gas being too strong to continue the work.

C. I. Burton.

Mr. Gurney's letter happens to be preserved, as Mrs. Burton attached it to her reply.

No. 68.—The *Bristol Times and Mirror* of October 9th, 1888, contains the account of water finding by Mullins at Cirencester, "under circumstances of great interest" according to the newspaper report:—

Some farm buildings at Bagendon, occupied by Mr. J. Hayward, had no water supply, except the runnings from the roofs. The buildings stand on the summit of the rolling Cotswold district, the ground level being on a level with Cirencester church tower, and 144 feet above the road from Cirencester to Cheltenham. Mullins undertook to sink a well, the depth he estimated as necessary being from 70 to 80 feet; whereas owners of house property in the vicinity situated on much lower levels have sunk from 120 to 150 feet, and then often failed to keep a supply of water in dry weather. By the terms of the contract, Mullins is to receive a certain stated sum on finding a supply of water, but if he fails he receives no payment whatever. His men have now been at work for seven or eight weeks, and have sunk just over 70 feet through the rock without coming to water, but they entertain no anxiety as to the result. The termination of the undertaking is being looked forward to with interest.

A subsequent report informs us that the men sunk the well to a depth of 101 feet, when an abundant supply of water was obtained standing 11 feet in the well. This case is quoted to show the absolute faith Mullins had in dowsing, as tested by a heavy pecuniary loss had he failed.

No. 69.—In the *Bath Natural History and Field Club Proceedings* for 1839 (Vol. VI., p. 411), is a lengthy paper on the divining rod, by Mr. T. Forder Plowman. In this paper the author gives the evidence of his friend, Mr. W. J. Brown, of Middlehill House, Box, Wilts, a gentleman occupying a high position in the county, and a member of the council of several public bodies. Mr. Brown states (p. 415): —

I employed Mullins to try for water near Box, the only well near, which was 180 feet deep, being often out of water from September to December after a dry summer. Mullins marked the track of four different springs, one of which, he said, was rather stronger than the others. I asked him how deep the best spring was under the surface, and he said about 110 feet. I then directed Mullins to search for an old well, which, when I was a lad, my father had discovered in an open quarry at the time the Box tunnel was being made. Although it had been filled up many years ago and there were no outward signs of it, I had an opinion as to where it was and directed Mullins to try. They worked all day, but came upon no trace of it, and the general opinion was that I was mistaken as to the spot. However, I ordered them to go on in the same direction next day, and in the afternoon, after working a little more westward, they suddenly came upon the well, and, on examining, we found that the marks Mullins had made in the first place to denote the position of the strongest spring pointed exactly into the centre of the well. [In another communication Mr. Brown says they found the depth of the old well to be 70 feet, and that he contracted with Mullins to sink it 50 feet deeper.] I then directed him to sink down further for water, and strange to say, at 111 feet, viz., within a foot of the distance he had stated at first, we found the spring come in, and just where he had marked it. The well now supplies twenty cottages and if, in a very dry season, they draw all the water out by night, there is plenty again the next morning.

Whilst this work was in progress, some friends and myself arranged to test Mullins' capacity for discovering metal. In his absence we took ten stones off the top of a wall, and having placed them on the road, we deposited a sovereign under three of them. Mullins passed his rod over the top of each stone, and without the slightest hesitation, told us at once under which stones the sovereigns were. When he came to a stone under which there was no sovereign, he at once said, "Nothing here, master," but when he got to the others, he remarked, "All right, master, thankee," turned the stone over and put the sovereign in his pocket.

He afterwards tried for water on the Cottle's House Estate, the then owner, Dr. Parfitt, being very anxious to obtain it, as there was none on the estate. Mullins, however, tried in vain, and, having given it up as a bad job, was leaving for home, when just as he passed the front of New House Farm, with his rod in his hand, it suddenly indicated the presence of water

He at once said there was a strong spring at a depth of only about 18 feet below the surface. He sank a well on the spot, and the water was found at the depth he stated. [In another letter Mr. Brown says the depth of the well was 20 feet.] The tenant told me it is capital water, and the supply never runs short.

After Mullins has indicated water I have blindfolded him and turned him round and round, but whenever after this he crossed the spring up went the rod directly. I conclude by saying I believe in him thoroughly.

The author, Mr. Plowman, bears testimony "to the open and straightforward manner of Mullins, and that he is without any of the outward characteristics of the professional charlatan." In answer to enquiries Mullins stated to Mr. Plowman that whenever he is dowsing and gets over a stream of water he feels a tingling sensation in his arms like a slight electric shock, and the strength of this sensation enables him to guess the approximate volume or depth of a spring.

Somewhat similar evidence of the success and accuracy of the dowser's art was also given to the author of the above paper by Mr. Malton Druce, of Abingdon, by Mr. W. D. Little, estate agent to the Earl of Jersey, (I have referred to this evidence elsewhere, (No. 65 p. 93), by Mr. W. H. Ashhurst, J.P., of Waterstock, by Mr. F. Webster, of the Queen's Home Farm at Osborne (whose testimony is endorsed by Mr. A. Blake, Her Majesty's Steward); Mr. Webster discovered to his surprise that he himself was a good dowser. The author also quotes at length the remarkable evidential cases furnished by Sir W. E. Welby Gregory, Bart., and by the Hon. M. E. G. Finch-Hatton, now the Earl of Winchilsea and Nottingham. (See Nos. 73 and 74).

No. 70.—Another interesting case is given in full by Mr. Forder Plowman, on p. 424, Vol. VI., of the *Proceedings of the Bath Field Club*. It is from Mr. H. D. Skrine, J.P., D.L., of Claverton Manor, Bath. Mr. Skrine writes:—

My first acquaintance with the divining rod was in January, 1865. I had heard that one John Mullins, a well sinker, who lived at Colerne, had the gift of finding water by the rod. I sent for him and took him to a field adjoining the village of Conkwell, where I had thought of building a cottage as a sort of sanatorium for my wife. On the way he tried the divining rod several times, and I was aware that in a line below the points where the twig turned with him, there was a spring in the wood which came to the surface. Arrived on the field, the twig turned with him in several places, and he set a mark on the wall opposite the spot.

A few days after I asked Mr. Earle, Rector of Monkton Farleigh, to meet John Mullins and myself on the field on January 20th, 1865; as I had heard that Mr. Earle had the gift, and had discovered water by it on his own land at Monkton Farleigh. He was not aware of the marks on the wall, but the twig turned with him at the same places as with Mullins; they differed only in the position in the field as to the best place to sink the well, both being in the same line. The well was sunk, and water was found at about 80 feet in yellow clay under the rock, but this not being of sufficient depth and the clay being a thin bed, Mullins went down about 25 feet lower and came on a good spring in the blue lias.

Mullins afterwards found some springs near the house and traced them up to the spot where, under the croquet lawn, a spring had been found some years before. Since then I have employed him at Claverton, and sunk two wells succesfully, and he has again traced several springs which have been verified. In two instances where the line of a drain had been lost, he recovered the spot and was always correct. My two sons, who have watched the operation, found they also had the gift. I cannot resist the conclusion that it is a real gift possessed by some persons, and that it may have been a natural provision to enable men to obtain that very necessary element (water) when there are no signs above the surface.

The following abstracts of cases already published in our *Proceedings* are added here for the convenience of the reader:—

No. 71.—Captain Henry Smith, J.P., of Horbling, Folkingham, Lincolnshire, writing on December 26th, 1882, states that his scepticism as to the practical value of the indications given by the divining rod, as used by Mullins, were overcome by what he himself witnessed and describes in full in *Proceedings* S.P.R., Vol. II., p. 95, etc. Mullins fixed on certain spots where water would be found, and again indicated the same spots when unable to see the previous places. Against Captain Smith's opinion, Mullins said an abundant supply of water would be found at a particular spot, and on sinking a well, this was found to be the case. Other evidence is also given.

No. 72.—Mr. G. Hancock, of Corsham, Wilts, writing on January 23rd, 1883, states he employed Mullins to find the best place for sinking shafts for mining operations, so as to *avoid* the inrush of water, which had previously hindered their work. Mr. Hancock says, "In every case Mullins was right." (*Proceedings* S.P.R., Vol. II., p. 96).

No. 73.—Sir Welby Gregory, Bart., formerly M.P., of Denton Manor, Grantham, writing on January 28th, 1883, states he employed Mullins to find water for a new country house he was building. As a test, Sir W. Gregory first tried whether Mullins could find water on the lawn, through a certain part of which a drain-pipe carried running water; the exact position was known to Sir W. G., but not to M.; the twig instantly moved whenever M. crossed the drain. After traversing the grounds, Mullins fixed on two lines, A and B (about 30 yds. apart), where he said water would be found, from 20 ft. to 30 ft. deep at A, and from 30 ft. to 40 ft. deep at B, the latter the more copious supply, the former small. A neighbouring hill, which Mullins thought likely to yield a better supply, was traversed, but no indications of water were given by the rod. Subsequently Sir W. Gregory consulted an eminent civil engineer, who stated from his geological knowledge of the country, that the hill was the best place to bore for water, but that none would be found at the places indicated in the grounds, A and B, at a less depth than 120 feet to 130 feet. This opinion was confirmed by another geological authority. Sir Welby's gardener having found the rod moved in his hands, tried his skill, and fixed on the same spots as Mullins had done; the rod, held by pincers, violently twisted itself over the spots, A and B. Sir Welby blindfolded the man, and at the same spots again the rod moved. Hence he decided to sink on both the lines indicated. In one (A), he found water at 20 feet, and in the other (B), as stated by Mullins, a much larger supply at 28 feet. Between the two lines Mullins said there was no water. Sir Welby sank a shaft midway, and went down 10 to 12 feet deeper than the deepest well, but found no water, although the formation appeared precisely similar; neither well was affected by this trial shaft. This is a striking ease, and is given in full in *Proceeding* S.P.R., Vol. II., pp. 97-99.

In a speech Sir Welby Gregory made at Grantham (reported in the *Grantham Journal,* September 28th, 1888) he refers to his experience of the practical value of the divining rod and remarks that in future he prefers to trust to the dowser rather than to the geologist in sinking wells.

No. 74.—The Hon. M. E. G. Finch-Hatton, then M.P. (now the Earl of Winchilsea), writing on February 29th, 1884, from 23, Ennismore Gardens, S.W., describes his own experience with Mullins, at Haverholme Priory, a place Mullins had no previous acquaintance with. (1) Mullins found and traced the water-supply pipe up to the house, though no indication on the surface was visible, nor had any information been given to Mullins. (2) He found a spring on the lawn, the existence of an old well at the very spot being afterwards proved, though unknown at the time. (3) He was unable to find another water pipe, when the distant tap was *not* turned on, but when the water was running he fixed the spot correctly. Mullins was then blindfolded, and though led round by a different route, again fixed on the same spot. "At first he slightly overran it a foot or so, and then felt round, as it were, and seemed to be led back into the exact centre of influence by the twig. All present considered the trial conclusive of two things : (1) of the man's perfect good faith; (2) that the effect produced on the twig emanated from an agency outside of himself, and appeared due to the presence of running water." (See *Proceedings* S.P.R., Vol. II., p. 101).

No. 75.—Mr. F. T. Mott, F.R.G.S., whom I know personally, writing from Bristol Hill, Leicester, states that on his estate at Charnwood Forest there was no spring water. The formation was metamorphic slate; several wells had been sunk, and no water found; in one case the boring went to 100 feet, but unsuccessfully. Mullins was employed, and by the movement of the twig, which Mr. Mott states he could not restrain, though he tried to do so, certain spots were marked. "Anywhere along that line," Mullins said, "you will find water if you sink about 30 feet." A well was sunk, and at 28 feet water was found. On sinking to 31 feet, a constant supply, standing 6 feet in the well, has been obtained. (See *Proceedings* S.P.R., Vol. II., p. 100).

I have, after considerable enquiry, met with two or three failures on the part of Mr. J. Mullins, which are narrated on a later page.

## (b) Mr. H. W. Mullins

Although no conclusive evidence exists to show that the faculty of "dowsing" is hereditary, yet in several instances one or more of the children of notable dowsers do possess the "gift." Mr. H. W. Mullins, of Colerne, Box, Wilts, son of the late J. Mullins, is a case in point, judging from the following cases of his that I have investigated.

No. 76.—Having been informed that Mullins, junr. had been successful in finding water for a brewery where an old well existed that was of no use, I wrote to the proprietor, Mr. Bean, and the following is his reply:—

Wothorpe House, Stamford, *May 24th*, 1896.

> I had Mr. Mullins, the water finder, some time last year down to my brewery at Ketton, in which there was an old well with only a very small quantity of water.
>
> Before Mr. Mullins came I had the well covered over so as to completely conceal it from view. Mr. Mullins walked up my yard and when he came to the spot marked B on sketch, said, "there is a very strong spring here, flowing in this direction," marked C. I then showed him the well, W, and he said the amount of water we got from it was not as large as the spring he found at B. He advised me to sink lower, when I should probably tap the spring which, according to him, ran in the direction of the wells. I asked how many gallons per hour did he think I should find; he said from 1,000 to 1,500. I did nothing to the well until three months ago, when I sank three feet lower in the well and tunnelled four feet in the direction of the supposed spring, when one day the men heard a rumble and a large amount of water broke in and rapidly rose in the well. I gauged the amount and found it about 800 gallons per hour (by pump).

## *The Credibility Of Dowsing*

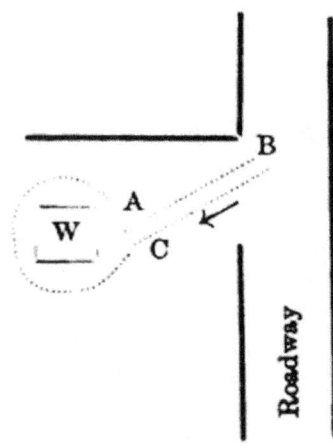

W, site of old well. B, position of strong spring indicated by Mullins, said to be flowing in the direction of C. Water broke into the well at the spot A, when tunnelling towards B.

This is all I can tell you as to water finding, but if you write to my friend, Mr. W. Barber, C.E., 22, Buckingham-street, Strand, W.C., he will give you some more information about water finding at different parts of the country.

W. Bean.

Mr. Barber kindly replied to my enquiries and gave me information that appears elsewhere.

No. 77.—The next letter furnishes a still more striking case of Mr. H. W. Mullins' success. In answer to my enquiries Mr. Bayley writes:—

Arnold's, Holmwood, Surrey, *December 29th*, 1896.

In reply to your communication of the 26th inst., I beg to inform you when I bought this property 10 years ago there was an old well about 60 feet deep on the premises which was said to have a good supply of water, but when I came to put it to the test I found it quite inadequate for the wants of my house, so consulted Messrs. Isler and Co. as to the best means of increasing the supply. On their advice I got them to bore through the bottom of the old well to a depth of about 100 feet, making in all about 160 feet, but found no water. Some time after, seeing an account of the divining rod, I sent for Mullins and he said there was water to be had at about 60 feet deep on the top of a hill 300 yards from the old well. He dug a well on the site and found water at a depth of 90 feet, and now we have an abundant supply. Holmwood is 28 miles from London and is under the Surrey Hills.

Edmond K. Bayley.

No. 78.—It is sometimes urged that only springs yielding a limited supply of water are found by dowsers, who fix on spots where more or less surface water can be got from shallow wells rather than run the risk of sinking a deep well. Many of the cases already cited refute this notion, and the following sent to me in answer to my enquiries bears on the same point. It is from Messrs. Beamish and Crawford, the well-known brewers of Cork.

Cork Porter Brewery, Cork, *December 30th*, 1896.

In reply to your letter of 26th inst. we beg to state:—

1. We had an old well yielding a small supply of water. It was about 30 feet deep.

2. No new well was fixed on by Mullins. He bored down to a depth of about 60 feet below the bottom of the old well, and therefore about 90 feet below the surface of the ground.

3. The supply of water now obtained from the new pipes sunk by Mullins is, as nearly as we can estimate, about 10,000 gallons per hour.

Beamish and Crawford, Ltd.

No. 79.—The next letter in answer to my enquiries is from the Rev. H. F. Ramsay, M.A.:—

Brendon, Lynton, N. Devon, *December 30th*, 1896.

In reply to your letter of the 26th instant, I beg to state that before commencing the building of the new rectory at Oare we sunk a well close to the site of the house to a depth of 28 feet. As hard rock full of fissures was there met with, and there was no sign of water, we decided to discontinue the sinking. It was at this stage that we called in Mullins, who went all over the ground in the usual way holding a hazel twig. He tried about the site and pronounced our well to be absolutely hopeless; afterwards he tried below the site and at the lowest spot on the field he pointed out a place where we should get 400 gallons a day at 35 feet deep and a big spring at 70 feet. We soon started to dig and came to a small spring yielding about 200 gallons at 26 feet. I find the supply insufficient, so I propose to deepen the well somewhat, as there is not more than three feet of water in it. The new well is about 40 yards from the old well.

I do not pretend to explain Mullins' modus operandi, but it does appear to me that he has a marvellous power of finding water underground. To test him we took him to two fields (far apart from each other), and in each case he discovered a hidden covered spring, of the existence of which he could not possibly have been aware beforehand. In the one case the water was drained off by underground drain tiles into the river Badyworthy, and in the other the water shows on the surface of the grass only when the springs burst after prolonged heavy rain.

H F Ramsay

P.S.—Perhaps I ought to mention that the house is in the Lynn Valley, but not quite at the bottom of the slope.

No. 80.—Mr. F. T. Elworthy, of Foxdown, Wellington, sends me the following:—

At the Parsonage Farm, Bishop Nympton, North Devon, the owners had expended large sums in the hope of finding a better supply of water, but all to no purpose. At last they determined to avail themselves of the assistance of Messrs. J. Mullins. and Sons, water-finders, of Colerne, Chippenham, Wiltshire. Mr. Henry Mullins (one of the firm) visited the farm, and, by the aid of a twig of hazel, pointed out several places where springs might be found at depths varying from six feet to twenty-five feet. He succeeded in finding one six feet deep at a short distance from the farmhouse, and two more a little further off, from eight to ten feet deep, each of which Mr. Mullins estimated would produce from 300 to 400 gallons of water per day.— From North Devon Herald, September 27th, 1894, communicated by Mr. G. M. Doe to the Devon Association, Vol. XXVIII. (1896) p. 90.

Mr. Elworthy adds:—

Parsonage Farm is well-known to me. It belonged to an uncle of mine up to and since his death, when it was sold to the present owners.

With reference to the foregoing, Mr. R. B. Crosse, solicitor to the trustees of the estate, writes as follows:—

25, Broad Street, South Molton, North Devon, *October 16th*, 1895.

I am pleased to say that the result of Mr. Mullins' experiments on Parsonage Farm, Bishop Nympton, Devon, has proved highly satisfactory. At the second place indicated by Mr. Henry Mullins a well has been sunk and water found at the exact depth he foretold. His judgment as to the quantity of water was also quite correct.

Reginald Stawell Crosse.

# The Credibility Of Dowsing

I wrote to the present proprietor for further information, and Mr. Crosse replies:—

25, Broad Street, South Molton, North Devon,
*January 6th,* 1897.

My tenant, Mr. George Rudd, has handed me your letter, and in reply I may say that the divining rod as used by Mr. Mullins was a complete success. I had spent (on behalf of my trustees) a considerable amount for sinking wells prior to Mr. Mullins' visit, and the places indicated by Mr. Mullins were not far away from where the first sinking operations took place.

I was with him at Oare, near Lynton, and he was just as successful there.

Reg. S. Crosse.

No. 81.—Writing on December 29th, 1896, in reply to my enquiries, Captain Hobbs states he is the agent for some property near Warrington, Cheshire, where a supply of water was obtained by sinking a well at a spot indicated by the dowsing rod, though several other wells had previously been sunk unsuccessfully without the use of the rod. In a subsequent letter, Captain Hobbs gives me the following details:—

8, King-street, Manchester, *January 7th,* 1897.

I have to-day been able to get all the information about the finding of water on the farm at Burtonwood, near Warrington. The property is owned by the executors of the late Wm. Bindloss, and is situated about five miles from Warrington. Up to the visit of Mr. H. W. Mullins, the farmer had used the rain water, filtered.

On November 29th, 1895, Mr. H. W. Mullins accompanied me and several ladies and gentlemen to the place (he had never been in that neighbourhood before), and after walking over the farmyard, garden, and field near the house, he fixed on a spot about 50 yards from the house, in the garden, where he said we should find a supply of water sufficient for the use of the house.

There a well has been sunk, and a supply of from 60 to 70 gallons (probably more, as we have never pumped it out quite dry) an hour was found. The water was first found at 40 feet from the surface, but sinking was continued for 5 feet more (through quicksand). There is now an ample supply at all times in the well.

In 1880 a well was sunk about 12 yards from the house; 48 feet were sunk and 18 feet bored (a total of 66 feet), but no water was found. No further steps were taken since that date until Mullins' visit

On the opposite side of the road from the farm in question, in or about 1877, three wells were sunk about 50 feet deep. In two of them no water was found, and hardly any in the third, but the supply was so small that it was useless. The farm on which these wells were sunk is in a north-west direction from the Forest Farm (that is the name of the farm where our well is), and about 80 to 100 yards distant.

These three wells were all in sand; our well was through 15 feet of clay, then sand, and lastly quicksand.

The river nearest to these farms is the Mersey, distant about four miles.

The following were present at the finding of the water [a lengthy list of names and addresses is here given.]

## Prof. W. F. Barrett

*We all* were, and are, convinced that the operation of the divining rod in Mr. Mullins' hands was perfectly honest and genuine, as well as very wonderful.

J. C. Hobbs.

Replying to my further enquiries Captain Hobbs writes:—

8, King Street, Manchester, *January 21st*, 1897.

The ground all round the house is nearly level. I give below a sketch, as you wish, of the relative position of the wells; but I am a bad hand at drawing.

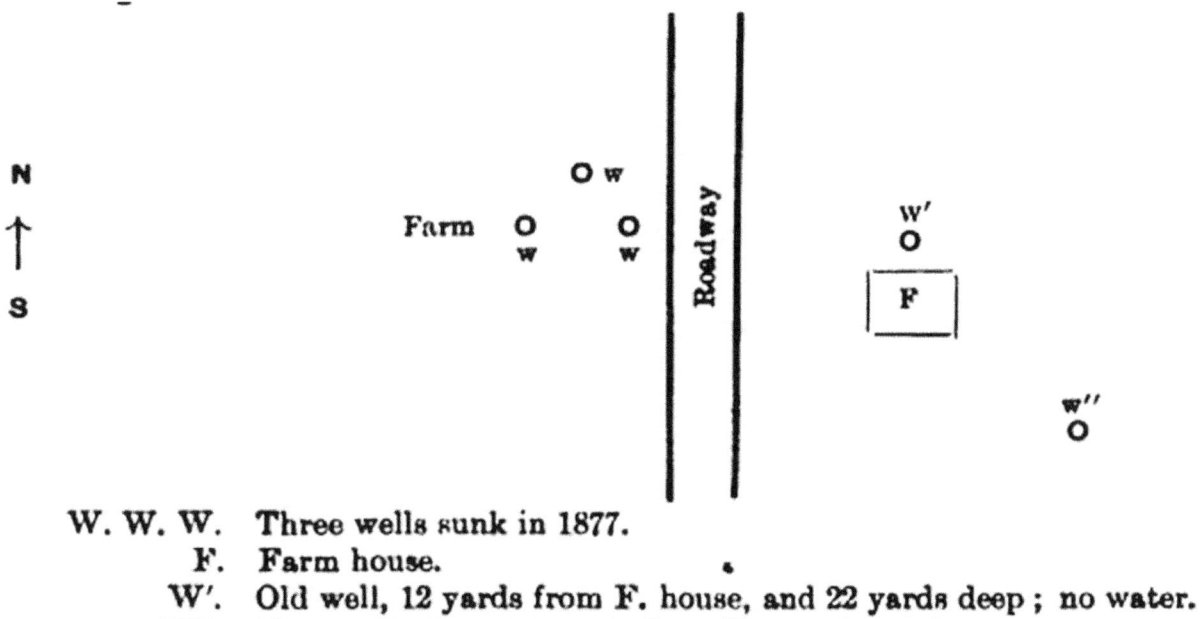

W. W. W. Three wells sunk in 1877.
    F. Farm house.
   W'. Old well, 12 yards from F. house, and 22 yards deep ; no water.
  W". New well, about 50 yards from F.; good supply.

No. 82.—Another illustration of young Mr. Mullins' faculty is given in the *Warrington Guardian* for the last week in April, 1896. The report states that a Mr. Beck Chadwick, J.P., having sunk borings and failed to find water, was led to employ Mr. Mullins, who from the indications given by the dowsing rod fixed on a certain spot, where he asserted an abundant supply of water would be found at about 70 feet deep. A well was accordingly sunk, and, at between 50 and 60 feet, a great inrush of water occurred and a copious supply has been obtained. The Editor of the *Warrington Guardian* to whom I applied, referred me to Mr. Chadwick's agent, Mr. J. Shaw Green, F.S.S., an accountant at Warrington, who could vouch for the facts. Mr. Shaw Green's reply to my letter is as follows:—

18, King Street, Warrington, *January 11th*, 1897.

The whole of the circumstances are very familiar to me. The spot is in the township of Kingsley at a place where a valley runs for a considerable distance. Two trial borings were made by an eminent firm of well-sinkers at places selected by them, but without result, and it was upon their failure that the services of the water diviner were brought in. In reply to the queries stated in your letter:

1. The facts [in the newspaper report] are correctly stated.

# *The Credibility Of Dowsing*

2. Two previous attempts, as stated above, had been made, one of them immediately before the water diviner was called in. I cannot give the exact depth.

3. The results are set out in the cutting. A well already existed with a small quantity of water in it at about 35 feet. The distance between place indicated by water diviner and well is about 18 yards. One of the trial borings was made at a distance of about 25 yards from the spot indicated by the diviner.

It is altogether a most interesting case and the full particulars of the search appeared in the Warrington Guardian, I believe, in the month of April last.

J. Shaw Green.

In reply to my inquiry, Mr. Shaw Green writes:—

18, King Street, Warrington. *January 20th,* 1897.

The gentleman who made the search for us was the eldest son of J. Mullins, who died nearly three years ago.

The date of the search was Friday the 24th April, 1896.

I will obtain and send you particulars of the abortive borings, but it may be a few days before I can do so, for the particulars are at Kingsley and not in my office.

J. Shaw Green.

No. 83.—The *Pall Mall Gazette* of February 20th, 1897, publishes the following letter from Lord Burton:—

We are situated in Needwood Forest, on the top of a mass of marl thrust up between the rivers Dove and Trent. Our water is derived from wells averaging from 140 ft. to 180 ft. deep, and owing to a series of dry years our supply has recently been very scanty. Our best well gives about 4,000 gallons in the twenty-four hours.

About three months ago I sent for Mr. Mullins, the well-known water-finder, who walked round the property with a small hazel wand or twig in his hands. Every now and then the wand seemed to twitch, and he indicated that water would be found in these places, naming an approximate depth and probable supply. At last we came to a field where the twig gave indications of a row of springs, and Mullins informed us that if we sank we should probably get a supply of nearly 40,000 gallons in the twenty-four hours. We have sunk, and at 140 feet to 150 feet we have a most abundant supply, quite equal to what was promised, and we expect to get more by driving adits right and left.

One curious thing was that when the twig was placed in another person's hands turning towards the ground, on Mullins grasping the hands the twig slowly turned up; but this happened only with two out of four persons experimented on. I cannot explain the phenomenon, but it appears to me to be perfectly genuine, and certainly in my case the result has been very successful.

Burton

*February 18th.*

I wrote to Lord Burton asking him whether any wells had been sunk on his estate unsuccessfully prior to young Mr. Mullins' visit. His reply is as follows:—

# *Prof. W. F. Barrett*

Rangemore, Burton-on-Trent, *March 9th*, 1897.

I fear I can add no facts to the short letter I sent to the Pall Mall. [Prior to Mullins' visit] we may have sunk a dozen wells in all, varying from 40 to 60 yards in depth; the supply is not copious in any of them; the stable yard is the best, about 4,000 gallons in the 24 hours at the most,—this well is over 60 yards deep. The supply at the new [Mullins] well about half a mile to the east of the above and about 300 yards below and south of the village, is so good that we are going to considerable expense in sinking and putting down pumps, erecting tank and tower and so forth. Mullins marked five springs in a line extending over perhaps 30 yards or more. We are driving side adits from the well and they seem to be producing a quantity of water.

Burton.

No. 84.—The *Essex Times* of January 29th, 1896, reports:—

Considerable difficulty has been experienced in finding a sufficient supply of water for the Bower House, Havering, the residence of Mr. A. Money Wigram, M.P. As Havering stands on very high ground, the only chance of finding supplementary sources of supply lay in the discovery of the course of the underground springs. Investigation in this direction by the ordinary methods having proved fruitless, Mr. W. H. Pemberton Barnes a few days ago invited Mr. John Mullins.[1] A field near the top of the hill was selected as the sphere of operations. Providing himself with the indispensable rod, Mr. Mullins began by walking slowly across the ground, holding one end of the rod in each hand with the point downwards, until he came across what he intimated was an underground spring, when the twig would turn in his hands in a half-circle. He indicated a certain spot as the place where the spring was strongest, giving as his opinion that water would be obtained at a depth of from 30 to 35 feet. Here a shaft was afterwards sunk, but before the specified depth was reached the water came in so rapidly that operations had to be suspended, owing to the impossibility of working the pumps fast enough to keep the well empty.

I wrote to Mr. Money Wigram for further particulars, and the following is his reply, which has been delayed for the reasons given:—

101, Eaton Square, S.W., *May 15th*, 1897.

I have left Havering, and for the last few months have been travelling in the East.

In answer, I would say the first experiment made at Mullins' suggestion failed through no fault of his. He said, "You will find water [at] 37 feet." We did, in a shifting bed of sand, but on going 3 feet lower we struck clay and lost it all. Afterwards he indicated two springs within a few feet of each other, and both were tapped with success.

I believe in him strongly for surface springs, and should always consult him were I building cottages, &c., where the supply required is small.

A. Money Wigram.

It will be seen that none of these cases, where Mr. H. W. Mullins was the dowser, afford such striking evidence on behalf of a dowsing faculty as was given by the portion of his father's work that I have been able to investigate. Though I have not heard of any distinct failures on the part of the son, beyond wrong estimates of the depth and volume of the underground water, (if the Richmond Experiments to be narrated later are excepted), yet this is not

---

[1] This is the name of the firm, but here and elsewhere in this group (b) the dowser is the son, Mr. H. W. Mullins.—W. F. B.

surprising, as Mr. Mullins, junr., has not long been engaged at this particular work. That he has had, or will have, occasional failures is likely enough, but what proportion they bear to his successes I have no independent means of ascertaining.

MR. H. W. MULLINS.

## The Waterford Experiments

In the group of cases under the head of the late Mr. J. Mullins will be found a very striking one, No. 52, (p. 58), the particulars of which were kindly sent to me by Mr. Christie-Miller. Subsequently my friend Mr. Kilroe, of the Geological Survey of Ireland, told me of a very similar case occurring at Messrs. Richardson's factory at Waterford. I begged Mr. Kilroe to put the facts in writing for me, which he did in the accompanying letter. Afterwards additional evidence of eye-witnesses was obtained and it then became evident the case was the same as that sent to me by Mr. Christie-Miller; this led to enquiry and it turned out that Mr. Christie-Miller, though not living at Waterford, is the proprietor of Messrs. Richardson's factory. As the case is of special importance it will be necessary to give some, I fear, rather tedious details.

Mr. Kilroe writes:—

Geological Survey of Ireland Office, 14, Hume Street, Dublin, *January 23rd*, 1897.

In or about the year 1888, Messrs. Richardson, bacon curers, of Waterford, required a considerable water supply and got professional advice, based upon geological grounds, as to where to obtain it by sinking. The amount procured on sinking proved entirely insufficient. This was surface water, and when the rock was reached it proved quite dry, giving a worse rather than a better prospect as the sinking progressed. The strata at the place are nearly vertical and the bedding much folded.

An English "diviner" was engaged, and to hinder collusion, the chief clerk of the firm met him at the boat on arrival in Waterford; who also brought him to the works. There the diviner was accompanied by the head of the firm and his staff of clerks, as he went around the premises. He carried in his two hands a forked hazel twig, holding a branch of the fork in each hand, the stem extending from him in front horizontally. He almost immediately came to a spot over which the rod bent slightly and quite spontaneously, as well as could be observed. This spot was marked and the search continued. Similar indications appeared at two or three other places. At one, the effect was so manifest that the rod twisted completely round and *broke!*—also of its own accord. (The man had several of these rods with him.) The firm sank at one of the places indicated and obtained a copious supply of water.

Mr. Budd, a local amateur geologist, ascertained the above particulars and communicated all to Mr. Clark, of the Irish Survey, who gave them to me.

J. R. Kilroe.

I wrote to Messrs. Richardson requesting them to give me a reply to a series of questions I enclosed. The following are my queries and their answer to each:—

*Query*. Name of the "dowser"? *Answer*, The late J. Mullins.

*Q*. Were any borings made or wells sunk prior to the dowser's visit? *A*. Yes; three.

Q. If so, how deep? *A*. One was 300 feet, one 1,011 feet, and one 52 feet deep.

*Q*. With what success as to water supply? *A*. Neither of the three wells yielded more than 120 gallons per hour.

*Q*. How far from the old well did the diviner fix on for a new well? *A*. 40 or 50 feet (shortest distance).

*Q*. How deep was the new well—sunk on the spot indicated by the divining rod? *A*. 82 feet.

*Q*. With what success as regards water supply? *A*. 3,000 to 5,000 gallons per hour; according to the rainfall.

*Q*. What was the date of the dowser's visit? *A*. 1889.

As I was anxious to get exact details of this case, I again wrote to Messrs. Richardson for further particulars and an accurate plan of the respective position of the wells. Their reply is as follows:—

# The Credibility Of Dowsing

*February 2nd, 1897.*

In reply to yours of the 28th January, I regret the delay, but owing to the dispute in our trade at present I am very pressed with work. I have had a rough sketch made out of the lie of the wells, and a description of same, and trust it is what you require. Should you want any further information I shall do my best to get it for you.

W.Richardson

*Memorandum from Messrs. Richardson and Co., Waterford.*

*February 2nd, 1897.*

In the year 1887, we received an estimate for boring a 2½ inch artesian bore from John Henderson and Son, Glasgow. He started to bore on the 18th May, 1887, with jumper steel drills. The first 15 feet was clay, the following 17 feet was slaty sandstone, after which the rock became harder with the result that the rate of boring slowed, varying from 2 to 5 feet per day. When going through extremely hard rock they bored (on Monday, the 18th June, 1887) only 4 inches. We continued boring until we had reached a depth of 292 feet, after which we widened the bore for 100 feet to allow a pump to be lowered, but the yield was not sufficient to justify our going deeper, so relinquished this bore.

We next started to bore, in 1888, a 7 inch bore hole at the bottom of a well 62 feet deep. This bore was executed by the Diamond Rock Boring Co., of London, and was bored by a revolving tube 7 inches in diameter having black diamonds set in a nose piece fastened to bottom of tube. We bored 612 feet with this size tube and then reduced to 6 inches and with the 6 inch tube bored 337 feet 7 inches, making a total depth bored of 949 feet 7 inches from the bottom of well, and from the ground level of 1,011 feet 7 inches. We had, during the process of boring, tested at intervals for yield of water but with no satisfactory result. We again tested at 1,011 feet 7 inches, and again failure, so relinquished this bore.

We then asked Mr. Kinahan [senior geologist of H.M. Geological Survey of Ireland] to come down—which he did, and suggested a spot to bore. This bore we started with a 4 inch tube diamond drill, and bored 40 feet through yellow sandstone when we came on blue slate for 8 inches; we then stopped and wired Mr. Kinahan what we ought to do. In the interval we tested for water;—result, 230 gallons per hour, not one-tenth part of what we required. Mr. Kinahan advised going on again. Went on 11 feet more, tested again, with the yield 180 gallons per hour, a loss of 50 gallons; wired Mr. Kinahan again; — reply, give up boring—which we did;—another failure. We then sent for John Mullins, the water diviner. He suggested that we put down a bore on a marked out line, which we did, with the result that we have an ample supply. See below for rough plan of wells.

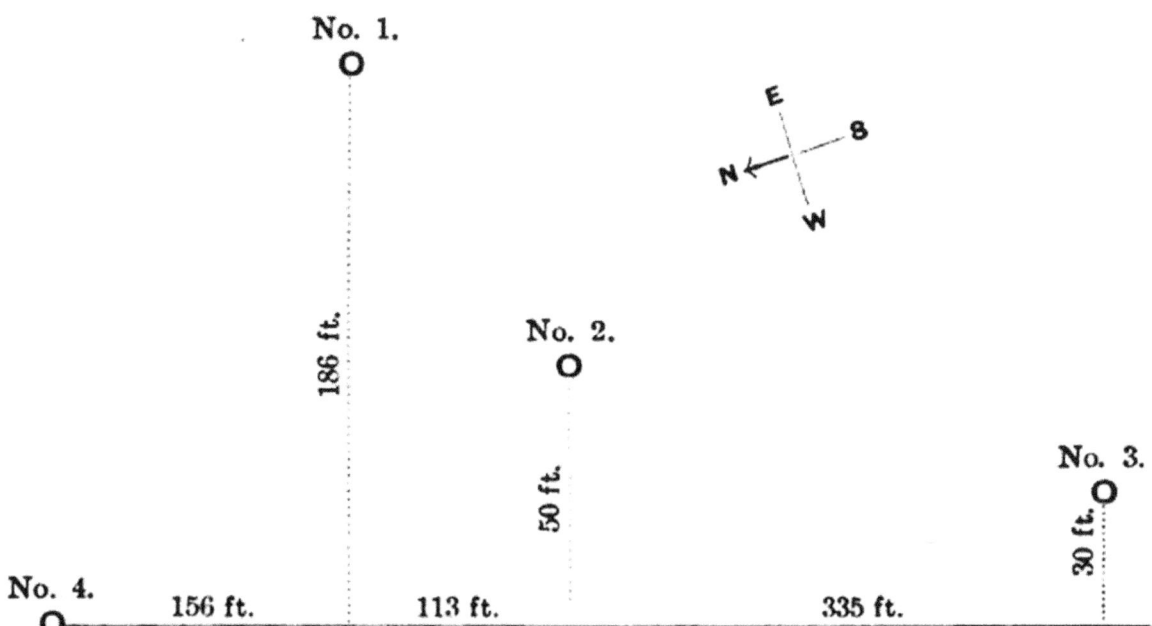

No. 1. First Bore Hole, sunk to a depth of 292 feet:—not satisfactory.

No. 2. Second Bore Hole, sunk to a depth of 949 ft. 7 in. from bottom of well 62 feet deep;—from ground level 1,011 ft. 7 in.:—another failure.

No. 3. Bore Hole suggested by Mr. Kinahan:—third failure.

No. 4. Bore Hole suggested by John Mullins, around which bore hole we sank a 6 ft. well, 82 feet deep. Yield from 3,000 to 5,000 gallons per hour depending on rainfall.

Line from No. 4 shows course of spring as suggested by Mullins, anywhere along which line, he says, water will be found. The line runs N.N.E.

The particulars sent me by Messrs. Richardson are obviously of great interest and evidential value in connection with our subject. I was therefore anxious to obtain the best geological evidence on this case. Happily Mr. G. H. Kinahan, M.R.I.A., who at the time was senior geologist of the Irish Geological Survey, had not only been called in by Messrs. Richardson, prior to Mullins' visit, but had kept the contemporary notes and correspondence relating to this case. The letters which Mr. Kinahan sent me (with an accompanying note from himself) are from Messrs. Richardson and from a local geologist, Mr. Budd, and, as will be seen, they were written at the time of Mullins' visit to Waterford.

Mr. Kinahan writes to me as follows:—

*January 25th,* 1897.]

I am glad to learn through Mr. Clark that you are taking up the Divining Rod question. I, therefore, through him, send you a rather interesting case. These letters [which follow] I give solely up to you, and you are at liberty to use them as you like. I should, however, let you know how I was connected with them. A bacon firm in Waterford (Messrs. Denny and Co.) were looking for water, and their trials were unsatisfactory. My friend, the late Mr. James Budd, advised them to apply to me. This they

## The Credibility Of Dowsing

did. and as their case was a simple one, I easily put them right. Then another firm, Messrs. Richardson's, was in a similar predicament;—they had a water supply, but not sufficient. They employed a borer who bored, I think, 1,000 feet, without finding water. They were then advised by Budd to employ me; when I visited their premises I found it was probably crossed by three water lines, one south, another at their well, and the third to the northward—as the strata was hard, impervious ordovician shale. It was evident that unless the bore hole was exactly on one of the water lines a bore was useless. I, therefore, advised sinking and driving. While they were considering my report, young Richardson heard of the water-man, and what happened afterwards you will know from the letters. I have my theory about their "water-finder," and would like to talk it over with you.

G. H. Kinahan.

The next letter is from Mr. Richardson, addressed to Mr. Kinahan in the year 1889:—

Waterford, *October 24th*, 1889.

In reply to your favour, re John Mullins, Colerne, Chippenham, Wiltshire, I will give you a short account of his doings here. The morning he came I had him met at the Milford steamer, in order to prevent his having communication with any one in Waterford, and making inquiries about our premises. I myself went with him when he began his searches for water.

He had in his hands a hazel fork of this shape  holding an end between his fingers of each hand. He then walked about until the hazel fork twisted suddenly in his hands. He did this over and over again to test it, and marked several places for us to bore where he said he was certain we should find water, and gave the depths. One place in particular he pointed out to us and advised our boring, saying we should find about 1,500 gallons per hour at a depth of 80 to 90 feet. We procured the boring people, and the result of it was we obtained water at the depth of 79 feet from the surface. We tested to 1,672 gallons per hour, but we are sure there is more, only our pump could not test a greater supply. He [told us he] has six sons, and not one of them has this power.

It is a most curious thing, but must be genuine without doubt. I know several people in the north who had Mullins there, and found water where pointed out by him. It was from them I heard of Mullins in the first instance.

The rod often breaks with the force it turns in his hands. The greater the movement the more water is there, and by this he tells the depth.

W. Richardson.

Mr. Richardson adds later:—

He holds the twig straight out in front of him, with the ends passing between his finger and thumb and coming out between his second and third fingers; backs of hands downwards.

The next letter is from Mr. Budd, addressed to Mr. Kinahan, and is interesting on account of its having been written whilst the boring experiments were in progress:—

Tivoli, Tramore, Waterford, *September 3rd*, 1889.

Your being interested in Messrs. Richardson's case here will be my apology for my inflicting on you the following authentic account of the late proceedings there.

## Prof. W. F. Barrett

Well, they pierced where you pointed out to a depth of about 40 feet, got a little water, and then came on our blue metamorphic rock. Then the boring machine was, I believe, out of order, and while waiting for some new parts from London the borers got some jobs in Clonmel; this delayed work here. Meantime young Mr. R. heard in the North of a man named Mullins, I think from Chippenham, who had been most successful in finding water with his hazel twigs. He is one of a few who possesses this " faculty." He cannot communicate it, for none of his own sons possess it. They sent for him, and to prevent any collusion or prefatory inquiries, one of their clerks met him at the Milford boat, and walked up with him to the concern. He carried with him about a dozen fresh forked twigs as thick as a quill, each side of the fork 12 or 15 inches long.

He traversed the whole of the premises, marking out four places where water might be got. The premises are about 700 feet long [see diagram].

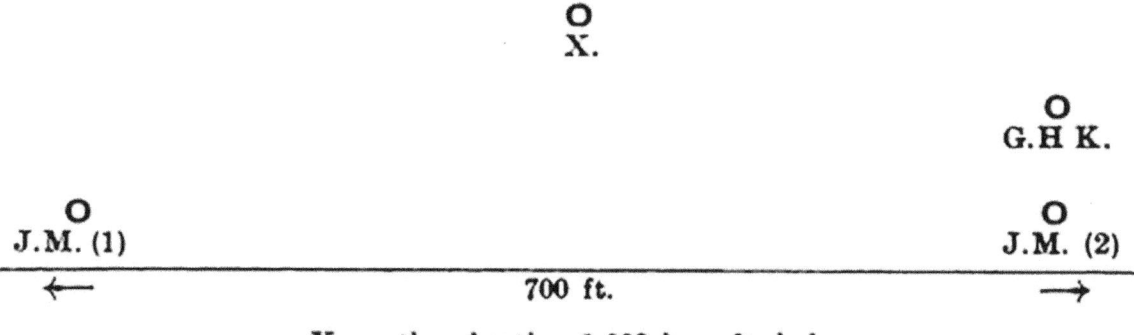

X = the abortive 1,000 bore ft. hole.

No. 1 he said was the best place. No. 2 was not 20 feet from the place that you marked out (marked G. H. K.).

He held the twigs near their ends, between his second and third fingers, as if you were going to write, the point of the fork pointing downwards. At No. 1 the point lifted itself up till it turned over backward and twisted itself till it broke! "Water here not more than 80 feet deep," said he. He used another and another twig. The clerks then held them with him, and held his hands, always the same effect. I saw to-day two of the broken twisted twigs.

Now for the result [at J.M. (1), which corresponds to No. 4 in Messrs. Richardson's drawing.]

The diamond borers pierced through 41 feet of boulder clay, then through 39 feet of our ordinary clay slate. Then on the 2nd [yesterday,] touched our old friend, the blue metamorphic rock, and stopped, sounded, and found 36 feet of water in their four-inch tube. They were told to pump, a steam one, which they did all night. 3 o'clock on 2nd to 9 o'clock on 3rd—18 hours —without any diminution of the supply, their estimate being 800 to 900 gallons per hour.

Arrangements were then made while I was there to pump into a cistern containing 270 gallons. After repeated trials the average was found to be 1,560 gallons per hour without the slightest sign of abatement. To-day it is reported to me to be 2,000 gallons per hour. Good water, temperature 52°, an important item to Messrs. Richardson's.

I would like to know what you think of this thing. To me it is wholly unaccountable. All I know is, they are singing "Jubilate " at Richardson's. What would Professor Huxley say?

J. Budd.

# *The Credibility Of Dowsing*

Mr. Budd gives additional particulars in the next letter, also addressed to Mr. Kinahan:—

Tivoli, Tramore, *September 11th,* 1889.

I have been not only considering the bearings of the case, and it is an extraordinary one, but I have been making myself up on all the facts of it.

Mullins was never in the South of Ireland before, and certainly had no idea of Messrs. Richardson's locality. As to reading faces: they had no expectation of success; indeed, the failure of your boring made them give up all hope, and one of their principal persons utterly scoffed at the idea of the twigs; their faces, they tell me, must have expressed only incredulity and curiosity. I can quite believe that some nervous or muscular force, voluntary or involuntary, affected the twigs, for certainly they could not move of themselves. But was this force derived from some innate faculty? Mullins made no pretence of magic; there was nothing about him of "See now vot you vill see." Quite in a business-like way he walked through the premises as each door was opened for him, most of the clerks following him, and stopping every now and then. Up to the present there has been no effect on other wells with them or elsewhere. As to his knowledge, he did not know whether there was any well in the concern, but he had the general idea, which every one in Waterford has, that they had bored and utterly failed.

The clerk who accompanied him from the steamer, and whom I cross-examined to-day, is a reliable man. He was warned to answer no questions as to wells, water, or strata. Mullins did not ask him a single question.

When M. was asked before he left about his successes elsewhere, he said he had often gone to places where there was no water, but when he had indicated water in any place, as far as he knew, it had always been found, but he made no boast of this, said only he could not account for it.

As to 80 feet, no one said this to him, nor did any one know the depth of the strata there. Your boring was only 41 feet deep. The well through which the 1,000 feet was bored was originally 60 feet deep, and it was only to-day that I learned for the first time, with some difficulty, that the steam pump well is 72 feet deep. This I learned from the clerk who manages the machinery; none of the others knew it, nor had ever asked.

As to the sailors[1];—as I said before, every one [here] knew of their boring, and failing, but no one outside the office but myself knows the particulars. They keep their business to themselves. I believe it was quite impossible that any sailor could know anything about their [Messrs Richardson's] concern, or, indeed, would care to know.

Well, he [Mullins] was written to, to come over and try his hand, as they were very anxious to get water.

He came, drove up to the concern, and they first brought him to the field you indicated. He walked about and said there was water in a spot about 20 feet east of yours. "Oh," said they, "We tried near this and failed." "No matter," said he, " There is water here." They then brought him through each of their yards and stores. In most of them he paused, and said, "There is no water here," but in two of them he said, "There is water here," and they marked them in red.

---

[1] In reply to my enquiry Messrs. Richardson tell me this probably refers to the sailors on board the steamer in which Mullins crossed over from England to Waterford.—W. F. B.

The last place they came to, to their surprise, he said, "This is by far the best place I have come to. Mark it No. 1." "Now mark the first place I went to No. 2, the others 3 and 4. I am sure you will get at least half the quantity you require at No. 1."

He has the look of an honest John Bull master mason, has picked up a good deal of information going about, and is of quiet manner, but answers any question he is asked promptly and in the most straightforward manner. He said he could not tell the depth at No. 1, but probably it would be within 80 feet. Their since finding it, at exactly 80 feet, was a mere coincidence. He left by the boat that evening. He asked no questions as he walked about, nor did they volunteer any information.

Jas. Budd.

In reply to my enquiry as to the exact direction of the spots marked by Mullins, and as to the cost of boring prior to Mullins' visit, Messrs. Richardson kindly send the following additional particulars:—

Waterford, *February 22nd*, 1897.

The Mullins line runs N.N.E. and almost in the direction of the bedding of the rocks.

This was merely a coincidence, as Mullins had no local knowledge whatsoever of the locality, it being his first visit to this part of the country, and we gave him no knowledge in any way, as to position of wells, or that we had bored. In fact we kept him in entire ignorance, until he had located his line.

The line as marked on our map, and position of well, is the correct position, and all the borings and old wells are to the east of Mullins' line except the final well, which of course is on the line.

Mullins' line was not theoretically straight, but was comparatively so. Mullins started with his twig (a light hazel fork) at the top of Hodges field, and worked down through the concern,[1] and when finished the marking and pegs were almost a straight line running N.N.E.

No. 1. Bore Hole,—sunk to a depth of 292 feet, cost £267 13s. 4d.; widening same down to a depth of 100 feet, cost extra £100, total £367 13s. 4d. [These numbers refer to the plan on p. 85.]

No. 2. Bore Hole,—sunk to a depth of 949 feet 7 inches from bottom of well, cost £916 16s. 6d.

No. 3. Bore Hole,—cost about £40, with pumping tests and delay, awaiting Mr. Kinahan's advice.

The cost of a bore hole depends on the size of the bore, and depth, as the contractors will not bore a 100 foot bore at the same rate as the first 100 feet of a 5 or 600 foot bore. Carriage of engine and gear, and pumping test have to be paid for, and add also to the comparative cost of the shorter bore hole.

The No. 4. Bore Hole—bored on Mullins' line—was composed as follows:—

First 38 feet clay, loose shingle 3 feet, yellow shaley sandstone 39 feet, last few feet slate and yellow shaley sandstone.

Mullins works his rod with the back of hands down, and holds each rod of fork between the second and third finger of each hand with the apex of the fork pointing to the ground, and each rod of fork passing over the second and first finger, and under the thumb, and held firm by thumb.

---

[1] The ground is covered with buildings and sheds, and I understand Mullins had to go in and out of these in the course of tracing out the water line.—W. F. B.

## The Credibility Of Dowsing

When the rod passes over any flowing water, the apex rises from the downward position, to a position with the apex of the fork in an almost vertical position and pointing upwards with a very perceptible jerk, although the diviner's hands are apparently inactive and without any movement whatever.

Exors. Of J. J. Richardson, Per C. F. Hopges.

It will thus be seen that the cost of the unsuccessful borings and well sinking prior to Mullins' visit was some £1,324,—an expensive experiment.

One other point required elucidation, viz., the level of the water in the Mullins' well compared with the level of the water in the adjoining tidal river. As to this Messrs. Richardson write as follows:—

*March 11th*, 1897.

In reply to your enquiry, the surface of the well is 95 feet above low water level; while the bottom is 13 to 14 feet above it. The level of the water in the well when not pumping is 44 feet from the surface.

W. Richardson.

So that the water level in Mullins' well is some 50 feet *above* the low water level of the river; the well is therefore not supplied by percolation from the river.

Mr. Kinahan has also sent me the following as to the geological aspect of the locality:—

*February 21st*, 1897.

The Waterford rocks are Ordovician with protrudes or intrudes of basic igneous rocks. From the wells above and below the premises there seemed to be two water lines crossing it, both of which our friend [Mullins] found by instinct, due either to his being able to smell water, or that water has such an influence on his nervous system that he can tell the distance and quantity when he is near it; unless he was a Sherlock Holmes who could draw conclusions from trifles that no one else could detect.

G. H. K.

Having submitted the foregoing case to the Geological Survey of Ireland, Mr. J. R. Kilroe was good enough to send me a memorandum on the subject, discussing the whole matter from a geological point of view, accompanied by a geological map and section of the locality. Mr. Kilroe's memorandum is as follows:—

H.M. Geological Survey of Ireland, Dublin.

## Notes on the Borings at Waterford

The rocks of the neighbourhood are of Silurian age (Ordovician), and are in great part concealed by glacial drift. The drift area is indicated by stippling on the accompanying map; the portions enclosed by chain (boundary) lines are those where the rock is devoid of drift, and appears at or comes very near the surface.

The strata consist of slates and grits in alternating bands; the former are comparatively impervious to water while the latter are more or less porous, and some may be sufficiently so to constitute reservoirs for underground water.

The beds of rock are set at a uniformly high angle—about 60° to the horizontal near Waterford,—technically called the dip: they are also much folded and contorted and dislocated by faults, as may

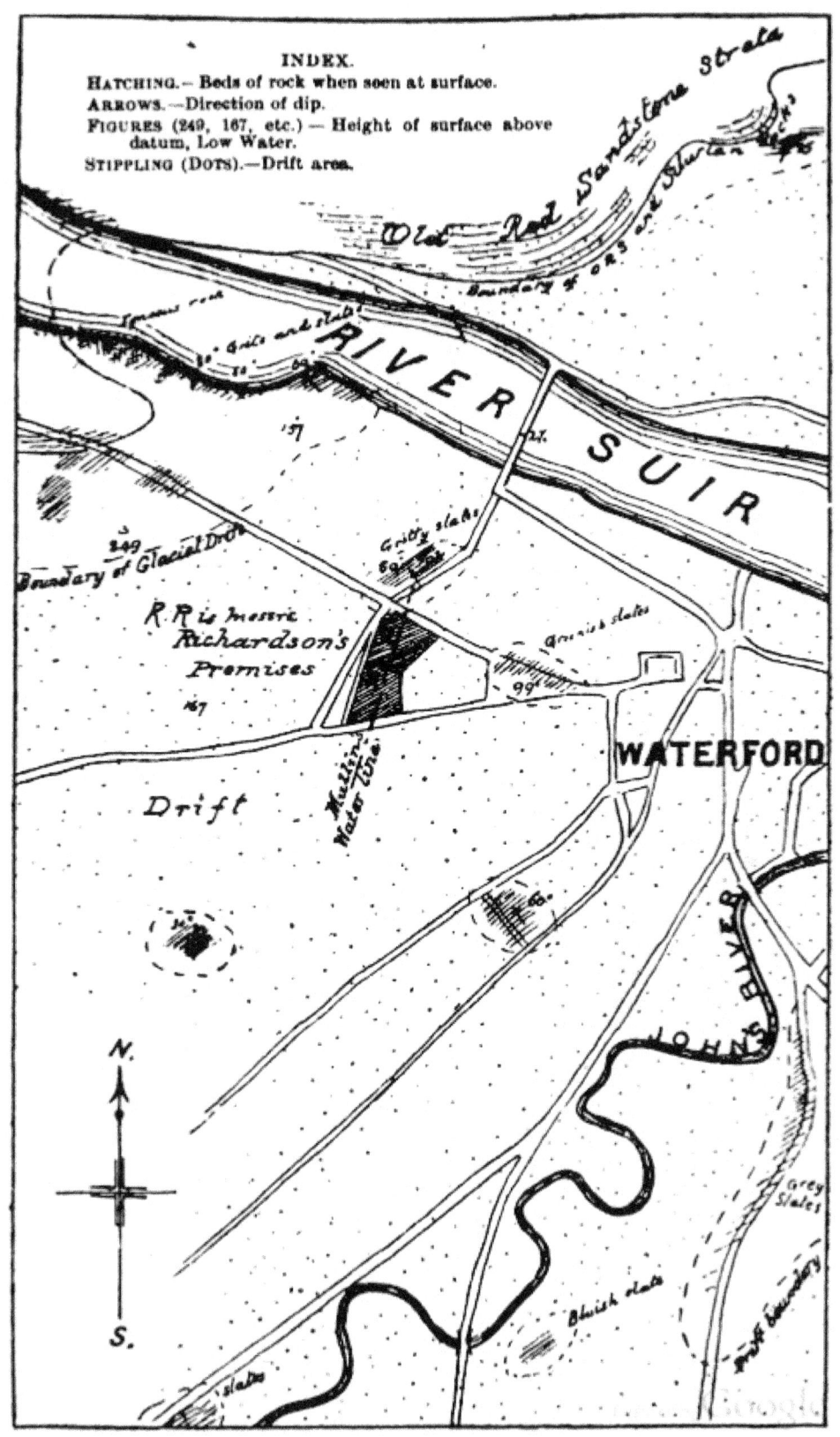

# The Credibility Of Dowsing

well be observed along the sea coast not far distant, though no faulting, and but little contortion of the strata, seems to have been noticed at, or near, Waterford city.

The strata at Waterford, moreover, are cleaved in a direction which accords with that of the stratification; but stratification and faulting, in general, affect the location of underground waters, rather than cleavage, so that the latter is not of apparent import in our case.

The futility of the first three attempts to find water proves the absence from the rocks pierced, of water-bearing strata, in other words, of porous sandstone or grit bands of any importance. A particular case in which a thick sandstone band might be supposed to exist, concealed, notwithstanding the unsuccessful sampling afforded by the first experiences, is discussed below; about this, however, one cannot speak confidently without a more intimate knowledge of the ground.

The lack of water in those borings does not seem to me to be accounted for by concealed faults or breaks in the strata; for if the rocks were thereby sufficiently shattered to admit of leakage, and descent of the water from the ground tried, it would not descend lower than the level of the Suir and the same conditions would with equal facility and greater probability admit of percolation from the river to the point reached by the borings.

The water in Mullins' well, however, stands at 44 feet from the surface, and is dependent on the rainfall. It cannot therefore be due to percolation from the river; and must collect beneath the more or less porous drift which covers the rock at Richardson's works (see section).

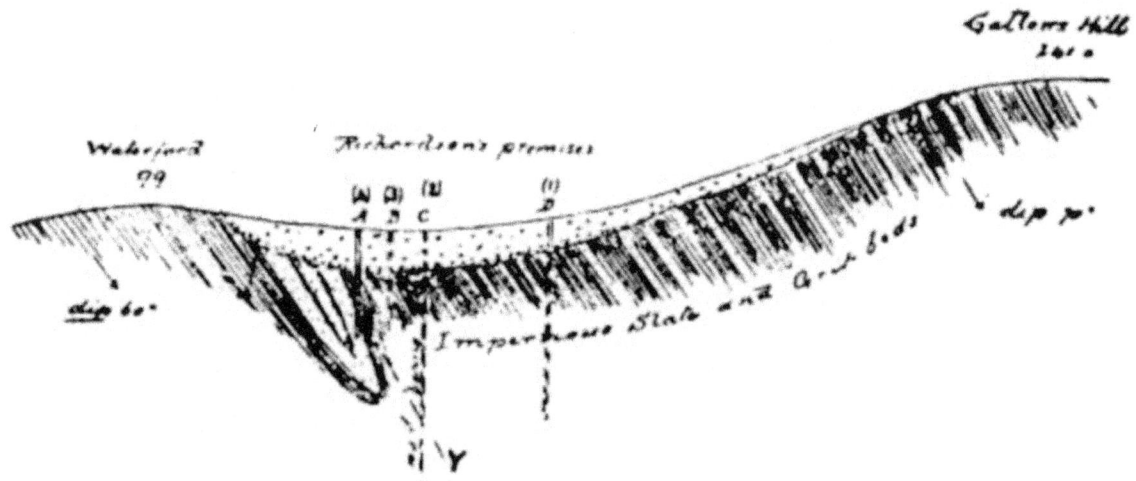

Diagrammatic Section along a vertical plane supposed to cut through strata at Waterford, at right angles to Mullins' water line. The wells are numbered as on page 85.

Assuming that water would be found at the other points indicated by Mullins, equally with that at which the successful boring was put down, we should have a wet zone stretching N.N.E.-ward, in which a copious supply would be, in fact was, tapped [at one point] at some 80 feet below the surface.

This zone might be coincident with a line of fault in which water falling upon the sloping surface northwestward would collect; and such a supposition is favoured by the circumstance that it is not coincident with the direction taken by the outcrop of the bedding.

On the other hand, a break of sufficient dimensions to supply over 1,500 gallons of water per hour would in all probability extend to and beyond the river, and admit of very great if not entire leakage of the water entering it, to a much lower level than 44 feet from the surface at all events; and no fault is represented here, on the published maps of the Geological Survey.

An alternative supposition is that of a porous stratum concealed beneath the drift, in the slight hollow at Richardson's premises. The only manner in which such a stratum could occur, consistently with the direction and amount of dip recorded for the beds in the vicinity, is such as that represented in the above section, drawn at right angles to Mullins' wet zone, and showing the relative distances from the latter of Kinahan's boring B, the 1,000 feet boring C, and the first one D. In this section the porous stratum and the thin grit beds are represented by dots, Mullins' boring by A, and the glacial drift by larger dots immediately beneath the surface line.

The stratum mentioned cannot be regarded as continuous (see line X Y) according to the dip of the beds, as seen at the surface, for in this case it would have been tapped by the 1,000 feet boring. It therefore should assume a synclinal curve, and form a trough-shaped reservoir receiving the rainfall between the point marked 99, Gallows-hill (241 A) and the water shed south-westward. Such folding of the strata is common in Silurian rocks throughout the country.

J. R. Kilroe

The bearing of this case on the general theory of a "dowsing faculty" must be considered in connection with the rest of the evidence.

# The Horsham Experiments

Reference to this remarkable case has already been made in the preceding group, No. 58, p. 65. The facts are briefly as follows:— The owner of an estate near Horsham, in Sussex, Mr. Henry Harben, found there was a scarcity of water on his property. He called in the aid of an experienced local well sinker and had a well sunk some 90 feet deep (well A, see p. 118), but got little water—in fact, this well, Mr. Harben states in a memorandum he sent me, is "absolutely useless." In an adjoining field, some 200 yards off, and at the lowest part of the estate, another well was sunk under the advice of another well sinker (well C); at some 55 feet down a small spring of water was met with running into the well, but the quantity was so small that the supply was quite insufficient.

Having spent a considerable sum uselessly in sinking these two wells, Mr. Harben determined to obtain from London the highest engineering and geological advice. His position, as one of the directors of the New River Company, and his ample means, rendered this comparatively easy. Acting under such advice another well was sunk (well B) not far from the first one (well A). This well was of large dimensions and sunk to nearly 100 feet, with, however, little result as regards water; tunnels were then driven in various directions, and finally, after £1,000 had been spent on this last attempt—made under the best scientific advice and with the most modern and approved engineering methods—the well B was abandoned.

Finally Mr. Harben was induced to send for the dowser, Mr. J. Mullins, of whom he had heard, and whom he had distinctly refused to employ before sinking well B, as he utterly disbelieved in him. Mullins came some time in the year 1893 (not long before his death), and, to prevent his gaining any local information, Mr. Harben met Mullins at the railway station and drove him to his estate, Warnham Lodge, some four miles off. Mullins said it was his first visit to that part of Sussex, and there is no reason to think otherwise. Arrived at Warnham Lodge, Mullins traversed the estate, said there was no water where wells A and B were situated, unless an immense depth were bored. As he came near well C he was narrowly observed. Mr. Harben tells me he and the well-sinker alone knew the exact direction of the streamlet of water which entered this well; no hint of any kind was given to Mullins. Suddenly the rod turned—" There is a small stream here," he said, "flowing in this direction." This was absolutely correct, I am informed; Mullins indicated the exact direction the streamlet was known to enter the well. Mullins told Mr. Harben that the depth of this well was between 50 feet and 60 feet, the actual depth being 55 feet. Dissatisfied with this supply, Mullins said he would try the higher ground. Mr. Harben tried to dissuade him, as that part had been examined and rejected by the scientific experts. "Never mind," said Mullins, "I am going to try it." At the top of the hill the rod turned vigorously, and the spot was marked; 30 feet further on (absolutely on the crest of the hill) it turned again. "Call this No. 1," said Mullins; 20 feet further it turned again. "Call this No. 2," said Mullins, "and the first No. 3." Mr. Harben then remarked that water doubtless existed everywhere at a certain depth beneath the hill. Mullins tried carefully and said "No. Nos. 1 and 2 are independent springs, there is no water between them, but you will find plenty of water at either of these places at 12 feet or 15 feet deep."

Mullins was then taken across the road to find a well for the supply of some cottages on the estate, about 250 feet distant from these last springs; he found a place where he said water would be obtained at a depth of about 40 feet. Here a well was subsequently dug, and at 35 feet deep a good spring was found, which, however, on analysis, proved to be chalybeate; accordingly this well was filled up. Mullins had indicated another place for a well, 75 feet distant from No. 2 spring, and some little distance from the cottages. Upon sinking here, water was found in this well in sufficient quantity for the requirements of the cottages (well G.).

The spots Mullins had marked as springs Nos. 1 and 2 on the crest of the hill were then dug; soon a hard limestone was encountered and after blasting and sinking at each spot to a depth of 12 feet from the surface, a copious supply of excellent water was suddenly met with (wells E and F). At No. 3 a good spring was also found at 19 feet deep (well D). Much to Mr. Harben's surprise, Mullins had proved right in each case.

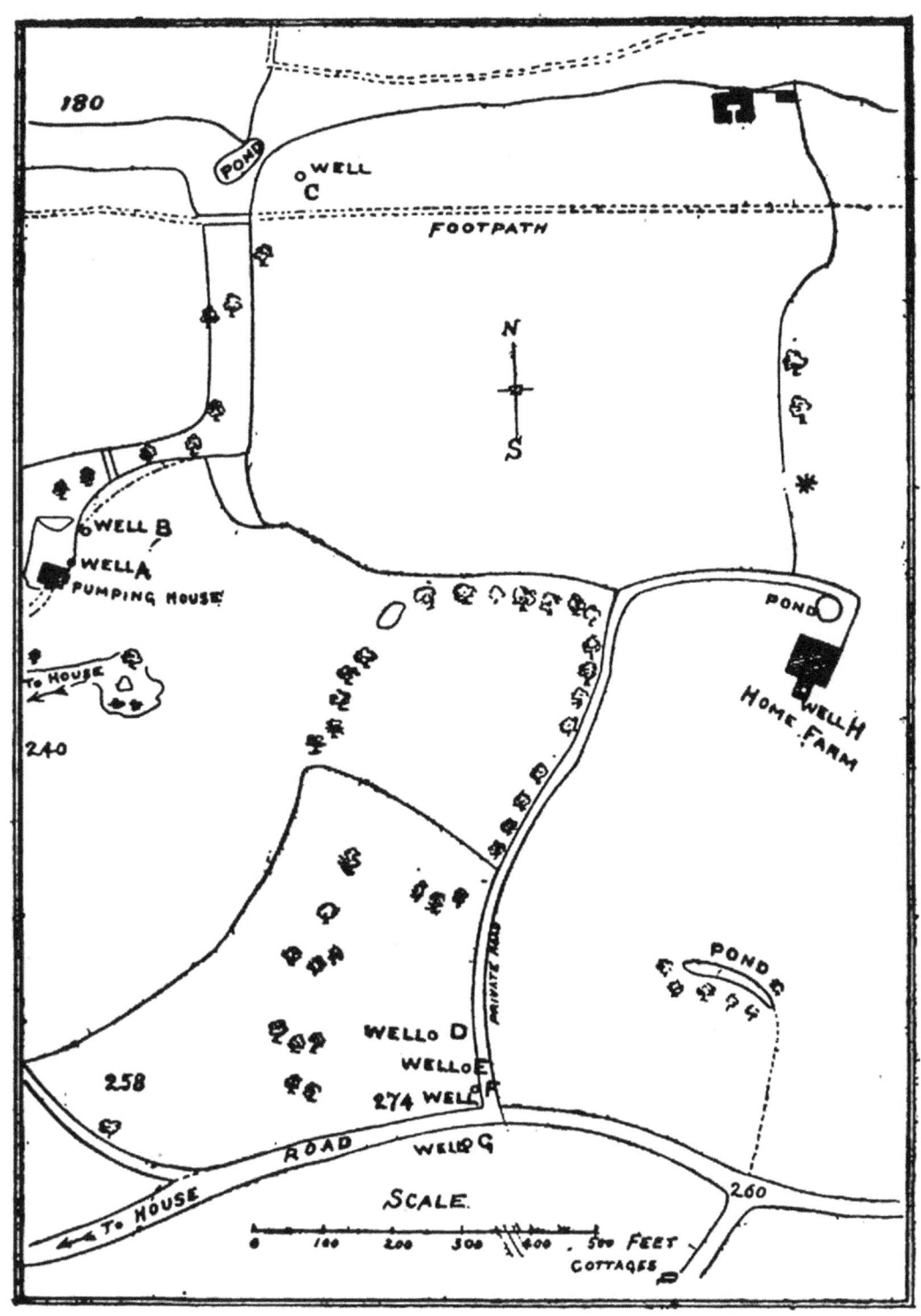

WARNHAM LODGE PARK.
*From 26 inch Ordnance Survey Map of Sussex (West), 1897, 2nd Edition.*
The numbers, 260, etc., indicate height above sea level.

# The Credibility Of Dowsing

Mr. Harben, fortunately for our enquiry, then resolved to go to the expense of testing Mullins' assertion that no water would be found between wells E and F, but that, both were independent springs. By means of a powerful pump he had one of the wells pumped nearly dry; the water level in the other was unaffected. To leave no room for doubt, however, Mr. Harben went to the expense of further testing Mullins' statement by tunnelling through the solid rock the intermediate 20 feet from the bottom of well E to the bottom of well F. Mr. Harben assures me from his own personal observation, corroborated by the overseer, whom I saw, that *no water* was found between the two wells, the intermediate rock being dry.[1] As the tunnel joined the water in the two wells a large storage tank has thus been formed some 5 feet in diameter and 20 feet long. "We have had," Mr. Harben writes to me, "ever since, even in the driest season, a most abundant supply of water, and Mullins was right not only in indicating the precise spots where water was to be found, but also in his assertion that water would *not* be found between the two wells E and F."

Writing to me on April 8th, 1897, Mr. Harben says:—

> I had forgotten to tell you of another illustration of Mullins' power. He was walking with me towards my Farm Buildings [marked Home Farm on the map] trying his rod occasionally; when he came to the spot marked with an asterisk [see right hand side of map], he stopped and said that here was another spring. I told him there was a well in the neighbourhood. Mullins then said, "I shall be able to tell you whereabouts it is." He walked to and fro with his rod and said, "The spring runs that way, and the well is probably behind that chimney" [see map, well H]. This was perfectly correct; a well with pump attached was in an outhouse behind the Farm building. There was no possibility of Mullins seeing the well or pump, as it was entirely out of sight and in a closed building; nor had he left my side to make any enquiries. We had not yet verified his other predictions and this incident, together with his discovery of the direction of the spring running into the well C, and the depth of that well, impressed me much.

On visiting Warnham Lodge, I found what Mr. Harben said was strictly accurate as to the impossibility of Mullins seeing the well and pump H from the position he occupied. In fact, I could not discover it until taken into the building where it was situated.

The foregoing account was compiled from information Mr. Harben gave me either in writing or verbally; it has been seen and revised by Mr. Harben, who writes as follows:—

Warnham Lodge, Sussex, *May 5th*, 1897.

> I return the account you have written, which is quite accurate, and have added one or two additional particulars. I have just heard of another feat of Mullins'. After doing his work at Captain McCalmont's, Mullins was in the dining-room. He said there was water below the floor. On opening the floor a disused well was discovered.[2]

H. Harben

---

[1] What is known to geologists as "jointing" in the rocks suggests itself as a possible explanation of this peculiar distribution of water. But I should be glad to have some competent geological opinion on the whole of this case; no geological explanation, however, can lessen the remarkable character of Mullins' water-finding faculty. A geological section of Sussex is given in the maps of the Geological Survey, and runs very close to Warnham Lodge; the district is Weald clay with Horsham stone; the latter is a sandstone often calcareous.

[2] I wrote to Captain McCalmont, M.P., who informed me that this incident did not occur at his house, but at a neighbour's in the country. The name, I learnt on enquiry, was Mr. Crawshay, to whom I wrote. It is, I find, a reference to the incident that occurred with the dowser Mr. Tompkins, related by Mr. Crawshay, particulars of which are given on a subsequent page. See latter part of No. 102 p. 122.—W.F.B.

## Failures

The evidence thus far presented shows that certain persons, among whom the late John Mullins was conspicuous, certainly possess some faculty which is not given to all men, and not recognised by the science of to-day. It would be interesting to know how many failures Mullins had in the course of his career; but this, I fear, it is impossible now to ascertain. There could not have been very many, or news of them would probably have reached me, as I have made numerous enquiries for this purpose throughout the districts visited by Mullins in England and Ireland. A few cases have, however, been reported to me which I will here detail.

The first was the case of the Hastings Board of Guardians, who engaged Mr. J. Mullins in 1888. A new workhouse had been erected and attempts to find an adequate supply had, I believe, been unsuccessfully made before Mullins was called in. The Guardians were subject to some criticism for asking a "dowser" to advise them where to sink a well, and this was increased when, after sinking some 80 feet at one of the spots indicated by Mullins and no water found, the case was reported a failure. Later on, however, after the well had been sunk some 200 feet, the architect reported (according to the local papers and the *Gas Journal* of June 4th, 1889), that a supply of 2,300 gallons daily was obtained. In a letter to Mr. Vaughan Jenkins, John Mullins writes that he marked three places where water would be found, and indicated the best, but "the Guardians chose to sink on the worst and had to go deeper than they expected, but they did, at last, get a good supply of water, though not sufficient for their wants, which were great." In the *Sussex Daily News* of May 23rd, 1890, a meeting of the Board of Guardians is reported, at which a discussion took place concerning the success that had attended Mullins. Councillor Perrins moved that whilst the Board believed in Mullins' sincerity they regretted their hopes had not been realized, as at the best spot indicated by Mullins they had sunk 80 feet and found no water. [This was evidently a second well.] Others raised some objection to Mr. Perrins' motion, and Councillor Chapman thought it only fair to say that at the first well they had a yield of 2,300 gallons a day and that they had not driven headings as Mullins recommended.

I wrote to the local newspaper and also to the Chairman of the Board of Guardians to know whether any greater success had been obtained later, as I saw by another newspaper report that such was the case. To neither of my letters was any reply sent. Through the kindness of a relative at Hastings who saw Councillor Perrins on my behalf, the following letter from Mr. Perrins was sent to me:—

157, Queen's-road, Hastings, *March 26th*, 1897

> The Hastings Guardians a few years ago purchased a piece of land for a workhouse site, and for the purpose of determining the best spot to sink a well, the late Mr. Mullins was engaged to test the land by means of the twig . . .

[Mr. Perrins then describes the *modus operandi,* and the evident sincerity and absence of trickery on the part of the dowser.]

> Mullins, at the end of his experiments, was able to indicate the best spot at which the well should be sunk, as being the place where the various springs converged nearest to each other; he also stated the probable depth at which the water would be found, but would not absolutely pledge himself on that point. Suffice it to say, water was ultimately found in fairly large quantity, and the well only needed the requisite headings to store the water to make it a complete success. The water was found at a depth of about 25 to 30 feet

W. Perrins.

It will be noticed that the foregoing letter gives a much more favourable account of Mullins than the statement made by the writer of the letter at the Board of Guardians in 1890, nor was I able to obtain from Mr. Perrins any explanation of the discrepancy.

## The Credibility Of Dowsing

This case cannot therefore be regarded as a complete failure, in fact I am informed by Mr. Percy Clive that it was hearing from a friend of his of the *success* which attended Mullins at this Hastings visit that led Mr. Clive to employ Mullins on his estate in Herefordshire (see p. 25).

F. 3.—The next case, however, is more properly a failure; here also I found it extremely difficult to obtain precise details. Mullins, it appears, was called in by the governors of the Berry Wood Asylum, near Northampton, to find a water supply, and as no water was found at the depth he estimated, he was considered an impostor. I wrote to the authorities at the Asylum for particulars, and eventually obtained the following information:—

Berry Wood, Northampton, *February 27th*, 1897.

> Mullins, father and son, were here in March, 1892. They said we should find water at a given place, and there we sunk a well about 70 feet deep right through the ironstone and drove headings in two directions without result.
> 
> I should say that water is often found under the Northamptonshire ironstone, and one of our wells draws its supply from that source.
> 
> The marlstone lies about 300 feet from the surface here. We knew we could obtain water at that depth, as numerous wells in the county get their water from this marlstone. Having failed with the ironstone we bored to the marlstone and found abundant water. Of course, Mullins had nothing to do with this, as it was well known the water was there.

Richard Greene.

With reference to this case Mr. H. W. Mullins writes that he went to Berry Wood with his father and that a very large supply of water was ultimately obtained, only at a greater depth than they had estimated. This does not, however, put any different construction on the result.

F. 4.—The next case is from Mr. Denny, of Waterford, whose large bacon-curing establishment is near Messrs. Richardson's premises, where Mullins had the remarkable success detailed under the head of the Waterford Experiments.

Mr. Denny writes to me as follows:—

Waterford, *February 5th*, 1897.

> Mullins indicated several spots on which he said water would be found, but in our case we got nothing practically but surface water. In fact with us here Mullins' plan proved as great a failure as it proved a success in Mr. Richardson's case.
> 
> Mullins also indicated a spot on our Cork premises where water would be found, and following his advice we dug a well and found a good supply at about the depth he mentioned.

E H M Denny

I wrote to ascertain some further particulars, and learnt that at Waterford they sunk through clay and slaty rock down to 57 feet, and then bored a six inch hole to a depth of 207 feet from the surface, but found no good spring, the water obtained from the well being mostly surface water.

When the Waterford case (p. 83) is read in connection with this, it will be seen how easy it is to miss the exact water line in this locality. Messrs. Denny tell me Mullins pointed out several places where they would find water, and they sank at one of these; it is, however, conceivable that a very small deviation by the dowser, or the well-sinker, would be fatal to success in this particular instance.

## *Prof. W. F. Barrett*

These are all the failures of the elder Mullins which I have been able to obtain; even if multiplied tenfold they probably would not amount to one per cent of the successes which he appears to have had; for it must be borne in mind that whilst I have printed all the failures of which I can get any corroboration, only those successes are given which I have heard of that appear to bear upon the main object of this paper.

# The Credibility Of Dowsing

## Group V — Mr. W. Stone

*Mr. W. Stone,* now residing at Bolingbroke Hall, Spilsby, Lincolnshire, is a native of Burbage in Wiltshire; he is a contractor for well-sinking, etc., and has had a wide and successful experience as a dowser. Though he has, I believe, risen from humble circumstances, his local standing is seen from the fact that he is Rector's Churchwarden and a District Councillor of his parish. I wrote to Mr. Stone and asked him to tell me how he found he had the art of dowsing, and to furnish me with evidence of his success and of any failures he has met with. He replies as follows:—

Bolingbroke Hall, Spilsby, *October 13th,* 1896.

> In reply to your first question in your letter of the 17th inst., I was invited by a friend who had some suspicion that I possessed the power of a "diviner" to try the rod; I did so, and when walking with the rod in hand I felt a peculiar twitching in the rod, and hearing that the rod would turn with any one who had this feeling. I was determined to stop it, if possible; but, to my astonishment, the rod twisted itself over until it broke in my grasp; a good spring of water was found to be running beneath. I was, of course, some time before I would take hold of the rod and try it, as I was an unbeliever, and after I found I possessed the power, I was a long time before I would practise it, though I had numerous invitations.
>
> Since then I have discovered thousands of springs of water with my divining rod, and can openly say that I have never failed to find water at the spots I have indicated. In numerous cases I have been called in after great expense had been incurred without success; also in many instances I have discovered water within a very few yards of the unsuccessful operations. I may say that I have discovered over a hundred springs within a radius of about 30 miles of where I am now living. I still feel a peculiar tingling sensation passing through my body, when standing immediately over springs of water.
>
> The power to use the rod is not, I think, hereditary. My father did not possess the power, but I have a little daughter who possesses the power to a slight degree.
>
> W. Stone

On my venturing to question Mr. Stone's statement that he "never had a failure," he replies, "I would frankly tell you, if I could recall a single failure, but I do not know of even one that I have had." This statement is, however, not quite correct, as Mr. Stone, like other dowsers, has had occasional failures, particulars of which have reached me and will be given in a subsequent section In another letter, Mr. Stone adds, "The sensation I experience when over an underground spring is very like what is felt when grasping the handles of an electric machine, often seen at railway stations."

The book of testimonials Mr. Stone sent me certainly contains a very remarkable and lengthy list of successes testified to by owners and agents of landed property, manufacturers, etc.; the following is one of these.

No. 85.—The manager of a brewery in Newcastle writes:—

Newcastle-on-Tyne, *November 7th,* 1894.

> The success which has attended the sinking and completion of our well affords another striking proof of Mr. Stone's marvellous power in the use of the divining rod. He visited us in May, 1894, and with his divining rod directed us to a spot where he said we would find water about 40 feet from the surface. His prediction was correct, for after sinking 41 feet, we came upon a spring of beautiful water, large enough to supply our wants at this brewery. We need scarcely say that our confidence in Mr. Stone's ability is beyond doubt, and he fully merits the fame which he has achieved in this
>
> Pro The Arthur's Hill Brewery Company,
> A. H. Higginbottom.

## Prof. W. F. Barrett

In reply to my enquiries Mr. Higginbottom writes:—

Post Office Chambers, Newcastle-on-Tyne, *October 23rd,* 1896.

Before engaging Mr. Stone no attempts had been made to find water by boring. I cannot believe Mr. Stone's success in our case was a mere chance. His prediction as to the depth at which we should find water was about accurate.

These replies answer your questions. I may now add that the experiments were made inside and outside the brewery; the strongest indication of the presence of water exhibited by the twig in the hands of Mr. Stone was in a cellar, the floor of which was covered with cement about three inches thick. Having in my own mind perfect confidence in the power of Mr. Stone I did not even bore, but at once proceeded with the sinking of the well with the result that at a depth of 20 feet we came across good feeders; but at 40 feet, predicted by Mr. Stone as the depth at which we should find a good supply, we found all the water we wanted and now can draw 3,000 gallons per day. In order to put Mr. Stone to a further test I took him to a back street about 25 yards from the brewery where very many years ago there was a pump (but of which Mr. Stone knew nothing) and on the very spot where it stood the twig denoted the presence of water, but not of sufficient quantity for our requirements.[1]

A. H. Higginbottom.

I wrote to Mr. Stone to furnish me with particulars of any cases where, as he stated in his letter of October 13th, he had been called in to find water by the rod "after great expense had been incurred without success." He replied he had not kept a list of all these cases, but quoted a few he remembered as follows:—

No. 86.—Colonel Grantham, West Keal Hall, Spilsby, dug to the depth of 50 feet for a water supply for a house, without success, and sent for me to come and test with my divining rod. I did so, and tested, and about ten yards of where his deep sinking had been carried out, I discovered a beautiful spring of pure water at a depth of 30 feet. The water came in so strong when tapped, that the men had great difficulty in bricking the well. I have had just the same results in other parts of the estate.

I wrote to Colonel Grantham asking him if the foregoing statement, which I sent, was correct. Colonel Grantham, I learnt with regret, had recently died. His son, Captain Grantham, who was present at the experiments and took much interest in them, writes:—

West Keal Hall, Spilsby, Lincolnshire, *October 19th,* 1896.

Mr. Stone is quite correct in saying that he has sunk two most successful wells for us in West Keal; the spring, or as it was in this case the run, of water, being found by use of the divining rod. Certainly in one case a well had been sunk to considerable depth, without success, within twenty yards of where Stone found a large supply at, as he says, about 30 feet. I do not know the depth of the well originally sunk without success, but could find out if you care to know. Not only did he find the stream of water, but could tell in what direction it was running. Having found two streams running at right angles he pointed out the spot where they would meet, and on walking over it with his rod proved to be right within a few feet. He also told us pretty nearly, if not quite, the exact depth of the water both times he has sunk for us. There is an under-drain running a small run of water across the drive in front of my house, with nothing to indicate the place; I got him to walk along the drive with the rod; as soon as he stood over the drain the twig turned over.

E. M. Grantham.

---

[1] This is referred to by another correspondent see No. 94.—W. F. B.

## *The Credibility Of Dowsing*

In reply to further enquiries, Captain Grantham writes:

West Keal Hall, Spilsby, *October 27th*, 1896.

> Mr. Stone assured us that we should get a sufficient supply of water by sinking on what he said was the strongest run. It being a suitable place we did so, with, as I have already told you, every success. That there is something in the indication of the rod, after seeing it used, is not in my mind open to question. I consider it is of the greatest use and saving in finding springs, and should not now think of sinking a well when I was not sure of water without the use of the divining rod. I have not as yet been able to ascertain the depth of the unsuccessful well you mention, as I have been away from home, but will do so and let you know.
>
> E. M. Grantham.

Asked the exact depth of the wells, in a subsequent letter Captain Grantham informs me that the unsuccessful well was 42 feet deep; 28 feet of this were dug and 14 feet bored. The successful well sunk by Mr. Stone was only 30 feet deep, and was 15 yards distant from the useless well.

No. 87.—The next "evidential" case Mr. Stone quoted was as follows:—

> Mr. Shirley, Ettington Park, near Stratford-on-Avon, had gone to great expense in a field this summer, and had to give up the same as Colonel Grantham did, without any success, and he sent for me to go and test. I at once went, and in the same field, only 15 yards from his expensive excavation, I discovered an abundant supply of water at 7 feet deep, and my men have just completed the laying on of the water, by natural gravitation, to the top of a very large mansion, gardens, stables, and yards. Many expensive trials had been made in trying to obtain a water supply to this house, but without success. Therefore the house could not be occupied through not having a water supply.

I wrote to Mr. Shirley, sending him the foregoing statement by Mr. Stone, and asking how far it was correct. Mr. Shirley replies:—

Lough Fea, Carrickmacross, Ireland, *October 23rd*, 1896.

> Mr. Stone's statement is correct. I was with him when he went over various portions of my English property. He marked five or six places where he said there would be water, but so far I have only had one actually tasted; this was, however, perfectly successful, the water was found where he pointed out and at the depth he stated. I had previously gone to considerable expense in sinking, but could not find a sufficient supply. I was quite satisfied with Stone.
>
> S. E. Shirley

In a subsequent letter, after reading the proof of the above, Mr. Shirley writes:—

Ettington Park, Stratford-on-Avon, *March 23rd*, 1897.

> We sank at various places looking for water before Stone's visit; the one nearest to the subsequent supply found by Stone was about 20 or 30 yards off and about 10 feet deep: Stone went a little deeper but there was water before we got to this depth. The supply has continued very good. . . . Stone found the main supply at once and without hesitation, and certainly saved me a great deal of expense.
>
> S. E. Shirley

## *Prof. W. F. Barrett*

No. 88.—The following is the next "evidential" case quoted by Mr. Stone:—

> A large hall called Preston Hall, Uppingham, Rutlandshire, had been standing empty for several years through not having a water supply. Major Codrington, of 110, Eaton-square, London, went to look at it with the view of purchasing, and when he found there was no water on the place he refused to purchase, but agreed he would wait and see if I could find water. I was, therefore, sent for, and upon my arrival I met Major Codrington and the agents of the estate. They had also a gentleman from London to meet me who is a leading geologist.
>
> I at once tested with my rod, and said a spring of water would be found flowing at about the depth of 60 feet. The geologist said water would be found at 20 feet anywhere about the place, and he said to the Major, "If you don't find water at 20 feet, don't sink deeper whatever you do, for you won't find water until you get to 150 feet." It was decided to have a trial for the water, and the well is now sunk; not a drop of water was found at 20 feet, so the well was carried deeper until it reached 60 feet. Just at this depth, to the inch, a beautiful spring of water was tapped, which yields an abundant supply for all purposes, and through this result Major Codrington has purchased the estate.
>
> Nine wells had been sunk on this estate before I visited it, without success, and useless wells are on each side of the well I have just sunk. My sinking plant is still on the spot and the well is just completed and open for inspection.

I sent the foregoing to Major Codrington and asked him how far it was an accurate statement. Major Codrington's reply and subsequent letters are as follows:—

110, Eaton-square, S.W., *October 19th*, 1896.

> Stone's account is substantially accurate. There are a few details which are not quite accurate, however. There was water on the place, but the supply was insufficient. The geologist did not imply that water was to be found at 150 feet, but he merely said, "The clay is 150 feet thick at least, and there is no water in it."
>
> At about 60 feet the clay was noticed to be very wet, and the actual supply of water comes from a point 66 feet below the surface of the ground, where there is a band of rock about 7 or 8 inches thick.
>
> I sent a piece of this rock to the geologist, and he pronounced it to be a band of limestone, such as frequently occurs in the upper lias clay.
>
> I may say that the soil which lies above this clay, and which is from 20 to 25 feet thick, is known as "Northampton sand." All the old wells are merely dug in this, but they have apparently been neglected for years. They nearly all contained some water, but, as I have said, the supply has not been sufficient for the place.
>
> As to the name of the geologist, I do not like to give it to you without his permission, but I will ask him, and if he has no objection, send his name to you.
>
> I had the water in the newly made well analysed, and the first analysis was not satisfactory. Being told that it frequently happens that new wells are contaminated, either by accident or design (men washing in them, etc.), I had precautions taken, and the well cleaned, and the water analysed again. The final analysis being satisfactory, I decided to purchase the property.
>
> A. E. Codrington.

# The Credibility Of Dowsing

110, Eaton-square, S.W., *October 22nd,* 1896.

Stone is a very decent man, and I am much struck with the confident way he works, and the practical knowledge he appears to possess. I saw him test for water; he walked very slowly, holding the rod thus Y, the point being about 12 inches from the ground. At one spot it curled up.

We tried again. This time he held one branch, and I held the other, and it curled up again.

Then I tried alone over the same spot, hut absolutely no result whatever. On the spot where the rod curled up we found water at 60 to 66 feet deep.

A. E. Codrington.

110, Eaton-square, S.W., *November 5th,* 1896.

My geological friend preferred that his name should not be mentioned. He said to me the other day that the presence of the water where it was found was a great surprise to him.

A. E. Codrington.

No. 89. — The next case quoted by Mr. Stone was as follows:—

I discovered a spring in an estate in the North of Ireland for a gentleman who lives at Newcastle-on-Tyne, after he had spent an enormous amount of money without success. Upon my arrival on the scene, I pointed out a spot where a spring of water would be found, after walking about five minutes. Water was found at this spot, less than 20 feet deep, and the previous sinking and boring had been abandoned after being put down to the depth of about 50 feet with no results. This had been done in the same field I discovered the spring in at 20 feet deep.

W. Stone

Having obtained the name and address of this gentleman, I wrote to him for particulars. He replies as follows:—

6, Brandling-park, Newcastle-on-Tyne, *December 23rd,* 1896.

In reply to your letter of the 13th, with reference to Mr. Stone and his "divining rod" (whom I employed on my place in county Down, in 1895), before employing him I had quarried through 17 feet of granite for water ,without success. I then sent a man from Northumberland with proper appliances to bore through the granite, still hoping to find water. He worked for several months. In December, 1894, he reported to me that he had found a good spring. In June, 1895, we had no water; after a great deal of expense it had turned out a complete failure. In December, 1895, I sent for Mr. Stone, and I must confess my faith in him was not very great at first, hut I was soon convinced he could point out where there was water. He did so on several places on my land, and on one spot where he said there was a good spring, we started and quarried down some 20 feet in hard granite; we found a splendid spring and we have a great supply of water. Through all the long drought last spring and summer, when most of the springs in the neighbourhood were dry, ours showed no signs of diminishing. Where Mr. Stone found the spring was not near where we thought we had a spring; in fact, I would never have looked for one in the place he pointed out.

I have great confidence in Mr. Stone and his divining rod, and I am very pleased to recommend him. He has been successful in finding water in several places in Northumberland and Durham to my knowledge.

I shall be very pleased to answer any more questions with reference to the finding of water on my land.

J. McKay.

I wrote again to enquire the exact depth of the unsuccessful boring and of the successful well, and the locality. Mr. McKay replies:—

*January 3rd,* 1897.

(1) The depth of the old well quarried was 17 feet deep. We then bored through hard granite 29 feet, in all 44 feet. There is a lake a little distance from where the well was sunk. We were 6 feet 6 inches below the level of this lake. We expected to have a good supply of water on account of this. The depth we quarried where Mr. Stone pointed out was 23 feet, and we got a good spring.

(2) The locality where the land is situated is in South Down, between Rathfriland and Castlewellan (about midway). Cabra Towers, Cabra by Newry, is the postal address, and the nearest railway station is Ballyroney via Scarva.

J. McKay

No. 90.—The next "evidential" case which Mr. Stone sends me is a remarkable one. The place, Woodside, is on the north coast of the Isle of Wight, between Osborne and Ryde; it is indicated on the geological map of the district. Mr. Stone's account is as follows:—

Woodside, Wootton, Isle of Wight.

The owners of this estate had never been able to obtain a supply of water, although they had gone to a great expense to try and find a supply. I was therefore sent for, and upon my arrival I cut a hazel rod and immediately commenced to work. I had not been walking ten minutes before I discovered an enormous spring of water, and being convinced by the action of my rod that there was an abundant supply for all purposes beneath the spot upon which I was standing, I did not trouble to test further. I was then asked, at what depth I thought the water would be found. I said at about seven feet. The agent said to me, "Mr. Stone, there's a well over the fence there, 80 feet deep and no water in it, and another well 30 feet deep, just behind you and no water." I said, "Never mind the old wells; you will find an abundant supply at the spot I indicate, at about seven feet deep." I was asked if I would undertake to carry out the necessary work, and agreed to do so. I started two of my sinkers to dig at the spot I had marked, and they had not been at work a day before they struck the water, which rapidly rose to the surface. I then laid on the water by gravitation to the mansion, garden, stables, etc., and after all was completed Dr. Morgan expressed himself entirely satisfied with everything I had done.

My first visit to the Isle of Wight was to a village called Arreton. Several attempts had been made, at great expense, to obtain a water supply to this village without success, and upon my arrival I was told by the old men that I should never find a spring of water in their neighbourhood. I said, "Well, you must wait and see, "and I started to work with my rod in hand, and in a few minutes I discovered a spot, beneath which a good supply of water was flowing, and all the company who were with me were astonished, and said that was a spot they thought water would never be found at; I, however, guaranteed a spring at 10 feet, and the work was entrusted to me to carry out, which I did, and my men tapped water at nine feet, which quickly rose to the top, and I laid it on to the rectory and village by gravitation. A well had been sunk within 20 yards of this spot, to a depth of about 50 feet, and not a drop of water was found.

## *The Credibility Of Dowsing*

An account of this case, I find, appeared in the Isle of Wight papers, and also, as follows, in *The Morning Post* for September 20th, 1892:—

> No little astonishment has been caused amongst the inhabitants of Fishbourne and Wootton, Isle of Wight, by the successful use of the divining rod. On the shore near Wootton Creek, overlooking the Solent, is a yachting estate known as Woodside, the residence of the Rev. J. B. Morgan, which has hitherto been without a good supply of water. Two wells have been sunk at considerable expense, but without success. It was thereupon decided to call in the assistance of Mr. William Stone, a well-known operator with the divining rod. On his arrival, Mr. Stone, after cutting his rod in the neighbouring coppice, set to work, and within ten minutes indicated a spot which every one seemed to consider the most unlikely on the estate. It was on the brow of the hill, and over 100 feet above the house, whereas the wells had been previously sunk in low-lying land. Men were, however, quickly set to work, and at a depth of 7 feet the water rushed into the well so fast that the men were obliged to get out, and the water came to the top of the well. This spring has been found an ample supply, and the quality is excellent. This is Mr. Stone's third visit to the Island. On his first visit he discovered a spring at Arreton, which yields enough water to supply the wants of the village, and he subsequently found water on another estate near Hyde.

On writing to Mr. Morgan for information, he replied to me as follows:—

5, Avenue Montaigne, Paris, *October 21st*, 1890.

> I do not know the details of the account of Mr. Stone's work at Woodside House, I.W.—which has reached you,—but it is quite true that he discovered an abundant supply of water where efforts had previously been made in vain.

J. R. Morgan

I then sent Mr. Morgan the above particulars and he replies:—

Paris, *November 6th*, 1896.

> The account which you sent to me of Mr. Stone's work at Woodside is substantially correct.

J. R. Morgan

Mr. Morgan, in answer to my request for further details, wrote to say Mr. Taylor, of Woodside, would be able to give me the facts desired. I, therefore, wrote to Mr. Taylor, at the same time enclosing him a copy of Mr. Stone's statement, and asking him if it were correct. Mr. Taylor returns Stone's statement, endorsed, *"Quite correct, William Taylor,"* and also sent the following letter and plan of the respective position of the wells. It will be seen that "quite correct" does not apply to the relative depths of the wells.

Woodside House, Wootton, Isle of Wight, *March 31st*, 1897.

> In reply to your letter as to Mr. Stone and his finding water, I beg to inform you his statements are quite correct. The good well is about 200 feet from the old supply, which was very scarce through the summer, and I am pleased to say the supply from the new well is abundant. I enclose a sketch of the land, with the wells marked. The well said by Stone to be 30 feet deep is only 12 feet, and the one said by him to be 80 feet deep is 120 feet deep.

William Taylor.

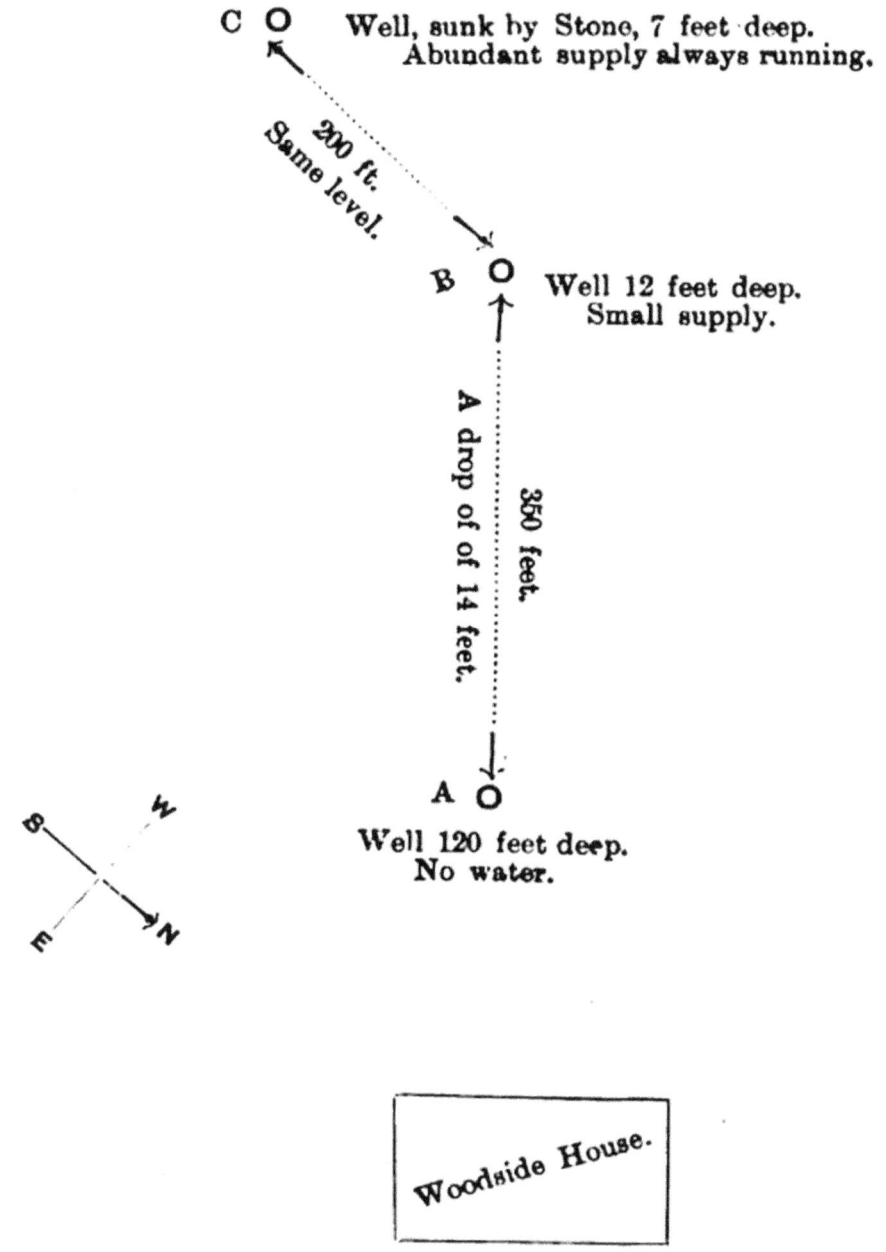

**Wells A and B were sunk before the diviner's visit. C is sunk at a spot selected by Mr. Stone. C and B are on the same level. A is 14 feet lower.**

In a subsequent letter, dated April 5th, Mr. Taylor says in reply to my inquiry—" The well that Stone sunk is only 7 feet deep and is nearly always running over; it is on the same level as the well with hardly any water, as you will see by the sketch, and 14 feet above the deep well with no water."

I should be glad if any friends living in the Isle of Wight would kindly make further enquiries into the Arreton case mentioned on p. 105. The various replies to my enquiries show that, after making due allowance for occasional exaggeration, the accounts of the various cases Mr. Stone has given me were substantially correct, and I have no

## The Credibility Of Dowsing

reason to think it would be otherwise in the case of Arreton. Subsequently Mr. Stone sent me some fine photographs that had been taken of the springs, one of which we reproduce (see next page), and which he describes as follows:—

> [It] shows me standing by the spring of water I discovered for the Rev. Mr. Morgan, Isle of Wight, and the rod I have in my hand shows me holding it just as I did when I tested for this valuable spring. The moment I put my foot over the water the rod turned in spite of me, broke itself, and left the two ends between my fingers and thumb. I was photographed with the same rod, but of course it was much shorter than when I first tested, as about three inches from each end had been broken off. I always hold the rod in the position you see. The photograph is taken near the house, the water from the spring having been "laid on."

No. 91.—The next case Mr. Stone sends me is an interesting one, but unfortunately, owing to the death of the gentleman for whom the work was undertaken, the account given is only imperfectly corroborated.

### The Hareby Estate, Spilsby, Lincolnshire

This estate recently belonged to, and was occupied by, the late Mr. F. Tooth; it is now occupied by Mr. George Morriner. It comprises about 1,000 acres of land, upon which is built a large mansion, several cottages,—forming the village,—farm premises and a church. No water was obtainable here, only by two water carts, continually being used to fetch water from a distance. In addition to the mansion, cottages, farm buildings etc., the cattle had to be supplied with water. In this case numerous well sinkers had been called in and they all failed. Hearing of me Mr. Tooth visited me when I was engaged carrying out some extensive work, and having satisfied himself, there and then specially engaged me for his estate. On my arrival there I found five wells had been sunk, from which no water was obtainable. I tested with my divining rod, and near one of these wells, I discovered a spring of water, at a less depth by some 80 feet; this was only within a few yards of one of the previous sinkings. When I discovered this spring, I guaranteed to bring the water to the surface and above it. Let me say at once that that spring now delivers itself into a reservoir rising four feet above the ground, and when tested was yielding 24,000 gallons per 24 hours: this same spring is now supplying the whole of the wants of the above named mansion, village, farm buildings, etc.

In connection with this, Mr. Tooth, since deceased, wrote to Mr. Stone as follows:—

Hareby, Spilsby, Lincolnshire, *June 12th,* 1893.

I am greatly pleased with the result of your discovery of springs by the "divining rod" on this farm in October last, and by the practical way you have since carried out the necessary works.

I have hitherto had great difficulty in keeping my stock supplied with water during the winter months, while in the yards, let alone the cost of leading; now I am pleased to witness a constant supply, which has begun at about 17,000 gallons per twenty-four hours, of clear, pure, spring water; an advantage to a stock farm that cannot be too highly estimated. I shall be pleased to answer any inquiry upon the subject; meanwhile the drainage work to my grass fields will have your attention.

Frederick Tooth.

I wrote to the present occupier of the farm, Mr. Marriner, and his reply is as follows:—

Hareby, Spilsby, January *13th,* 1897.

The water discovered on the Hareby estate has proved most satisfactory, and I can faithfully substantiate the late Mr. Tooth's testimonial, for the water discovered by Mr. Stone has proved abundant all through last summer, which as you know was exceptionally dry.

G. T. Marriner.

## Prof. W. F. Barrett

Mr W. Stone.

## *The Credibility Of Dowsing*

In reply to further enquiries from me, Mr. Marriner writes:—

Hareby, Spilsby, *January 20th,* 1897.

> In answer to your first question: Was a well or wells sunk prior to the diviner's visit, and if so with what result and at what place?
>
> Only one new well had been sunk by Mr. Tooth, and that one proved a failure; he had sunk 28 feet. Mr. Stone then commenced operations and said there was water three yards away, and he sank 15 feet and found plenty of water; this well is some distance from the house and buildings and simply supplies a tank in the field for stock. There are several old wells about the place which Mr. Tooth had opened into, but from information learned from present foreman, who was here before Mr. Tooth came into possession, I gather that the above well was the only one sunk by him.
>
> Second question: How deep were the useless wells, and how deep the well or wells successfully sunk by Mr. Stone, and how far apart?
>
> One old well is 80 feet deep. The well sunk by Mr. S., which supplies house and buildings, is near one which supplied same before Mr. Stone did anything, but which used to run dry in summer. The well sunk by Mr. Stone was only seven feet deep; it proved and has all along proved, a never-failing supply; the water here rises to the surface, and is conveyed into three circular reservoirs.
>
> I myself think that Mr. Stone could very well do without the "divining rod," it being simply a visible sign of the effect which water has upon his body.
>
> G. T. Marriner.

Writing again in explanation of the difference between Mr. Stone's statement and the foregoing letter, to which I called his attention, Mr. Marriner says, "I am afraid my last letter was misleading, as I understood from the foreman only two wells had been sunk; he now tells me that several others were dug before Mr. Stone's visit; our water supply now never gives us any trouble."

I sent the proof-sheets of the above, with Mr. Stone's statement, to Mr. Marriner for revision. In his reply Mr. Marriner states that further careful enquiry led him to make one or two slight corrections in his letter of January 20th, which I have incorporated, and he adds:—" I find *eight wells* had actually been sunk on this place prior to Mr. Stone's visit, but no satisfactory water supply was got until Mr. Stone came. Three or four of these wells had been dug by Mr. Tooth and filled in again. Stone discovered a spring at 15 feet below the surface, only three yards from the useless well sunk to 28 feet by Mr. Tooth, as shown by Mr. Tooth's letter, a copy of which I enclose." The letter enclosed is from Mr. Tooth to his agent, Mr. Parish, dated October 23rd, 1893, and corroborates Mr. Marriner's statement. The subjoined plan and explanation were also sent to me by Mr. Marriner.

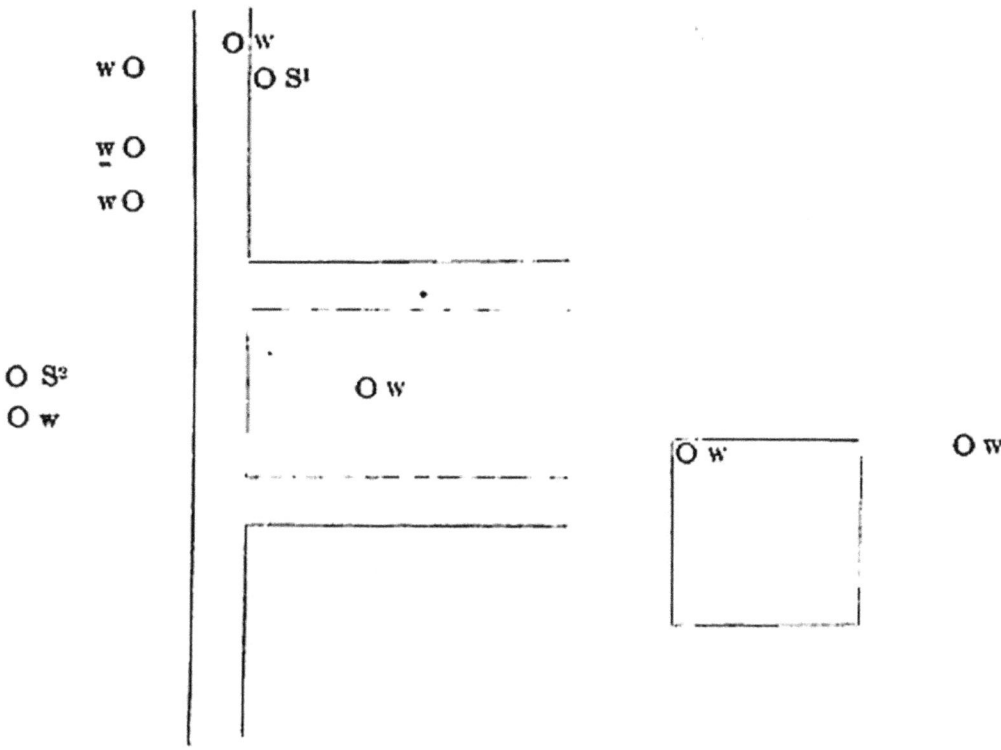

w, w, etc., are the wells sunk before Mr. Stone came and are practically useless, and considerably deeper than $S^1$ and $S^2$, the wells sunk by Stone. $S^1$ supplies the house and buildings. $S^2$ is the 10 feet well, 3 yards from the well, w, which is 28 feet deep and has no water.

No. 92.—Mr. Stone also sends me the following:—

The Blyth and Tyne Brewery, Blyth, Northumberland.

At this place they had a well which had been sunk, and they only got a very little water. I was called in and tested with my divining rod. I found a spring from six to eight feet from the well. I suggested I should send some of my skilled men and that they should cut a drift from the side of the well in the direction of the spring. My suggestion was adopted; the men cut the drift and immediately the spring was tapped it commenced to flow into the well and the supply was and is sufficient (and amply so) for all the purposes of brewery, etc. I have heard nothing from Mr. Carmichael, the manager's director, lately, but he would, no doubt, furnish you with the plain facts of the case.

I wrote to the managing director, Mr. Carmichael, enclosing the foregoing account, and he replies as follows:—

Blyth, Northumberland, *February 11th*, 1897.

In reply to yours of the 12th inst., I have to say that what Mr. Stone has informed you about his work here is practically correct.

The date when the work was done was in May, 1894. The site was in the brewery yard. Depth of old well 24 feet; it was by no means useless, as we had a regular supply of water, although small. The well is now 28 feet deep, and the supply is what I would call fairly good but not large.

# *The Credibility Of Dowsing*

The place in the rock where Mr. Stone found the spring would be about 6 feet from the bottom of the old well in a drift which had previously been made by us; this was where we were getting the water from, and when the rock was cut away it so relieved the spring as to give us a much larger quantity and a quicker supply.

James Carmichael.

In subsequent correspondence with me, Mr. Stone remarks that he thinks Mr. Carmichael's recollection of the facts is not quite as favourable as the case deserves, and mentions some additional particulars. I forwarded Mr. Stone's remarks to Mr. Carmichael, who replies that, though Mr. Stone's recollection of certain particulars is not quite accurate, yet "both I and my co-directors were very pleased to get the increased supply."

No. 93.—The *Lincolnshire Chronicle* of November 7th, 1896, describes some experiments in water-finding by Mr. Stone in front .of the Sessions House at Spilsby; at a certain spot the "little twig which had been held horizontally, rose perpendicularly and curled towards the operator." Digging was commenced, and at 15 feet a, copious supply of water was met with. I wrote to the magistrate's clerk at Spilsby—Mr. Thimbleby, a solicitor,—to enquire whether previous attempts to find water near the Sessions House had been made without the dowser's aid, and with what result. But this question Mr. Thimbleby does not answer; he replies:—

Magistrates' Clerk's Office, Spilsby, *January 9th,* 1897.

Mr. Stone's power to find water is something marvellous. The only instrument he uses is a branch of hazel or willow. He can tell at once where the water is, and approximately the distance to bore. I saw Mr. Stone " divine " for water at the Sessions House at Spilsby with great success, -and his prediction of depth, namely 15 feet, was exact. I have seen what he has done at Hareby on the estate of Mr. Tooth and he was most successful. He found water at Newcastle for a laundry company on a space between two -disused coal pits. Every one thought he was mad when he stated that there would be water, as each of the pits showed no signs of the presence of water, but by the aid of his rod he struck a spring which has supplied the laundry company at a saving; I believe, of some £500 or £600 a year.[1]

Thos. Wm. Thimbleby.

No. 94.—Reference is made in the foregoing letter to water-finding at Newcastle-on-Tyne. I have had some correspondence with the Laundry Company referred to and obtained full particulars from them, though the facts named by Mr. Thimbleby are not mentioned; possibly he was mistaken.

A long account of the Newcastle experiments was given in the *Newcastle Daily Leader* for April 12th, 1894. The reporter minutely describes Mr. Stone's appearance and mode of using the rod, "merely a small V-shaped branch of a sapling, the legs not more than nine inches long and the sixth of an inch thick,"—and how it rose up and pointed to the dowser's chin whenever "he had struck water." The positions were marked and then trials were made at the Moor Edge Laundry, where a spot was marked as likely to yield a large supply "about 50 feet below." The reporter states that "the keenest scrutiny could not see a persuasive movement of his [the dowser's] fingers."[2] Then other persons tried their hands but the rod "would not rise, not even for a reporter." The dowser's hands were swollen by the strain, the report adds.

The *Newcastle Daily Journal* gives a very similar account, and in its issue of May 17th, 1894, states that after digging a well a powerful spring was struck at only 15 or 16 feet deep, at the precise spot marked by Mr. Stone.

---

[1] The secretary of the Laundry Co. (see next case) informs me this should be £50 or £60 a year.-W. F. B.
[2] To this statement one of the directors of the Laundry Co., Mr. R. J. Charleton, who was present at the trials, replies in a letter he has kindly sent me. I will quote this letter subsequently,—when dealing with the question of unconscious muscular action in the motion of the rod.

## *Prof. W. F. Barrett*

The secretary of the Newcastle Laundry Co., in reply to my enquiries, writes as follows:—

The American Steam Laundry Co., Ltd.,<br>
New Bridge-street, Newcastle-on-Tyne, *March 5th*, 1897.

> I had the pleasure of reading your letter of enquiry before my directors on Monday last, and one of them who took notes at the time of Mr. Stone's visit, promised to look them over and communicate his impressions to me. The notes he has evidently mislaid, but I enclose you his letter that you may peruse and judge of his opinions.[1]
>
> In reply to your queries—
>
> (1.) No previous attempts had been made to find water within my knowledge.
>
> (2.) The well we sunk at the identical spot marked by Mr. Stone and only went 15 feet deep.
>
> Personally, I consider the extract from Daily Leader a very true report of all that took place.
>
> Perhaps another instance may be of interest to you:— Some little time after the experiment at our works I was invited to meet Mr. Stone whilst he tried the ground at a brewery here. After indicating one spot inside the building where water would be found, he was conducted over some adjacent property and stopping short at a spot some 50 yards off, he indicated another find. The principal of the brewery then stated to Mr. Stone that the ground he was upon was not theirs, but that he had conducted him thither to test him, adding that "the ground you are now on is the exact spot where an old public well was closed by the Newcastle Corporation years ago, owing to the unfitness of the water for drinking purposes."
>
> I should add that Mr. Stone was a perfect stranger to this part of Newcastle and I cannot see that he could possibly have known of the existence of this old well.
>
> W. Bird.

The description given by Mr. Bird, in the latter part of his letter, appears to refer to the incident already mentioned in No. 85.

In the beautifully illustrated pamphlet issued by this Laundry Company, there is a reproduction of a photograph taken of Mr. Stone in the act of discovering the spring which now supplies this laundry; the picture, which we have to thank the directors for allowing us to reproduce (see next page), is prefaced by the remark:—

> An important item in Laundry-work is to get pure water and plenty of it. An abundant supply, fulfilling its requirements, we are pleased to say, has been found on the premises at the spot indicated by Mr. Stone. It will be noticed in the photograph that the rod is pointing upwards, indicating the presence of water below.

No. 95.—Mr. Bolam, the agent to the Duke of Buccleugh, writes to say he has employed Stone for several years, and that he is most successful in finding water by means of the divining rod. Mr. Stanton, a contractor, gives several instances of Stone's success. Here is one in a letter addressed to Mr. Stone:—

Geddington, near Kettering, *October*, 1891.

> I have sunk the well on Acreland Farm, where you found the spring, and got a good supply of pure water at 54 feet. This is a great success, as there have already been three wells sunk and no good

---

[1] This letter, from Mr. Charleton, will be quoted later on, as already stated.— W. F. B.

## The Credibility Of Dowsing

water. In fact there never has been any good water on the farm before. All the old men on the place said there would not be this time.

Arthur Stanton.

## Prof. W. F. Barrett

In answer to my enquiries, Mr. Stanton writes:—

Geddington, Kettering, *March 20th*, 1897.

Acreland farm in about half way between Geddington and Grafton-underwood, by the roadside; the old wells were about 20 feet deep, the new one sunk was about 80 feet [distance] from one of the old ones which I filled up; one is in use now for the cattle, and the other was filled up some years ago.

I have also sunk wells after four men using the divining rod, but most after Mr. Stone and Mr. Mullins. In every case I found water, but in some cases a very short supply where the springs were shallow. At Barnwell Castle where I sunk a well, after Mr. Stone's trial, in a field for the use of cattle, I found a strong spring about four feet below the surface. At Burton Latimer I deepened an old well 40 feet, which was 35 feet before, making the total depth 75 feet. I came across the spring exactly in the line as Mr. Stone indicated.

Arthur Stanton

Mr. Stanton's reply shows the importance of ascertaining the relative depth of the old and new wells. It appears that at Acreland the old wells were "about 20 feet" deep and the new one 54 feet, and as there is no evidence to show water might not be found anywhere in this locality at 50 or 60 feet deep, the case ceases to be of the evidential value it first appeared.

No. 96.—Having heard that attempts to find water had been made unsuccessfully at the Oakworth Mills, Keighley, Yorks., prior to the use of the rod and that Stone had found an abundant supply, I wrote to Messrs. Haggas and Co., the owners of the Mills, and the following is the reply of the managing director:—

Oakworth Mills, Keighley, *March 24th*, 1897.

In reply to your questions: 1. We have made attempts to get water previously by boring without success. 2. We bored 50 feet without finding water in one place, and 60 feet in another, about two years ago.

Recently Mr. Stone has had men sinking on places indicated by himself with the following results:—

(1) A well sunk 10 feet and found water to fill a half-inch pipe.

(2) A well sunk 14 feet and found a small supply, fill perhaps quarter-inch pipe.

(3) A horizontal drift into a hill perhaps 25 to 30 yards long, and 25 feet deep at far end, yielding water about equal to a one inch to one and a-half inch pipe.

(4) A well sunk about 25 feet; the water rose to within 10 feet of top, and then ran off. This will necessitate our drifting the water off at 10 feet down.

(5) A well 30 feet deep without result, and we have abandoned this, as we think we have got the underground stream in about 100 yards distant (6), where at a depth of 18 feet we have got a strong run, perhaps 250 to 300 gallons per hour. This will not rise in the well, but will require drifting off at 18 feet down, or pumping. We shall drift, as the ground falls rapidly, and we shall have a short adit only.

For W. Haggas, Sons, And Co., Ltd.
William W. Vint, Director.

# The Credibility Of Dowsing

No. 97.—The *Liverpool Daily Post* of March 12th, 1897, has the following. Holywell is in North Wales, Penymaes is a village near Holywell.

> A remarkable instance of the finding of water by means of the divining or "dowsing" rod has just occurred at Holywell. The governors of the intermediate school now in course of erection at Penymaes were desirous of obtaining a supply of water, and with that end in view sank a well, but although the excavation reached a very considerable depth and was a very expensive undertaking, there was not the slightest trace of water. In their difficulty the governors decided to employ a "water finder," and Mr. William Stone, of Spilsby, Lincolnshire, was consulted. He duly appeared upon the scene, and, having procured the usual hazel twig, went with it over the grounds of the school, and ultimately indicated a spot where water would, be found. On this spot accordingly a borehole was made, and at a depth of about twenty feet an abundant supply of water was discovered, and yesterday there were fourteen feet of water in the hole, with every indication of a, splendid supply.

A very similar report was also published in many other Lancashire and Welsh papers. I wrote to the governors of the school at Penymaes, but received no reply. I then wrote to the solicitor to the board of governors (whose name I obtained from Mr. Stone), who had engaged Mr. Stone and again had no reply. Hearing that Mr. S. K. Muspratt, Grove Park, Liverpool, was chairman of the board of governors of the school, I asked my friend. Professor Oliver Lodge, F.R.S., if he would kindly make enquiries. Professor Lodge had an interview with Mr. Muspratt, who is also mayor of Flint, and forwards me the following notes of Mr. Muspratt's replies to his enquiries.

"The newspaper account is correct, except that they had not previously sunk for water (an important exception). But there is not a full supply of water yet. The dowser asserted a depth of 70 to 100 feet, and the boring is going on and has reached 45 feet about at present. No previous boring was made, but advice from local men and others was got, and not being very satisfactory, was not acted on.

"The general impression, however, is that there is a good deal of water about Holywell altogether. The dowser indicated four springs, and on one of these spots the boring is being made and seems likely to be successful. There is no supply to the town, except surface water. The town and school are near top of the hill."— O.J.L.

Here I may remark by way of caution that newspaper paragraphs on behalf of the success of any particular professional dowser are often mere paid advertisements of the man; so that little value should be attached to them until corroborated by independent testimony.

The rivalry of the professional dowsers and the network of correspondents who are in communication with me from all parts of England, enables me to hear of *failures* as well as successes in the use of the rod. In fact, it is my practice specially to ask for information as to any failures. One correspondent gave me a list of three or four failures Stone had made. I wrote to each of the persons concerned. One or two appear to be failures, and are given in the list of "failures" below, whereas another writes that, though he does not like Stone personally, he would certainly employ him again if he wanted to find water elsewhere on his estate.

No. 98.—Again, another of these reported failures turns out to have been more or less a success, and brought the following letter:—

Conheath, Bellingham, *March 24th*, 1897.

> There is not the slightest doubt of his (Mr. Stone's) powers to find water; the only objection I have to him is that his rod is too susceptible and finds water in too small quantities to be of practical value in all cases; although in justice to him it is only right to say that when I had him the weather had been extremely wet, so that at the time small springs were running abundantly.
>
> He gave one remarkable instance while sitting in the room at an inn with a piece of steel in his hand; he said, "there is water here," and on taking the hazel twig and walking round the room he indicated

the spot where it could be found. An old man in the room at the time then spoke up and informed the company that he could remember a former tenant of the place having a well in the cellar below the room where we were sitting.

R. Riddle.

In reply to my further enquiries, Mr. Riddle writes:—

Conheath, Bellingham, *March 29th*, 1897.

The incident of Stone finding the water in the inn is quite correct, and there was no possibility of him getting any previous knowledge, as I met him at the place and was in his presence during the whole time. Another incident of the same nature occurred in one of the fields, where he indicated a supply of water which had been drained away at some time, and no indication of such was visible; another old resident that I had with us to mark the places called out, "I believe in him now, I have carried water from this place when I was a boy."

The scheme [of well sinking] was not carried out properly; the part that was done was at my own expense, and as the other proprietors did not join with me in going to a source where I have every confidence plenty of water could be found, I, of course, gave the thing up.

Robt. Riddle.

In reference to this case Mr. Stone says, "the ratepayers complained that the sinking was not done skilfully, which is the usual cause of these so-called failures."

In the case of another failure of Stone's that was mentioned to me, I could get no reply to my repeated enquiries addressed to the gentleman named.; but from other enquiries I have made it appears that in this case a supply of water was obtained, only not of the volume, nor at the depth anticipated.

F. 5.—The next letter, however, records a more distinct failure. Mr. Hodgson writes to me as follows:—

Redesdale Cottage, Otterburn, Northumberland, *March 24th*, 1897.

I have yours of the 23rd inst., respecting Mr. Stone. He made a good many tests for me, and on one estate I followed up three of them, and in each instance got a good supply of water, though generally at a greater depth than that named by Mr. Stone.

I tried two places on another estate, at each of which Mr. Stone said I should get water at about 45 feet. I sunk a well of about 5 feet in diameter to over 50 feet in depth in each case. I then bored from the bottom of the well—in one case over 100 feet, and in the other about 70 feet, and never got a drop of water in either of them. When "divining" Mr. Stone pronounced the last mentioned to be the best and strongest spring he had found in Northumberland. After the two trials above referred to, I lost faith in Mr. Stone, and several other places which I have marked out remain untried.

William Hodgson.

I sent the preceding letter to Mr. Stone and asked what he had to say to it. He replied that the well sinking and boring was not done by him, that the work was badly carried out, and he was in no way responsible for the failure. I sent Mr. Hodgson Stone's explanation, and he replies as follows:—

Otterburn, Northumberland, *March 29th*, 1897.

I tried by boring at one place, and went deeper than Mr. Stone said, but did not get sufficient water to be of any use. This boring, I must say, was not very satisfactorily conducted, as it was done for me

## *The Credibility Of Dowsing*

gratuitously, and I could not have the same command of the men as I should have had if they had been employed and paid by myself.

William Hodgson.

It will be noticed that Mr. Hodgson now speaks of boring at *one* place, and getting some water. I do not understand the discrepancy between his two letters. Mr. Hodgson adds that Stone was a complete failure at Otterburn. On the other hand Mr. Reynard, a gentleman who formerly resided at Otterburn, states that it was owing to Stone's success which he witnessed in that town, that he recommended his employment elsewhere. Without attempting to reconcile these different points of view, it is sufficiently clear that, even after wide enquiry, and making allowance for cases that have not reached me, the ratio of Stone's failures to his successes is a very small fraction.[1] For here, as elsewhere, it must be borne in mind that, whilst all the failures I have been able to substantiate are cited, only such successes are given as are needful for the main object of this investigation.

---

[1] Albeit one correspondent holds a very poor opinion both of Stone's success and of his veracity; but there appear to be extraneous personal reasons for this opinion. I have never seen Stone: judging only from the evidence before me, he certainly seems one of the best dowsers now living.

## Group VI — Mr. B. Tompkins

The next group of cases relates to Mr. B. Tompkins, of Pipsmore Farm, Chippenham, Wilts, whose experience as a professional dowser only extends from 1890. Prior to that time Mr. Tompkins was a tenant farmer, and gives me the following account of how he discovered his dowsing power.

On his farm he had been to some expense in trying to obtain a good supply of water for his cattle and at last was advised to send for Mullins and get the aid of the divining rod. This he did; Mullins came and found a spot where he said a plentiful supply of water existed at a depth of less than 30 feet. A well was sunk and at 15 feet deep a strong spring was tapped, which has yielded an unfailing supply ever since. After Mullins left Tompkins tried his own skill, and found the forked twig also moved in his hand. He traversed another part of his land, and found three spots where the twig turned vigorously. Mullins was asked subsequently to try the same ground; he came during Tompkins' absence from home, tried over the place, and fixed on the same spots that Tompkins had found, and privately marked, unknown to Mullins. This led the former to test his own powers in other ways, and, having gained confidence, he was asked by Messrs. Smith and Marshall, of Chippenham, the agents to the late Lord Methuen, to try if he could find a spring on Lord Methuen's estate, as a well already sunk had proved useless. Mr. Tompkins tried, and after a long search the rod moved at a certain spot on a hillside, where he predicted a good supply of water would be found. A well was sunk, by blasting through 9 feet of solid rock, and at 18 feet a spring was struck, which rose some 9 or 10 feet in the well. Messrs. Smith and Marshall afterwards wrote as follows to Mr. Tompkins:—

Chippenham, Wilts, and 7, Whitehall Place, London, *November* 24th, 1891.

> The decision you arrived at was perfectly correct, and it is our opinion that if we had made the well six feet either way to the right or left of the spot you marked, we should have missed the water, which is now abundant.

Smith and Marshall.

I wrote to Messrs. Smith and Marshall, sending them a proof of the foregoing paragraph and letter, and begged them to make any corrections that were necessary. They replied from Chippenham that "the statements in the proof are perfectly correct," both as regards their own letter and the facts mentioned in the preceding paragraph.

No. 99.—Mr. Charles Maggs, who is a Wiltshire county magistrate, and proprietor of the Melksham Dairy Company, required a large supply of pure water for his butter factory, and, after ineffectual attempts to obtain it, wrote to Mr. Tompkins to come over and try the divining rod. This was done, and subsequently Mr. Maggs writes to Mr. Tompkins as follows:—

Melksham Dairy Company, *November 10th*, 1890.

> We found water at 30 feet, as stated by you at time of finding the spring — a very strong spring. Our hopes had almost gone and faith was all but spent. I have written an article thereon in the Wiltshire Times.

Charles Maggs.

The following is an extract from the article Mr. Maggs refers to:—

> Proof positive of the efficacy of the divining rod has been recently supplied in this town for water in the paddock in the rear of Mr. Charles Maggs' Butter Factory. To obtain a good supply of cold water for the dairy, a well had been sunk in close proximity to the buildings; but after going down 21 feet and boring a further 18 feet, no water of any consequence was met with. This led Mr. Maggs to request Mr. B. Tompkins, of Chippenham, to come over to ascertain if water was present in the field. After considerable search, the twig began to rise, and the upward movement was so strong that the rod bent considerably in its frantic endeavour to turn over, which it at once did on coming over the

spring head, and broke. Sinking operations were shortly commenced; but the faith of the workers, after going down 25 feet without any results, was well nigh gone. However, they were instructed to continue, and on reaching a depth of 30 feet, the axe "pricked" the spring, and up came the water straight in a column of about 9 inch circumference with great force. It continues to rise, and Mr. Maggs has now a good supply of cold spring water, which rises to within three feet of the surface level and as fast as the powerful centrifugal pumps carry it away to the Dairy; during the extreme drought of 1893 this spring has stood the test and yielded a plentiful supply for our use.

MR. B. TOMPKINS.

## Prof. W. F. Barrett

I wrote to Mr. Maggs, and had the following interesting letter in reply:—

Bowerhill Lodge, Melksham, *March 8th*, 1897.

Briefly the facts are:—

I sunk a well to find water for my dairy, and found none. Then I wrote to Mr. Tompkins, who came the following day; he cut a forked stick out of the hedge, and having placed it over the well, said, "There is no water here," but found a slight spring within 10 feet, too small to be of any service, he reported. He walked all over the field, and said he had not come across any spring at all. However, in the extreme corner of the field a bunch of nettles was growing, and he entered this, and instantly exclaimed, "Here it is; and a good head of water, too! Not running away, but just ready for tapping, and as soon as you strike it, it will come surging up." "How deep?" "Not over 25 feet." He cut out a turf to indicate the spot, and we commenced sinking next day. The person employed was an old well sinker, and he came to me two or three times whilst engaged in sinking, showing specimens of the soil or marl, assuring me there never was water where such existed, and it was worse than useless to go further. I told him to go on if he had to get to New Zealand—it was my money, and he need not regard me nor my pocket. When he had gone about 22 feet, his pickaxe tapped the spring and the water came up like a fountain, and at such a rate he feared he should be drowned before he could get pulled up—his mates being away! The water rose rapidly to within twelve or fifteen inches of the surface. We put on pumps and kept the water down whilst he went a little deeper, but the rush of water was such that we had to desist going lower. Since then we have had a splendid supply. This was the beginning of his [Mr. Tompkins'] public career, and since then he has found water in several English counties, and has been doing like work in the African Bush, also with equal success.

Chas. Maggs.

No. 100.—Following the preceding case, the local newspapers give an account of Mr. Tompkins' success in finding a strong spring on the estate of Sir Gabriel Goldney, Bart., at Bradenstoke Abbey, Wiltshire. Having heard that the agent to Sir Gabriel Goldney could give some evidence bearing on our subject, I wrote to Mr. H. B. Napier, the agent, who replies as follows:—

Chippenham, Wilts, *May 11th*, 1896.

In reply to yours of the 6th inst., on the subject of water finding or "dowsing," as we call it:—

I have employed Mr. Tompkins on several occasions, and up till now he certainly has not been at fault, except in his estimate of the depth of the spring. Undoubtedly there is a great deal of humbug about the practice of these water finders, but at the same time I am satisfied that they have the power of detecting a spring, but I am driven to the opinion that beyond this their powers do not extend.[1] I remember an interesting case where Mr. Tompkins traced gold. When the Bath and West of England Show was held at Gloucester some years ago, a sovereign was lost under the board floor in the Finance Office. The members of the Council did not themselves know exactly where to find it, and sent for Mr. Tompkins, who indicated a particular spot on the floor, and on a carpenter being sent for, the sovereign was found to be immediately beneath the spot. In conclusion I may say that I am so satisfied of the "dowsers'" power, that I should never dream of sinking a well without their assistance.

H B Napier

---

[1] Mr. Napier probably means that their powers do not extend to finding the depth and volume of water.—W. F. B.

## The Credibility Of Dowsing

With reference to the finding of the sovereign, this is certainly an interesting fact, and appears inexplicable by the hypothesis hitherto advanced of sign-reading or possible thought-transference. I am disposed, however, to consider it merely a chance coincidence. It is true Mr. Tompkins gives a detailed account of his finding concealed coins on other occasions; see pages 16 and 17 of a little book on the "*Theory of water finding*" which he has published.[1] Here, however, the persons present knew where the coins were hidden: the experiment narrated by Mr. Napier is much less common and the result probably due to the cause I have assigned.

No. 101.—Mr. Cowper Coles, who is agent to the Duke of Beaufort and Sir Joseph Bailey, at Crickhowell, near Abergavenny, informed me in May, 1896, that he was sinking two wells at spots where Mr. Tompkins predicted water would be found, and would send me the result when the work was complete. Writing a few months later, Mr. Coles tells me the result in both cases was successful. I wrote to ask in either case had prior attempts to find water been made, and with what result. Mr. Coles replies:—

Penmyarth, Crickhowell, *September 19th*, 1896.

> In the case of Penprisk, Crickhowell, two wells had previously been sunk; both were failures. Tompkins said water would be found at a certain spot at about 100 feet deep. After going through 98 feet of rock we came on a gravel bed, and partly lost the water; we are going deeper now into the next rock. The rock is a very hard stone
>
> The other case, at Easton Court, near Tenbury, no prior attempt to find water had been made. The rock here is sandstone. The well was sunk 50 feet, and is doing well. We are now pumping with a windmill.
>
> I am sinking several other wells now under Tompkins' guidance, and believe in the man.
>
> S. H. Cowper Coles.

I wrote to Mr. Cowper Coles again this year to ask whether they had yet sunk deeper at Penprisk. Mr. Coles replies, under date March 22nd, 1897, that, "owing to the continued wet weather, they had not been able to do anything more to Penprisk well."

No. 102.—The next case, from Mr. Codrington Crawshay, D.L., J.P., of Abergavenny, is instructive from the precautions taken by Mr. Crawshay to avoid any local knowledge being gained by the dowser. The letter is quoted from Mr. Tompkins' list of testimonials.

Llanvair Grange, Abergavenny; *August 29th*, 1893.

> For the last four months I have been almost without water (and in consequence could not have my family home), and I now find that my predecessors were short every summer. Having ascertained from Mr. Tompkins his fees, I wired for him to come, and met him at the station myself, so as to prevent him speaking to anybody who knew my place. He at once started work, cutting a V-shaped twig from a white thorn in the garden. He soon came on a stratum of water, and, following it up through my smoking-room, eventually came on the spring at a distance of 80 yards from the house. As my readers may imagine, I did not believe him, and told him I wanted to see the water. He immediately offered to sink the well on the condition of no water, no pay, which offer I closed with. After arranging terms, which were the ordinary well-sinking charges, plus the fee for finding the

---

[1] Like all the other pamphlets and booklets issued by the various professional dowsers, this is simply a trade advertisement of Mr. Tompkins, and is not so remarkable a collection of testimonials as some others of the same kind. The late Mr. Mullins' little book, *e.g.*, is far more striking, and contains numerous instances of his success which I have not quoted in Group IV. On asking Mr. Tompkins what his "theory" was, for it is not mentioned in his brochure, he replies, much as I expected, as follows : — "My theory is, it is the action of the water naturally which produces electricity and magnetism in the body; this acts upon the twig, which serves to indicate the presence of water, and the greater the strength, the stronger is the pressure on the operator, who is of a sensitive nature."!!

water, he started sinking the well, and at a depth of 14 feet struck a very strong spring—so strong that it was impossible to sink deeper than 18 feet, as no pump was able to keep the water down so that the men could work. Since then I have connected my engine, etc., to the well, and I am glad to say that I now have an abundance of water, and I find it impossible to lower the well more than 2 feet 6 inches. The water never rises more than 5 feet at the most.

Codrington Crawshay.

I wrote to Mr. Crawshay to ask if he had sunk any wells unsuccessfully prior to Mr. Tompkins' visit; Mrs. Crawshay replies to me from Llanvair Grange, under date of February 10th, 1896, that her husband was at the Cape, but she believes that no previous attempt to find water had been made by them. Mrs. Crawshay kindly sends me her own recollection as to the particulars of Mr. Tompkins' visit, which coincides with the facts stated above. Mrs. Crawshay adds that Mr. Tompkins has been most successful elsewhere, but "he is not always correct as to the probable depth of the spring; he said we should have to sink between 30 and 40 feet, and instead of that it was only 14 feet."

I wrote again subsequently to Mr. Crawshay with reference to the incident mentioned by Mr. Harben at the end of the "Horsham Experiments," p. 94, and enclosed the printed account of what is there said. Mr. Crawshay replies:—

Llanvair Grange, Abergavenny, *May 25th*, 1897.

Mr. B. Tompkins, of Chippenham, Wilts, was the water-finder I employed, and I can't speak too highly of the work he did for me. He came here a perfect stranger, and after casting round with his twig he came on a stratum of water, which he eventually ran to ground under our kitchen. This afterwards proved to be true, as the following November the spring burst through the floor, and nearly flooded us out, and I had to cut a drain to run the water off. He, after having found the above stratum, carried the line through the house, and found the heart of the spring about 80 yards away. At his advice, we sank the well, and at a depth of 14 feet came on water in marly rock, and on driving the crow bar through, we came on a spring, enough to supply a large town. We had the greatest difficulty in sinking the well to a depth of 23 feet, which we eventually did. From that day to this we have had a most abundant supply of water, and although I have an engine, I don't think we can pump the well out, as the water comes in with a regular stream.

One of the curious things in sinking the well was, at a depth of 12 feet, we came across several green frogs in the marl, and as soon as they were exposed to the air they turned black and died.

I see by the paper you enclosed me that Mullins is the name mentioned as having found the water in the dining-room; I don't know anything about this, but the facts I have told you happened under my own eyes. Captain McCalmont, M.P., has an estate about 25 miles from me. Any other information that I may have I shall be only too pleased to give you.

Codrington Crawshay.

In a subsequent letter Mr. Crawshay writes in reply to mine:—

Llanvair Grange, Abergavenny, *May 28th*, 1897.

Prior to Tompkins' visit we had a well sunk over 60 feet deep, which always ran dry in the summer. Tompkins knew nothing about this well, nor its position: 20 yards from the old well he came on the stratum of water I have previously described; this led him to the spring where we sank the new well. The depth of this well is only 23 feet, and it gives us, as I have said, an abundant and never-failing supply of excellent water.

## *The Credibility Of Dowsing*

I am sure there are many people who, like myself, would greatly benefit if they only believed in water-finding by the so-called divining rod; in fact, I can never repay Tompkins for the service he did me at Llanvair. You are quite at liberty to publish anything I have told you.

Codrington H. Crawshay.

No. 103.— Another spring was found by Mr. Tompkins for the Rector of Llanvair, under circumstances of considerable importance in connection with the theory of the dowser's art, for the ground was covered with snow at the time. This was the case also with the experiments recorded on page 83, No. 62, where the dowser was the late J. Mullins. The Rev. W. J. C. Lindsay writes to me as follows:—

Llanvair Rectory, Abergavenny, *September 7th*, 1896.

The snow was on the ground when the "diviner" came here the first week in February, 1895. There was the usual walking over the grounds round the house, with the forked hazel rod in his hands, which occasionally gave an upward movement that, he said, indicated the presence of water. At last the evolutions of the rod became so marked and vigorous, that it almost skinned the fingers of the holder, and he said a strong spring would be found here. This was at a distance of some 250 yards from the house, and at an elevation rather above the level of the top of the house.

A well was sunk and water found at a depth of 34 feet, the water rising to as high as 29 feet in the well. During all the dry weather we have had an abundant supply, and little pumping, as the cisterns are mostly filled by gravitation.

W. J. C. Lindsay.

In reply to certain specific enquiries I made, Mr. Lindsay writes as follows:—

Llanvair Rectory, Abergavenny, *September 11th*, 1896.

My gardener will give you answers to your questions. Mr. Crawshay's well is about a mile and a-half from this. The diviner was anxious in my case to find a good spring as near the house as possible, to save the expense of pipes to convey the water to the house. He knew nothing of the surroundings, and made a diligent search all round, and found this splendid spring in a place where we should have never thought of looking for it.

W. J. C. Lindsay.

The gardener's letter is as follows:—

Abergavenny, *September 11th*, 1896.

(1) We had not tried to find water before Mr. Tompkins came. (2) It is therefore impossible for me to say whether a spring would be found anywhere on the grounds. (3) I am sure the diviner had no knowledge of the place to guide him. (4) Mr. Crawshay's place is about two miles from here, but I had not seen Mr. Tompkins before he came here.

James Hughes.

No. 104.—Of more value, from an evidential point of view, is the following letter, sent to me in reply to my enquiries. It is from the proprietor of the "Western Counties' Creamery Company":—

Marston House, Marston Magna, Bath, *May* 28th, 1896.

In reply to yours, I beg to say that previous to Mr. Tompkins' visit I had sunk two wells, one 20 feet, and the other, plus boring, 50 feet, with the result of only a very limited supply of water.

After a careful search by Mr. Tompkins, he assured me he had found a good spring at less than 30 feet. I agreed to let him sink the well, and at 18 feet he struck on a rock more than a foot thick, which, by the bye, we had not found in the other two instances. The water came in so fast that for several months I hoped I had sufficient, but some time after I found the supply was not enough, and I was then induced by a friend to bore at the bottom of Mr. Tompkins' well. This we did, and went down 130 feet, but then came on salt water, and had to plug down the bore hole. I then consulted some civil engineers, and they advised me to tunnel at the bottom of the 18 feet where Tompkins stopped. This I did; and followed the springs 10 feet each way, with (I am pleased to say) success. We now have plenty of water for factory, and I have just connected the well to the house besides.

E. Marden.

In reply to my enquiries as to the nature of Mr. Tompkins' search, and the position of the useless wells, Mr. Marden writes:—

Marston House, Marston Magna, Bath, *June 1st*, 1896.

The search by Mr. Tompkins was with the divining rod. The other two instances were wells we had previously dug nearer the factory. Perhaps I should add the first well was sunk as close as possible to the building for the convenience of machinery, but we found no water. No. 2 is only 6 feet from No. 1, and I dug down 25 feet with this; I here bored at the bottom of it, 25 feet more, making a total of 50 feet from surface. In neither of these wells did we come across any material rock, and at the bottom of No. 1 we drove a pipe to connect the two wells for storage. Why I made the two wells so close together was on account of an amateur twig-man assuring me that although there was no water in the first well, yet there was some within 6 feet of it. This proved true, but when Mr. Tompkins (the expert) came down, he informed me that the real spring was exactly under the engine. Of course it was not practical to sink there, so Tompkins started to find a spring elsewhere. After a search of about an hour he came upon No. 3, which, as before said, he told me was within 30 feet from the surface. Tompkins sank No. 3 himself, and at 18 feet came upon a thick rock, and a good supply of water.

E. Marden.

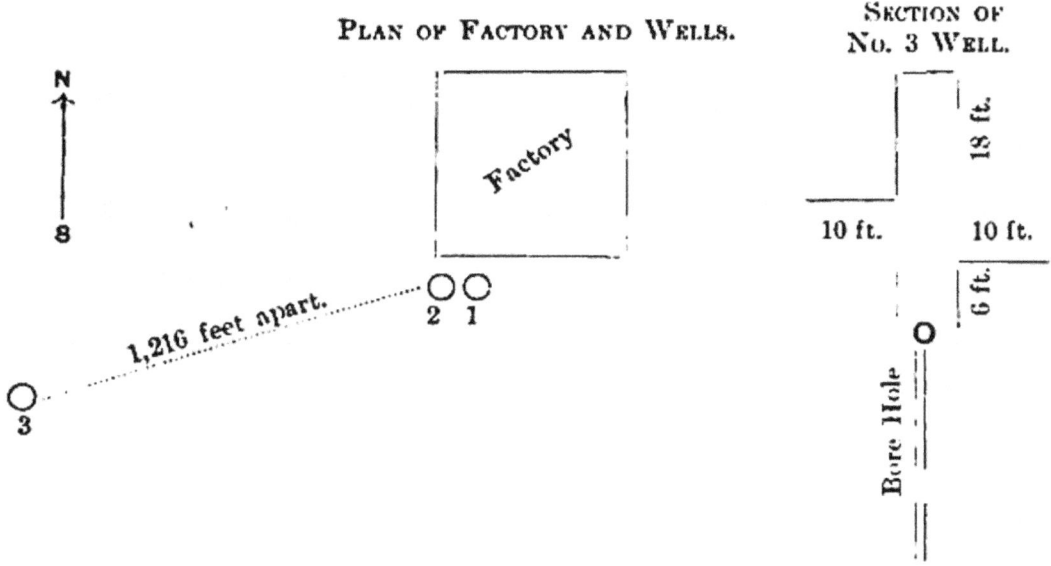

# The Credibility Of Dowsing

No. 105.—I am indebted to Captain the Hon. T. S. Brand, R.N., a son of the late Viscount Hampden, for the following evidence. Mr. Brand writes to me as follows:—

Home Farm, Glynde, Lewes, Sussex, *May 28th*, 1896.

In reply to your letter, I have made the enquiries asked for, and am now able to enclose a statement of what happened on this estate with regard to "water finding."

Thomas S. Brand.

Statement Enclosed.

(1.) An attempt was made to find water about 30 years ago. After sinking some distance, air came into the well. This was then abandoned. After this another attempt was made, and a well dug 167 feet deep, but no water was found. This was given up.

(2.) In 1893, Tompkins of Chippenham was engaged. The spot selected by him was 450 feet from the old well, the ground rising from 8 to 10 feet. He went over the ground, tracing all the springs to one point, saying that water would be found at a depth of 70 feet. We dug at the spot selected, and found indications of water at 70 feet, and struck the spring at 124 feet below the surface. We have since run a bore something like 20 feet, to obtain a better supply, but I do not think it has improved it.

(3.) Site of well, Southdown Hills, in white chalk, with flints. When Tompkins visited the place, he was taken over the old well, which was then covered up, and according to him there was no spring in the old well, or anywhere near it.

Some further particulars of the case (2) were given at the time by Mr. Pickard, the steward of the estate, in the following letter addressed to Mr. Tompkins:—

Home Farm, Glynde, Lewes, Sussex, *October 2nd*, 1893.

You will be interested to hear that water has been found at the Toy Farm; at a depth of about 118 feet a spring was found, and within a few inches from an opposite direction a second has broken forth, giving a strong supply. The digging operations were carried on for a day or two, gaining an additional 6 feet before the water gained the upper hand. We have, therefore, a well of 124 feet in depth, with 12 feet of water in the well, which certainly is very satisfactory. Water has been found where you indicated. The spring flows from the directions you named from either end of the Plantation, and I am very thankful for the supply.

I think as you have found a spring of water on the Toy Farm, you will find one anywhere. I should not have a well dug unless I employed you.

T. W. Pickard.

No. 106.—The next letter is addressed to me from the Rev. G. Booker, M. A., and gives particulars of Mr. Tompkins' dowsing for water at Woolhope, Herefordshire:—

5, Norfolk Terrace, Brighton, *May 11th*, 1896.

In reply to your queries, my brother in his lifetime tried to deepen a small well at his lodge gate; and he lost the very insignificant quantity of water which he had. There was on a high level, not far from the stable yard, a small well; but there was no quantity of water in it; quite insufficient for the supply of the house, and much more of the stables and gardens. The principal supply of the house and stables, &c., was drawn from two ponds used as reservoirs to collect the surface water from the rain, and a so-called land spring on a neighbouring estate. There was trouble about the water supply almost every summer. Under these circumstances, I being a trustee of the estate, had Mr. Tompkins' work as a water-finder brought under my notice. I communicated with him at once, and he came, and without any trouble or delay found two springs, one of which, more convenient in position, we adopted, and found water, sinking through the hardest bluestone, at 51½ feet. Mr. Tompkins, in reply to an enquiry of mine when he found the spring, named 50 to 55 feet as the probable depth we should have to sink; you will see that the actual distance was between his two limits.

As to your third question [whether any prior attempts to find water in the neighbourhood had been made without the aid of a dowser] I have heard of attempts being made to sink wells and get water in the immediate neighbourhood of my son's property; but without success.

The latter part of the sinking in our well had to be done with dynamite. The water came in too quickly for the use of gunpowder, When last I enquired, there were 25 feet in the well, and the workmen are now fixing a wind-pump to lift the water from the well and force it to the house and stables. There may be charlatans amongst the so-called water-finders: but Tompkins is a genuine man and may be trusted.

Geo. Booker

Two days later, the Rev. G. Booker kindly sent the following further details:—

*May 13th*, 1896.

The spring was found on the 19th September, 1893; but the well was not sunk for some months after that date, as Tompkins was very busy; and when he got to work he had to proceed by blasting with large charges all the way down. It was past midsummer in 1894, I think, before he finished the well, and had a head of water of 30 feet. I said 25 in my last, but it is recorded as last mentioned. The parish where the well was sunk is that of Woolhope, which is in County Hereford, and distant (speaking roughly) equally from Hereford, Ledbury and Ross. It is, you may be aware, well known to geologists from its presenting a sample of the silurian formation; and is, I believe, mentioned by Sir Roderick Murchison in one of his works. Tompkins' success on my son's estate got him employment on the Earl of Chesterfield's, which is close at hand. If you were to see him at work you would not doubt him. It is most interesting to see him following the run of the spring.

Geo Booker.

No. 107.—I am indebted to Mr. Eastes, the Clerk to the Parish Council at Yelling, Huntingdon, for the following statement. I have also to thank Mrs. Rowley, of The Priory, St. Neots, who, at my request, kindly made enquiries at Yelling, and confirmed the facts narrated below:—

Yelling Parish Council, Yelling, Huntingdon, *January 24th*, 1896.

Yelling is a village and parish on the borders of Cambridgeshire, six miles from St. Neots, and seven and a-half from Huntingdon. The inhabitants have suffered much at times from scarcity of water, there being in reality no supply. What was procurable was from ponds and brooks, and was known to be contaminated with organic impurities. There are several surface wells in the place, but their

## The Credibility Of Dowsing

position at once indicates that the water which percolates into them would be unsatisfactory[1], and a chalybeate spring situated at some distance from the village is useless for domestic purposes.

In February, 1895, the water-supply question was brought before the Parish Council, and it was decided to seek the services of a water-finder. Mr. B. Tompkins, of Pipsmore, Chippenham, Wilts, was communicated with and engaged to visit Yelling. This he did on April 8th. Mr. Tompkins carried a white thorn twig in front of him. Following quickly its lead, Mr. Tompkins was soon [as he alleged] upon the spring-head, when round and round went the twig, over and over, twisting below where it was being held firmly, and eventually breaking off on one side. Mr. Tompkins then stated that here was what he termed "a water-flat"; the spring pointed out was the strongest point. It was [he said] about 80 feet down, and capable of supplying 2,000 gallons of water a day. (Spring No. 1.) This was satisfactory, but it was hardly in the right position. Another start was made from the centre of the village, and shortly round went the twig again, over and over; this was in the right place, near the centre of the village; he said, about 20 to 25 feet down [we should have a] supply of about 1,000 gallons a day. (Spring No. 2.) A third spring was also afterwards found in the same manner.

The Parish Council then set to work. Had a well dug over Spring No. 2. Found water at 23 feet 8 inches. Water analysed and found good. The Council have laid pipes from the well to the roadside, and there erected a pump to supply the central part of the village. They have also dug over No. 3 Spring, found good water and erected a pump. The rock over the Spring No. 2 was 2 feet 8 inches thick; the soil consisting of blue gault. The rock over the Spring No. 3 was thicker. There appeared to be two rocks to get through, between which was a layer of blue gault.

J. P. Eastes.

In reply to enquiries Mr. Eastes writes, "No definite attempt to find a spring by sinking a well beyond the surface wells had been made before Mr. Tompkins came." In a subsequent letter, Mr. Eastes tells me that the depth of No. 2 Spring was 23 feet 8 inches, and of No. 3 was 80 feet.

Further particulars were also sent to me, in answer to enquiries, by Mr. Anthony, of Yelling, who, Mr. Myers informed me, could also use the dowsing rod. Mr. Anthony writes:—

Yelling, Hunts, *December 24th*, 1896.

The water-finding here has proved very satisfactory. Although no attempts had been made to find water by sinking wells in Yelling prior to Mr. Tompkins' visit in 1895, yet I am quite satisfied that we should not find a spring of water by sinking a well anywhere in Yelling.[2] For there are several old wells in the village which have been sunk many years ago, not with the idea of finding a spring of water (as no such spring was ever found in those old wells), but the idea was to sink wells and lay drains in the land 2 or 3 feet deep so that the surface water might be drained into them, and so storing water in winter for summer use; frequently, however, the supply fell short in summer and great inconvenience was caused thereby. Since [Mr. Tompkins' visit in] 1895, we have had a plentiful supply from two wells sunk last summer, and which proved to be two good springs.

I find I can also tell where there is water [even] without the use of the rod, but the rod indicates more distinctly the spot or strata where water may be found.

---

[1] In a subsequent letter Mr. Eastes informs me that the Parish Council emptied the best of these surface wells, and after it had refilled had the water analysed. The result showed "it was highly charged with organic impurities," and unfit to drink. No spring therefore existed in the well.

[2] Mr. Anthony tells me he means "anywhere at random," as will also be seen from the latter part of his letter.

I would further say here, that I know instances in the neighbourhood where boring, or rather digging and boring operations, have been carried on to a depth of some 200 or 300 feet without success. I am quite satisfied if we sank wells in Yelling, in many places we should find no water, and yet by means of using the rod it is possible to find water within a few yards of such wells without going many feet down.

R. Anthony

In a subsequent letter, Mr. Anthony replies to my inquiry as to the depth of the surface wells which existed prior to Tompkins' visit:—

*January 11th,* 1897.

The surface wells are various depths, from 30 to 40 feet. The success which attended the sinking of two wells in the neighbouring village of Croxton is satisfactory, although water was not found at the depth Mr. Tompkins expected. In one case it was found at about 12 feet, in the other at 80 feet. Mr. Tompkins said they would find water about 35 or 40 feet from surface. Those two wells are sunk where the surface is about level, but in our case [at Yelling] one is on a hill, the other in a valley.

R. Anthony

In a recent letter I am informed that, Mr. Anthony having found that the rod (in his own hands) moved strongly at one particular spot on his farm, he determined to sink a well there, and has just obtained a good supply of water at a depth of 65 feet. The last sentence of Mr. Anthony's letter of December 24th should be read in connection with this result.

No. 108.—The next two letters are from a tenant farmer and fruitgrower, Mr. Beaven, of Hereford. I had heard of the use which the dowsing rod had been to his fruit farm, and wrote to Mr. Beaven.

He replies:—

Highfield House, Holmer, Hereford, *May 9th,* 1896.

In answer to your questions, in the summer of 1893 we had not a drop of water on the premises—a farm of 50 acres—other than what was carried from a road-side spring. Though the house well was 80 feet deep, it was dry, and never could be depended on in a drought. No attempt [besides the above named well] had been made to obtain water here prior to the visit of the "diviner," nor should we have been at all likely to sink for water without some certainty of finding it, as the whole formation of the subsoil is of a very dry nature. The farm lies on a bank, and the dwelling-house is at the foot of the bank. The spot where Mr. Tompkins discovered water is some 50 feet above the level of the house, exactly on the highest point of our fruit plantations. The spring had two subterranean outlets,[1] and by means of one of these the water finder traced the head of the spring, the twig pointing and leading him in a zigzag course till at length it revolved rapidly in his hands. There, he said, water would be found, probably at a depth of 60 feet. The well sinkers, however, had to go to 97 feet, through dry marly strata, before they tapped the spring, which has since yielded at the rate of 2,000 gallons per day. No sooner had the confined water been properly released, than the rod refused any further action, though up to that time it had been tried almost daily, not only by Mr. Tompkins himself, but by a workman on the farm who discovered he had the power, and the twig indicated, and turned over the spot up to the very hour the full flow commenced. A windmill pumps the water for us into a 5,000 gallon tank, and at the present hour we are using it on a freshly planted strawberry plot of 1½ acres, the water being conducted through pipes, and from taps at intervals by means of hose.

E. W. Beaven.

---

[1] Mr. Beaven, I understand, means "the spring supposed to be indicated by the rod."—W. F. B.

# The Credibility Of Dowsing

Highfield House, *May 21st*, 1896.

(1) No attempt was made to find water previous to the arrival of the diviner, for the simple reason that we should not have thought of attempting anything of the kind. It was only on the guarantee that water would be met with, and, in fact, the absolute certainty of the rod's indicating power, a power that every unprejudiced mind must admit to be undoubted and genuine, that induced us to sink for water. I am convinced that a thousand pounds might have been laid out in boring, &c., with no successful result. It would have been entirely chance work without the divining rod.

(2) As I said before, a workman on the premises discovered, quite unknown to us at first, that the twig would turn in his hands just over the spot indicated by Mr. Tompkins, and this was the only instance, although many ladies and gentlemen tried their hands.

E. W. Beaven.

Mr. Beaven, it will be seen, is (as, in fact, he tells me) "a thorough believer in the divining rod," and has, I understand, published a book called "Tales of the Divining Rod." Although the dry well was 80 feet deep and the well sunk at the spot indicated by the dowser was 97 feet deep, the surface level of the dry well appears to be 50 feet lower than the other. Geological opinion on this case would be important.

No. 109.—Mr. Tompkins has recently returned from a visit to South Africa, where he was engaged in sinking for springs by the rod. The accompanying picture, from a photograph taken on the spot, shows him at work in British South Africa, and the following letter, addressed to Mr. Tompkins, is from the same quarter:—

Prieska, Cape Colony, South Africa, *October 19th*, 1896.

We have struck water at the spot indicated by you, 57 feet deep. The news came in yesterday. You can imagine we are all delighted with the success. The mining work was completely at a standstill for want of water. We are sinking at three other spots you marked, and we believe we shall get lots of water in the "Bult,"[1] and make the property a valuable one. The drought is still very severe, and the difficulties of obtaining water for the men and cattle are very great.

Hedley Bros.

Mr. Tompkins, in a letter to me, states that "The syndicate which owned this large South African property had spent some £7,000 in the attempt to find water, but completely failed. Within 100 yards of one of the borings made I found a good spring." This statement must be taken for what

MR. TOMPKINS DOWSING IN SOUTH AFRICA.

---

[1] [A 'BULT' is the name giving to a belt of rising ground in this region. Ed]

it is worth, for I have no independent information whether any unsuccessful boring for water had been made previously at this place.

I wrote to Prieska, and also to Mr. Hedley's brother, who lives in England; the latter can give me no further information, and from the former I have not yet heard in reply.

No. 110.—Mr. R. C. Warner writes to Mr. Tompkins as follows:—

Oaksey, Malmesbury, *October 27th*, 1892.

> We have sunk the well in the rick-yard, and at 49 feet we found the water. There is now 9 feet standing in the well of 6 feet diameter, and I believe we shall have a sufficient supply for my requirements. We have also sunk the second well for the garden and house supply, and believe that both will prove very successful. At the second well the water rose quickly to within 4 feet of the top, the well being 25 feet deep. At the first well we have 12 feet of water now, and from this one we can draw 400 gallons per day continuously, and this quantity is as much as we are likely to require in any one day.
>
> R. C. Warner.

I wrote to Mr. Warner to ascertain whether any prior attempts to find water had been made; he does not reply to this, but writes:—

Eversley. Oaksey, Malmesbury, *April 14th,* 1897.

> In reply to yours I have very little to add to the testimony already given us to the utility of the divining rod in finding springs of water; in my case the result is still very successful, for during the last two seasons, which, as you know, were extremely dry, we had quite sufficient water for my use.
>
> R. C. Warner.

In a subsequent letter, Mr. Warner adds that "many failures had occurred in my district in sinking wells at hap-hazard."

I have not space to quote the replies to other enquiries I have made in this group, as they merely indicate that a copious supply of water was found at the various places indicated by the dowser; the Rev. G. Platt Dew, of Shirenewtown Rectory, Chepstow, and others, write to me to that effect. The Press Cutting Agency has also sent me newspaper reports of similar results in other places, including some Parish Councils who have engaged this dowser to find water in their localities. Mr. Tompkins also sent me a lengthy list of different persons for whom he has found underground springs by the rod, and no doubt among the list evidential cases are to be found.

Whether the dowser's estimate of the depth and volume of the underground spring be pure guesswork, or is arrived at by some instinct or experience, only a careful examination of the evidence can establish. As I have quoted some letters which mention that Mr. Tompkins was often incorrect as to the depth, it is only fair to say other correspondents tell me he was singularly accurate in his prediction of the probable depth of the spring.

No. 111.—Here, for example, are two letters which reached Mr. Tompkins unasked, and the originals of which he has sent me:—

Parnacott, near Holsworthy, Devon, *July 22nd,* 1896.

> I should have written to you sooner to say how extremely gratified we are with the result of your "findings" here. The spring I sank upon last year which we found at 34½ feet (you guessed 33 feet I think) keeps the 5 feet diameter well even now supplied with 20 feet of excellent water. I am now sinking for the deeper spring you found (the first) for my fruit plantations.
>
> D. C. Cousins.

# The Credibility Of Dowsing

Stapeley House, Knighton, Radnor, *January 27th,* 1897.

I am pleased to inform you that we have found a good supply of water in my meadow at the spot indicated by you in September last. You reported the spring to be about 30 feet below the surface, and as we "tapped" it at 33 feet, I have every reason to be satisfied with the result of your waterfinding.

A. H. Wainwright.

In answer to my enquiry as to whether he experiences any sensation when over an underground spring, Mr. Tompkins replies:—

I feel a tingling sensation, and the twig begins to quiver when I get on to a running stratum of water, and when over it the twig rises immediately. It does not move for surface water nor water in pipes or drains, only natural live water, as I term it. The moment I cross a stratum of water I feel a sort of bracing sensation, which passes up my legs, back, and shoulders, and down the arms to the twig; when I get off the water course I feel the loss of this power, till I cross the water again. When I get over the exact spot the twig revolves over and over, and I am powerless to keep it still.

Whether this tingling sensation which is described by most dowsers is due to their imagination or not, I have no means of knowing; and meanwhile we must not attribute too much importance to it. Every dowser believes electricity moves the rod, and the chief effect of electricity is popularly believed to be this tingling sensation. Hence it is possible enough that if the dowser thought electricity always produced a peculiar taste, we should find *taste* substituted for *tingling* when over a spring. I shall, however, return to the question of the physiological effect alleged to be produced when dowsing for water.

## *Failures*

F. 6.—Mr. G. F. Lambert, of Bridgend, Glamorganshire, informed me on September 10th, 1896, that Tompkins had been engaged by the Urban District Council of Porthcawl, to find a supply of water for that favourite seaside resort.

Tompkins fixed on a certain spot where he said "an ample supply of water would be found at a depth of 80 feet." A well was sunk here and on September 18th, 1896, in reply to my enquiries, Mr. Lambert informed me that water *was* found at the spot indicated at a depth of 50 feet; and he adds, "the water collects in the well, which is 8 feet in diameter, to a depth of 20 feet in one night." Subsequently, however, I heard that the supply was insufficient and that the Local Government Board had disallowed the expenditure involved, which was stated to amount to £800.

In response to my further enquiries, Mr. Lambert kindly went over to Porthcawl, and writes to me on June 24th, 1897, that he had seen the clerk to the District Council, who explained that, hoping to get a larger supply, the well was sunk to a depth of 140 feet, but though some additional springs were intercepted, the total yield was quite inadequate to the requirements of the neighbourhood. The well was sunk through a conglomerate magnesian-limestone (well known to exist round Porthcawl).

Mr. Tompkins had previously, in answer to my enquiry, frankly given me particulars of three cases where he had not been successful. He states these are the only failures of his he had heard of; quite possibly, but the dowser's estimate of the number of his own failures, as well as the usual attempt he makes to explain them away, must obviously be taken *cum grano salis* [with a grain of salt - ED]. After ascertaining where the failures occurred in these three cases, I wrote to each person concerned, and asked for further particulars.

F. 6a.—From the agent to the Kemble Estate, Cirencester, I received the reply that they "bored to a considerable depth at the spot indicated by Tompkins, but found no water."

F. 7.—The only other information of these failures I have been able to obtain is from Sir Henry Mather Jackson, Bart., D.L., etc., who kindly gave me full details of his case, and to whom I sent Mr. Tompkins' own account of this failure. After some correspondence, Sir Henry gives me permission to publish the following letter:—

Llantilio Court, Abergavenny, *April 6th*, 1897.

> I am obliged to you for allowing me to see Mr. Tompkins' statement in reference to his attempt to find a water supply for Buguderi—a house of my mother's near to here.
>
> Mr. Tompkins advised sinking on the top of a hill, and stated that in his opinion there would be water enough to supply a cottage.
>
> Boring was first adopted, and at one period there was, as Mr. Tompkins states, a certain amount of water in the bore-hole, but whether this was spring or surface water it was impossible to say.
>
> After boring to a depth of 87 feet without any satisfactory result, Mr. Tompkins came over to see the place again, and he then said that it was a mistake to have bored, that sinking should have been adopted, and that though a considerable quantity of water had been allowed to escape, enough was left for the purposes for which it was required. Sinking operations were then commenced on the same spot, and after going down 122 feet without any sign of water, or evidence of there having been any water, the whole thing was abandoned. Mr. Tompkins is mistaken in stating that the boring was continued in the hopes that the "water would rise to the top of the well;" no such hope was ever entertained, and had any quantity of water been found in the bore-hole, sinking to that point would at once have begun.
>
> In my opinion Mr. Tompkins failed entirely in this instance, but I know of so many cases of success that I do not myself doubt the existence of the "gift"; moreover, as you say, the fact of his giving my name to you, though he failed here, shows his honesty.

Henry Mather Jackson

In concluding this group I have to acknowledge the readiness with which Mr. Tompkins has offered to assist me. He writes: "I will gladly submit to any test or experiment you may like to impose, in order to arrive at the truth of the enquiry you are engaged in." Not only so, but Mr. Tompkins, at his own expense, came from Chippenham to the meeting of our Society in London, when this paper was read, to meet me and also to show the members of the S.P.R. the method he adopts in dowsing.[1] Since then he has been to Cheltenham to submit to a series of experiments which Colonel Taylor has made for the purpose of this enquiry, the results of which will be given later on.

---

[1] Mr. Chesterman, another professional dowser, also did the same, kindly coming up from Bath to London.

# The Credibility Of Dowsing

## Group VII —Mr. J. Stears

Mr. Stears' name has already been mentioned in connection with the very interesting case sent me by Mr. Clark (No. 7, p. 22). Mr. Stears is now living at Westholme, Hessle, Yorkshire, and was until recently engaged in business as an engineer in Hull. For some time he was hon. sec. of the Hull Field Naturalists' Society, and is much respected by all who know him. My attention was first directed to Mr. Stears' use of the divining rod by the following letter which appeared in the *Pall Mall Gazette* and the *Leeds Mercury* for October 9th, 1890. The writer is the Rev. W. Spiers, M.A., F.G.S., of Hull:—

> Recently in the company of a few geologists on the Yorkshire Wolds, it was stated that one of our company (Mr. John Stears, engineer of Hull) was able to discover hidden water or metals by means of the rod. Our friend cut out of the hedgerow a fork of hawthorn, shaped like a long V. Holding a prong in each hand with the apex downward, we soon had an opportunity of seeing "there was something in it." Here and there, as he slowly walked along, the apex of the branch curled upwards as if alive. I know the gentleman too well to suspect that he was cheating us; but in order to see that he was not self-deceived, I placed my hand around those muscles which must have moved had the contortions of the rod been due to unconscious muscular contractions. I quite satisfied myself upon that point.
>
> I then requested him to close his eyes, and I led him over a small stream that was running down the hill on which we were walking, and the moment we reached it, the rod commenced its remarkable movements. As soon as I touched it with my fingers it resumed its natural position. For water, it moved away from the operator, but for metals it swung round in the opposite direction.

I wrote to Mr. Stears, and the following is his reply:—

> My experience has been most satisfactory (extending over 20 years), and I have always found water where the rod indicated it, also iron pipes. In some towns I have mapped out their position for the purpose of repairs, and the pipes have been found exactly where I stated, some even left deep where a road had been raised.
>
> I may say that I notice a different sensation with waters and metals; there is a chilly feeling creeps up my legs when the rod shows water.
>
> My powers vary with health; if tired I lose the power; provide the animal system with a fresh supply of food, and back the power comes. I do not like blindfolding. It seems to interfere with that calmness which is desirable, but I have tried it on roads where I denoted water; having been taken backwards and forward I have been started in the middle of the road and stopped at the part previously marked. Darkness does not interfere with the power in the least.

Mr. Stears then relates how he finds the nature of hidden metals by trying various metals in his hand along with the rod, the corresponding metal stopping all movement. This is referred to in Appendix C; it is the survival of an old tradition, but is nothing more than the effect of the dowser's own idea. Experimental proof of the fallacy of this among other superstitions connected with the divining rod will be given subsequently.

Mr. Stears states that it was after watching the noted dowser, Adams (see No. 25, p. 35), that he found he also possessed a similar power, and he adds that In 1870 he and Adams, quite independently of one another, located the same spot as the source of a good underground spring. On sinking a well a strong spring was found some ten feet beneath the surface in the magnesian limestone. When in Brazil in 1872, Mr. Stears says he occasionally tried his powers as a dowser and found a good supply of water for a resident, who sank a well at the spot indicated by him through the motion of the rod.

## Prof. W. F. Barrett

Mr. Stears has at my request furnished me with a tabular statement showing the places and the depths at which he has found water by the rod within the last two years only, at the same time furnishing me with references to those who had engaged him for this purpose. The list includes several local boards, noblemen, landowners and their agents, mill-owners, farmers, &c., a lengthy list. From many in this list I have received several letters in answer to my enquiries, and there can be no doubt of the success Mr. Stears has obtained as a water finder.

No. 112.—At a farm belonging to Mr. J. Letts, at Rillington, near Malton, in Yorkshire, a previous bore of 120 feet had been made unsuccessfully, not a drop of water being obtained; nevertheless, close by Mr. Stears found, by the use of the rod, a tremendous spring which he informs me "fires up as high as the house and continues to do so when the pipe is open." I wrote to Mr. Letts and had the following reply:—

Rillington, Yorks, *January 23rd,* 1897.

1. Boring for water had been made prior to Mr. Stears' visiting the farm at my recommendation, but without success, although they bored a distance of 120 feet.

2. The place where Mr. Stears selected to bore would be about 30 yards distant from the previous place. Mr. Stears found a very good supply at 84 feet.

3. The site of the farm is in the valley between the Moors and the Wolds.

I may add Mr. Stears selected another spot for boring on my other farm.

Although he found water, it was not nearly a sufficient quantity, consequently I didn't consider in that case he was so successful. I know several other places where he was most successful.

John Letts.

In correspondence Mr. Stears informs me that in addition to the 120 feet useless boring, there was also another well close by, some 70 feet deep, which was contaminated with sewage, and that by the rod he traced an underground stream, which fed this well, to a spot where the new and successful well was sunk. It was important to know the exact position of the useless deep boring, and in reply to my enquiries Mr. Stears sent me the accompanying sketch plan (next page). The dotted lines marked "underground streams," Mr. Stears has put in solely on the faith of the indications afforded by the rod; they must therefore be taken as merely hypothetical. Moreover, as the well A is contaminated, if a stream flows towards the river in the direction indicated by Mr. Stears, one would expect the well C to show signs of contamination also. I sent this plan, with the foregoing remarks, to Mr. Letts, and asked him if he had any corrections to make. Mr. Letts returned it with merely a verbal correction, and marked "correct."

I am indebted to Mrs. Williams, of Temple House, Great Marlow, Bucks, for a list of places in Aberdeenshire, where it was stated Mr. Stears succeeded in finding water by the rod after other attempts had been made in vain. This latter statement, however, is not shown in the correspondence that follows. Mrs. Williams says, "The facts were related to me by my brother-in-law, Mr. Muirhead—Lord Aberdeen's estate-agent—who would tell you about his experience with Mr. Stears. Mrs. Irvine, of Drum Castle, tried the rod, but it made her quite ill and exhausted."

## The Credibility Of Dowsing

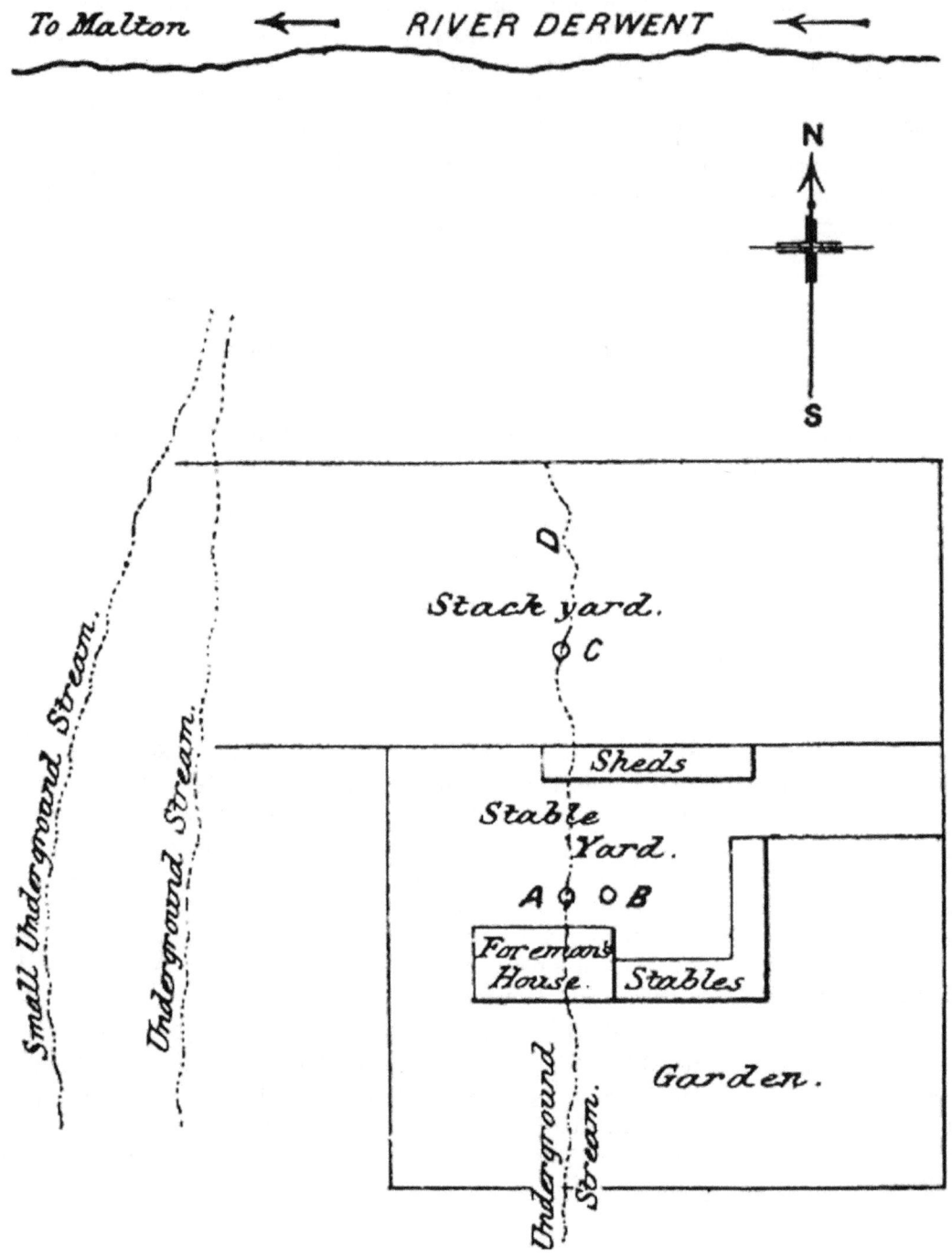

PLAN OF MR. JOHN LETTS' STABLES AT RILLINGTON, YORKS.

A—Old bore, strong but contaminated with manure, about 70 feet deep.
B—120 feet bore, 5 feet off A; no water found by Halliday.
C—Bore ordered by J. Stears; plenty of good water with pressure at 84 feet.
D—Stream which feeds A and C.

## Prof. W. F. Barrett

No. 113.—In reply to my enquiries, Mr. Muirhead writes:—

Estate Office, Haddo House, Aberdeen, *March 23rd,* 1897.

On July 7th last, accompanied by Mr. Stears, water-finder, I visited the farm of Braiklay, on the Haddo House estates of his Excellency the Earl of Aberdeen, in the parish of Tarves, and county of Aberdeen, the tenant of which is Miss Elizabeth Bean. The object of our visit was that Mr. Stears might indicate a place on the farm where a supply of water might be found, which could be introduced to the buildings on the farm by gravitation.

The farm lies entirely, according to the Geological Survey Map, on the gneiss formation, and slopes generally to the east and south, from about 380 to 250 feet above sea level, the farm buildings lying about half-way down the slope.

Mr. Stears proceeded from the farm buildings up the slope, and very soon indicated by means of the rod a stream of water whose course he followed to the highest point on the boundary of the farm. Leaving this stream he proceeded along the boundary until he found another stream, which he followed down the slope until he reached a point where he said that this second stream joined the first, which he had followed upwards from the farm steading.

The crop on the field at the time of the visit was turnips, and as the tenant did not wish the crop interfered with until the turnips were ready to be consumed by cattle, it was not until the month of November last that boring operations were commenced. After boring 21 feet water was found, which flowed at the rate of four gallons per minute, with steady pumping. The boring was continued to a depth of 40 feet where a great supply was found and which has never been pumped dry.

The water was recently introduced to the farm buildings.

Mr. Stears also, about the same time, visited the farm of Newton, in the parish of Methlick, also on his Excellency's estates; the tenant of which is Mr. Robert Wilson.

Here Mr. Stears also indicated a spot where water might be found, and, on boring operations being carried out, water was found at a depth of 10 feet. The boring was continued to 25 feet, where a satisfactory supply was got.

I will be glad to afford you any further information in my power.

George Muirhead.

In a subsequent letter, Mr. Muirhead writes, in reply to mine:—

No attempt either by boring or sinking for water had been made in the neighbourhood of the place where Mr. Stears indicated that water would be found, prior to Mr. Stears' visit.

There was no evidence of there being any water at hand either at Newton or Braiklay, both farms being on hills, and water had previously to be carried some distance. There is now a good supply.

George Muirhead.

## *The Credibility Of Dowsing*

No. 114.—I wrote to Mrs. Irvine and the following is her reply:

Drum Castle, Aberdeen, *March 16th*, 1897.

In reply to your note I beg to state that in 1893 we had the late Mr. Lawrence of Bristol to find us water, which he did successfully in three or four different places. In 1897 Mr. Stears came twice and marked a great many places. Some for future use we have not yet tried, but in seven cases we have found water on the exact spot marked by him. Both with Mr. Lawrence and Mr. Steers I tried the divining rod several times, but on each occasion it made me feel so ill that I do not care to repeat the attempt.

M. A. F. Irvine.

I asked Mrs. Irvine if any previous attempts to find water, without the aid of a dowser, had been made on her property. Mrs. Irvine writes in reply.—

Drum Castle, Aberdeen, *March. 30th*, 1897.

We had been obliged to provide water for various cottages and farms prior to the diviners' visits, as there was not a good supply, and one that was very apt to fail in the summer. Our attempts were not very successful, so hearing that Mr. Lawrence was coming to our neighbourhood, we decided to have him before making any fresh attempts in new places, with the result that I have told you. I am afraid that is all the information I can give you.

M. A. F. Irvine

No. 115.—The following report I abridge from the *Bury Times* of August 15th, 1896:—

Some interesting experiments, in regard to the search for underground water, took place on land occupied by Mr. J. Eddleston, farmer, Wrigley Carr, Birtle, yesterday. The experiments were occasioned owing to a well which had supplied the wants of the farm since 1888 having recently become dry. In consequence Mr. Eddleston has been put to some inconvenience in obtaining an adequate supply of water, and he decided to invite Mr. John Stears, of Hull, to visit the locality for the purpose of ascertaining by means of a "divining rod" where water could be found. About twenty persons, including farmers and others interested, witnessed the experiments. . . . After proceeding for some little distance, the "divining rod" (a forked branch of hawthorn) held in the hands of Mr. Stears about three feet from the ground, began to turn, and Mr. Stears announced that a good stream of water would be found underneath where they were standing, some distance below the surface. Wooden pegs were driven into the ground, in places indicated by Mr. Stears, to mark the course of the stream. . . While tracing this stream the current indicated was so strong that the twig was snapped in two, and a little further on a second twig which had been obtained was also "broken. . . . The well which had previously supplied the farm, and which had been worked by one of Mr. Webster's wind-power pumping engines, was next visited, but no satisfactory result was obtained in the vicinity of the well. A route was then taken in the direction of the farm, and it was soon apparent that another stream had been struck. This was traced for some distance and eventually found to cross the stream first discovered, although the two water-courses were, according to Mr. Stears, at different levels. He found the junction of the two streams, and a number of pegs were driven into the ground. Boring operations will be commenced in due course, and if these are successful the wind engine will be removed to the place from the well previously referred to. The spot indicated is on rising ground.

I wrote to Mr. Eddleston to ascertain if the foregoing report were correct and whether water had been found as indicated. The following is his reply:—

## *Prof. W. F. Barrett*

Wrigley Carr Farm, Birtle, near Rochdale, *September 15th*, 1896.

> I gladly comply with your request for report of the water found by means of the divining rod. Having been very much troubled this dry summer for good water, at the suggestion of Mr. Jonas Webster, water engineer, of Bolton, I agreed that he should get Mr. Stears from Hull. At the time appointed Mr. Stears came, and on a very dry hill above the house he found a good stream running in a west to east direction, and another smaller stream crossing the same north and south.[1] We considered [it] best to take the crossing point, so I at once engaged men to sink a well there; they went on sinking, and bricking as they went on, through the different minerals as dry and hard as possible until they got to the depth of 30 feet; then they came to the stream [running] north and south, which made a fair supply of water. But I kept them sinking on till they came to the next stream at the depth of 42 feet, which was an excellent stream running across the bottom of the well, just in the direction the diviner indicated, I should think we get as much water as would supply four or five farms; and it has risen in the well ten feet. I am glad to say the result is very successful, and Mr. Webster is now going to put up one of his wind pumping engines.

Joseph Eddleston.

No. 116.—Another case, which needs further investigation, is given in a letter to a journal called *The Carpenter and Builder*, of November 18th, 1892. Mr. W. Smith, of Atherby, Malton, Yorkshire, writes:—

> "In order to supply a small cottage property with water, I dug a new well, and got to a considerable depth, when to our dismay, we struck solid rock, when on account of the cost it might entail, we were compelled to cease further operations, and in despair, filled it in again.

> "I was relating my experience to Mr. Nelson, the courteous surveyor of the Norton (Malton) Local Board, who suggested Mr. John Stears, of Hull, with his divining rod. . . .

> "Mr. S. proceeded to cut out of the hedge a forked thorn, which he held by the forked ends, with both hands straight out before him, and walked leisurely across the ground. Immediately he came across the spot underneath which he said lay water, the rod, which he held firmly with both ends, began to move upwards until it touched his breast. At that spot we have dug, and found water at a depth of only seven yards, which has set at rest any doubt as to the success or otherwise of the experiment."

No. 117.—The following is from the *Peterborough Express* of September 12th, 1895.

> As we briefly announced in a recent issue, the Arborfield Paper Mills at Helpston, owned by Messrs. A. Towgood and Sons, are being provided with a fresh supply of water, a spring having been discovered by means of the divining rod in the yard at the rear of the premises. A plentiful supply of water is highly necessary for the manufacture of brown paper, and the finding of the spring will give to the mill that which has long been required. The services of Mr. J. Stears, water expert and engineer of Westholme, Hessle, near Hull, were called into requisition. He found water in the yard, and it was eventually decided to bore at a spot behind the mill. The boring operation was placed in the hands of Mr. J. E. Noble, builder and contractor, of Bourne. Boring proceeded steadily for several days, various strata of earth, including rock, being passed through. At a depth of 49ft. rock was again reached, and at 52ft. a steady stream of water was discovered. The operations were still continued, the rock being again pierced, and at 69ft. the main spring was tapped, a volume of water of tremendous pressure shooting up. The boring was intended for a two and a-half inch pipe, but it has

---

[1] Mr. Eddleston, of course, means that Mr. Stears stated these underground streams existed.—W. F. B.

## *The Credibility Of Dowsing*

since been decided to have a four inch pipe. The quality of the water is to all appearances exceedingly pure, and the volume of water is estimated to be between seven and eight thousand gallons per hour. The method of passing the water into the mill has yet to be dealt with.

Mr. Stears sent me the following letter from Messrs. Towgood to him:—

Arborfield Mill, Helpston, *May 14th*, 1896.

The boring for water which we made here at the spot indicated by you by means of the divining rod has proved entirely successful; a continuous supply at the rate of 10,000 gallons per hour is now rising to the surface.

Alfred Towgood And Sons.

I wrote to Messrs. Towgood asking if the above newspaper report were correct, and if a previous boring had been made, and, if so, how deep. They reply:—

The printed report you send is quite correct. No previous boring had been made. We quite believe in the divining rod.

Alfred Towgood And Sons.

No. 118.—Mr. Stears, writing to me, states that he was also engaged by the local authorities at Helpston, who were in want of a better supply of water, and that he succeeded in finding an abundant supply by the indications of the rod. This is described at length in the local papers. I abridge the following from the *Peterborough Express* of August, 1896:—

The question of the water supply of Helpston has been the one absorbing topic for some time, and the villagers have been in sore straits owing to the inadequate supply. So short was water in the village a few weeks ago that the inhabitants trooped to the pump in the early morning, but many had to return disappointed. A well sunk last year proved to be of little use. Mr. Howes, the representative on the District Council, interested himself to a great extent, and his efforts resulted in the matter being placed in the hands of the Parish Council with power to act. This body called in the service of a "diviner," Mr. Stears, of Hull, who successfully operated in the case of the water supply at the Paper Mills. One of the spots tried was at the four cross roads in Woodgate. Here so strong was the current that the divining rod was broken, and Mr. Stears recommended that boring operations should take place. The work was placed in the hands of Mr. Noble, of Thurlby, and boring operations were commenced. By Saturday night a depth of 37 feet had been reached, 6½ feet of rock having been passed through at the top, followed by a thick layer of clay. By Monday a depth of 46 feet had been reached, a second layer of rocks being pierced at about 43 feet. The water was " struck " on Tuesday and rose to the surface in great quantities. The flow from the top, notwithstanding that the drill had not been removed, was more than a six-inch pipe could take away, and the immediate locality was flooded. Immediate steps had to be taken to open the drains. There is every reason to believe that a supply has now been tapped which is more than sufficient to supply the whole of the village, besides providing an unlimited quantity for flushing and other sanitary purposes.

Mr. Stears has sent me a copy of Mr. Noble's letter to him which is as follows:—

Thurlby, Bourne, Lincolnshire, *September 4th*, 1896.

I am pleased to tell you the bore on the Village Green at Helpston, marked out by you, has given very great satisfaction. At a depth of 50 feet, the water rushed up, the overflow being measured at 7,000 gallons per hour; the Helpston people are delighted at the success, having been without water so long.

J. E. Noble.

No. 119.—The next case was described by Miss A. W. Richardson, of Moyallon House, Gilford, Co. Down. She wrote to Mrs. Sidgwick in 1885, as follows:—

> On one occasion, being with my father on business at one of our homes in Ireland, Mr. Stears offered to tell him if there were water beneath a certain part of my father's property, in which he wished to build, and in which being very rocky, it was troublesome to bore.
>
> The idea was quite novel to us then, but upon his assuring my father that water existed there, it was proved to be the case. This is the only instance where the process was at all removed from the possibility of thought-transference. At our other home (he had never been to either before) he was led over a piece of ground where several of us knew that drains at periodical distances existed, and his rod went up quite correctly as he passed over them.
>
> In this case, of course, it could at once be referred to transference of thought. Of course in these cases it is almost impossible to devise a plan by which it may be tested without the knowledge of some spectator.
>
> I have observed that the very slightest muscular motion sends up the vertex of the rod; but, of course, the ambiguous part of the process is the coincidence of the sensation which produces this movement with the presence of water.
>
> My sisters were interested in finding that the custom commonly obtains in a remote part of the South of France, in which they spent a winter, lately.

A. W. Richardson.

Mr. Stears is now on a "water-finding" visit to the West Indies, where he has been professionally engaged.

## Failures

I have heard of a few failures in connection with Mr. Stears; others doubtless exist which have never reached me. (As before, the numbering F. 8 is consecutive, following on from p. 163.)

F 8.—Here is one where the failure has led the Parish Council to a very heavy and useless expenditure:—

Bardney, Lincoln, February 16th, 1897.

Bardney Water Supply.

> Mr. John Stears, of Westholme, Hessle, Yorkshire, diviner, was employed by our Parish Council to find water. He tried many parts of the village, and indicated several places where he was sure water would be found, particularly in one spot, where he was satisfied a very copious supply would be found. At this spot we commenced boring about three months ago, and have got to a depth of about 240 feet still in blue clay, but at present without any signs of water. No engineer has been consulted. As soon as water is found I will let you know.

J. R. Hird,<br>Clerk to the District Council.

In reply to my subsequent enquiry, Mr. Hird writes:—

# *The Credibility Of Dowsing*

Bardney, Lincoln, *April 13th*, 1897.

A depth of 340 feet has now been reached, but unfortunately without any signs of water. They are still in blue clay. At a depth of 286 feet they came to rock 2 feet 9 inches in thickness, and at 300 feet the like 3 feet in thickness.

J. R. Hird.

From the following which arrived as this paper is going to press, it will be seen the boring has been made still deeper. I enquired who was the Chairman of the Parish Council.

Bardney, Lincoln, *May 21st*, 1897.

A depth of 390 feet has now been reached, without at present any signs of water. They are now in rock, and have got about 16 feet into it. Mr. John Sharpe, of Bardney Manor, is our Chairman.

J. R. Hird.

F. 9.—In the next case my informant, Mr. Bradley, gives me evidence of Mr. Stears' success as well as failure. Here is his letter:—

Estate Office, Ebberston, York, *May 20th*, 1897.

I heard of Mr. Stears being at Heslerton, Ganton, Knapton, etc.; several parties bored where Mr. Stears said there was water, and were successful. I went over to some of the places, and saw for myself.

I recommended Mr. Stears to the managers of Trainton School, and they sent for him. He came over, and pointed out where there was water, and they sunk a well and bored about 80 feet, and got plenty of water.

I also recommended Mr. Stears and Mr. Gataker to the Parish Council at Appleton le Moors. They sent for Mr. Stears, and he went over and pointed out to them that there was water in a certain field, a very high point. They also sent for Mr. Gataker, and he sent his assistant, named Wills, and he fixed on the same place that Stears did. But some of the Parish Council thought that Mr. Wills had overheard them say, "That would be the best place if there was water." Mr. Wills said there was water, and a good supply could be got.

The Parish Council sunk a well about 45 feet, and bored 36 feet (81 feet altogether) and then stopped because there were no signs of water. They had been told they would get water at 60 feet, or might have to go 80 feet.

The Parish Council then asked me to go over and see the place. I went and inspected the well, etc., and the whole district, and I have not the least doubt in my mind they would have to go down a great depth. At the place where the well is sunk there is at least 280 feet of limestone before they get to the clay bed.

Joseph Bradley

Mr. Bradley adds a geological section of the district, which confirms his statement. Mr. Bradley informed Stears and Gataker of this failure, and both say the water is there, only somewhat deeper than the Parish Council has bored!

F. 10. - I have also had some correspondence with reference to another case of failure on the part of Mr. Stears, which occurred at Flamborough in Yorkshire. Here a well was sunk at the spot indicated by Mr. Stears, and sinking or boring carried down to 170 feet through the clay into the chalk, and no water reached. My correspondent, however, does not wish his name or letters published. Mr. Stears, in reply to my enquiry, gives as his explanation that "the boring was not carried deep enough, as the chalk is upheaved and the strata contorted at the place."

Doubtless, if a boring goes deep enough, water might be reached, but failure is the only name to be given to cases where water— predicted at a certain spot and limit of depth—is not found, after sinking to this depth, or, say, 20 per cent, deeper than was indicated by the dowser.

## Experiments In Kingstown

Mr. Stears happening to be on a visit to Ireland, in July, 1892, I requested him to submit to some tests of his powers, to which he readily consented.

*Experiment I.*—The experiments were made in the private pleasure grounds opposite my house, at Kingstown, a place entirely new to Mr. Stears, who had never been in this neighbourhood before. Cutting a forked twig, Mr. Stears started from the point marked A in the accompanying plan, and walked to and fro until he reached the point marked with an asterisk, when from the sudden and vigorous movement of the twig he asserted that a considerable spring of water was underneath this spot. There was nothing whatever to indicate that such was the case, but on enquiry from the gardener (who was not present during the experiment) I learnt for the first time that the very spot upon which Mr. Stears had fixed was the site of an old well, now completely hidden beneath the level greensward. I now begged Mr. Stears to walk slowly over the ground, and if the rod indicated any other springs, to allow me

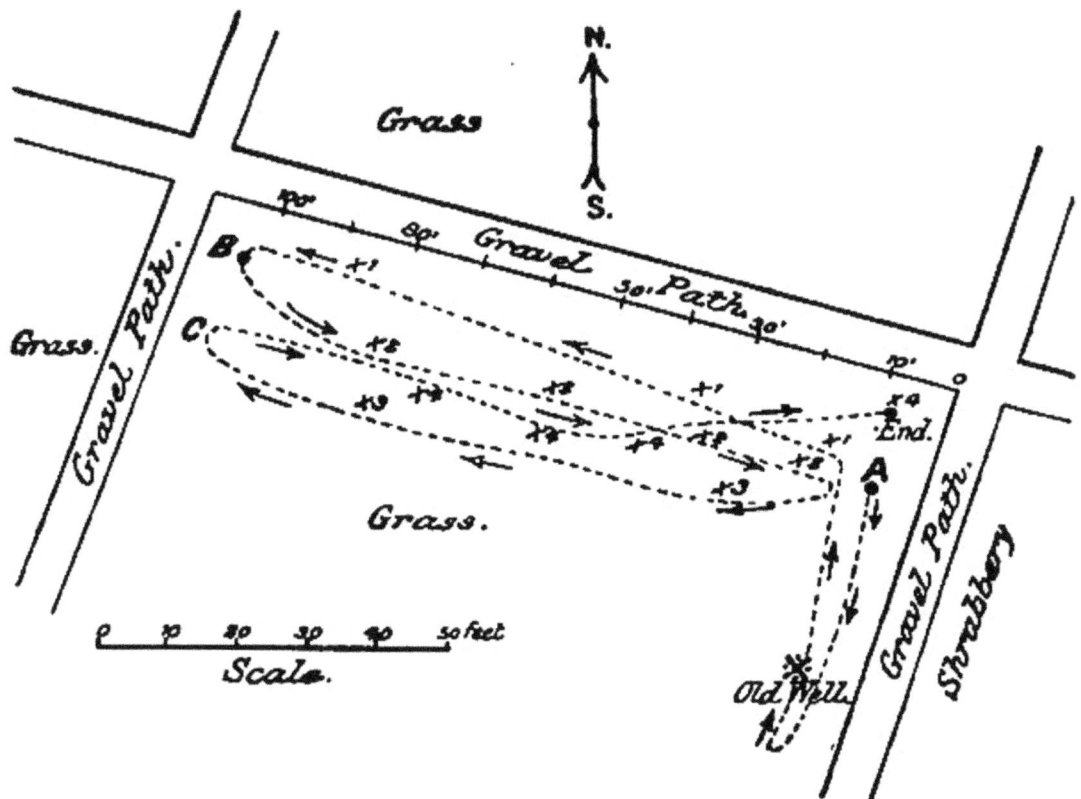

then to blindfold him and so retrace the ground. Mr. Stears consented, and with this object he moved in the direction of the dotted line. The rod moved at the points marked $x^i$ on the plan. At the point B., Mr. Stears, notwithstanding the very reasonable objection he had made in his letter to me 18 months before, (p. 134), was carefully blindfolded, and endeavoured to retrace his steps: the rod moved at the points marked x². He now asked me to let him try the same course with his eyes closed and the bandage removed. This I did, and the rod moved at the points marked x³. Finally, at C, he consented to be again carefully blindfolded, and once more he retraced his steps, the rod moving at the points marked x⁴. It will be seen that these points do not coincide, but in two or three places they are nearly in the same straight line,—approximately N. and S. It is possible that there may be underground water in this direction, as Mr. Stears subsequently declared there was from the movement of the rod, and tracked out the supposed course of two or three imaginary streams.

*Experiment* 2.—Mr. Stears having stated that the rod moved over comparatively small masses of metal, I procured nine bandboxes and removing their lids, put large lumps of iron beneath some of them, and nothing under others; Mr. Stears did not see this arrangement I made on the lawn till it was completed, when, as the boxes were all inverted, it was impossible to tell under which one the iron weights were concealed, nor was I quite certain in each case myself, so that thought-transference need hardly be considered. The result was that out of the nine boxes Mr. Stears indicated five correctly; that is, he was certain from the movement or non-movement of the rod that iron was or was not beneath the box; three indications were wrong, and one was doubtful. The trial was therefore inconclusive, as the number told correctly was not beyond the probability of chance coincidence.

*Experiment* 3.—Another trial was made with three bandboxes, a mass of iron, unknown to Mr. Stears, being placed under No. 3. On testing with the rod, Mr. Stears asserted from the movement of the rod that the iron was beneath No. 2, and nothing under No. 3. This was therefore a complete failure.

*Experiment* 4.—Finally I chose two exactly similar boxes and put a half cwt. [56 pounds - Ed] beneath one and nothing beneath the other; recalling Mr. Stears, I begged him to make a succession of trials, at short intervals, on the two boxes, whilst I noted the results. I got some one to change the position of the iron each time (or not change it), and then go away without letting Mr. Stears or myself know what had been done. On adding up the number of successes and failures, I found that the result was just what chance coincidence would have given, that is to say, there was almost exactly an even number of successes and of failures.

With the exception, therefore, of the location of the old well, the first experiments with Mr. Stears were inconclusive, and the latter, metal-finding, distinctly adverse to the existence of any such alleged power. At the same time I am perfectly satisfied of the *bona fides* of Mr. Stears, and have cordially to thank him not only for so readily acceding to every test I proposed, but for having put himself to some expense and inconvenience by prolonging his stay in Ireland to enable me to carry out these trials.

## Group VIII — Mr. Leicester Gataker

One of the younger water finders is *Mr. Leicester Gataker*, formerly of Weston-super-Mare, now residing at Crescent-gardens, Bath. He is a gentleman by birth and education; his father was a captain in the Bengal Staff Corps, and the son, after leaving Bath College, where he was educated, discovered to his surprise that a forked twig revolved in his hands in the same way as it did with a local "diviner." Mr. Gataker states that whenever he is over

a spring of water a sensation not unlike a slight shiver comes over him, chiefly in his arms, and the forked twig, or wire, he sometimes holds, continues to revolve—independently of his volition—so long as he remains over the bed of the stream or spring; running water alone affecting him.[1] Judging from his sensations, or the movement of the rod, he asserts that by practice he has been able to estimate the depth and volume of the underground spring or stream. Repeated trials having satisfied Mr. Gataker that his success was not due to a mere "fluke," he determined

---

[1] In conversation, Mr. Gataker told me this sensation was most marked, and usually began at the pit of the stomach: a feeling of sickness often being produced. This is what some other professional dowsers have also told me, quite independently of each other. How far this experience is due to a preconceived idea, I do not know.

## The Credibility Of Dowsing

to make water finding his profession, his health not permitting him to continue the sedentary life of a London office. In addition to finding water, Mr. Gataker, like many other professional "diviners," employs workmen to sink the well; like others also, he agrees to the terms of "no water, no pay," but charges 25 per cent extra for his work if carried out under these conditions!

Unlike other dowsers, Mr. Gataker does not, ordinarily, use a forked twig or any kind of rod. An eye-witness thus describes his proceeding. The rod, it will be seen, is discarded:—"His procedure seems to be a rapid survey of the ground. He walks along with a quick step, with his hands hanging by his side, until (according to his statement) he strikes a stream of water, when he at once becomes visibly agitated. With outstretched hands he appears carefully to feel his whereabouts, until he ascertains the direction the stream is flowing and follows it up. Then he marks the spot of greatest supply and estimates the depth and quantity likely to be obtained."

The accompanying woodcut (taken from *Black and White*) shows Mr. Gataker at work (see previous page).

Again, Mr. G. F. Tregelles, of Barnstaple, gives me the following description of Mr. Gataker's procedure:—

> On October 28th, 1896, I went down to Ilfracombe to join a party of members of the Ilfracombe Local Board, who had engaged Leicester Gataker, of Weston-super-Mare and Bath, to look for additional supplies of water for their reservoir.
>
> Gataker, who is a young man, did not use the forked twig, but walked about with long strides, holding out his hand, or hands, palm down, and every now and then making a dash or lurch to one side, diverging right or left, sometimes walking straight, and sometimes in a circle, and at last, if satisfied, digging his heel into the turf at the chosen spot. He seemed to be following a sensation, which is what he professes to do, and he looked very like a dog following the traces of a rabbit over the grass.
>
> On questioning him he said that when over a hidden spring, even with arms folded, he felt a tingling all through his body, and still more so when one or both hands were extended. The depth and quantity of water he estimated by the intensity of this feeling, coupled with experience.

I wrote to Mr. Gataker and asked him to furnish me with a summary of any cases where he had been called in to find an underground spring, by the exercise of his dowsing faculty, after previous attempts to find water in the ordinary way had failed. In reply, Mr. Gataker sent me brief particulars of some two dozen cases—drawn up in a business-like and excellent manner,—and writes as follows:—

Bath, *January 12th,* 1897.

> I think I am right in saying that water was sought for unsuccessfully prior to my visit, in each case. However, clients can substantiate my claim or not. If the latter, I should like to know of it.
>
> I can give you other cases, only my own time being so much occupied, I came to the conclusion that the few I have sent will be sufficient.

Leicester Gataker.

The particulars given by Mr Gataker were, in nearly all these cases, followed by a copy of a letter from the person who employed him, supporting in general terms Mr. Gataker's statement; these letters, some of which I here quote, did not, however, indicate that previous attempts to find water had in each case been made.

## *Prof. W. F. Barrett*

No. 120.—Mr. Ashworth, agent to Mr. Arkwright, of Hampton Court, writes as follows to Mr. Gataker:—

Hampton Court Estate Office, near Leominster, *October 30th*, 1895.

Referring to your visit to Bodenham on August 3rd, 1894, I am writing to inform you that a well was sunk at the spot indicated by you at the back of the keeper's cottage, and water was found at a depth of 53 feet, being 13 feet lower than the extreme depth as estimated by you.

The supply of water is sufficient for the purposes for which it is required, the water rising about 3 ft. 6 in. in the well, and being of excellent quality.

Henry A. Ashworth.

Respecting this, Mr. Gataker states he was employed on this occasion to find water in consequence of a deep well formerly in use having run dry; and he succeeded in locating the above supply within a few yards of the old well.

I wrote to Mr. Ashworth asking if Mr. Gataker's statements were correct, and received the following reply:—

Hill House, Bodenham, Leominster.

In reply to your letter of the 5th inst, Mr. Gataker visited Hampton Court Estate in the summer of 1894, and asserted, after searching, that water would be found at a certain depth—about 20 ft. east of the old well which has been sunk for the use of the cottage, for which a supply was required— the old well proving dry. An excellent supply of water was found on sinking at the spot he indicated, but at about 10 ft. lower than he thought it would be found.

No attempts [beyond the old well] to sink had been made previous to his visit.

H. A. Ashworth,

*Agent, Hampton Court Estate, Near Leominster.*

In reply to my enquiries Mr. Ashworth writes further:—

Hill House, Bodenham, Leominster, *April 26th*, 1897.

The following are the particulars you require:—

(1) Depth of new well, sunk at the spot Mr. Gataker indicated, 53 feet.

(2) Character of ground sunk through: hard marl, with the exception of a thin bed of stone 6 inches thick, 6 feet from surface.

(3) Depth of water in well: from 36 to 42 inches.

(4) Depth of old well, which was situated 8 yards west of new well: about 72 feet.

H. A. Ashworth.

No. 121.—The next letter is addressed to Mr. Gataker, from Mrs. Holloway, of Stroud:—

Farm Hill, Stroud, Gloucestershire, *December 13th*, 1894.

Your search for water at Farm Hill, Stroud, was most successful, the water being found at the spot indicated by you.

## *The Credibility Of Dowsing*

The men told me there were 18 feet of water in the well, which I have had analysed twice, and it is found very good.

Ann Holloway.

Here Mr. Gataker states that, prior to his visit, boring for water had been made to a depth of 70 feet, but no water found. I wrote to Mrs. Holloway and asked if this statement were correct; the following is the reply:—

Farm Hill, Stroud, Gloucestershire, *March 16th*, 1897.

The statement made by Mr. Gataker is correct. The distance between the unsuccessful and the successful bore was a gradual ascent of about 300 yards. Mr. Gataker gave the limit of depth at 50 feet, but a good spring of water was actually found at 45 feet.

Ann Holloway.

No. 122.—In the next case Mr. Gataker writes to me as follows:— "I was engaged on the estate of Mr. Geake, near Launceston, and after searching for water in Mr. Geake's field, I was brought to an old well (dry), and which was looked upon as useless. Full particulars of the work carried out following my advice will be found in the letter I received, as follows ":—

Millways, Launceston, Cornwall, *October 4th*, 1895.

You will be pleased to hear we found the spring, after sinking one well to 65 feet, and driving a heading about 15 feet, exactly as you predicted. This we had to do to get at the spot marked by you.

The find was more remarkable because you said we ought to come to this spot very soon, and you could not see how the well should go quite dry, considering the spring was so near. The well was not straight, and was sunk the opposite way.

We have now 10 feet 6 inches of water deep, 15 feet long, and about an average of 5 feet wide, which has kept to the level through September.

John Geake.

In reply to my enquiries, Mr. Geake writes:—

Millways, Launceston, *April 1st*, 1897.

The well was sunk many years ago to supply 20 acres of grazing land. Originally it was about 25 feet deep. It was taken in hand from time to time by different men, and put down to 55 or 56 feet. Even after that it went dry for three and four months, according to the summer weather. When we sent for Mr. Gataker, we did not open the well; it had been quite dry, as usual, for some time. Mr. Gataker came upon it suddenly. He had been going over other ground. We had hoped he would find a shallow spring somewhere else. After asking a few questions about the well, he walked on one side of it, and simply said, "I have it." He turned and said, "There should be a certain quantity of water at the bottom of that well, if it is 55 or 56 feet deep; there is a spring running near," pointing to one side of the well, "and it should have touched the top of it." We found out afterwards that if the well had been sunk straight down, as we supposed it to be, this should have been the case, but in order to escape some hard ground, the men, years before, had gone all on one side, quite the opposite side to where Mr. Gataker was pointing. He gave instructions to sink the well 10 feet deeper, and drive to the place he marked. When it was accomplished we had a room of water, about 15 feet long and 10 feet deep, at the bottom of the old well; the water rose to the level of the bottom of the old well.

An old Cornish miner, who went down, said that at the spot Mr. Gataker pointed out, and depth, there was a lode, about 12 feet wide, showing "Manganese." The water is of excellent quality, and we have raised the rent accordingly. [!]

John Geake.

In answer to my enquiry whether Mr. Gataker's predictions were verified upon actual trial, and whether it was probable water might have been found elsewhere on the estate, or by sinking the existing well deeper, Mr. Geake replies : —

Millways, Launceston, *April 13th*, 1897.

We verified Mr. Gataker's predictions. The spring was found at the very place he indicated. We [probably] should not have found a similar supply by sinking deeper, or anywhere about but the place he marked. In my last to you, I quite forgot to mention that we had gone to great expense by having two holes bored at the bottom of the well, 20 and 30 feet, which made the well and holes 86 feet deep. We had given up trying a year or two before Mr. G. came to us.

John Geake.

No. 123.—Mr. Gataker states that being engaged by Messrs. Ruscombe Poole and Son, the well known solicitors of Bridgwater, he found a spring less than 14 feet deep, and within 3 or 4 yards of a useless well, 20 feet deep, sunk prior to his visit. In corroboration, he encloses the following letter:—

Bridgwater, Somerset, *July*, 1896.

We have sunk a, well in the garden, and a copious spring has been found at 13ft. 6in., which amply verifies your prediction.

J. Ruscombe Poole and Son.

I wrote to Mr. Ruscombe Poole, and asked him if Mr. Gataker's statement were correct, and he replies:—

Bridgwater, *January 15th*, 1897.

We return the paper you sent us. As regards the statement that there was a well about 20 feet deep which was useless, this is perfectly true, because the water in it was foul, and smelt badly. The supply found is a very much more copious one than the old well, which contained very little water.

J. Ruscombe Poole and Son.

No. 124.—In the next case, Mr. Gataker states he was engaged by the Messrs. Pacey, of Melton Mowbray, who, prior to his visit, had sunk a well on the advice of a water-finder, but the supply proved useless; that he found a spring close by, and agreed to sink a well on the terms of " no water, no pay."

I wrote to Messrs. Pacey, who replied on September 17th, 1896, that they had not yet got to the depth of 50 or 60 feet, predicted by Mr. Gataker, but would write later. In December they wrote to Mr. Gataker they had found "abundance of water at the depth of 58 feet." In reply to my specific enquiries (1) Whether Mr. Gataker had been successful? (2) Who was the unsuccessful diviner previously employed? (3) What was the distance off and depth of the old well? Messrs. Pacey write:—

Egerton Brewery, Melton Mowbray, *December 19th*, 1896.

Replying to yours of the 17th, we beg to say, in answer to your questions (1) Very successful. (2) No other diviner was employed by us. (3) There is a well 5 yards distant from the site the diviner indicated. The new well has 14 feet 6 inches of water, the old well only 2 feet 6 inches.

Adcock, Pacey, And Co.

## *The Credibility Of Dowsing*

I had to write again to get the depth of the wells, when I was informed the unsuccessful well was about 45 feet deep, and the successful one 56 feet. After all, therefore, this case is not of evidential value.

No. 125.—The next letters are addressed to Mr. Gataker from the agent to Sir J. de Hoghton, Bart., of Hoghton Tower, near Preston, Lancashire:—

Hoghton Estate Office, Walton-le-dale, Preston, *April,* 1895.

> Several farms on these estates being short of water, your advice was obtained, and you pointed out places where water would be found, giving the depth.
>
> In a field close to Hoghton Station, at one of these spots, where the depth was estimated at from 10 to 15 feet, a boring was made and water reached at 10 feet; a well will probably be sunk there at some future time.
>
> At Hardshaw Hillock, Walton-le-dale, you indicated a place where water might be found at from 20 to 25 feet. Here, in March, 1895, water was found in a bed of sand, after sinking through 22 feet of stiff marl, and a large supply is being yielded.
>
> In this latter case, you used your hands only, without any rod.
>
> Walter De H. Birch.
>
> *July 30th,* 1895.
>
> Another well has been sunk at a neighbouring farm, Leigh House, Walton-le-dale. Here you had indicated a spot where water would be found at from 30 to 35 feet deep.
>
> After getting down 30 feet of exceptionally hard clay and marl, the well sinkers were beginning to lose heart, and the tenant suggested that a rain-water tank would answer his purpose, but continuing to sink, they struck a vein of sand at about 31 feet, with a good supply of water.
>
> At 34 feet, clay was again reached, and boring 10 feet more at the bottom of the well showed only hard clay, so it was decided to "let well alone," as the result was so satisfactory.
>
> Walter De H. Birch.

I wrote to Mr. Birch to inquire if any previous attempts to find water had been made, and what was the result, and whether Mr. Gataker had any failures. The following is the reply I received:—

Hoghton Estate Office, Walton-le-Dale, Preston,

*April 12th,* 1897.

> Mr. Gataker certainly has been remarkably accurate in his estimate of the depth at which water will be found, though sometimes he has been wrong. I do not place much reliance upon his estimate of quantity.
>
> His most notable failure was the last. Here he gave the depth at from 12 to 18 feet, but after sinking that in quite dry sand, he came again and said there must be a quicksand, which threw him out, and that it was about 60 to 70 feet deep. We bored through dry sand, and found a quicksand at a depth of 72 feet, so that he redeemed his character in this. This is a list of his predictions, and the results:— [1]

---

[1] Mr. Birch explains that the lettering indicates different places on the estate where the trials were made.—W. F. B.

|     | Estimated.       | Actual.                                                                                                       |
|-----|------------------|---------------------------------------------------------------------------------------------------------------|
| a.  | 20 ft.           | 22 ft. good supply.                                                                                           |
| b.  | 20 ft.           | 8 and 37 two springs one above the other.                                                                     |
| c.  | 25 ft.           | 10 ft. very small spring.                                                                                     |
| d.  | 30 ft. to 35 ft. | 34 ft.                                                                                                        |
| e.  | 10 ft. to 15 ft. | 10 ft.                                                                                                        |
| f.  | 15 ft.           | about 15 ft.                                                                                                  |
| g.  | 20 ft. to 30 ft. | about 11 ft. a fair stream.                                                                                   |
| h.  | 30 ft.           | Here water was found on boring and rose in the bore to 22 feet from the surface. Exact depth of spring not ascertained. |
| i.  | 12 ft. to 18 ft. | No water, but on boring deeper, a quicksand struck at the depth of 72 feet, as already mentioned.             |

In "g" there was more water lower down, and you will notice that in the least accurate estimates there were two springs at different depths.

Walter De H. Birch.

No. 126.—Lord Llangattock writes as follows to Mr. Gataker:—

The Hendre, Monmouth, *June*, 1896.

Mr. Gataker, at my request, has been searching for water in several places on this estate, and has been most successful.

Water has been found wherever he has indicated, and at the depth mentioned by him.

I cannot speak too highly of him and the wonderful skill he shows as a water finder.

Llangattock.

With reference to this case, Mr. Gataker informs me that, prior to his visit, attempts had been made to find water by digging deep trenches in many directions, but without success. I wrote to Lord Llangattock for corroboration, and he replies as follows:—

The Hendre, Monmouth, *April 12th*, 1897.

I sent your letter to Mr. Lipscomb and asked him to give you all information. I have great faith in Mr. Gataker. I wanted to find springs in the Park to strengthen a pond, and he marked several places, and told me exactly the depth we should find the water, and he was always correct.

Llangattock.

Mr. Lipscomb writes:—

The Hendre, Monmouth, *April 12th*, 1897.

Mr. Gataker was asked to find water to strengthen the supply of water to the lake in the park. He located five springs, near the lake, within a 100 yards of the margin of the lake at separate points, and varying from 11 to 20 feet in depth. There was no sign of water on the surface at these points. In every case his predictions as to depth and yield were correct. This is as far as we have proved him. No sinking had been done previous to his visit, the lake being fed by natural surface streams. In Pearson's Magazine, p. 311, you will find some account of Gataker's work here. He is there depicted

## *The Credibility Of Dowsing*

hunting for springs in the bed of the lake. He had let the water out of the lake to repair a hole in the bank. I shall be glad to answer any questions you may wish to ask.

C. Lipscomb.

No. 127.—The Rev. A. T. Fryer, of Cardiff, who has frequently given most valuable assistance in the course of this research, sends me the following letter addressed to him by Captain Stansfeld, in answer to Mr. Fryer's enquiries:—

Dunninald, Montrose, N.B., *September 18th*, 1896.

On the 24th of July Mr. Gataker visited this estate, and as he was rather pressed for time on that occasion, he is to give me another call. We, however, walked over two fields, in each of which points were marked where Mr. Gataker said springs of water at various depths would be found. I have up to the present only experimented on one, and this at about 9 feet deep, which is well within the estimated depth made by Mr. Gataker, and the apparent water supply is nearly as stated by Mr. Gataker, viz., about two gallons a minute. Mr. Gataker, when pointing out this supply, told me that in a previous digging I had just missed the proper spring by about 4 or 5 yards, and in this he seems to be correct. The excavation was almost entirely through rock.

I shall be happy to report further if you desire it, but work is necessarily slow, as there is so much rock to go through.

John Stansfeld.

Subsequently I wrote to Captain Stansfeld, who stated he was expecting another visit from Mr. Gataker, and that the spring the water-finder had previously found continued to give a plentiful supply. Later on, I received the following:—

Dunninald, Montrose, *October 24th*, 1896.

Mr. Gataker did not use the rod in discovering water, but in order to show the working, he took a forked hazel rod, and this rod twisted round in his hands. A gentleman then tried the rod, but in his hands it did not move, till Mr. Gataker put his own hands on the wrists of the gentleman, when the rod immediately turned round.

John Stansfeld

No. 128.—The *Bath Chronicle* of January 7th, 1897, has the following:—

Mr. Leicester Gataker was recently engaged by the Belfast Brewery to put them in the way of obtaining a good supply of water. They had previously sunk four wells, and had also some time before had the services of another diviner. Acting upon Mr. Gataker's advice, they have sunk two wells. In the case of the second one, he advised the company that at a depth of from 120 to 150 feet they would obtain what they required. After going 80 feet they tapped a spring. This did not come up to their requirements, so they asked Mr. Gataker to come again, doubtless in view of their previous failures. He accordingly went, and informed the company that they must go on to the depth originally given—150 feet. They went on, and at the depth named they secured a second spring of large power. While in Ireland last month he again visited the place, and after descending the well, he predicted that by going nine feet deeper they would obtain an even stronger (third) spring. They no longer had any doubt as to what course to pursue, and by doing as last advised, they have increased the supply by 2,000 gallons a day.

A subsequent issue of the same newspaper states that:—

Well No. 2 has now been carried out, and Mr. T. R. Caffrey, the proprietor, gives the yield at 7,000 gallons per 24 hours. He has also stated that "it would have been a saving of many hundreds of pounds had I known Mr. Gataker when I first started looking for water." Both wells are 197 feet deep.

I wrote to the proprietor of the brewery as to the accuracy of the foregoing newspaper reports, and asked for further particulars. Mr. Caffrey replies:—

The Brewery, Belfast, *February 26th,* 1897.

The enclosed cuttings are quite correct, save and except the No. 2 well is now giving over 9,000 gallons in the 24 hours.

I had a water-finder before I met with Mr. Gataker, who marked out four places. I got water in one of the four, none in the other three. Mr. Gataker marked the two wells I have opened and found the water all right.

Thomas R. Caffrey.

I could not ascertain from Mr. Caffrey the name of the previous unsuccessful dowser.

The next letter is from Dr. A. A. Mantell, of Bath:—

The Elms, Bathampton, Bath, *July,* 1894.

On June 4th, 1894, I took Mr. Leicester Gataker to a neighbour's tennis lawn in Bathampton, which was made by him, and during the excavations a spring of water was found, which now runs diagonally across the lawn.

Mr. Gataker had not entered the premises before, nor had he the slightest knowledge that there was any water there; I therefore proposed to the owner of the lawn to put him to a severe test as to his powers of divining. I carefully blindfolded him, and in order to prevent his injuring himself fastened a rope to his arm, and held it loosely in my hand; he was then asked to walk about and see if there was any water to be found. Immediately, when he walked over the spring, which lies about three or four feet deep, the rod revolved, and whilst still blindfolded he traced its passage most accurately across the lawn. At a recent meeting of the Bath Field Club to witness some experiments by a "Water Dowser," we asked him to walk on a row of bottles, which were placed over a spring, and which was known to be there. When he was quite insulated by these bottles, the rod ceased to revolve, and several members of the Club were under the impression that the bottles acting as non-conductors prevented the current of electric fluid, or whatever it may be, from passing into the dowser's body. I therefore put Mr. Gataker to a similar test, but with him the rod revolved as well with as without the intervention of the bottles; this seems to indicate Mr. Gataker's great susceptibility to the influence.

My neighbour and those present on this occasion feel convinced that Mr. Gataker has the power of water-finding in a remarkable degree, and we hope that he may be successful in making it his profession.

A. A. Maxtell, M.D.

The foregoing letter illustrates how necessary it is to guard against giving unconscious indications and suggestions, which may account for the dowser's success on this occasion. The failure of the insulation test corroborates what has already been said about the fallacy of this experiment.

No 129.—The next letter to Mr. Gataker is the result of work done on the Duke of Devonshire's Estate.

## The Credibility Of Dowsing

Chatsworth, Chesterfield, *June 22nd*, 1895.

You stated that you believed we should find water at a depth of between 60 and 70 feet. We found a supply at 69 feet, and there is every probability that it will be sufficient for the requirements of the farm.

You are no doubt aware that we had previously sunk a well to a considerable depth without success.

I was much surprised to find that you first indicated the locality of water with your hands and no rod, only using the rod as a secondary aid to confirm your indication.

Gilson Martin.

In reply to my enquiries Mr. Martin writes:—

Chatsworth, Chesterfield, *January* 14th, 1897.

Mr. Gataker's statements enclosed are quite correct. The well which was sunk before he came was, so far as I remember, about 45 feet deep; the well which proved successful was about 300 yards from the useless one, and upon much higher ground.

Gilson Martin

Mr. Martin adds that he has increased the cheque due to Mr. Gataker, as he was so gratified with the success attained.

## Failures

I have received reports, but no details, of several failures on the part of Mr. Gataker. I spoke to Mr. Gataker about these when he called upon me in Dublin, and he frankly said there was no doubt he was occasionally wrong, but he did not think his failures averaged more than 10 per cent, of his total engagements. He told me he kept a careful record of all his work, and he had, as I had requested, gone over all his cases to find the number of failures of which he had heard, with the result stated. This statement I have, of course, no means of verifying.

The Rev. A. T. Fryer sends me some particulars of the failure of Gataker and H. W. Mullins to find water for a Brewery near Bath, but I cannot ascertain which of the two dowsers was really at fault, as it appears the well was sunk, not on the spot where both dowsers — independently of each other—agreed there was a spring, but at a spot where one said there was a spring and the other said there was not. In the Richmond Experiments which follow, Gataker and H. W. Mullins were also employed, with the result described below.

It will have been noticed on the preceding page, that Mr. Gataker sends an assistant when he cannot go himself. These assistants Mr. Gataker professes "to train " for a fee. If there is a peculiar instinct, or faculty, for finding underground water, such as the dowsers themselves claim to possess, this so-called " training " is a piece of the charlatanism which crops out in so many of these "water experts." Here, for example, is an extract from the *Richmond Times,* of January 11th, 1896, where an account is given of Mr. Gataker's dowsing for water at Richmond, as fully detailed in the "Richmond Experiments," which follow. The account, the editor informed me, was written by an experienced reporter, who states that

> "Mr. Gataker was closely questioned as to whether the stream of running water in the channel of the adit might not affect his judgment. To this he replied most positively in the negative, saying that it might affect the twig, but that by 'a new dodge' which he had discovered about ten months ago, in working with his hands, he could absolutely eliminate that disturbing influence. He could also discriminate between natural and artificial currents, and could even tell if there were two springs, one immediately beneath the other, and could divine the depth and quantity of each."

This is the sort of thing that can only provoke well-deserved contempt.

## The Richmond Experiments

Among the more extensive and costly series of experiments made to test the value of the "divining rod" as a means of finding underground water, must be included those carried out at Richmond, Surrey, in the spring of 1896. Though the results were only of transient success, the experiments derive additional interest from the following facts:—

(1) Prior to the "diviners'" visit, a series of borings for water had ineffectually been made; (2) the independent opinions of two different "diviners" were obtained; (3) a full record of the experiments, as they took place, was published from time to time in the local newspapers; and (4) the opinion of the highest geological authorities on underground water was also obtained and borings made according to their directions. It will be necessary, therefore, to consider this case at some length, the more so as public attention was widely called to these experiments by the reports in the London papers which will be quoted presently.

It appears that the water supply of Richmond is derived from wells, but was found inadequate to the growing needs of the township. Attempts to increase the supply were made, whereupon a correspondence arose in the local newspaper suggesting that the aid of the "divining rod" should be called in. The whole question was discussed by the "Water Supply Committee of the Borough, who, however, could not officially take so novel a course: but the chairman of the committee, Mr. T. H. Watney, acting upon the suggestion of the editor of the *Richmond Times*, undertook in his private capacity to defray the cost of putting the "divining rod" to the test. Arrangements were therefore made for two "dowsers" to come to Richmond. The dowsers selected were unfortunately two young and comparatively unproved men.

In the *Richmond Times* of January 11th, 1896, a lengthy and admirable report is given of the search for water by the two young "diviners," who were first Mr. H. W. Mullins and afterwards Mr. Gataker. From this report I condense the following:—

> The water hitherto obtained from the chalk at Richmond is taken from a depth of over two hundred feet, and as there appeared to be no record of the divining rod being influenced at so great a distance, it was determined to take the diviners or dowsers down the Borough well and along the adits, of which there are some miles. It was decided that the two "dowsers" should make independent examinations on different days, and that the first report should be kept secret till after the other had been obtained. Accordingly on December 11th, 1895, "Messrs. Mullins" came as requested. Before going down the well Mullins showed the use of the rod on the surface of the ground. At one spot it was found to twist violently, Mr. Mullins stating that water was to be found not far from the surface at that spot. Mr. Peirce, of the Borough water works, confirmed this, stating a water pipe passed under the ground there only a few feet down. Mr. Mullins had no previous knowledge of this fact. The party then went down the well and spent some hours exploring the adits, Mullins walking in front carrying the forked twig. The indications of the rod, he said, were against a good supply. One place, however, was better and the quantity promised went as high as 1,000 or 1,500 gallons a day, the other places much less. In all some thirty places were indicated by the "diviner," but Mr. Mullins repeatedly said, "I cannot hold out any hopes of large quantities of water." The depth to be sunk he estimated at from thirty to seventy feet. Mr. Peirce marked the places indicated.

> Three weeks later Mr. Gataker made his examination. Here a noticeable difference was observed in Gataker's method of working, as compared with Mullins'. He discarded the twig or any other artificial aid whatever, and simply walked about with his arms held stiffly down by his sides, the palms spread outward. There were consequently no outward manifestations to indicate the supposed presence or absence of water beneath the ground, and it was necessary to take his word entirely for the matter. A twig, however, was carried by his pupil who accompanied him, and by its lively dippings and twistings

## The Credibility Of Dowsing

sustained the divinations of the master. As before, the party, after descending the well, tramped for some hours through adit after adit, until Gataker had explored every portion of the workings. The results were rather startlingly different to those obtained per Mullins. Gataker marked many more points than the other, and he predicted for each a vastly larger flow. The range of depth at which water would be obtained was, in his opinion, from 50 to 200 feet below the floor of the adit. In one or two cases his points tallied almost exactly with those of Mr. Mullins, and in several other cases they were within a few feet, but this could not be said of the great majority. Altogether he marked 55 places where a good supply could be obtained at an average depth of 60 feet; the points marked were distributed pretty equally all over the present headings. The total daily supply he predicted would be 277,000 gallons. It should be added that one of the members of the Richmond Town Council, who accompanied the party, found the "twig" moved in his hands, also at some of the points which were indicated by Gataker as likely to yield the best supply.

In the *Thames Valley Times* of January 15th, 1896, a week after Mr. Gataker's visit, is a report of a meeting of the Richmond Town Council, when the chairman of the water committee announced that borings had been made at a spot indicated by both the diviners, working independently of one another, one stating water would be found at a depth of 50 feet, the other 30 to 50 feet, the former naming 800 gallons a day as the yield, the latter 7,000. Water to the extent of 8,000 gallons a day was actually found here at a depth of 21½ feet. Public attention was directed to the matter by the following notice in the London *Times* of January 17th, 1896:—

> A supply of water, estimated at about 8,000 gallons a day, has just been tapped at Richmond in somewhat remarkable circumstances. For some time past extensive borings have been made in the adits of the Richmond-terrace-gardens well, but with comparatively little success. Last week two "water diviners," named Gataker and Mullins, visited the well, and both predicted that water would be found at certain indicated spots, the former alleging that by making 50 borings, at a cost of about £800, an enormous supply might be obtained, worth to the town about £5,000 a year, on the Southwark and Vauxhall valuation. On Monday last it was decided to begin boring at a point where both the "diviners" predicted a find, from 30 feet to 50 feet below. At a depth of about 20 feet a spring was tapped which is yielding 8,000 gallons a day. The experiments have been carried out at the expense of Councillor Watney, and he has undertaken to bear the cost of further borings at other points indicated by the water-finders.

The *Standard* of the same date also had the following:—

> A remarkable discovery of water by the aid of professional water-finders has just occurred at Richmond, Surrey. The Corporation have had wells sunk to a considerable depth to procure water sufficient to meet the requirements of the borough, and a supply, which for the past five or six weeks averaged 233,000 gallons per day, was discovered. Further borings for a greater yield have, however, been attended with little success. Last week two water diviners, named Gataker and Mullins, visited the Terracegardens Well, and indicated a number of places in the adits at which they alleged water would be found. The former stated that by making about 50 borings at indicated spots a supply of water would be found worth about £5,000 a year to the town, on the valuation of the Southwark and Vauxhall Company. This suggestion was acted upon, and when the boring reached about 20 feet, a spring of water was tapped yielding about 8,000 gallons per day.

The local newspaper, in commenting on these facts, states that the finding of the water may be merely a coincidence, though a large number of borings had been previously made with practically no result. It also points out that the "dowsers" worked under conditions entirely new to them, not on the surface of the ground, but in tunnels far underground, with water probably all round them.

## *Prof. W. F. Barrett*

The editor and proprietor of the *Richmond Times,* Mr. F. W. Dimbleby, J.P., in reply to my enquiries (1) as to the accuracy of the reports in his newspaper, and (2) as to evidence of any previous boring for water being made prior to the use of the "divining rod," writes:—

Richmond, Surrey, February *5th,* 1896.

> (1) You may entirely rely upon the reports referred to. Being interested in the matter (as a former member of the Water Supply Committee of the Corporation), I went down the well with Mullins myself, so that the part of the report referring to his visit is my own work. The part relating to Gataker was written by my chief reporter, an experienced and reliable man.
>
> (2) By this post I send you another paper of mine, the Thames Valley Times of January 15th, which answers your question as to previous unsuccessful attempts to find water, and shows that a supply has now been obtained at the spot indicated by Gataker and Mullins. I should add, however, that since that date the yield of 8,000 gallons a day has greatly diminished. This usually happens when a fissure is tapped, and the water "backed up" in it has had time to run away.
>
> (3) Gataker paid us another visit on January 23rd, as reported in the Richmond and Twickenham Times of January 25th, also sent by this post. We have now had three visits in all, at a cost (including expenses) of from ten to fifteen guineas each, and as the work has been done very thoroughly by two independent men, both well-known as expert " water-finders," it does not appear to me to be necessary to go further until the reports of Mullina and Gataker have been fully tested.
>
> Fredk W. Dimbleby

The newspaper of January 15th, referred to in the above letter, contained the following extract from the official report of the Borough Engineer to the Town Council as to previous borings to find water:—

> During the past five weeks the workmen have been engaged boring in the adits in various directions 624 feet, viz., 179½ feet horizontally, six holes from 7 to 70 feet, 248 vertically (downwards), seven holes 13 to 80 feet in depth (since increased to 88 feet), 196½ feet inclined upwards, thirteen holes 8 to 20 feet, yielding a very little water.

The local paper of January 25th states that the supply of 8,000 gallons from the boring made at the place indicated by both Gataker and Mullins had diminished, as was usual in newly tapped chalk springs, to 5,000 or 6,000 gallons. Concerning Gataker's second visit on January 23rd, the *Richmond Times* of that week gives a detailed account which I here condense:—

> At more than one point Gataker's "divinings" were in close proximity to the places previously marked by Mullins and the depths given approximately equal. At two points where bore holes had been sunk and only a moderate supply obtained, Gataker advised deepening the holes to the limit named in his former predictions, viz., about 80 feet. In the south adit Gataker estimated the depth of water as greater, reaching from 100 to 150 feet, and in one place as probably 200 feet. At the next point reached, five men were then engaged in sinking a bore hole at the place Gataker had previously marked, a depth of 63 feet had been reached and no spring as yet tapped. Gataker advised going down to at least 80 feet, which was also the limit he had given on his previous visit. Two other places where borings were going on Gataker also advised that the bore holes should be carried deeper.

Commenting on this visit the same paper remarks:—

> The result of the inspection may be described as fairly satisfactory. There are certain points of difficulty in connection with the experiments, which cause a critical test to be arrived at less easily

# The Credibility Of Dowsing

than would otherwise be the case, and tend to lessen the practical value of the method. Chief amongst these may be mentioned the apparent impossibility of fixing the exact spot, to a foot or two, where water may be found, and as the diameter of the bore-hole is only about four inches, a slight error in giving the precise point might render that particular bore-hole useless. But notwithstanding these difficulties, a sufficient prima facie case has been made out to justify Mr. Watney proceeding with these experiments, which he is carrying out at his own expense.

My friend, Mr. W. Whitaker, F.R.S., F.G.S., who is well known both as an eminent geologist and authority on underground waters, writes in answer to enquiries as to his opinion of the foregoing reports[1]:—

Southampton, *January 28th*, 1896.

I know the Richmond waterworks, having been all along the underground galleries, etc, on two occasions. ... As the two "rodders" were more or less surrounded with water, their rods ought to have been twiddling everywhere! I enclose the Engineer's answer to a letter of mine which lowers the reported success.

The enclosure is as follows:—

Borough Waterworks Office, Richmond, Surrey, *January 22nd*, 1896.

With regard to the divining rod reported in the London press, too much has been put forward. The truth is our new chairman has engaged both Mr. Mullins and Mr. Gataker at his own expense, to prove whether there is any power of proving water springs, as had been suggested in our local paper by one who had seen the rod used. We have not yet had much from the experiment; that reported was at a spot where both the diviners said there was water and so we bored a three-inch hole; it has now very sensibly diminished. We have benefited most by the adit driving and must go in for more, that being the only sure method of getting water here.

W. G. Peirce.

The next information comes from the local newspapers of February 8th, 1896, as follows:—

We are compelled to mention to-day, and we do it with no small regret, that the prospect of obtaining any greatly increased supply of water from the Richmond well through the assistance of the "water diviners " has darkened this week considerably. The bore-hole in the south adit, at which during each of his visits Mr. Gataker has so confidently promised that a supply of five to six thousand gallons a day would be found within the extreme limit of a depth of 100ft., has been abandoned after being driven to a depth of 125ft. without producing a drop. This is the second of Mr. Gataker's points that have been tested, the first being that at which an additional supply of 8,000 gallons a day was tapped, but quickly ran itself off. However, in the absence of any other guide as to desirable localities, some more of the points indicated by Mr. Gataker and Mr. Mullins, where borings have already begun, will be thoroughly tested.

Probably the bore-hole referred to above was the one at which the five men were working in the previous report which Gataker advised to be sunk to at least 80 feet; otherwise there seems a discrepancy in the statements, as in the south adit the reporter stated previously that Gataker advised boring to some 150 feet or even deeper in one place.

A month later, at a meeting of the Richmond Town Council, reported in the *Thames Valley Times,* of March 11th, 1896, the borough engineer reported as follows:—

---

[1] I am indebted to the Rev. Osmond Fisher, M.A., for this information.

## Prof. W. F. Barrett

> During the past four weeks the workmen have been engaged boring in the adits at various places indicated by Messrs. Mullins and Mr. Gataker, 409½ft. in all, viz., thirteen bore-holes completed and in hand, varying from 10½ft. to 125ft. in depth, yielding 220 gallons of water per day. Messrs. Mullins estimated 1,500 gallons per day, and Mr. L. Gataker 30,000 gallons per day, at the places selected and depths bored during the past month.
>
> Six feet of adit driving in the North-East Adit has been completed, and a bore-hole put down to the depth advised by Mr. L. Gataker, but without result as regards an increase of water.
>
> The total quantity of water pumped from the Terrace Gardens and Waterlane wells during the past four weeks has been 6,464,670 gallons, averaging 230,881 gallons per day.
>
> Councillor Watney said he was afraid he had very little to report in regard to the work at the well. He regretted that there was a decreased supply this month of water pumped from the well. They had been most unsuccessful during the past month in tapping any new fissures or supplies of water. He was not going himself to be a prophet, or to predict what would happen in the future. He desired to remind the Council that, although not mentioned in his report, the period of his three months' holiday at the well would expire before the next Council meeting. He thought if they would allow him, he would go on with his experiments until the next Council meeting, when he would ask leave to continue for another three months.—It was resolved that Councillor Watney's application should be acceded to.

In *Notes and Queries* of April 25th, 1896, there is a letter from the Borough Engineer, who writes as follows to a correspondent of that journal:—

> The diviners' success was of short duration; the one bore-hole that yielded 8,000 gallons a day on the first day, gradually fell off and was exhausted at the end of the week. About 22 bore-holes have been driven to the directions with a very small increase in the quantity of the water.
>
> W. G. Peirce.

Writing to me on October 2nd, 1896, Mr. Dimbleby says, in answer to my enquiry:—

> Mr. Watney is still carrying on the boring operations at his own expense, pending an application to the Local Government Board by the Corporation, for power to borrow more money for these works. Small fissures, yielding very small quantities of water are frequently met with, but no large increase in the supply has been obtained.
>
> Fredk. W. Dimbleby

Finally, the same kind correspondent, in reply to my recent enquiries, writes on May 24th, 1897:—

> 14, King Street, Richmond, Surrey, *May* 24th, 1897.
>
> The Richmond Corporation have now resumed the boring works on their own account; the Local Government Board having, after a public inquiry, sanctioned a further loan of £5,000 for this purpose.
>
> No reliance is now placed on the advice of the so-called "water-finders." I send you the last report of the Water Committee, dated May 4th, 1897, and also the one for the previous year.
>
> Fredk. W. Dimbleby

In the last report of the Water Committee it is stated that the total length of adits driven is 6,991 feet; "one fairly good fissure, passed on April 8th, still keeps up the yield of 5,846 gallons per day . . . The total quantity pumped

## *The Credibility Of Dowsing*

from the wells during the past four weeks averaging 225,848 gallons per day." Though this is a less amount than that given above for the preceding year, yet, as the report shows, a regular increase in the water supply has been obtained in proportion to the length of adits driven. The cost of the wells and adit driving at Richmond has been considerable. The Water Committee's report shows that the Water-lane wells and bore-hole cost £20,753; the Terrace Gardens well, adits and boring, cost £16,590, or a total of £37,343.[1] Of this, Mr. Watney has refunded £670, the expense only incurred up to March 31st, 1896, in his public-spirited experiments.

With regard to these experiments, it is greatly to be regretted that John Mullins was not available. But Mullins was not living when his "firm" were invited, and nothing could be more misleading than the practice adopted by "Messrs. J. Mullins and Sons," of sending out a book of testimonials, which chiefly relate to their father's success, and not stating the fact that their father is dead. The public ignorance of the whole subject, which ignorance this paper will, I hope, in some measure dispel, is, however, the most fruitful source of errors like the preceding. The respective qualifications of various dowsers should be ascertained from independent evidence, or their work paid for in proportion to the success achieved.

---

[1] Nevertheless, as the report shows, the actual cost to the ratepayers is less than if they had bought the water from the London water companies.

## Group IX — (a) Mr. H. Bacon

I heard of this dowser, who lives at Newport, Essex, through Mr. F. W. H. Myers. In reply to my enquiries, he sent me several testimonials from those for whom he had successfully found water by the divining-rod. In some of these cases Mr. Bacon tells me that attempts to find water by sinking or boring had been made unsuccessfully before his visit to the place. Stagnant water he cannot detect, only running water, and he says it is a matter of indifference to him whether he goes over the ground at day or night; or whether blindfolded or not. Having seen a dowser at work some five years ago, he tried, and found the forked twig moved with him; hence, he was led to take up this business. According to his own statement,—which must be taken for what it is worth,—he has never had a failure, though he admits he is sometimes mistaken in estimating the depth and the volume of the spring. When over an underground spring he states that the rod revolves strongly, and "I begin to shake from head to foot; in fact, I shake so much that often my knees begin to knock together."

Among Mr. Bacon's testimonials are letters from Lord Calthorpe's agent, from Sir Walter Gilbey, Bart., from Hudson's Breweries, &c. Mr. Hudson writes that he was "previously very sceptical, but the proof of the pudding is the eating," a good supply of water being obtained on his premises at 19 feet deep; whereas in the immediate neighbourhood (according to Bacon's statement to me) a deeper well had been sunk prior to his visit with no result.

No. 130.—I am indebted to Mr. J. Christian Smith, the Clerk of the Works on Colonel Houblon's estate in Essex, for the following interesting facts:—

Great Hallingbury. Bishop's Stortford, Essex, *December 1st*, 1896.

> I have pleasure in giving you some particulars of water-finding by the divining rod on the estate of Col. G. B. A. Houblon, Essex.
>
> We were making extensive alterations in the year 1893 at Threenhall Priory, Essex, which necessitated a new water supply. We looked about for what we thought was a suitable place to have a well sunk; we proceeded to a considerable depth without any signs of a supply. We then resorted to the divining rod, and sent for a Mr. Stone out of Northamptonshire.[1] By the aid of his rod he informed us where we should find a good supply of water; the depth he could not give, but did not think it was very deep. He also traced the direction the spring took. We sunk at the point indicated, at the depth of 38 feet. The spring proved to be so strong that it rose and filled the well nearly full. It was only about twenty yards from the well we had previously sunk and failed; the nearer Mr. Stone went with his rod to this, the weaker the latter became.
>
> The latest experience we have had was with Bacon. I took him to several places where we were anxious to obtain a supply of water. I am pleased to say that those places we have tried have been most successful. The first well we sank was 20 feet deep; at this depth we obtained an excellent supply, indeed, it has been up to the top. The second well we obtained a bountiful supply at 53 feet deep; standing supply, 17 feet. This well was sunk within 200 yards of the old well, where there was an inefficient supply after being bored (depth of sinking, 30 feet).
>
> Bacon informed me that he invariably finds that the springs run from east to west, or vice versa; he, therefore, carries in his pocket a small compass, so that he may be enabled to cross the spring; walking as the spring runs, he says, punishes him more than he can bear.
>
> If I can be of any further service, I shall esteem it a great pleasure.

John Christian Smith.

---

[1] (Now of Spilsby, Lincolnshire. See Group V.)

## *The Credibility Of Dowsing*

In answer to my further specific enquiries, Mr. J. C. Smith writes:—

Great Hallingbury, Bishop's Stortford, *December 7th*, 1896.

Bacon is, I understand, a clever mechanic, and at the present time acting as foreman to a local builder, unknown to me, until this year, when his services were required. Living near, and hearing of his successes, we were induced to try him.

(No. 1.) The exact locality of this estate is about 28 miles north-east of London, 20 miles south of Cambridge, 5 miles west of Great Dunmow, 1 mile east of Bishop's Stortford.

(No. 2.) Bacon's trials were on the same estate, about four miles distant from Threenhall Priory, where Stone was. I do not think water is likely to be found anywhere.

(No. 3.) The well [at Threenhall Priory] was sunk to the depth of twenty eight feet only, with no signs of water, nothing but boulder clay coming out. Stone went over this, "said we should never find any water there;" the nearer he came to it from the present spring, the weaker did the crutch [effect] become.

(No. 4.) I cannot say how deep the old 30ft. well had been bored. When we were anxious to get a better supply here we examined this, and found that a false bottom of wood had been put in and the bore hole plugged up; we concluded that the boring had taken away the little water there was, and had to be plugged up again. Bacon went all round this, but could find no trace of water.

John Christian Smith.

Again my correspondent kindly replies:—

Great Hallingbury, *December 12th*, 1896.

I have no hesitation in saying that my experience proves that the indication of the rod has enabled us to find water when other means had failed.

I am trying to get at the depth of the boring of that well; if I succeed I will inform you. [In a subsequent note I am informed it was 50 feet deep.] I mentioned in my previous letter to you that I took Bacon all round this old well, in hopes that we might find water near to the dwelling house, but there was not the slightest indication of his rod moving.

The 28 feet well does refer to the one we sank at Threenhall Priory without success. The 38 feet well, sunk where Stone indicated, where an abundant supply was obtained, was about 20 yards distant. At the 28 feet well Stone went over and around. He said, "You may go as deep as you like, you will get no water there." We therefore abandoned it.

The nearer he came to the unsuccessful one, the weaker the indication became, losing it entirely before he got to that well.

## Prof. W. F. Barrett

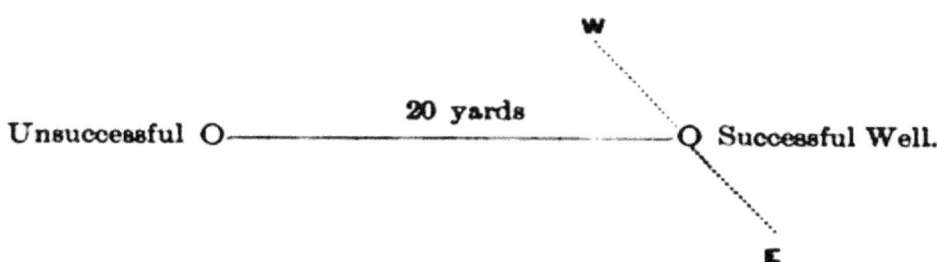

I can only add my experience of this method of finding water has been highly successful on this estate. In the future there is not the least doubt we shall resort to the same methods; not having a single failure gives us every confidence.

John Christian Smith.

No. 131.—Through the kindness of Mr. Salisbury Baxendale, who has sent me several letters on the subject, I have received the following information regarding Bacon's success on his estate at Henham in Essex. Bacon informed me he had found a considerable underground spring at 18 feet deep, not far from a useless well which was deeper than this. Mr. Baxendale's reply to my enquiry is as follows:—

1, Sloane Gardens, S.W., *December 2nd*, 1896.

In answer to yours of 30th, Bacon was a very satisfactory "water diviner."

I went down to see him "divine," and he "found water" at about the depth he mentions, on the top of a hill, which looks down east and west on the source of the Cam, the "Bench Mark" at the top being 321.5. There was a waterless well very near.[1]

After this we went to look for water near some cottages, and he marked a spot where he said water would be found, but in my absence my tenant thought that he could make one well do for two sets of cottages—sunk a well some 70 yards to the north of the place marked by Bacon, and found much chalk and no water. As he was an honest fool I declined to sink another well, and told him to use the chalk for "top dressing."

Since then Bacon has been divining in Hampshire for Lord Calthorpe— and successfully. He was very modest as to his powers, there was no "conjuring" about his manner;—nor could any of my party do the same— though we tried it.

Salisbury Baxendale.

In reply to my enquiries, Mr. Salisbury Baxendale sent me the following plan and memoranda concerning the second place that Bacon fixed on for a well, and adds, "my father sank many wells without finding a reasonable water-supply."

---

[1] Subsequently Mr. Baxendale tells me this was not a well, but a very deep pond, 18 feet deep. By "found water" is meant on a well being sunk water was found at about the depth indicated by the "diviner."—W.F.B.

## The Credibility Of Dowsing

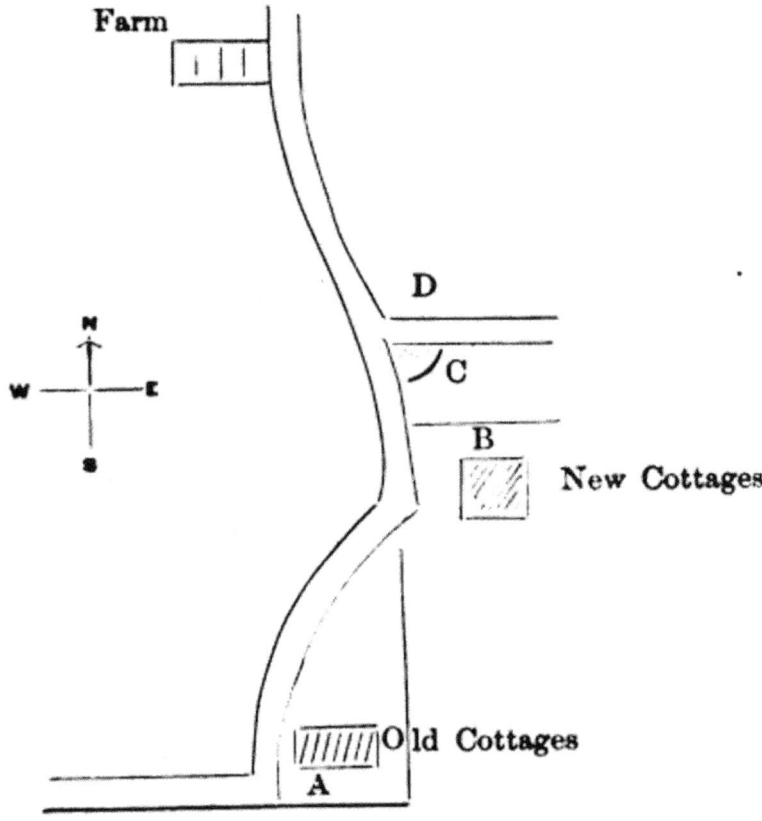

D. Situation of well—70 feet deep—that held chalk, and not water.

C. Small pond at corner of road that always, or nearly always, held water,—not more than 3 or 4 feet deep.

B. Well—50 yards from C - sunk by my father and his agent, guided only by the light of nature, and not by the light of Bacon. My tenant tells me that it is 100 feet deep (I think not so deep, but cannot go and measure it), that it holds 2 feet of water in winter, and is dry in summer.

A. The place that was suggested to me by Bacon, and where the well should have been sunk.

Salisbury Baxendale.

In answer to enquiries whether a well or boring could be made at the spot A, marked by Bacon, and also as to the exact locality, Mr. S. Baxendale writes:—

1, Sloane Gardens, S.W., *December 17th,* 1896.

In answer to yours of yesterday, I do not feel inclined to spend any more money in search of water at present—although I have a benevolent wish to give any kindly person permission to do it at his own expense. Times are hard with landowners.

Henham is 6 miles N.N.E. of Stortford, and about 6½ miles S. of Saffron Walden. Brayshots is one-third mile from Little Henham Hall—where the unsuccessful well was sunk by my father at (B).

Salisbury Baxendale.

F. 11.—In the *Herts and Essex Observer* for December 19th, 1896, is an account of the employment of Bacon by the Malden District Council to find a water supply for that neighbourhood. The rod indicated a strong spring at a certain spot where it was decided to sink a well. I wrote to Mr. Blyth, of Tolleshunt D'Arcy, who had taken an interest in the matter, who replies as follows:—

Oxley Lodge, T'Darcy, Witham, Essex, *May 17th,* 1897.

> We have not yet bored, but have driven a tube to a depth of 27 feet with no result. It is a difficult matter to move a Parish Council to bore where they have always been told there can be no water. They fear a failure and also a surcharge by the auditor. But if they will not move, I shall try on my own account, and will then let you know the result.
>
> Fred. W. Blyth.

So far, therefore, this may be taken as a *failure* by Bacon: other like cases of his doubtless exist of which I have not heard.

## (6) Mr. H. Chesterman

Among the many West of England dowsers is Mr. H. Chesterman, of Bath, who states — in the course of a lengthy account he has sent me — that 30 years ago he found he had the "gift" of dowsing, and has been, to some extent, engaged as a "water expert" ever since, though it is not the business of his life, his occupation being keeper of some recreation grounds in Bath. Mr. Chesterman, like the late Mr. Lawrence, prefers to use a loop of wire instead of a forked twig when dowsing, and states that when approaching an underground spring he experiences "a peculiar sensation, like an electric shock, creeping up the hands and arms, becoming more violent when directly over the hidden spring; the wider the space over which the shock is felt the nearer the spring is to the surface, and the smaller the space the deeper the spring." Mr. Chesterman also adds that he has made a scale by which he can approximately tell the depth of the spring; this he has described at length to me; an account of it is also given in the *Gentleman's Journal* for October 1st, 1896, but it is of no value to any one but himself, and not much to himself, judging from Mr. Cree's experience given below.

Like other dowsers, Mr. Chesterman states that the rod ceases to move, and the sensation he experiences is completely cut off, when he is insulated on glass vessels. Again, like others, Chesterman finds that when he holds the wrist of a person, in whose hands the rod would not previously move, then the rod or wire instantly revolves if over a spring. This transference of what is apparently involuntary muscular action is doubtless an effect of suggestion, which plays so large a part in the present as in the past history of the divining rod. Like other dowsers, also, Chesterman believes the faculty of dowsing is hereditary; out of his seven children he tells me five have the "gift." He claims to have "trained" Mr. Gataker in the proper use of the gift he possessed, just as Mr. Gataker offers to train other apprentices—for a substantial fee. The utter nonsense of this so-called training is obvious enough.

I am indebted to Mr. Cree, of Over Moigne, near Dorchester, for giving me particulars of an abundant supply of water found for him by Chesterman; but though geological information had been obtained, and a well dug unsuccessfully prior to the dowser's visit, yet the case is of no evidential value, as the unsuccessful well was only a third of the depth of Chesterman's well. Moreover, Chesterman's prediction of the depth of the spring was completely wrong, the prediction being 20 feet, the actual depth double this. At the same time I believe Chesterman has been much more successful in other instances.

I have to thank Mr. Chesterman for kindly coming to London from Bath at his own expense to exhibit his method of dowsing before the members of the S. P. R., when this paper was read.

## (c) Mr. F. Rodwell

Another dowser is the lad who bears the appropriate name of Fred Rodwell, and who came into some notoriety a few years ago through the animadversion [strong criticism - Ed] of Professor Ray Lankester.

# *The Credibility Of Dowsing*

Rodwell is the son of a mining engineer and surveyor, living in Wensley, Yorkshire, and in this case the use of the rod has chiefly been for the purpose of finding mineral veins. I shall, therefore, reserve the evidence of Rodwell's success in this direction to the next part of my paper. I have before me an extensive correspondence,— partly addressed to me and partly to Mr. Vaughan Jenkins,—from the father and other friends of young Rodwell, relating the tests to which the lad was subjected in his search for minerals, till at last he was regularly employed by the Grinton Mining Company to prospect for mineral lodes on their property. The *Graphic* of November 2nd, 1889, gave an account of the lad and a wood cut illustrating his method of procedure. From this account the following extract is taken.

> "Not long ago there was a long and animated correspondence in the Standard on the use of the 'divining rod' for finding water and minerals. A good many of the writers held that it was a mere superstition, handed down from the dark ages, and that the belief in it was due to a few accidental successes on the part of the water-finders. On the other side, however, a multitude of evidence was adduced showing that there are certain persons who do possess this peculiar faculty. One such is the lad named Rodwell. He is in the employment of the Grinton Mining Company in the North of England, and according to the chairman of the company has never failed when tested. Wherever he has indicated the presence of water or minerals, at that very spot a spring or lode has been discovered. He proceeds thus. Taking in his hands a light rod, or, if he has no rod, with his hands, clasped in front of him, Rodwell walks about in likely places. As soon as he steps over water or a mineral-vein the rod springs up to his breast, or the hands clench themselves immovably, and he cannot unclasp them till he moves from the spot. The lad in whom this strange faculty has developed, is about 14 years of age. We are not told whether his peculiar employment has any effect upon his health."

For the above wood cut, which illustrates young Rodwell at work as a dowser, I am indebted to the kindness of the proprietors of the *Graphic*.

No. 132.—The following letter relates to Rodwell in his capacity as a dowser for water.

The Grange, Aysgarth, Yorks., *May 13th,* 1893.

> It may be interesting to you to know that there is a youth (Fred Rodwell by name), who has on three separate occasions found the exact locality of underground water on my property. The first occasion was the location of water pipes underground, of the existence of which he could not possibly have had any previous knowledge. The other two instances were the discovery of two powerful springs of water, one of which has since been taken for a village for the supply of 500 people, and in neither of

these two cases was there suspected or was there the least external appearance to indicate the presence of underground spring. These facts speak for themselves.

James C. Winn.

I sent Mr. Winn the printed proof of the foregoing letter and asked him to correct any inaccuracies. Mr. Winn replies:—

The Grange, Aysgarth, R.S.O., N. Yorks, *June 10th*, 1897.

The proof of my letter is absolutely correct in every particular. I believe Rodwell is now residing at West Witton, near Leyburn, but I have no particulars of him recently.

J. C. Winn

The evidence in my possession respecting Rodwell's water-finding power is very meagre and inconclusive; he may have had more success of late, but of this I have not heard.

The following account of experiments I made with Rodwell at Wimbledon were conducted and recorded in the year 1890. Had I then the information I now possess, I should hardly have selected this young dowser for the purpose of experiment.

## The Wimbledon Experiments

I was anxious to obtain some direct experimental evidence of my own as to Rodwell's ability to find hidden water or metal. Accordingly I wrote to Dr. McClure, who is the Chairman of the Grinton Mining Company in Yorkshire, and from whom I learnt that the lad was not only employed by this Mining Company to seek for mineral lodes, but according to Dr. McClure he was also under an engagement to go to Australia to "dowse" for water and minerals. Hence I arranged to examine the alleged powers of the lad before he left England; for this purpose instead of going to Yorkshire, on ground with which Rodwell was acquainted, my friend, Mr. R. S. Donkin, M.P., kindly allowed me to make use of his extensive private grounds on the edge of Wimbledon Common, where it is needless to say the lad had never been before. The experiments I am about to describe were made on July 17th, 1890.

Before Rodwell arrived from Yorkshire I went over the place carefully with the head gardener, and the various buried water pipes, drains, disused wells, and underground springs were pointed out to me. On the arrival of Rodwell, who was a fat heavy-looking youth, and who was accompanied by Dr. McClure, I begged the lad to try first of all the lawn beneath which (unknown of course to the lad or Dr. McClure) a troublesome spring was known to exist.

*Experiment I.*—Pulling from his pocket a bundle of small forked hazel twigs, he selected one and holding it in the usual way marched to and fro across the lawn; presently the twig turned up and he declared there was a small spring below his feet. This was within a foot of the right place and looked promising.

*Experiment 2.*—He then endeavoured to trace the course of the -stream, which ran through drain pipes in a direction that had previously been pointed out to me, but here he blundered a good deal.

*Experiment 3.*—Next I told him to see if he could find any of the water mains, and for this purpose to walk all round the grounds on the pathway. He did so. I observed that as he walked along his eyes were constantly on the alert, and when he came to a part of the gravel walk that had lately been disturbed he said a pipe occurred there, but that there was none under the path he had traversed. As a matter of fact the pipe ran under his feet to the stables all the way he had gone, and a branch had recently been taken off to a greenhouse at the only spot he stopped at. The test was therefore a complete failure; he was correct only where it was probable that plumbers had been at work.

# The Credibility Of Dowsing

*Experiment* 4,—He then tried the archery ground and orchard; in the latter an Abyssinian well[1] had been sunk for water, but had been removed, as a supply had not been obtained; here the result was doubtful, as I was unable to test his assertion.

*Experiment* 5.—He then went to the paddock, an extensive field where an old and long disused well existed. The grass had so completely covered the site of the well that its position was hidden Rodwell wandered over the field, but found no water. He was told to walk in the direction where I knew the well existed; he did so and crossed and recrossed the site of the old well, but found no indications of water, though it is highly probable there was an abundance below; a little further on, however, the twig bent strongly upward and he declared that there was a large supply of water under that spot. The place was marked, and was subsequently tested by digging.

*Experiment* 6.—I now took the lad into the kitchen gardens where a sunken tank full of water existed; the tank was so well concealed beneath the ground that its position could not be detected by the eye. He walked twice over the place where the tank was buried, but gave no indication. I then told him what we were looking for and suggested he should try again; after moving slowly about, presently at a certain spot the twig turned and he said the tank was under that spot, but it certainly was not. This trial also was therefore a complete failure; it is fair to say dowsers state they cannot detect stagnant water.

*Experiment* 7.—I now proposed to blindfold the lad and take him again to the lawn and paddock to see if he indicated the same spots as when unblindfolded. But both Dr. McClure and Rodwell strenuously opposed blindfolding. At last they gave way, but only upon my insistence.[2] For the purpose of blindfolding a quantity of cotton wool was placed over his eyes and on each side of the nose, and an ample cloth tied round his head. I then led him to the paddock and brought him near to the spot where he had found water before (Experiment 5); he traversed and re-traversed the spot where he had previously located water, without giving any indication, and walked some distance in the wrong direction, when he pulled the bandage off saying he was too hot. I readjusted the bandage and told him to try again; this time the twig moved violently very near the spot he had before indicated. His hands appeared locked in a convulsive effort; he declared that he was perfectly sure that water was below, and he thought near the surface. With the permission of my host I caused a well to be dug next day; two men were employed, but after several hours' work, and a depth of about eight feet had been reached, no water was found; an unusual fact, as in that gravelly soil water springs abounded very near the surface.[3]

*Experiment* 8.—Finally I took the lad back to the lawn and told him, when blindfolded, to find the spring he had previously discovered (Experiment 1). He crossed the lawn two or three times, going over the right spot without giving any indication, and then fixed on another spot where it is true there might be a spring, but its existence was not known, nor could it be ascertained without injury to the lawn.

This ended my experiments with Rodwell; as will be seen the result was unsatisfactory, or to say the least inconclusive, and if I were to generalise from this one day's experiments, I should agree with Professor Ray Lankester, who, the year previously, had—after a similar but rather hasty trial with the same lad—come to the conclusion that the boy was a rank impostor, and "the divining rod business of the same order as fortune telling." To generalise from a single instance is, however, unphilosophical at all times and is absolutely forbidden in dealing with those problems which come within the scope of this Society.

---

[1] [A TYPE of well which consists of a perforated pipe sunk into the ground. Chiefly used for pumping up groundwater. - Ed.]

[2] Rodwell's father, in a lengthy letter which he addressed to Mr. Vaughan Jenkins, and the latter sent on to me, explains the reluctance of the lad to be blindfolded as due to the harsh treatment he received at the hands of Prof. Ray Lankester, who, according to Mr. Rodwell's statement, almost frightened the boy to death! Hence Mr. Rodwell says, "I charged my son never to submit to anything of the kind again, and told Dr. McClure I would not allow it." It was for that reason, thinking I was about to treat him as a rogue and impostor, that they objected to the blindfolding.

[3] Subsequently I had the hole dug deeper and about two feet of water came into the hole, but the gardener, an experienced man, told me that in the light sand and gravel soil that exists there, water would probably be found in any spot that was dug; 10 or 12 ft. deep. It would, of course, have been better to sink deeper, but it seemed hardly worth going to the further expense involved by so doing.

# Group X
# Welsh Dowsers — (a) Mr. Thomas Heighway

Mr. J. F. Young, of Llanelly, kindly sent me the name and address of Mr. Heighway, who is a Welshman, the proprietor of the Park Pump Room, Llandrindod Wells. His father, John Heighway, was, I believe, most successful as a dowser, but he does not write English.

Mr. Thomas Heighway tells me when he is dowsing and gets over an underground spring his nervous system is so much affected that he does not recover from it for some hours; he therefore does not care to use the rod much; his father does not suffer in the same way. I have not much information of Mr. Heighway's experiences, but the following letters are interesting, and present a new aspect of the subject, viz., dowsing for mineral springs.

No. 133. — Mr. Heighway having referred me to Captain Penry Lloyd, for whom he had recently found a sulphur spring, I wrote to Mr. Lloyd, and the following is his reply:—

Glasbury, R.S.O., Radnorshire, *February 27th*, 1897.

> I have only one fact of evidential value regarding the use of the rod, and that is in the case of Mr. Thomas Heighway, of Llandrindod, Radnorshire, who, in November last, discovered a sulphur spring on my land at Llanwrtyd, Breconshire, at a depth of 75 feet from the surface, 68 of which was solid, tough clay. Directly we struck rock, we struck water, and, curiously, on the very side of the well which Mr. Heighway had predicted, the water bearing lode crossing the diameter (6 feet) of the well on the south half. From a profound sceptic, I am now a firm believer in the power of the rod.
>
> P. Lloyd

Captain Lloyd kindly sends the following additional particulars in reply to my enquiries:—

Glasbury, R.S.O., *March 15th*, 1897.

> (1) I had been seeking for sulphur mineral water previous to the dowser's visit, and failed to find the spring.
>
> (2) Mr. Heighway was engaged, and I went with him over the ground. He, with the twig, soon found three several springs, and I selected the most suitable for sinking, and found the water at 75 feet; the vein of rock carrying the water crossed the bottom of well from west to east, and if we had sunk 3 feet more to the north, should have missed it. When about 35 feet down he came again, and went down the well, and told me to mind and sink well to the south side, as the water was there. And he was quite right. He was confident from first to last, when I had given up all hopes. I am now sinking, on his advice, for a chalybeate spring, and we are now down about 25 feet, but have not yet come to the rock. He also traced the springs across the river, which runs near the well.
>
> There is no doubt whatever as to his power, and he can distinguish between fresh water and mineral water.

I enclose rough sketch and section. P. Lloyd.

# The Credibility Of Dowsing

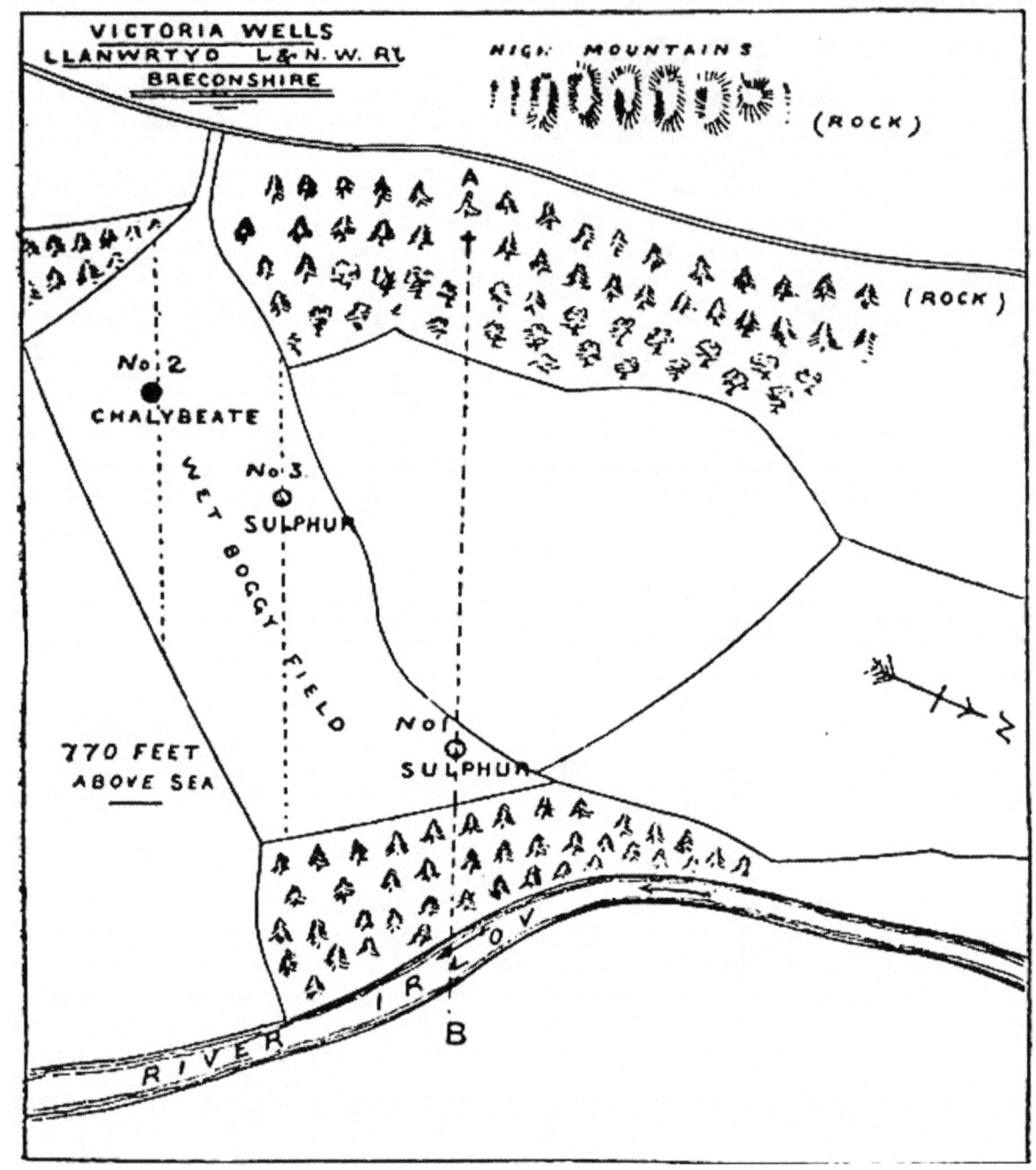

Note.

† is where Mr. Heighway found sulphur spring, and followed it to No. 1 well.
No. 1. Sulphur, 75 feet deep.
No. 2. Chalybeate, 35 feet deep, running over.
No. 3. Sulphur. Now sinking

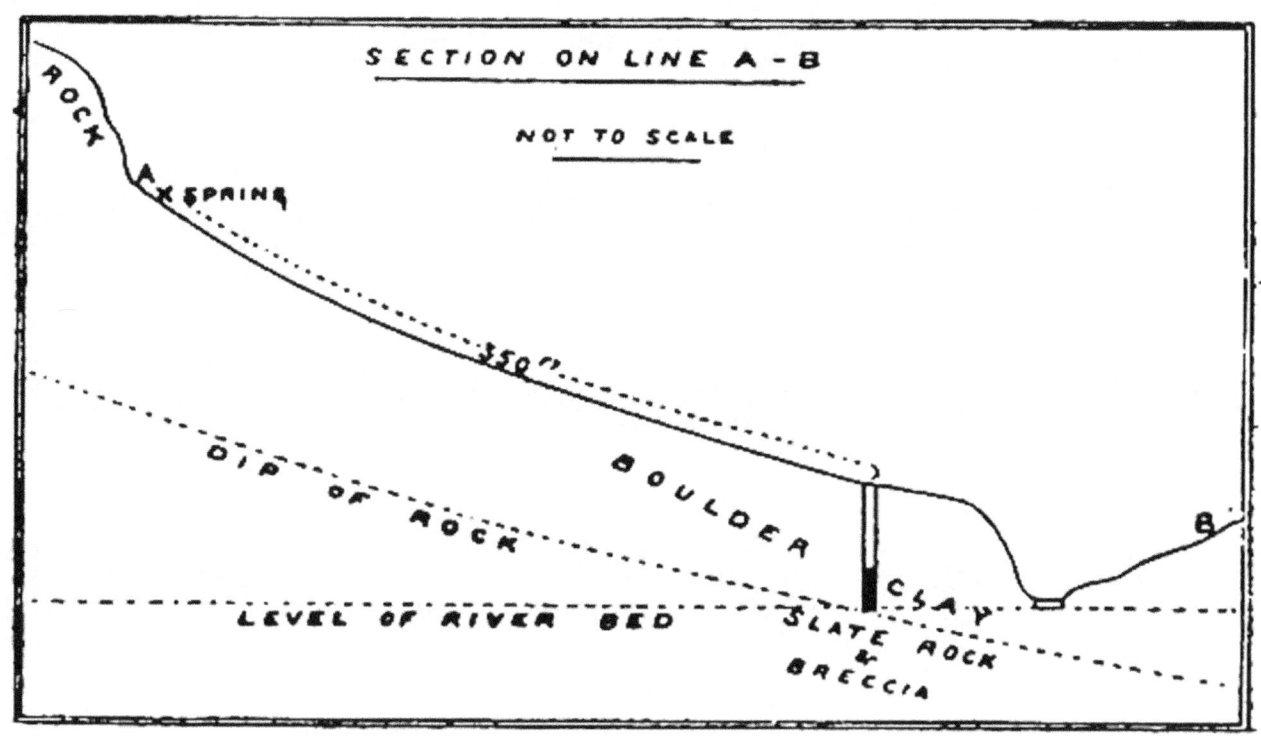

Subsequently, Captain Lloyd writes:—

Glasbury, R.S.O., *March 23rd,* 1897.

You will be interested to know that Mr. Heighway has again been successful; we have struck water at 32 feet from the surface, in a rock full of minerals, mainly iron, I believe. Mr. Heighway's prophecy was, "Chalybeate water, very strong spring," and he has proved himself to be correct.

I quite believe he has the power of distinguishing between mineral and plain water; at all events, he has succeeded in many instances, and I have not heard that he has been wrong once. He tells me he acquired the power by practising over known mineral springs, and finds that he is affected in different ways. Mineral water, he says, has much more power over him, and "draws stronger," and is more difficult to determine as to depth. He also says that plain water intervening would not affect him, owing to the greater strength of mineral. It is indeed a wonderful attribute of the human body, and he certainly is an exceptionally good subject.

Penry Lloyd

Writing again on May 14th, Mr. Lloyd says:—

Glasbury, *May 14th,* 1897.

We have just completed sinking No. 3 well, on the spot indicated by Mr. Thomas Heighway, and found sulphur water 52 feet below surface, and 6 feet down in the solid rock.

P. Lloyd

## The Credibility Of Dowsing

One interesting feature in the above letters will be noticed, namely, that the prediction of the dowser in two of the cases was communicated to and received by me before the actual discovery of the mineral springs.

### (6) Mr. R. Rothwell

Rothwell is a gardener living at Cardiff, (65, Upper George-street, Cathays, Cardiff), and is, I believe, over 60 years of age. Our friend and fellow-worker, the Rev. A. T. Fryer, of Cardiff, to whom I am mainly indebted for the evidence concerning this dowser, knows Rothwell, and was favourably impressed by his evident straightforwardness. The Vicar of the parish also writes in answer to enquiry, "I know Rothwell well; he is an excellent gardener, and quite trustworthy as far as I know."

Rothwell states that he experiences "a slight tingling sensation when the rod bends, just the same as he has felt with an electric battery." He determines the depth at which the water will be found by walking away from the supposed stream at right angles to its course; the rod invariably bends with lessening force as he moves away. Directly the rod is stationary, Rothwell stops, and then measures the distance, from the spot at which the rod ceases to act, to the stream. This, he asserts, gives him the distance down.[1]

No. 134.—Mr. Lyddon, Rothwell's employer, sent Mr. Fryer the following account of Rothwell's first essay at dowsing:—

Bute Docks, Cardiff, *July 5th*, 1893.

> A well had been sunk by the builder when my house was being erected, but on my occupying the house the supply of water was found to be insufficient; not knowing where to sink a well, I was advised by a member of a large firm in Bristol to let one of his engineers, who had the power of discovering water by the aid of a divining rod, see if he could find water by the aid of the rod. This person, a complete stranger to the neighbourhood, came, and accompanied by W. Rothwell, my gardener, went over my field. He told me I should find water in two places, at the extreme north end, and at a spot in the south end, and nowhere else. There was nothing to show that water was underneath. The Bristol man advised me to bore in the north corner of my field. I did this, and found water, but not a good supply.
>
> Rothwell, when accompanying the Bristol man, thought the whole thing ridiculous, and had no faith in it, but after the departure of the man Rothwell tried the rod, and to his surprise found that in his hands it moved as it did with the other person. With the aid of the rod he discovered another spring, and considered I should find water, about 40 to 45 feet down. I found some, I think at about 55 feet, and I believe a better supply was obtained at 62 feet.
>
> Rothwell has been in Cardiff many years, has worked for me three years, and is, I believe, a perfectly truthful man.
>
> The 4½ inch bore to the spring did not give us sufficient water, so on Rothwell's advice I sank a well, and have now a good supply.
>
> E. T. Lyddon.

---

[1] [THIS IS an example of the 'Bishop's Rule' for finding depth. - Ed.]

## Prof. W. F. Barrett

No. 135.—The next letter is from Mr. James, of the Malting House, Cardiff, and Chepstow.

Cardiff, *June 30th*, 1893.

Some years since, I called in the services of a man named Lawrence, a "diviner," in order to find, if possible, indications of water on property adjoining our Maltings, at Cardiff, with the result that he pointed out a spot at which water would be found at a depth of 20 to 25 feet.

Two years since I made the acquaintance of Rothwell, a gardener, in Cardiff, who had very recently found out he possessed this "gift." As I was anxious to test his powers and see if he could find the same spring which was indicated by Lawrence, he came up, and after carefully walking over the field, in a few minutes found the precise spot, but fixed the depth at 28 to 30 feet. Since then, we have followed up the course of this spring, which runs into property belonging to the Bute Docks Gas Works, the manager of which informed us that when erecting a new gasometer two years ago, when about 26 feet below the surface, they were unexpectedly flooded out by some spring breaking up, which necessitated a steam pump to keep the water down whilst certain work proceeded.

We have to-day finished sinking a well at the place indicated by the two diviners (Lawrence and Rothwell) and found a good spring—even in this severe drought—in the upper strata of marl, at a depth of 18 to 24 feet. The main spring is 18 feet below surface.

You will note the Bute Dock Gas Works found water at about 26 feet. This may be explained by the stratum dipping very considerably as it nears the sea-board.

Being successful at Cardiff, I took Rothwell up to Chepstow, at which place we also have maltings, with result that he has pointed out a spot at which we may expect to find water at about 28 feet.

We commence operations next week, and shall be pleased to inform you of result later on.

A. A. James

I wrote to Mr. James to enquire whether Rothwell had any means of ascertaining beforehand the site of the spring fixed on by Lawrence.

Mr. James replied that the only information Rothwell had was that Lawrence had somewhere indicated a certain spot where he said a good spring of water would be found; Rothwell was then left entirely to himself to locate the place, which he found within a few minutes, after walking to and fro over the ground. Mr. James adds that Rothwell, so far as he knew, had never been in Chepstow before. Subsequently, in answer to enquiries whether water had been found at Chepstow at the place indicated by Rothwell, Mr. James writes:—

The Cardiff Malting Company, Limited, East Moors, Cardiff, *September 10th*, 1896.

As regards the result of Rothwell's "divining" for water at Chepstow, in 1893, we found, by sinking a 30 foot shaft of 4 foot diameter, water coming through the limestone at about 26 feet below the surface.

The rock is hollowed out by the action of the water, which no doubt at one time was a very strong spring — but owing to the drought of the last two years the supply has become limited, but the water is there.

I may mention a fact which I learned a few days after his visit, the existence of a disused well near the river Wye, within the old fortified town wall, on a direct line from our present well to the river, the course of which he indicated exactly.

A. A. James

# *The Credibility Of Dowsing*

The following letter was sent to the Rev. A. T. Fryer in answer to his enquiries:—

Severn Side Brewery, Wick, Bridgend, *May 22nd,* 1897.

I am in receipt of yours of the 20th inst., and in reply have to say that Mr. Rothwell visited my place for the purpose of finding water, and hit upon a spot where he told me I should find a large supply at about 36 feet deep. I then engaged a sinker, and when he got to the 36 feet a very weak spring was discovered. Wet weather then set in and prevented any further working, and nothing has since been done. I feel quite certain that there is water at no great distance, and should we have a dry summer I intend going a few feet lower.

I may state that I put a test to Mr. Rothwell, and that was to ask him to trace the spring from a distance before reaching the spot by the Brewery; this he did, and followed it for about a quarter of a mile across the road, under the buildings, and across the fields to an old disused parish well. Mr. Rothwell, to the best of my belief, had never been in the neighbourhood before. Not being altogether a believer in the art, I took care that everything was fairly carried on, and I am now a firm believer in it.

W. J. M. Herbert.

In the following letter the Rev. A. T. Fryer kindly gives me an account of some experiments he made with Rothwell. Though the results obtained are of no evidential value in connection with a "dowsing faculty," yet several points of considerable interest are referred to. The use of a wet pad on the rod to test whether the motion of the rod be due to water or metal, is identical with the device employed in America and elsewhere, see Appendix C. It is undoubtedly an entire fallacy, the effect being in all probability merely due to suggestion. It is possible Rothwell heard of it through Lawrence, but it is curious how these traditions spread. Much the same remark applies to the experiment with the glass bottles and insulation.

13, Dumfries Place, Cardiff, *September 14th*, 1893.

We went this morning to a small estate at St. Briavel's, Gloucestershire, named Woodside, and occupied by a Mr. Cuthbert, retired sea-captain and merchant, of Cardiff. He has been without water for some time, and at last determined upon sinking a well near where a spring had hitherto given a good supply. Having gone down 30 feet and meeting with no reward, he felt in a fix. [This well was marked D on an accompanying plan.] He then made up his mind to give Rothwell a trial. R. had never been to the place before he went with me to-day. We started the search in the field behind the house, Rothwell having cut a hazel forked-twig from the wood, and water was found in a very few minutes. To test the find, R. placed on the top of the twig a piece of paper which he had wetted with water. The rod remained quite unaffected, and did so also at other points. I have not heard of this test in any other case, but R. is satisfied with it. I may mention here that at another spot where R. said he felt the influence of iron, the water test was also resorted to, and the paper made no difference, it remained on the stick, and the stick bent down as for iron, all the same.

The water was traced up the field, into the wood above. Here we applied the bottle test. I had two champagne bottles stuck into the earth, and when R. stood on their broad, uppermost bottoms, the rod ceased to act. Then we followed the indications of water across a wall, and into the next field. At [a point marked A on the plan] the source was found; no trace of water above it, or anywhere else, in the same field. Then R. descended the well, D, and held the rod over the water at the bottom of the well (a little accumulation of surface drainage), and reported, "No spring there." Then I blindfolded him and made him walk towards A; the rod was quiet until we came to A, when it dipped. It was settled that the well should be sunk at C [a certain spot on the course indicated by R.], and Mr. Cuthbert has promised me that I shall have the news of the result as soon as possible.

## *Prof. W. F. Barrett*

Writing to me six weeks later, Mr. Fryer says, "I sent Rothwell over to Woodside the other day to see if they had begun sinking, and he has reported to me that they are sinking 6 feet away from the spot which he indicated! Mr. Cuthbert is rather a self-willed man." On November 4th, 1893, Mr. Cuthbert writes to Mr. Fryer, in a letter which is before me, stating that he "has sunk 58 feet through very hard rock, and according to my [Mr. C's] measurement of depth have only to go two feet more, for the water is certainly under where we are sinking. This is nearly the same place as Rothwell fixed upon. . . . Had I not been able to use the rod, I would never have reached water by Rothwell's advice." From which it would appear that Mr. Cuthbert believed that he was a better dowser than Rothwell, and so preferred to trust his own opinion. Upon subsequent enquiry I learnt that Mr. Cuthbert had died, but had not found any water in the well, which he had sunk to a considerable depth.

These particulars are given, as it is not improbable the case may be quoted in the neighbourhood as one where great expense was uselessly incurred on the strength of the advice given by Rothwell. At the same time Rothwell's success as a dowser is not so marked as many others. I have before me a letter from a Mr. Stacey, who lives near Cardiff, dated July 5th, 1893, stating he sunk a well 12 feet deep at a spot where Rothwell said a good spring existed, and "only a little water was found, which went off in a few days; it cost me £12, and as there is now no water, I do not believe in the man at all." Rather a sweeping conclusion for one trial only 12 feet deep.

Rothwell frankly informed Mr. Fryer that he had been asked to find water at Vaynor Rectory, near Cardiff, but there he had partly failed. This spontaneous admission on Rothwell's part is some evidence of his undoubted honesty. Mr. Fryer wrote to the rector of Vaynor, and the following is his reply:—

Vaynor Rectory, *May 22nd,* 1897.

> Mr. W. Rothwell found water in our village two years ago, and was paid by the local authority for his work, and his train expenses paid by myself and another gentleman.
>
> There was no failure, but we had him here twice. The men after sinking down about 20 feet at the spot pointed out by Mr. Rothwell, came to a hole or a fault, and there was no sign of water at the depth suggested. Fearing that this hole or fault had something to do with it, we asked Mr. Rothwell to come up again. He came and held his twig over the shaft, and said that water was there, but had been thrown downwards by some convulsion or fault. We asked him to point out another spot on the same [invisible] stream, and he did; we found beautiful soft water at a depth of 22 feet, and it still runs a splendid [supply]. Mr. Rothwell had not been to Vaynor before. He found another stream and followed it for a mile until he got to the well.
>
> Since that time I have practised the art myself, and can find water anywhere where there is water. I found water on my own land here, in the midst of lime-rock. I have not yet finished the well, but the men have gone down 25 feet, and have found already nearly 3 feet of water.
>
> I read in an old book that there was a stream of water running under the old Castle of Brecon. I was there last Tuesday, and with my twig found the stream.
>
> I am writing a pamphlet on water-finding, which will include my questions to Lord Kelvin.
>
> J. G. Jenkins

F. 12.—Mr. Fryer also sends me the accompanying letter, addressed to him, which gives an account of a distinct failure on Rothwell's part:—

Steam Flour Mills and Ship Biscuit Works, Cardiff, *May 24th,* 1897.

> In answer to your letter of the 20th inst, Mr. Rothwell's water finding was not at all satisfactory. We did not come to water at the depth he predicted, but had to go a good deal lower, and then, as far as

we can judge, only came to surface water. We think we should have come to the same surface water wherever we had sunk the well, which is about 36 feet deep. We could find no trace of a lead pipe in another place where Mr. Rothwell said we should find one. Altogether, we regard his experiments with us as a complete failure; but we have heard that he has been very successful elsewhere.

Spillers And Bakers, Ltd.

Mr. Fryer, in a recent letter, tells me Rothwell has signed a contract to go to Australia to dowse for water there.

### (c) Mr. R. W. Robertson

In the early part of this paper (p. 30) I referred to two enthusiastic amateur water finders, Messrs. Robertson and Young, of Llanelly, South Wales, several of whose children have inherited their fathers' faculty. Mr. Robertson's son has now become a professional dowser, and has sent me a copy of the testimonials he has received in this capacity. One of these is as follows:—

No. 136.—The following letter from Mr. G. S. Richmond, hydraulic engineer, is addressed to Mr. R. W. Robertson:—

Llanelly, *November 23rd*, 1895.

> My sinkers struck the spring on Wednesday last, at Goodig, at 28 ft. 6 in. from the surface, and considering that this spot is less than 100 feet from an old quarry, the rock in which shows no signs of water, and also that the surface of the ground where the well is sunk is about 50 feet higher than the farmyard only 107 feet away, I think it extraordinary that you should have found a spring at all, and more so that you should have estimated the depth at which it would be found, so near, being only 3 feet beyond your estimate. The position of the well is quite unique, and I do not think a pump will be necessary
>
> G. S. Richmond.

Mr. Buckley Roderick, a solicitor of Llanelly, for whom the well was sunk, also writes to the same effect, and states that before the spring was found, all the water for the farm had to be carried a great distance. I wrote to Mr. Richmond, and he replies:—

Llanelly, *September 22nd*, 1896.

> Goodig is a farm near Pembrey, South Wales. The place chosen by Mr. Robertson was a very remarkable and unique spot for a well, which is sunk on the side of a steep hill; the bottom of the well being higher than the farmyard. Water rose some 18 feet in the well, and a plentiful supply was obtained, which I have laid on to the farm by a siphon. No indications of water existed anywhere about, nor for 300 yards distance before this spring was found.
>
> I have sunk a good many wells in Monmouthshire and South Wales at spots marked by the divining rod, and in every case with success.
>
> G. S. Richmond.

Mr. R. S. Seymour, the agent to the Earl of Ashburnham, also testifies to the fact that great difficulty has been found in providing a sufficient water supply to Pembrey House, the property of Lord Ashburnham, and in 1895, the springs that supplied the house having run dry, Mr. R. W. Robertson was called in, and by the rod fixed on a certain spot; here a well was sunk, and at a depth of 13 feet from the surface a copious spring was struck, yielding, by measure, 8,000 gallons a day.

Other letters are before me also testifying to Mr. R. W. Robertson's success, whilst on the other hand I have heard of his being less successful, particulars of which it is hardly necessary to give, as there is not yet a sufficient body of evidence on behalf of young Mr. Robertson's powers to enable a fair estimate to be formed of the percentage of his successes.

No. 137.—Mr. G. Blake, the agent to the Stradey Castle estate, writes to me as follows respecting Mr. Robertson, the father of Mr. R. W. Robertson:—

New Road, Llanelly, Carmarthenshire, *February 14th*, 1897.

On the estate of C. W. Mansel Lewis, Esq., at Llanelly, three springs were found at spots indicated by Mr. Robert Robertson (Steward). There was not the slightest surface indication of wetness.

By means of the divining rod these three spots were suggested by Mr. Robertson as likely to afford a subterranean supply. Tubes were driven down from 18 to 23 feet and 1 with pleasure certify that a continuous supply of water of great value to the cottagers on this estate has been regularly pumped up since. As a result the expense of carting water has been saved.

G. Blake,
*Land Agent for C. W. Mansel Lewis, Esq.*

Mr. Robertson informs me that one of the above springs he discovered on the Stradey Castle estate is 25 yards from a bore hole that was sunk haphazard prior to his visit to a depth of 50 feet. The bore hole was a complete failure, not a vestige of water being found; whereas the spring discovered by the rod was struck at a depth of only 18 feet and continues to yield a copious and undiminished supply. The Rev. A. T. Fryer has verified this.

## An American Dowser — Mr. Cyrus Fuller

After the greater part of this paper was in type, I received from our friend, Mr. Hodgson, Secretary to the American Branch of the S.P.R., the following account of a successful American dowser, Mr. Cyrus Fuller, of Plymouth, Wayne County, Michigan. Mr. Fuller was a farmer and Quaker by birth, and died at the age of 85, three years ago. An article was published about him in the *ReligioPhilosophical Journal* of December 9th, 1893, by Mr. Giles B. Stebbins, who in reply to Mr. Hodgson's enquiries, writes:—

143, Pitcher Street, Detroit, Michigan, *November 22nd*, 1894.

Cyrus Fuller is over eighty years old, and his reply and handwriting may be imperfect, but his mind was clear as ever when I last saw him. His integrity, judgment and ability are of high order. He is of Quaker birth— a spiritualist of the higher grade, but has no theory as to his water finding save of a subtle rapport in his temperament—no miracle in the case, but natural law. He has found some 200 wells, with no single failure. Some years ago he sent some twenty names, signed to a statement that he had found water for them on the first trial, and a lasting flow, to the Detroit Tribune, which had flippantly treated previous statements. Men of solid influence, Hon. Mr. Penniman, ex M.C. of Plymouth, now departed, among them. The Tribune published the list, and became respectful. I have looked out from his home windows and seen a dozen windmills drawing water to feed human beings and cattle from wells of his finding. It has never been a money-making work, as he is not a poor man.

Giles B. Stebbins.

Mr. Stebbins attempted to find for Mr. Hodgson the *Detroit Tribune* containing the statement referred to, but unfortunately without success. He quotes the following from a letter from Mr. Fuller to him, dated April 19th, 1894:—"Two of my neighbours have just opened wells which I located with my rod, both a success." He also sent Mr. Hodgson a letter written by Mr. Fuller to the *Religio-Philosophical Journal* to correct some inaccuracies in their account, part of which we print.

# The Credibility Of Dowsing

Plymouth, Michigan, *December 13th,* 1893.

We have nine flowing wells in this school district, all located by the divining rod, and not one has been found by putting the wells down at random.

There are very few wells in this vicinity but those located by the divining rod. I, myself, have located between four and five hundred. The depth of the wells in this vicinity on the timber land is, as near as I can calculate, on an average of forty-five feet. I have located a good many wells since I saw Mr. Stebbins.

I went to Hudson, Lenawee County, 170 miles south, on the solicitation of the water board of that village, and located a vein of water where they put down five wells. The pump [with which] they tested the wells threw two hundred gallons per minute. Each well would produce that amount of water without being exhausted. The village contains fifteen hundred inhabitants; they got all the water they wanted.

I have located wells every season, I think, for the last fifty years, and I never solicited a job of that kind, — they all come to me. I commenced on this farm that we live on sixty-one years ago, and it's our home yet. There are four wells I located this last season, that were to be put down this last fall; hard times prevented. One of these wells I located when the snow, last winter, was a foot and a-half deep. The man was putting up a barn, and wanted to build the barn by a well, instead of digging the well by the barn, so as to have it handy. In the dry time this season I went to the place and found it located all right.

I located a well at Plymouth that may prove celebrated. The medical properties are said to be superior to almost any in this county. They sent off twenty-five gallons of the water to be tested at Detroit. Since then I met a load of jugs of the water going in the cars, destination Cincinnatti,

Cyrus Fuller.

Mr. Fuller having died a few months later, Mr. Hodgson was, by the kindness of Mr. Stebbins, put into communication with his son-inlaw, Mr. Ransom L. Alexander, who writes to Mr. Hodgson as follows:—

Plymouth, Mich., *March 5th,* 1895.

I am sorry to say that I have not the newpaper article to which you refer, and cannot obtain it, several years having elapsed since its publication. Cyrus Fuller found many wells in this section of the country; I believe something over 100, but I do not find among his papers any list of the names of those for whom he found them. I send you a few names that occur to me. He found three flowing wells for himself, which are still running. Two of them have run 50 years, the other 30. He found wells for the following named persons:—

| | | |
|---|---|---|
| William Hake | Plymouth P.O., Mich | Flowing |
| Grant H. Joslin | Since deceased | Flowing |
| Otto Melon | Plymouth | Flowing |
| Albert Durfee | Grand Rapids | Flowing |
| William E. Fry | Northville | |

## *Prof. W. F. Barrett*

| | |
|---|---|
| William Riddle | Plymouth |
| William T. Rattenbury | Stark |
| Joseph Clizbee | Bell Branch |
| Otis Warner | Wayne |
| Robert Rhead | Hudson, Lenawee Co. |

He used a forked peach tree or witch hazel twig, commonly the former.

R. L. Alexander.

Mr. Hodgson wrote to the persons named by Mr. Alexander, but received only the following replies:—

No. 138.—The first is from Mr. Durfee.

103, Ottawa Street, Grand Rapids, Michigan,<br>*March 25th*, 1895.

Mr. Cyrus Fuller did locate not one, but two wells on my farm in Livonia Township, Wayne Co., Michigan; one is 50 feet deep, the other $87\frac{1}{2}$. The first-named is a flowing stream running into a tank, from which stock may drink. The other, water rises within 20 feet of the surface, to which a windmill is attached, and by letting the mill run continuously for forty-eight hours I was only able to lower the water two feet, and within a few minutes after mill was stopped water came to the same level (namely, twenty feet from surface). I have known Mr. Fuller all my life, having lived neighbour to him, until five years ago I came to Grand Rapids. During the past year Mr. Fuller has departed this life. I know of eight wells located by him within a radius of one mile, all flowing ones, together with a great many that wore good ones, but not flowers.

Mr. Fuller's method of locating underground streams was by the "divining rod." Those he used were either peach, witch-hazel, yellow or swamp willow. He has told me no other kinds of wood that he had ever tried would turn in his hands.

Some other things I can remember his having told me; in following veins, as he called them, through forests, that they would lead directly under many of the largest trees, and one other thing was that if a tree was stricken by lightning, he was sure to find a stream leading very near to it.

Within the past ten years he was called to many places to locate wells, some out of the State, one in Canada, I think for a railroad company.

I will conclude by saying, I know Mr. Fuller to be a man honest in purpose, and one whose name was above reproach. Deceived he might have been, but dishonest never. If time and space would permit I could add much more, and if of interest to you may do so at some future time.

A. B. Durfee.

No. 139.—The next is from Mr. Hake.

Plymouth, Michigan, *March 25th*, 1895.

Mr. Cyrus Fuller located five wells for me, and all are good ones. We had no one else to locate them but Mr. Fuller. Two of those wells are flowing wells, the others are plenty of water.

# The Credibility Of Dowsing

William Hake.

No. 140.—The only other reply received by Mr. Hodgson was from Mr. Riddle as follows:—

Plymouth, Mich., *March 25th*, 1895.

> I went 112 feet in the ground where Mr. Fuller did not locate and found no water. Then I went 56 feet in a four foot well, and got 30 feet of water in 30 minutes after I struck it. This last well Mr. Cyrus Fuller, who was a neighbour of mine, located. This was about eight years ago, and the well has never failed. Mr. Fuller died last summer.

William Riddle. Mr. Riddle writes again as follows:—

Plymouth, *April 12th*, 1895.

> I had a well in my barnyard, but it was dry, and Mr. Fuller told me that there was water if I would dig for it. I tried to, but it caved in, and I had to abandon it. Then I moved about 10 feet from the old well, and dug about 112 feet, as I told you before, and found no water. This last well was not located by anybody. I dug there merely for convenience.

William Riddle.

It is to be regretted further details cannot now be obtained of Mr. Fuller's work as a dowser. There is, I find, a letter of his published in *Light* for August 30th, 1884, the substance of which is as follows:—

> (1) The "Michigan Central" officials invited Mr. Fuller to try at Esse Centre, 15 miles south of Detroit. They had previously bored nearly 1500 feet to get water, but without avail. Fuller located a certain spot with the rod where an abundant supply of pure soft water was obtained at 110 feet deep.
>
> (2) At Wayne, 18 miles west of Detroit, a large sum had also been spent by "the officials" in boring for water, but in vain. Water was, however, found at the spot fixed on by Mr. Fuller at 137 feet; moreover a good supply was also obtained at a second spot he located here a few years after.
>
> (3) At Northville, Michigan, W. Foy (Fry?) had spent 200 dollars digging and boring to 97 feet, but got no water. A short distance from this useless well, the rod indicated a spot, where a good supply of water was obtained at 20 feet from the surface.

It would be useful to have independent evidence of these statements. Several other instances of the success of dowsers in finding underground water, often when other means had failed, are to be found in the columns of *Light* from 1882 to the present time; but as the majority of the correspondents do not give their names, their evidence cannot be corroborated. A dowser of whom I had not heard before, Mr. Child, writes from Norwich in *Light* of October 8th, 1887, stating he had repeatedly found water by the rod within a few yards of wells that had been sunk unsuccessfully. I wrote to Mr. Child asking for particulars of these places, but my letter was returned marked "present address unknown."

Evidence has already been given showing the wide area of distribution of the dowsing rod. This fact also comes out in the correspondence on the subject that appears from time to time in various journals. I have not heard of its use in Asia or South America, though the North American Indians are said to have long known and practised dowsing. The London *Times* of December 27th, 1881, refers to its use in Dakota, as Mr. E. T. Bennett has pointed out.[1] In an article on "Farming in Dakota," reference is made to a farm near Valley City belonging to a Mr. Kindred, and according to the *Times*:—

> Water is got in abundance from a bed of sand 30 feet deep, and brought to the tanks by a pump worked by a windmill. An effort had previously been made only 100 yards further north to find water; a shaft, 138 feet, had been ineffectually dug. The bending of the willow twig carefully carried over the surface is said to have afforded indications which justified the present successful opening.

In Italy the rod has been in use for over three centuries. Lieut.Col. Cocks, in a letter to the *Times*, states he has seen certain Italians travelling through the Riviera locating the site for wells with a twig of olive bent into the form of a loop. The loop turns upwards with jerks, often striking the breast of the operator when over a hidden spring; Colonel Cocks gives instances that came under his own observation, of the success of these dowsers. This form of rod is, I observe, pictured in a work on Practical Mining published in Bologna in 1678, and is also described in various Italian essays on the rod of a century ago; a loop of wire is used by some English dowsers. In parts of Switzerland the rod has also long been in use; in the neighbourhood of Lucerne the dowser appears to be called the *Brunnen-Schmecker* (spring-taster);[2] in the United States he is often called "water-smeller."

---

[1] See *Light* for January 7th, 1882, where Mr. Bennett asks for authentic instances of water-finding by the rod and originated the correspondence on the subject which followed. Some remarkable cases of the use of the rod in Jersey, by a local dowser, are given in *Light* for February 11th, 1882.

[2] See *Light* of January 28th, 1882, where a good instance of the Swiss dowser's success in water-finding is given.

## *The Credibility Of Dowsing*

# Part IV
# GEOLOGICAL OPINION

Before bringing to a close the evidence for or against the dowser's success, in the search for underground water, I wish to cite the opinion of a few geologists.

### *PROFESSOR SOLLAS, F.R.S.,*

It is certainly a singular fact how very few attempts have been made by competent scientific men to put the dowsers' claims to the test of experiment. One such is recorded in our own *Proceedings,* Vol. II., p. 73, *et seq.*[1] This is a report by a distinguished geologist, Professor Sollas, LL.D., F.R.S., etc., which was made at the request and at the expense of our Society in the year 1883. The experiment consisted in sinking two adjacent similar wells in an alluvial plain at Locking, near Bristol; one well was sunk at the spot indicated by the dowser, and the other at a spot 15 feet distant where the "rod" did not indicate water.[2] At the former, which Professor Sollas called the + well, the dowser predicted that water would be found; at the latter, or - well, that it would not. Professor Sollas, as a geologist, predicted water would be found in both or neither. Wells were sunk, and when the + well was 16 feet deep, Professor Sollas reports, "it contained a good deal of water, 8 or 9 feet. . . . The - well was 20 feet deep and contained 4½ feet of water. Water was trickling into it, but not so fast as into the other. The well-sinker said this 4½ feet was merely surface water." A fortnight later the bailiff to the estate visited the wells, and reports that the + well was only sunk to a depth of 17½ feet, but the - well was sunk to 20 feet, nevertheless the former had 9 feet of water in it and the latter 4½ feet. Ten days afterwards a pupil of Professor Sollas visited the wells and reported that the water stood at the same level in both wells, and a similar report was given some time later.[3] A month after this last Mr. E. R. Pease visited the spot and had both the wells emptied of water. "The + well I found (he remarks) now to be a mere hole some 10 feet deep, whilst the - well was a carefully timbered shaft 24 feet deep." Measurements of the rate at which water flowed into the two wells "seem to show that the + well filled more rapidly than the - well, although its depth was so much less. The tenant of the farm told me that the water in the + well was of better quality than that in the - well."

The conclusion Professor Sollas draws from this experiment is that "The case for the dowser has conspicuously failed "; any success dowsers may have he believes due to their possession of much mother wit and a large experience of the behaviour of underground water. Mr. Pease, however, remarks "I cannot feel his [Professor Sollas'] complete confidence in the conclusive nature of this particular experiment." An opinion from which, with all respect to my friend, Professor Sollas, few, I imagine, would be disposed to dissent; even although the - well certainly could not be called "dry."[4]

---

[1] Reprinted, as already mentioned on p. 30, with some additions and maps in the *Proceedings of the Bristol Naturalists' Society* for 1881.
[2] The dowser was Mr. Thomas Young, since dead, see No. 29, p. 39.
[3] The dowser and his assistants attributed the water in the - well to an outflow from the + well, and the tenant of the estate said he had seen it flowing in from the side nearest the + well; Professor Sollas confirms this from his own observation, but adds it trickled in from the other sides also, and remarks that if the rock between the two wells were so porous as to allow percolation from one well to the other, then the rock would be water-bearing and furnish water to both.
[4] At the close of his paper Professor Sollas draws attention to the incompatibility of the dowser's pretensions, in this and like cases, with the assumption that some physical effect is produced on the dowser by underground water, *provided* this effect be assumed to radiate from the water and decrease as the square of the distance increases. I shall return to this argument subsequently when discussing the suggested explanations of the " dowsing faculty," if such there be.

## *Prof. W. F. Barrett*

# MR. T. V. HOLMES, F.G.S.

Mr. T. V. Holmes, F.G.S., the President of the Geologists' Association of London for 1889-90, who read a paper on the divining rod before the Anthropological Institute on March 30th, 1897,[1] writes to me as follows:—

28, Grooms Hill, Greenwich Park, S.E., *June 23rd,* 1897.

A priori conclusions seem to me absurd and unscientific, whether put forward by the President of the Royal Society, or by a village cobbler. As regards the water diviner, I am only anxious that he should be brought from the realm of disorderly mystery, which is ignorance, to that of orderly mystery, which is science—to use a phrase of Huxley's. That a somewhat abnormal nervous organisation may make given persons specially sensitive in special ways, where ordinary persons remain unconscious, is a perfectly possible, and not improbable thing to me. It is simply a matter of evidence.

Whilst geology as a science is very modern, a knowledge of water-bearing surface beds is extremely ancient, as the evidence afforded by the sites of ancient towns and villages amply demonstrates; in fact, the presence of a water-bearing stratum, such as a flat of old river gravel, was one of the strongest attractions.[2] Nowadays, the existence of water companies allows the extension of London over thick clay. But the ancient London, " the City," is on the first high terrace of old river gravel to be met with on going up the Thames from the sea. Innumerable instances of a similar kind might be given. This perception of water-bearing surface beds is therefore a knowledge quite independent of a knowledge of geological structure, and one which has existed from time immemorial.

Indeed, (as I have elsewhere remarked), the rise of geology as a science tended to put this older knowledge of water-bearing surface beds into the background. The Geological Survey had been at work many years at the deep-seated geology of England and Wales, before any "drift-maps," or those showing the superficial beds, which lie indifferently on the older rocks of various ages, were even thought of. But at a later period it was discovered that to ignore the superficial beds in such a district as the Eastern Counties was to ignore the strata forming four-fifths of the surface to an average depth of thirty or forty feet. So drift-maps became more common. But geologists seldom bestow much thought on these various drift-beds, unless interested in flint implements. Again, with the rise of geology as a science came, pari passu [side by side with it - Ed], a distrust of water from surface beds as a source of domestic supply, and a preference for deep wells and water companies. In short, the tendency of the great bulk of geologists is to ignore utterly surface beds as a source of water supply, and to care but little for them from any other point of view; while, as regards older rocks, most would be found interested in them rather as showing deposition under marine, estuarine, fresh water, warm or cold water, conditions, than in their relations to water-supply.

Consequently, I am not surprised to learn from one of the cases you cite, (No. 73, p. 74), that a "geological authority " had said that no water would be found at a less depth than 120 to 130 feet, and that Mullins found water at 20 feet in a surface deposit. Whether the geologist ignored the surface deposit, or thought water from it unwholesome, I know not.

In another case (No. 42, p. 51) the geologist is not so wrong as he seems. Limestone is a water-bearing rock, and water would tend to flow to the lowest level in that rock, impervious clay beneath preventing it from getting lower. But while water tends to percolate evenly through gravel and sand,

---

[1] I am indebted to my friend, Mr. E. Westlake, F.G.S., for this information, which reached me too late for insertion in the earlier part of this paper.
[2] This fact was pointed out some time ago by Professor Prestwich.—W.F.B.

# The Credibility Of Dowsing

it flows through sandstones and limestones mainly along their lines of jointing. Hence it is by no means rare to find that little if any water comes into a shaft driven into a limestone or sandstone to a supposed sufficient depth, and a very common practice of practical well-sinkers to run headings in various directions to tap joints and fissures when such is the case, with results as successful as in the above example.

In certain Essex cases north of Chelmsford and between Braintree and Bishop's Stortford, where the diviner's success was thought wonderful, there is a plateau of Boulder clay intersected by valleys

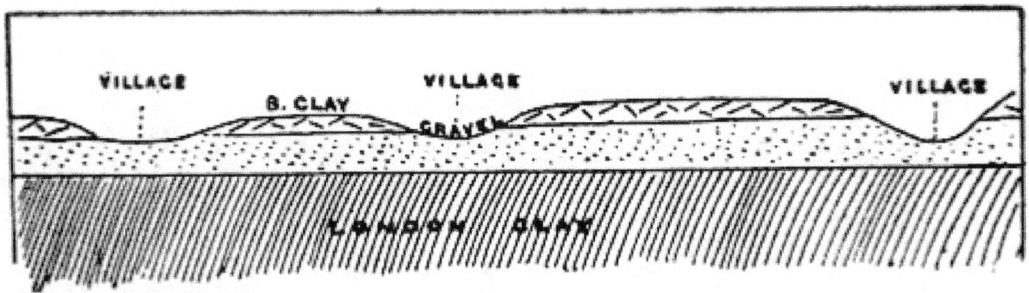

FIG. 1.

which show the underlying Glacial gravel and sand, London clay underlying both. The villages are on the gravel and sand of the valleys, and any practical well-sinker would see at once that water would be attainable at a moderate depth on the plateau on sinking through the Boulder clay into the underlying gravel, see Fig. 1; the London clay, of course, prevents the water from getting lower. The valleys thereabouts are very close together, in addition. Non-drift maps of Essex ignore almost everything above the London clay; hence a Government official, reporting a year or two ago on Essex agriculture, stated that most of the soil of Essex was London clay. Much more of it is Boulder clay than London clay. But drift-maps are of recent date, and all geological maps of less scale than one inch to the mile necessarily ignore drift for the sake of clearness in more fundamental points of structure.

With regard to Lady Milbanke's and Dr. Button's experiments (p. 31); the "new college" was evidently the Royal Military Academy on Woolwich Common, at which Dr. Hutton was Professor of Mathematics (1773-1806.) Now the surface of Woolwich Common between the Military Academy and the Artillery Barracks and Rotunda (northward) consists of Blackheath Pebble Beds; while from the Academy (southward) the Pebble Beds become covered with a gradually increasing thickness of London clay. Whether the spot at which the lady discovered the water had Pebble Beds at the surface, or they were covered by a few feet of London clay, is immaterial, as the water would be found only towards the bottom of the Pebble Beds. And as water percolates evenly and freely through them, and they are lying almost perfectly flat, water would be found thereabouts at very nearly the same depth wherever the Pebble Beds are uncovered, and at a greater distance from the surface as the thickness of the London clay above increased. It is therefore obvious that whatever influence may have caused the lady's agitation and the twisting of the rod in her fingers, it could not have been a peculiar and special nearness of underground water at that particular spot. In this instance, too, there can be no suspicion that she was trying to give herself a reputation for an abnormal faculty; nor that her movements were the result of knowing that water was almost certain to be found at no great depth in a bed of gravel. We learn also that the most perfect integrity is quite compatible with complete, though unconscious, self-deception. In short, this case is one best explained by the conclusion of Paramelle, that "the wand turns in the hands of certain individuals of peculiar temperament, and that it is very much a matter of chance whether there are, or are not, wells in the places where it turns." Records of experiments with the divining rod show many apparently similar cases.

In my paper I spoke of myself as a field-geologist, because having worked on the Geological Survey of England and Wales about 11 years, in Yorkshire and Cumberland, I have often since felt the advantage of having been compelled from official duty to note much about superficial, and other beds, which the non-official geologist almost invariably neglects. And when president of the Geologists' Association, at a later date, (1889-90), it often struck me how little many otherwise accomplished geologists saw in the field of those points which would be instinctively noted by the Geological Survey, who had to map the various beds in detail. But many of these points would equally attract the attention of the professional diviner. But the geologist—on water being found at a certain depth, whether in Carboniferous sandstone, or river gravel, or anywhere else—would not call water so found "a spring." A spring is a natural fountain. Where a permeable bed of sandstone—for example—lies above impermeable shale, water will flow downwards through the sandstone in the direction of its dip. Where the sandstone becomes saturated to a level above that of the surface, there may be one strong spring, many slighter ones, or a belt of wet ground, according to local circumstances.

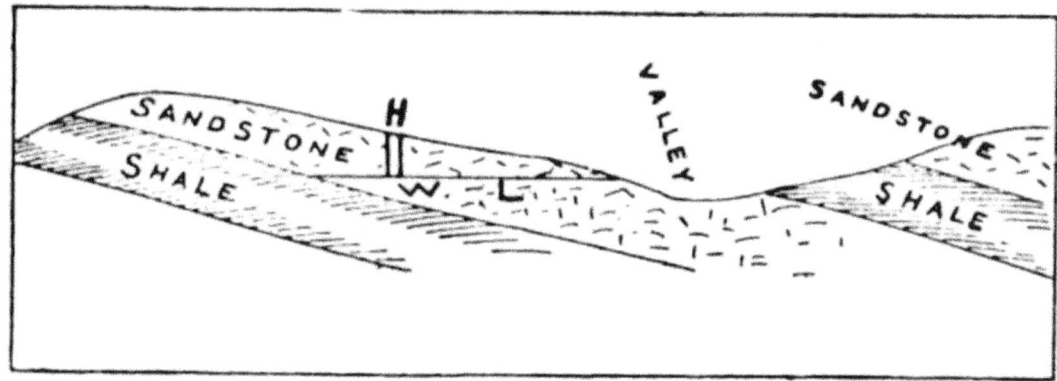

Fig. 2.

If the permanent level of the water is at W.L. (see Fig. 2, representing a section) then there will be springs along the line of the valley. But if I sink a well at my house at H. and find water 30 or 40 feet below the surface I cannot call water so found a "spring." A geological surveyor or a practical well-sinker would see the dip of the sandstone, and note any spring or belt of wet ground in the valley, the latter telling him that the sandstone being full of water there, he need not go very deep for it at H. In a map the sandstone would probably be traceable for miles, and have a breadth of perhaps a quarter of a mile. Anywhere towards the bottom of the slope water might be expected at a moderate depth. In short, where water may be found at a moderate depth is a question of acres or square miles, not of feet or inches, as the diviner absurdly thinks. And when the finding of water by diviners is, nevertheless, treated as though it were equivalent to the finding, in each case, of a pot of ancient coins, six feet below the surface of a ploughed field, belief in his abnormal powers follows as a matter of course.

# *The Credibility Of Dowsing*

Nevertheless I may add, that to me abnormal sensitiveness to the proximity of water seems quite as possible as abnormal sensitiveness to the action of some special drug, or to the presence of some particular animal, of which many curious examples are known.

As to the nature of the nervous sensibility which produces these performances with the divining rod; how much its possessors resemble in nervous organisation persons subject to hypnotic influences, or those who speedily become convulsed at fervid religious meetings,—that is a question of much interest, but one into which I have not entered.

I am amused at the fee demanded (note p. 4 of your paper) for training. For on the hypothesis that the diviner depends solely on his inner sensations, "training" seems likely to do harm rather than good. The usual dislike of diviners to be blindfolded also becomes unintelligible. For, if blindfolded, he would be much more likely to be governed solely by his inner sensations. I know that they do not always object. If I were a diviner, I would object or not according to the nature of the ground. If I were in the midst of a large flat of river or other gravel, I would cheerfully consent. But if progress in a certain direction for 100 or 200 yards might lead to a mistake, I would prefer to see. So far as I can make out, the diviner acts in this way.

As to the question of sensitiveness to the nearness of mineral lodes, I have not touched upon it. It seems to me that the two things are better treated separately. And mineral lodes being confined to special lines of country, to definite and very limited areas, it would be much more easy to obtain satisfactory evidence in their case of abnormal sensitiveness than in that of so broadly diffused a thing as water. Indeed, as regards water, I cannot think of any country in which the matter could be tested satisfactorily. And with regard to mineral lodes, it must not be forgotten that the practical observer sees much in his own line where very able men, in other walks, see nothing particular, as regards surface indications. The "Savage" is a far better observer than most of our "educated" people, who see little and argue much. Had I known you were writing on the subject I should not have written my own paper, but have sent you my notes thereon. But I heard of it only about two months ago.

T. V. Holmes.

Mr. Holmes had not seen the whole of the sheets of my paper when he wrote the foregoing letter. After receiving the rest of the paper, Mr. Holmes writes to me as follows:—

I think no intelligent person can doubt the practical successes of dowsers. The question with me is: Does a recognition of them involve the recognition of an abnormal faculty in the dowser? It seems to me too much forgotten that a man may become a "Sherlock Holmes" as an observer of the special natural phenomena in which he is interested, and remain a very average observer in other departments. I am very far from thinking that dowsers are guilty of conscious deception when they attribute their successes to an abnormal power. But people who owe little or nothing to education, so far as education means "booklearning," are particularly apt to believe themselves the possessors of special abnormal gifts, simply because they know that their success cannot be the result of what is commonly called education.[1] In his special sphere a gamekeeper may point out many things to a Darwin which the latter would not otherwise have noticed.

---

[1] This is very true. I have already referred to the dowser's liability to self-deception.—W. F. B.

P. 35.—Adams. Blindfolding should have helped him by preventing any confusing of his sensations—on the sensations hypothesis.[1]

P. 40. — Stokes doubtless was "an excellent dowser," but his sensations deceived him very decidedly. Should like to have his views as to the origin of "spring water."[2]

P. 42.—As to Hale Park, I note on looking at the geological map that in Hale Park Bagshot-sands come on eastward above Lower Tertiary clays, etc. I have not visited the spot, but have no doubt that the sands occupy higher ground than the Lower Tertiary beds. As the sands occupy a large area of the surface east of the house at Hale Park, they must contain a large amount of water, which is "surface" water as coming from surface beds. Any discovery more simple and less "uncanny" it would be hard to mention. It makes one suspect that many other cases which seemed extraordinary to the narrators would prove equally simple if one could get a similar knowledge of the geology.[3]

P. 81. — Close to Bower House, but higher up, Edward the Confessor had a palace. The patch of Bagshot-sand on which it stood gave a water supply.

P. 184.—The Bacon cases are in the Boulder clay district of Essex. The thicknesses of the Boulder clay forming the surface of the plateau and of the underlying glacial sand and gravel, seen in the valleys of the various streams, vary considerably within certain moderate limits. But the water is diffused through the gravel, and obtainable when the gravel is reached. Perhaps the usual depth to which it would be necessary to sink through the Boulder clay is from 20 to 40 ft. (See Fig. 1, p. 223.)

The Horsham Experiments (p. 94).—The position of Warnham Lodge is not shown on the old Ordnance map on which the geological surveyors worked, but it evidently stands where the words "Lit. Mays " appear on that map, about a mile N.W. of the village of Warnham, which is about 2½ miles N.W. of Horsham. Horsham stands on the Tunbridge Wells Sand of the Hastings Beds, while Warnham and Warnham Lodge are both on the overlying formation known as the Weald Clay, as the great bulk of it consists of clay. Topley, in the "Geological Survey Memoir on the Weald District " (p. 101), gives a section of a "well at Warnham, near Horsham."

|  | ft. | in. |
|---|---|---|
| Bluish clay | 7 | 0 |
| Red sandstone | 0 | 9 |
| Bluish clay | 20 | 0 |
| Red sandstone | 0 | 8 |
| Blue clay . | 49 | 7 |
| Water-bearing bed | 1 | 0 |
| Clay, chiefly blue | 73 | 0 |
|  | 152 | 0 |

[This is slightly condensed, the names of varieties of clay being omitted.]

---

[1] This is quite true, blindfolding *ought* to help the dowser as it does the quasi thought-reader, like Stuart Cumberland, whose performances are due to slight and ordinarily imperceptible variations of muscular pressure unintentionally imparted by those who know what has to be found or done. At the same time, if the rod be an *autoscope* (p. 7) one can quite understand how unexpected blindfolding might disturb, rather than induce, that passive state of mind which seems necessary for success in the whole group of sub-conscious phenomena.—W. F. B.

[2] This particular experiment of Stokes is recorded to illustrate what is said at the bottom of p. 40; it ought not to have had a number, but should have been classed among failures of a specific kind.—W. F. B.

[3] Possibly this case, like some other successes of the dowser, is readily explicable on geological grounds. I wrote to Major Goff to enquire why "everyone was astonished" at water being found. His reply is given on p. 42. Mr. Westlake, F.G.S., writes, "I know Hale. The well referred to is near the top of the London clay and not, I think, as shown in the old Geological Survey map, actually on the Bagshot-sand."— W. F. B.

# The Credibility Of Dowsing

Topley notes (p. 396) that of 97 towns and villages on the Hastings Beds (which consist of alternations of sands and clays, neither decidedly predominating as regards the area they cover), 79 are on sandy sites. To obtain a water supply by means of shallow wells and pumps has been the chief cause of this selection, clay yielding no water. In the Weald Clay district, the most important of the subordinate beds of stone is the Horsham Stone, on which the village of Warnham and Warnham Court stand. The presence of one of these beds of stone, where it attains a thickness of a few feet, will be marked by the existence of a ridge, which will make higher ground than that where the surface beds are almost wholly clay. As water supply in such a district depends so largely on the presence of these beds of stone, the dowser naturally has a keen eye for the elevated ground, and will go there, to the horror of his backers at first, and to the enormous increase of their wonder at his powers, when a well is successfully sunk at the top of a hill, after failures down below.

There are signs of the presence of a bed of stone on the high ground where Warnham Lodge and farm buildings stand, and Topley mentions (p. 92) a bed of sand and sandstone ranging by Hurst Hill, Gearing's, Little May's, Charman's, and other spots to Rudgwick, which is evidently the stone in question.[1] Whether in Yorkshire, Sussex, or anywhere else, where beds of stone alternate with others of clay or shale, the high ground is composed of the beds of stone, and the lower of the shales, and the former are waterbearing, the latter not.

I do not wonder that the non-dowsing advisers ignored the surface stone bed, and thought of (I suppose) going down to the Horsham Stone, or even the Tunbridge Wells Sand; or, perhaps, of tapping a sufficient number of waterbearing beds, which individually insignificant might collectively prove sufficient, and be free from possible dangers arising from surface pollution— dangers by no means uncommon in similar cases. The dowser's triumph is to find water, and to find it as near the surface as possible; he has no further responsibility. But the geologist who should recommend water from a source easily polluted, and which gave rise to disease in persons using it, would be deemed to have shown a most culpable recklessness—at the very least.

However, the dowser in this case, after "blasting and sinking " in hard limestone, obtained a supply of water at a depth of 12 feet, at spots known as E and F, and at 19 feet at D (p. 95), all these wells being only a few yards apart. The dowser, however, insisted that no water would be found between wells E and F, as "both were independent springs." One of the wells was pumped nearly dry, and the water-level in the other was unaffected. But this merely showed that there were no lines of bedding or jointing giving an easy passage to the water between the two wells. And the water from the stone for some distance around having been collected into the two wells, the space between them was likely to be a spot comparatively free from water. Of course, ultimately, a well midway between E and F would have become as full of water as they were. But the days necessary for this to take place, in the absence of a good system of jointing, were not allowed, but a tunnel was at once made connecting the wells E and F, and ensuring a better supply than could otherwise be obtained.

This stone was evidently an extremely hard and compact rock, very much more so than the chalk, but the best illustration I can think of to show the difference between the restricted circulation of water in jointed rocks, and its free percolation in gravel and sand is from the chalk.

In the Essex Naturalist, Vol. I., p. 254, (1887) there is a brief account of some "chalk wells" in Buckinghamshire. These chalk wells were situated at a tile works, and consisted of some five or six shafts, about 70 ft. deep, which after piercing through the surface beds, entered the chalk to a depth of about 6 ft., and then widened out into bell-shaped chambers. The object of their makers was to

---

[1] It is called a *limestone* in your paper. Probably it is more calcareous than usual at Warnham Lodge.

obtain chalk for lime from the ground beneath the limited area of the tile works. The chalk being locally full of water almost to the top, these chambers were hollowed out as near the top of the chalk as possible. After a considerable amount of chalk had been removed from one of these chambers, it would become unpleasantly wet, and would ultimately be abandoned and another shaft sunk, and so on. The important point is that these chambers became unpleasantly wet only after some time had elapsed, though from their size, as compared with that of a mere well, they must have been comparatively far more likely to be speedily flooded. I have no doubt that the Warnham well between E and F would eventually have had water in it, had sufficient time been allowed, just as in the case of the chalk chambers at the tile works. That Mullins fixed upon the spot midway between two wells as a dry place, seems to me simply caused by his experience of the behaviour of water in jointed rocks, not as showing the veracity of his sensations. The dowser in the case reported by Professor Sollas no doubt fancied that he was directed by his sensations. But he probably thought also that water circulated as irregularly through the sand of an alluvial flat as through a jointed rock—and consequently deceived himself.

T. V. Holmes.

Mr. Holmes' criticism of some of the cases which I have cited is extremely interesting and useful, and I am much indebted to him for the trouble he has taken. Regarding the Horsham experiments, the explanation suggested by Mr. Holmes presumes that Mullins had not only local knowledge, but also a *geological* knowledge of the locality. This is in the highest degree improbable. I never met John Mullins, but every one who has done so testifies to the fact that he never troubled himself in the least about gaining the advantage to be derived from even an elementary acquaintance with geological facts. Whatever information of water bearing strata he has gained by experience was probably not consciously drawn upon, but may have aided him in a kind of *instinctive* selection of the right spot where to sink a well. The question to be discussed presently is whether this instinct gained by experience is sufficient to account for the dowser's success in the whole of the cases I have cited. At Warnham Park there was absolutely nothing in the surface of the ground to indicate which was stone and which Weald clay. The hill and its slopes as well as the rest of the ground were covered with vegetation, under which was a thick layer of alluvial soil. Moreover the water found, though from a shallow well, is an excellent, abundant, and perennial supply. If its discovery was so very obvious, as Mr. Holmes points out, why did not the experienced local well sinkers and the eminent engineers who were consulted,—aided as they were by geological maps and geological advice,—indicate the fact to Mr. (now Sir Henry) Harben and save him the fruitless expenditure of over £1,000? If Mr. Holmes visited the site, he would see the source chosen is the highest point on the estate; it is not easily polluted and in fact it furnishes the whole of the drinking water which is used in the establishment. It is, as we all know, very easy to prophecy after the event, but in this case not quite so easy beforehand, apparently.[1]

With regard to the absence of water between wells E and F (p. 118) if I understand Mr. Holmes aright, he argues this is merely relative, water would gradually have percolated into the intervening space, if time were allowed for it to do so. Possibly, but that is not the point in question. How did Mullins find the exact spots where bedding or jointing allowed an abundant supply of water to be tapped? And how did he know that between E and F in the solid rock 12 ft. below him there was "an absence of a good system of jointing," to use Mr. Holmes' words? He did

---

[1] Writing to me on July 8th, 1897, after the above was in type, Mr. Holmes says :—
I visited Horsham on June 30th. As you say, there is no evidence of stone on the surface, but that would not matter to the dowser. He would see, as I saw, that there was a ridge capped by stone of some sort there, *i.e.*, by something harder than clay, which would be enough for his purpose. And the information which he would inevitably gather from Mr. Harben and others would suffice without asking many questions. I did not notice the Waterford case, because I do not know the country at all. The majority of recorded cases cannot be discussed by a geologist. from the absence of sufficient geological details.
T.V. Holmes
It was extremely good of Mr. Holmes to take the trouble to visit Warnham specially; he is, however, entirely mistaken in his assumptions, as Sir Henry Harben would inform him; how, except by trial, or from some geological knowledge, was Mullins to know the ridge was "capped by stone of some sort," when Mr. Holmes himself says "there was no evidence of stone on the surface"?

## *The Credibility Of Dowsing*

not remove the trees, the shrubs, the grass, and the surface soil, and explore the rocks beforehand. Had Mr. Holmes himself been in Mullins' place, he must have been more than a geological Sherlock Holmes to have discovered all this in a rapid walk over entirely new ground.

No, Mr. Holmes' criticism leaves the solution of the question *as a whole* as far off as ever. Many individual cases are, no doubt, readily explicable; but nothing Mr. Holmes has said explains the Waterford experiments, nor, I venture to say, the Horsham experiments, nor the numerous cases I have cited where useless wells or borings had previously been made, and where water was found by the dowser at a less depth, or at a corresponding depth close by.

The next letter may be contrasted with Mr. Holmes' instructive criticism, or with the opinions given on pp. 4, 5, and 51.

## MR. J. H. BLAKE, F.G.S.

I wrote to several well-known geologists to ask for any information they could give me either favourable or unfavourable to the pretensions of the dowser. Among other replies, my friend, Mr. W. Whitaker, F.R.S., referred me to Mr. J. H. Blake, F.G.S., of the Geological Survey, who has had considerable experience in hydro-geology. I wrote to Mr. Blake, and the following is his reply:—

*Re* "The Divining Rod."

16, Polstead-road, Oxford, *October 1st,* 1896.

I have received your letter of September 26th, desiring some information as to the non-success of the above. When was it ever successful?

The late W. J. Palmer, of the Biscuit Factory, Reading, wanting a water supply at Kingwood House, Lambourn, Berkshire, employed a divining rod man, who walked over the ground and stated water would be found at a few feet beneath the surface over a certain area which he pointed out. I was afterwards consulted, and having inspected the site, and made some calculations, informed Mr. Palmer that no water would be met with until the plane of saturation in the chalk was reached, which at the locality mentioned would be about 300 feet from the surface of the ground. Mr. Palmer then decided to have a well dug, six feet in diameter, which was carried out by a man I know very well, and who supplied me with all particulars, and no water was found until the plane of saturation in the chalk was reached at about the depth I stated. This well was sunk in 1892.

To mention a more recent case, last June, the owner of "The Hollies," Burghfield, near Reading, called upon me, and stated that her tenant — a General, who believed in the divining rod — had employed a well-known divining rod man, who went over the ground, and told him water would be found at about 40 feet beneath the surface. After making some calculations, I informed the owner that no water would be met with until the basement bed of the London clay was reached, which at the site of the house would be about 183 feet beneath the surface. This information was communicated to the General, who shortly afterwards called upon me, when I explained to him how I arrived at my conclusions, and that the divining rod business was absolute nonsense! I advised a boring to be made, which was completed a few days ago, and no water was met with until the waterbearing basement bed of the London clay was reached at a depth of 190 feet from the surface.

I will mention one more case to show the fallacy of the divining rod, or "dowsing fork," as it is sometimes called, but better known on the Geological Survey as the "chousing fork!"

A well-known divining rod man visited Reading a few years ago, when Mr. Walker, the waterworks manager, took him along a street, at a certain spot beneath which the Holy Brook (which used to supply the old Abbey) flows in a culvert. When they came to it, all those present watched the hazel twig, or fork, which he carried in the usual manner, and not the slightest movement occurred, although all those present, excepting the divining rod man, knew perfectly well there was running water beneath them!

In conclusion, I consider those who profess to find water by means of the divining rod, and receive money[1] for their erroneous information, ought to be prosecuted for fraud, quite as much as a fortune-teller, for deceiving her Majesty's subjects.

J. H. Blake

As Mr. Blake mentions two specific instances of failure, it was desirable to obtain information about these at first hand, so that they might be recorded with other adverse evidence. Upon enquiry, I ascertained the name of the General referred to in the foregoing letter, and wrote to him. General Buck kindly replies as follows:—

The Hollies, Burghfield, Mortimer, Berks., *October 5th*, 1896.

In reply to your letter of October 2nd, 1896, I have to inform you that Mr. Mullins, the diviner, came here and pointed out places where I should find water, but I did not sink a well at the place pointed out, as he said I should have to go down 70 or 80 feet. I subsequently consulted Mr. Blake, Government geological surveyor, who informed me that I should get no water nearer the surface than 186 feet. As a matter of fact, I had to bore 210 feet before I got a supply. No doubt I should have found water at that depth at the place pointed out by the diviner, as I was aware that if I went deep enough I should get water.

L. Buck

The dowser in this case could not have been John Mullins, who was dead, but must have been one of his sons. Mr. Blake, it will be observed, is not quite accurate in his statements as to the depth predicted by the dowser, or that at which water was actually found. This, however, is immaterial, as the well was not sunk at the place indicated by the dowser. Nevertheless, the geological evidence shows that the dowser employed was probably mistaken. It would, however, have been rash to make any such prediction in the case of a spot fixed on by John Mullins, as the Waterford experiments, the Horsham experiments, and other evidence already cited demonstrate.

With regard to the first case mentioned by Mr. Blake, that of the late Mr. W. J. Palmer, of Reading, I wrote to the address given by Mr. Blake, and received the following reply from Mr. G. W. Palmer:—

Elmhurst, Reading, *February 25th*, 1897.

In reply to your letter, I write to say you have been entirely misinformed; my experience with the divining rod has, I am glad to say, been eminently satisfactory.

Geo. Wm. Palmer

Upon explaining that the reference was to the late Mr. W. J. Palmer, I was informed that the latter had been dead some years, and no information was possessed by my correspondent as to the facts narrated by Mr. Blake. In reply to my enquiries as to any one who could give me the requisite information, Mr. G. W. Palmer's private secretary states that he has submitted my letter to Mr. Palmer, who had to leave home on account of illness, and that "he is unable to throw any light upon the matter." Whilst I do not in the least dispute Mr. Blake's statement, it will be observed that his information in this case does not appear to be first-hand. Certainly, Mr. G. W. Palmer's letter disposes of Mr. Blake's assertion in another letter which is before me, viz., "The Palmers now are no longer believers in the divining rod, but strong believers in Geology and Hydro-geology."

---

[1] The General alluded to paid a fee of £3 3s., [i.e., three guineas —Ed.] and Mr. W. J. Palmer, I believe, *considerably* more, — J. H. B.

# The Credibility Of Dowsing

The *parti-pris* [bias -Ed] with which the investigation of our subject is approached by most geologists is seen in the first sentence of Mr Blake's letter, when the question is asked, "when was it ever successful?" By this is evidently meant, "when was a dowser ever successful in discovering underground water?" Even without reference to the bulk of the evidence collected in this paper, an answer to this question is given by an experienced and practical man like the bailiff to the Merchant Venturers' estates, who remarks (No. 28, p. 50) that he "would as soon think of planting a tree with its root upwards as of digging a well for water without employing a dowser."

## Mr. C. E. DE RANCE, F.G.S.

Among English geologists who have made the question of water supply their special study, few are more qualified to speak than Mr. C. E. De Rance, Assoc. Inst. C.E., F.G.S., of the Geological Survey of England and Wales.[1] Mr. De Rance was secretary to the British Association "Underground Water Committee," and drew up the whole of their twenty annual published reports. In a letter to Mr. E. Westlake, which I am permitted to print, Mr. De Rance, like most other geologists, speaks of the divining rod as a fraud, though he thinks many of its operators are honest and deceive themselves; and adds, under date, November 16th, 1896:—

> With an experience of a quarter of a century I know of no public water supply, or first class pumping station for trade purposes, which originated with a dowser. As regards shallow wells for domestic use, sunk by local well sinkers, it is very seldom that a small supply of water cannot be got for the limited requirements, and failures are few. The dowser is in the same general condition; for a small quantity he can hardly go wrong, and one never hears of his failures in the newspapers!

How far the evidence I have presented confirms this opinion of Mr. De Rance I leave the reader to judge; certainly local well sinkers do frequently sink without finding water, as a large number of the cases I have cited prove. I wrote to Mr. De Rance, and asked him if he could supply me with a*ny facts* as to the relative success, or non-success, of a good dowser on the one hand, and a good geologist on the other, in determining the correct sites of wells for various private properties. I received the following interesting letter in reply:—

55, Stoke Road, Stoke-on-Trent, *December 15th,* 1896.

> Divining rod.—I agree with you that facts, and not belief or unbelief, should be the basis of the enquiry. But the difficulty is to get facts on both sides that are comparable. It does not follow, because a man is an eminent geologist or civil engineer, that he has studied "Hydro-geology"; the chances are that he has not. There are at the present time barely twenty underground water-experts in the British Islands, so the "personal equation" is of the greatest importance. There are probably 1,500 geologists, including geologically inclined civil and mining engineers, but twenty would be the outside who could give a reliable opinion on underground water, any more than on fossil insects, or fossil fish.
>
> It is a matter of common experience that local authorities do not know who are the underground water specialists, and call in a leading geologist, who may, or may not, respond to the call, just as some surgical experts may, or may not, advise, when asked for an opinion outside their special branch. The opinions of such geologists rest upon chance, and I should not be surprised to hear that their success, or non-success, was on all fours with that of "the dowser."
>
> Then again, as regards comparing successes, it is important to remember an underground water-expert is hardly ever called in, except a daily supply of from 100,000 to 4,000,000 gallons is required.

---

[1] See Appendix B, where Mr. De Rance's work on the Water Supply of England and Wales, London, 1882, is referred to. Mr. De Rance kindly sent me a number of press cuttings on the divining rod of older date than those I had.

## Prof. W. F. Barrett

So far as I am aware, no public or private supply of over 100,000 gallons per day has ever been advised by a "dowser," though such, of course, may be the case, unknown to me.

Underground water travels in sheets and not lines, and though underground "channels," or "courses," occur in limestones and impure limestone—like the chalk,—occasionally, they are wholly absent in other rocks; though, of course, these throw up lines of springs, where the flow of water is intercepted by faults, throwing in some impermeable material, forming a water-tight barrier. Such lines are well marked by melted hoar-frost at daybreak, on a. frosty morning.[1]

C. E. De Rance.

Mr. De Rance is doubtless right that no large *public* water-supply is due to a dowser; this is one of the special functions of the hydrogeologist, who will on scientific grounds accurately advise where to sink *deep* wells. Here I should expect the dowser would be quite useless. Mr. De Rance is, however, mistaken in thinking no water supplies of over 100,000 gallons a day (say 4,200 an hour) have ever been found by dowsers, see *e.g.*, No. 49, where 20,000, and No. 78, where 10,000 gallons *per hour* were obtained; but as a rule the supply found is not so enormous, though ample for private purposes.

It is necessary to bear in mind that there are two distinct kinds of wells, viz., *shallow wells,* sunk into a superficial permeable stratum; and *deep wells,* sunk through the superficial stratum and through an impermeable stratum beneath, until the underlying water-bearing stratum is reached. Shallow wells are often contaminated and yield as a rule moderate supplies of water; deep wells generally yield a much larger supply of pure water. Though the evidence in this paper shows that some deep wells have been successfully found by dowsers, an analysis of the whole of the cases shows that the success of the dowser evidently lies in fixing the best spot where to sink comparatively shallow wells, the average depth of the dowser's wells mentioned in this paper being a little over 40 feet, and the average supply found being sufficient for the purpose required, though insufficient for a public water supply. There is, however, abundant evidence to prove that in these wells, as a rule, the quality of the water, even in the 12 foot well (p. 94) sunk by Sir Henry Harben, is excellent for drinking purposes. The dowser, it must be remembered, is rarely employed in towns, where shallow wells are undoubtedly a source of danger.

Again, in estimating the success or failure of the dowser, it should not be forgotten that the most experienced geologists are sometimes mistaken in the advice they give as to water supply. Mr. De Rance goes so far as to say that even the opinion of leading geologists (the *result* of their opinions is probably meant) "rests upon chance." There is a well-known case of the serious and costly failure of scientific advice in well-sinking recorded in the *Encyclopcedia Britannica*, (Art. Water Supply, p. 405). This was at the deep well on Southampton Common, "which has only yielded a small supply of water, though carried 852 feet into the chalk." This well has since been sunk, by boring, to a depth of 1,317 feet, and was ultimately abandoned after the ratepayers had been put to an expense of £13.000.[2] Other cases of failure on the part of scientific experts in sinking deep wells have occurred. A French engineer congratulates himself that out of 16 deep borings he has made, only two were unsuccessful; that is, his failures were rather over 12 per cent. The writer of the work in Weale's Series already cited, an experienced hydraulic engineer, states "the non-success of these borings is worthy of remark, as illustrating the uncertainty of this class of operations." Nor do these deep wells always yield a large supply; according to the same writer, the artesian well sunk at the "Model Prison, Caledonian-road, London" to a depth of $370\frac{1}{2}$ feet only yielded 800 gallons per hour. The artesian well at Chichester is sunk and bored to a depth of 1,054 feet, but does not yield 100 gallons an hour and "the water is of a repulsive taste and smell." These, I suppose, would be cases which Mr. De Rance would

---

[1] This is an interesting observation and one to which I shall return in discussing the theory of a possible "dowsing faculty." In mining districts the melting of hoarfrost and the peculiar growth of herbage have long been known to afford some indications of the direction of mineral lodes beneath.—W. F. B.

[2] Treatise on *Well-digging and boring* in Weale's Series, 7th edition, p. 89. Mr. Westlake, F.G.S., informs me the total cost of this well was £19,600; it did yield from 2 to 5,000 gallons per hour, but this was a failure for the object intended and the well was abandoned as useless in 1882; though now used for road watering.

maintain illustrate his contention. Whether this be so or not, the significant point is that, when a failure on the part of a dowser occurs, an outcry is immediately raised and his successes are ignored; whereas similar treatment is not accorded to the engineer or geologist. This is, no doubt, inevitable, though the problem being to *obtain* a water supply, it is a matter of supreme indifference to the user whether the process by which it is obtained be rational and explicable on scientific grounds, or irrational and inexplicable.

As these sheets are passing through the press a sheaf of newspaper cuttings has reached me, containing comments on the surcharge of the Urban District Council, at Ampthill, in Bedfordshire, of the fee paid by them to the dowser.[1] The geological reasons for this surcharge are fair enough, the site being on the Oxford clay, which it is said has been bored 700 feet without finding water; albeit it appears that a fair yield of water was obtained at a moderate depth, on the site selected by Gataker; but the supply was quite inadequate for public use.[2] A similar dispute has recently arisen at Porthcawl, in Glamorganshire, which is referred to on p. 132. In both these cases I am informed that the newspaper comments are based on misleading reports. The solicitor to the Porthcawl District Council and Clerk to the Board, in answer to my enquiry writes to say that the dowsing experiment was not, as stated in the papers, a complete failure, but the quantity of water found was less than anticipated and insufficient for public purposes.

The action of the Local Government Board auditors in surcharging some District Councils for fees paid to a dowser is closely connected with the hostile, a priori, geological opinion that is now current. And rightly so, for our administrators cannot go behind the recognised and authoritative exponents of any branch of science and enquire whether their views are based on a wide, patient, and unbiassed examination of the evidence for and against the possible existence of a "dowsing faculty." It must be assumed that no competent scientific authority would unhesitatingly give an opinion on any subject without having scientific grounds for so doing. The a priori improbability of any alleged phenomena, or the difficulty of finding any immediate explanation, are grounds for demanding ample and trustworthy evidence, but are not reasons for rejecting such evidence, or science would not have accepted the aid to surgery given by the Rontgen rays —among other instances that might be cited. On the contrary, it is the received dictum of scientific investigation, as long ago pointed out by Sir John Herschel, that "The observer ... in any department of science . . . will have his eyes, as it were, opened, that they may be struck at once with any occurrence which, *according to received theories, ought not to happen*; for these are the facts which serve as clues to new discoveries,"[3]—a sentence that might well form the motto of our Society.

---

[1] One of the legal reasons given by the auditor for the surcharge was based on a decree of the High Court to the effect that " the pretence of power, whether moral, physical, or supernatural, with intent to obtain money, was sufficient to constitute an offence within the meaning of the law." Some sensible remarks on this case are to be found in one or two papers, but the bulk of the Press make merry over "the superstition," "the mediaeval ignorance," "the corporate blindness," etc., of the District Council.

[2] In justice to Mr. Gataker I append the following extract from a letter of his which appeared in the Pall Mall Gazette for July 3rd, 1897 :— "Two misstatements have appeared in the papers in relation to my work for the Ampthill Urban District Council. The first misstatement is that a boring to 700 ft. without result was made on my advice. This is not the fact. A boring to a depth of 700 ft. was, I believe, made at considerable expense, for a brewery company, long before I was consulted by the Council, and in a totally different locality to that in which I located the springs for the Council. . . . The second is that test borings were made on my advice by the Council, and that my predictions were not verified. This, again, is not the fact. At the monthly meeting of the Council held on Tuesday, June 15th, the chairman of the Council, as reported in the *Bedfordshire Mercury* of Saturday, June 19th, said: 'The Council had really tested but one of his spots (that is, the spots at which I had located springs for the Council), and there, where he said they would find a yield of 2,500 gallons, they had actually found 2,800. He contended that Mr. Gataker had been treated in a very un-English way.'

"It would be a matter of great gratification to me were the whole question investigated by some well-known scientific person, or scientific body."

Leicester Gataker.

[3] *Discourse* on *Natural Philosophy,* section 127, p. 132. The italics are mine.

## Part V
# BRIEF SURVEY OF THE EVIDENCE

To those who have had the patience to toil through the wearisome body of evidence which has so far been adduced, two things are sufficiently clear. One is, that the absurd and preposterous idea entertained by many advocates of the divining rod in the present day, as in the past, that the indications afforded by the "rod" are *infallible* for whatever special purpose it is employed, has, it need hardly be said, no foundation in fact. The other is, that the current view entertained by most men of science, especially by geologists, that there is nothing to investigate but "absolute nonsense," "a miserable superstition," "a pestilent heresy," "a bit of clever legerdemain," that dowsers "ought to be prosecuted for fraud,"—if not so absurd, is equally erroneous.

Whatever be the explanation, the evidence shows that failures in the use of the rod *for the discovery of underground springs* is a small percentage of the total number of trials *when a skilful dowser is employed*. How large the actual percentage of failure is, it is difficult to estimate. It varies undoubtedly, and very largely, with different dowsers; with some, like the late John Mullins, the number of failures seems to have been very few; with others, failure is far more frequent. This is what might be expected if there be a peculiar instinct or faculty in certain persons which is not common to all. Moreover, as an easy way of earning a living without the trouble of any education, the class of professional dowsers is sure to be recruited by a number of rogues and charlatans, and also by ignorant fools, who, because a forked twig turns in their hands, without any apparent muscular action on their part, call themselves "water experts," and, as such, demand big fees from the credulous public who employ them. Such men are pretty sure to quote in large type the first sentence of this paragraph to advertise themselves. An emphatic caution is therefore necessary in advance, to warn the public against putting the smallest faith in the puffs of a dowser, unless his work has stood the test of thorough and independent investigation.

It must not be assumed that all the professional dowsers whose careers I have endeavoured to investigate are equally satisfactory. The evidence shows that this is *not* the case; on the contrary I have grave doubts whether some of them are not self-deceived and their successes due to mere chance. What is needed is a record of every trial they have made for, say, a couple of years, and an exact statement of the results in each case; supplemented by a report from a competent geological authority, as in many districts water-bearing strata are easily reached over a wide area.

But how any reliable statistics of this kind are to be obtained I do not know. All that was possible in the present investigation was to make the range of evidence as wide and unbiassed as possible, and not exclude a single case of failure that was substantiated. This has been done, and I may add here that among other enquiries as to failures, I addressed a letter to *Notes and Queries*.[1] For many years past this useful and carefully edited journal has published a large number of letters from various correspondents on the divining rod. Accordingly I asked to be informed by letter or otherwise of any cases adverse to the pretensions of the dowser. But I did not receive either publicly or privately a single reply in the direction asked for, though fresh instances of its successful use were given by subsequent correspondents, and other similar replies were sent to my private address.[2] It must, however, be borne in mind that (especially among amateur dowsers) one is more likely to hear of success than of failure[3]; and therefore an extensive and searching enquiry is necessary before any safe induction can be drawn. This must be my apology for the tedious length of the evidence cited, and the long delay in the publication of this paper. Protracted as this enquiry has been, it does not pretend to be a final one, but only the starting point for further and more exhaustive investigation.

---

[1] *Notes and Queries,* Eighth Series, No. 248, p. 255. The case of a failure in Northumberland, quoted by an anonymous correspondent in the previous volume of *Notes and Queries,* p. 336, probably refers to the one I have given on p. 117.

[2] The *Waterworks and Investment Review* for May, 1897, contains an unsigned article on the divining rod in which reference is made to a complete failure on the part of some dowser; but no names or localities are given. I wrote to the editor to ask for these particulars, but received no reply.

[3] Of course professional dowsers give their "hits" and not their "misses" in their pamphlets, but their failures get sooner talked about for obvious reasons.

## The Credibility Of Dowsing

Two points adverse to the dowser must be noted. One is that their general idea of the distribution of underground water is absurd. As a rule, they imagine springs exist like a buried treasure, or as Mr. Holmes says "like a pot of ancient coins," located to an area of a few square inches beneath the surface of the ground : or they believe these springs to be the source of narrow underground rivers, which they profess to trace to within an inch on either side. Underground water usually exists in wide saturated areas, as is fully explained in Appendix B. Nevertheless, the evidence cited in this paper shows, as is well-known, that narrow streaks of permeable water-bearing strata,—sand, or gravel, or rock, — or water-bearing fissures, do often occur in waterless localities, so that while water may not be found in one spot, it is found in another a few feet away, see e.g., Nos. 11, 27, 42, 89, etc. I am not a geologist, and may be wrong, but it seems to me that geologists have not sufficiently recognised this fact in their discussion of the subject.

The other fact adverse to the dowser is the failure or inconclusive character of test experiments: e.g., those I have made with Stears and Rodwell, the one Professor Sollas made with Young, and those Mr. Watney made at Wimbledon with Gataker and H. W. Mullins. To this it may be replied that none of these dowsers are really in the first rank—like the late W. S. Lawrence and J. Mullins, (or Bleton of the last century); and, except Young (whose case has already been discussed) and Stears, they are all comparatively young and inexperienced. Moreover,—and this, I think, is the more cogent reply, — the conditions of the experiment did not sufficiently resemble the actual operations of the dowser in the discovery of underground springs.[1]

After all, the best test that can be applied is the result of actual trials in finding water where water had not been found before the advent of the dowser. And here the evidence is so clear that I have not the least hesitation in saying that, had I to sink a well, I should prefer to have the precise spot selected by a good dowser rather than general advice given by a geologist,—*provided* that the depth of the well did not exceed, say, 50 feet, and the quantity of water required was for a private and not for a public supply.[2] Deep wells and large water supplies should always be left to the hydro-geologist.

As a practical and commercial test, the evidence afforded by the owners and agents of landed property who have employed an expert dowser is of considerable value. In several of the letters I have received this opinion is incidentally expressed. Thus the Treasurer of the Merchant Venturers' Society, Mr. G. H. Pope, writing to me from Bristol, p. 51, says:—

> On the estates which I look after we always employ a dowser, and I do not recollect any instance of failure to find water; we never sink a well before using the rod.

The forcible opinion of the experienced bailiff to these estates (p. 37) has already been quoted. If these witnesses be considered biassed by local custom, this objection could hardly apply to an extensive Wiltshire land agent and surveyor like Mr. H. B. Napier, who writes, p. 121 : —

> I am so satisfied of the dowsers' power, that I should never dream of sinking a well without their assistance.

Or again take the opinion given on pages 65 and 96 of Mr. Harben, (now Sir Henry Harben), whose judgment as one of the directors of the New River Company and a business man of wide experience is certainly entitled to no little weight. Or the opinion of Sir Welby Gregory, Bart.,(p. 74) who states that he prefers to trust to the dowser

---

[1] If, as is asserted, dowsers can discover water running in pipes underground, the experiment ought to be capable of easy disproof or verification. This experiment I propose to try, though dowsers not being indigenous to Ireland makes the trial somewhat more difficult for me to bring about. It need hardly be pointed out that, if established, the fact adds enormously to the difficulty of whatever explanation be adopted. I am inclined to believe, in spite of the remarkable success which Bleton had in this particular experiment, that the results are due to indications unconsciously given by those who were conducting the experiment.

[2] The dowser will also, in most cases, take the risk of sinking a well on the condition that if the promised supply be not found the loss will fall on himself.

rather than to the geologist in sinking wells; or that of the Earl of Winchilsea, given on the same page. Or of Captain Grantham (p. 102) who writes:—

> I should not now think of sinking a well, when I was not sure of water, without the use of the divining rod.

Or of Mr. Clifford Gibbons (p. 67), who says:—

> The thing is altogether a mystery to me, but certainly if I were to sink another well, I should get Mullins to select the spot, as I have spent very large sums of money almost fruitlessly before I knew him.

Again, there is the opinion of a man of affairs and large landed proprietor like Mr. Christie-Miller, whose wife writes, p. 58:—

> We are unable to quote an instance of failure with the divining rod, and can therefore speak most confidently in favour of water finding by the twig. We have seven wells sunk after marking by Mullins with his rod.

An astronomer, Mr Leeson Prince, writes, p. 61, "I confess I have been converted to belief in the divining rod," and then gives his reasons, and the same opinion is expressed by others, *e.g.*, Mr. Crump says (p. 6 2), "I became a convert against my will and so did others." Mr. H. D. Skrine, D.L., states (p. 74), "I cannot resist the conclusion that it is a real gift possessed by some persons." Captain Penry Lloyd writes, (p. 169), "From a profound sceptic, I am now a firm believer in the power of the rod," and other similar expressions of opinion founded on experience might be cited, e.g., Mr. F. T. Elworthy on p. 4 .

It may be useful to contrast with the foregoing the opinion of a leading English scientific journal. In *Nature* of June 10th, 1897, the following comment appears *a propos* of the employment of a dowser at Ampthill, Bedfordshire.

> It is depressing to think that there exist not only private persons, but public bodies, who put more trust in the wild assertions of charlatans than in the matured conclusions of science. The latest instance of gullibility of this character comes from Bedfordshire. . . . The decision [of the Local Government Board auditor] will assist perhaps in reducing the number of believers in the water-diviner's art.

The editor of *Nature* will have cause to be still more depressed when he hears from the distinguished Bursar of Trinity College, Cambridge, Mr. R.T. Glazebrook, F.R.S., that his College has employed with success a dowser on one of their estates. Mr. Glazebrook kindly put me in communication with Mr. Reginald Woolley, of Lincoln, the College agent, who, in reply to my request for some particulars, writes as follows:—[1]

Minster Yard, Lincoln, *June 20th*, 1897.

> We determined to try the dowser,—who had been successful for my firm elsewhere,—before undertaking experimental boring.
>
> I met John Mullins at the Farm (Walkeringham), alone with the tenant, on May 16th, 1893. I took him to the place which would be convenient as the site of a windmill pump to supply the farmstead. He soon passed a point at which the twig turned up strongly. He estimated the spring as fairly good, and from 60 to 70 feet deep. He marked other points, but we bored only at the first. A spring was

---

[1] Owing to Mr. Woolley having been abroad for his health, his reply reached me too late for the insertion of this case in its proper place, Group IV.

# *The Credibility Of Dowsing*

found at 45 feet 9 inches, and others at about 80 feet, the depth to which we went. These springs yield an ample supply.

A point of interest is that the contractor for the boring, who was a local man quite unconnected with Mullins, stated that if the boring had been driven a few inches from the point fixed, the first spring would have been missed.[1]

Reginald Woolley.

Mr. Woolley's brother also wrote to me as follows:—

South Collingham, Newark, *June 24th*, 1897.

We have employed the late J. Mullins for other clients than Trinity College, Cambridge, with satisfactory results.

I made use of his services in Gloucestershire on Lord Leigh's estate, where he found us an excellent and invaluable spring of water.

It may interest you to know that in one spot where he indicated water, I took the twig in my own hands and went over the same spot with no result.

He then took hold of my wrists without touching the twig himself and when we together walked over the same place, the twig turned up in my hands. This was, I suppose, caused by muscular action on my part, but if so, it was certainly, as far as I was concerned, perfectly unconscious action. My mental attitude was one of neutrality!

T. Cecil S. Woolley

The fact mentioned by Mr. Woolley in the latter part of his letter is also described by others, see p. 199.

It will be noticed later on that in *the discovery of metallic veins* there also exists a considerable body of evidence in favour of the practical value of the indications afforded by the rod; evidence that stretches back from the present time to the year 1540. But when we come to the other multifarious uses to which the rod has been applied in the past, such as the finding of buried treasure, of lost property, of strayed cattle, the settlement of disputed boundaries, the tracking of criminals, and other uses in the moral world,—all of which were rampant two centuries ago,—its history will be seen to have been a very chequered one, ever apt to degenerate, as it once did, into a mischievous superstition. Even at the present day, owing to the impulse that moves the rod being apparently derived from an unseen external source, some perfectly honest dowsers will tell you they can find the difference between a bucket of spring or rain water *(e.g.,* No. 30), can discover hidden coins, buried treasure and buried objects of all kinds, can trace underground gas pipes and electric cables, find the place where you intended to hide an object, or the spot on which you have breathed, or on which a ray of light has fallen, etc.! In a few of these things the reading of natural signs, such as the disturbed surface of the ground, or of unconscious signs or thought-transference from those who knew the position of the object searched for, will explain such success as is observed; but otherwise, needless to say, failure is absolute, when chance coincidence is excluded and a rigid investigation made; proof of this will be given subsequently.

---

[1] How the contractor knew this is not stated: I do not dispute the fact, as similar statements by others abound, but the reason should in each case be given.—W.F.B.

## PART VI
## THEORETICAL CONCLUSIONS

These remarks will help to clear the ground, and enable me presently to give a brief enunciation of the provisional laws which appear to me to embrace the whole of the phenomena of the divining rod. It is, however, desirable that the reader should bear in mind that the subject before us is necessarily a most entangled one, and that the usual rough and ready explanations, given by the scoffer on the one hand and the believer on the other, are wholly inadequate from any rational point of view. Problems of considerable scientific interest appear to be involved.

(i.) Few will dispute the proposition that the motion of the forked twig is due to unconscious muscular action. When the rod is held in the manner described by Cookworthy (see Appendix C), as was the custom up to recent years, it is more or less in a *sensitive state* (p. 7), and an unintentional and almost imperceptible approach of the two hands will cause it to turn upwards. But this is not the case when the rod is held as J. Mullins used to hold it, or as many other dowsers hold it at the present day. I have tried, and asked many friends to try, to rotate the rod under these circumstances, and it is certainly most difficult to produce any motion of the twig without a very visible motion of the hands. This, however, is not all. Both with practised professional dowsers like Lawrence and J. Mullins, and with amateurs like the Rev. J. Blunt, Lady Milbanke, and others, the forked twig not only rotates, but one limb is frequently twisted completely off by the force with which it is driven round and round; see *e.g.,* Nos. 1, 4, 12, 18, 45, 53, 60, 107, 115. How is this to be explained? A good deal depends on the thickness of the twig. This varies; some dowsers use a thickish forked stick, others a much more slender one. The twig that Colonel Waring, M.P., sent me, which was the actual one he had seen thus twisted and broken in the hands of Mullins, is about as thick as a cedar pencil in the thickest part and tapers off; the exact dimensions are given in the foot-note to p. 60. Using this twig neither I, nor any muscular friends who tried, could in the least imitate the effect produced by Mullins. One side must of course be rigidly held and the other allowed to rotate, and the fists must be kept practically still. Any one can cut a forked twig and try the experiment; the only advantage of hazel is that the two limbs are more symmetrical in size, and the wood is tough. One witness states that even when the rod was held between pincers (bottom of p. 66) "the contortions still went on."

Certainly no voluntary effort, without long and laborious practice at legerdemain, could produce an effect corresponding in kind or degree to that which actually takes place in the cases cited. We may compare it, as regards the kind of motion, to the involuntary pressure exerted by the "medium" or agent, which guides the percipient in the "willing game," or the quasi thought-reader in writing down the number of a bank note,—a sub-conscious pressure that cannot be intentionally imitated by voluntary effort. And so also, in degree, the amazing force with which the twig is sometimes twisted, without apparent cause, is like the extraordinary and involuntary spasm of muscular power, which often occurs in cases of hysteria or in moments of great excitement, and which cannot be repeated at will in the ordinary state.

(ii.) There is also another curious point which cannot he disputed, for it rests not only upon the testimony of numerous credible witnesses at the present day and in England alone, but, as historical investigation has revealed, goes back to a remote period and was as noticeable with Bleton, in Dauphiny, in 1780, as with Mullins, in Wiltshire, a century later. This is the apparent transmission of the power to twist the rod from the dowser to another person whose wrist he grasps. The twig, hitherto passive, immediately begins to move in the hands of the second person, without conscious effort on his part, and in a manner he could not imitate at will; among other instances which are given, see Nos. 53, 61, 83. Here also the directive action may be analogous to the faint sub-conscious muscular pressure that is transmitted from the agent to the quasi thought-reader. In any case the phenomena described in this and the two preceding paragraphs seem worthy of more careful investigation by the trained physiologist.

(iii.) The same remark applies to another interesting characteristic of dowsing, which is as follows. A successful dowser has to "set" himself (as some term it), when he uses the rod or trusts to his sensations in dowsing. By this he means rendering himself as far as possible oblivious to the ordinary stream of sense impressions; making his

# The Credibility Of Dowsing

mind as passive, as effortless, and as much a *tabula rasa* as he can.[1] A psychical state appears to be set up, analogous to that which a good subject in the "willing game," or in telepathic experiments, is able to bring about. This is a well-known condition of automatism. Just as when the sun sinks the stars become visible, so the dark continent within us, the large unconscious background of our life, only emerges when the light of consciousness is dimmed. A good dowser is largely an automatist and the rod is a convenient form of autoscope.[2]

Further it is occasionally noticed in the so-called willing game[3] that a sense of *malaise,* a faintness and trembling, sometimes even a, more serious nervous shock, is exhibited by a successful subject (see *Proceedings* S.P.R., Vol. I., p. 57, etc.). A similar physiological disturbance is still more frequently exhibited by the dowser. For one of the curious and well-attested facts revealed in the course of this enquiry is that an obscure pathological or sensory effect, sometimes resulting in a convulsive action either of the limbs or epigastric region, is exhibited by the dowser when he is on the "scent."[4] This cannot be a stage effect, nor a traditional idea transmitted from one dowser to the other, for it crops up in all parts of Europe and will be found amongst the most illiterate dowsers, from the time of Jacques Aymar in 1692 to Bleton a century later, and is exhibited to-day by dowsers in the country districts of England. I have given historic and contemporary evidence of this in Appendix D, but the reader will have noticed how this sensory effect is referred to incidentally in some of the evidence already cited. The asserted sensations may be due to causes purely imaginary on the part of the dowser, but to what association of ideas is this widespread illusion due? It seems more probably a genuine physiological disturbance, due to a psychological cause common to the group of sub-conscious phenomena of which the divining rod is a remarkable type.[5]

(iv.) Another point that appears worthy of enquiry is, why should the rod move in the hands of some persons and not with others? In the answer to this there is, of course, involved the whole phenomena of automatism, and the general theory of autoscopes, like planchette, etc. Reliable statistics are wanting as to the number of persons in every hundred who can use the rod. Amoretti, working in Italy towards the close of the last century, states, in his *Storia della Rabdomanzia,* that he found 20 per cent, of the persons he tried had the "gift." Sementini, Professor of Chemistry in the University of Naples, who published a short treatise on the rod in 1810,[6] thinks this estimate too small, and that probably in 4 out of 5 persons the rod will move successfully: but I prefer Amoretti's estimate. The children of dowsers almost invariably can manipulate the rod; they have "caught the trick," or "inherited the instinct" from their father,—the reader will take which view he pleases: probably there is some truth in both points of view.

(v.) We have now to consider *what determines* the automatic motion of the rod; what pulls the trigger? The first point to be noticed is the *prior intention of the dowser.* As Malebranche pointed out two centuries ago, the rod moves only for that particular thing the diviner has the intention of discovering. When Jacques Aymar was in search for underground water, his rod was unaffected by the track of a criminal, or *vice versa*. And so to-day, if a mineral lode be the object of quest, a sheet of underground water may be passed over without any effect on the dowser or his

---

[1] That a partial hypnosis occurs with some dowsers is very probable. I have referred to this elsewhere.

[2] A device for recording or magnifying small or involuntary movements of the body.

[3] [THE WILLING game was so-called from selecting one person from a group who then left the room while the rest decided upon a task to be performed by that person. It could be anything from a specific movement to touching an object or finding something hidden. Upon re-entering the room, the group members concentrated on the task, 'willing' if you like, the chosen person to perform it. The game was considered successful if the task was accomplished quickly. –Ed.]

[4] The sympathetic nervous system, especially the solar plexus, appears to be the chief seat of the disturbance with the dowser, as it is also frequently asserted to be among so-called clairvoyantes in the hypnotic state.

[5] In an article published in *Light* for August 4th, 1883, p. 349, it is stated that Professor Lochman, of the University of Christiania, who is described as a distinguished physiologist. recently read a paper on the divining rod before a scientific society in Christiania, in which he stated that his scepticism on this subject had lately been overcome by the discovery that he himself could use the rod successfully. He had personally tested its indications over and over again, and was now convinced that a peculiar gift, of which he could give no explanation, was possessed by certain persons that enabled them to find underground water. He thought the phenomenon was of a *physiological* nature, an opinion with which Professor Monrad, "an eminent *confrere",* agreed. I should be grateful if any friends at Christiania could send me particulars of the foregoing report.

[6] *Pensieri e Sperimenti sulla Bachetta Divinatoria*, p. 24

rod. The object to which the dowser "sets" himself is the determining factor in the unconscious movement he imparts to the rod.

Precisely similar is the preconceived idea that *electricity* is the cause of the motion of the rod, an idea entertained by most dowsers and by others ignorant of physics. Dr. Thouvenel was the first to suggest this explanation in 1781, nor did the complete experimental disproof of his explanation, given by some distinguished physicists in Paris at the time, much affect his belief. "I strongly suspect it is the devil; but if not, it must be electricity" is still the explanation given by multitudes who encounter any phenomena outside the daily range of their somewhat limited experience. Hence it is improbable anything I can say will disturb so widely cherished and so simple a faith. Lest, however, I myself should be accused of sacrificing truth to a preconceived idea, I made some direct experiments on this very point, visiting the N.E. of Ireland for the purpose of meeting an unsophisticated amateur dowser, who, with his master, strongly held to "electricity." It is needless to detail my experiments; suffice it to say that when the dowser believed I had insulated him from the earth, the rod ceased to move; when he believed he was electrically connected with the earth, the rod promptly moved. Nevertheless, in the former case he was, unknown to himself, uninsulated and in the latter insulated. It was the dowser's idea, and not electricity, that moved the rod.

That the motion of the divining rod is determined by a fixed but sub-conscious idea is seen again and again in a historical study of our subject. The most striking example of this will be found in the precisely opposite behaviour of the rod claimed by some now, and by those who used it in the search for metals 150 years ago. Some assert when a *similar* metal to that in the vein was held in the hand, it arrested the motion of the rod; others that a similar metal held in the hand had no effect, but a *dissimilar* arrested the rod.[1] Again take the following from Dr. Mayo, F.H.S., who, in 1847, made some experiments with the divining rod when he was staying at a watering place in Russia. Four or five persons were found in whose hand the forked twig moved, though they had, presumably, never seen a divining rod before. With one of these the rod moved in the orthodox way whether he walked backwards or forwards, with others the rod reversed the direction of its motion when they walked backwards.[2] Dr. Mayo then says:—

> I tried some experiments, touching the point of the rod with a magnetic needle. I found, in the course of them, that when my man knew which way I expected the fork to move, it invariably answered my expectations; but when I had the man blindfolded, the results were uncertain and contradictory. The end of all this was, that I became certain that several of those in whose hands the divining rod moves [unconsciously] set it in motion. In walking forwards the hands are unconsciously borne towards each other; in walking backwards, the reverse is the case.[3]

A curious example of the influence of unconscious intention is to be found in Priestley's old work on *Electricity*. A distinguished scientific man, Dr. Grey, in 1736 thought he had discovered the fact that light bodies, when suspended and electrically attracted, always moved from west to east. This Grey thought was the secret of the mechanism of the heavens and he sent his results to Dr. Mortimer, the Hon. Secretary of the Royal Society. Dr.

---

[1] In a little work on the divining rod by an American engineer, Mr. Latimer, C.E., it is stated that a Mr. Sangster, of Tennessee, wrote to the author in 1870, that he had been 50 years experimenting with the rod, and added "I can tell to a certainty whether I am over any substance, either water or mineral. ... I find out by taking a sponge and saturating it with ordinary water, putting it on the top of the rod; if the substance beneath be water of the same kind, it will turn much stronger. If the rod should not turn at all, it will be some other substance, either mineral or metal. The tests are made in the same manner for metals. I put a piece of metal on the top of the rod, — iron, lead, silver, copper, etc.,—until I find one of these that will cause the rod to turn in a manner sufficiently strong;—that indicates the same metal underground." Mr. Latimer, who could also use the rod, says that after receiving this letter he made similar experiments, and arrived at the conclusion that Mr. Sangster's statements were quite correct!" I took a wet rag," he remarks on p. 81, "and fastened it on to the top of the twig or divining rod; I found the rod turned over a cistern of water, but would not turn over iron pipes. I then put a key at the end of the rod over the wet rag; now the rod at once turned over the iron pipes." Contrast this with the opposite results given by Cookworthy, etc., in Appendix C Mr. Latimer also says, "Upon insulating myself there was no motion of the rod, which proves the motion is due to electricity." Contrast Mr. Blunt's experience, given on the top of page 27, when he was insulated by thick rubber shoes.

[2] See also an example of this I have given in No. 13, p 28.

[3] Mayo, *Truths contained in Popular Superstitions*, p. 19.

# The Credibility Of Dowsing

Mortimer repeated the experiments and obtained similar results.[1] Dr. Wheeler, however, repeated with great care the experiments and showed that a preconceived notion or the desire to produce this particular movement of an electrified body, really determined its direction, unknown to the experimenter. For the movement was only produced when the body was suspended from the experimenter's hand, but *not* when it was suspended from a fixed support. It was in fact a form of *pendule explorateur*,—usually a ring suspended by a thread and thus held by the fingers in a glass; this will often strike the hour of the day or oscillate in a determined direction. The motion of the divining rod and of the *pendule* are equally due to a latent prior intention and unconscious muscular action.[2]

What then, it may be asked, remains to be investigated if this be the key to the mystery? The answer to this has already been given in the survey of evidence cited, where the success of the dowser remains to be explained. Is this merely due to his practical knowledge of the signs of underground water?

(vi.) The opinion that certain appearances on the surface of the ground do indicate the site for shallow wells,—i.e. the existence of underground water comparatively near the surface —as other appearances also indicate underground metallic veins, has long been entertained, and with more or less justice. Mr. De Rance, on p. 196, has already referred to one of these signs, and Paramelle, in his work on the Discovery of Springs, to which reference is made in Appendix B, quotes several of these traditions. In the treatise on Wells in Weale's series, 7th edition, 1877, p. 22. it is stated, as a guide to the well sinker:—

(1.) That when the grass is of a brighter colour on one part of a field than another, or when in ploughed ground the earth is of a darker hue in one place, water may be suspected below.

(2) That when gnats hover in a column at a definite height above the ground, a spring will probably be found below that spot.[3]

(3) At all times of the year a greater humidity is said to exist over the places where subterranean springs exist, and hence in the early morning or evening a denser cloud of vapour will be seen at those spots. It is said well sinkers in Northern Italy determine the site for a well by lying on the ground and looking towards the sun in the early morning; wherever the exhalation of vapour from the ground is seen to be more copious, that spot is selected.

This last appears to have been an ancient practice; the power of detecting the vapour doubtless varies with different people; moreover some appear to have an abnormal sensitiveness and it has even been supposed that they are able to perceive it by other methods than sight; see *e.g.*, the letter quoted at the end of Appendix D.

Thus also the learned Jesuit Dechales, in his *Mundus Mathematicus*, which was published in Lyons in 1674, states in Vol. II., p. 190, that a certain noble person, whom he knew, could not only find springs by the bending of a forked twig of hazel, "so surely that he could trace the whole course of the underground water; but he had also other signs, for he used to detect a vapour issuing from the earth, and by this means immediately pointed out the head of the spring." Owing to the wonderful power of discernment of this ancient amateur dowser, Dechales says:—" At first I suspected he had a compact with the devil, but when I observed no incantations nor sorcery, I suspended my judgment, as there are many things we know to be true, but cannot explain." [4]

This philosophical remark of Dechales may also be applied to the well known idiosyncracies of certain persons which afford an instructive parallel, the faintest trace of certain odours or the presence of certain animals, etc, being

---

[1] See Priestley's *Electricity*, London, 1775, p.. 60, *et seq;* also *Phil. Trans*, of the Royal Society (abridged edition), Vol. VIII., pp. 404, 405, and 418.

[2] [IS THIS idea not similar to the programming of pendulums? – Ed.]

[3] There is also a curious tradition referred to by the late Dr. Brewer, and used by Thomas Moore in one of his poems, that in Arabia the lapwing indicates the presence of an underground spring. I have not, however, been able to obtain any confirmation of this tradition. In "Lalla Rookh" Moore sings :—"Fresh as the fountain under ground,
When first 'tis by the lapwing found."
A note explains: "The *hudhud*, or lapwing, is supposed to have the power of discovering water under ground."—W.F.B.

[4] This passage translated from Dechales is the earliest account I can find of the successful use of the divining rod for the discovery of springs. (See Appendix C.) Dechales was a man of marvellous erudition, as seen by his folios on mathematical physics.

instantly detected by, and often causing extreme discomfort to, such persons, who are abnormally sensitive in one direction. Probably a divining rod held by these sensitives would be unconsciously and vigorously moved by them, in the presence of the obnoxious object, and thus reveal it, even before the sense of discomfort had risen to the level of a conscious impression.

Doubtless in all these cases the impression comes through one of the recognised channels of sense; in the same way as acute vision enables some persons to detect distant objects, invisible to others, or an acute sense of smell enables the bloodhound to trace the footsteps of a fugitive. The Zahories of Spain were credited with a miraculous sense of vision[1]: a writer in the *Quarterly Review* (Vol. II., p. 264) says, "The Zahories, by attending to indications which escape the less experienced eye, are able to give a tolerable guess of underground waters. Something similar is told of the Arabs of the desert . . . who have the faculty of discovering distant wells by signs which do not affect the senses of Europeans." The camel is said to have a similar power of discovering unseen water.

According to Professor Milne, who was for many years Professor at Tokio in Japan, and has devoted his life to a study of seismic phenomena, the faint preliminary tremors of an earthquake, detected by extraordinarily sensitive apparatus, are perceived by pheasants, geese, ponies and some other animals. Professor Milne states that "the late Professor Sekiya, of Tokio, kept pheasants in order to observe their behaviour at the time of earthquakes, with the result that he found they gave him a few seconds' warning of shocks of local origin by screaming."

In the United States dowsers are often used to find mineral oil springs and are called *oil-smellers;* though it is probable keen observation rather than a keen sense of smell is employed. So, too, in parts of Ireland I am informed that the local fishermen term the look-out man who apprises them of the approach of fish the *herring-smeller,* though I imagine in this case it is unquestionably the sense of sight, and not of smell, that is concerned.

It is possible, therefore, that the professional dowser has the power of detecting signs of underground water which escape the ordinary observer, and as this power would be trained by long practice at one employment, part of their success may fairly be taken to be due to this. But it does not cover all the ground. The supposition of Mr. Holmes that professional dowsers have a hereditary practical knowledge of the geological features which indicate the presence of subterranean springs has no support; Lawrence was a stonemason, so was Mullins, Tompkins was a farmer, Stone a drainage artizan, Stears a gas engineer, etc. The fathers of none of these were dowsers, nor did they know any of the secrets of their craft, if such exist, when they scored their early successes. Mr. Holmes, however, very justly points out that uneducated persons, as many of these dowsers are, usually imagine themselves the possessors of abnormal gifts when they find they can discern natural signs overlooked by the ordinary observer, and further they exaggerate their success by regarding the underground water, which may really extend over acres or square miles, as if it were only a few square inches in area, and located at one spot like a buried treasure. But, as already remarked, the striking successes of the dowser in finding water where none existed in adjacent wells is probably due to his discovery of fissures, or jointing, or water-bearing veins. But the same problem meets us: how is he able to discern from a superficial inspection of ground, often entirely new to him and sometimes covered with snow (No. 103), the signs which indicate these interruptions of continuity in the strata below? See *e.g.,* Nos. 57, 88, etc.

(vii.) The question then before us is whether the success of a good dowser is only due to his practical knowledge of surface water-bearing localities, indications being perceived by him that escape an ordinary observer; or to some peculiar instinct or faculty, the explanation of which involves considerations new to science. Mr. Holmes, F.G.S., writes to me to say that, "looking at the professional dowser as the possessor of an ancient practical knowledge of

---

[1] The only authentic reference in history to the Zahories which I have been able to find is in Delrio's Latin folio on Magic, published 300 years ago. In a passage which will be quoted in the subsequent historical paper, Delrio says in 1575 he met one of these Zahories in Madrid, and that the man could see underground metals, water, and buried corpses. No evidence is however adduced, but it appears to have been a long standing tradition with this tribe of Spanish gypsies, as they probably were. Delrio says the facts are "most fully received and well known," and he adds, "the Zahuris probably know veins of water from the vapours exhaled at those places morning and evening, and veins of metal from the kind of grass growing there; but treasure and corpses I consider are indicated by demons." (!) Delrio spells the word Zahuris, and says, "the redness of their eyes is particularly to be observed."

surface water-bearing beds, I should expect him to be right in detecting them 19 times out of 20 . . . but when they trust to their sensations to 'locate springs' in the water-bearing bed, they become the victims of delusion."

Four methods suggest themselves at first sight in order to test whether the pretensions of the dowser have any more solid basis than chance coincidence, or shrewdness gained from long experience at one vocation. The successful issue of any of these tests would go far to prove the dowser was not a charlatan, but the tests 1 and 3a would only show that his success might be due merely to a useful practical knowledge of water-bearing localities. The suggested tests are:—

(1) Separate and entirely independent examination by different dowsers.

(2) Blindfolding the dowser with care and taking him over the ground again; or repeating the trial on a dark night.

(3a) Geological opinion as to whether water is, or is not, likely to be found on the spots and at the depths indicated by the dowser; *i.e.*, agreement of geologist and dowser. Or, more conclusive (3b), dowser *versus* geologist,—water actually found at the spot and about the depth predicted by the dowser, in spite of geological opinion to the contrary.

(4) A well or boring made to a corresponding depth in the immediate neighbourhood of where water has been found by the dowser, but at a spot where no spring was indicated by the dowser.

All of these tests, successfully made, are to be found in the course of the evidence in the foregoing paper, *e.g.*,

Test 1 in Nos. 6; 7; 17; 23; 46; 54; 63; 70 and 135.

Test 2 in Nos. 2; 6; 17; 25; 45; 69; 73; 74.

Test 3b, in Nos. 42; 52; 58; 73; 88.

Test 4 in upwards of 50 of the cases cited.

But these tests are of very different value. Tests 1 and 2 are liable to be vitiated by sign-reading or thought-transference from the bystanders (assuming telepathy to be a *vera causa*). Test 3a is occasionally quite misleading, as the Horsham and Waterford experiments, and other cases of 3b, illustrate. The most reliable test is the last named, namely, borings in adjacent places made either before or after the advent of the dowser. The existence of such borings has chiefly influenced me in the selection of the evidence presented in this paper.

Let me, therefore, enumerate the cases where adjacent wells or borings, which yielded little or no water, had been made to at least the same depth as the successful wells or borings located by the dowser. So far as I am able to judge, 40 of these may be regarded as good evidential cases; these are:—

| | | | |
|---|---|---|---|
| *With Miscellaneous dowsers* Nos. 3a; 9; 10; 11; 17; 23(?); 24; 25; 26; 27; 28 | Total, | | 11 |
| „ *W. S. Lawrence* Nos. 42; 43; 47; 48 | | „ | 4 |
| „ *J. Mullins* Nos. 52; 55; 57; 58; 60; 62; 65; 67; 73; 75 | | „ | 10 |
| „ *H. W. Mullins* Nos. 77; 81 | | " | 2 |
| „ *W. Stone* Nos. 86; 88; 90; 91; 96 | | „ | 5 |
| „ *B. Tompkins* Nos. 99; 102; 105 | | „ | 3 |
| „ *L. Gataker* Nos. 120; 121; 122 | | „ | 3 |
| „ *Other dowsers* Nos. 130, 140 | | " | 2 |
| | | | 40 |

It is quite possible that further local or geological examination may lessen the significance of some of these cases; but on the other hand, the evidence presented is only a small portion of what might be obtained by a wider and more exhaustive enquiry. It will, I think, be admitted by every candid and careful reader that the evidence on the whole affords a strong *prima facie* case on behalf of the existence of some peculiar instinct or faculty in certain individuals, the explanation of which is not to be found in the narrow region of the dowser's conscious experience, but in the wider realm of his sub-conscious life.[1] Whether this faculty, which we may provisionally assume to exist, is so rare as it appears, whether it is hereditary, or whether it can be exalted by cultivation, are questions to be answered in the future.[2]

The explanation of the divining rod is therefore probably a complex one, and its full discussion cannot be appreciated until the reader is in possession of the historical evidence to be adduced in a subsequent paper.[3] Here it will suffice to say that doubtless a *subconscious suggestion,* of some kind, evoked in the dowser's mind, excites the reflex action to which the actual movement of the rod is due. The evidence shows that this suggestion cannot come only from a capricious idea in the dowser's own mind, but is also derived from an impression he gains from without: how far that impression is correlated to the object of his search, and if so, how much is due to practical knowledge, and how much is due to some unknown cause or unrecognised instinct, are questions which can only be solved by a careful study of ample and trustworthy evidence. Cases such as the Waterford and Horsham experiments, where special precautions were taken, and the ground was entirely new to the dowser, or some of Stone's cases, such as those on pages 104 and 105, and others, tend to exclude the idea of any information being derived from surface indications or practical knowledge, and suggest either a novel and useful instinct on the part of the dowser, or that his perception is due to some physical effect associated with underground water. The recent discovery of a new type of obscure radiation from certain bodies, such as uranium salts, and also from numerous common bodies with which we are surrounded, renders it conceivable that a radiation, to which opaque bodies are permeable, may be emitted by water and metals, which unconsciously impresses some persons. The great difficulty in the way of this, or any physical hypothesis,—a difficulty which would be insuperable but for the fact that no hypothesis can be purely physical where human automatism plays so large a part—is that which Malebranche pointed out 200 years ago, viz., that exposed running water and exposed metals ought to produce a still greater effect than those that are underground and further off, and yet the dowser appears for the most part insensible to these.

Assuming the actual motion of the rod to be caused by involuntary muscular action, a summary of the causes determining that motion, excluding of course cases of fraud or self-delusion, may, in my opinion, be given as follows:—

(1) In every case the *direction* of the motion of the rod, upwards or downwards, and probably in all cases the motion itself, will be found to arise from a suggested or preconceived, but usually latent, idea in the dowser's own mind. It is the unconscious emergence of a fixed or derived idea registered in, or made upon, the sub-conscious self.[4]

(2) In some cases (such as those already alluded to, finding coins, etc., an idea is unconsciously conveyed to the dowser's mind by almost imperceptible signs, unintentionally made by those present; or by (3).

(3) In many cases, an impression from without, derived through the ordinary channels of sensation, appears to be unconsciously made upon the dowser by faint indications associated in the dowser's mind with the particular object of his search. These indications,—usually visual, or it may be a vague diffused sensation,—would probably entirely escape the bystander: the impression that comes in through the sensory apparatus going out through the hands of the dowser without recognition or conscious effort on his part. Added to this we have the ordinary

---

[1] "The sum total of our impressions never enters into our *experience,* consciously so-called, which runs through this sum total like a tiny rill through a broad flowery mead. Yet the physical impressions which do not count are *there,* as much as those which do." Prof. W. James' *Text-book on Psychology* p. 217.

[2] It must not be assumed, let me repeat, that ability to twist the rod necessarily indicates the existence of a dowsing faculty in the operator. The motion of the rod is an outward and visible sign of an inward and psychical state due to various causes.

[3] [THIS COMPRISES the second half of the book - Ed.]

[4] An amusing illustration of the effect of suggestion in determining the motion of the rod is given by Mr. E. B. Tylor, D.C.L., F.R.S., *(Nature,* May 17th, 1883, p 58); the suggestion in this case arising purely from an association of ideas. Mr. Tylor remarks that he does not believe that the dowser fraudulently moves the rod, but that slight movements of his hands unconsciously cause the twig to turn, and he adds, "I noticed that, when I allowed my attention to stray, the rod would from time to time move in my hands in a way so lifelike that an uneducated person might well suppose the movement to be spontaneous."

observing power of the dowser, trained by years of continuous practice at one particular occupation, and constantly confirmed or corrected by the results of his previous trials.

(4) In other cases, however, an impression from without appears to be gained, *not* through the ordinary channels of sensation. Thought-transference will, I believe, be found to receive remarkable confirmation from experiments with the dowsing rod. But only here and there can this agency be even supposed in the evidence cited in this paper: it may occasionally come into play in finding hidden coins, or tracing the direction of underground pipes conveying water.[1]

(5) There appears to be evidence that a more profound stratum of our personality, glimpses of which we get elsewhere in our *Proceedings*, is associated with the dowser's art; and the latter seems to afford a further striking instance of information obtained through automatic means being often more reliable than, and beyond the reach of, that derived from conscious observation and inference.[2] The whole of the evidence cited, in my opinion, cannot be explained away merely by the practical knowledge of the dowser, nor by the explanations given in 1, 2, 3, and 4.

In some cases a peculiar pathological effect is produced upon the dowser, often strong enough to rise to the level of consciousness and even discomfort; or it may be so weak that it is not perceived, though sufficient to start the motion of the rod.[3] This effect *appears* to be associated with the object of the dowser's search, and may be merely due to nervous excitement, or a secondary result of some hitherto unsuspected impression made upon the nerve centres of certain individuals. Whether, if this latter be the case, it can be traced to an abnormal sensibility of one or other of the recognised channels of sensation, resembling the hyperaesthesia of hypnotised subjects, or is due to some more transcendental psychological condition, or, far less probably, to some physical cause, can only be conclusively ascertained by a persevering and unbiassed investigation, which this paper may perhaps help to stimulate.

---

[1] The fact that the water must be running and not stagnant (see Nos. 50. 74, etc.), suggests that hearing, or possibly a slight tremor produced by the running water, may be the means whereby the desired information is picked up by the sub-conscious or secondary self. Sir Philip Smyly, M. D., told me of a hyperaesthetic patient of his, who heard and related to him the words he had uttered in a low voice two floors below, and with closed doors between. Hearing in such cases is beyond the normal power of strained attention, as any one can prove. The most remarkable instance of the dowser's power of tracing underground water pipes, conveying running water, occurred with Bleton and will be given in the subsequent historical paper.

[2] Numerous cases of extraordinary subliminal perception are given by Mr F. W. H. Myers in his essays on the subliminal self published in our *Proceedings*. The frequent success of the dowser in forecasting the approximate *depth* of springs is remarkable (see pp. 62, 76, 109, 119, etc.); but it needs somewhat more evidence to eliminate local knowledge and chance coincidence.

[3] See Appendix D.

*Prof. W. F. Barrett*

# APPENDIX A

## The Words "Dowse" And "Dowser"

The origin and derivation of these words is at present unknown, according to all our best dictionaries.[1] I have applied to Dr. Murray, editor of the new *Oxford English Dictionary,* for the latest results of etymological investigation upon the word, and he tells me that these results are at present absolutely *nil.* The part of the dictionary containing the word, though printed, is not yet published, and I am indebted to Dr. Murray for kindly allowing me to see the proof-sheet and for liberty to make the following extract here;—

"Dowse (dauz) also *dowze, douse,*—Derivation unknown; apparently a dialect term. To use the divining or dowsing rod in search of subterraneous supplies of water or mineral veins. Hence *Dowsing* vbl. sb.; Dowser, one who uses the divining rod, or water diviner; *Dowsing* rod, the rod or twig used by dowsers. 1691. Locke *(Lower. Interest,* p. 40) 'Not of the nature of the *deusing rod* or virgula divina, able to discover mines of gold and silver.' 1838. Mrs. Bray *(Tradit. Devonsh. III.,* p. 260), 'The superstition relative to the *dowsing* or divining rod, &c.'" [A series of later examples of the use of the word follows down to 1894.]

It will be noticed that the word in a slightly altered spelling goes back to the end of the 17th century, but that no quotations are given of its use in the 18th century. Dr. Murray has asked me if I can supply any, but I cannot.[2] There is a long account of the divining rod and its manner of use in Hooson's *Miner's Dictionary* (1747), and in Pryce's great work on Cornish mines (1778), but in neither work is any mention made of the word "dowser" or "to dowse." Neither is there in Borlase's *Natural History of Cornwall* (1758,) where the divining rod or *virgula divinatoria* is referred to; neither is there in the *Gentleman's Magazine* of 1751, where there is a lengthy description of the rod; nor are the words used in the account of the divining rod in North Wales, given by Pennant in his *Tour in Wales,* 1770, nor in a similar work by Mr. Evans in 1800, nor in Emerson's account of the rod in New Hampshire (U.S.) given in 1821, nor in the lengthy and detailed paper on the rod given in the *American Journal of Science* for 1826. Moreover in the earliest English accounts of the divining rod which my investigations have recently brought to light, viz., Childrey's *Britannia Baconia, or Natural Rarities of England,* 1660, G. Platte's *Discovery of Subterranean Treasure,* 1638, and the extract from Boyle's works, 1663, to be given later on, there is no mention of the word deusing, or dowsing rod, or dowser. The use of the word *deusing rod* by Locke in 1691, is therefore remarkable and apparently unique, until we come to 1830, when the word is used freely in the *Quarterly Mining Review* of that date, Vol. I.

In the glossary of Pryce's work already mentioned, and also in the glossary to Borlase's *Cornwall* (1758) occurs the Cornish word *"dizzue,* to discover unto; to dizzue a lode is to discover or expose the good ore." Looking at Locke's " deusing rod," I thought that possibly a "dowser" might originally have been a "dizzuer" of a lode. But Dr. Murray tells me that this word *dizzue* is entirely irrelevant, and neither in sound nor sense allied to *dowse.*[3] The same remark, Dr. Murray says, applies to the well-known word "douse," which is common in Cornwall for dipping or lowering, as "douse the sail." Dr. Murray also points out that we must not make too much of Locke's spelling, since the word occurs in a single passage, and may be merely a misprint for *dousing,* which in the case of an unknown word might easily happen. Such instances are not at all uncommon. But it may also be founded in the Somerset and Devon

---

[1] The *ws* in dowse is pronounced like the same letters in *browse*. The word dowse must not be confounded with the word *douse* (pronounced to rhyme with house) which has various meanings in our language, and, according to Dr. Murray, has no etymological connexion with dowse or dowser.

[2] Since this was printed, I have found the word *josing* mentioned at the close of the 18th century by Billingsley in his *Survey of the County Somerset,* Bath, 1797; he says the miners in the Mendip Hills use the divining rod, "which they call *josing,* etc."; he goes on to speak of their complete faith in its efficacy,—a faith which is as strong among the miners in the Mendips to-day as it has been for the last 250 years. Locke's acquaintance with the word *deusing rod* may be accounted for by the fact that he was a native of Somerset and born under the shadow of the Mendips. The published copy of Locke's letter on *Lowering of Interest* in the British Museum is dated 1692, and the page on which the word "deusing rod or Virgila *(sic)* Divina " occurs is 127, not 40, as given above.

[3] An incidental evidence of the marvellous range of Dr. Murray's Dictionary is shown by the fact that this word "dizzuc" and Pryce's references thereto are all quoted in this Dictionary, as I see from the proof sheets Dr. Murray sent me when I ventured to suggest this origin of the word "dowse."

# The Credibility Of Dowsing

pronunciation, since in these dialects *ou* or *ow* is often sounded in a way that a "foreigner" might mistake for *eu* or *ew*. De Quincey and some other writers of the present century have spelt the word *jowser* or *jouser*, and we learn from the *West Somerset Wordbook*, by Mr. Fred. T. Elworthy, in which there is an interesting article on the word *Dowse*, that this is a real dialect pronunciation in some parts of the county. De Quincey's suggestion that the slang word *chouse*, to swindle, may be derived from the "jowser," regarded as a charlatan, is absurd and baseless (see CHOUSE in *Oxford English Dictionary);* but it may be responsible for the fact that (as I am informed) in the *Geological Survey of Great Britain,* the *dowsing rod* is called the *chousing-fork.*, which has certainly no local support in any dialect.

Two conjectures as to the possible etymology of the term *dowsing rod* occurred to me, but I fear they must be dismissed, as the distinguished philologists to whom I ventured to submit these conjectures regard them as valueless.[1] It may, however, be useful briefly to refer to them here, as collateral questions of interest are opened up.

It is well known that the English language was not spoken in Cornwall till the middle of the 16th century. At the close of that century, when the *virgula divina* was introduced by the German miners into Cornwall, the Celtic Cornish language was still widely used. The Cornish miners might therefore naturally call the rod by the nearest Cornish equivalent to the Latin name. In Williams' *Lexicon Cornua-Britannicum,* a dictionary of the ancient Celtic language of Cornwall, as Mr. E. Westlake first pointed out to me, the Cornish word for "Divinity, Godhead," is "*Dowses*" and Williams gives also another form, "*Dewsys.*" Pryce in his glossary of Cornish words gives "*Deuyse*" for goddess. One might conjecture, therefore, that the "divining rod" or, as some early writers called it, the "divine rod," might to the Cornish miners become the "dowses-rod" or "deuyses-rod," which would accord with Locke's "deusing-rod" in 1691.[2]

Professor Rhys, the Professor of Celtic in Oxford University, to whom this conjecture was submitted, advised that Dr. Jago (one, I believe, of the best living authorities on the Celtic Cornish language), should be consulted, though the term "dowsing rod" is not, Professor Rhys adds, in Dr. Jago's *English Cornish Dictionary.*

Accordingly I wrote to Dr. Jago and have received in reply a series of lengthy and interesting letters, of which I regret that space only allows me to give a few extracts. In his second letter to me Dr. Jago writes:—

13, Ham Street, Plymouth, *November 26th*, 1896.

> I cannot but think that the rod was looked on as a sacred instrument, hence " virgula divinatoria" for its name, and so would the Cornish in their tongue apply a term as meaning what is sacred or God-like. . . . In Cornish we have for God these forms:—Dew, Deu, . . . etc , etc., the plurals ending in various ways, as in ow, ou, etc., etc. Williams (Lex. Corn. Brit.).has for "Divinity (Godhead)" Duses,

---

[1] I have specially to thank Dr. Murray, who, though overwhelmed with his *magnum opus,* kindly took immense trouble in explaining to me the reasons for his opinion, which, of course, I do not venture to question.

[2] I had remarked in writing to Dr. Murray that though "dowses" is "divinity," and not "divining," yet the Latin *divinitas* has the double meaning of "divinity"and "divining." In his reply Dr. Murray writes fully on this point, and coming from so high a philological authority, the following extract from Dr. Murray's letter is of interest:—Oxford, November 21st, 1896."Certainly, in Latin, *divinitas* has the twofold meaning; that is the initial fact on which we have been going all along, and upon which, as I understood it, your conjecture as to *dowse* started. For it is *only because of this Latin fact* that there is, in any language *descended from* or *borrowing from Latin,* any connexion of notion between *god, godhead,* and *soothsaying.* And it is precisely *because* it is a *Latin* fact, and so far as I know, a Latin fact only, that I, as a philologist, consider it irrelevant."In Latin, *divinus* meant not only 'of or pertaining to the divus or deity,' but also 'inspired by the deity, hence 'prophetic," soothsaying.' Consequently *divinitas* meant not only divineness. divine nature, but also divine inspired-ness, prophetic character; and *divinare* to act the prophet, to 'divine.' *Divinare* became in French *deviner,* and the French word became in English *to divine;* hence English inherits *through* French, *from* Latin, an *etymological* connexion between the notions of '*divine,* godlike ' and the verb to 'divine, to guess supernaturally,' with its noun of action *divination.* To us, it is only an *etymological* connexion, for I think no one feels any connexion of idea between 'divining what a person would be at, and the 'divine nature,' any more than he feels between sealing a letter, and seal fishery. But the fact is only a *Latin* one; there is nothing analogous in Greek, in Germanic, or in Celtic; in none of these languages has the word for 'god' happened to give birth to a derivative meaning 'soothsay'; they *might,* perchance, have done so as well as Latin, but they *did not.* Now ' the illegitimate process ' of your reasoning a that you take a fact which is true of Latin only, and apply it without proof to a *Celtic* language. . . . But *this is the very thing to be proved;* and investigation shows that there is no evidence for it, that all the words connected with divination in the Celtic language are quite different and have no connexion with the word for *god* or *divine.* Thus to the philologist, the conjecture is one that lies outside the lines of scientific notice, and is for him no solution. "J A H Murray"

Dewsys, Deusys, terms nearest to Dowser, and Dowsing. . . . My own opinion is that dowsing is in its origin from the Latin Deus, through the Cornish forms duses, deusys, dewsys.

*December 5th,* 1896.

For Goddess we have in Cornish, Dues (Lex. Corn. Brit.) Deuyse (Pryce), Duwies (Welsh), Douees (Armoric). Borlase gives as Cornish "rhodl, a branch." All trees and plants are in the feminine gender in Cornish.

In a letter dated December 7th Dr. Jago sends me a long and carefully compiled list of changes in words and names of places brought about by the mingling of the ancient Cornish with English.[1] Writing again on December 14th, Dr. Jago says:—

*December 14th,* 1896.

I sent you the list of compound words to show how dewsys and rhodl, the ancient Cornish for goddess and rod may easily be changed by passing from the Cornish to the English, and for want of a better term, I call such changes "phonetic." The terms used by the Cornish miners are mostly of great antiquity, and so far as I know, the dowsing rod was in use in Cornwall long before the Cornish language became extinct. This being so, the Cornish miners must naturally have had a CORNISH name for the rod. . . .

It was not till towards the end of the reign of Henry VIII. (1509 to 1547), that English was used in any of the Cornish churches. Before this time Cornish only was known or spoken. . . . But the Cornish was so well spoken in the parish of Feok (near Falmouth), in 1640, "that the Rev. William Jackman, chaplain and vicar of Pendennis Castle, Falmouth," at the siege thereof by the parliament's army, was forced for divers years to administer the sacrament in the Cornish tongue; but, says Drew, "So late as 1650 the Cornish language was spoken in the parishes of Paul and St. Just (near Penzance), the fish-women and market-women in the former and the miners in the latter for the most part conversing in their old vernacular tongue." . . . Old Dolly Pentreath who died, aged 102, at Mousehole, near Penzance. in January, 1778, was the last known person whose mother tongue was Cornish; she could not speak English till she was a grown woman....

I am of opinion that the modern dowsing rod was with the Cornish miners, before the old Celtic tongue died out, known as the Dewsys Rhodl, and corrupted by English-speaking people into dowsing (or deusing) rod, and that it is a sacred term in origin.

Fred. W. P. Jago.

On the other hand, no evidence is forthcoming in support of this conjecture, and the highest philological authorities, such as Dr. Murray, of Oxford, and Professor Skeat, of Cambridge, to both of whom I submitted Dr. Jago's letters, are entirely opposed to the foregoing conjecture, and state that it is "not even a possible suggestion of the etymology of the word *dowsing rod.*"[2]

The other conjecture, suggested by a historical investigation of the rod, seems more plausible, but to it there are also philological objections. In the earliest references to the use of the dowsing rod, it is called (written in Latin or German) "the striking rod," and it is always spoken of as "striking" when it comes over a hidden vein of ore. Thus

---

[1] See Appendix in Jago's *English-Cornish Dictionary,* "English changes of Celtic-Cornish words," containing a long list of curious changes of Cornish into English, *e.g., Men Eglos,* the Chapel Rock, changed to "The Manacles:" rocks near Falmouth.

[2] I sent the proof-sheets of this note to Dr. Jago, who writes, "With the highest respect for the authorities you have referred to, I am still of opinion that *dowzin-rod* is only a corrupted form of *Dewsys rhodl,* the rod of the goddess; this is not more strained than the Cornish *pen-y-bal,* head of the mine, into the corrupted form 'penny ball' or *men eglos,* church rock, into manacles.'"

# The Credibility Of Dowsing

Basil Valentine, in his *Novum Testamentum* (date uncertain, assigned to 1440, probably later), speaks of the dowsing rod as the "*Furcilla, oder von der Schlag-ruthen*"; in the English translation (1657) of this alchemist's work this is given as the "Furcilla, or striking rod," and we are told "if it *strikes*," the ore is beneath. The phrase *Die Wünschel-ruthe schlägt* (the divining rod strikes) occurs continually in works of the 17th century. Beyer, in his work on mining (1749), discusses why the rod *strikes* (schlägt) with some persons and not with others. Formerly the motion of the rod was always downwards; it turned until it struck, or nearly struck, the ground; and it is still called in parts of Cornwall "the dipping rod." Now, one meaning of the word *dowse*, or *douse*, is to strike, and another, to dip; thus Professor Skeat, in his Etymological Dictionary, under "Dowse," gives "middle English (13th to 15th centuries), *duschen*, to strike; Cf. O. Dutch, *doesen*, to strike." It seemed possible, therefore— to one who is not an etymologist—that the "deusing rod" of Locke, and the "dowsing rod" of to-day, might simply be the "striking" or "dipping rod."[1] On the other hand, Dr. Murray says the two words are no more related than to "seal" a letter is to "seal" fishery. Professor Skeat writes, "That *dowse* means to strike, especially in the face, is well authenticated, so that the etymology suggested is not phonetically impossible, and this is something." But in a subsequent letter Professor Skeat says, "I did not know the *dowse* you refer to is pronounced *dows*; it makes a great difference, and to my mind completely severs it from the verb *douse*, to strike, which rhymes with *house*. To *douse* means to slap, rather than merely to strike."

Here I leave the question still in obscurity; if, as Professor Skeat remarks, "people *will have* etymologies, 'Recte si possint; si non, quocunque mode,'" then the perusal of this Appendix may be instructive.[2] [Rough translation is, "You are right if they agree, and, if not, you could be right anyway." – Ed.]

---

[1] Dr. Jago, though opposed to this derivation, tells me that in Cornwall *douse* means to dip or lower *suddenly* or forcibly; this is precisely what occurs with the dowsing rod when it "strikes" the vein or spring. The Rev. W. Jago, of Bodmin, independently suggests the same etymology as his namesake. It will be interesting to see what the *Oxford English Dictionary* has to say on the word "strike," and the history of its many meanings.

[2] It is a curious coincidence that one George Dowsing, a schoolmaster of St. Faith's, near Norwich, used "magic" to find treasure in the early part of the reign of Henry VIII., (1521). A license had been given to Sir R. Curzon to search for hidden treasure in Norfolk, and the aid of George Dowsing was sought, he being considered an expert "hill-digger," as those were called who searched for minerals and buried treasure, an uncanny occupation in those days. See Dr. Jessopp's Random Roamings, p. 103. Oddly enough, one of the very earliest uses of the divining rod was in the search for hidden treasure. This superstition became the subject of one of Sheppard's Epigrams on the Virgula Divina, published in London in 1651, p. 141:

"Some sorcerers do boast they have a rod, Gathered with vows and sacrifice,
And (borne about) will strangely nod, To hidden treasure, where it lies.
Mankind is (sure) that rod divine, For to the wealthiest (ever) they incline."

# APPENDIX B

## *Geological Opinion Upon Underground Water*

The available sources of underground water depend mainly on the rainfall.[1] The rain water which sinks into the earth, or the water which has leaked from the bed of a river or lake, passes through more or less porous strata, which it gradually saturates, until it meets with a more impermeable layer: here it accumulates underground, "until by the pressure of the descending column, it is forced to find a passage through joints or fissures upwards to the surface. The points at which it issues are termed *springs*. In most districts the rocks underneath are permeated with water below a certain limit which is termed the [underground] *water level*. This line is not a strictly horizontal one, like that of the surface of a lake. Moreover, it is likely to rise and fall according as the seasons are wet or dry. In some places it lies quite near, in others far below, the surface. A well is an artificial hole dug down below the water-level, into which the water percolates. Hence, when the water-level happens to be at a small depth the wells are shallow; when at a great depth they require to be deep. Since the rocks underneath the surface vary greatly in porosity, some contain far more water than others. It often happens that, percolating along some porous bed, the subterranean water finds its way downward until it passes beneath some more impervious rock. Hindered in its progress, it accumulates in the porous bed. ... If a bore hole be sunk through the impervious bed down to the water-charged stratum below, the water will rise in the hole, or even gush out as a *jet d'eau* above ground. Wells of this kind bear the name of Artesian, from the old province of Artois in France, where they have long been in use."[2]

A spring, therefore, depends for its supply upon the extent of the underground reservoir furnished by the permeable stratum. Owing to their permeability, "the old red sandstone, the triassic sandstones, some beds of millstone grit, the jurassic limestones, the lower greensand and chalk formations constitute the more important water-bearing formations of the British Isles." [3] Rocks absorb varying quantities of water, from the oolite, which reaches up to an absorbing power of 2.2 gallons per cubic foot, down to the carboniferous limestone; one gallon of water absorbed per cubic foot corresponds to over 80 million gallons per square mile of rock for every yard of its thickness.[4]

It must not be forgotten, however, that there *is* a circulation of underground water, the direction of its flow depending on the dip of the impermeable strata, or on the direction of the faults and fissures of the rocks, which act as ducts for the underground water. Thus Dr. Ansted in his *Physical Geography* writes:—"It is certain that water must be constantly circulating through natural fissures in the earth at all depths." As Sir A. Geikie points out:—"That the water really circulates underground and passes not merely between the pores of the rocks, but in crevices and tunnels, which it has, no doubt, to a large extent opened for itself along numerous natural joints and fissures, is proved by the occasional rise of twigs, leaves, and even live fish in the shaft of an artesian well. Such evidences are particularly striking when found in districts without surface waters, and even, perhaps, with little or no rain. ... In these and similar cases it is clear the water may, and sometimes does, travel for many leagues underground away from the district where it fell." [5]

---

[1] Mainly, because from the bed of the ocean, water is continually filtering downwards. Moreover, Mr. I. Roberts, F.R.S., has shown in an admirable series of experiments *(Proc. Brit Association,* 1878, p. 397), that sea water filtering through the Bunter sandstone is, by a purely mechanical and physical process, deprived of the salts it contains, and issues as potable water; this action continues until the sandstone is saturated with saline particles, which can be washed out by fresh water. As a matter of fact, this filtration from the salt water of the Mersey is the source of fresh water in numerous wells in Liverpool, which "yield daily several million gallons of water, the yield having been continuous for years." Of late, however, the water in many of these wells had mysteriously become more and more brackish, and in some was as salt as its source. Mr. Roberts' experiments have now cleared up this mystery; the sandstone is becoming saturated with salt.
[2] Sir A. Geikie, F.R.S. "Geology," in *Encyc. Brit.,* 9th Ed., p. 269.
[3] Dr. Hull, F.R.S. Text Book of Physiography, p. 203.
[4] Report of British Association Committee 18S2, p. 237.
[5] Sir A. Geikie. "Geology," *Encyc. Britannica,* p. 270.

# The Credibility Of Dowsing

In certain districts, moreover, actual subterranean rivers exist. Thus in the limestone district of the West of Ireland, Professor Hull remarks:—"The limestone itself is often penetrated by underground rivers, which create hollows arched over by the rocks, but when these give way a chasm is created, and the commencement of a lake may be the result."[1] But prior to this, Mr. G. H. Kinahan, M.R.I.A., in his excellent *Manual of the Geology of Ireland*, published in 1878, devotes a section of his book to subterranean streams and rivers, and gives the various localities where they are to be found in Ireland. In most cases Mr. Kinahan believes the origin of these rivers to be due to "dykes of incoherent fault rock, through which the water flows as through shingle;" in other cases they are passages "dissolved out along the joints in the peculiar limestones of the district." Similar phenomena exist in Fermanagh and in the limestone districts of Derbyshire and Yorkshire, the underground river channels being dissolved out by water beneath the surface.

The "diviner" has, therefore, some reason for speaking of underground rivers; but the place in which he locates them is often where geologists assert they do *not* exist, and there is no geological evidence to show that there is anything in nature analogous to his peculiar notions of the distribution of water underground. Albeit, in justice to the dowser, the following remarks of a distinguished geologist, the late Professor Ansted may be quoted (it occurs in his *Geological Gossip*, p. 17); speaking of underground water, he remarks:—"It will exist sometimes in open cavities, and sometimes under great pressure in crevices to which the day never penetrates, and of whose position no one can guess *who is not endowed with the peculiar second-sight of the dowser.*" (The italics are mine.)

This brief notice of geological views on underground water would be incomplete without special reference to De Rance's comprehensive work on the *Water Supply of England and Wales*, published in 1882. It embodies the author's experience as one of the staff of the Geological Survey of Great Britain, and also as secretary of the B.A. Committee on underground water. The mass of statistics which Mr. De Rance has collected are arranged on a geological basis; some 215 catchment basins are given, and 985 urban sanitary districts are dealt with.[2]

The neighbourhood of London has obtained most attention from the *hydro-geologist*,—the name now applied to experts in this special branch of applied science. The principal works on this are Prestwich's *Water-bearing Strata around London*, 1851, and Lucas' *Horizontal Wells for Supplying London*, 1874; important papers on "Water Systems," by the latter author, will be found in the *Proceedings* of the Institute of Civil Engineers, and also of the Institute of Surveyors, from 1877 to 1880. The ordinary reader will find in the second chapter of Huxley's *Physiography* an admirable account of the origin of springs, with especial reference to the London basin.[3]

In connexion with the subject of underground water, I wish in conclusion to draw special attention to the remarkable treatise by M. l'Abbé Paramelle, called "*L'art de découvrir les sources.*" This bulky volume was first published in Paris in the year 1827, several editions have been issued, the last appearing in 1896. Paramelle, so far as I know, was the first *hydro-geologist*, and the first, I believe, to use that term. His book is the result of a careful study of the geological conditions which determine the presence or absence of water-bearing strata, more especially of the district in which he lived,—the Department of Lot, in the south-west of France. So successful was Paramelle in his prognostications that he was appointed the official "Hydroscopist" to the Department. Towards the close of his book a series of documents are quoted from the Prefecture of the Department, these being the official records of

---

[1] Dr. Hull. Physical Geography of Ireland, p. 234.

[2] As Mr. De Rance has pointed out, the sea bottom near coasts can also yield fresh water,—for the sea bottom, like the land, consists of permeable and impermeable strata; the former receive the water from the land, which travels down the line of dip, and issues as fresh water springs beneath the floor of the sea,—when intercepted by faults or penetrated by well-borings. An instance of the latter is seen at Spithead Forts, where a well sunk beneath the sea bed supplies sufficient fresh water for the large garrison stationed there.

[3] Those interested in the subject of underground water should consult Daubrée's *Les Eaux Souterraines,* or any standard work on geology or physiography. Much information will also be found in the series of reports presented to the British Association by the Committee on Underground Waters from 1875 to 1894. For the non-scientific reader I have met with nothing so admirable on this subject as a little book by Professor Ansted, M.A., F.R.S., called *Lectures on the Application of Geology to the Arts and Manufactures:* the second lecture is devoted to an exposition of Springs and Water Supply. Prof. Ansted also published a paper on *Subterranean Water Storage* in the Journal of the Royal Agricultural Society for 1866. A chronological list of works referring to underground water (England and Wales) is given by Mr. W. Whitaker in the *Proceedings* of the British Association for 1895 and 1897; in all, 695 works are cited, ranging from the years 1656 to 1895.

his work in that immediate neighbourhood. The last document, dated February 1st, 1843, certifies that out of 338 wells sunk at places indicated by Paramelle, 305 continued to yield an abundant and excellent supply of water, which in all cases was found at the depth which the Abbé had predicted. M. le préfet du Lot, writing to the prefect of Versailles, remarks:—

> Aujourd'hui l'expérience a confirmé la realité du pouvoir de M. l'Abbé Paramelle pour découvrir les sources: les faits sont tellement nombreux, tellement accumulés que le doute n'est plus permis. On évalue a pres de six mille le nombre des sources découvertes par ce savant hydroscope dans plus de trente départements. . . . On ne peut porter à moins de quatre ou cinq millions [francs] la valeur des sources déjà mises au jour d'aprés les avis de M. l'Abbé Paramelle.[1]
>
> [Translation: "Experience today confirmed the reality of the power of the Abbe Paramelle to discover the sources (wells): the facts are so numerous, so accumulated that doubt is no longer allowed. It is estimated that the number of sources discovered by this scientist hydroscopist in over thirty departments is nearly six thousand…The value of these can not be less than four or five million (francs)" Ed.]

Though Paramelle professed to be guided solely by scientific reasoning in his discovery of underground water, yet his manner in locating the site for a well was more like intuition than scientific deduction, and strongly reminds one of the ordinary dowser. It is possible that if the faculty claimed by the latter really exists, Paramelle may unconsciously have possessed it. Be that as it may, his book, from the early date at which it appeared, seems to deserve a wider recognition in England than it has received.

---

[1] Quoted in an article on Paramelle, published in the *Journal d'Agriculture pratique,* Avril, 1845, p. 459.

# APPENDIX C

## *How The Rod is Held*

A writer in the *Gentleman's Magazine* for 1751, p. 507, gives a description of the method he had found best for holding the rod, and says, "after numerous experiments he has good reason to believe the effects of the divining rod to be more than imagination," remarking that he believes all persons could use the rod, though "some have the virtue intermittently."[1] He uses either a forked hazel twig or two straight twigs tied together in the shape of an X, and continues:—

> "The most convenient and handy method of holding the rod is with the palms of the hands turned upwards, and the two ends of the rod coming outwards; the palms should be held horizontally as nearly as possible, the part of the rod in the hand ought to be straight, and not bent backwards or forward. The upper part of the arm should be kept pretty close to the sides, and the elbows resting on them; the lower part of the arm making nearly a right angle with the upper, though rather a little more acute. The rod ought to be so held, that in its working the sides may move clear of the little fingers. The position of the rod when properly held is much like the figure annexed (Fig. 1.) where the distance between the four downward lines is the part that is supposed to be held in the hands.

FIG. 1.

The best manner of carrying the rod is with the end prolaided (sic) in an angle of about 80 degrees from the horizon, as by this method of carrying it the repulsion is more plainly perceived than if it was held perpendicularly. But after all the directions that can be given, the adroit use of it can only be attained by practice and attention. It is necessary that the grasp should be steady, for if, when the rod is going, there be the least succussion or counteraction in the hands, though ever so small, it will greatly impair and generally totally prevent its activity, which is not to be done by the mere strength of the grasp, for, provided this be steady, no strength can stop it.

It is interesting to note that the foregoing description of the way of holding the rod closely resembles that given by Agricola, in his famous folio, *De Re Metallica*, published in Basle in 1546. Agricola's work is the earliest detailed account we have of the use of the *Virgula divina*, and refers, of course, only to its use in finding mineral lodes. In like manner the learned Jesuit Dechales, in his great work *Mundus Mathematicus*, Lugduni, 1674, Vol. II., p. 190, gives a similar description of the way the rod is held. The following is a translation of the passage, which is of great interest, as it is the earliest reference I can find to the successful use of the rod in finding underground water (the emphasis is mine):—

---

[1] The writer in the *Gentleman's Magazine* does not give his name; the Editor calls him an "ingenious gentleman, who has revived with great success the use of the rod." There can be little doubt, however, from internal evidence, that the writer was William Cookworthy, of Plymouth, who, in the obituary notice published of him in 1780, is described " as an eminent Minister of the people called Quakers, and one of the greatest chemists this nation has ever produced." This latter statement is of course merely local colour; Cookworthy was, however, a notable, learned, and high-minded man; to him is due the discovery of the existence of china-clay in Cornwall, a discovery which has so largely enriched that part of England.

> They hold it [a forked branch of hazel] with both fists, in such a way that the outer part of the fists turns downwards, i.e., the two little fingers face each other. Thus each branch being grasped firmly in each fist, they walk to and fro. . . . When they come perpendicularly over underground water, the branch, however strongly it is held, turns upside down; that is, the vertex points downwards, so that the forked sides are twisted; but it does not succeed with all persons. . . . Once on a certain occasion I purposely hid some money in the earth, which was found by a certain noble person by the hazel twig in my presence. The same person used to find springs so surely that he would trace the whole course of underground water.

One of the earliest *English* references to the use of the rod for finding underground water, is contained in the article before quoted from *the Gentleman's Magazine of* 1751 : the writer says, "The hazel, willow, and elm are all attracted by springs of water; some persons have the virtue intermittently, &c."

A detailed account of the manner of holding the divining rod is also given by Pryce in his *Mineralogia Cornubiensis*, p. 118. The date of this folio is 1778. Pryce, or rather, again, Cookworthy, who, we are told, wrote this part of the work, says:—

> "It is very difficult to describe the manner of holding and using the rod: it ought to be held in the hands, in the position shown, the smaller ends lying flat or parallel to the horizon, and the upper part in an elevation not perpendicular to it, but 70 degrees, as shown (Fig. 2).

> "Alonzo Barba directs the rod to be fixed across the head of a walking stick in the form of a T, and the end which is nearest the root will dip or incline to the mineral ore.[1]

Fig. 2.

> "The rod should be firmly and steadily grasped; for if, when it hath begun to be attracted, there be the least imaginable jerk, or opposition to its attraction, it will not move any more, till the hands are

---

[1] I can find no mention of this in Alonzo Barba's interesting old Spanish work on mining called *Arte de los Metales,* Madrid, 1639. I am greatly indebted to the ever ready and kind help of my friend and colleague, Professor J. P. O'Reilly, Foreign Secretary of the Royal Irish Academy, for examining on my behalf this and other Spanish works to which I have had occasion to refer in the preparation of this monograph. There is a reference to a T shaped extemporised rod in a book by Gabriel Plattes, called *The Discovery of Subterranean Treasure,* viz., of *All Manner of Mines and Minerals,* London, 1638. This is the earliest English reference to the use of the divining rod for finding mineral veins which I have been able to find.—W.F.B.

## *The Credibility Of Dowsing*

opened and a fresh grasp taken. The stronger the grasp the livelier the rod moves, provided the grasp be steady, and of an equal strength.

"A little practice by a person in earnest about it will soon give him the necessary adroitness in the use of this instrument : but it must be particularly observed that, as our animal spirits are necessary to this process, so a man ought to hold the rod with the same indifference and inattention to, or reasoning about it or its effects, as he holds a fishing rod or a walking stick; for if the mind be occupied by doubts, reasoning, or any other operation that engages the animal spirits, it will divert their powers from being exerted in this process, in which their instrumentality is absolutely necessary; from hence it is that the rod constantly answers in the hands of peasants, women, and children, who hold it simply without puzzling their minds with doubts or reasonings. Whatever may be thought of this observation, it is a very just one, and of great consequence in the practice of the rod.

The remark in the last paragraph is interesting, and Cookworthy's observation is confirmed by the quite independent testimony of others. Thus the German writer, Beyer, makes a similar observation on the divining rod in Chapter 12 of his folio on Mining, published in 1749. If the dowsing faculty be some intuitive sub-conscious sense perception, possessed by certain individuals, of which the rod is the outward and visible sign, we should expect to find "doubts or reasonings" fatal to the successful use of the rod, as they would be in the case of any other autoscope.

Cookworthy then goes on to describe how the motion of the rod may be stopped by various objects held in the hand or put under the arm. In other writings of his, he tells us that "a piece of the same matter with the attracting body, held in the hand, or applied to any part of the rod, prevents its attraction. Its attraction to springs of water is prevented by spitting on the hands or moistening them with water." Thus, he explains, the diviner can discover whether it be metal or water, or what kind of metal is indicated.[1] This is another of the numerous illustrations with which the history of the divining rod abounds, of the effect of *suggestion* on the motion, or arrest of motion, of the rod. For in 1663, exactly the opposite effect is assigned by no less an authority than Robert Boyle, who in his Philosophical Essays states that he has been informed "the wand will bow more strongly" when a piece of the similar metal to that underground is held in the hand.[2] See also the letter quoted in the foot-note to p. 201.

I have already referred (p. 12) to the excellent picture by A. Crowquill, of a dowser at work, given in Mr. Phippen's *brochure* on the rod, published in 1853. Here also the arms are held tightly to the sides of the body, but the prongs of the fork pass between the index and next finger of each hand.[3] Miss Cox in her paper on the rod, shows Stokes, the dowser, holding the rod pointing downwards with the prongs grasped by the fists. (See Fig. 3).

---

[1] So also the writer of *La Verge de Jacob*, a little work on the rod, published at Lyons in 1693, states that a wet rag will stop the rod when it turns for underground water, but not when it is turning for metallic ore; similar assertions are made to-day by Tompkins and other dowsers, so this belief is wide-spread and long lived!

[2] Vol. I., p. 172, in the complete edition of Boyle's *Philosophical Works:* the whole passage will be given in the historical part of my paper.

[3] I had intended quoting the careful description Mr. Phippen gives of the way the rod is held, but it is hardly necessary, as it closely resembles that already given.

Fig. 3.

The late J. Mullins, however, whose success as a dowser was the most remarkable in modern times, always held the rod as shown in Fig. 4.

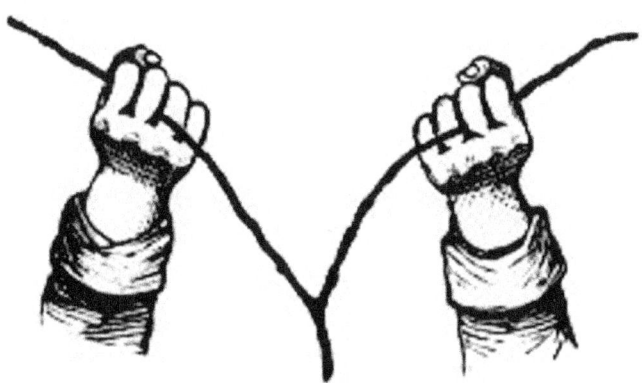

Fig. 4.

This is much the same way as Tompkins is shown holding the rod on pp. 120 and 130; this might indeed be expected, from the narrative given on p. 119. On the other hand, W. Stone, who is also a successful dowser, is seen on p. 109 to be holding the rod in quite another manner. Again, in the *American Journal of Science* (Silliman's Journal) for 1826, p. 201, in the course of a lengthy article on the rod, a picture is given showing how the rod must be held, and here the prongs of the fork pass between the thumb and forefinger of each hand. Messrs. Young and Robertson, in their little book on the divining rod, mentioned on p. 12, give illustrations showing their way of holding the rod: they have sent me a little waistcoat-pocket forked rod made of aluminium, which they recommend to be held in the way shown in Fig. 5. They also use a straight rod or wand some three or four feet long, which they hold inclined in the right hand, the thinner end

# The Credibility Of Dowsing

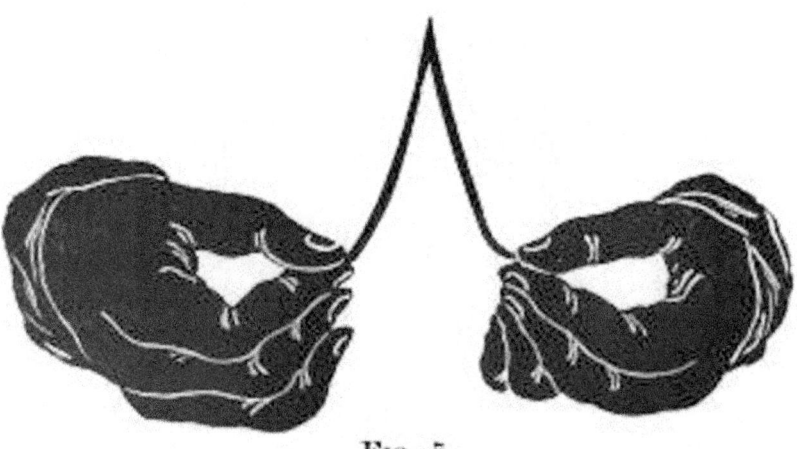

FIG. 5.

being held in the hand and "the eye resting on the top of the thick end." This, they assert, dips down over an underground spring. This "dipping rod " is a return to an old form of divining rod, a picture of which is given in an Italian work on the rod, published in 1678, and will be reproduced in the subsequent historical part of this paper. The Abbé de Vallemont gives pictures of straight rods in his *La Physique Occulte*, published in 1693; and Bleton, as already mentioned (p. 14), in the last century used a nearly straight rod placed horizontally on the index fingers of the two hands. This slightly-curved rod revolved from 30 to 80 times a minute when Bleton came over underground water. Here (Fig. 6.) are some other ways of holding the rod in use in the 17th century.[1]

FIG. 6.

---

[1] I am indebted to the editor of *Pearson's Magazine* for this woodcut. Though not stated the picture is a copy of one of the plates in Lebrun's *Lettres . . sur la baguette*, 1693. Aymar sometimes used a straight rod held in one hand.

## *Prof. W. F. Barrett*

It will thus be evident that the manner of holding the rod varies with the individual dowser, and obviously cannot be of much consequence. Some positions in which the rod is held doubtless render it a more sensitive indicator to the muscular tremor which determines its motion. It may be held in a position of tension or poised equilibrium (as mentioned on p. 7), and it then becomes a very sensitive *autoscope;* in this position it is desirable some experiments on thought-transference should he made with the holder of the rod.

# APPENDIX D

## *The Sensations Alleged To Occur In Dowsing*

The assertion is made by numerous dowsers that when they are over underground water they experience a peculiar sensation,—which some describe as felt in the limbs, like the tingling produced by a mild electric shock, others as a shivering or trembling, and others as an unpleasant sensation in the epigastric region, etc. It is unnecessary to quote the various statements made by different dowsers, quite independently of each other. But these sensations seem to be only experienced when they are dowsing; when off duty, underground water seems to have no effect. This fact, coupled with the apparent absence of any feeling produced by the much greater masses of visible water in lakes, rivers, or the sea, indicate the purely psychological origin of the asserted sensations. The interesting point is, however, that this psycho-physiological disturbance in the use of the divining rod can be traced back at least two centuries, and exists among diviners in different countries.[1]

Among the most remarkable symptoms were those exhibited by the French dowser, Bleton, in the last century. A careful medical examination of Bleton was made by Dr. Thouvenel, who was a distinguished French physician, and in his *Mémoire Physique et Medicinal,* Paris, 1781, page 53, he describes these symptoms as follows:—

> La première impression que fait éprouver au corps de Bleton la presence de l'eau souterraine, se porte sur le diaphragme, en s'étendant vers ses appendices supérieurs ou ses attaches avec le sternum, et produisant un serrement avec de l'oppression, dont le siège paroît borné à la partie antérieure et supérieure de la poitrine. Un saisissement, un tremblement et un refroidissement général s'emparent en même-tems de lui. Ses jambes chancellent. Les tendons des poignets se roidissent et entrent en convulsion. Le pouls se concentre et diminue peu-à-peu. En un mot, cet état représente et caractérise l'invasion d' une véritable attaque de spasme convulsif. Il subsiste, avec des nuances cependant et des variations du plus au moins, tant que cet homme reste sur la source, et disparoît presque subitement lorsqu' il se place à côté si ce n'est, à ce qu'il dit, un sentiment intérieur de froid et de serrement légers, au devant de la poitrine. Ce sentiment ne cesse totalement qu'à une certaine distance de l'eau; et cette distance exprime selon lui la profondeur de cette dernière, comme nous le verrons ci-après."

> [Trans. "Bleton, on first approaching underground water is affected first in his diaphragm, extending into his chest. There is a shock and a general cooling which affect him at the same time. Wrist tendons stiffen and convulse and the pulse decreases. This state is characterized by convulsive spasms which remain as long as he is over the underground source and disappear when removed from it. He feels cold and as if his chest is being squeezed. This feeling ceases completely at a certain distance from the water, and this distance on the ground is converted to the depth of the water." Ed.]

Dr. Thouvenel states Bleton did not feel any effect from stagnant water; a headache and lassitude were, however, produced by a river, when in a boat, "mais point du tout ce qu'il appelle sa *commotion* dans la poitrine, ni le contre-coup de cette commotion dans les extrémités." [Trans. "…but not at all what he calls his concussion in the chest, or the *commotion* in his extremities." Ed.]

It is said that when Bleton was a child, the discovery of his "gift" was accidentally made from perceiving that a feverish attack seized him whenever he happened to be at a certain spot where a subterranean, spring was subsequently discovered. In one of the numerous *pièces justificatives* and *procès-verbaux* attached to Thouvenel's book,

---

[1] That nervous excitement is partly at the root of these sensations seems to be indicated by the case of Jacques Aymar. In a copy of the *Journal des Sçavans* (Savants) for January 1693, for the possession of which I am indebted to the zeal of Mr. Holland's excellent book agency in Paris, it is stated by a contemporary witness, Dr. Chauvin, that when Aymar, who had gained repute as a spring finder, was taken with his *baguette* into the cellar where the Lyons murder had been committed, Aymar "n'y fut pas plutôt entré qu'il se sentit tout ému, et que son poux s'eleva comme une grosse fievre." [Trans. 'He no sooner entered the room than he was affected and acted like he had a fever.'- Ed] )

the following evidence is cited. The writer of the certificate, after stating that numerous persons in Burgundy can testify that Bleton is neither an impostor nor a charlatan, goes on to say:—

> C'est un pauvre paysan qui a été élevé par charité dans une des Chartreuses de Dauphiné, et voici comment ce talent, si c'en est un, lui a été connu.
>
> A l'âge de sept ans, portant le diner à des ouvriers, il s'assit sur une pierre, où la fièvre le prit: les ouvriers l'ayant fait mettre à coté d'eux, la fièvre cessa; il retourne à plusieurs reprises sur la pierre, toujours la fièvre. On raconta cette histoire au Prieur de la dite Chartreuse, qui voulut par lui-meme en voir l'expérience. Convaincu par le fait, il fit creuser sous la pierre; il s'y trouva une source qui, à ce que l'on m'a assuré, fait moudre aujourd'hui un moulin.[1]
>
> [Trans. "He was a poor farmer, raised on charity in Chartreuses Dauphiné, and that's how this talent, if it is one, came. When he was seven years old, taking dinner to the workers, he sat on a stone and the fever took him. Removed from it, the fever ceased. He returned to the stone several times, always he had the fever. We told this story to the Prior of Chartreuse, who wished to see the experiment for himself. Convinced by it, he dug under the stone; where he found a spring which, I am assured, is now a grinding mill." Ed.]

Several witnesses of high standing are cited by Dr. Thouvenel, who testify to the pathological effect which underground water had upon Bleton; the curious point being that Bleton's prognostications were so rarely wrong, water being found, according to the evidence, even in the most unpromising places when Bleton was affected in this manner. M. le President d' O____ , who made numerous experiments with Bleton, relates that, a generation before Bleton, in 1735, another *sourcier*, or water finder, had said when there was a difficulty in finding him a proper rod or *baguette*:—

> N'importe, Monsieur, ce n'est pas la baguette qui me dirige, c'est un sentiment que j'éprouve au dedans de moi-même.
>
> [Trans. "Never mind, sir. It isn't the wand that directs me, but the feeling inside myself." Ed.]

On p. 263, Dr. Thouvenel gives an account of a visit paid by M. C____ to a Prior at Autun who possessed the "gift" of water-finding, which he had gratuitously exercised for the benefit of his commune.

The Prior states that he detected an underground spring by a peculiar *malaise* it produced upon him, which was more marked in following the spring upwards than downwards. He stated a shivering was produced in his shoulders and muscles of the arm and leg, and if he continued following an underground spring, extreme and abnormal fatigue was produced; the sensation was stronger after fasting than after meals.

Dr. Thouvenel also refers to Parangue, a young girl, born in 1760, who from her infancy appeared to have the faculty of detecting underground water by the terror she displayed when over an underground spring. According to the Abbé Sauri, Parangue apparently *saw* the water below, "the earth becoming transparent to her vision." A similar case is related by Dr. Ashburner of a girl who, when hypnotised, declared she "saw" a spring at a certain depth below a certain spot; upon digging, a spring was found at the spot and at the very depth stated.[2] But these

---

[1] *Memoire physique et médicinal*, etc. (Paris, 1781), p. 251.

[2] The incident as related by Dr. Ashburner is as follows: A respectable girl, a lady's maid, was found to pass into a mesmeric sleep on holding for a few seconds a hazel twig; when asleep the twig was so tightly held that in spite of using much force, a bystander could hardly turn it. Her mistress wrote in July, 1845, "We made a curious experiment with Harriet. We have very bad water here and have long been unable to find a good spring. Mr. G. has dug and dug in vain. I proposed the divining rod; Harriet was willing, so we went to a field . . . put Harriet to sleep, with the hazel stick. She grasped it so tightly we were obliged to use the gold chain. She then held it only in one hand and began to walk very carefully for about 20 yards, then suddenly stopped; not a word was uttered, we all looked on, and were not a little surprised to see

# The Credibility Of Dowsing

cases of clairvoyance obviously need confirmation and critical examination; the same may be said of the following. In an article on *Modern Magic* by M. Shele de Vere, published in 1873, it is stated that Catherine Beutler, of Thurgovia in Switzerland, and Anna Maria Briegger, of the same place, were both so seriously affected by the presence of water that they fell into violent nervous excitement and became quite exhausted when they happened to cross places where water was concealed underground.

We have also the evidence of Dr. Mayo, F.R.S., who states in his essay on the divining rod[1] that when in Russia he met with a youth who had not handled a divining rod before. Instructing him how to hold the rod and to walk over some ground where Dr. Mayo believed underground water to exist, the forked twig instantly began to ascend. Dr. Mayo goes on to say that the lad

> Laughed with astonishment at the event, which was totally unexpected by him, and he said that he experienced a tickling or thrilling sensation in his hands... The experiment was repeated by him in my presence with like success several times during the ensuing month. Then the lad fell into ill health and I rarely saw him. However, one day I begged him to make another trial with the divining fork. He did so, but the instrument moved sluggishly and when it moved .... the lad said he felt an uneasy sensation, which quickly increased to pain at the pit of the stomach, and he became alarmed.

This, doubtless, was a purely nervous effect, but the coincidence is curious, as Dr. Mayo seems to have been wholly ignorant of Thouvenel's experiments with Bleton, and of course the Russian lad knew nothing about them.

On the other hand, the profound effect of *suggestion* in producing or arresting pathological disturbance comes out very clearly in Thouvenel's experiments. Believing that the motion of the divining rod was due to some unknown electric agency, Thouvenel experimented upon Bleton with what he calls "electric compositions," and also "compositions magnetiques récemment électrifées." [Trans. "magnetic compositions recently electrified" Ed] When Bleton was over underground water, if he were touched with one of these compositions, the usual symptoms and the rotation of the rod were instantly diminished by three-fourths, and (p. 91)—

> Dès l'instant même que le retirois mes préparations, les phénomènes de l'eau sur Bleton réparoissoient dans toute leur force.
>
> [Trans. "The moment I ceased my preparations, Bleton's reactions returned in full force." Ed.]

Now it is absurd to suppose any physical effect could have been produced upon Bleton by these compositions, which were probably bits of sulphur or of iron that had been sparked upon by an electric machine; the result was undoubtedly an effect of sub-conscious and possibly telepathic suggestion. The latter (telepathy) seems indicated also in the subsequent experiments with Bleton to test the effect of insulation, for Thouvenel appears to have taken the precaution not to let Bleton know the fact nor the object of the experiment.

Coming to the present day, an old amateur dowser, Mr. Robert Young, of Sturminster Newton, Dorset, writes to say that whenever he comes over an underground spring, so violent a trembling seizes him that he has to be supported or he would fall. Mr. Young, I am assured, is entirely ignorant of the literature of this subject, so that he has not been affected by what others have said. His daughter writes:—

> One day I asked father to point out to me the spring in Gough's close; he walked to and fro, and when he came to a certain spot he reeled and staggered and said the spring was below. To test the

the rod slowly turn round until her hand was almost twisted backwards. Suddenly she exclaimed 'There, there, don't you see the stick turn? The water is here, under my hand. I see it, I see it.' 'How deep is the water?' said Mrs. G. 'Oh, about 3 feet.' We marked the place, and after a few moments awoke her. Mr. G. caused a large hole to be dug and just at the depth of 3 feet the water was found. A brick well has been constructed and we have now a good supply of excellent water. When awake Harriet knew nothing of the circumstance."—Note added by Dr. Ashburner to his translation of *Reichenbach's Researches (London,* 1851), pages 100-103.

[1] Truths contained in Popular Superstitions, (London, 1856) p. 18.

reality of his indications, I privately marked the spot where he said the spring was. I then took him to the far end of the field and blindfolded him carefully, then led him about the field by a circuitous route. Directly he came on the spot I had marked, he reeled as before and would have fallen if I had not held him up. Directly he came off the place he was all right.

As perhaps might be expected, the son of Mr. R. Young, Mr. J. F. Young of Llanelly, (also an amateur dowser) feels somewhat similar sensations when he is dowsing. I have already referred to Mr. Young in the foot-note to p. 13; though a hard-working tradesman with little time at his disposal, Mr. Young has devoted his leisure to an investigation of the rod, and I may add, the extensive correspondence Mr. Young has had with me has impressed me with his sincere love of truth. Mr. Young writes:—

> I have noticed, when divining, unpleasant and peculiar symptoms always occur when I am over an underground spring; often a convulsive feeling and staggering comes on. My father, though never otherwise sick, staggers and vomits when over a spring. These unpleasant symptoms only occur when we are "set" on divining."

Writing to me again on November 29th, 1896, Mr. J. F. Young says:—

> The sensation I experience when I get over a spring in divining is very like that experienced at the epigastrium when on the downward stroke of a swing, together with a peculiar tingling of the fingers. There is no mistaking this and I have also seen the fingers of Mr. Robertson [a friend of Mr. Young's, also an amateur dowser] severely contracted when he gets over a spring.

Mr. Thomas Heighway, the Welsh dowser referred to on p. 169, also sends me an account of the very similar sensations he experiences, and so with other dowsers quite independently of each other.

These symptoms may only be the result of nervous excitement, but as Bleton a century ago trusted to his "sensations" in finding water and as some dowsers still do so to-day, it would seem as if they had some psychical root deeper than mere imagination. In connection with this I will quote the following interesting letter, which has recently appeared in the columns of *Truth* (July 22nd, 1897); the writer is personally known to me, he is an F.R.S., and a distinguished London physician:—

> Although the great majority of people disbelieve in the power of a man to detect the presence of water even a few feet under the ground upon which he is standing, they readily credit the story of a camel scenting water half a mile off in the middle of a desert. I believe that the almost incredible acuteness of sight, scent, and hearing, which are found universally in certain classes of the lower animals and are not uncommon in savage races, are *occasionally* possessed by certain individuals amongst civilised races. For instance: the presence of water-vapour in the air over certain spots makes itself evident to every one as a visible fog in early morning. *Now I am acquainted with a rheumatic patient who, on passing over such a spot during the day, when no vapour is visible, feels pains in her joints.* Of course, such a condition of hyperaesthesia is very rare indeed. I think, however, that the diviner detects water by some sensation which affects either his nostrils, or his body generally, when he is standing in a place where there is water below the surface. The only use of the divining rod is to magnify involuntary muscular motions, and thus convert what might otherwise be a vague sensation into a definite and perceptible action. But the moving of the rod in a diviner's fingers depends simply upon the bodily condition of the diviner himself, just as the rigidity of a pointer's tail when scenting game depends entirely upon the excitement of the dog.

The part I have emphasized is interesting in connexion with what is stated on p. 202.

## *The Credibility Of Dowsing*

The comparison of a dowser to a pointer, though inadequate in my opinion, is quite as far as the present state of scientific knowledge will be disposed to admit. From this point of view it is a very just analogy; the wonderful scent of the dog, in its sensitiveness far beyond any instrumental means of detection which science could employ, corresponding to the dowser's "scent" for underground water; the nervous excitement of the dog, corresponding to the dowser's psycho-physiological disturbance; and the index afforded by the rigid tail of the dog when pointing, being the analogue of the involuntary motion given to the indicating rod of the dowser.[1]

---

*1* Dr. Carl du Prel, in a brief essay on *Die Wünschelruthe,* believes the explanation of the rod will be found "in the domain both of transcendental physics and transcendental psychology, the rod being the historic fore-runner of the modern practice of 'questioning the oracle' by automatic writing." But this was an ancient use of the rod, as will be seen in Zeidler's *Pantomysterium* (Magdeburg, 1700), where the prescience displayed by the rod is attributed to the spirit of nature, the *anima mundi,* "the Soul needing the rod as an instrument." Of the theories of the rod held in successive centuries by the learned world, Zeidler's was one not discordant with certain views of psychical phenomena set forth in our *Proceedings.*

# APPENDIX E

## Note On The Horsham Experiments

Since this paper was printed, Mr. E. Westlake, F.G.S., who has devoted attention to hydrogeology, has visited Sir Henry Harben's estate, Warnham Lodge, and sent me some geological notes on the Horsham Experiments, detailed on pages 94-98. These notes are interesting in connection with Mr. T. V. Holmes' remarks on pages 183-9, and also as correcting some slight inaccuracies in the statement originally given to me. Mr. Westlake went over the ground with Mr. Ogilvie, the bailiff, and with Mr. Edwards, the head gardener, (called the overseer by me), who superintended the work of the well-sinking. It seems the rock mentioned on p. 94 was not a limestone, as Sir Henry Harben thought, but a "white, fine-grained, close-jointed, compact *sandstone*" nor was it so hard as to require blasting: a sand pit some 300 feet to the west of the well G shows the same stratum. Some 3 to 4 feet of soil and sand or sandy loam covered the stone, which rests on an impervious "blue marl" (the Weald clay), the latter being found some 14 feet below the surface in the case of well D, which penetrated 5 feet into this marl. Most of the water comes from little veins in the sandstone and runs into the wells from the direction of the pond (see map, p. 94) "as Mullins had said it would." Mr. Westlake says, "The main source of the water thus appears to lie to the east of the wells, though what should confine its flow to certain lines in a tolerably pervious bed is not easy to understand, nor yet the large flow from what seems a small collecting ground. It is possible the direction of the flow may be determined by the patchy character of the bed, which is soft in certain places, as may be seen in the sand pit, and was said to be also in the wells. The depth of the water in the wells varies from 4 feet in summer to 9 or 10 feet in winter. The water is soft and good in all respects; the analyst who examined it said he had never seen a better."

An additional fact was ascertained by Mr. Westlake, which is of considerable importance in connection with Mr. Holmes' remarks. In order to run the water from the wells to the pumping house, which is on lower ground, (near well A, see p. 94), a trench was sunk to within a foot of the bottom of the wells E and F, and carried 85 yards to the north of well E; 24 yards from E an offset, 8 yards long, connects the 2 inch water pipe, which was laid in the trench, to the well D. Mr. Westlake says: "These trenches, Edwards assured me, were all dry to the bottom and no springs were intersected, except the one supplying D; at that time, October, 1893, the water in the wells E and F stood more than 6 feet deep, but it was kept down by pumping when the trench was being brought near to the wells. It was not a 'tunnel,' but a trench, subsequently arched over, 4 feet wide, that connected the bottom of the wells E and F, and here also no spring was met with in the stone between the two wells, as is stated on p. 96."

I regret that no mention is made of the length of time that elapsed before the trenches were covered in, but whether a few hours or days, it is obvious the water-bearing character of the surrounding sandstone was very different in different places, through jointing or otherwise. Even allowing for possible looseness of observation on the part of Edwards, the broad facts remain that a copious supply was found in certain spots indicated by the dowser and not in others closely adjacent. Sir Henry Harben confirms the fact that, prior to connecting the wells E and F, one of these wells was pumped "continuously while the work was proceeding, "during which the level of the water in the other well did not sink perceptibly.

Sir Henry Harben also informed Mr. Westlake that the engineer whom he consulted, and whose advice failed, was a leading water engineer of large experience. He walked over the whole ground and his attention was specially directed to the pond and to the fact that water was sometimes seen on the higher ground; but he decided to reject that locality, and the high ground generally, and fixed on the site where the well B was sunk, with adits, at a useless expenditure of £1,000. Mullins was told exactly what the engineer was told, though he did not see the pond; on trying with the "rod," he utterly scouted the place the engineer had fixed on, and decided on the higher ground.

It seems that Mullins (who is now dead) came twice; at first he "located" the wells D and E, and on the second visit the wells F and G; it was then he stated no water would be found between E and F. Having contracted for the well-sinking, his son, Joseph Mullins, carried out the work and also, it is said, independently found by the "rod" the spring at F.

# The Credibility Of Dowsing

The bed of stone in which the wells are sunk is about 100 feet above the outcrop of the Horsham Stone at Warnham (Geological Survey, sheet 8), and is the "No. 2, Sand and Sandstone" of Messrs. Topley and Drew—viz., the second of seven subordinate permeable beds that occur in the Weald Clay, of which the Horsham Stone is the first and lowest. (See Topley's *Geohgy of the Weald*, 1875, pp. 102, 104.)

Mr. Westlake suggests that one of the best tests of the claims of the dowser would be a series of experiments in connection with suitable engineering works, such, for example as a projected deep cutting for a new railway. The dowser should be taken over the ground before the cutting was begun, and his report as to the existence, the exact location, and the probable depth of any underground water that might be met with should be carefully noted. The cutting should then be watched and reported on during construction in respect of any springs, or lines of flow that might be encountered. The expense of such a test would not be great, and I think it is most desirable it should be made; two dowsers should, however, be employed, independently of each other, to examine and report beforehand.

My best thanks are due to the Editor, and to Miss A. Johnson, of Cambridge, for the careful reading of the proof-sheets of this paper, and for many valuable suggestions.

BOOK II., on the use of the divining rod in the search for Mineral Veins and for other purposes, together with the Historical Survey and a Bibliography compiled by Mr. E. Westlake, F.G.S., will not be published till next year.

## END OF BOOK I

*Prof. W. F. Barrett*

# The Credibility Of Dowsing

# Part 2

*A PSYCHO-PHYSICAL RESEARCH ON A PECULIAR FACULTY ALLEGED TO EXIST IN CERTAIN PERSONS LOCALLY KNOWN AS DOWSERS:*
*By W. F. Barrett, F.R.S., Etc.,*

*Professor of Experimental Physics in the Royal College of Science for Ireland.*

(Presented in 1899)

# BOOK II

# The Credibility Of Dowsing

## TABLE OF CONTENTS

### PART I

*Introductory* — 233

*Objects of Investigation* — 238

### PART II

*Experiments by the Author § 1. The Carrigoona Experiments* — 241

*§2. Experiments at Kingstown* — 256

### PART III

*Cases Where the Dowser Found a Good Supply of Underground Water near to a Useless Well or Boring Previously Sunk to as Great or Greater Depth:*
    e.g at—(1) Shanklin p.258; (2) Errol p.264; (3) Lytes Cary (Somerset) p.266; (4) Sherburn-in-Elmet p.267; (5) Tiddington House (Oxford) p.267; (6) Chelford (Cheshire) p.269; (7) Welwyn p.272; (8) Minting p.273; (9) Haddington p.273; (10) Aspley Heath (Bedford) p.274

### PART IV

*Experiments with Two or More Dowsers Independently Tried on the Same Ground:*
    at—(1) Cheltenham p.277; (2) Westbury-sub-Mendip p.280; (3) Thomastown p.281; (4) Claverton Manor p.283; (5) Pontyberim p.284; (6) Mayfield p.284

### PART V

*Experiments in Blindfolding the Dowser:*
    by—(1) the Author p.288; (2) Mr. Pease p.289; (3) Lord Winchilsea and others p.289; (4) Mr. Hoskyns, p.289; (5) Mr. Westlake p.291; (6) Mr. Denison p.292; (7) Dr. Thouvenel p.293; (8) Judge Spinks p.295; (9) Mr. Withnell p.295; (10) Mr. Emerson p.297

## PART VI

*Details of a Few Further Cases of Amateur Dowsers :*
(1) Sir R. Harington, Bart. P.299; (2) Mr. E. Hippisley p.301; (3) Mr. J. H. Jones p.301; (4) Mr. J. D. Enys p.302; (5) Mr. J. F. Young p.303; (6) Mr. R. G. D. Tosswill p.306; (7) Mr. G. H. Ward-Humphreys p.306; (8) Mr. G. F. Attree p.307

## PART VII

*Miscellaneous Cases :*   309
From the Rt. Hon. Sir Edward Fry, Colonel King-Harman, &c

## PART VIII

*Professional Dowsers in England and Wales and Their Probable Percentage of Failures :*
§ 1. List of Dowsers   p.315; § 2. Recent Cases of Complete or Partial Failure in Water-finding by English Dowsers p.317; § 3. Percentage of Failures p.320

## PART IX

*Continental, Colonial and Californian Cases of the Use of the Rod in the Search for Underground Water:*
§ 1. Continental Dowsers   p.322; § 2. Californian Dowsers   p.327; § 3. South African Dowsers p.329; § 4. Australian Dowsers p.330

## PART X

*Bleton, the Notable French Dowser of the Last Century*   333

## PART XI

*Involuntary Muscular Action and the Motion of the Rod, Pendule, or Other Autoscope. Motor-automatism:*
§ 1. Evidence of the Automatic and Uncontrollable Motion of the Rod p.346; § 2. Evidence of Physiologists   p.353; § 3. Consideration of Bleton's Case   p.356; § 4. Apparent Transmission of Motor Automatism p.357; § 5. Historical Note   p.358

## PART XII

*The Malaise of the Dowser and Its Origin*     363

## PART XIII

*Origin of the Stimulus That Gives Rise to the Motor-automatism of the Dowser:*
§ 1. Is it Derived through the Ordinary Channels of Sense? p.366; § 2. Is it mere Chance, or a Supernormal Perceptive Power? p.368; § 3. Is a Physical Cause Likely? p.369; § 4. Probable Explanation of Outstanding Cases. p.369; CONCLUSIONS p.373

## APPENDICES

| | |
|---|---|
| A. Report on some Cases of Water-finding by the Divining-rod, by E. Westlake, F.G.S | 374 |
| B. Note on the Geology of Somerset, by E. Westlake, F.G.S. | 391 |
| C. Use of the Rod in the Search for Mineral Lodes. | 393 |
| Mr. Westlake's Experiments in Dowsing for Minerals at Sidcot | 396 |
| D. Paramelle | 400 |
| E. Evidence of Clairvoyance in Dowsers | 404 |
| F. The Zahoris | 409 |
| G. Scientific and Literary Opinion | 414 |

---

"In the sciences, that also is looked upon as property which has been handed down or taught at the Universities. And if any one advances anything new, .... people resist with all their might; they act as if they neither heard nor could comprehend; they speak of the new view with contempt, as if it were not worth the trouble of even so much as an investigation, or a regard; and thus a new truth may wait a long time before it can make its way."

(*Conversations of Goethe with Eckermann and Soret*, translated by J. Oxenford;
Bohn's Standard Library, 1874, pp. 47-8.)

*Prof. W. F. Barrett*

# PART I

## *Introductory*

After my previous lengthy paper "On the So-called Divining Rod," published in Part XXXII. (Vol. XIII.) of our Proceedings, [The first part of this volume - Ed.] some apology is due for a second paper on this subject; the more so as the subject itself, to most intelligent people, appears a contemptible one and unworthy of prolonged and serious scientific inquiry. It certainly is not one I should have chosen for investigation. However, having been urged to undertake it, those who may have had the patience to read the mass of evidence given in my former paper will probably have come to the same conclusion as that to which I have been led,—in spite of very different preconceived ideas,—namely, that the whole subject is one eminently worthy of careful investigation; not only as a question of folk lore and of historical interest, but also because several problems of considerable psychological and also physiological interest appear to be involved. In addition to which the main problem before us is a settlement of the disputed point whether mere shrewdness, an "eye for the ground " and experience on the part of the so-called "diviner" afford a sufficient explanation of the success which he so often achieves.

It is true that the subject at first dispirits and repels the investigator from the quantity of rubbish that overlays it and the credulity and ignorance that surround it, and which characterise so many of the enthusiastic votaries and writers on the divining rod, both in ancient and modern times But this is equally true of many other obscure questions which this Society was founded to investigate, and it is our business to try and discover, with the divining rod of science, the treasure that is buried beneath any soil. As Sir John Herschel has truly said of scientific research in general :—"He that has seen obscurities, which appeared impenetrable, suddenly dispelled, and the most barren and unpromising fields of inquiry converted into rich and inexhaustible springs of knowledge on a simple change of our point of view, or by bringing to bear on them some principle which it never occurred before to try, will be the last to acquiesce in any dispiriting prospects."[1]

Before entering upon the discussion of the fresh evidence I have collected, it may be convenient to those who approach this subject for the first time if I briefly state by whom, and the purpose for which, the divining rod is at present employed, and how it comes to pass that what appears at first sight to be a mere relic of a superstitious age survives amid the scientific light of the present day. Readers of my previous report will, I hope, forgive the repetition.

There are in the country districts of England a certain class of persons who profess to be able to discover, without geological or local knowledge, the exact location of any underground "spring" or subterranean course of water supply.[2] For this purpose they usually, but not always, employ a forked or Y-shaped twig, generally of hazel or some pliant wood. Grasping the ends of the fork in a particular manner,—to which great importance is usually attached, albeit the mode of holding has varied in late years in an amusing manner,—the holder fixes his attention upon the slightly raised point of the twig, and thus becoming as far as possible oblivious to the world around, he traverses the ground. When supposed to be approaching the hidden source the twig is seen to quiver, and when the "diviner" believes he is vertically over the "spring," so vigorous is the motion of the twig that it forcibly strikes the holder's body, and, if short enough to escape the body, rotates rapidly, though the holder appears to be doing his utmost to restrain its motion; a fact that he will emphatically corroborate, and which seems to be undeniably proved by one limb of the twig being often snapped across, under the strain of the opposing forces. The holder of the twig generally appears much exhausted by the effort; in some cases he complains of sickness or giddiness, occasionally the pulse rises, he breaks out into a violent perspiration, and trembles all over. As a rule (but not always) he asserts that he experiences singular sensations, resembling muscular cramp, when he is over an underground water-course. These

---

[1] *Discourse on the Study of Natural Philosophy*, p. 8.

[2] I put the word spring in inverted commas, as this term is invariably employed by the "water-finder." As so used, it is, however, often a very misleading expression. In order to remove misconception on the part of non-geological readers, I have given the reason why this expression is usually incorrect in an Appendix on "Geological Views of the Distribution of Underground Water," which will be found in my previous Report. See also Appendix B. in the present Report.

## The Credibility Of Dowsing

sensations are so well marked that in some cases he discards the use of the twig and trusts to his sensations alone.[1] If now the place be carefully noted beneath which the hidden water course is asserted to exist, the probability is that, however often the spot be crossed by the holder of the twig, the same phenomena recur, even when his attention is distracted, or another and independent diviner employed. Further, if a well be dug at the spot so indicated, water will usually be found at no great depth below the surface. These water-finders, or diviners, are widely and regularly employed, not by ignorant folk, but by some of the most distinguished and clever people in England, by Cabinet Ministers and Judges,[2] by shrewd business men and large landowners —men not likely to waste their money on a silly superstition. In parts of the south-west of England, in Somersetshire particularly, these waterfinders are held in high esteem, and are known as "dowsers," and their rod as the "dowsing rod."

This alleged power of finding underground water, when to an ordinary observer there appears nothing to betray the presence of a spring below, is not confined to a professional and paid class of men, but is found among amateurs, young and old, male and female, and in all classes of society. Nor is the dowser only met with in England; he is found to-day in some parts of France, Italy, Switzerland, Germany, Denmark, Scandinavia, and Finland, and flourishing in the United States, Canada, Australia, and doubtless in other places of which I have no direct evidence. Many instances of the wide distribution of the dowser were given in my former paper, and others will be given in the evidence to be cited later on.

In my previous paper I gave an account of fourteen contemporary English dowsers, all of whom make or add to their living by this means, and, in addition, evidence was given of the practical use of the rod by upwards of thirty amateurs of both sexes and ranging over every class in society, from elderly magistrates to young children. Since then several other dowsers, both professional and amateur, have come under my notice (see Part IV). I have not, however, found any Scotch or Irish professional dowsers, though these countries regularly invite the services of English dowsers. I should say there are at the present time in England at least a score of these men engaged in the business of water finding, and a very profitable business some of them find it to be. Curiously enough I have come across no women professional dowsers, though this is contrary to what one might expect.

The etymology of the word dowsing rod is uncertain;[3] it is first mentioned by the philosopher Locke in 1691, who speaks of the "deusing rod or virgula divina." Locke was a native of Somersetshire, born under the shadow of the Mendips, and for upwards of two centuries the Mendips have been, and still are, the radiating point and stronghold of the dowser. The term "dowsing rod" is preferable to "divining rod," as the latter, or rather its Latin equivalent *virgula divina*, was used by Cicero, Tacitus and other writers of antiquity to denote a wholly different thing, namely, divination by rods or bits of stick; and no doubt a good deal of the prejudice which the term divining rod creates at the present day is due to the fact that it suggests to most people some form of rhabdomancy[4]. The forked divining rod, or *virgula furcata*, our modern dowsing rod, is not much older than the age of printing, and was first described in one of the earliest treatises on mining, Agricola's *De re Metalliaa*, published in 1546; for its original use was in the search for metallic ores, and, thus used, it spread from South Germany to the South of France and thence over Europe, reaching England towards the end of the 16th century.[5]

---

[1] For a fuller account of the sensations alleged to occur in dowsing and the evidence thereon see the discussion of this subject in my previous paper, Proceeding) S.P.R., Part XXXII., Appendix D.[The first part of this book. - Ed]
[2] For example, Lord Salisbury, Lord Lansdowne, and others; see also the testimony of the Rt. Hon. Sir Edward Fry, D.C.L., F.R.S., etc..
[3] See Appendix A to my former paper. With great deference I am inclined to believe the etymology suggested on p. 261 of that Appendix, viz., from the middle English *duschen*, to strike, is after all the most likely: the objection raised to this by Professor Skeat on the ground of the pronunciation being dowz is much weakened if not destroyed by the fact that it is very frequently pronounced in other ways. Moreover I find that when the rod was first brought to England at the end of the 16th or beginning of the 17th century, it was called "the striking rod," *schlag-ruthe*, by the German miners who brought it over.
[4] [DIVINATION BY rods or wands - Ed.]
[5] In Germany the word *wünschel ruthe* (wishing rod) was, and is still, used as the equivalent both of the old divining rod, *virgula divina*, and the more modern dowsing rod, the *virgula furcata*, though, as mentioned in the previous foot-note, the German miners of the 16th century called the latter *schlag-ruthe*. Several German writers, long before the age of printing, speak of the *wünschel ruthe*, and a *forked wünschel ruthe*, it is true, is referred to by one Nithart, a German writer of the 14th century, but in these early cases it was the ancient magic wand, or *virgula divina*.

## Prof. W. F. Barrett

Not until the 17th century was it used in the search for underground, water, but whether for ores or water, the business-like way in which it was employed[1] distinguished it from the ancient *virgula divina*, the efficacy of which was supposed to depend on the ceremonies and Kabbalistic words which accompanied its use. But among the superstitious and ignorant some of the practices of rhabdomancy clung to the new rod along with the old name; hence it is that in several descriptions of the divining rod from the 16th century down to the present time we find special importance attached to the day of the month the diviner was born, the particular kind of twig employed, the day or hour on which it was cut, or the way it turns for underground water or metallic ores, etc.

Here, for instance, is an illustration of the survival of this superstition, and also of the use of the rod in Jutland. In Kristensen's *Jyske Folkeminder* (Popular Traditions of Jutland), published at Kolding, 1888, Vol. IX., Section 822, under the heading, *Folketro und bonde regler* (Popular Beliefs and Farming Rules), the following passage occurs:—

> It has been a general custom that, when a well was to be dug, word was sent for a "water-shower" (*vand-viser*), who went over the ground with a forked (*klöftet*) willow-wand. If the twig began to twist about in his hand, there was water near the surface, and digging could be begun with confidence.

> Much the same procedure was followed to discover ore. A two-year-old willow-shoot was taken, which was forked in growth. If water was to be found it must be of a different age. One who can find ore may not be able to discover water: it depends upon what month they are born in.[2]

Those who have had experience of an investigation of this kind, where people are afraid of being laughed at for giving their testimony, will understand the labour of obtaining accurate evidence of eye-witnesses who are willing to append their names. The correspondence entailed in this inquiry has been endless; not far short of 6,000 letters had to be written for the purpose of my previous report. Upwards of 200 cases of water-finding by dowsers in recent years have been investigated; in each case the independent evidence of disinterested persons who had witnessed the experiments was sought. Generally speaking such evidence was obtained, the witnesses allowing their names and addresses to be given. Altogether, 152 cases of dowsing were cited in my previous paper; of these 140 were successful,—that is, the predictions of the dowser were verified, a well was sunk on the spot and water found at the place indicated,—and 12 were failures.

As one is far less likely to hear of the failures than of the successes of amateurs, let us confine our attention only to the professional dowser. Omitting a remarkably successful series of cases by an American dowser, which Dr. Hodgson kindly investigated, 105 cases of British professional dowsers were given in my former paper; of these 95 were successful and 10 were failures. That would make the record of failure less than 10 per cent., which is certainly remarkably small. I have endeavoured to find the percentage of failure which skilled geologists or other scientific experts have made when they are consulted as to water supply,—for failures, and sometimes very costly failures, they have,—but it is difficult to ascertain. I doubt if their percentage of failure is less than the average dowser's; probably it varies very much with the individual employed in each case.[3] As might be expected, some professional dowsers, especially those who are fond of advertising themselves in newspaper paragraphs, have a poor record, and some are unadulterated humbugs. These do their best to conceal their failures, and their success is probably no greater than would have been obtained had a well been sunk at haphazard without their aid. For in many districts of England, the water-bearing area, for shallow wells, lies over a large extent of country, and in such districts one cannot go far wrong in sinking anywhere.

---

[1] This is well seen in pictures from Agricola's work and from Sebastian Munster's *Cosmography*, 1550, one of which we give later on.

[2] I am indebted to Mr. W. A. Craigie of Oxford for kindly searching Kristensen's works for me, and for the translation of the foregoing passage. Kristensen is an authority on Danish folk-lore, though his books are not to be found in the British Museum. The use of the divining rod in another part of Scandinavia is referred to in my previous paper, p. 200. Professor Lochman, of the University of Christiania, recently read a paper in that city in which he said his scepticism on the subject had been overcome by his own personal experience with the rod.

[3] The geologist, however, labours under restrictions which the dowser is free from; see on this Mr. Holmes' letter, p. 237.

# The Credibility Of Dowsing

I may remark here that, whilst the idea of the illiterate dowser concerning the distribution of underground water is often most grotesque, yet, if I may venture to say so, it is not impossible that the geologist has a good deal to learn on this subject. Although, as Mr. T. V. Holmes, F.G.S., remarks, many dowsers think water exists here and there beneath the surface of the ground, like a pot of buried coins, instead of, as is often the case, in sheets, wherever a permeable stratum, like sand or gravel, meets an impermeable one like clay or slate; yet on the other hand the wide practical experience of those dowsers who are well-sinkers has been too much overlooked by geologists.[1] Underground watercourses do exist, under certain geological conditions, and it is here, where an error can easily be made, that the true test of the dowser comes in. In deep artesian wells skilled geological knowledge is always necessary, but even this sometimes fails completely. Now it must be remembered that the professional dowser is sublimely ignorant of geology and has, in general, a contempt for science, —as a rule, he is an illiterate man. It was noticed more than a century ago, both in Germany, France, and England, that "peasants who do not puzzle their minds with doubts or reasonings" (I quote from Pryce's famous mining work of 1778) are the most successful dowsers. This is true to-day. The well-known dowser, the late J. Mullins, was a working mason and well-sinker, and his success as a dowser in the discovery of underground water was really phenomenal; he rarely was at fault, and I think we may take it he was the most remarkable dowser this century has produced.

Two cases of John Mullins' success were critically and fully investigated in my former paper—one at Horsham, on the estate of Mr., now Sir, Henry Harben, and the other at Waterford, for the large factory of Messrs. Richardson. In both of these, as might be expected, the best geological and engineering advice had been obtained prior to calling in the dowser. It was only when the resources of science were exhausted,—over £1,000 having been spent in each case in fruitless sinkings and borings in different places on the estate,—that Mullins was at last sent for, in 1889 to Waterford, and in 1893 to Horsham. He was an entire stranger to the neighbourhood in both cases, and was received, not unnaturally, with a good deal of suspicion. At Horsham he quickly pointed out two places where an abundant supply of water would be found within a moderate depth, and his predictions were verified to the letter. I have visited the spot and obtained the evidence of eyewitnesses, including Sir H. Harben, and at my request the place has been visited by competent geologists. The case was ably discussed from a geological point of view by Mr. T. V. Holmes, F.G.S., past President of the London Geologists' Association, and Mr. E. Westlake, F.G.S., in my previous Report, pp. 94-98 and Appendix E (pp.225-226).

The case of Waterford is still more remarkable; I will not repeat the details, which will bear careful study, as it is, I think, one of the most remarkable cases in the whole voluminous literature of the rod. Suffice it to say, that the rock there is of a hard slaty nature called Ordovician, it is hidden beneath a surface bed of some 40 ft. of boulder clay and in the search for water various wells and borings had been fruitlessly made, one boring being over 1,000 ft. deep. Not far from this deep and useless boring, made under the best scientific advice, Mullins found the twig turn vigorously; he traced what he said was a line of copious water supply—either a line of jointing or a "fault" in the hidden rock—and fixed on one point as being the best to sink the well, asserting water to the extent of 1,500 gallons an hour would be found at a depth of some 80 or 90 ft. I need not say that no one believed him, but in despair a boring was made at this spot, when suddenly, at the depth of 81 ft., water burst up the bore tube and rose half way to the surface. After pumping day and night, the supply could not be run dry; it was measured and the yield was found to be 2,000 gallons per hour, which has been maintained with but slight fluctuations from 1889, when the experiment was made, to the present time, a period of eleven years. These statements have the advantage of being corroborated by eye-witnesses and by letters written at the time, not by gullible, ignorant people, but by educated men, including a well-known local geologist, Mr. Budd, who held as it were a watching brief against Mullins; and by Mr. Kinahan, a distinguished geologist of H.M. Irish Geological Survey, as well as by Mr. Richardson himself. In fact Mr. Kinahan (who, as one of the best Irish geological authorities, was consulted by Mr. Richardson), writes to me: "As far as the actual results went I failed, and the diviner 'wiped my eye.' " No surface observation nor experience, nor "an eye for the ground " can explain this Waterford case, nor some others I shall refer to in the sequel.

---

[1] In support of this view, see Dr. A. R. Wallace's letter (Appendix G)

## Prof. W. F. Barrett

On the other hand, in the opinion of competent geologists who have kindly given me their aid in this inquiry, several cases where the dowser has had a striking success, and which at first sight appear to suggest some power transcending any recognised faculty, were found, upon geological observation on the spot, to be capable of explanation by the rapid detection of surface indications of underground water by the dowser. This will be seen from the useful geological notes Mr. T. V. Holmes, F.G.S., has kindly appended to some of the cases in the previous and also in the present Report. A fuller investigation of several cases was, at my request, undertaken by Mr. E. Westlake, F.G.S., who has made a special study of hydro-geology, and whose valuable co-operation throughout this inquiry I have already acknowledged. Mr. Westlake selected a group of cases, given in the previous Report, which appeared to be evidential of some special faculty possessed by the dowser, and visited each of the places; the result of his investigations is given in the able paper which forms an Appendix to the present Report. It will be observed that Mr. Westlake is of opinion that many of these cases can be explained without calling in the aid of any novel faculty or instinct on the part of the dowser—merely a sharp eye for the ground was required. At the same time we must remember it is much easier to prophesy after the event than before it, and it remains to be seen whether our geological friends would have thought the location of the site in these cases quite as obvious before the well had been sunk, or the dowser had visited the spot, as it seemed to be afterwards. However that may be, I gratefully accept the opinion of geological experts, and will here quote a letter which expresses Mr. Holmes' views on the subject.

28, Crooms Hill, Greenwich Park, London, S.E.,
*December 18th*, 1899.

I may add that I am attracted, not repelled, by the supernormal, for our senses must give us extremely limited perceptions of things as compared with the perceptions possible to more highly gifted beings. Hence, among ourselves, there is no improbability in the existence of powers of special perception in individual cases, even though the total range of perception may not be supernormal. Thus if the line A.B. represents the normal range of a sense, there may be abnormally gifted persons whose range is not greater, but is more extensive at one end of the scale, if correspondingly less so at the other, like the line CD.

However, it has always struck me that while stories of apparitions, &c., are treated with a curious ultra-scepticism in many cases, the dowser's claims to supernormal powers have been admitted with the most extraordinary alacrity.[1]

As the position of our old towns and villages testifies, the men who knew where water might be attained at a depth of from 5 to 50 ft. have always been with us. Geologists generally do not trouble themselves with water, as regards supply for dwellings, though anxious to know whether the superficial formations are deep sea, shallow sea, estuarine river, glacial, etc. And the cholera in the first half of the century so discredited water from superficial deposits that supplies from those sources have not been trusted, even when sufficiently good. The dowser's supply is voted excellent, and he is triumphant where a hydro-geologist would feel that he would be deservedly blamed for recommending it, should it become polluted and cause disease.

All I feel is that an eye for ground can do very much and can be immensely developed by experience. The dowser needs no geological knowledge beyond what he might have had a century ago. The most remarkable successes of dowsers are those in which sensitiveness to the proximity of water cannot

---

[1] By some persons, certainly not by geologists, nor by the Council of the S.P.R. nor by myself.— W.F.B.

have helped them, while their views as to its distribution seem fatal to the hypothesis that they are influenced by special sensitiveness. Somehow, the more one looks into cases, the more the supernormal recedes.

I quite agree with you that the twisting of the twig—though a most interesting phenomenon—has no (direct nor invariable)] connection with the nearness of underground water.

T. V. Holmes

The dowser asserts that he does not concern himself with the nature of the ground, but is guided solely by the twisting of his forked twig or by some peculiar sensation he experiences. In this case one would have expected to find some *blind* dowsers, as the blind are peculiarly sensitive in some directions, but—though I know the extensive literature of the divining rod pretty thoroughly—I have not been able to find a single blind dowser in any country in the world during the four centuries the dowsing rod has been employed. It may be urged that blind people could not engage in the peregrinations required of a dowser, nor properly hold the forked twig if they had a guide. This may be so, but I do not think it is the true answer, for I can find no account of the sudden and involuntary twisting of the rod in the hands of any blind person under any conditions: blind people may not have been tried, and I intended, had time permitted, to have tested the inmates of a blind asylum. The true explanation, I believe, will be found in the fact that the rod only moves in the hands of a novice when he has seen it "work" in the hands of somebody else; it would no doubt move with many blind people if they had previously felt the hands and the twig of a dowser when the latter is twisting. In any case the absurdity of imagining there is any direct connection between underground water and the motion of the so-called divining rod is seen from the fact that the first use of the rod was for finding underground ores, then for finding buried treasure, then for tracing lost cattle or boundaries, then for a multitude of uses in the moral world (until its employment for this latter purpose was forbidden by the Inquisition in 1701), and at the present day dowsers profess to discover, not only underground water and mineral lodes, but hidden coins, water or gas pipes, etc., by the twisting of their rod. Obviously, therefore, the peculiar involuntary motion of the rod and what causes this motion is one thing, and the existence of an alleged dowsing, or water-finding, faculty is quite another.

## *Object Of Our Investigation*

This brings us to an important point in our investigation. We must know clearly what we are seeking for. Is it for the cause of the motion of the dowsing rod, or for a proof or disproof of an alleged "dowsing faculty," or for a particular explanation of that faculty, assuming it to exist? Now it will be found that nearly every scientific investigator of the divining rod during the last 100 years has set out with some theory of the action of the dowsing rod, which, when he has satisfactorily demolished, he has asserted the whole thing was a fraud. Some of the most famous names in French scientific history a century ago, when they showed that electricity afforded no explanation of the movement of the divining rod, asserted they had disproved the existence of the alleged faculty itself. Had they been versed in the history of the subject, they would have found that a century prior to their day equally eminent French savants asserted the same thing, because they had demonstrated the devil was not the cause of the twisting of the forked twig. And now, in our own day, no less eminent French, American, and English men of science assert,—electricity and the devil having been laid,—that involuntary muscular action on the part of the dowser finally disposes of the divining rod and the mystery of an alleged dowsing faculty. This, of course, is equally erroneous. Assuming this explanation to be established, all that it explains is the twisting of the rod. Here is an instance of this fallacy.

Mr Emerson, to whom I have already referred[1], published in the *American Journal of Science (Sillimans Journal)* for 1821 a series of remarkable cases, showing how underground water had been found by dowsers where it had previously been sought for in vain. Five years later he was led to an ingenious theory of the motion of the rod as due to involuntary muscular action, an explanation we may readily admit: then after blindfolding a young boy, in

---

[1] See previous Report, p. 32. Not Ralph Waldo Emerson, but a contemporary and namesake.

whose hands the forked twig moved, albeit he had never been tested as a dowser, Mr. Emerson draws the following sweeping conclusions from the failure of some fallacious experiments which we have given later on :—

> The pretensions of diviners are worthless. The art of finding fountains and minerals with a succulent twig is a cheat upon those who practise it, an offence to reason and to common sense, an art abhorrent to the laws of nature, and deserving of universal reprobation.

I venture to say that the majority of scientific men who have read Emerson's papers will imagine he has proved his assertions, and that the question had been finally settled by him, just as in Europe it was considered that Chevreul in 1854 had settled the question by a similar explanation, forgetting that the astronomer Lalande had also given a similar explanation in 1782. What a hardy perennial this superficial and easy dismissal of the whole subject is may be seen in a recent letter in the scientific journal *Nature* (January 6th, 1898). Here, once more, an American professor tells us "the whole secret of the divining rod" is to be found in the involuntary muscular action of the operator.

And so also with regard to blindfolding. If well-conducted experiments, with a good dowser, show that blindfolding prevents the dowser from fixing on the same spots that he did when he could see,— places where he alleged underground water to exist,—all we have proved is the extreme improbability of any direct influence of the water on the dowser, or any clairvoyant perception on his part. Failure when blindfolded does not prove the dowser to be a charlatan, but merely that a particular physical or psychical explanation is improbable. For the success of the dowser under normal conditions may still be due to some instinct or faculty, derived from a rapid but subconscious observation and interpretation of the surface indications of underground water or mineral lodes, or his success may be due merely to experience and shrewd observation, which, from habitude, has almost ceased to excite a conscious effort. As eyesight would be necessary in either of these cases, the dowsing faculty, if there be such, would in this event take its place along with other familiar illustrations of keenness of perception in men and animals.

Let us therefore clearly recognise in our experiments what is the aim we have in view. A particular theory may be proved to be wrong, but the important point is to obtain trustworthy evidence of all the facts in each case, and when a sufficiently wide range of evidence is before us, to endeavour to arrive at some explanation. It is for this reason that I have been compelled to burden this and the previous Report with such an accumulation of cases, for the subject is full of difficulties from a scientific point of view, and any explanation we may give must be based upon an extensive survey, and is likely to be either a tentative or a complex one.

We may summarise the objects of our investigation as follows :—

I. Whether the alleged claim of the dowser to a special faculty, or even facility, in the discovery of underground water or mineral lodes has any basis in fact, and if so :—

(i.) Whether this is due merely to knowledge acquired by the dowser from experience and careful observation of the ground; or

(ii.) Whether such information is derived by some instinctive and sub-conscious process of observation on the part of the dowser, or perhaps hyperaesthetic discernment of surface signs too faint to be perceived by the ordinary observer; or

(iii.) Whether there is evidence of any supernormal perception by the dowser—that is, information derived subconsciously otherwise than through the ordinary channels of sense.

II. The evidence for and the explanation of:

(i.) the sudden and often uncontrollable movement of the rod in the hands of the dowser;

(ii.) the apparent transmission of this power of motor-automatism from a sensitive to an insensitive person; and

(iii.) the singular malaise and convulsive spasm which is associated in so many dowsers with the involuntary motion of the rod.

## *The Credibility Of Dowsing*

III. The History and Bibliography of the subject. These have been prepared, but the matter is so voluminous that it must be published later on.

I propose to begin with No. 1—further tests as to the alleged claims of the dowser.

*Prof. W. F. Barrett*

# PART II

## *Experiments By The Author*

### § 1. The Carrigoona Experiments

It has been suggested[1] that the most satisfactory test of the alleged claims of the dowser would be to carry out some experiments under my own personal supervision, boring or sinking wells in places where the dowser indicated water would or would not be found. As I have said elsewhere, this can only be a very restricted test, owing to the expense involved, and, unless care be taken, may be as inconclusive as were Professor Sollas's two test borings described in the previous Report, pp. 182 and 183. However, I determined to make the attempt, and have done so this spring and summer, with the results I will now give. In order that an impartial judgment may be arrived at by my readers a somewhat detailed account is, I fear, unavoidable.

Certain precautions were necessary if any satisfactory evidence one way or the other was to be obtained. (1) The place chosen must be one entirely unfamiliar to the dowser, and no opportunity must be allowed him of knowing beforehand where the experiment is to be made, otherwise the dowser might make a prior careful examination of a geological map of the district (assuming he had access to such maps and could understand them — a possible assumption); such examination would doubtless yield a good deal of valuable information to a clever man. (2) The district selected must be one geologically suitable, that is to say, not a large water-bearing or waterless area, the character of which he might discern at a glance, and where he could not go wrong anywhere in predicting water or no water. (3) The dowser should be taken direct to the place and not allowed to get any information from persons living in the neighbourhood as to the position of any existing springs or wells. (4) The persons who accompany the dowser should also be ignorant of the likeliest spots where water would or would not be found, lest they perchance consciously or unconsciously convey their knowledge to the dowser.

These conditions were all successfully met, the place I selected —a mountainous region in the co. Wicklow, four miles from Bray— admirably fulfilling the geological conditions required, and a region I believe no dowser had ever visited. I wrote to two or three of the best known English professional dowsers, asking them if they could come over, and as Mr. Stone replied he was shortly coming to Ireland, I arranged to see him. On his arrival he had no idea where the experiment was to be made, nor did I tell him, but took him straightway to the place. My friend Mr. B. St. G. Lefroy accompanied us to take notes as an independent careful observer, and the memorandum he has written will be given directly. It was Easter week, 1899, and the day was fine. Mr. Stone told me he had never been in co. Wicklow before, and I have no doubt that is quite true. Leaving our car in the Rocky Valley, we ascended the mountain road leading round a hill called Carrigoona, on the lower slopes of which there are patches of cultivated ground, but the quartzite rock of which the hill is composed juts out here and there, though the hillside is generally covered with two or three feet of alluvial soil, on which gorse and heather and bracken grow, clothing the mountain with a garment of beauty. The panorama from the mountain-side is also one of unsurpassed beauty, and stirred the emotions of my geological friends who afterwards visited the spot with me.

For the accompanying geological map of the district I am indebted to the kindness of H. M. Geological Survey. The field we first went to is on the eastern side of Carrigoona and is marked E on the map. The upper part of the map is due north. A general view of the surrounding country is shown in the picture opposite, Fig. 2; this is taken from a rocky eminence on the south-eastern corner of the field E and is therefore looking nearly west: Carrigoona mountain is seen on the right hand side of the picture; only the summit of the quartzite knoll in the middle distance is visible when in the field, where the boring operations are seen going on as described subsequently.[2]

---

[1] In a review of my previous Report in *Nature*, October 14th, 1897.
[2] I have to thank Mr. Kendrew for the photograph of which Fig. 2 is a reproduction; unfortunately the reproduction does not do justice to the original photograph.

# The Credibility Of Dowsing

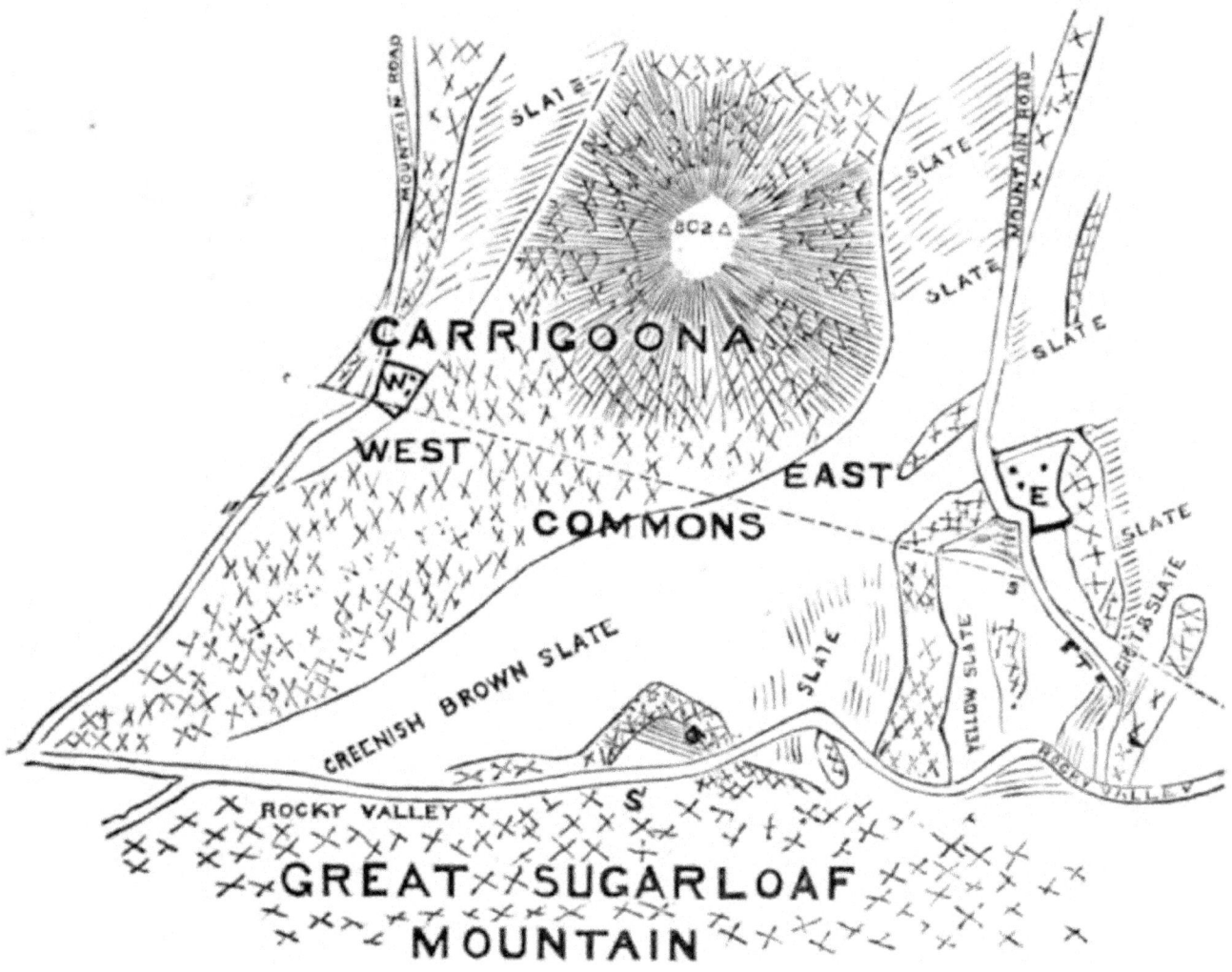

Scale: Six inches to the mile. Quartzite marked thus, x x x.

Fig. 1.

Fig. 2.
LOOKING WEST.

# The Credibility Of Dowsing

## Experiment I

Having secured the necessary permission, I took Mr. Stone first to the field, E, Fig. 1, rather over an acre in extent, and asked him to begin operations. He pulled out a slender forked twig from his pocket, and immediately walked round the field; at one spot the twig forcibly revolved, and he said we should find plenty of water there, less than 15 ft. deep. The spot was marked, and after traversing the field two or three times he asserted that water was flowing from north to south along a line or region he traced out, but that at the side of the field very little, if any, water would be found.[1] "Bore anywhere along this line," he said (see dotted line in Fig. 3), "and you will get plenty of water, but very little or none over there," i.e., on the east side of the field. The places were marked and subsequently fixed by measurement, so that the marks could be removed. All round the field was a rough stone wall, overtopped to a height of 8 ft. or 9 ft. by a thick gorse hedge, so that it was impossible to see a plateau of rock that flanked the east and west sides of the field beyond the boundary wall; I mention this for a reason that will appear presently. The field was on the mountain side, it sloped downwards from north to south, was uniformly covered with grass, and had no trace of water anywhere on the surface.

## Experiment II

From this field we crossed the mountain and went to an enclosed piece of the commons on the western side of Carrigoona, marked W on the map, Fig. 1. Here, again, I asked Mr. Stone to select two test places. He walked round the field, but there was no motion of his forked twig. It so happened a friend had purchased this field in order to erect a summer cottage, and particularly wanted to find a spring. Noticing a patch of rank and very green grass I asked him to try that spot. "No good," he said; "it's no good boring anywhere in this field; there is little or no water." Pressed to try once more, he fixed on one spot as best to bore, but said only a little water, "of no use," would be found: this place was marked. It is the more northerly of the two dots marked in W, Fig. 1.

## Experiment III

Three weeks later a country gentleman, Mr. J. H. Jones, of Mullinabro House, Waterford—who some years ago accidentally discovered that the rod moved in his hands, and had had some success in his own neighbourhood as an amateur dowser—kindly agreed, at my request, to try the same fields. Mr. Jones had never been in that district before, and knew nothing of the places marked by Mr. Stone. These marks had been carefully removed prior to Mr. Jones' visit.

As before, Mr. Lefroy accompanied us, and we agreed to let Mr. Jones go round the fields alone, so that no hint could be derived from any involuntary indications on our part. Mr. Jones used a small, slender forked twig, which he held in the same way as the elder Mullins. We went, first, to the larger field on the east of Carrigoona. On completing his perambulation of the field we examined the places marked by Mr. Jones. The spot where the twig moved most vigorously with him, and where he was confident we should find water, was not a foot distant from the place selected by Mr. Stone, as we found subsequently by measurement with the tape. This was at No. 1, in Fig. 3. Mr. Jones alsp asserted the watercourse ran from north to south in the field, in the same direction as marked out by Mr. Stone; but from the movement of the twig he asserted we should also find water a few feet on the east side of the place marked No. 1, but flowing towards Stone's line. We then crossed the mountain to the smaller field on the western side; after Mr. Jones had traversed it with his "rod" he said much as Mr. Stone did, that very little, if any, water would be found there.

## Borings

It was not until July, 1899, that the boring apparatus arrived. Mr. Stone had kindly placed it at my disposal, so that the only expense incurred was for labour and the services of his brother, Mr. E. Stone, who was a skilful working engineer. A four-inch bore-hole was made in each case; a hardened steel "jumper" and the usual boring tools being

---

[1] The three dots on the field E, Fig. 1, indicate these places, and where the boreholes were subsequently made. The dotted line across the map is supposed to indicate a line of "fault" in the rocks: but this is only a geological surmise.

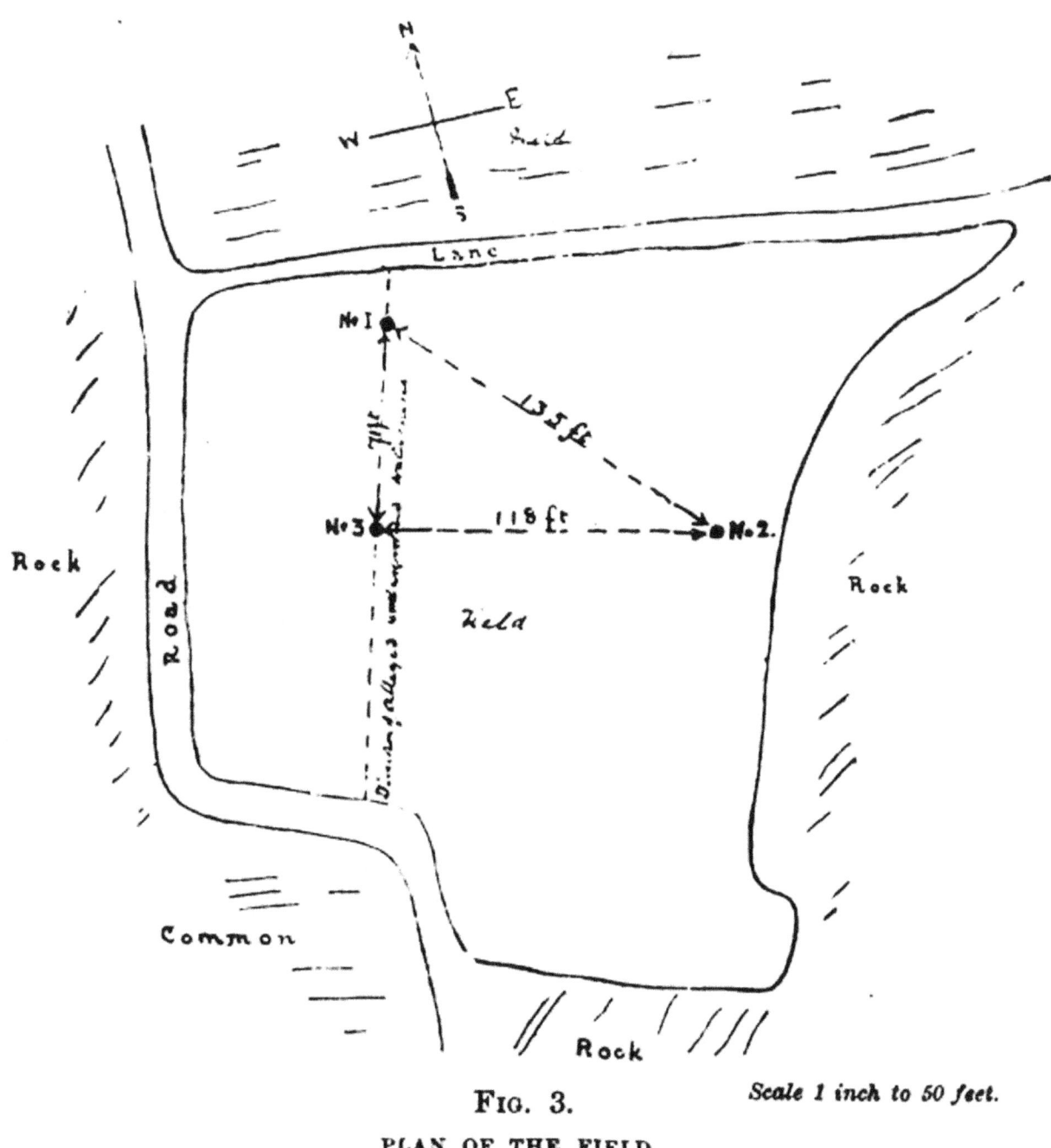

FIG. 3.   *Scale 1 inch to 50 feet.*

PLAN OF THE FIELD.

employed. Fig. 4, p. 246, shows the boring apparatus at work. Mr. E. Stone is standing on the left of the picture, and the men are boring with the jumper. The thick gorse hedge is seen round the field. From conversation with the farmer who had tilled the eastern field for many years, we expected to reach the bed rock some 6 ft. below the surface, and I anticipated a laborious and costly boring if we were to get anything better than surface water. As I had taken a farmhouse for the summer on the northern slope of Carrigoona, I was able daily to inspect the result of the boring operations. We commenced at the spot marked No. 1 in Fig. 3, and a foot below the surface struck

**Fig. 4.**

IN THE FIELD, LOOKING NORTH.

a very hard dry clay; this went on for a depth of 8 ft., with slow progress, until suddenly, after two days' work, a bed of sand was encountered, through which the "jumper" sank, and water rushed up the bore-hole to within 4 ft. of the surface. After 4 ft. of sand a bed of gravel was reached, but the quantity of water was so great that the sides of the lower part of the bore-hole were constantly washed in, and we could not sink deeper until a lining tube was obtained. As this could only be procured in London, we proceeded to test the east side of the field, where Mr. Stone said little or no water would be got. Here No. 2 bore hole was sunk, and nothing but a hard clay, with stones

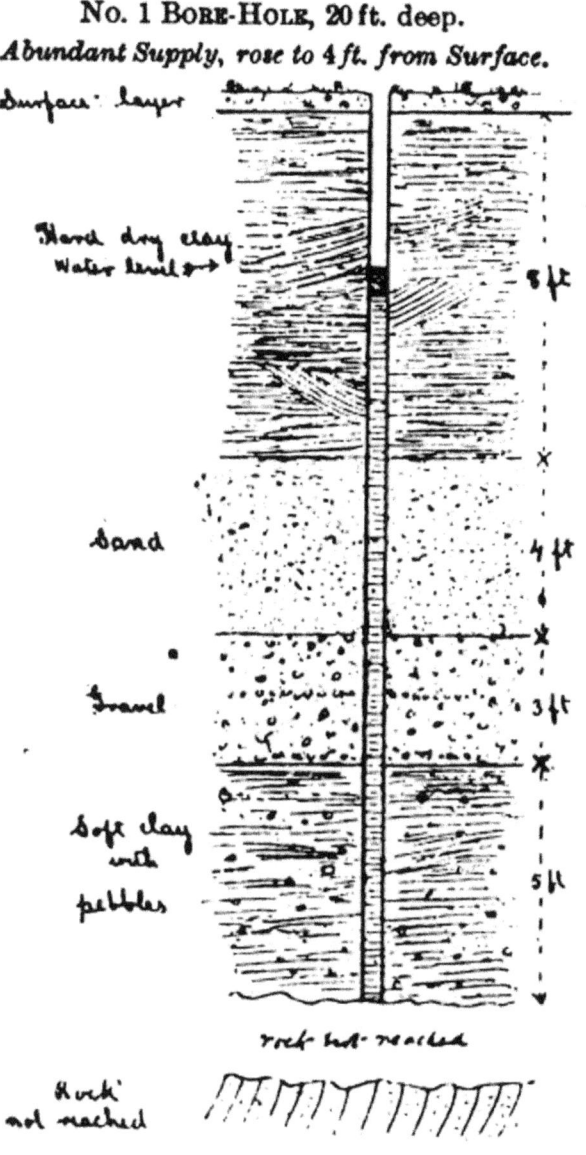
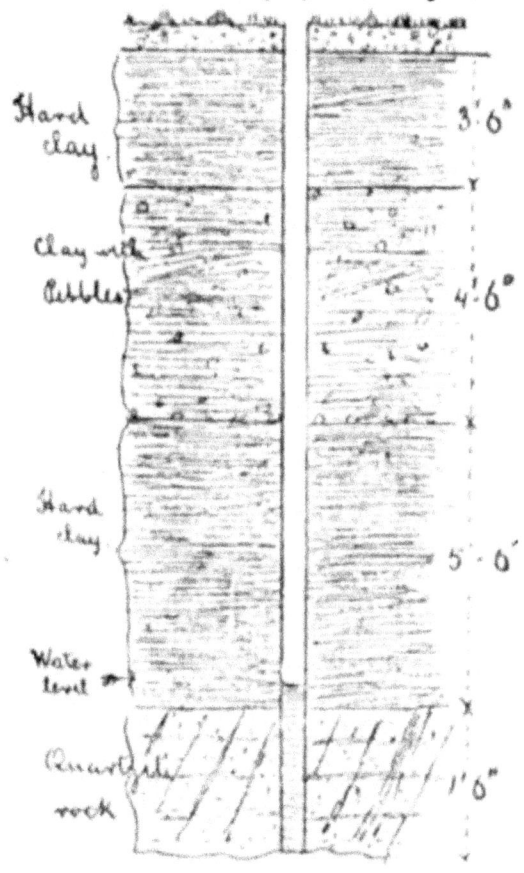

intermixed in one part, was met with till the rock was reached at a depth of 12 ft., when a little water was found between the rock and the impermeable stratum above it. I made them continue boring to a depth of 1 ft. 6 in. into the solid quartzite rock, but no more water was obtained. We then began No. 3 bore-hole, on what Mr. Stone called the " water-line." The boring was similar in its results to No. 1, the water-bearing permeable stratum being struck 6 ft. below the surface, and abundant water rose in the bore-hole. The boring was continued when a bed of soft plastic clay was reached, and after this a hard clay mixed with pebbles. I was astonished at not reaching the rocky bed, and determined to continue the boring; after we had gone to a depth of 22 ft. we were still in the clay, and were so impeded by the constant washing in of the sandy stratum that we had to abandon the boring, the lining tubes not having arrived.

**Fig 5.**
*The two diagrams above and the one on the following page*

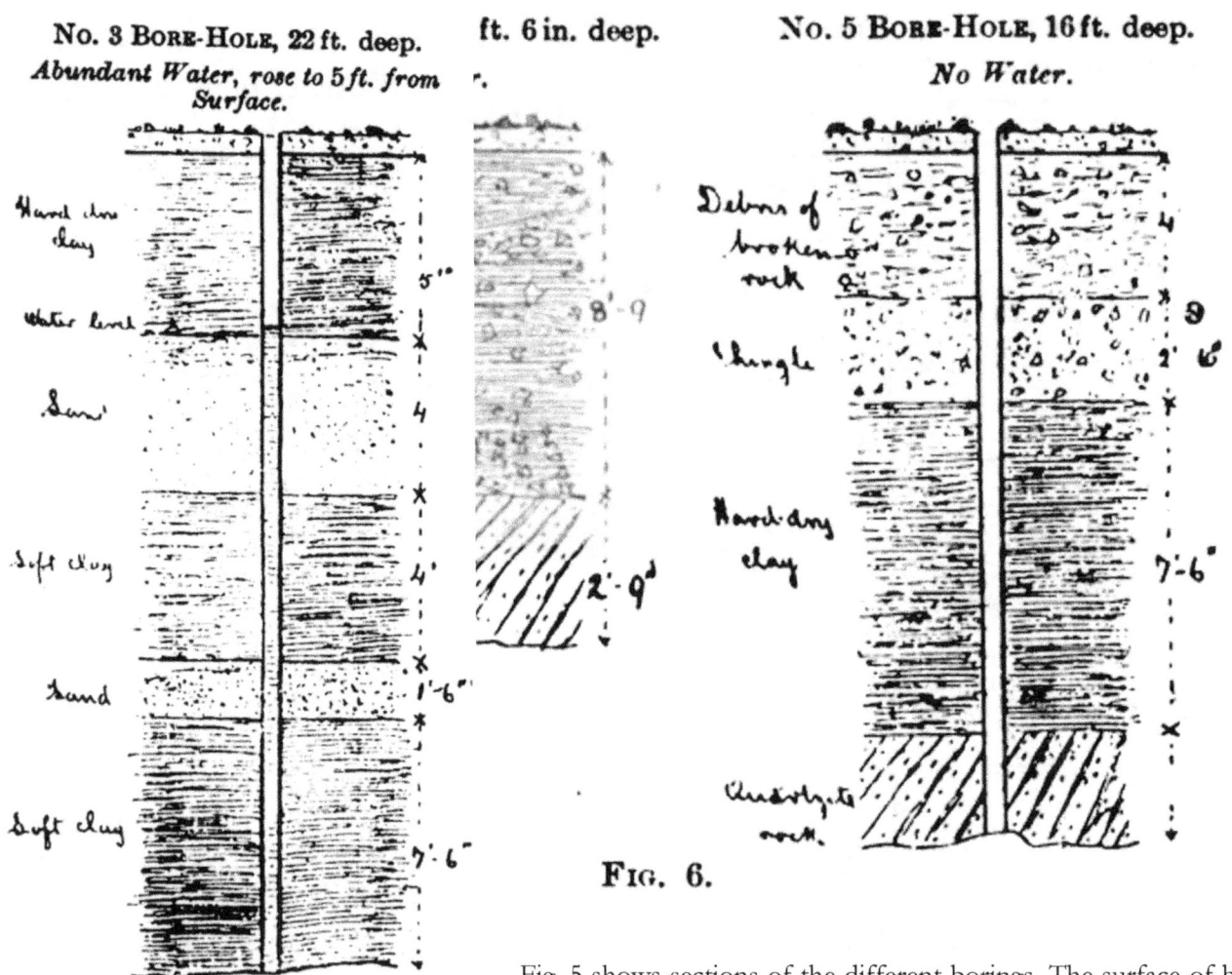

Fig. 5 shows sections of the different borings. The surface of bore No. 1 is 6 in. above the level of bore No. 2, and 3 ft. above the surface of bore No. 3, as will be seen subsequently in the cross section of the field, Figs. 8 and 9.

So far, then, Mr. Stone's prognostication had proved perfectly correct, and we now moved the boring apparatus to the field on the western side. Here I made them sink a bore-hole at a spot that seemed to me most likely to yield water, where the ground appeared moister, and was covered by a patch of rank grass. The boring, No. 4, in Fig. 6, proved difficult and very tedious. Instead of clay a rocky debris mixed with clay was encountered below the surface-soil; at 9 ft. deep the bedrock was reached, and, thinking we might strike a fissure it was bored to a depth of nearly 3 ft., but not a drop of water was obtained. Then I had a bore-hole sunk at the spot fixed on by Mr. Stone as likely to yield a little water, but "no use," as he remarked, (this is No. 5 bore-hole); here, after the shingle, we reached a hard dry clay, and continued boring through this until the rocky bed was encountered at a depth of 14 ft. from the surface, but no trace of water was found. This field slopes sharply down from east to west, and No. 5 bore hole is at some 10 ft. lower level than No. 4, which is on the upper eastern side of the field. Finally, I had a small trial bore made at the lowest point in the field adjoining the mountain road, but only dry shingle, and no sign of water, was met with. Here, again, Stone's predictions were verified; there might have been a little water between the impermeable clay and the rocky bed when he made his trial at Easter, as it was then in the early spring, after rains.[1]

---

[1] Subsequently, after the summer drought, Mr. Lefroy noticed a little water at the bottom of this bore-hole, see P.S. to his memorandum, p. 250.

## *Prof. W. F. Barrett*

The borings were all made in the long drought we had during the summer of the present year; it was, therefore, all the more astonishing to find such a good supply of water in the No. 1 and No. 3 borings in the eastern field.

After the perforated lining tube had arrived we were able to go on boring in No. 1 hole, but found a second bed of clay below the gravel, and reached no rock, though we went down 20 ft. All the water was therefore supplied by the permeable layer between the two impermeable clays. In order to test the quantity, I procured a pump and 15 ft. of iron tubing, and found that No. 1 bore-hole yielded five gallons a minute, which, if the supply held, would be equivalent to over 7,000 gallons in the 24 hours. After pumping 10 minutes, however, the pump choked, and the water was then found to stand 8 ft. from the surface; it had been lowered about 4 ft. in the four-inch bore-hole. The water was flowing in all the time through the perforations in the lining tube, but not sufficiently rapidly to maintain a constant level, as the pump was a powerful one. The temperature of the water was some 20 deg. F. below that of the air. No. 2 bore-hole contained so little water that we were able, in a few minutes, almost to empty the borehole by ladling out the water with a small tin can. The pump had to be sent back to Dublin for repair, and another trial was postponed till early in November, as my geological friends thought a more crucial test would be afforded at that period of the year.

I will now give the account of Stone's visit, which Mr. Lefroy kindly sent to me.

August, 1899.

On April 2nd, 1899, Professor Barrett invited me to accompany him and Mr. Stone, an English "dowser," to a field in the Rocky Valley, co. Wicklow. We drove directly from Bray station to the field, which is enclosed by a high stone fence, partly covered by a gorse hedge. The configuration of the immediately adjacent land cannot be seen from the field, owing to its situation and the height of this fence and hedge. The area is between one and two acres in extent. Mr. Stone had no opportunity afforded him of examining the surroundings of the field except upon the side of approach, nor did he, I fully believe, receive any information on that subject, to which he made no reference in my hearing, and was apparently indifferent. I watched him closely, but saw no sign of attention on his part to surface indications, if any existed.

He traversed the field in various directions, holding a fork of the divining rod between the forefinger and thumb of each hand. His manner was that of easy confidence, and he readily maintained a conversation at the same time. At certain points the rod in his hands was violently twisted. One of these points, marked "No. 1" on the plan, Fig. 3, he stated to be that most suitable for boring purposes and he declared that a sufficient supply of water for domestic use would be found there at a very moderate depth. To the best of my recollection he said not more than 15 ft., but of this I am not now certain. The other points at which the rod was notably contorted were in a line south from this, which he attributed to the existence of an underground watercourse. The direction of this is shown on the plan by the dotted line.

The positions of these points Professor Barrett and I measured at once and noted on a rough plan. The line of the asserted watercourse was marked by taking the distances from the side of the field. Except on that line, only very slight movements of the rod were anywhere observable, and an area in the eastern portion of the field was designated by Mr. Stone as practically waterless. The test boring subsequently made in this area is marked "No. 2" on the plan.

On April 22nd, I again visited the place with Professor Barrett and Mr. Jones, of Waterford, an amateur "dowser." The same conditions were repeated. He saw no more of the surrounding land than was strictly unavoidable and appeared to pay no attention to that or to any indications other than those furnished by the "rod." No marks had been left by which the places selected by Mr. Stone as yielding water could have been identified or guessed at. Mr. Jones walked over the field as Mr. Stone had done, the "rod" behaved similarly in his hands, and his results were practically the same. The difference of a foot or so in the "best" point selected may be reasonably attributed to his crossing the line of the watercourse referred to at a different point.

From this field, which is on the eastern side of Carrigoona Hill, we went, on the day first mentioned, to the western side, and Mr. Stone was asked to find a spring in a small field on that side. He walked over this field in the same manner with the rod, and said that no water, or so little as to be useless, would be found in it,—that there were traces of water at a certain spot, but that it would be "no good boring." Mr. Jones also went with us to this other field and he confirmed what Mr. Stone had said of there being little water to be found there.

B St. G. Lefroy.

P.S.—Since the borings have been made, I have measured and verified their positions with Professor Barrett, and on November 5th, 1899, I again visited Carrigoona, and made a careful examination of the borings. In the field on the eastern side, the one first tried by Mr. Stone, I found the water in boring marked No. 1 in the plan [see Fig. 3] standing 6 ft. from the ground level. The water in boring No. 3, on the line of the watercourse alleged by Mr. Stone to exist, stood 6 ft. 3 in. from the surface of the ground. The boring No. 2 was dry. In the field on the western slope of the hill I found the upper boring [No. 4] quite dry, and the lower boring [No. 5] had four or five inches of water in it [Fig. 6]. These results agree with the predictions made by Mr. Stone, and also by Mr. Jones, before the borings were made.

B. St. G. L.

Although the excellent maps of the Irish Geological Survey had given me a general knowledge of the suitability of the locality chosen for the experiments before they were made, it seemed desirable that the opinion of some recognised geological authorities should be obtained. For this purpose I asked some of my geological friends, who were intimately acquainted with the geology of that district, to visit the fields where the experiments were conducted, and I gratefully acknowledge their kindness in doing so and furnishing me with the accompanying valuable reports. It would have been fairer to the dowser had I asked the geologists to come before the borings were made, as the depth (which I informed them) to which borings Nos. 1 and 3 were made, and yet no rock reached, revealed the unsuspected fact that the field was on the site of an ancient and deep V-shaped depression or narrow valley between the rocks, probably an ancient river bed now filled with drift. The first report is from my friend and colleague Professor Grenville Cole, F.G.S., the professor of geology in the Royal College of Science, Dublin.

# *Prof. W. F. Barrett*

August 20th, 1899.

(i) The Rocky Valley is cut by denudation through the ancient series of shales and sandstones, altered to slates and quartzites, which occur in the Sugar Loaf area,[1] at Bray Head, and at Howth. Unless a fissure were fortunately struck, it would be very difficult to find water in this series. It is not a water-bearing series in itself, as is well known to residents at Howth, who are in the habit of collecting rain and surface-water.

But in the Rocky Valley area, considerable deposits of glacial drift occur, varying from clays to permeable sands, filling all the ancient hollows carved in the slates and quartzites. A trained eye readily picks out, by contour and the green or cultivated patches, the position of the sands and gravels where they abut on the older series.

The heights are formed of slate and quartzite, on which heather and some thin bogs accumulate.[2] The rainfall on these is considerable, and soaks off down into the old waterways, carved before glacial times, in the rocky bed. As these hollows are full of drift, the drift, where sand and gravel prevail, absorbs the water. The supply at any point, by tapping the drift, must depend greatly on the extent of the impervious gathering ground round about, and would, in any case, probably diminish in autumn after a dry summer.

(ii) The field selected for boring in the Rocky Valley shows a marked green surface, with the hard quartzite sloping steeply down close at hand on either side. It falls towards the valley, and so, evidently, does the old rocky bed under the infilling of drift. Water would accumulate in the infilling, and would probably flow slowly down along the middle line of the old hollow. Its constancy may be doubted, but can be tested satisfactorily after the present dry season (August, 1899). A trained eye would certainly select the central line of the field, along the ancient stream-hollow, for boring

Grenville A. J. Cole.

In a subsequent letter Professor Cole says :—

I think a professional engineer would undoubtedly bore two or three holes along the line under which the two rock slopes at either side meet; this line might or might not be along the lowest line of the hummocky surface of the field above, where the borings were made. I am clearly of opinion that a casual visitor who knew anything about general conditions of water supply would proceed a good distance from the obvious rock on either side before he predicted a fair water supply. But I also feel with you that the rapid survey and determination in two minutes or so [by the dowser] show either exceptional powers of observation or confidence in some power not possessed by ordinary engineers.

With all deference to my friend Professor Cole, I am quite sure that the rocky contour immediately on each side of the field was not observed by Mr. Stone, nor could it be seen from the side that we approached. It requires a trained geological eye, after traversing the ground round about, to arrive at the conclusions stated by Professor Cole. I myself had been over the place dozens of times, having spent two summers in the neighbourhood, and I confess that before the borings were made there appeared to me no evidence that the "hard quartzite sloped steeply down close at hand on either side," leaving a deep ravine filled in with glacial drift. As can be seen to some extent from

---

[1] The "Sugar Loaf" is the miserable modern name given to one of the most beautiful and impressive mountains in the Co. Wicklow, a mountain rising to nearly 1700 ft. high, and flanking one side of the Rocky Valley as Carrigoona does the other.—W. F. B.

[2] This refers to the Sugar Loaf, as there are no bogs on Carrigoona.—W.F.B.

# The Credibility Of Dowsing

FIG. 7.
LOOKING EAST.

the photograph reproduced in Fig. 7, to all appearance the local opinion seemed probable enough—that the field was simply a layer of a few feet of clay over a rocky bed which was nearly level from east to west.[1]

It was desirable, in order to decide the question as to the exact levels of the respective bore-holes, that a careful survey of the field should be made For this purpose my friend and former student, Mr. J. A. Cunningham, B.A., kindly assisted me in taking the levels shown in Figs. 8 and 9 on the next page. In these diagrams the vertical scale is exaggerated five times the horizontal, the surface depression shown in Fig. 8 not being perceptible in the field. These diagrams illustrate the probable geological sections of the field from bore-hole No. 1 to No. 2, nearly west and east, and also the section from north to south. It will be observed in Fig. 8 that the nearly dry bore hole No. 2 is actually a little lower than the water-bearing hole No. 1. Possibly water might be found between Nos. 1 and 2; in fact, Mr. Jones predicted it would be a few feet to the east of No. 1. But this can only be settled by boring at intervals across from west to east; I hope to be able to do this eventually. As the bed rock was not reached in bore holes Nos. 1 and 3, its representation in both sections is in part imaginary, as is the lateral extent of the layer of sand in Fig. 8.

---

[1] I am much indebted to Mr. Kendrew, of Dublin, for the photographs here reproduced. Mr. Kendrew happened to be taking some photographs in the neighbourhood whilst the boring was in progress.

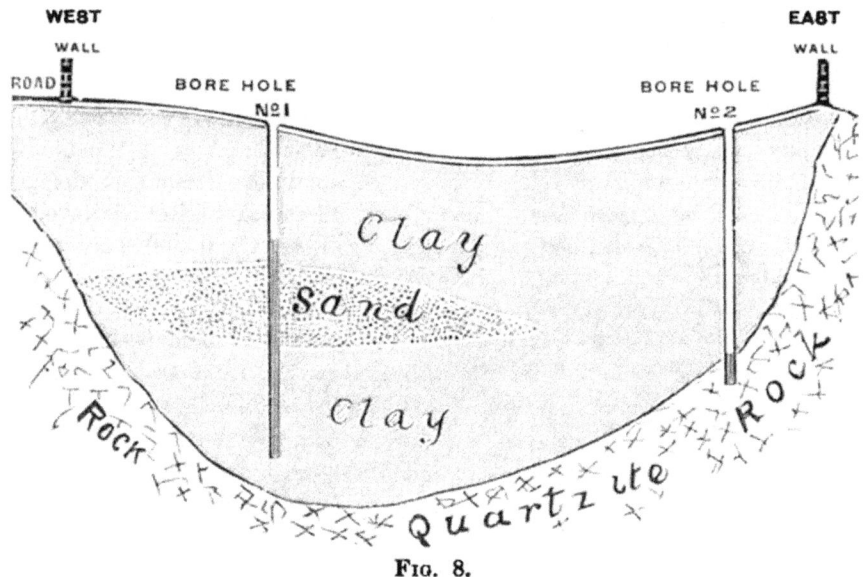

Fig. 8.
SECTION OF FIELD, EAST AND WEST.
Horizontal scale 1 in. = 60 ft.
Vertical scale, *exaggerated five times*, 1 in. = 12 ft.

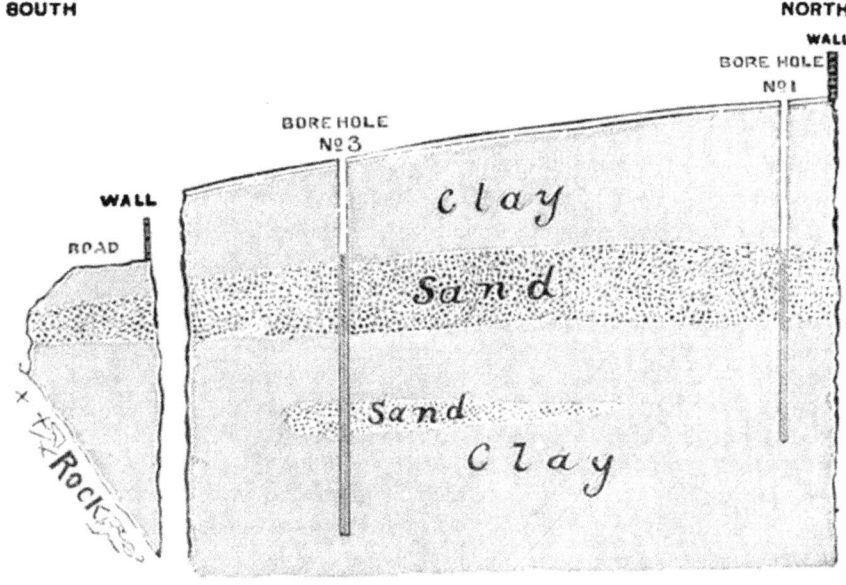

Fig. 9.
SECTION OF FIELD, NORTH AND SOUTH.
Horizontal scale 1 in. = 60 ft.
Vertical scale, *exaggerated five times*, 1 in. = 12 ft.

For the next memorandum I am greatly indebted to my friend Mr. J. R. Kilroe, of H.M. Geological Survey of Ireland. Mr. Kilroe, it will be remembered, gave me the benefit of his geological knowledge in the famous Waterford case described in the previous Report, and on the present occasion he at once responded to my request and, at considerable inconvenience, came from a distance on purpose to inspect the field.

# The Credibility Of Dowsing

Carrigoona Hill, rising to the moderate height of 802 ft. above the sea, commands one of the most attractive and varied panoramas in Wicklow. From its foot, eastward, spreads the park-like country containing and adjoining Kilruddery, the Earl of Meath's demesne, to the town of Bray and the sea beyond. North-westward the hill overlooks the Dargle Valley which separates it from the Dublin and Wicklow Mountains. Southward the eye is attracted by the valley of Killough, from which, on its east side, rises almost precipitously the Great Sugarloaf Mountain to a height of 1,659 ft.—this beautiful conical hill being separated from Carrigoona by the narrow, weird gorge known as the Rocky Valley. Further eastward the Little Sugarloaf Mountain bounds the landscape beyond the vale of Kilmacanoge.

The hills named above—Carrigoona, with the Great and Little Sugarloaf —constitute a group standing above the general level of the surrounding country, a circumstance attributable to the greater resistance offered to disintegration by quartzite, which forms the hills, than by the slate rock which prevails in the lower ground. Bands of slate also occur with the quartzite; and the results of unequal denudation are apparent in the uneven—in some places, rugged—aspect presented by the higher ground.

The rocky bed is largely covered with a mantle of glacial drift, which, though chiefly occurring in the low ground, is of fairly general distribution, resting in various places on the hill-sides, and partially filling hollows between crags.

In these latter cases, the drift consists of local rock detritus, chiefly a mixture of sand, clay, and pebbles of slate and quartzite. Limestone pebbles also are interspersed in the drift which skirts the hill slopes; but few, if any, are to be found at higher elevations. The drift in the latter positions usually contain lenticular layers of sand and gravel, which form favourable reservoirs for underground water.

Alluding to the immediate topography of the ground experimented upon (E, Fig. 1), it is situated on the south-eastern slope of Carrigoona Hill, adjoining the Commons, that is, the heathery and rocky portion of the hill near its summit. Descending the slope, one observes crags of quartzite jutting up on either side of a hollow, which is partially filled with drift of the character described above. The south-eastern drainage of the hill would naturally in part flow along this hollow, and would rapidly disappear, were there no drift. The drift, however, intercepts the drainage, and would merely retard its flow were it quite porous in texture; but it is comparatively impervious, with the exception of the sand and gravel layers; and whatever drainage-water percolates through, reaches and is retained by the layers, which consequently are ready sources of supply when tapped. These are almost horizontal, probably dipping more or less from the sides towards the centre, and somewhat basin-shaped when spreading to any extent over the area occupied by the field. Hence, when such a stratum is pierced, the water rises to a height in the boring corresponding to its head in the basin-shaped layer—higher than the layer at its centre; and practically to the same height in borings which tap the same source—as in the case of the two successful borings with which we are concerned here.

Judging, then, from geological data, the nature of the ground would suggest as the most promising site for a water-boring, a point, say, midway between the quartzite crags—perhaps a little nearer to the western crag than the eastern, say 40 yds. from the former and 60 from the latter. The successful borings [Nos. 1 and 3] have, on the dowser's advice, been put down some 22 yds. from the west side of the field (lying immediately between the crags) and some 70 yds. from the east side.

It is very improbable—at least, very difficult to understand—that a merely casual visitor to the place, however shrewd, if not versed in geological facts, could divine the existence of water in the field by a cursory inspection, much less indicate with any accuracy the spot and depth at which it would be found. The success attending the experiment here is rendered the more striking by the dowser's additional prediction that water would not be found in the other field at the west side of Carrigoona (W, Fig. 1); though, to the ordinary observer, there would appear to be at least as much probability of finding a supply in this place as in the one above described.

J. R. Kilroe.

Mr. Kilroe's opinion is all the more valuable as he is a recognised authority on the "drift," and it will be seen, from the last sentence in his interesting and full report, that he regards the dowser's prediction as very curious and remarkable, and, a fortiori, still more striking as having been given before any knowledge of the nature and slope of the underlying ground had been obtained.

For my own part, I do not think geological knowledge, nor even observation of the rocks of the neighbourhood, has anything to do with the dowser's success. If a plausible explanation is to be found, it is much more likely to be in the impression made upon the dowser by some surface indications of water. This impression may be an entirely subconscious one, and probably is more effective when it is so, and it ultimately evokes the involuntary motion given to the twig: for it certainly is involuntary—a purely reflex action—in a genuine dowser.

Although there were absolutely no indications of water in the experimental field, E, Fig. 1, yet on the way up to it there is a small spring (marked S in the map, Fig. 1) emerging from the rock, and flowing over the grass beside the road. This spring is not derived from the field, but comes from quite another direction, though a casual observer could not tell this.[1] A little beyond there is also evidence of some feeble springs.[2] Mr. Stone may have rapidly, and more or less unconsciously, perceived all that I have described, and when he traversed the field his subconscious self may have made good use of this information, and drawn a very happy but accidental conclusion therefrom. It could hardly have been his conscious self, for he was talking to me of other matters all the time, and appeared quite as astonished as I was when the twig forcibly leapt up and twisted round as he crossed the dotted line on Fig. 3. There was a barely perceptible contraction of the muscles of the hand when the twig thus vigorously turned; the movement is one that I never yet found any one able consciously to imitate without a good deal more visible muscular exertion. But that matter I will refer to again later on.

As regards Experiment II., where it will be remembered no water was found, there is in one corner of the field a hole some 6 ft. deep, with the debris from it lying about. This hole is quite dry, and, of course, the nature of the surface-soil can be seen from the sides of the hole and the debris, which consists of shingle and rocky debris. Mr. Stone passed sufficiently near the hole to have examined it if he wished to, but he seemed to pay not the least attention to it. Again, however, this dry hole may have been the means of setting his subconscious self to work, and have led to the result already described. It would, however, have been an unsafe induction from any conscious process of reasoning, for the boring No. 5 revealed quite a different material beneath the surface from that in the hole and in No. 4 boring, which was on the same level as the hole.

I have now placed on record all the information about these experiments which my geological friends and careful observation have enabled me to obtain, and I leave the matter to the judgment of each reader.

---

[1] There is a famous spring, known as Silverwell, that gushes out of the quartzite rock at the foot of the Great Sugarloaf Mountain, about a quarter of a mile further up the Rocky Valley; it is marked S' in Fig. 1.

[2] Which probably have their origin in the outcrop of the layer of sand shown in Fig. 9; but this is not obvious, as the turf at the spot is simply swampy, and a stretch of dry ground intervenes between this spot and the field.

## § 2. Experiments at Kingstown

### Experiment IV

When Mr. Stone was in Ireland he came to Kingstown, and I asked him to see if he could find any underground water in the De Vesci grounds which are in front of my house. This place had already formed the subject of experiment, see Part XXXII., p. 175. Though I did not inform Mr. Stone of this fact, he might possibly have read of it in the previous Report, and hence I do not attach much, if any, value to this experiment, though, even assuming he had a vague recollection of the plan given in the former Report, it would have been of very little service to him. Referring to that plan (p. 175) the site of a disused well is marked: it is entirely concealed beneath the lawn, and only one or two persons know of its existence. The rod moved vigorously directly Mr. Stone passed over this spot, and he asserted a spring existed below, which he traced across the gravel path to the centre of the wood marked "shrubbery" on the plan; here, he declared, a plentiful supply of water would be found. To fix the place a snap-shot photograph was taken of Mr. Stone at this moment, see next page. Mr. J. H. Jones also tried the same place before he visited Carrigoona with me, and he, too, from the prompt motion of the "rod," fixed on a spot very close to that selected by Mr. Stears and Mr. Stone. There is no doubt water does exist below this spot, at no great depth; but whether it is generally diffused surface-water or not I have no means of knowing. There is a famous ever-flowing spring on a lower level not far from the grounds, but this was unknown to the dowsers. More to the point is the fact that by careful observation one can see a very slight circular depression on the evenly-covered sward, where the mouth of the well once existed. This possibly may have started a similar subconscious suggestion in each case; any information or involuntary suggestion from myself or others was guarded against. In any case the experiment cannot be regarded as of much value, though the triple coincidence is certainly curious.[1]

### Experiment V

One other experiment I made with Mr. Stone. He told me that he had been able to detect buried water pipes or drains when water was flowing through them, and he at once consented to try the experiment in my presence. I therefore asked him to come into my garden, under the surface of which ran a water pipe, and tell me when the water was running or not. In the present case a water tap was turned on and off at the back of the house, completely out of ear-shot of Stone, who was in the front, and a system of signals was arranged so that I knew when the water was or was not running; the signals could not be seen by Stone, nor would he have known their meaning. As the house water supply comes through the buried garden pipe, when the tap was turned on at the back a flow of water was at once set up in the garden pipe. The result of this experiment showed that the number of times Stone proved to be right was very little different from the number given by pure chance coincidence. Hence this experiment, so far as it goes, was adverse to the dowser's belief that he could detect whenever water was running in a pipe.[2] The elder Mullins, now dead, was often successful, I am informed, in a similar experiment, though I do not know what precautions were taken; except in the case narrated by my friend Master Bruce, and given on p. 83 of the previous Report, and in the experiment by Mr. Finch-Hatton given in Proceedings S.P.R., Vol. II., p. 102; but a good many instances of success, under strict conditions, would be required to be at all conclusive. A series of experiments of

---

[1] As these pages were passing through the press a curious incident occurred in the De Vesci grounds, which removes all doubt of there being a watercourse at one of the very spots marked by all three dowsers. Here, after long continued heavy rain, the earth suddenly fell in, to the consternation of the gardener who was driving a lawn-mower over the spot; a deep hole was left, on examination of which by myself and the gardener it was seen that an ancient-built watercourse (still carrying water) ran some 5 ft. below the surface, and had broken in. The "oldest inhabitant" knew nothing of this watercourse (for it was not a mere surface drain), and apparently led to the old well which is supposed to be there.

[2] The pipe was only a small leaden one, about ¾ in. bore. The experiment is such a very simple one, and precautions to avoid misleading inferences can so easily be taken, that I hope some of our members may be induced to test any dowser in their neighbourhood who may be willing to try. I should be grateful for any information on this point. Care must, of course, be taken that no other taps are turned on in the house whilst the experiment is in progress, and that no sound of the running water, either in the pipe or from the tap, reaches the dowser.

this kind were, however, tried a century ago, with the famous French dowser Bleton, and the results were certainly very remarkable (see p. 269).

This ended my experiments with Mr. Stone, and I have to thank him for his ready courtesy in submitting to any test I wished, not only without fee, but at some inconvenience to himself, as he put off an engagement in England in order to stay a night in Kingstown at my request. I intended to have tried blindfolding him and taking him over the same ground the following day, but neither he nor I could spare another day just then; he promised, however, to submit himself to that test when I or any friend could carry it out, either in England or over here. An account of a successful experiment of this kind with Mr. Stone is given in Part V.

FIG. 10.
SNAP-SHOT OF MR. STONE DOWSING.

# PART III

## Cases Where The Dowser Found A Good Supply Of Underground Water Near To A Useless Well Or Boring Previously Sunk To As Great Or Greater Depth

### *No. 1. The Shanklin Experiments*

Without multiplying the evidence needlessly, I will now give a few more cases that have reached me where a useless well or boring having been sunk without the aid of the dowser, the latter found a good supply of underground water hard by, and at a less depth. Some forty cases of this kind were given in the previous Report; and although at first sight such cases appear to afford strong evidence of some supernormal, or at any rate some peculiar, faculty possessed by the dowser, a critical investigation on the spot reveals that this conclusion is unwarranted in many cases. Assuming that the dowser has a keen eye and considerable experience in his business, such successes could often be explained by shrewd guesses on his part. Most geologists who have so far overcome their prejudices as to believe the dowser may, to some extent, be an honest man, would explain all his successes in this way, attributing them to a conscious exercise of his power of observation. For my own part, I venture to disagree: the geologist speaks from his own experience, and rarely has he seen a dowser at work or investigated the evidence on his behalf. It is certainly not by a conscious exercise of his powers of observation that the dowser usually succeeds; sub-conscious observation and interpretation of surface indications there may be, and doubtless often is—we may call this instinct if we like. The question before us is, can we stretch this explanation to cover the whole ground?—for we are bound first to exhaust every known or possible explanation. To enable the reader to arrive at the geological evidence in the cases I am about to cite, I am greatly indebted to my geological friends, Mr. E. Westlake, F.G.S., and Mr. T. V. Holmes, F.G.S. The former has in several cases conducted a critical investigation on the spot, and the latter has in many cases appended valuable geological notes.

In the previous report (Proceedings S. P. R., Vol. XIII., p. 60 [p 46 in this volume -Ed]) a brief account is given of the success of two amateur dowsers at Shanklin, in the Isle of Wight. Subsequently I visited the spot and obtained fuller particulars at first-hand. As the case seemed one eminently worthy of careful geological investigation, I requested Mr. Westlake, F.G.S., to make an independent examination and report. Accordingly he did so, and the accompanying able report which he has drawn up is the result of his inquiries.

### Report By E. Westlake, F.G.S.

> On visiting the Isle of Wight in 1897 at Professor Barrett's request, for the purpose of examining the cases at Wootton and Arreton, criticised in the columns of Nature, I took occasion to inquire into some experiments at Shanklin, cited on p. 60 of his former paper, which were exceptional as having been made by members of the Local Board, who were themselves the dowsers. I found that, though three or four eminent geologists had been previously called in, they had altogether failed to find water, while the three dowsers had been as uniformly successful. As the strata at the point in question are as well known to geologists as any in England, this result was rather unexpected, and I have therefore taken some pains to get at the circumstances. After visiting the place on four occasions, and through the kindness of Mr. Milman Brown, the Chairman of the District Council (who has revised this account), and others concerned, I am now able to give the main particulars, which to make intelligible I will preface by a few words on the geological situation.
>
> The Shanklin reservoirs are in the Gault Clay a mile south of the town, at the sources of the small stream which issues in the Chine. The collecting ground is the southern mass of the Chalk and Upper Greensand, the water issuing at the base of the latter where it rests upon the Gault. The valley is a right-angle facing the north and east, due to the main joints in the Greensand, which run E. and W.

and N. and S. The dip of the strata is 1 in 45 (1¼°) south. Along the sides of the valley the Greensand has a local inward dip of from 2" to 8°, due to the slipping out of its base upon the Gault, forming fissures which increase in size as they descend. On account, however, of the tendency of the water to run southwards, the valley is unfavourably situated for springs, and on its sides one only has been utilised, viz., on the south side just below the top cottage, The Retreat; the remainder are in the copse at the head of the valley.

Greatwood Copse, the scene of the water-finding, occupies a semicircular hollow a quarter of a mile wide at the angle of the valley. The effect of this hollowing is that the Greensand, which extends for a quarter of a mile to the north, obtains in the copse a slight southern face traversing the fissures aforesaid, and it is here that the springs take their rise. The well (to be described presently) which was sunk at a spot indicated by J. Mullins, the late famous dowser, is placed in this southern face—the very best place, geologically speaking, i.e., on the above theory that the main supply comes from the north-east corner of Shanklin Down. As the consumption of water in the town has been continually increasing (in 1898 it was about 50,000 gallons a day), while the supply has never been large (about 40,000 gallons in September, 1898), there have been continual efforts to augment it, which, as far as they relate to our inquiry, are as follows :—

The first wells in the copse, Mr. Brown informed me, were sunk in 1875 by the London engineers, Messrs. Quick. The east well, 150 yards west of the road, is 55 feet deep, and held (September, 1898) 9 feet of water; its cover is 411 feet above Ordnance Datum (i.e., above sea-level). The west well, 20 yards further in, is 420½ feet O.D., and 65½ feet deep, with 10 feet of water. There is thus a difference of only 1 foot in the bottoms of the wells. They are connected by a sub-water heading so as to form virtually one well, and by a middle heading for syphoning purposes, the floor of which averages 383 feet O.D. They supply, I am informed by Mr. E. C. Cooper, the town surveyor, about 4,000 gallons a day. The water, when syphoned, stood (September, 1898) at 365 feet O.D. When not syphoned it stood (December, 1899) at 382 feet O.D.; in winter it rises till it overflows the outer sill of the middle heading at 388 feet O.D.

The upper heading, which is close by, was driven without expert advice above a wet place in the copse, and followed the water in a westerly direction for a distance of from 400 to 500 feet. This heading starts at a level of 401½ feet O.D., at a point 15 yards west of the middle heading and 18 feet above it. (See Fig. 12.)

About 1878 Mr. H. Bristow, F.R.S., F.G.S., of the Geological Survey, was consulted by the Board, and visited the spot. On his advice the upper heading was extended to a point about 900 feet west of the entrance directly under the old chalk pit on Shanklin Down, but without getting any appreciable addition to the flow of water. When I measured it in December, 1899, the quantity was 9,000 gallons a day, which, however, is below the average; the turncock, Mr. Whittington, said when the flow was good it was double this. That hardly any water was found in Bristow's extension is probably due, as pointed out by Mr. Topley, F.R.S., in a subsequent report, to its having been driven "at too high a level"; "water," he adds, "might be found by a well or boring at the far end, but would probably not rise into the heading."

In 1885 the Board consulted two other geologists, Mr. W. Topley, F.R.S., of the Geological Survey, whose report in May of that year I have just cited, and Mr. Mark Norman, author of a geological guide to the Isle of Wight, but their schemes of sinking to the Lower Greensand were not only costly but problematical.

# The Credibility Of Dowsing

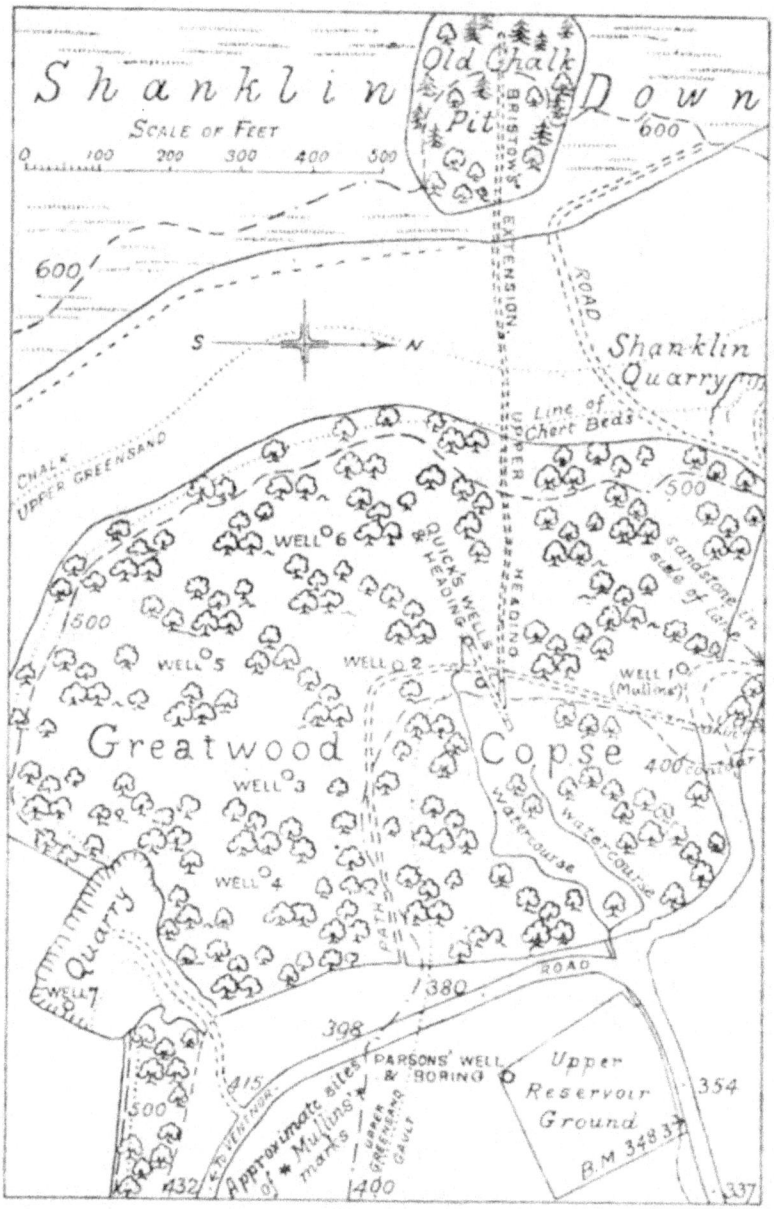

Fig. 11.

*From the 25 in. Ordnance Survey Map of the Isle of Wight, 1865, with additions from the Geological and local Surveys.*

The numbers, 337, etc., indicate height above sea level. Strong dotted lines are the 400, 500, and 600 ft. contours; faint ditto are geological boundaries. Asterisks are Mullins' marks as remembered. The watercourses are the natural drainage.

In 1893, as a last resort, the Board called in Mr. John Mullins, the well-known Wiltshire dowser, who marked several spots in the field to the south of the reservoirs, but the conditions were too onerous for them to sink there. On their own land, however, by the S. W. corner of the upper reservoir, which was from 50 to 100 yards to the north of Mullins' marks, they sank a well 30 feet deep, but without getting water. Then they got Mr. Parsons, the Brading harbour-master, to bore at the bottom of the well for 97 feet—i.e., to 127 feet from the surface—but he got no water, only bad air, which suffocated him, his son, and his men, who were all found dead in the well one morning in July. Mr.

Thom, of Manchester, continued the boring from 200 to 300 feet deeper into the Lower Greensand, but after diminishing the bore from 8 to 4 inches the Board refused to sanction a further reduction and the boring was abandoned. The borehole is now disconnected. The well has a supply from surface soakage of from 400 to 800 gallons a day, which is not used. I may remark on the foregoing that Mullins' marks, being on the outcrop of the Upper Greensand, offered a reasonable prospect for finding water, whereas the site chosen for the well at a level of 373 feet O.D., being on solid Gault clay, could have only a little from surface percolation.

In 1895 the Board consulted Mr. A. Strahan, F.G.S., of the Geological Survey (who had re-surveyed the district), on the prospect of obtaining a supply by a deep boring on the same site. In his report of September of that year he says, "I do not think there is a more favourable site, from a geological point of view, in the immediate neighbourhood." His plan, like that of Messrs. Topley and Norman, was to sink some 400 to 700 feet, and pump from the Ferruginous Sands below the sea-level; "but this," said Mr. Brown, "would have cost us a great deal, and he could not promise us anything certain when we got there."

Returning to Mullins' operations, it appears that after he came, early in 1893, two members of the Board, Messrs. Brown and Bailey, who had found the twig turn in their hands, started dowsing in the copse on their own account. They each found the twig turn at certain places nearly coincident; one of these places they found to be the same spot previously fixed upon by Mullins. At this spot (No. 1, see map, Fig. 11) they sunk a well 26 feet deep, and at two points of their own (Nos. 2 and 7) they sank wells 28 feet and 64 feet deep. Though No. 1 is only 100 yards to the north of the headings and No. 2 only 40 yards south, a good supply of water was found in the three wells. No. 1 supplied, at first, 7,000 gallons a day; No. 2, about 10,000 gallons. No. 7 required, at first, nine days to pump it out; at the present time, however, it only supplies about 2,000 gallons a day. In 1895, again following the

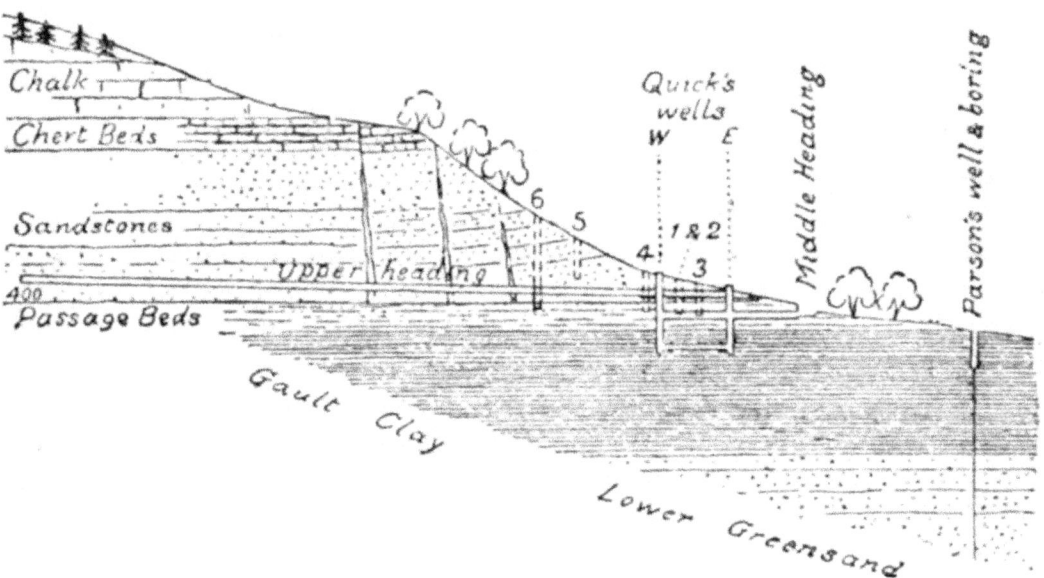

FIG. 12.

**Diagrammatic Section through Greatwood Copse: vertical scale (exaggerated twice) 208 feet to one inch.**

**The dowsers' wells, shown by dotted lines, are numbered as in Fig. 11.**

**Parson's boring extends to double the depth shown in the above diagram.**

## The Credibility Of Dowsing

twig's indications, they sank four more wells (Nos. 3, 4, 5 and 6), in all of which water was found. Nos. 3 and 4 have supplied from 1,500 to 2,000 gallons a day. No. 5, when dug, had 2 feet of water which ran freely, but has since failed. No. 6 (72 feet deep) has not been connected to the reservoir. These additional supplies, though quite inadequate for a growing town, had, said Mr. Brown, kept them going for the time being. The height of the ground at these wells (Nos. 1 to 7) I found, by levelling from St. John's Church, to be 415, 415, 413, 419½, 447½, 465 and 466 feet O.D. All the wells are now covered over, except No. 7, but I have ascertained their respective depths to be, approximately, 26, 28, 28, 30, 33, 72 and 64 feet; their bottoms are, therefore, approximately, 389, 387, 385, 389½, 414½, 393 and 402 feet O.D. Hence, except in No. 5, the water lies at levels between the middle and upper headings, showing the dowsed water to come from the same stratum as that in the other wells and headings. In No. 7 the water stands at 416½ feet O.D., so that the exhaustion of No. 5 is probably due to its not having been sunk deep enough.

The geological position of Parson's well is in the Gault clay, which is penetrated after the first 100 feet, the remainder of the boring being in the sandstones of the Lower Greensand (Neocomian). Quick's wells and the middle heading are in the passage-beds between the Gault and Upper Greensand, which pass into one another insensibly. The upper heading is mostly in the Upper Greensand, the base of which, according to the Geological Survey, is a little below the path in the copse, and coincides nearly with the 400 feet contour. The dowsed wells start in the Upper Greensand, and, except No. 5, penetrate to the passage-beds.

Tabulating the results obtained by the professionals and dowsers respectively, we have :—

### Engineers' and Geologists' Results.

| | | Supply when good. | Supply at worst. |
|---|---|---|---|
| Quick's east well ... ... | 55 ft. ⎫ | | |
| ,, west ,, ... ... | 65 ft. ⎬ syphon, 4,000 gals. per day | | |
| Submerged heading ... | 60 ft. ⎭ | | |
| Middle ,, ... | 120 ft. ⎫ flow, 20,000 ,, ,, | | 9,000 gals. |
| Upper ,, about | 900 ft. ⎭ | | |
| Parson's well and boring, not connected | ,, 300 ft. | | |
| Total | 1,500 ft. | 24,000 gals.[1] ,, | 9,000 ,, |

[1] This estimate agrees, Mr. Brown tells me, with a measurement of 25,000 gallons made by the surveyor, Mr. Colenutt. Parson's well is surface water and not used.

## Prof. W. F. Barrett

### Dowsers' Results

|  |  |  | Supply when good. | Supply at worst. |
|---|---|---|---|---|
| No. 1 well (Mullins's) | 26 ft. flow | 7,000 gals. per day | 1,250 gals. |
| ,, 2 ,, (B. and B.'s) | 28 ft. ,, | 10,000 ⎫ | |
| ,, 3 ,, ,, | 28 ft. ,, | 2,000 ⎬ ,, ,, | 0 ,, |
| ,, 5 ,, ,, | 33 ft. ,, | 1,000 ⎭ | |
| ,, 4 ,, ,, | 30 ft. syphon | 2,000 ,, ,, | ? |
| ,, 6 ,, ,, | 72½ ft. not connected | ? ,, ,, | ? |
| ,, 7 ,, ,, | 64 ft. pump | 2,000 ,, ,, | ? |
| Total 281 ft. | | 24,000 gals. ,, | 1,250 ,, |

The dowsers' first total includes the first flows (always exceptionally large) for Nos. 1 and 2; in the second total, which I took in December, 1899, after a very dry season, most of the wells had gone dry. Thus, for comparison with the engineers' total, the dowsers' first total is too large, and the second too small. To compare the water found by them respectively, we ought properly to have figures either for all the first flows, or for some time when the springs were high enough to get flows from all the wells. Mr. Cooper writes (July 11th, 1900): "I think if you put the value of the [dowsers'] wells at their best as a third the value of the headings, you will then be stating their [relative] value very fairly." According to this estimate, and taking the amount of excavation into account, the dowsers obtained nearly twice as much water per foot as the other water-finders. Of the success of the latter, five-sixths was due to empirical means, one-sixth to the engineers, and none to the geologists who went either above or below the proved water-bearing bed. The dowsers on the other hand went straight to the point by putting their wells into the water-bearing bed itself.

The relative professional failure, however, does not entitle the dowsers' results to pose as mysterious. The top of the Gault is typically water-bearing: the well-known landslip at East End, a mile or two distant, is due to the water in this very bed, the level of which in the copse was known from Quick's two wells. The probability, therefore, of some water at this horizon no geologist would doubt. What they did doubt was whether a useful quantity would be found in the copse by driving or sinking at haphazard : thus in his report Mr. Topley says, alluding to Mr. Bristow's attempt, "Galleries have been driven into the Upper Greensand for the purpose of intercepting springs . . . and I cannot recommend any further experiments in this direction." The subsequent experiments of the dowsers, introducing ex hypothesi a new method of discovery, do not throw light on the problem of haphazard sinking, except in so far as the doubtful utility of wells Nos. 5 and 6 tends to show that a useful quantity of water is not to be met with everywhere. The results of the experiments may be considered under their (1) qualitative and (2) quantitative aspects:—

(1) The finding of some water in all the dowsers' wells if claimed as evidence for dowsing involves the assumption that water could not be found everywhere by sinking into the passage beds. Between this and the geological deduction that it probably could, there is no direct evidence to decide. Quick's wells, though supporting the geological view as far as they go, are close together, and inadequate for comparison with the dowsers' seven distributed over the copse.

# The Credibility Of Dowsing

(2) The 50 per cent superiority of the seven dowsed wells assumes that Quick's wells represent the average of as many trials by ordinary methods; granting this, the superiority seems too slight to exclude accident. In support of the dowsers' opinion that they had a faculty for pitching on the right places, Mr. Brown mentioned that in one or more wells they came on loose rubble like that filling the fissures in the adjoining quarries, which made him think they had hit on a "vent" (water-bearing fissure): this was confirmed by Mr. Young, the sinker of wells Nos. 2 and 7. Failing an examination of the wells at the time, we can now only judge of the extent of this feature from its probable consequences in an increased supply, so that it does not add to the evidence. Hence the dowsers' success cannot I think be pressed in either aspect, for want of proper terms of comparison.

There remains the broad result that for equal amounts of work the dowsers got twice as much water as the engineers, while the geologists got hardly any. As regards surface signs of water in the copse I did not notice any in relation to the dowsed wells, and have given the dowsers the benefit of assuming there were none. But the absence of a reason for digging somewhere in particular may lead to digging nowhere, and in such cases the rod may succeed by supplying a motive for digging. The sceptic may urge, "the dowser turns the twig and fortune does the rest." We see, however, that geological explanations of dowsers' successes do not necessarily show that the geologists would have found the water themselves.—E.W.

## No. 2. The Errol Case

The following case is of interest, as it was first published in the columns of one of the leading engineering journals, The Engineer, for October 8th, 1897, after an editorial note on the Divining Rod. The writer of the accompanying letter to The Engineer is a member of a well-known engineering firm in Perthshire :—

Errol Works, Errol, Perthshire, *October 1st,* 1897.

Referring to your article on the above subject, as you say of yourself, "There was no one in the world more anxious to believe that these divinations were hoaxes than I was." The worst of it is, they will keep on succeeding. I will give you my own experience. A. gentleman in this parish—Mr. Clark, of Taybank—started above where he thought he would get water. He went down, I think, over 460 ft., and got none. He heard of a water-finder, now deceased—Mullins by name. Of course, he did not believe in him, but thought he would give him a trial. A lot of folks turned out to see him, amongst them the Rev. Robert Graham, LL.D. My father and I were also present. I was quite sure there was nothing in it. Mullins was first taken to the bore Mr. Clark had in progress. He was not told it was a failure. He was taken over it with his V-shaped hazel twig, and asked how much water would be got there. He said, "You may go down hundreds of feet, and you will not find any water." He—Mullins—discovered water not fifty yards from this bore. He indicated its course, and marked it by pegs driven into the ground. He told Mr. Clark if he went down 40 ft. to 50 ft. he would get so many gallons of water, and, if what he said was not true, he would pay for the digging of the well. Mr. Clark dug it, and got the supply named at the depth stated. Mullins held the ends of the V-shaped twig in his hands—an end in each hand—firmly. Whenever he came over running water the twig turned round and round, and, if held long enough, the twig twisted till it broke. When Mullins had the twig in his hands, he more than once allowed me and another party to take an end each, where the twig projected past his hands. We held on as hard as we could, and with the turning of the V part of the hazel twig, it was twisted till it hung by the bark. Yet another proof. I took the V-shaped wand in my hand, and passed it over running water without any result. Mullins laid his hands on my wrists, and grasped them firmly, when the twig instantly began to turn, and continued turning till he removed his hands. He never touched the twig while it was in my hands. Whatever folks may say to the contrary, there is something in it. "Facts are chiels that winna ding, and darna be disputed."

Duncan A. Morton.

## *Prof. W. F. Barrett*

In reply to my inquiries Mr. Morton writes :—

Errol Works, Errol, Perthshire, *October 11th,* 1899.

Yours of 9th inst. came duly to hand. I regret that I never replied to yours of October 14th, 1897. As I have not much time at my disposal, I will reply as briefly as I can to your queries. Before Mullins came, Mr. Clark had made a bore 430 ft. deep, and got little or no water, and that little he did get was bad and generally supposed to come from some drains or something of the kind. Mullins came and was taken over the bore with his rod, and said, "You can go down a thousand feet and you will not find any water there." He discovered a spring at once 100 yards from the bore at a depth of 40 ft. — an abundant supply of good water—first-rate water, indeed. Mr. Clark uses it yet, though there is a district supply now! Mullins said water would be got at a depth of 36 ft. to 40 ft., and if not, he would pay for the digging of the well.

I was as determined against the rod as any man alive till I saw it, but I could not shut my eyes to facts.

I took the V-shaped hazel wand in my hand, and passed over where Mullins said there was running water. The twig never moved, but whenever Mullins grasped my wrists the twig turned round and round till it broke and hung by the bark. I explained all this in my letter to the Engineer, October, 1897.

I saw Mr. Clark, of Taybank, last night, and he gave me the particulars. Mullins indicated the course of the running water, and we put in pegs, and they just looked like (in an uneven line) the wriggling of a stream, and came out right in line on the face of the rising ground with a drain which Mr. Clark had made, and which he said cut through a stream of water.

I shall be glad to reply to any further inquiries from you.

Duncan A. Morton.

I have also heard much to the same effect from Mr. Clark, and, in a subsequent letter, Mr. Morton informs me he has, at my request, seen Mr. Clark again, and sends me the following additional particulars. The exact depth of the useless boring was 432 ft. This bore first went through a stiff blue clay or marl, turning to red when deeper; the water that was eventually obtained was insufficient and not good. Mullins' well was dug 40 ft. and then bored to a total depth of 80 ft., when the water rose to within 12 ft. of the surface; in spite of very dry weather and continual use it has never fallen below 17 ft. from the surface. It was the old Mullins, now dead, who was employed.

Mr. Holmes' geological comment on this case is as follows:—

Looking at the general geological map of Scotland by Geikie, I find Errol on the " Old "Red Sandstone " Series. The beds pierced in the deep boring were, however, it is said, clay or marl. (It may be worth remarking that a name such as Old Red Sandstone only implies a series of rocks of a certain relative age in which red sandstone is the predominant rock.) Of course clay and marl are not likely to give a decent water supply at any depth. But close to Errol come the alluvial deposits of the Carse of Gowrie, and these (or any other alluvial deposits) would give a flat surface, contrasting in the most marked way with ground where Old Bed Sandstone formed the surface beds, and might furnish a good supply of water at 35 ft. or less. I don't know the place, but the rough diagram below will explain the general difference. If the river Tay ran through soft clay, the slopes outside the river deposits would be more gentle in contour than would be the case with harder rocks, but the practised eye would hardly fail to distinguish between slope and flat whether on the Tay, the Trent or the Thames.

T V H

# The Credibility Of Dowsing

The diagram showing the conjectured geological section, which Mr. Holmes kindly adds to his note, is not reproduced, as it is of course only a conjecture. I should be extremely obliged if any of my readers in Perthshire would make further geological inquiries into this case, as it is evidently one of considerable interest. It will be remembered that it was old John Mullins who was the dowser in the famous Waterford case, which was so fully discussed in the previous Report. The useless bore in that case was over 1,000 ft., and there were absolutely *no* surface indications to guide him.

## No. 3. The Lytes Cary (Somerset) Case

The following is a very interesting case. The dowser, in this instance, was an amateur, the late Mr. E. M. Hippisley, a leading surveyor and land agent in Wells, Somersetshire, who was singularly successful as an amateur dowser. In a paper on his own experiences in dowsing that he read at the Bishop's Palace, in Wells, in April, 1892, he stated :—

> At Lytes Cary [near Kingsdon, Taunton] there is an interesting old English house with a chapel in good preservation, which, with some modern [farmhouse] buildings, enclose a large courtyard. I found [by dowsing] on the south side near the garden, indications of water, and had a well sunk 25 ft. deep, in which the water rises to within 13 ft. of the surface, and here a singular incident occurred. During the past year part of the paving on the opposite side of the yard gave way, when an old well was discovered 45 ft. in depth, but no water in it, and only 30 ft. from the new well.

Mr. Westlake kindly went over to Lytes Cary and made a careful examination of the surroundings, and of the geological conditions as well as the facts of the case. He reports to me as follows:—

*May*, 1900.

> "Lytes Cary is in the southernmost bend of the river Cary, in Somersetshire. The farmhouse is in the occupation of Messrs. Porter and Porter, who aided my inquiries in every way. I was first shown the sites of the wells, both quite covered over and concealed; they are about 40 ft. apart. The old well was carefully built, and is 60 ft. deep (not 45 ft., as Mr. Hippisley thought) so I was informed by the estate builder, who had measured it himself. He told me also that Hippisley's well is 25 ft. deep, sunk in the marl all the way down, and the sides are strong enough to stand without masonry.[1] It still continues to give an abundant supply to the house, and contained 9 ft. of water when last opened. There are also three other wells on the N. and W. of the premises, about 190, 140, and 80 ft. distant from Hippisley's well; one of them, the furthest off, is 22 ft. deep, and yields a small supply of "suspicious" water; the second, which once contained a few feet of foul water, has been filled up; and the third was long ago abandoned and used as a cesspool.

> "The farm premises are all on level ground. The strata at the farm, according to the geological survey, are Lower Lias, which, as seen in quarries about a mile to the north, consists of the usual thin limestones with partings of marl, and has little permeability except in the vertical joints. The beds at the farm appear to underlie the above, but there are no surface indications, geological or otherwise, to show that water is more likely to be found at one spot than another. Had the existence of the old well been known a geologist would have been chiefly concerned to avoid its proximity. In finding water so near it Mr. Hippisley certainly achieved the improbable, though, as agent for the estate, he was thoroughly acquainted with the place, except the existence of the old dry well, which had been lost sight of by all. A characteristic of the Lower Lias is to hold water in unsuspected fissures. This places the hydro-geologist at a disadvantage, and renders this formation a suitable ground for dowsing, or chance discovery, as the case may be. I have referred to other cases of the dowser's success in the Lower Lias in my Report, p. 315. - E. W."

---

[1] This does not necessarily show the strata were different.

## No. 4. The Sherburn-in-Elmet Case

I heard that Mr. Stone had been engaged by the owner of some property at Sherburn-in-Elmet, Yorkshire, to find a water supply where a well, over 150 ft. deep, already existed, but had run dry, and that Stone had predicted by the " rod" that an abundant supply would be found less than 50 ft. from the old well at a depth of 60 ft., and that, upon boring, Stone's prediction was verified and a good supply obtained. I wrote to the owner of the property, Mr. Lolley, for an exact statement of the facts, and had the following reply:—

Northfield House, Lovell Road, Leeds, *December 6th*, 1899.

> It is quite true we had a well 70 ft. deep, and had bored about 90 or 100 ft. from the bottom of the well without finding water. The well had been in use about fifteen years, and always had a good supply until an artesian well was sunk in the low-lying part of Sherburn, after which we seemed to lose the water.
>
> Seeing Mr. Stone's testimonials, I applied to him. Mr. Stone visited Sherburn and said that there was a good supply of water some 60 ft. deep beneath a place he indicated, about 15 yds. from the old well, and on the boring being carried out the water was found at 62 ft. deep.
>
> Walter Lolley.

This case is of interest, and I should be glad of some further information concerning it, especially of the geological character of the locality. Sherburn-in-Elmet is midway between Leeds and York, and Mr. T. V. Holmes, F.G.S., informs me it lies near the bottom of the slope of the Magnesian Limestone, which here dips down to the Old Red Sandstone that overlies it in the valley. I wrote to Mr. Lolley to ask if he had kept a record of the strata bored through, and he replies:—

Leeds, *December 28th*, 1899.

> The borehole at Sherburn was through limestone and clay, the rock is the " Magnesian " limestone, and my property is on the eastern slope of this; in fact, the lower part of the village further east is on the alluvial clay of the Vale of York. The water was found in a layer of gravel and clay in the borehole after getting through the limestone.
>
> Walter Lolley.

## No. 5. The Tiddington House (Oxford) Case

The following letter appeared in the Farmer and Chamber of Agriculture Journal for October 18th, 1897. The case is interesting as the artesian well borers were attempting to bore through the Oxford clay, whilst the dowser, as in many other cases, evidently found a permeable surface stratum, of sand or gravel, above the clay.

Tiddington House, Oxford, *October*, 1897.

> Being without water for my garden and stable, except what was fetched by water cart some distance day by day and caught from rainfall, and this altogether unsatisfactory, I experienced a great difficulty in getting a proper water supply, and eventually decided to employ a firm of artesian well borers to bore for water for my use in 1883. A spot was decided upon, and a boring put down to a depth of 312 ft., which cost me over £300, and no water whatever was obtained; all I have for my money is the piece of parchment containing the sections of the boring and a few samples of the formation...
>
> I engaged Mr. Tompkins to search my property for a water supply... and instructed him to carefully test my stable yard, as this was the site I was most anxious to find water on. After carefully searching this property he reported that no water existed there, and that it would be simply useless to attempt

# The Credibility Of Dowsing

to obtain water here. I then informed him of what I had previously done, and the amount of money I had uselessly spent. Thus the water-finder proved correct in his first test.

A move was then made into the gardens, and, after going over them, the water-finder reported a stratum of water was running across the corner of the garden, and was an overflow from a spring above. Ho traced up this stratum of water. The twig he was using was a white thorn cut in the shape of a V, which he held by the two prongs apex downwards. As he walked over this stratum of water, the twig kept rising in front of him until he came to the head of the spring[1] in the upper part of the paddock above, when it turned completely over and over, and so strong was the upward movement of the rod that it bent considerably in its frantic endeavour to turn over, and on being held firmly by the water-finder, it broke off in his hand. Naturally, we were all surprised and astonished at such a remarkable occurrence.

I instructed Mr. Tompkins to prepare me an estimate to sink a well four feet diameter in the clear, and to supply and erect a wind engine and storage tank. The well was put in hand, and at a depth of 30 ft. water was struck. The well was steined up[2] before sinking deeper, and a strong pump put down to keep the water under, and before sinking many feet it became necessary to put on seven men to keep the water going. From the inrush of water the bottom men were working up to their knees in water, and the moment the pump and buckets stopped they were in danger of being drowned out. The work proceeded under these circumstances for a week or so, until it became useless to continue the work owing to the abundance of water; 10,000 gallons per day being the yield of the spring at a depth of 37 ft., and this site is at a higher elevation than my stable yard. I cannot speak too highly of Mr. Tompkins' practical success, both as regards his finding water and the satisfactory way in which he has carried out the work.

G. W. Bennett.

In reply to my inquiries Mr. Bennett confirms the statements in his published letter and adds :—

Tiddington House, Oxford, *October 9th*, 1899.

My well has never gone dry, neither this summer nor last, though it gets low generally about November or December. The only drawback to the windmill is, I find, we have not always enough wind to pump, and sometimes we are four or five days without wind for pumping for drinking purposes. There are [not] and never have been any wells near where Mr. Tompkins found the water with the divining rod.

G. W. Bennett.

Mr. Holmes' comment on this case is as follows :—

Oxford stands upon "Oxford Clay," the thickness of which varies from 300 ft. to 600 ft. (Woodward). But over the greater part of the site the Oxford clay is covered by gravel, which is usually from 8 ft. to 20 ft. thick. And gravel on a higher level is often found to cap the plateaux of the district. I do not know whether Tiddington House is in or near Oxford. The unsatisfactory boring of 312 ft. was evidently in the Oxford Clay. But the satisfactory supply was evidently from sand and gravel lying above the Oxford Clay. But the gravel on which Oxford stands is not that deposited by the rivers Isis and Cherwell, but is of the higher level and older date. Where in Oxford and its

---

[1] This is an absurd but favourite expression of Mr. Tompkins, who is under the delusion that underground water originates in a reservoir, and that the higher up you trace the " spring " the more copious the supply.—W. F. B.

[2] [THIS EXPRESSION means to line the excavation to prevent soil being washed away or to prevent a cave-in. Ed]

suburbs, between the Isis and Cherwell, the ground is covered by a thick mass of superficial sands, gravels, etc., there the ground is likely to be higher than where the Oxford Clay is bare. And the contours of the ground will tell at once to the practised eye where there is bare clay and where there is a gravel-capping above it, or river-gravel at a lower level. Of course, if, in this case, the successful sinking had been in the gravel of the Cherwell or Isis, and the house on the Oxford Clay, it would have been at a lower level than the house. It appears, however, to have been at a higher level than the house—or at least the stable yard. Gravel seems to have the same way of capping the highest ground in the Oxford Clay country that it has in the London Clay districts.

T. V. H.

Mr. Holmes' geological diagnosis of this case is confirmed by the following letter, which I received in reply to my inquiry as to any surface indications, and as to the nature of the boring and also the distance apart of the useless boring and Tompkins' well. The sand or gravel bed was evidently thicker than intimated by Mr. Holmes, and no doubt the rush of water came when the well-sinkers got close to the underlying impermeable clay. All the same, this does not explain how Tompkins hit on the right spot, for "the practised eye" of the well-sinkers who put down the useless bore, and that of Mr. Bennett's gardener, failed to discover the right spot.

Tiddington House, Oxford, January 3rd, 1900.

The Tompkins well is on rather a higher elevation than where we bored in 1883, and is quite 150 yards from that boring. The Oxford clay is certainly capped by sandy grit or gravel. We first took off about 3 or 4 ft. of turf mould; then went into a red sand which continued some 25 or 30 ft., when the water came in so fast they could not go on digging the well. To the ordinary eye, no one could possibly have said where to hit upon the spring. Mr. Tompkins went backwards and forwards in a zigzag course with the twig till he came to what he calls "the fountain head," where he cut a sod out of the turf to show the well-sinkers where to begin to dig the well.

I should say we are about 40 ft. above the level of the river Thames, which connects with the Isis at Dorchester, Oxon., and there it is called "Thamisis" or Thames. We are nine miles from Oxford, and nearly two from the river Thames.

G W Bennett.

## No. 6. The Chelford (Cheshire) Case

The following letter appeared in the Manchester City News for October 23rd, 1897. The writer is the head of a well-known firm of chartered accountants in Manchester.

Bella Vista, Heaton Moor.

Having noticed the great amount of controversy that has of late been manifested, together with the number of articles that have appeared in various contemporaries, on the so-called divining rod as a means of discovering water supplies, I venture to give you an account of my recent experience with a water-finder and his work.

Having had occasion to obtain a new water supply for a house in Cheshire, the opinion of a firm of artesian well borers was obtained. They recommended that at a certain spot an artesian well should be sunk, with the idea of tapping a spring of water, and at the same time to have the advantage of an artesian well to ensure absolute purity. Accordingly a contract was obtained and a well [boring] made, with the hope of finding a supply of water at a reasonable depth; and after several months' work, entailing considerable expense, boring was carried to a depth of about 480 ft. But the long looked for supply of water was not obtained, and after trying for some time to get a supply of water from this

## *The Credibility Of Dowsing*

deep well, I found that it was almost useless, and in the end had to be abandoned as a failure. I then, for the first time, sought the advice of a firm of water-finders who use the divining rod, and having made an appointment with Messrs. John Mullins and Sons, Colerne, Box, Wiltshire, I met a member of their firm on the estate.

In the simplest way possible he began to prospect the grounds for what he called a spring, or water-bearing strata. Carrying in his hands a V shaped hazel twig, holding the point downwards, with one fork in each hand, he began to walk across the lawn, and after walking a distance of about twenty yards he suddenly stopped, with the twig automatically twisting in his hands. He declared that here a spring existed at a depth from the surface of not more than 40 ft. To convince me that he could not govern the action of the twig in his hands, he requested me to grip the ends of the twig, and so try to keep it from turning, but in trying to do so I was quite powerless. After trying for some minutes to gauge the volume of the spring, which he professed to do by the action of the twig, he then gave what he considered to be the approximate yield of water per day, and proceeded to trace the direction in which the spring was running. Having gone into the kitchen garden, he said the spring was only 10 ft. from the bore which had previously been made to so great a depth.

In order to prove that he had faith in his own method, he asked to be allowed to undertake the necessary work, and to obtain the supply of water which he had predicted, at the same time undertaking that if his predictions were not substantiated, the work done by him would not be charged for. A contract was entered into on these terms. As a result, the well has been made, and, at a depth of 36 ft., a good supply of water has been found. The water is of excellent quality.

I venture to trouble you with these facts, because I think that this method of discovering springs of water deserves to be better known.

Charles William Nasmith.

I wrote to Mr. Nasmith for some additional particulars and received the following reply :—

69, Princess Street, Manchester, *June 6th*, 1898.

In reply to yours of the 31st ult. *re* the water supply at Mereleigh, Chelford, I have very little to say beyond that which I gave in my letter addressed to the City News of October 22nd, except that Mullins was quite a stranger in the neighbourhood, and had no knowledge of the subsoils. He first found the spring of water on the lawn, and traced its course from the lawn to the kitchen garden, and the site he selected for the well was 10 ft. from the deep bore, and at this site the well has been made, with the result given in my letter, and the supply is still satisfactory.

The subsoil where the spring was found was sand, with about 13 ft. of clay on the surface and clay below the level of the spring, but it appears that in the old deep bore it was all clayey.

No other authority was previously consulted beyond the firm who did the boring. They, I believe, worked by the geological chart of the neighbourhood.

Charles William Nasmith.

Mr. Nasmith also sent me a plan of the estate with position of the useless boring and Mullins well, but this adds nothing to the information given in his letter. In reply to Mr. Nasmith, the artesian well borers, Messrs. Timmins, wrote to the local papers to say that the well sunk by Mullins merely yielded surface water and was therefore unsafe to use for drinking, that the surface soil was sand and an old disused well sunk in this sand existed close by. Mr.

Nasmith, however, maintains that the Mullins well does not yield surface water, but is sunk below an impermeable stratum of clay. I submitted the whole correspondence to Mr. T. V. Holmes, who writes in reply as follows:—

28, Crooms Hill, Greenwich Park, London, S.E., *June 11th*, 1898.

> As to the discrepancy between the accounts of Timmins and Nasmith as to the strata at Chelford, I can offer only the following remarks :—My experience of the sections obtained from well-sinkers and borers is that they are extremely careful as to details, and go into more detail than a geologist usually would. The well-sinker will not mistake darker-coloured sand, which owes its special hue to saturation with water, for clay.
>
> Then, if we suppose that there were *locally* 13 ft. of clay at the surface, the water found in both old and new wells evidently came from the same source, the lower part of the sand; and if the occasional surface clay did not protect the old well from surface pollution, it would not protect the new one.
>
> As regards the deep boring, the new red marl would be mainly what might be termed clayey, and its top would probably be not many feet below the level of the water in the sand.
>
> I enclose a rough diagram to illustrate the general nature of things. The alternatives as regards water in the district are evidently that you either get it from the surface sand and gravel, or from the new red sandstone hundreds of feet below. Any surface clay (supposing it not to be *made* ground; see subsoils memoir), being of no practical importance.
>
> T. V. Holmes.

It is clear, therefore, from Mr. Holmes' letter that he regards the clay as occurring in patches on the surface and affording no real protection from possible pollution from surface drainage. In reply to my further inquiries Mr. Nasmith informs me that the old condemned well was 18 feet deep, the useless boring is 480 feet deep, whilst the new well, the supply from which he informs me is still "very satisfactory," is 36 feet deep. Chelford is near Alderley Edge in Cheshire.

Shallow wells, certainly, often yield safe potable water, as is seen from the following letter which I received from the Rev. J. G. Geare in reply to my inquiries :—

Farnham Rectory, Bishops Stortford, *May 26th*, 1897.

> In reply I beg to say that Mullins, junr., found on my rectory of three acres a splendid spring of good water with his divining twig on September 28th, 1893. He found water at less than 20 ft. depth. A boring was made and a well (brick) was sunk to 15 ft. depth. The water was analysed, and found good, and since then I have had a bountiful and unfailing supply through a rotary pump action.
>
> I may add that Mullins was always correct as to depth to sink a well and the best place to bore. His was a first visit, and no test previous to his had been made.
>
> J. G. Geare, Rector.

Upon which Mr. Holmes remarks :—

> Whether the water from surface beds is wholesome or not depends largely on the density of the population around any given well. Nobody can get water absolutely pure. But the poor geologist would hardly venture to recommend surface supplies, for finding which the dowser is hailed as a supernormally gifted benefactor.
>
> T V H

# The Credibility Of Dowsing

## No. 7. The Welwyn Case

The writer of the next letter is known to Mr. F. W. H. Myers, who kindly sent me the letter.

*The Node, Welwyn, Herts, October 30th, 1899.*

> I sent for a water diviner last summer, as I wanted advice about the water supply here, our well not being satisfactory. When the diviner came he at once found out the direction of the spring supplying my well and advised me to make a heading in a certain direction which he marked, and which I afterwards carried out, 150 ft. below the surface. The well-sinkers found, before they had carried this heading 6ft., the inrush of water was so great they had to stop, in spite of a steam engine which kept going night and day with powerful pumps.
>
> After trying every device for keeping water out of an accumulator house, which always seemed to be rising, in spite of a concrete floor 6 in. thick, the same diviner told me exactly where a spring caused the trouble. We tapped it from the outside, and now the place is perfectly dry.
>
> I held one side of the forked rod myself and the "diviner" the other, and when we came to water [alleged underground water] the strain was so great on my fingers I was obliged to ask him to stop. From the position of the rod it was absolutely impossible for him to produce the pressure, which increased with the strength of the stream.
>
> Montague Price.

The last paragraph of this interesting letter I will refer to again when dealing with the motion of the rod. In reply to my inquiries as to the name of the dowser, the geological strata, and whether any surface indications or other wells existed to guide the dowser's choice, Mr. Price replies as follows :—

*The Node, Welwyn, Herts, November 7th, 1899.*

> Anthony, of Huntingdon, was the "diviner" we employed here last June. Nobody knew where the spring came from supplying the well. When the "diviner" arrived, being Saturday afternoon, the workpeople had gone and I certainly did not know where the water came from. I was with him all the time he was here, and he did not go down the well, which is over 150 ft. deep.
>
> There is no well anywhere near the existing one, and, so far as I know, there was no surface indication to guide the diviner. In fact, he found the spring on adjoining property, 50 yards from the well. We drove the heading in the well (already existing) 150 ft. below the surface in pure chalk. Other springs he found on my property, but I had no occasion to try them.
>
> Montague Price.

Mr. Holmes explains this case as follows :—

> In this case the supply from a well in the chalk 150 ft. deep being unsatisfactory, the dowser simply recommended a heading. This is a common and well-known contrivance in such cases. Water in the chalk, the great water-bearing formation of S.E. England, circulates by the lines of bedding and jointing, especially the latter. Where the lines of jointing are feebly developed the supply of water from the chalk is usually feeble—the permanent saturation level being of course reached. The usual plan then is to drive a heading or headings in order to tap additional joint lines; one direction being about as good as another,
>
> T V H

Mr. Holmes' comment on the geological aspect of this case is that the dowser simply advised doing what a skilled engineer or geologist would recommend. But it must be remembered on the other hand that the dowser probably knew nothing of geology or engineering; I doubt if he even knew that the well was in the chalk, as he came from Huntingdon. Assuming, however, he knew all this, and was a geologist in the bargain, how did he find out the direction in which to make the heading which reached so large a supply "before 6 ft." had been driven? The Richmond headings[1] were driven great distances in the chalk under the advice of the best geologists and engineers, and yet to a large extent failed to accomplish their purpose. Was it by a mere bit of luck that here, as in many other cases, the dowser succeeded?

## No. 8

The next is a letter addressed to Mr. Stone, the dowser, from a Mr. Stevenitt.

Minting, Horncastle, Lincolnshire, *February 7th*, 1898.

> I beg to inform you that I dug a well at the second place marked by you, viz., about 20 yds. from the stockyard in grass field, and found water. I dug a well 42 ft. deep, so that I should have a good supply for the yard. We have plenty for ourselves and several neighbours, who fetch it regularly for drinking purposes. I feel sorry I did not know of you sooner; it would have saved me something like £200 in boring 290 ft., where I only found salt water at 135 ft. deep.

T Stevenitt

I wrote to Mr. Stevenitt, who confirms the above statement and tells me the useless bore is only 45 yards from the well. He was for twenty-five years Superintendent of Police in the County Constabulary. As regards this case Mr. Holmes remarks:—

> In Lincolnshire the gratitude for good water at 42 ft. on the part of Mr. Stevenitt is most intelligible. May it never be polluted by soakings from the stockyard to any injurious degree.

T. V. H.

## No. 9

The next letter is from the Managing Director of the Bermaline Maltings, Haddington, where Mr. Gataker was the dowser employed.

> We may state that, previous to our communicating with Mr. Gataker, we had decided to put down an artesian bore at a different part of our ground. On arrival Mr. Gataker started over the ground at a fair speed with the palms of his hands towards the earth. After proceeding some distance he was able to locate a spring at the end of our new maltings. He then proceeded over a strawberry field belonging to us, and at about 70 yards from where he located the first spring he located another. He guaranteed that from either of those springs we would get a supply of about 20,000 gallons per day at a depth of from 100 ft. to 150 ft. We put down a 4 in. bore at the first spring, and are pleased to say that at a depth of 102 ft. we are getting a supply of about 100,000 gallons per day, and the water is coming up with great force. We believe it will rise to about 40 ft. above the surface. We tested it at 13 ft., when it overflowed with a strong pressure.
>
> We challenged the editor and readers of an Edinburgh evening newspaper, who seem to think that water was to be found in any part of our ground, to put down a similar bore half-way between the two springs located by Mr. Gataker in our ground, and if the same quantity of water was found at the

---

[1] See previous Report, Vol. XIII., p. 195. [p 157 in this volume - Ed]

## The Credibility Of Dowsing

> same depth we would pay the expense of putting down the bore, and if not found, the party challenging was to pay the expense; but up to now the challenge has not been taken up by any one.
>
> It might interest your readers to know the strata the bore went through, and we have much pleasure in enclosing you a copy of the journal, from which you will see that it was after piercing 14 in. of the fourth layer of sandstone that the water was struck, and as soon as the crust of this layer was broken, the water came away with a rushing noise.
>
> Montgomerie And Company (Limited),<br>John Montgomerie,<br>Managing Director.

It is to be regretted this challenge was not accepted, as it would have been a very crucial test, though, from geological considerations, we are disposed to think the newspaper would have won. Mr. Montgomerie, however, in his letter to the Edinburgh newspaper, states his reasons for believing that water would not be found "at any part of the valley of the Tyne." He says :—

> Bermaline Maltings, Haddington, *January 14th*, 1899.
>
> During the excavations for the new bridge here, there was dug out a hole 40 ft. square by 13 ft. deep alongside our mill dam, with only about 3 ft. of an embankment between the water and the hole. We naturally expected that this hole would be filled up with water rising through the gravel bed; but to our surprise there was not a drop of water came up. Any water that found its way into the working came in at the north-east corner—that is, the corner furthest from the river.
>
> There is a firm in East Lothian, not far from Haddington, who put down a bore without calling in the aid of a "water-finder." They have, I believe, sunk it to a depth of 660 ft., and, failing to find water, have had to abandon the bore.

I should he glad of any further information regarding the deep bore-hole here mentioned, as neighbouring artesian wells do not usually vary like this.

In reply to my inquiries Mr. Montgomerie states that his successful borehole is about 100 ft. above the sea level; he sends a "journal of the bore," showing the strata passed through. First, 20 ft. of sand and gravel, then 6 ft. of boulder clay, followed by 19 ft. of fire clay, after that 45 ft of sandstone and what are called "faikes" [sandy shale - Ed] in alternate layers, then 8 ft. of marl, and, finally, sandstone, the depth of the bore being nearly 103 ft.

## No. 10. The Aspley Heath (Bedford) Case

The next case is also one where a deep, unsuccessful bore had been made prior to the dowser's visit. The account here given was published in the Midland Counties Herald for April 7th, 1898.

> A Bedfordshire gentleman, Mr. Plater, wanted water for his house, so got a firm to sink a well 60 ft. deep, this being the depth at which it was expected water would be found. However, none was found, and then sinking was continued to 100 ft. deep, but still without success. A bore was then put down at the bottom of this well a further 66 ft. deep, making a total depth of 166 ft., but still no water. At Mr. Plater's request a water expert visited the place, and said it was useless to continue working at that spot, for no water would be found; but he felt absolutely confident that by sinking a well at a spot only 39 ft. from there, there ought to be a plentiful supply of water at about 100 ft. or so. Mr. Plater acted on his advice, and at 116 ft. an abundant supply was found. The old well, although so close, is said to be still as dry as a bone.

# Prof. W. F. Barrett

I wrote to Mr. Plater, enclosing the above report, and obtained the following reply:—

Silver Birch, Aspley Heath, Woburn Sands, R.S.O., *October 16th*, 1899.

I return the press cutting which was enclosed with your letter to me of the 9th inst. It is correct. In reply to your three questions :—

1. As stated in the newspaper cutting, an unsuccessful attempt was made to a depth of 166 ft., at which we had bored several feet into Oxford clay.

2. No further useless wells or borings were made near the successful well.

3. There is an ample supply of water obtained from the well sunk on the spot indicated by Mr. Gataker.

I may state that my property at Aspley Heath, Bedfordshire, where the wells were sunk in 1896, is about 500ft. above sea level.

Mr. Gataker stated that water would be found on the spot indicated, but not under 100 ft. from the surface.

Arthur C. Plater.

Mr. Holmes remarks: "The boring in Oxford clay was unsuccessful, and Mr. Gataker was successful. The interesting point is the statement in the newspaper cutting that the useless well was only 39 ft. from the good one. Mr. Plater, however, does not seem to confirm this statement.—T. V. H."

I wrote again to Mr. Plater with regard to this latter point and also to inquire whether he was present when the dowser visited the spot, and whether he could tell me the strata bored through in his new well. Mr. Plater replies as follows:—

Silver Birch, Aspley Heath, Woburn Sands, R.S.O., *December 14th*, 1899.

In reply to your letter the distance between the two wells, about 39 ft., is quite correct. The new well is 116 ft. deep. I was present when Mr. L. Gataker expressed his opinion that water would be found at a depth of about 100 ft, I have lost my record of the strata through which we bored in the old well, but to a depth of about 90 ft. sand, with occasional layers of ironstone, formed the principal feature; at about 130 ft. we bored through 6 ft. of fuller's earth, and after more sand we bored into the clay several feet, and then ceased work. I think the water in the new well is on a bed of fuller's earth. The level of the mouth of the new well is about 14 ft. lower than that of the old. The latter is now used as a rainwater tank.

Arthur C. Plater.

Though I am not a geologist, the explanation of this case appears to me simple. The bed of fuller's earth found at a depth of 130 ft. in the old well evidently forms the bottom of the new well, which is 116 ft. deep and 14 ft. lower level = 130 ft. As fuller's earth (a silicious clay) is a nearly impermeable water bed, when this was pierced, as in the old well, the water would escape into the sand below the bed. If the record of the old boring was shown to Mr Gataker, or known to him, the explanation of his successful prediction is also easy; though I have no doubt it would be rejected by all concerned, as dowsers trust more to themselves than to any information given them.

It will be seen from the notes which Mr. Holmes and Mr. Westlake have so kindly added to many of these cases, that a geological explanation of why the dowser found water in the places he indicated is clear enough. The important point is, would these places have been selected by a shrewd observer, or even by a skilled geologist, before the

## The Credibility Of Dowsing

dowser had visited the spot? In some cases this might, as in No. 10, have been so; on the other hand a considerable body of evidence exists to show that the dowser, though ignorant of geology and an entire stranger to the locality, succeeded, where expert geological or engineering advice, aided by careful local observation, completely failed. Those who have taken the trouble to read the previous Report will recall several cases of this kind, notably the Waterford case on p. 83 et seq., the Horsham case, p. 94 et seq., the Uppingham case, p. 103 et seq., Sir Welby Gregory's case, p. 74, etc.

Then again, if merely shrewd observation and considerable experience as well-sinkers afford a sufficient explanation of the dowser's success, how are we to explain the achievements of young dowsers and other complete novices? Take the case of the French charity boy Bleton recorded in Part X of the present report, or, referring to the previous Report, take the cases of the eleven-year-old Cornish lad given on p. 36, Vol. XIII. [p. 26 in this volume -Ed], or the young daughter of an estate agent given on p. 24 et seq., or the daughter of an English clergyman on p. 28, or the young son of another clergyman on p. 28, etc., etc. Then, too, we have other amateur dowsers of all ages and in all ranks of life, whose successes in the discovery of underground water certainly appear at first sight to be greater than mere observation or good luck would account for. Numerous instances of this were given in the previous Report, and a few additional cases of successful amateur dowsers, such as his Honour Sir Richard Harington, Bart., are quoted later on.

One of the four methods suggested by me to test the pretensions of the dowser (see p. 251 of last Report [p.204 in this volume - Ed]) is "separate and entirely independent examination of the same ground by different dowsers." The evidence on behalf of this test I will now proceed to cite.

# PART IV

## Experiments With Two Or More Dowsers Independently Tried On The Same Ground

### No. 1. The Cheltenham Experiments

I am indebted to our fellow-worker, Lieut.-Colonel Le M. Taylor, of Cheltenham, for the following interesting report of his own and other experiments at Cheltenham. It appears that in 1896 the Directors of the Cheltenham Steam Laundry, anxious to obtain a supply of water for the laundry, at Colonel Taylor's suggestion and by arrangement with him, employed two dowsers, independently of each other, to locate the best site whereon to sink a well. Colonel Taylor arranged first to take Mr. Tompkins to the laundry, and after he had fixed on the place or places where water would be found, the laundry directors were to employ a second dowser and the results were to be compared. The following is an abridged account of the proceedings given in a local newspaper :—

> A "diviner" went over the ground a week or so ago in company with several of the directors. He subsequently wrote a report which, according to an arrangement unknown to the diviner himself, the directors sealed and kept strictly secret. As business folk, the directors were not going to trust to the decision of one expert, and, therefore, another was engaged to go over the ground on Wednesday in company with other directors, who did not know what the result of the former experiment was, in order that there might be no unconscious collusion or "thought reading," Mr. Chesterman, of Bath, the chief huntsman on this occasion, seemed to think that his task was none too easy, as it is not always that a reliable supply of water can be found in a small field of clay soil, such as that at the side of the laundry to which his prospecting was restricted. Taking one of his small, slender twigs, he held it in front of him with his arms lowered and one end of it in each hand, so that the angle of the fork pointed very slightly downwards, about three feet from the ground. Thus he commenced to walk slowly in a straight line across the field. Suddenly the twig gave a turn in the operator's hands, began to revolve, and continued to do so while he remained within the area in which he experienced the "shock" of water. The two directors attempted to stay the revolving motion of the twig while the operator carried it over the affected area, but though each seized one end of it, they could not do so, the ends of the twig, in fact, slightly lacerating their fingers as it turned in resistance to all the pressure they could employ. Similar results were obtained with the wire. Then Dr. Cardew walked across the affected spot with the twig in his hands, but the simple apparatus remained quite stationary until Mr. Chesterman placed his hands on the doctor's wrists, when it began to revolve.—Cheltenham, Echo, December 10th, 1896.

How far the sites fixed on by the two dowsers coincided will be seen from Colonel Taylor's report and drawings, which I now append.

### Lieut.-Colonel Taylor's Report

On December 8th, 1896, I was informed that Mr. Chesterman, of Bath, had been engaged by the Directors of the Hatherley Laundry to "douse" for water on their property, and that he was to arrive the next day. I wrote him a note and asked him to call on me when he had finished, which he kindly did. On his arrival I showed him my plan of the laundry ground and asked him to point out where he had found water. The dotted lines on the plan, Fig. 13, show the places indicated by him, and these agree also with the information I subsequently got from Mr. Wilkins, one of the directors, who accompanied Mr. Chesterman during the experiment. Mr. Wilkins also told me that Chesterman had found indications of water about the place I have marked E, but as it was not a strong stream, no more was done about it. Mr. Chesterman has been for years in the Indian D.P.W., and therefore quite understands a plan. No one who was at the former experiment at Hatherley was present on December 9th, and Mr. Wilkins did not open the envelope containing the record of what Mr. Tompkins had done till the trial was over. Mr. Chesterman

# The Credibility Of Dowsing

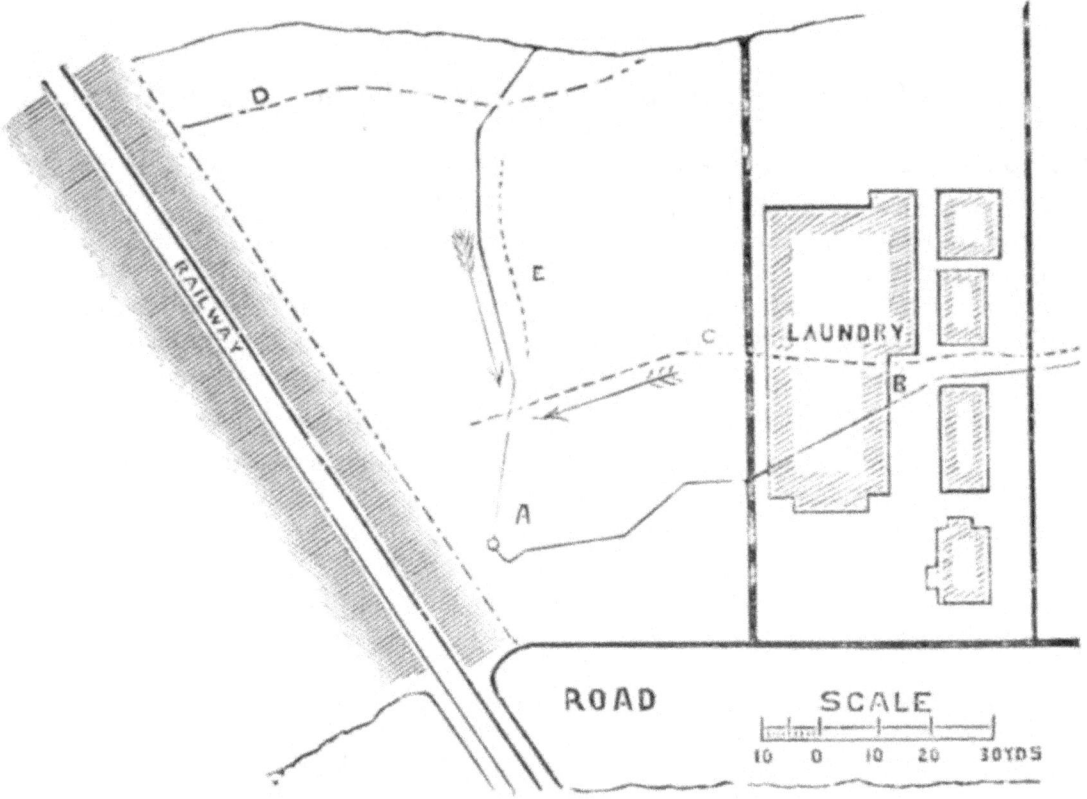

FIG. 13.

**Rough plan of Hatherley Laundry, where water-finding experiments were tried, November and December, 1896.**

**Tompkins on November 25th traced the streams marked in continuous lines and recommended Well at A, estimated at 80 ft. to yield 3,000 gals. in 24 hours, and also one at B, but not so strongly.**

**Chesterman on December 9th traced streams marked in dotted lines and recommended Well at B, 108 ft., to yield 3,600 gals. in 24 hours, or Well at C, 90 ft., to yield the same quantity, or one at D, 85, to yield, however, less.**

was not told that another man had gone over the ground, though, as he told me, he suspected it after he had completed his search from being asked what he would say if another finder had indicated other places.

All parts of the field near the laundry seem equally open to their choice, but it might be said that a desire to make things pleasant for the Laundry Company may have influenced each of them to locate water near the engine house, well knowing that water would most likely be found everywhere.[1]

Previous to Mr. Chesterman's visit Mr. Tompkins had been to my place to conduct the experiments on finding coins already sent you,[2] and I had also asked Mr. Tompkins to indicate any place in my garden where underground

---

[1] Colonel Taylor sends a geological map of a section of the district, taken from Murchison's Geology of Cheltenham. Sand occurs in patches up to 30 feet in depth, over the lias formation, which latter is probably some 300 or 400 feet thick at Cheltenham; shallow wells sunk in the sand would yield surface water, and wells sunk 70 to 130 feet about Cheltenham frequently yield water, which, however, is more or less saline. But the laundry experiment is, if anything, adverse to the dowser. —W. F. B.

[2] These experiments will be given in a subsequent paper.—W. F. B. [This report was never completed - Ed]

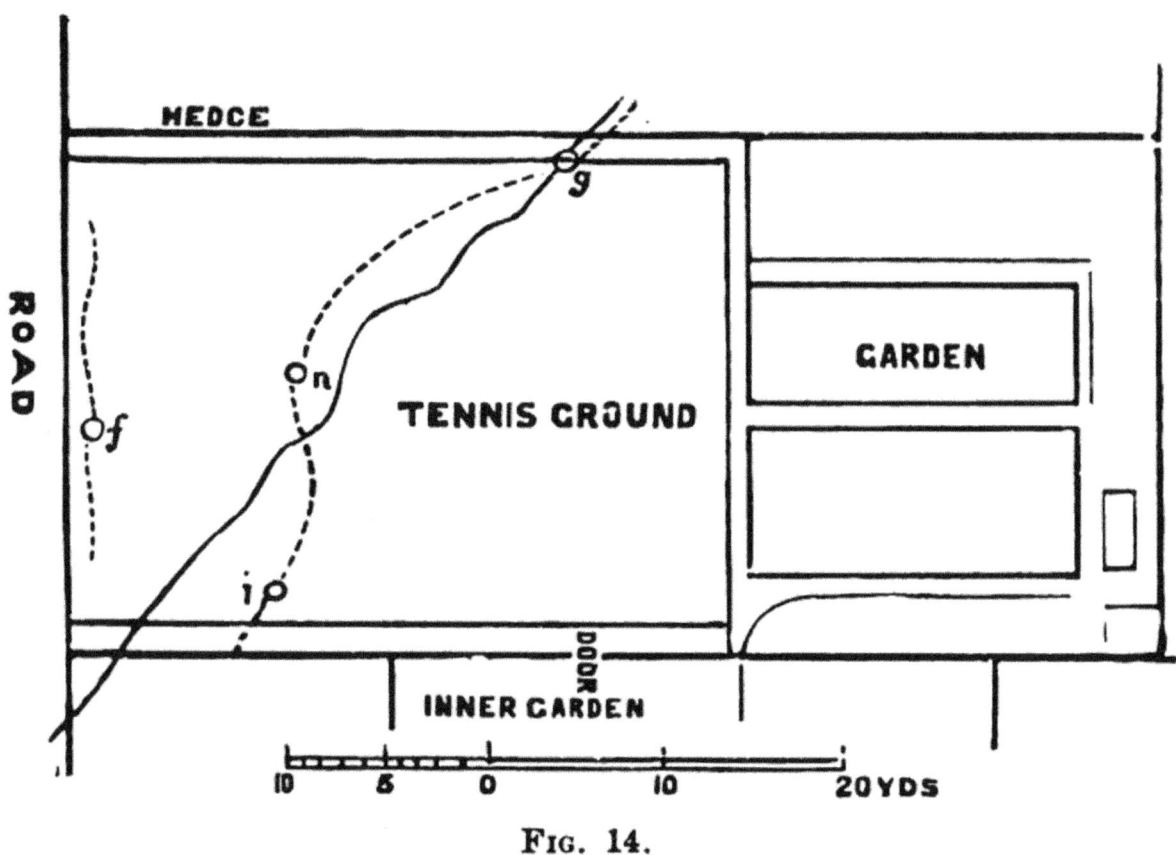

Fig. 14.

Rough plan of Garden behind Colonel Taylor's house.
The continuous line indicates the stream found by Mr. Tompkins, November 23rd; the dotted line those found by Mr. Chesterman, December 9th.

water would be found. He traced the line of an underground stream and I marked it with pegs (about four inches long) driven in quite to their head; one spot *g*, Fig. 14, he specially noted.

I told Mr. Chesterman about my experiments with Mr. Tompkins and asked him if he would go into my garden and try to locate a stream found by the latter. He kindly consented. It was quite dark when we went out, but it made no difference; in a short time he found water at *f*, Fig. 14, and said the stream ran parallel to the road. He then, passing up by the hedge, found the rod turn at the point *g*, when he said he was crossing a stream. I put down my hand to mark the place with a peg when it came into contact with the end of the peg I had previously put in to mark the spot Tompkins had selected. It was much too dark for either of us to see the pegs even if we had searched for them. Chesterman then walked down the centre and afterwards the inner edge of the tennis ground and crossed the stream at *n* and *i* respectively. The dotted line on the plan of my garden will fairly represent the flow of water underground as indicated by Mr. Chesterman.

How far, from these experiments, it may be considered that the subterranean streams influenced these two men I cannot say; I think, however, something more than chance must have dictated their choice of ground.

Mr. Tompkins follows his stream when he has once struck it, the "wand" pointing the way when the stream takes a turn, and he estimates the distance underground of the water and the yield by the position assumed by the rod and his feelings generally.

# The Credibility Of Dowsing

When Mr. Chesterman discovers a stream he does not attempt to follow it, but steps back, and then again approaching it at right angles marks the spot where he first feels the indication of water. He then goes some paces forward so as to cross the stream, turns round, and again approaches it, marking the spot where the water is again first felt. By dividing the distance between his two marks he gets a point directly over the water, and by a scale, which he has worked out from experience, he judges the distance below at which the water is flowing by the distance between one of the points where he first feels the water and the point immediately over it.

For example, when the horizontal distance is 15ft, the water will be 20 ft. below, and when the distance on the ground is 5 ft. 3 in. the stream should be 85 ft under the surface.[1]

Every dowser, however, uses the method which he feels answers best; a water-finder whom I saw at work two or three years ago found the distance of the water underground by raising his rod above his head and then lowering it slowly till he felt "first contact" of influence and then he calculated by a scale he had made.

*December 13th*, 1896. - Le M. Taylor.

On inquiry I learn from Colonel Taylor that the directors of the laundry have not sunk a well, after all, at the place indicated by the dowsers, as they feared, Colonel Taylor says, "that the water, when got, might turn out to be 'Monkey Brand.' "

## No. 2. The Westbury-sub-Mendip Experiments

Among the numerous letters and evidence of various kinds relating to the divining rod, which Mr. Vaughan Jenkins (to whose painstaking zeal this inquiry owes so much) has kindly sent me, there is a good deal of correspondence relating to a dowser named Thomas Pavey, of Cheddar. I will only refer to one case where the late Mr. Nalder, of Westbury-sub-Mendip, Wells, Somersetshire, employed Pavey and another dowser quite independently of each other to go over his ground at different times. I condense what Mr. Nalder says in a couple of letters to Mr. V. Jenkins written so far back as October and November, 1882 :—

> "I got the two men [Mr. Nalder writes] at a month's interval apart—quite unknown to each other or of what the other had done—to test my field for water, and though there was nothing to guide them, the rod moved within two yards of the same spot in each case; moreover they each traced the same direction as the line of the underground watercourse. In other parts of the field the twig would not work (or only very slightly), but it moved strongly where they asserted the 'spring' existed. I had a well sunk at this place and came upon a splendid water supply at 39 ft. Below the surface soil we passed through a bed of gravel, 2 to 2½ ft. deep, then came upon a very hard dry substance called by the well sinker 'wark.' The water rose in the well up to within 2 ft. of the top and remains so. The well-sinker told me he had sunk five wells at different places where Mr. Pavey found the twig moved strongly, and in each of the cases he had found abundance of water."

In a subsequent letter Mr. Nalder writes :—

Westbury-sub-Mendip, Wells, Somerset, *November 21st*, 1882.

> I was at Cheddar this morning speaking to my butcher, Mr. John Branch, and he reminded me of a circumstance I had quite forgotten. It seems he came over to Westbury to see me shortly after Mr. Pavey had marked out the spot for my well, and as Mr. Branch said he could "work the twig," he cut a forked twig from the hedge, and went to the same spot marked out by Mr. Pavey, and of which there was not the least sign whatever, as I had not begun the well. So this made three persons who had found the spring by the twig.

Frank J Nalder

---

[1] Colonel Taylor here gives a plan of Chesterman's method, but it is hardly necessary to reproduce it, as it is purely imaginary and exactly opposite to the system described by Mr. Emerson in the American Journal of Science and followed by some dowsers in England.—W.F.B.

There was some correspondence on this case in the London Times during October, 1882. The former owner of Mr. Nalder's place pooh-poohed the thing and said the dowsers were only joking, to which Mr. Nalder properly says: "If so, it was a capital joke for me."

## No. 3. The Thomastown Experiments

It has been already mentioned in the Carrigoona experiments that a friend living near Waterford, Mr. J. H. Jones, was an amateur dowser. Mr. Jones tells me that, having seen Mullins locate the site for a well in his neighbourhood, which turned out remarkably successful, he was astonished to find the rod also moved in his own hands and he writes to me as follows:—

Mullinabro, Waterford, *November 29th*, 1897.

> I began experimenting with the rod as a sceptic—and thoroughly prejudiced against it, and thinking that its action in a diviner's hands was a mere trick or sleight of hand—but I am now convinced that the thing is genuine, and that the rod is moved in consequence of some action or influence produced in persons susceptible when near or over subterranean water.
>
> J. H. Jones.

It will be remembered that Mr. Jones, in our Carrigoona experiments, independently pointed out the same places that Mr. Stone indicated as water-bearing or waterless. Mr. Jones has had several experiences of this kind, and a recent one is worth referring to. Water was much needed for a new convent, in Thomastown, co. Kilkenny, and, after some unsuccessful attempts to obtain a supply had been made, an English dowser was sent for; he pointed out a certain region in the convent grounds where a supply of underground water existed, estimating the depth at about 80 feet; an unlikely place it seemed, as the convent field was at some altitude. Mr. Jones was asked to try his hand independently, knowing nothing of the place pointed out by the English dowser and having nothing to guide him. The result was that he fixed on the same place, and I learn that any possible telepathic influence was also out of the question. Accordingly a well six feet in diameter was sunk at the spot indicated as best by both dowsers. After passing through a layer of surface soil and rocky debris, the solid rock was encountered at the depth of 15 ft. from the surface, and (at a cost of several hundred pounds) the well was sunk in a hard micaceous quartzite. The Administrator of the parish writes as follows to Mr. Jones:—

Thomastown, Co. Kilkenny, *September 21st*, 1899.

> I am happy to say that we have got water on the exact spot pointed out by you and Mr. Wills [the English dowser]. We are now 70 ft. deep, and since we reached 60 ft. water has come—so far, however, in small quantities insufficient for our needs; we are therefore continuing the boring. The well-sinkers declare they never encountered a harder stone. It is getting soft at one side, and sand is coming up with the water, a good sign. All the springs are very low now, and we expect a good increase of water during the winter.
>
> John Roe, Adm.
>
> P. S.—I should mention the water is increasing every day for the past week.

In reply to my inquiry the Rev. J. Roe writes:—

Thomastown, co. Kilkenny, *December 8th*, 1899.

> In your letter of the 9th ult., you have asked me three questions: 1st, "Is water difficult to find in Thomastown, etc.?" I may state that water is not very difficult to find here, but as the convent is

## The Credibility Of Dowsing

situated in a rather elevated position, we anticipated considerable difficulty in finding water. The site of the house is really charming, but the great drawback was water; in fact, some wise heads told us we should never get it. However, we were determined to try our luck, and as the tradesmen were putting the finishing touches on the building, we began sinking operations. The spot selected at first was about 12 yds. from the kitchen door. The men worked on for about 15 ft. when we came upon the rock. We were very doubtful at first about our success, and having come upon rock so soon we nearly lost courage, and dreaded the great expense necessary even in trying to find it. I consulted Mr. Hynes, architect, Cork, and he advised me to bring over Mr. Gataker or his man. At first I laughed at the idea, and though I had heard and read a little about the divining rod, I was most sceptical as to its results. After some persuasion I communicated with Mr. Gataker and he sent over his partner, Mr. Wills, at a cost of of £10. When he arrived he looked at the site already selected, and after some evolutions of his rod said he should abandon it, as there was only a very, very small ripple, and at great depth. He then went through the whole field with his rod and marked out two or three places where an abundant supply of water could be obtained, but selected a rather elevated spot in preference to the others. He said we would most certainly get water at about 80 ft. and so many gallons per hour. By a most singular coincidence Mr. Jones came on the scene accompanied by a mutual friend, Mr. O'Connell (engineer), Kilkenny, and this brings me to your second question. We invited Mr. Jones to have a try with his rod, and he pointed out the exact spot, and traced out the water in the same line as Mr. Wills had done. They were quite independent of one another, and Mr. Jones knew nothing about the coming of the English dowser, or what he had already done. Mr. Jones could not tell the depth, nor the quantity, etc., but he was certain there was a strong current of water. I noticed in the operations when they came over the places where water could be found, Mr. Wills' rod jumped up and Mr. Jones's down.

Third question. We have now gone down about 75 ft. and the men have ceased to sink any deeper, as we consider we have got a sufficient supply of water for the convent. To-day the pumping apparatus, etc., has arrived from some English firm, and I expect it will be in working order by the first of next month. I need not tell you how difficult it was to bore through the rock and how expensive it has been upon us. The architect was anxious that we should go deeper, but the men found it very difficult to carry on the blasting operations, because of the constant flow of water. I must ask you to excuse me for the long delay in writing this, but I have been very busy. I may add that I am now convinced that the divining rod is no sham, but genuine, and I cannot explain its influence on some susceptible people when they come over or near water.

John Roe, Adm.

In a concluding letter, Father Roe, in reply to my question why he did not in the first instance consult a geologist, writes as follows :—

Thomastown, co. Kilkenny, *December 11th,* 1899.

It would have been wiser to have consulted a geologist before beginning the sinking operations, but I was obliged to act very economically. I did not mean by "boring" a small borehole, for the well is 6ft. in diameter at least from top to bottom; I only used the word as a pumping phrase. I did not intend that my letters should be published, as they are not very fit, but if you think they can be of any service to you in your valuable researches, you have my permission to use them.

John Roe, Adm.

## No. 4. The Claverton Manor Experiments

In the previous Report [p. 73 this volume- Ed] a case is quoted from the Proceedings of the Bath Field Club where two dowsers independently fixed on the same spots in an estate belonging to the Deputy-Lieutenant of Gloucestershire, Mr. H. D. Shrine, J.P. As one of these dowsers was an amateur, and an Archdeacon, the case is above all suspicion of collusion, and through the kindness of Mr. Vaughan Jenkins I obtained the following fuller account of the experiment contained in a letter written to Mr. V. Jenkins by Mr. Shrine, who was an eyewitness. The date is somewhat remote, but the facts are not disputed.

Claverton Manor, near Bath, *December 20th*, 1882.

In reply to your questions relating to my experience of the use of the divining rod for the discovery of water, the facts are these :—About twenty years ago, intending to build a cottage residence on the top of Warleigh Hill, adjoining the hamlet of Conkwell, I employed a man named John Mullins, a reputed spring-finder and well-sinker living at Colerne, Wilts., to find water, which he did by means of a forked twig of hazel or thorn. He was, so far as I know, an entire stranger to the place, and could not have known anything about the springs. I took him to the top of the wood in a flat field, the subsoil of which for a great depth was known to be oolite rock. He pointed out by means of his forked twig where water was, in his opinion, to be found under the surface, but at what depth he did not pretend to say. In every instance where he said he found water, there was to my knowledge a spring low down in the wood in a line with the spot indicated.

He afterwards made some attempts to find water on the lawn in the front of the house, and traced a spring upward to a spot on the grass plot in front of the greenhouse where, some years before, in moving a large arbutus tree we had found a spring of water. To test the man's water-finding powers more closely, before I allowed him to sink the well, I invited my friend and neighbour Mr. Earle—late Rector of Monkton Farleigh, and now Archdeacon of Totnes, who had the gift himself, and who had found several wells by this process—to meet Mullins in the field near Conkwell. He did so, and though unaware of what places Mullins had selected, they both agreed in a very remarkable manner in the spots where the hidden springs were; the forked twig turned with him at the same places as with Mullins. On this conjunction of their discoveries I decided to sink a well, and at a little over 80 ft. deep we came to a bed of yellow clay and found water. The bed was, however, too thin, and the men sank the well to over 100 ft. deep, when they came to a blue marl or lias, and we have a fair supply of water about 4 ft. deep.

Since then and quite recently Mullins has found for me several springs in Claverton and sunk two wells, in one of which the water was found not more than 6 ft. below the surface, where we had no idea there was any. In each instance of his finding by the twig a spring on the hill, he traced it down to an existing spring unknown previously to myself. He also found for us the course of several drains, the lines of which had been forgotten by the workpeople, and in every case was right and saved us much trouble in digging.

It certainly appears to me that Mullins is himself a believer in the divining rod, and if it is a mere trick or deception, it is strange that he could not communicate it to his own son who works with him. The twig on the approach to a spring curved upwards in his hands without the least appearance of action on his part.

Henry D. Shrine.

# The Credibility Of Dowsing

## No. 5. The Pontyberim Experiments

Another case where two dowsers, in this case both were amateurs, independently fixed on the same spot is given me by Mr. J. F. Young, of Llanelly. A friend of Mr. Young, a contractor, was building some cottages at Pontyberim, a mining village noted for its anthracite coal, eight miles from Llanelly. Wishing to select a site for a well, the contractor asked Mr. Young (who is well known in the locality as an amateur dowser) to come over and fix the best spot. Mr. Young tells me he had never been to the place before, and on arrival, after casting about with his twig, he fixed on a certain line along which he asserted underground water would be found. Having done this, he begged the contractor, Mr. Williams, to try the rod himself. This he did, and to his surprise Mr. Williams found the rod moved vigorously, and apparently spontaneously at the same place found by Mr. Young. Then Mr. Young went out of sight of Mr. Williams, and having traced the course of the water-bearing fissure, as Mr. Young believed it to be, he returned and asked Mr. Williams to do the same. Aware of the influence of unconscious guidance by hand or look, Mr. Young informs me that he took special care to avoid this, and kept out of sight whilst Mr. Williams tried. On subsequently comparing notes, the same line was found to have been traced by both Mr. Williams' sister, Mrs. Rees, to whom the cottages belong, was present, and adds her testimony. I have received independent reports from both Mr. Young and Mr. Williams. Here is the account given by the latter; after relating what I have stated above, Mr. Williams says:—

Pontyberim, *October 20th*, 1899.

> Mr. Young then asked me to stop where I was, while he went to the side of the building in order to trace the course of the underground water. In a short time he returned and begged me to try if I could find it. I did so, and had not gone far before the curious "electrified" sensation again returned, and the action of the twig could be seen moving over a certain spot, which proved to be the same as that located by Mr. Young.
>
> But still I was in doubt as to the probability of the existence of water there until a couple months after that, and in the worst of the last dry season, I resolved to put it to the test, and commenced sinking a well at that spot. On reaching a depth of 14ft. from the surface, I had the gratification of striking on a strong spring of clear and beautiful water, rising since to 5ft. and 6ft. in the well and so it now continues, a result of much importance to my sister, Mrs. Rees.

John Williams.

> I have read the above account of the finding of the spring on my premises, and the account is true in every particular.

Martha Rees

## No. 6. The Mayfield Experiments

I am indebted to Dr. Leadam for kindly sending me the following detailed account, accompanied with a map, of his experiments with two dowsers, whom he tested, independently of each other, on his estate in Sussex. Mayfield and Stone Mill are both on the " Hastings Beds," a series of sands and sandstones alternating with clays; see Topley's memoir on the Geology of the Weald.

167, Gloucester Terrace, Hyde Park, W., *December 7th*, 1899.

> I have a small property near Mayfield, in Sussex, a hilly district principally soft sandstone formation with hard sandstone strata, as at Tunbridge Wells.
>
> In 1895, as I wanted a further water supply, I sent for Mr. Gataker; he stated he had never been in the place before, and I accompanied him throughout the experiment. As my primary object was to

have an increased convenient supply for the farm buildings adjoining Stone Mill, I took him over there, and he soon marked a spot, C, as promising a good supply at 70 ft. depth. He then indicated spots D and E, giving from 50 to 70 ft. as the probable depth; a smaller but satisfactory supply at F, but, as he remarked, it was altogether out of the way of the farm.

As I also wanted a supply for the small house at the Stock-yards, I then took him round there, and he pitched upon A as a spot for a good supply at 80 ft. I then told him that I believed there must be water somewhere near the surface, as an underground dairy could not be kept satisfactorily dry, so he walked round the house, and outside the garden gate, about 30 yds. from the house, he marked a place, B, where he said we should find a sufficient supply for that small house at 12 ft. from the surface. I may say that the pond drawn near there is a surface pond and nearly dry in summer.

I determined to try first at B, and set an ordinary well sinker to dig a well; exactly at 12 ft. he came upon water in a stratum of blue marl. I had this dug down to 20 ft., brought the pipe for a house pump into it, and it has been in constant use ever since, and stood steadily at about 12 ft. from the surface during the late dry summer; though neighbours were allowed to use the well, the water did not sink more than 1 or 1½ ft.

Being well satisfied with this, I then set the same men to dig a well at E, and, after digging through varying strata, the man below, whilst digging in rather firm rock at 61 ft., suddenly called out to be hauled up as the water rushed up in volume at his feet. This flow was estimated at 300 gallons per hour, but there is a stratum of broken rock and rubbish about 1½ ft. above, through which the water

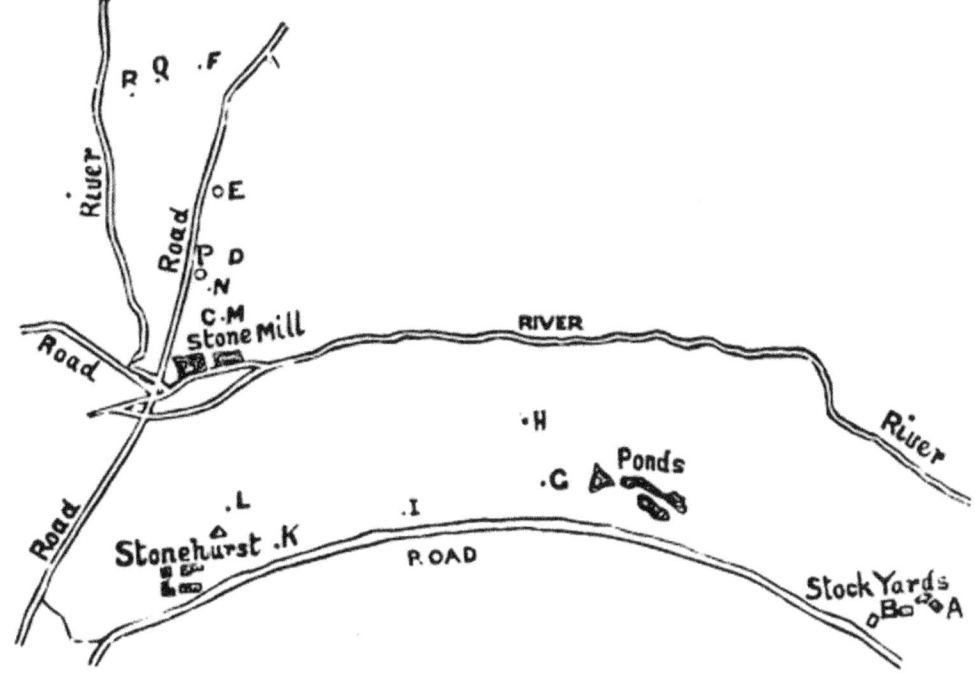

Fig. 15.

A to F positions marked by Mr. Gataker.
G to R ,, ,, ,, Stone.
Wells sunk at B, E and P.

*Scale*—About 1 in. to 850 ft., approx. 6 in. to the mile.

## The Credibility Of Dowsing

flows away; for that reason and its distance from the house, and a suspicion that the broken stratum in some way rendered the water unsatisfactory, I have not taken it into use, and my farm people have continued till now to supply themselves from the small stream shown in the map.

Having determined this summer that I would dig or bore somewhere nearer the farmhouse, I thought, before doing so, that I would have another diviner over to see, as a matter of interest, to what extent his opinions agreed with Mr. Gataker's. You were kind enough, in answer to my inquiry, to recommend Mr. Stone, and he came in August. He also had never been in the place before, and I met him on arrival and accompanied him round.

I took him first to the field near some ponds on the map; the ponds were certainly hidden by trees, and are in a dip in the ground so that Mr. Stone could not have noticed them. He marked a spot at G, then at H, and traced that flow back towards G, all at about 70 ft. depth. Also at I, and at K, and at L, a large flow, "bubbling up," as he expressed it, at about 50 ft. depth, and flowing in both directions from there. L is about the highest point in the field (A having been an ordnance survey station). He then marked M exactly where Mr. Gataker had marked C four years before, and N, O and P, which he considered one stream at about 60 or 70 ft. depth or rather less, and when I afterwards told him of Mr. Gataker's markings ho said he thought his own places better, and that they were branches of the same supply. Similarly he marked Q and R, which appeared to be the stream which Gataker had marked at F on its way to the meadow at the bottom, and I was already aware that somewhere about there a good supply was coming down to the stream and percolating into it.

Mr. Stone recommended boring at P, and I accordingly allowed him to send his foreman and boring tools to do it. They went through 5 or 6 ft. of mould, then about 30 ft. of sand rock, unfortunately a very hard seam, then about 3 ft. of blue clay. At 42 ft. 6 in. they again got into sand rock, and in that at 47 ft. reached water, which rose about 6 in. up the bore hole. It remains at about that level and is estimated at 200 gallons per hour, but I have not yet got a pump fitted. Before writing to me Mr. Stone advised that the boring should be carried deeper (I think there was no justification for this, as I considered it simple speculation and stopped it), his view being that by going deeper we should strike a stronger spring and perhaps have the water fill the bore hole to the surface. The boring showed that the water-bearing rock (or sandstone) reached to 58 ft. 6 in., then blue clay to 61 ft., rock to 65ft., and blue clay again to 69 ft. We therefore have, in my opinion, run a great risk of losing the water altogether. The layer of clay from 40 ft. to 42 ft. 6 in. was peculiar, almost black, and I am sending you by parcel post a sample of it, and if there is any peculiarity about it, I should like to know.

I will report later to you the working of the supply when it is fixed.

W. W. Leadam.

P.S.—With two streams of water on the map you may perhaps wonder at the need for boring, so I must explain that in the summer time the mill stream is so small that it takes three days to refill the millponds after use, and the water is very irony. The other stream is only just enough in summer to supply my house by a hydraulic ram. It is good water, and appears in summer entirely supplied by percolation from the water stratum indicated by the diviner at F, Q and R.

    The foregoing case is instructive, not from the coincidence of the spots C and M chosen by Gataker and Stone independently, a coincidence that was possibly accidental, but from the illustration it affords of the dowser's notion of underground water. With the utmost assurance, wherever he goes (if his rod turns) he proceeds to trace out narrow streams of water flowing underground, just as streams flow on the surface. Now in the foregoing case the geology of the district is perfectly well known and underground streams, such as are imagined by the dowser, are out of the question.

Mr. Holmes makes the following remarks on the foregoing case :—

> Mayfield and Stone Mill are not on the same subdivision of the Hastings Beds, but they agree in being both on sandy, not clayey beds. Topley gives the details of a quarry showing 36 ft. of stone "at the curve of the main road half a mile West of Mayfield." (p. 77.) He also mentions some fine natural exposures of sandstone rocks (between Mayfield and Stone Mill) as "continued down the valley towards Stone Mill." Thus the dowser thereabouts would have not only the evidence of hard rock interbedded with clay or other soft stuff, deducible from the contours of the ground, but the actual sight of the sandstone. I note that Dr. Leadam told the dowser that there must be water somewhere near the surface (par. 3), as an underground dairy could not be kept dry, near B, and that then the dowser decided that there was water, at B, 12 ft. from the surface—a very simple deduction therefrom.
>
> Granting the dowser's honest faith in himself and his rod, it is easy to understand how he might say to himself when in a farm yard, or other enclosure near a house,—" That would be a convenient spot for a pump or well, if there is a stream of water there." Any other dowser would probably take the same view and hence both would try that spot in the first place and give it an unconscious preference.
>
> T V H

Other cases of two or more dowsers tried on the same ground independently of each other are given both in the present Report and in the previous Report eight or nine such cases were referred to and some particulars given. All of these were successful, but in many of these cases the exact conditions of the test or of the ground are insufficiently described. There is, therefore, a considerable body of evidence of a certain value, but of what value it is hard to say, existing upon this instructive point.

# The Credibility Of Dowsing

# PART V

## Experiments In Blindfolding The Dowser

In the previous Report I described some experiments made by myself on carefully blindfolding two dowsers and noting whether they were able, by the movement of the rod, to indicate the same spots when blindfolded as when not blindfolded. If there be, as all dowsers and most of their supporters believe, a subtle influence exerted by underground running water upon the dowser, then blindfolding should make no difference. The same remark applies if the dowser be psychically sensitive, possessing, e.g., some kind of clairvoyance,—provided always the dowser is at his ease, i.e., if he joins heartily in the experiment.

In all experimental work it is essential for success that the instruments you employ are suitable for the purpose in view and also in good order. Having selected the proper instruments, the mental atmosphere in physical experiments does not affect the results, as we are dealing with non-living matter, but the physical conditions are all important. In experiments with living beings, the physical surroundings (except in so far as they produce discomfort) are unimportant, but, as we are now dealing with living instruments, our experiments are sure to fail or be inconclusive if the instrumental appliances we have to employ are out of order; and they are very apt to be deranged by a sudden change in the psychical conditions. Modern physical and chemical research has taught us the profound influence exerted by an imperceptible difference in the materials we are dealing with; the tendency of all psychical research is to reveal that an influence quite as profound is exerted by an imperceptible difference in the mental apparatus we employ. Though this may seem quite reasonable and obvious to most of us, it has taken physicists 200 years to learn the former truth, and we should not therefore be surprised if those to whom psychical research is new overlook, or even ridicule, the latter.

It may be remembered that some years ago Professor Ray Lankester, F.R.S., published an account of some experiments he had made in blindfolding a dowser, a lad named Rodwell, and a good deal of public interest was excited by what Professor Lankester and many others considered to be his complete exposure of the trickery of dowsers in general and of this lad in particular. Now, whilst I have no wish to be an apologist for this dowser, as similar experiments which I made with him (p. 205 of the last Report [p. 168 in this volume - Ed]) were inconclusive, and in one instance adverse, yet it must be remembered that Professor Ray Lankester, though a distinguished naturalist, is not an equally distinguished experimentalist. His scepticism regarding phenomena that do not lie within the range of his experience might almost be termed ferocious, and, on the occasion referred to, it can hardly be said he dealt with the living instrument—the dowser— as gently as he would have dealt with his microscope. Upon this point I may perhaps quote a sentence from a letter which I received some time ago from Mr. T. V. Holmes, F.G.S., who is quite as keen a critic as Professor Lankester, but somewhat better informed in all that relates to the subject of the present research. Mr. Holmes writes:—

> With regard to the experiments of Professor Ray Lankester on the alleged power of Rodwell, I am very decidedly of opinion that no result of any value could be obtained unless the boy was quite at his ease, and that he would require much more tact and geniality to put him at his ease than a man would. Now the impostor, or semi-impostor, shows his hand to the genial man, and is rigidly on his guard in the presence of the ungenial, as though "sweetness and light" never co-existed in the same person.

This is a sagacious observation, and bears out what I have already said with regard to those who are engaged in any experimental work connected with our Society.

## *No. 1. Experiments by the Author*

Returning to my own experiments, described in the previous Report, those narrated on p. 175 were made at Kingstown with Mr. Stears, who readily consented to be blindfolded, but who only approximately fixed on the same spots when he could not see as when he could see. The other experiments were made at Wimbledon (p. 178) with the lad Rodwell, who strongly objected to be blindfolded, for the reasons there given, but who at last consented: in two experiments he was completely wrong and in a third he was fairly correct. It may be urged that, Rodwell being blindfolded against his will, the experiment was not a fair one, as he was not at his ease; this I quite admit. Hence I can only regret that, taken as a whole, my own experiments were, as I have said, inconclusive.

## No. 2. Mr. Pease's Experiments

Mr. E. R. Pease made two experiments with a blindfolded dowser, which are described in his report on the divining rod, published in Vol. II. of our Proceedings, p. 85. These, like my own experiments, were inconclusive, and even had the dowser been successful, the result would have been of little value, as it is stated the dowser was "led over the same ground" in both cases. Unconscious muscular suggestion might well have vitiated the experiment.

## No. 3. Experiments by Lord Winchilsea and others

But there is a good deal of evidence by other experimenters on the blindfolding of dowsers. Eight cases in addition to my own experiments were given in the previous Report. Some of these are with amateur dowsers, as Mr. Golding, of Booking, Essex, p. 28 [In all the following cases pages refer to the previous Report, Proceedings S.P.R., Vol. XIII - Ed]; and Colonel Aldworth, D.L., of co. Cork (p. 31), and also a young farmer he mentions; another case is given on p. 40. A careful experiment made by Mr. J. E. Marshall, of Leeds, with the dowser Adams, is described on p. 48; an experiment with Lawrence, on p. 70; and with the late J. Mullins, on p. 95; an experiment made by Sir Welby Gregory, also on Mullins, on p. 97; and one by the late Earl of Winchilsea (then the Hon. Finch Hatton, M.P.) also on Mullins (same page). Here Earl Winchilsea states :—

> Mullins was then blindfolded, and though led round by a different route, again fixed on the same spot. At first he overran it a foot or so and then felt round, as it were, and seemed to be led back into the exact centre of influence by the twig.

This experiment is more fully described in Proceedings S. P. R., Vol. II., p. 102. In this case it was the discovery of a pipe of running water, but the success of the dowser may have been due to involuntary muscular suggestion, as Mr. Finch Hatton states he "led" the dowser. The same explanation may also account for the success that is asserted in several of the other cases mentioned in the previous Report, though unfortunately the particulars respecting them are too meagre to be of much value, except perhaps in the case given by Mr. Marshall.

I will now quote some further cases of blindfolding which have since reached me. The first of these is a very interesting case, and here again J. Mullins is the dowser. The introductory part of this case is also of interest, and might have been added to the cases given in Part III.

## No. 4. Mr. Hoskyns' Experiments

In the Somerset and Dorset Notes and Queries for June, 1897, the Editor publishes a letter from a Mr. H. W. Hoskyns, written to him on January 2nd, 1889. Mr. Hoskyns, whose letter, together with information he has subsequently sent me, I abridge, says :—

> Having an impure supply of water on his estate, North Perrott Manor, Crewkerne, Somersetshire, he sent for the late John Mullins, the well-known dowser, who, by means of the rod, fixed upon the best site for sinking a well, estimating the water to be about 25 ft. below the surface. The well was sunk, solid rock was soon encountered, and after 25 ft. below the surface had been reached, and a considerable thickness of rock pierced, still no water was found. Suddenly, however, when 25½ ft. had been reached, an inrush of water took place, so rapid that the men had to be hurriedly withdrawn from the well, and the water rose 23½ ft., or 2 ft. from the surface, and has given a constant supply ever since, even in the driest summers. An old well near contained water that was so polluted that it

# The Credibility Of Dowsing

could not be used, though the well had been cleaned out several times. The spring found by Mullins has given a constant supply of pure water. Not far off, Mullins indicated the site of a second well, which proved equally successful. Mr. Hoskyns adds that one of his labourers found he also had the power of using the rod, a fact corroborated by the Editor, the Rev. C. H. Mayo, M.A., who visited the spot.[1]

There is an interesting sequel to this. In consequence of Mr. A. Lang's notes on my previous Report, in Longman's Magazine, Mr. Hoskyns wrote to Mr. Lang upon the subject, and the latter forwarded me the letter. Mr. Hoskyns writes :—

North Perrott Manor, Crewkerne, *December,* 1897.

With regard to the tests suggested by Professor Barrett in order to ascertain the reality of a dowsing faculty, the following appears to satisfy Nos. 1 and 2, i.e., separate examinations by different dowsers independently of each other, and blindfolding the dowser. Mullins having on his visit here, in 1888, given several (half-a-dozen or so) indications of water in the lane by the two cottages, I had pegs put in on the strip of grass land opposite these indications, and thrust in very low, so as only just to be seen when looked for, and not showing above the grass, so that the cottage children should not pull them up or displace them. Some rather long time after, when I had made up my mind to go to the further expense of making a draw-well (not a deep one) for the cottages, having meanwhile heard that a labourer on my estate, one George Elson, had the dowsing power, I went with him myself, had him bandaged tightly and deeply, well over the nose, and in addition made a steady man keep his hands over the bandage, whilst Elson walked down the lane in question, holding the twig. At each halt that he made, the twig turning downwards for water, I looked for Mullins' peg, but the grass had grown over them and they were all quite undiscernible. So I made Elson and his guide (for being completely blinded, he stumbled occasionally) scrape a mark on the road surface with their boots. When we had come to the end of the lane, I returned with these men and one or two others (Elson being then unblinded) and we all made close search for the Mullins' pegs, every one of which, without exception, proved to be immediately opposite one of Elson's boot-marks on the road. This uneducated labourer could have had no geological, or even rule-of-thumb, knowledge of water-bearing strata, for the place was quite strange to him.

The only objection, so far as I can see, that can be raised to this extremely interesting test is that the guide, who kept his hand on the bandage over the labourer's eyes, might have known where the pegs were placed, and unconsciously tended to arrest the dowser at the right spots, in fact, a case of "muscle-reading," as in the so-called willing-game. This is likely enough if the pegs were discernible, but Mr. Hoskyns distinctly says they were not, and as some time had elapsed since Mullins visited the place, no one seems to have remembered the exact spots where the pegs had been put. I have had some correspondence with Mr. Hoskyns about this interesting experiment. He informs me that Elson's guide knew nothing whatever about Mullins' pegs; involuntary guidance is therefore excluded.

---

[1] My best thanks are due to Mr. Hoskyns for giving every facility to Mr. Westlake, F.G.S., who, at my request, kindly visited the spot and made a careful geological examination and report on this case. Mr. Westlake reports that the old foul well was probably between 20 and 30ft. deep. Mullins' well, about 18 yds. distant, is sunk in the Inferior Oolite, and at a depth of 25½ ft. water rushed rapidly in through a joint in the rock. This well gives a splendid pure supply, even when the river is nearly dry; the water is probably dammed up by a downthrow of Fuller'searth, which passes close to the farm. The second well indicated by Mullins is 50 yards further west, is only 18 ft. deep, and does not give so continuous a supply. All three wells are at nearly the same surface level.—W. F. B.

## No 5. Mr. Westlake's Experiments

I asked Mr. Westlake, who was living near Crewkerne, to repeat, with Mr. Hoskyns' permission, the blindfolding experiment with Elson. Mr. Westlake reports :—

> On April 24th, 1900, I went with Mr. Hoskyns and his agent, Mr. Slade, to Pipplepen farm. I walked down the same lane with Elson to a little stream at the bottom, a distance of 1,050 ft., in the course of which his twig turned seven times. I then carefully blindfolded him, and on retracing our steps, the twig turned ten times, five of which corresponded nearly or quite with his first marks, as under :—

| Elson's first marks when not blindfolded. | His second series when blindfolded. | | Difference. |
|---|---|---|---|
| 206 feet 2 inches | (1) | 206 feet 8 inches | + 6 inches |
| | (2) | 326 feet 7 inches | |
| 406 feet 6 inches | | | |
| | (3) | 429 feet 5 inches | |
| | (4) | 564 feet 3 inches | |
| 648 feet | (5) | 651 feet | + 3 feet |
| | (6) | 680 feet 6 inches | |
| | (7) | 742 feet 9 inches | |
| 762 feet | | | |
| 872 feet | (8) | 877 feet | + 5 feet |
| 931 feet | (9) | 934 feet | + 3 feet |
| 985 feet | (10) | 985 feet | none |

Elson was not held, and was only told (to prevent accidents) to keep to the right or the left. The results may have been somewhat impaired, first, by the steward, Mr. Slade, who accompanied us, having touched Elson with a stick (with a view to guiding him straight) at the points 1 and 5, immediately after which the twig turned; and, second, there was more or less conversation, at Nos. 8, 9, and 10, Slade informing Elson that he had passed the cottages (a landmark between 7 and 8), that the point 8 he had just indicated was the well (by the roadside), and so on.

In view of such sources of error, I think Mr. Hoskyns' experiment much better than mine, but, as I understand that some of those who took part in it had seen Mullins' pegs when they were put in, one cannot feel certain that the experiment was an absolutely conclusive one.

In the afternoon, I made a further trial with Elson in an orchard at North Perrott, where he had previously indicated two springs. Slade remained at a distance. Elson having found the points, I blindfolded him and, starting him from a little distance and directing him by voice, I got him to cross his marks. He thereupon re-found the spots three times, his marks at one of them being only a yard apart. It is possible he may have been able to reckon the distance; and I noticed also towards the end of the experiment that the bandage had slipped a little, and I could see the upper corner of his left eye, so that he may have been guided by the trees. Thus the result was probably inconclusive.

## The Credibility Of Dowsing

Elson's hands and arms are very muscular; he uses stout hazel forks and grips them very hard, and they turn downwards with corresponding strength, usually breaking, sometimes at the fork, but generally on one side; he then takes a fresh grip nearer the fork, and so on, till the stick may be used up to within an inch or so of the fork. When it turned over the stream his forearm muscles were strongly contracted. He says it usually makes his left thumb numb, and that he feels the effects in his biceps the day after. Mr. Slade said Elson had found water for many of the neighbours, and had never had a failure. The farmer also told me Elson had predicted water at another point half a mile to the east at 30 ft., and that it was found at 27 ft., and rose to within 5 or 6 ft. of the surface.—

E. W.

## No. 6. Mr. Denison's Experiments

For the next very interesting letter I am indebted, to my friend, Mr. B. St. G. Lefroy, who informed me that a Canadian scientific friend of his—Mr. Denison, of the Toronto Meteorological Observatory—had been making some experiments in blindfolding an amateur dowser. At my request Mr. Denison kindly sent the following account:—

Denison Square, Toronto.

With regard to the experiments with the "divining rod," I made a full note of them at the time and copy the following from my note-book :— June 19th, 1898. Rode over to Mr. Harris' residence at Clarkson, 18 miles west of Toronto. At dinner Mr. H. told the following story. "Last year my well near the house became dry, I sent for a well-digger to increase depth. Before doing so he asked permission to explore with a hazel wand to ascertain if another spring would be found deeper before going to expense of digging. He said he had discovered a stream which would flow into the well from west to east, a few feet below present level. The well was then deepened, and, when down 3 ft., water did flow in from the west, so rapidly it was difficult to pump fast enough to enable men to lay the bricks. Ever since there has been a good supply of fine water. It was at this time I found the hazel wand would turn in my hands also. The stick was Y-shaped, and held firmly by both hands with thumbs turned outwards."

After dinner I got Mr. Harris to cut a forked plum stick about 20 in. long—he had used a hazel before and felt sure plum would not work; however he grasped the plum switch firmly, as explained, holding it vertically before him. As he approached the well, the stick began to turn down in jerks until when over the stream to west of the well the rod turned so much that the bark was twisted near his hands. Mr. Harris is a powerful man and endeavoured to hold the rod in its original position. I then got him to explore other parts of the lawn and at 100 ft. from latter the rod again turned down. I then blindfolded him and allowed a sceptic in the party to turn him round about several times and then lead him in different directions; but when he came over the first and second spots, where the rod turned before, it again twisted down. He was once more turned about and asked to walk as requested not in contact with any one, but the same results occurred. He then tried an ordinary willow, and also a lilac twig, with good results. When a dry stick was used he obtained no action. Finally, I bent a galvanised wire thus :- When Mr. Harris held this like the twig, it not only moved downwards but twisted round to such an extent as to form a loop thus :- which assumed its natural shape as he moved away from stream.

I also got him to follow a stream for several hundred feet. Mrs. Harris tried without any result, but when Mr. H. grasped her wrists as she approached the spring, the rod turned forcibly. One daughter, aged 15, had also the power. When Mr. H. held the rod and Miss H. grasped his wrists, there would be a momentary increase in the vigour of the rod twisting, and when the daughter held the rod and her father grasped her wrists, a similar action occurred.

Out of the twelve persons who tried the above experiments, two had the power well developed, two slightly, while the remaining eight almost nil. When the weaker members used a rod over 4 ft. long, their slight muscular action was clearly shown by the far end of rod turning down. When Mr. H. held the rod exactly perpendicularly, it sometimes turned inwards until it pressed heavily against his chest. At the end of the experiments Mr. Harris' hands were considerably blistered.

I will try to follow up these experiments.

F. Napier Denison

It is to be hoped that Mr. Denison will do so, as the letter shows him to be a very careful observer, and I am greatly obliged to him for the trouble he has taken in the matter. It will be observed that Mr. Denison distinctly states that in his second experiment the blindfolded dowser was not in contact with any one, and yet was equally successful. This is therefore an important and excellent experiment, and more evidence of this kind is much to be desired.

In these experiments with about 2 in 12 persons, or say 16 per cent., the divining rod "worked," i.e., the forked twig suddenly revolved independently of volition of the holder. I should say this is not an improbable percentage, although in 1810, Professor Sementini (the Regius professor of chemistry in the University of Naples)—in an essay he published entitled, *Pensieri e Sperimenti sulla Bacchetta Divinitoria*, asserts that with five out of six persons on the average he found the "rod" would move, that is over 80 per cent. This large percentage was doubtless due to the position of unstable equilibrium in which the rod was held, though it is possible this class of automatic action may be more common in some countries than others. Another savant, Amoretti, who had a wide experience, states that he found about 20 per cent, of those he tried were susceptible; this fairly agrees with my own estimate above. If any of my readers who are interested in the subject will try, and get their friends to try, the "rod," or autoscope, as I have suggested it should be called, and let me know with what success, I should be grateful. The method of holding the rod is fully described in Appendix C to the last Report.

It will be noticed that Mr. Denison says a dry stick would not work, but any forked green twig would do and also wire. This is the experience of many others who can use the rod and who usually attribute it to the dry stick being a non-conductor of electricity; it is very improbable that electricity has anything to do with the matter; the reason is doubtless that the green twig is more supple and elastic, for whalebone is used by some dowsers in preference to a twig.

## No. 7. Dr. Thouvenel's Experiments

The next evidence is a remarkable statement made a century ago by a distinguished and learned French physician—Dr. Thouvenel.

This statement refers to the young French dowser, Bleton; the evidence relating to Bleton's powers as a water-finder is given in considerable detail subsequently, pp 257 et seq. Here I need only say that Dr. Thouvenel, having heard of Bleton's alleged powers, determined to test them thoroughly from a scientific standpoint. He did so, and published the results in a work called *Mémoire physique et médicinal, montrant des rapports entre les phénomenes de la baguette divinatoire, du Magnétisme el de l'Electricité*. Paris, 1781. A second memoir was published later, and though his theory of the divining rod was, I believe, mistaken, that does not affect the evidence I will now cite. On pp. 77-80 of his first *mémoire* Thouvenel gives a summary of the tests he made with Bleton in Lorraine. The following is a translation of the passage :—

> I took the precaution to repeat several times all the experiments just described in detail, after having carefully blindfolded Bleton; in addition his arms were sometimes fastened behind his back leaving

his forearms only just sufficiently free to hold the baguette at the extremity of his fingers, sometimes even confining these in order to hinder, if possible, all mechanical movement. These precautions were not taken for my own satisfaction, as I was already entirely convinced.

I conducted Bleton to places which he had never seen; I took him towards springs of which I knew, but which he could not know of, at other times over ground where neither of us knew what might be found. Whenever he experienced his peculiar sensations—and the baguette had repeatedly turned at the same spot,—I then led him far away, bringing him back by quite different roads, still with his eyes bandaged. . . . When he had followed the course of an underground spring—sometimes for more than a quarter of a mile, across mountains, rock, or forests, and indicated on the way numerous sub-divisions of the same spring—I made him return. He then re-conducted me himself, though still blindfolded, only supported by one arm, to the point from which we set out, without straying a single step from the line previously traced and marked by pegs, which were often hidden beneath the surface. He re-found all the subterranean rivulets already pointed out, and followed exactly the sinuosities of the underground stream. It frequently happened that we came across springs whose course was interrupted by walls, terraces, or wide ditches, so that in order to enable Bleton to overcome these obstacles, I had to procure ladders, or take long détours, or in some way get him conveyed across; nevertheless, although blindfolded, he soon regained the course without the aid of his eyes. Sometimes in order to try and deceive him, if his senses were concerned, I placed false marks as if to indicate a spring; sometimes after he had followed a spring across several fields, I moved the pegs some feet away without his knowledge. Nevertheless, he was never led astray and always rectified such errors. In fine I tried all sorts of ways to deceive him, and I can testify that *in more than six hundred trials,* I did not succeed in doing so one single time.

M. Jadelot, the Professor of Medicine in Nancy, Thouvenel states, was a witness of, and co-operated in, all his experiments, which extended over a space of two months, and was no less struck than he was with the strength and importance of the evidence obtained.

In addition to the foregoing we have successful blindfolding tests made with Bleton by a small committee of *savants* quoted in No. 15 of Part X.. What are we to say to the above evidence? It is true that Dr. Thouvenel mentions that he "led" Bleton when bindfolded, and therefore involuntary muscular suggestion may possibly account for most of the success of Bleton, but the results appear too remarkable and too uniformly successful to be wholly explained in this way; nor is it clear that Bleton was always touched by Dr. Thouvenel, who, it must be remembered, was a man of scientific training and habit of mind. Moreover, if the blindfolded dowser succeeds, as in Nos. 4, 5, and 6, when involuntary muscular action appears an inadequate cause, another explanation must be sought, and this explanation may, if established, be the true cause of success in some of the other cases where muscular guidance is possible.

No dowser of whom we have any knowledge in the present century seems to have rivalled Bleton, though it is much to be regretted no scientific man ever took the trouble carefully to test the remarkable powers of the late Mr. W. Lawrence, of Bristol, and Mr. J. Mullins, of Chippenham—names that will be familiar to readers of my previous Report. It will be noticed that Bleton, like Stone and other dowsers, mentions the peculiar sensations he experienced when over underground water; this may be a delusion, but the coincidence is remarkable, as it is wholly improbable the English dowser ever heard of Bleton, or had obtained the idea from him.

As already remarked, I do not know of any blind dowsers; if such exist, it would be most interesting to ascertain what degree of success they achieve. Of course, if there be any supernormal power possessed by a dowser, it is improbable that blindness would be prejudicial to its existence.

I will here add two or three cases which, though startling at first sight, may be capable of explanation by muscular guidance, and therefore I will not weary the reader with multiplying other instances of this kind that have reached me.

## No. 8. Judge Spinks' Experiments

A striking case of the success of an amateur dowser when blindfolded is narrated by a judge in British Columbia; this was also given in the previous Report, p. 27. His Honour Judge Spinks writes to Mr. F. W. H. Myers as follows :—

Vernon, Okanagan, B.C., *February 27th,* 1893.

> The rod works in my hands. I was rather sceptical, and thought that my own mind might work in some unknown manner on the rod and cause it to turn down where I fancied there ought to be water. I was blindfolded and led about with the wand, for about an hour at least, until I could not hold the wand upright without great pain. Each time the wand dipped, a peg was driven into the ground to mark the spot. I was walked in all directions, and passed over the same ground again and again, but in no instance did the rod fail to dip when it came to a peg. I have sunk two wells on the credit of the wand, and in both instances have found water, in both these instances contrary to the advice of the well-sinking experts. The power appears to increase rapidly with use. When experimenting with the rod over a water hose, I had the water turned on and off several times, and could distinctly feel the jar that one hears in such cases.
>
> Ward Spinks,

In a subsequent letter Judge Spinks gives some additional evidence. A third well was sunk upon the indications afforded by the rod and also proved successful; between two of the wells the rod would not move; there the foundations of his house were subsequently dug and proved dry, though "only a few feet from being immediately between wells 2 and 3." I wrote recently to Judge Spinks to inquire whether the pegs were put in before he was blindfolded and if some one led him all the time he was unable to see. To this I received the following reply:—

Rossland Club, Rossland, B.C., *January 12th*, 1900.

> It is some years since Mr. Streatfield and I experimented with the "wand," and my memory may be at fault. As well as I can remember, the facts were as follows:—I found several places where the "wand" dipped and marked them by driving pegs into the ground. Afterwards Mr. Streatfield led me blindfolded over the ground and the "wand" moved over every peg, I believe; I then led him and the "wand" dipped in his hands as it did in mine; he was blindfolded also. We led each other by the arm, so there *was* contact. Of late years I have been travelling too much to make experiments, but I tried the "wand" last Fall, and was surprised to find that it did not work with me as it use to.
>
> Ward Spinks.

It will thus be seen that in this case the amateur dowser was touched, or led, by a friend who could see, and hence the evidential value of the case is destroyed, as unconscious muscular guidance might account for the success achieved when blindfolded.

## No. 9. Mr. Withnel's Experiments

The next case relates to the blindfolding of Mr. W. Stone, evidence of whose success as a dowser was given in the last Report and also in the preceding pages. The following Report is abridged from Morton's Lincolnshire Almanac for 1899 :—

> Some two years ago the late Mr. J. B. Dunham, of the firm of Messrs. Dunham and Sons, Horncastle, commissioned Mr. Stone to find a supply of water at his farm, High Toynton, near Horncastle, where it was needed badly. On reaching the farm Mr. J. B. Dunham declared his intention of putting the dowser to a severe test. With a V-shaped hazel twig cut from a hedge close by, the diviner went over the ground in question, a field located on an incline some 200 yds. from the

# The Credibility Of Dowsing

main road, and soon indicated a spot where he averred a plentiful supply of pure water would be found at a depth of about 25 ft. As he passed and re-passed over this particular spot, the dowsing twig, held in the manner before described, turned and bent completely over towards him. The two spectators, watching every movement, candidly informed the diviner that they believed the turning of the twig was due to some sharp movement on the part of the holder, and Mr. Stone readily acceded to the request that each in turn should be allowed to hold the mystic twig, as he himself held it, over the same place. But do as they would, the twig never moved in the slightest with either. Mr. Stone then suffered himself to be completely blindfolded and led away from the spot which he had indicated as the place where water would be found. His two guides, holding his arms (in the hands of which the twig was loosely held), led him about in a circle and then in a zig-zag fashion, managing by devious ways to lead him over the located spot, previously marked by a stake, and each time as the diviner crossed it the twig curled as before. At the same time those on each side of him distinctly felt a twitching in the diviner's arms, such as might be caused by an electric shock. When the coverings from his eyes were removed, Mr. Stone remarked that he knew from the sensations he experienced that he had crossed the place he had pointed out two or three times. Our previous doubts were removed; and more particularly was this the case when a short time afterwards a well was sunk on the site, and a most excellent spring of pure water found at a depth of 24 ft. In September last the writer journeyed to the same locale and found that the supply of water was as good and as strong as ever, being even more than was required on the farm.

Having ascertained that the writer of the above report was a journalist named Mr. F. Withnell, who took an active part in the experiment, I wrote to Mr. Withnell to inquire whether he had blindfolded Mr. Stone effectively, and received the following reply :—

News Office, Horncastle, Lincolnshire, *September 15th*, 1899.

The Divining Rod was a thing unknown to me before I came into Lincolnshire. Therefore, as a journalist (of fifteen years' standing, and a member and officer of the branch of the Institute of Journalists for ten years), combined with a scepticism born of a rough life and much travel abroad, I determined to investigate the matter for myself. I will vouch for the particulars contained in the report, and if necessary can give you the names and addresses of other persons (men of standing and experience) who have put Mr. Stone, in his water finding, through a similar ordeal, and assure me they are, as the result, fully convinced of Mr. Stone's power of finding water, and even gauging the depth at which it is to be found in apparently the driest of places.

I blindfolded Mr. Stone personally; closely folding a silk handkerchief and tying it tightly over his eyes, afterwards pulling a close texture bag, made of canvas, over his head and twisting the mouth of it round his neck. There was no mistake, therefore, that the blindfolding was thorough, and that he was totally unable to see downwards. Mr. Stone assured me, and those who were with me, that he had never before been over the ground, and that it was purely on account of the hazel twig turning over in his hands that he was able to say that water would be found at that spot. I was thoroughly satisfied with the experiment and said so, and my companions also expressed themselves in similar terms.

I have been with Mr. Stone on other water-finding excursions since then, and I have never known him fail in his findings or be wrong in his calculations as to the depth, which he approximately estimated in each case. He informs me that he has had failures, but these are of rare occurrence and separated by long intervals. May I add that I have only been brought into contact with Mr. Stone professionally. He resides at Old Bolingbroke, which is nine miles distant from Horncastle, where I live.

Fred. C. Withnell.

As Mr. Withnell knew the spot fixed on by Mr. Stone, and it was "marked by a stake," it is quite possible to explain Mr. Stone's success in this blindfolding experiment by some involuntary muscular action on the part of "his two guides holding his arms;" albeit both Mr. Withnell and Mr. Stone have written to me subsequently, stating that no guidance was possible, as touching was excluded. This may have been another trial at the same place. Here is Mr. Withnell's letter:—

> 27, Bridge Street, Horncastle, Lincolnshire, *June 8th*, 1900.
>
> As regards my account of the blindfolding of Mr. Stone, I certainly wish it to be understood that Mr. Stone proceeded alone and untouched after being blindfolded when searching for water on Mr. Dunham's farm at High Tointon; the only place where I personally have submitted him to a test. After Mr. Stone was blindfolded, I and the late Mr. Beavis Dunham simply led him away from some paraphernalia that was on the ground and against which he might have stumbled, and then, releasing our hold, we allowed him to take whatever course he chose to take, assuring him, on his own request, that we would carefully watch him and give him a warning shout if in his peregrinations he appeared likely to blunder against the hedge. As he walked about free from obstruction, we neither touched him nor called out to him. I have only this week verified this by conversation with two others who were on the ground at the time, viz.: Mr. Dunham's foreman and another.
>
> Fred. C. Withnell.

## No. 10. Mr. Emerson's Experiments

So far I have quoted the dowser's success when blindfolded, but there are cases of failure. I have mentioned one, when I tested Rodwell at Wimbledon in 1890. Professor Ray Lankester's test of the same lad is a well-known instance of failure, and the following case of failure is so little known that I refer to it at some length, as it appeared in the leading scientific organ in America, the *American Journal of Science*, now called *Silliman's Journal*, and doubtless had much influence on scientific opinion in America. The investigator is the Rev. Ralph Emerson, who five years previously had published a paper in the same journal on some successful experiments with the divining rod. Mr. Emerson's paper is so very long that I am compelled to summarise what he says with regard to the blindfolding experiment.

> In 1821 he found at a farm in Ohio that a successful well had been sunk at a spot indicated by a "diviner," where no sign of water previously existed. One of the farmer's sons, a lad of 12, discovered the rod "worked" in his hand.s, and it was this young lad Mr. Emerson tested. In the first instance the young dowser, with his eyes open, professed to trace the course of an underground vein of water, the position being marked by Mr. Emerson; the boy was then blindfolded, led a short distance away from the spot and told again to trace the course of the water. He did so and the rod moving, he declared he was over the spot; this turned out to be perfectly correct. But on a second and a third attempt he failed, and afterwards "incessantly," so that, Mr. Emerson adds, "there could be no mistake, the illusion of all attraction underground vanished at once. The motion of the rod remained, but it must be accounted for some other way." Mr. Emerson then shows how the motion of the rod may be caused by a very slight muscular action on the part of the dowser;—this part of his paper is worth notice and is given subsequently. He explains the success of the blindfolded lad on the first occasion by his probably keeping count of the steps he took, but that his incessant failures afterwards were due to his losing count, and hence Mr. Emerson concludes that the boy was a "young fox" and "the pretensions of the diviner are worthless." [1]

---

[1] The *American Journal of Science and Arts* (Silliman's), Series 1, Vol. XI. 1826, p. 201

## *The Credibility Of Dowsing*

A singularly illogical and unscientific conclusion, but one very characteristic of the numerous "exposures" with which the history of this subject abounds. The surprising thing is that a precisely opposite conclusion was not arrived at, viz., that the lad was not right every time, and that Mr. Emerson did not as triumphantly assert that he had conclusively established the truth of a mysterious influence exerted by the "veins of water" on the boy, and so "set the question for ever at rest" on behalf of the dowser. For, on reading the account carefully, it seems that Mr. Emerson in every case was holding the blindfolded boy: "I took him lightly by the elbow"; "I guided him back "; "I led the lad to the next spot and he missed it again"; "I led him to and fro, but he failed incessantly," etc. Now, if the boy had been a "young fox," he might with perfect ease have been right every time, simply by allowing himself to be guided by the muscular indications which Mr. Emerson might have given involuntarily whenever he crossed the right track, just as successful finds are made in the "willing game." The whole series of experiments made by Mr. Emerson are absolutely valueless, and hence his conclusion is equally so. There is, further, no evidence to show that this young boy was a "dowser" at all; not only, therefore, was the experimenter unskilled, but the instrument he employed was probably defective, and a confusion of thought existed in the experimenter as to the object *sought for*.

# PART VI

## Details Of A Few Further Cases Of Amateur Dowsers

Those who may have read the previous Report will remember the numerous cases of amateur dowsers that are there cited, particulars being given of upwards of twenty-five individuals of both sexes, and in all ranks of life, who had discovered by accident that the forked twig twisted round in their hands, and had used its indications with some success in the discovery of underground water. It may be of interest if I now give somewhat fuller details of a few of the additional cases of amateur dowsers that have reached me.

### No. 1. Sir K. Harington, Bart.

Among notable persons who have found that they could successfully use the divining rod, and who have made use of its indications with advantage, may be mentioned his Honour, Sir Richard Harington, Bart., Chairman of Quarter Sessions for Herefordshire. In the County Council Times, for July 17th, 1897, Sir R. Harington published the following interesting letter of his experience with the rod :—

Whitbourne Court, Worcester, *July 11th*, 1897.

> I discovered, quite by accident, and at the age of fifty-seven, that I possessed this power [of using the divining rod]. I was building a new lodge to this place, and, desiring to find a water supply, I sent (more from curiosity than from any belief in its efficacy) for the gardener of a neighbour, who was said to be able to use the divining rod. He came. I watched his proceedings, and then requested him to allow me to try the rod myself. I did so, and, to my great surprise, found that with me it assumed the vertical position in the same places in which it had done so with him. He discovered water, but the place which he assigned to it turning out inconvenient, I proceeded to investigate on my own account. I had in the meantime been told the method employed to estimate the depth of the water beneath the surface. I found indications of water at a depth which I estimated at about 17 ft. to 20ft. I caused a well to be sunk, and a small supply was found at about 18 ft. This, however, was at the beginning of a long drought, and late in the summer the supply failed. I tried again at the same place, when my rod told me there was water about 10 ft. deeper. I had the well deepened, and found more, fortunately just within the 28 ft. limit, and there has since (this was five years ago) been a sufficient and unfailing supply for the use of the lodge.
>
> The most practical use I have since turned my power to is the discovery of leaks in a large artificial piece of water round my house. This for some distance runs parallel to the course of a brook at a much lower level, a road passing along the top of the embankment, the slope of which is covered with wood and undergrowth. Occasionally a rat or rabbit makes a hole, which draws off the water, and is difficult to find by ordinary search. I always find it easily with the divining rod.
>
> I have never been at the trouble to ascertain how many kinds of wood are serviceable, but the peach and Spanish chestnut will serve with me as well as hazel.
>
> As may be supposed, I am not constantly searching for convenient places to dig wells; but I occasionally use the rod for the purpose of showing friends how it acts, and they generally try it themselves. I very rarely find any one who possesses the power which I do alone, but almost invariably when the person who cannot use it alone holds one end of the fork and I the other, it works; in some cases more strongly than with myself alone. But I do not find that I have the power claimed by Mr. Gataker of estimating the volume of the water. The effect on me is the same, whether it is a mere trickle or a copious current.

## *The Credibility Of Dowsing*

That the power exists, and that it depends on some natural cause connected with the physical idiosyncracy of the individual possessing it, the operation of which is not yet understood, I cannot, after the evidence of my own senses, doubt. To stigmatise the action of those who do possess it as charlatanry appears to me a specimen of that arrogant ignorance which despises what it cannot understand.

I may add that the extent of the power seems to vary in individuals. For example, I cannot calculate the volume; my original instructor could not calculate either depth or volume, and, although the rod usually acts when held by another person and myself as above described, one of my daughters appears to have a kind of neutralising power, and when she holds one end of the fork and I the other, it will not act at all.

If the Local Government Board official, who, I understand, threatens Mr. Gataker and his fellows with prosecutions under the Vagrant Act, will do me the honour of calling here at any time when I am at home, I shall be happy to try the experiment with him, and let him try for himself—first, whether he possesses the power alone, and, secondly, if not, whether the rod acts with him jointly with me. His scepticism will not affect its action. The power is obviously purely physical.

Richard Harington,
Chairman of Quarter Sessions for Herefordshire.

In reply to my inquiries Sir Richard Harington was good enough to write me at length confirming the facts mentioned in his published letter, and he also states that, on the other hand, the rod seemed to give him a wrong indication on one occasion.

In a chalk soil in Essex two or three years ago it indicated water on a friend's property near the surface. My friend dug down to the depth guessed, but found none, and I dissuaded them from incurring further expenses, lest I should be mistaken.

The principal practical use to which I have put the power is to fix the locality of leaks in the bank of an artificial piece of water, and in determining the course of underground drains and leaks therefrom. For these purposes I have found the power practically useful.

Sir Richard Harington in reply to my question as to whether he could give me any further particulars of the use of his power, or the dates, etc., at which he found the leaks in the bank, writes as follows; after giving some details which are contained in his published letter, he adds :—

Whitbourne Court, Worcester, *October 29th*, 1899.

It has occasionally happened that leakage into the brook has taken place through rat holes and the like, the locality of which my servants have been unable to discover. When this has been the case, I have used the divining rod, which has always told me correctly where the leak was. I cannot give dates, but the event has occurred on two or three occasions during the last ten years.

The piece of water in question is supplied at one end from the above-mentioned brook by means of a culvert of some length.

It appearing that there was waste of water in this culvert, I tried the divining rod, walking parallel to it. It told me, as the fact turned out to be, that the leaks were numerous, so many, indeed, that it was useless to repair the culvert, inside which I had to lay glazed pipes. This took place in the year 1898.

Richard Harington, Bart.

The use of the " rod " to find a hidden leak in a culvert or reservoir has been successfully tried by others; see, e.g., p. 41 of my previous Report, [p 39 - Ed] where the amateur dowsers, Messrs. Young and Robertson, independently fixed on the same spot. Mr. Westlake, F.G.S., has recently informed me of another case, where the dowser, R. Pavey, of Cheddar, did the same thing at the moat round the Bishop's Palace at Wells. An engineer was first employed, and had spent £20 in trying to find the leak, but failed. Pavey, though a stranger, found the leak at once, and it was then stopped at a cost of a few shillings. Mr. Westlake visited the place and ascertained the facts; he states the engineer was much impressed by Pavey's success, as he, after careful and costly examination of the place, had failed. Experiments of this kind are worth careful repetition under strict scientific supervision.

## No. 2. Mr. E. Hippisley

One of the most successful amateur dowsers of whom I have heard was the late Mr. Edwin Hippisley, a leading man in Wells, Somerset. Mr. Hippisley was a member of the Institute of Surveyors, and his firm, Hippisley and Sons, are the principal surveyors and land agents in Wells. At a meeting of the Wells Archaeological Society, held at the Bishop's Palace, in Wells, in April, 1892, Mr. Hippisley read a paper on his experiences with the dowsing rod. A verbatim report of that paper appeared in the Wells Journal for April 21st, 1892, together with an interesting discussion that followed, in which the Bishop of Wells, who was in the chair, the Dean, and others took part. Mr. Hippisley's paper is too long to quote, but the following are some abridged extracts from it. Though his theory (a common one) is improbable, his facts are of considerable interest.

> In using the rod I always find the point turn upwards to a nearly vertical position when approaching an underground spring, and it reverses its action after the spring is passed over: upon turning round and walking over the same spot the same thing occurs. The only theory I can form is that those persons who have the "gift," as it is called, are more susceptible to electrical action, water being a good conductor of electricity, and that the rod is moved owing to some sensation in, or electric influence on, the body of the operator.

Mr. Hippisley then proceeds to give details of numerous instances of his discovery of underground water by means of the rod, which proved of great practical value.

For instance, at the Lodge to the Cemetery at Portway, at the Sanatorium near Axbridge, at cottages near East Horrington, at Burcot, at Wookey Hole, and at two or three other estates in Somerset. At Cotford Farm, near Taunton, a well was being sunk for the Western Somerset Asylum, and after 50 ft. had been sunk, Mr. Hippisley, by means of the rod, directed the men to drive a heading west of the well, when a largely increased supply of water was obtained. Another and remarkable case at Lytes Cary I have already given on a previous page (see p. 266.)

## No. 3. Mr. J. H. Jones

The next case is that of a country gentleman to whom I have already referred, and who is well-known to me, Mr. J. H. Jones, of Mullinabro, near Waterford. In answer to my request for a brief account of his experience, Mr. Jones writes as follows : —

Waterford, *January 3rd*, 1900.

> Some few years ago, a friend and neighbour of mine, after trying in vain to obtain an unpolluted water supply for his house, decided on enlisting the services of Mr. Mullins, the dowser. I was asked to witness the experiments and was glad to do so.
>
> Mr. Mullins, on his arrival in Waterford, per steamer, drove rapidly to his client's house and in a few minutes indicated an underground water supply near the house quite unconnected, as he alleged, with the flow to a polluted pump-well in the stable yard; he pointed out a favourable spot for sinking, where subsequently a splendid supply of pure water was found at about 30 ft. deep. On the evening

of Mullins's visit, I, for curiosity, cut a forked rod similar to the one he used, and experimenting in a field at home, found, to my surprise, that at one place the rod turned vigorously in my hands. Walking onwards in a zig-zag direction (similar to the way Mr. Mullins proceeded in tracing an underground flow of water), I traced the line of flow detected by me until I found its outcrop in a never-failing spring at some distance from the place where I first found the rod to turn. The direction of the flow to this spring greatly surprised me, for I had hitherto imagined that the spring was fed from a lake, the water from which, at about half-a-mile from the spring, disappeared under the face of a limestone cliff, emerging in a short distance. Here, I imagine, there could be no "subconscious" influence derived from my knowledge that a spring existed some distance from where I first felt the influence of the rod, inasmuch as the line of flow traced out by me by its means was in a direction nearly at right angles to my preconceived notion of the direction of the supposed feeder of the spring.

The ensuing evening I tested myself where Mr. Mullins had found the line of flow for my friend, and I found I could trace it exactly as he had done. Here it might be said I was unconsciously influenced by Mr. Mullins's action, but, as I traced the flow for some fields beyond where he stopped and where neither of us had any idea the line ran, the theory of the influence of his findings on me seems to break down.

The above experiments converted me (in spite of my determination at first to doubt the bona fides of the dowser's indications) from being a prejudiced sceptic to being a confirmed believer in the genuineness of the dowser's claims to point out underground flows of water.

What is the mystic influence emanating from water, and why it should produce the effect I have described is a problem for scientists to solve.

It is marvellous to find a flow of water, as I have proved, exercising a strong influence through 70 to 80 ft. of a dense quartzite rock.

The influence is in my case independent of contact with the ground. It effects me though insulated by standing upon a support resting on glass. I can feel the influence of underground water in a house as readily in the topmost storey as on the ground floor. I can also feel it—apparently as strongly as when standing on the ground,—when I am riding, driving, or travelling by rail, and this not over predetermined places, but over untried ground.

Mr. Jones then goes on to describe how he endeavoured to verify the accuracy of the indications given by the rod by going over ground that had been previously traversed by other dowsers before he was acquainted with the places they had fixed upon as water bearing; the result, he says, convinced him that some peculiar effect was produced upon him by underground water, an effect that caused a certain spasmodic muscular contraction in his arms and hands, thus producing an involuntary movement of the rod. Mr. Jones states that on approaching the spring, the point of the rod begins to creep upward and is more or less violently jerked into a vertical position when directly over the water; the rod he recognises as merely an index of some peculiar impression produced upon himself.

## No. 4. Mr. J. D. Enys, F.G.S.

In the preceding Report (Vol. XIII., p. 7 [p 5 this volume - Ed]) it was mentioned that the President of the Royal Geological Society of Cornwall, Mr. J. D. Enys, F.G.S., was an amateur dowser. In a recent letter to me Mr. Enys says :—

## Prof. W. F. Barrett

Enys, Penryn, Cornwall, *May 6th,* 1900.

In answer to your questions I may say (1) that only a slight feeling is produced in me when the rod commences to move over underground water, but a distinct feeling of relief when I let it go. (2) In a place I indicated (which place was also chosen by the dowser who showed me how to use the rod) an abundant supply of water was reached at 96 ft., which has stood the test of the late dry season.

The clerk of my Parish Council here (St. Gluvias), Mr. J. Lowry, tried the rod, at my request, over a place where I knew a spring existed; suddenly I heard him cry out, with genuine surprise, "It is alive, sir; it is alive." This exactly describes the sensation when the rod moves. I am unable, however, to form any opinion of scientific value on the action of the rod.

John D. Enys.

The interest of this letter is in the fact that not only is Mr. Enys a gentleman of high standing in his county, but he is also an able geologist. I asked Mr. Enys if he would try some blindfolding experiments, with precautions to avoid unconscious muscular guidance and other possible sources of error, but he has not as yet had time to do so. I hope he will pursue the subject.

## No. 5. Mr. J. F. Young

In the previous Report, I referred on page 40 [p 30 this volume -Ed], to two amateur dowsers, Mr. J. F. Young and Mr. Robertson, of Llanelly, S. Wales, who have written a little book on the divining rod. Mr. Young has had an extensive correspondence with me, and has also in person related to me the numerous experiments he has made with the rod in the attempt to arrive at some solution of its perplexing movements. I have been much struck with Mr. Young's enthusiasm, intelligence and scientific spirit, and it may be interesting to put on record the following account which Mr. Young has sent me of his own experience. The account is of greater interest from the fact that Mr. Young was unaware, until he subsequently read my previous Report, that the divining rod, like planchette, was an autoscope, and therefore its movements were profoundly influenced by any predetermined idea or suggestion. Mr. Young's experience is very similar to that of some early writers on the rod, such as Zeidler, who in his *Pantomysterium* gives an account of the manifold objects which excite the motion of the rod, and hence suggested the title of his book.[1] Mr. Young writes to me as follows:—

Llanelly, South Wales, *July 3rd,* 1897.

I will, with your permission, place before you some of my personal experiences with the "rod," trusting you will understand I am only a struggling tradesman, with but little learning and very little spare time, but with an earnest desire to search for the truth, and with that object I have been for years an ardent reader of mental physiology, and psychological books of all kinds.

I soon became convinced that the movement of the rod was due to an involuntary action on the part of the "diviner." To prove this I have watched carefully my own hands (and others') and in every case when the subject sought for has been found, I observe a difference in the relation of one hand to the other; there is in my own case a slight advance of the right hand. In other cases with larger rods, I note the arms at the elbows, which are usually fixed to the side, give greater indications of a closer grip, and the hands are clenched together; others watching have confirmed my views.

---

[1] I have added this quaint book of Zeidler's to our S.P.R. Library. Its title is *Pantomysterium oder das Neue vom Jahre in der Wündshelruthe, etc.*, Magdeburg, 1700. It has eleven plates and thirty-one figures of different kinds of "divining rods," made of every kind of forked article, such as tongs, snuffers, etc Later on, I will make further reference to this book, an excellent abstract of which has been made for me by Miss Stokes.

# The Credibility Of Dowsing

What causes this involuntary movement of the muscles I cannot say, but I will give a series of cases where it is produced and where I have used the rod successfully.

Water-finding was the first which engaged my attention; finding the rod turn in my hand, I tried every available means of proving the reality of a water-finding faculty. At last I was convinced of its truth and its usefulness to mankind. Electricity is generally put forward to explain mysteries we know nothing of, and I fell into this same trap. I set to work, and made many electrical appliances (which gave me great pleasure, as it revealed what I previously knew but little of) to test the matter, both in relation to the soil, the atmosphere and my own personality, and at one time I thought I had it within my grasp, but alas, with more knowledge, events transpired which toppled my electrical theory over. I left electricity for the study of "Odic Force," Animal Magnetism, Telepathy, Clairvoyance, Automatism, etc., and latterly the Spiritualist hypothesis, including in its wide range our "subliminal consciousness," and I look upon this last as one that meets the questions at all, or nearly all points; and here I may add in opposition to some arguments which have been put forth by some, it seems to me, taken on the lines of this latter theory, it becomes a proper subject for investigation by the S.P.R., as it is a question of the study of human personality and not of the rod.

I take it that the different sensations and experiences of different water finders is a matter of idiosyncrasy, as in my own person these vary according to conditions, from a strong convulsive feeling at one time, another a state of ecstasy, at another a peculiar, unpleasant feeling at the pit of stomach, and latterly a quick shock, darting, as it were, through the nervous system at the moment of the perception. This sensation belongs especially to Class G of experiments (see below).

In a number of the experiments the rod seems indispensable, but even then merely as an indicator, its motion being a notification to my brain that the influence has taken place, which otherwise would not have reached my consciousness, and for these especially delicate tests I use the form of instrument enclosed. It is a small aluminium fork, light and delicate to the touch, and, being nearly void of elasticity, no tension can be put on. The instrument I hold lightly between finger and thumb of each hand, and when it acts, it either slowly creeps up or suddenly twists at the moment of the impression.

The experiments for convenience of reference I will classify, commencing with Class A, which includes all experiments with water, the feet in every case coming directly or indirectly in contact with the soil, the latter through the medium of a horse, or some form of conveyance, or anything that touches terra firma. The so-called insulation by bottles and other nonconductors, or even rubber boots, may be traced in their several effects to imagination on the part of the water-finder.

I have made some very critical tests in this direction, and have found all so-called insulation a failure.

I may here remark that in all investigation in this matter (with a good sensitive) that suggestion, thought or spoken, of the agent plays a very important part.

Class B includes the finding of metals of all kinds, either hidden, buried, or lying on the surface. A coin or two may be (by another person) hidden with some opaque covering. The hands of the sensitive, with or without the rod, being merely passed above the table, its whereabouts is at once localised and the finger goes down straight upon the coin. Telepathy cannot explain this, as it can be so arranged that no one can know where the coins lie. With the case of coins I must not omit to include the singular fact that where metal has lain, it leaves an influence for many hours, which can in the early hours be detected as well as the coin. Or, on a country road, say, but seldom used, I can locate the track of the wheel and the spots where the horse has trod. A wonderful variety of experiments can be made under this group.

Class C.—The finding of heat rays that have fallen on earth, stone, wood, etc.; of a shadow or line of light, etc.

Class D,—The localising of a given spot, say a square inch, on which sound has been projected closely; this vibration soon passes away, and cannot be done unless tried at once.

Class E.—Currents of electricity in a wire; but this is difficult to prove, as the influence might be due to the metal and not electricity, as in the case of water flowing through metal pipes.

Class F.—The finding of a locality where friction has been made, say rubbing a floor, carpet, etc., if dry. On a dry walk it is successful; on a wet one, not so.

Class G.—Under this heading the experiments are so numerous that my naming two or three will give you an idea how easy it would be to extend them; the phenomena taking place here are really the same that underlie the whole of the phenomena connected with the divining rod faculty.

Mrs. Young (my wife) whom I shall hereafter call the agent, and myself the subject.

Expt. 1.—Picture to yourself Mrs. Y. sitting at one end of a room; a certain line is indicated on which I shall walk down the room from her and with my back toward her; she has a watch before her, and at a given moment, only known to herself, wills me to stop; that moment the rod moves and I stop. Sometimes when in good form I can do so minus the rod.

Expt. 2 —Mrs. Y. in same position fixes mentally, unknown to me (my back always toward her) on a sprig, flower or pattern on the carpet in a given line. I start on the quest; as soon as my foot "touches the spot," the rod moves.

Expt. 3.—I now walk along near the wall. Mrs. Y. has fixed on a spray, flower, picture, bracket, vase or some such small object, say the height of my shoulder or head. As soon as I get opposite the signal comes. Many of these are conducted by the agent in one room and the subject in another. You will observe here also there cannot be any bodily contact.

Expt. 4.—Cut, say, a dozen pieces of paper all alike, an inch square, mark one only, as you like, say pencil initials or a number. After stirring and mixing up, place all on floor in different parts, not knowing the marked one. The subject walks about, and ultimately finds the marked paper. In this way you cut out thought-reading or telepathy.

Expt. 5.—A hair from head or beard is placed on the floor, the subject, of course, being absent. The agent leaves the room, accompanied with a stranger (who is not in the secret) to see fair play; or the subject may be blindfolded or walks backward. As soon as he reaches the spot his rod moves. I won't trouble you with more, as you can picture to your mind's eye scores of similar experiments, those above narrated, with others quite as extraordinary, all indicating an intelligence—call it what you will—not under our control. It is almost needless to add that times occur with me and also with the agent when this cannot be done, and there are times when the power, whatever it may be, appears to be overflowing. It is, however, exhausting, and, after half-a-dozen experiments, a rest is required. I will do my best to carry out any other experiments you may suggest, and hope what I have recorded may be of some use.

# The Credibility Of Dowsing

The foregoing experiments must simply be taken for what they are worth; they are not quoted as of evidential value, for we do not know, e.g., how far any involuntary and unintentional signs from the "agent" may have reached the "subject" of these experiments. The detection of *points de repère* [landmarks - Ed] by hypnotised subjects, usually attributed to hyperaesthesia, resembles Mr. Young's detection of the track of a horse, etc., by the use of rod, and I am inclined to think the explanation in both cases is similar. I have given this letter at length, as it demonstrates the all-important part played by any suggestion or idea in producing the involuntary muscular action that causes the twisting of the rod. It further shows how absurd is the dowser's notion that underground water must be indicated when the forked twig twists round in his hands.

## No. 6. Mr. R. G. D. Tosswill

Through watching Mr. Young's use of the forked twig in Devonshire, a gentleman at Budleigh Salterton, Mr. Tosswill, found the twig also moved when he held it. He soon became an enthusiastic amateur dowser, and sent me the following account of his experience after reading my previous Report:—

Budleigh Salterton, Devon, *October 13th*, 1897.

> The first time that 1 saw the "hazel rod" used in seeking for water was on August 11th, 1897.
>
> My friend who used it was searching for the spot underneath which a small stream of water was flowing through the adit of an old disused copper mine. He asked me to walk alongside him and closely observe the movements of the rod as he passed over the water. I did so, and soon observed the top of the rod quiver, and then move slowly forward and outwards away from his body, until the point of the rod pointed downwards to the ground at his feet.
>
> He then asked me to try it, and walk over the same course that he had taken, holding the rod in precisely the same manner. I did so, holding the rod perpendicularly, with the end of either branch laid on the palm of each hand, with fingers and thumbs tightly closed, and back of the hands downwards.
>
> On advancing, I fully expected to find that if the rod moved at all in my hands, it would do so in precisely the same manner as it did with my friend. To my astonishment, however, I found that on coming to the same spot, the rod quivered slightly, and then moved towards my own body, inwards, and then downwards, pointing to the ground. This was exactly in the opposite direction to which it had previously moved when in my friend's hands.
>
> Since then I have used the hazel rod or some other "autoscope" nearly every day in seeking and tracing underground springs, water pipes, drains, hidden coins, etc. Hazel, willow, beech, thorn, elm and honeysuckle twigs, as also copper and other wire rods or forks that I have used, holding them perpendicularly either in the closed hands or between the thumbs and forefingers, move always in the same direction, i.e.. inwards and towards my body, and then downwards pointing to the ground.

Robert G. D. Tosswill.

## No. 7. Mr. G. H. Ward-Humphreys

In the *Cheltenham Examiner* for March 24th, 1897, Mr. G. H. Ward-Humphreys gives a lengthy report of his first experience with the divining rod, which affords a good illustration of the genesis of an amateur dowser and the amazement—shared by educated as well as illiterate persons—excited by the apparently automatic motion of the twig.

## Prof. W. F. Barrett

The night before, Mr. Gataker had expressed the belief that I was likely to possess the power of "divination"; and he was now very anxious for me to try my luck at once. He cut several twigs and armed me with one, and then, taking me down to the side of the lake where water already found was pouring in, he suggested I should walk across the covered-in stream. This I did three or four times in succession, holding the twig, but I was conscious of nothing, nor did I see any movement of the twig. He then, however, laid his hands upon the back of mine, and he walking backwards in front of me, we together crossed over the flowing water. Immediately the V-shaped twig turned completely round in my grip. Perhaps it is unnecessary to say anything about the astonishment with which I regarded this extraordinary movement of the inanimate twig. But what happened afterwards was even more remarkable: for, on going round to unbroken ground upon the other side of the lake, at one spot I felt the twig, which I was carrying with its point downward, so turn in my hand that the point was raised through an angle of 90 deg. Inquiries elicited the fact that this spot was exactly over a stream which had been found twelve months ago. But even now I was not convinced: though I could not believe that the others were deceiving me, I thought it possible that I might be deceiving myself. So I suggested that I might be blindfolded, led some distance from the spot where I was then standing, and then should be guided in such a direction that I must cross the line of the same stream. This was done, and I started my walk at a distance which I afterwards found to be about 60 yds. away. Walking then in the direction I have indicated, I suddenly became aware that the twig was commencing to move. This tendency became stronger at every step. I cast to the right and to the left, and finally guided by the stronger movements of the twig, walked some 15 yds. to the left of my original path and then stopped, the twig having now moved through an angle of 180 deg. My companions, who had hitherto been silent, were greatly amused at the sceptic [the writer]—who found, when able to see, that he had stopped about 3 ft. away from a peg which had been put in to mark the site of one of Mr. Gataker's springs! After this, scepticism vanished.

It will be observed that Mr. Ward-Humphreys states that when blindfolded he was "led," so that the explanation of his success in that ease may be due to the involuntary guidance exercised by those who were touching him.

## No. 8. Mr. G. F. Attree

In the Estates Gazette for February 3rd, 1900, Mr. G. F. Attree, an auctioneer and estate agent of Brighton, gives a lengthy account of his experiences as an amateur dowser. He points out how prejudiced he was against the whole subject until, after watching a dowser at work, he discovered to his surprise that the twig moved in his own hands, twisting round whenever he came to the places marked by the dowser. He goes on to say :—

> The operator holds the two ends of the twig so that the point of the V is at a right angle with his body and the thumb of each hand is in contact with one end of the twig. In this position he walks over the land where he wishes to ascertain what springs exist. On coming over running water (no matter how deep it may be from the surface) the operator feels a tingling sensation in his hands and arms, and the twig immediately twists over until its point has completed more than half a circle.

> During the year 1898 I spent much of my little spare time with the twig, frequently testing springs which I could prove through existing wells, and by this means, and by measuring the width of the influence on the surface of the ground, became able to gauge accurately the depth and strength of a number of springs. ... I cannot say why so few persons possess the power, nor what the current is that passes from running water through the body of the operator, causing the twig to twist. All I have been able to ascertain is, that it is not an ordinary electrical current, for insulation by glass or indiarubber, which will stop the one, has no effect upon that which is brought into force in water-finding.

# *The Credibility Of Dowsing*

Mr. Attree is an enthusiastic believer in the "rod," and objects to the term "divining-rod " and " water-diviner," as he affirms there is no guessing or divining or pretending practised by an honest waterfinder, the motion of the rod being due to some cause beyond the control of the operator: he states that he has successfully made use of the indications of the rod in finding "springs" for the benefit of his friends and neighbours. Several of these instances are given by Mr. Attree, and I have recently received some interesting additional evidence of Mr. Attree's faculty as an amateur dowser.

The interest of this case is the additional illustration it affords (1) of the involuntary muscular action that causes the motion of the twig; (2) of the accompanying peculiar sensation affirmed by so many dowsers; (3) of insulation not affecting the motion; (4) of the implicit belief of the operator that whenever the rod twists the presence of underground water must be indicated; and (5) of the readiness with which incredulity becomes credulity when something (such as the twisting of the rod) happens contrary to the sceptic's expectation; the dowser's erroneous views about "springs" and " head of the spring " being forthwith accepted without examination.

## PART VII

### *Miscellaneous Cases*

I will here add a few stray cases that do not come under the previous classification. The following was kindly sent me by the Right Hon. Sir Edward Fry, D.C.L., F.R.S., etc. To those who imagine that dowsers are only employed by the credulous and ignorant, this testimony, from one of the highest judicial authorities in our country, who is also a man of science, is a sufficient reply.

Failand House, Bristol, *October 15th*, 1898.

I have sunk in four places for water near here. The first time was some twenty-five years ago at Failand House Farm. There I was guided by Mr. Lawrence, a well-known dowser, who lived somewhere in Gloucestershire. I sank for water and got some, but subsequently, under Mr. Merryweather's advice,[1] I deepened the well, and have now a very good supply, which has shown no signs of failure even during the prolonged drought of this year.

I sank a well about 20 ft. in Faulkner's garden—on my own selection of the spot—got no water, and gave up the pursuit.

About six years ago I sank a well near this house, and got water at, I think, 36 ft. This now supplies this house and the garden, stables, etc., etc. The site was chosen by a dowser, who came over with my architect, Mr. Price, of Weston-super-Mare.

I was not here either when Lawrence dowsed for the farm well, or Mr. Price's friend for the well near this house, and know nothing in particular about their proceedings.

I consulted Mr. Merryweather same years ago about sinking a well near this house, and he dowsed and thought he could find a line of water, but I did not act on that suggestion.

Last year, wanting to get a water supply for a farm (Lower Failand Farm—Parson's) I again consulted Mr. Merryweather. He came with his two sons, to one of whom he attributes the power of dowsing, and I went over the ground with them, and he ultimately advised me to drive a tunnel into the hill. He did this work for me, and found water, though it has failed during the long drought. I am not sure whether there is not a leak in the tunnel.

There is no doubt a good deal of water in the hill on which all the land in question lies, but how far it is to be found everywhere I cannot say. I rather incline to the belief that the old red sandstone, which is the rock, is traversed by faults or lines of weakness, and that down these the water passes.

In the search for water of last year Mr. Merryweather certainly did not rely on the watch spring alone.[2] He considered also indications of water on the surface (from the character of the herbage) and the presence of small springs or droppings of water in the rocky sides of the lane, from which we drove the tunnel. He has been a well-sinker for years before he took to dowsing, and would, I am sure, scout the notion that he should neglect other indications of water. I may add that I have known him for many years—that I have employed him not only as before mentioned, but on other matters relating to drains, etc., and that I believe him to be a thoroughly honest man.

Edward Fry.

---

[1] Mr. Merryweather is another dowser. See previous Report, p. 72. [p 55 this volume - Ed] He died recently.
[2] Mr. Merryweather, like the late Mr. Lawrence, always preferred to use a long piece of flexible steel rather than a forked twig as an indicator, or "autoscope."— W. F. B.

## *The Credibility Of Dowsing*

The fact mentioned by Sir Edward Fry that Merryweather is in part intentionally guided by surface indications is very interesting. This, however, is not usually the case with other dowsers, so far as I know. The value of surface indications is referred to more fully in another part of this paper. Sir Edward Fry also sends me the following extract from a volume called *Memorials: Part II, Personal and Political,* by the Earl of Selborne, Vol. II., p. 384-5.

> In a letter to his daughter, the Countess of Waldegrave, under date September 25th, 1893, Lord Selborne writes, after referring to the effects of the drought:—" Willie" (i.e., the present Earl of Selborne) "brought a water-finder from Wiltshire to see if he could find near the reservoir any underground water which could be used for increasing the supply there, and he did find it as he said, but till this is verified by sinking to the necessary depth I shall suspend my belief, though the same man has been successful in finding it at Hatfield and for Lord Jersey." To this a note is added, "The divining rod proved successful."

There are, I believe, no professional dowsers in Ireland, though English dowsers are in considerable request in certain parts of the country, and there are a few amateur dowsers. The following case of an amateur dowser, who is a farmer in the co. Tyrone, has lately reached me through a friend :—

Mullantean, Stewartstown, *October 17th*, 1899.

> The water-finder, William M'Crea, who lives near Stewartstown, was here to-day, and found two springs for us. It is really wonderful the way the rod turns in his hands; it broke nearly in two, though it was a strong piece of ash. He says he sleeps badly the night after he does much of it, and at the time it feels as if the sinews of his arms were being torn out. He first tried the rod about twenty years ago, when an uncle of his came from America, who had made a good deal of money there by finding springs, so he tried if he had the power, and found he had. He can tell how far the spring is down by counting the feet from where the rod begins to tremble until it turns over,—double that distance is generally right, but he won't engage that, though he says in most of the wells sunk he has been right to a foot or two. He has found a fine spring lately for the creamery at Moy, and it has done well ever since. He can tell of no failure, so far, that he has had. He is a man about fifty years of age, and has a good farm near this, so he does not do it for money. We will begin, I hope, to dig our well soon, and I will let you know how it gets on. The spring, he asserts, begins on a hill, and continues all down the field and up to the house, I suppose 400 yards or more, and that it could be tapped anywhere we choose.
>
> C. M. Kennedy.

I have also received other cases where McCrea was successful, but he dislikes using the rod, as he says "it seems to take such a lot out of me."

Through the kindness of friends I have received some particulars of the successful use of the rod for finding underground water by one or two other amateur dowsers in Ireland, such as the late Mr. Thos. Purvis, of Wexford, of whom Mr. J. Haughton, of Ferns, co. Wexford, informs me that Mr. Purvis enabled his family to obtain a splendid supply of water on their premises, "as abundant to-day as forty years ago when the well was sunk."

Colonel King-Harman, of New Castle, Ballymahon, Ireland, is another Irish amateur dowser, and in reply to my inquiries told me that a former steward of his had been a successful dowser in America; Colonel King-Harman having kindly obtained the man's address, I wrote to him and had the following reply in answer to my questions :—

Whitfield Farm, Kilmeaden, Co. Waterford, *October 30th*, 1899.

> My experience of the divining rod was in Manitoba, Canada. There the rod proved successful every time but once, and I have every confidence would have done so then, but we struck on a vein of sand, and the well would not hold out.

I dug one well where other twelve were dry, and this one had abundance [of water]; it was finished by Government. Other six wells I dug myself out there, on the condition that if no water, no wage. All that I had to guide me was the rod, and in all those places water was scarce.

I cannot give the addresses of all I dug for, but by writing to Mr. Angus, postmaster, Logoch, Manitoba (for whom I dug the first well), you can have the names of all the places.

I have tried the rod in Co. Waterford for Major Chavasse on very dry hilly ground; he has not yet dug.

I have no special feeling in my hands or body when the rod turns.

George Mitchell.

In *Bibby's Quarterly* (a farming journal) for November, 1897, is an illustrated account of a Cornish dowser named George Williams, who lives at Falmouth. It seems he accidentally discovered that the rod moved in his hands, and was successful in tracing a lode by its means. Subsequently he used it for water, and several cases of his success are quoted. I wrote to the author of the article for further particulars, and had the following reply :—

Rosvean, Falmouth, Cornwall, *January 26th*, 1898.

George Williams has recently found a spring for me in the country near Falmouth. It was not where I had hoped or wanted, but his hazel rod pointed where the spring was. I was present while he walked all over the field. The work, he says, is always very exhausting to him. The spring, a fine jet of water in the rock, was found 28 feet below the surface. No one present knew anything about a watercourse there, and there was nothing to suggest it.

The spring at the vicarage (built on the hill at Budock) was 70 feet below the surface; it was also found by Williams.

Susan E. Gay.

In a subsequent letter Miss Gay tells me that in sinking her well, a solid slaty rock was encountered and dynamite had to be used; the water, when reached at a depth of 28 ft. was so abundant that "even through the drought of last summer it was never below 6 or 7 ft."

I visited Falmouth and saw the place where Williams found a water supply for Miss Gay. It certainly seemed an unlikely spot, on dry rocky ground between Budock and Penjerrick: the geological formation is a clay slate (Devonian), near its junction with the granite; as Mr. Westlake remarks, "water tends to run off the granite into the fissures of these slaty rocks, affording an excellent testing ground for the dowser"; here and there the water makes its way to the surface as seen by certain "springs" marked on the map not far distant. I had an interview with Williams; he is a working man, a mason, and, like other dowsers, has the most childlike faith in the indications of his "rod": he showed me several testimonials from gentlemen in Cornwall who spoke highly of his services in finding water on their estates. But I had no opportunity of making a personal investigation of any of these cases. Miss Gay states that Williams has been engaged by the Great Western Railway Company to "dowse" at Truro for water and that he has worked with success for the Ecclesiastical Commissioners on various occasions.

Among the dowsers with whom I have had some correspondence is Mr. H. A. Canning, who is a sanitary and hydraulic engineer at Market Lavington, Wiltshire. Mr. Canning tells me that seeing a dowser at work some twenty-five years ago he tried his hand, and discovered that the forked twig "worked" equally well with him. He encloses me a list of names of gentlemen for whom he has been successful in finding water by the indication of the twig. In one case the twig moved at a spot between two wells 100 ft. apart, which gave little or no water; on sinking at the spot indicated, an abundant supply was obtained. This may be so, but I have not verified the statements. Mr.

## *The Credibility Of Dowsing*

Canning, in a letter to the Standard in January, 1889, states that upon finding the rod suddenly move at a certain spot he was then blindfolded, and again on traversing the same spot the rod moved. He adds there was an unmistakable but indescribable feeling upon approaching the spot beneath which underground water existed, a sensation that could not possibly be avoided, even though an effort was made to do so. It is certainly a remarkable circumstance, whether this sensation be illusory or not, that for 200 years the great majority of dowsers in all parts of the world have quite independently asserted the same thing, and as a rule believed that this peculiar sensation, or malaise, existed only in their own case.

An interesting account of an East Anglian dowser, Mr. Child, recently appeared in the Eastern Daily Press. Mr. Child, who was formerly in business in Norwich, now lives near Hadleigh in Suffolk, and, like the majority of dowsers, was originally a Somersetshire man. When living near Wells in Somerset he saw a dowser at work, and was greatly astonished to find the rod twisted round in his own hand at the same places. Several instances of his success are given in the newspaper report referred to, but these I have not attempted to verify.

I have already mentioned a Cheddar dowser named Thomas Pavey (p. 280).[1] The son, Rowland Pavey, of Cheddar Mill, is also a dowser, but has lately abandoned the use of the forked twig, and trusts to what he calls a "New Science" in his water-finding expeditions. What this mysterious science is he does not tell the public. I have had some correspondence with Pavey, and his letters are full of rhodomontade [boastfulness – Ed]. Though he will not tell me what his wonderful secret is, he assures me it is "a science of sciences, and to keep it secret is keeping hid a field of wonderful discoveries that cannot be exhausted by scientists, as it is, I believe, the outcome of a higher state of civilisation." (!) In a printed circular he sends me he states that, though his science is in a crude state, yet the "science of geology will be surpassed, the uplifting of mountains and what lies hidden far beneath will be understood. There will be no more secrets in water-finding, and the human body will be understood as it never was before," beside a multitude of other revelations, which he enumerates, ranging over the universe! In spite of all this nonsense, the Rev. H. H. Streeten, who writes to me from Easton Vicarage, near Wells, tells me, in answer to my inquiries, that "Pavey certainly has a remarkable knowledge of the earth. How he has acquired this knowledge is a different question, but in localities he has never before visited he will in a short time tell you where the springs of water are, and generally he will say at what depth water is to be found underground. He is a quiet, nice-minded man." Mr. Westlake, who has visited Pavey, says he is a genuine enthusiast, with a firm belief in his "gift." The following report of an eye-witness describes how Pavey usually goes to work in determining the depth at which water would be found underground. In this particular case—

> He knelt down on one knee with his head resting on one hand, and gazed downwards for about half-a-minute, afterwards giving it as his opinion that it would be necessary to go down approximately 60 ft. As he predicted, a good spring was struck within a few inches of the depth mentioned. The supply is plentiful, as is evidenced by the fact that, after it had been left during the night, three hours were occupied in getting sufficient water out of the well to enable a commencement to be made in lining it with brick.

There is, however, no evidence to show he was not aware of the depth of other local wells.

However striking some of these cases of the success of the dowser may appear to the lay mind, to an expert field geologist, who knows the district, the explanation is often simple enough. Here, for example, is a case in point. Mrs. Hollands, of Dene Park, Tonbridge, kindly sent me an account of the success which attended the dowser (Mr. Gataker) at her place, but informed me they had not made any previous attempts to find water, and adds :—

Dene Park, Tonbridge, *October 17th*, 1899.

> We dug in two places, and found water about the depth he [the dowser] told us—fifteen to twenty-five feet. Two of these wells are now most valuable, in these long seasons of drought. Without them we should not have enough water to supply the house at all.

Minnie Hollands.

---

1  F. H. Pavey, p. 326, another Cheddar dowser, is a connection of these Paveys.

## *Prof. W. F. Barrett*

Mr. Holmes, F.G.S., remarks on this case:—

> At Dene Park, near Tonbridge, a gravel patch capping the Weald Clay seems to have been tapped. I learn from Topley's Geological Survey Memoir on the Weald (1875) that there are many outlying patches of gravel at high levels in that district. Dene Park is rather more than two miles north of Tonbridge. Gravel patches are mentioned (p. 185) as existing near Starve Crow Farm (about half-a-mile south-east of the house at Dene Park) and east of Little Park (about a quarter of a mile north of Dene Park). The dowser would need simply a good eye for contours, as in the Oxford case.

In addition to the cases which I have already cited, I have before me a number of other illustrations of the dowser's success in finding water, and very often correctly estimating the depth at which it would be found. In these cases, however, the replies I have received to my inquiries have shown that no previous attempt to obtain a water supply had been made, and several state that water would probably have been found without the dowser's aid, only they wanted to "make sure" before sinking a well. This correspondence has also shown how misleading are many of the reports appearing in some of the provincial newspapers. These reports doubtless give the dowser's own version of the matter. To quote a typical instance, the Bath Chronicle, which appears to be Mr. Gataker's favourite organ, contains two misleading statements in its issue of October 22nd, 1896. One is as follows:—

> Another striking testimony to the ability of Mr. Leicester Gataker, the water expert, of Bath, has just come to hand. In the face of much scepticism he recently undertook to supply Mr. Smith Barry, M.P., Cordangan Manor, near Tipperary, [with water] for the purposes of a dairy, on special terms of "no water, no pay." He foreshadowed 300 gallons an hour at from 25 to 35 ft. deep. On this he at once started his men to carry out the sinking of the well. At a depth of 32 ft. a supply of 400 gallons has been obtained as a result.

I wrote to the Right Hon. Smith Barry for information, and his estate agent (Mr. G. C. Townsend) replies that "the results of Mr. Gataker's work here have not been sufficiently successful to justify me in giving you the information you ask."

The other statement, a few lines above in the same paper, is as follows:—

> Mr. G. Marshall, of Sarnesfield Court, Herefordshire, was getting pretty well tired of well-sinking at the time he engaged the services of Mr. Leicester Gataker, but his latest move has been most successful.

In reply to my inquiries Mr. Marshall states that he sunk no wells before Mr. Gataker's visit, but simply made "catch-pits" to collect surface water. In further correspondence Mr. Marshall informs me:—

> Heralds' College, London, E.C., *October 16th*, 1899.
>
> In reply to your questions—
>
> 1 and 2. Before Mr. Gataker found water for me at Sarnesfield I had built a large tank and attempted to collect surface water, which failed me in a dry season.
>
> 3. Mr. Gataker came and indicated two spots within a short distance of my tank, telling the number of feet to sink the wells and the amount of water I should find. His estimate was perfectly correct, and since I have had the wells sunk I have had a most satisfactory supply. The late dry summer has been a severe test, but there has been a full supply of water, and I have no reason to believe there will ever be otherwise. It is curious how many people appear to have the power of water finding did they know how to use it. Several of us tried when Mr. Gataker was at Sarnesfield, and when he placed a

## *The Credibility Of Dowsing*

twig in their hands it moved, but with myself, although Mr. Gataker gripped me firmly by the wrists, there was no movement.

George W. Marshall.

Sarnesfield is near Weobley, about ten miles north-west of Hereford. I asked Mr. Marshall what was the need of a dowser, as probably surface water would be found anywhere in shallow wells at Sarnesfield. He replies :—

Heralds' College, London, E.C., *October 19th*, 1899.

Of course, on a soil like ours at Sarnesfield, which is on stone, you can get water anywhere when you get down to the rock; but the point which shows Gataker's skill is that being told whereabouts (a mile and a half from my house) I wanted water found, he fixed the spots to sink the wells, and told accurately the depth to go and the quantity of water which would be found.

George W. Marshall.

Mr. Holmes remarks :—

The Gataker cases are an excellent illustration—as you remark—of the deceitfulness of newspaper reports. Mr. Marshall's second letter reduces very considerably the atmosphere of wonder enveloping the first.

T. V. H.

Much of the wonder which the dowser creates, in the unscientific mind, arises from the notion which he invariably fosters that underground water is found in narrow streams or "springs," and that without his aid in hitting upon the exact spot where to sink a well, the chances are you would have missed the water altogether. It is true that in certain districts the geological formation causes underground water to be found in fissures or narrow streams, and there, as I have said before, the real test of the dowser is to be found. Such a formation prevails in the county of Somerset, as Mr. Westlake has shown in his instructive Appendix [Appendix A - Ed]). In the next Part, I have cited some failures of dowsers and the probable percentage of successes they obtain. It must, however, be clearly understood that neither in this Report, nor in the previous one, have I selected favourable cases and omitted others which were adverse. Every case that has reached me has, as far as possible, been investigated, either by correspondence with the person who employed the dowser, or by a visit to the spot by my geological friends.

# PART VIII

## Professional Dowsers In England And Wales And Their Probable Percentage Of Failures

### § 1. List of Dowsers and Hints as to their Employment

It may be convenient in concluding this part of our work, to append a list of professional dowsers in England and Wales. The stronghold of the dowser is to be found in those districts where the geological formation renders it difficult to discern underground sources of water, such, for example, as in the Lower Lias and amid the limestone regions of Somerset and Gloucestershire and in the South of France. In and around Cheddar there are numerous professional dowsers; to some of these I have already referred. With the help of Mr. Westlake I have drawn up the following list of professional dowsers now living in England and Wales. No doubt there are several others of whom I have not heard, and there are, of course, in addition numbers of amateur dowsers, some of whom have been remarkably successful. It will be noticed that even in this imperfect list no less than eighteen professional dowsers are found in Somersetshire, more than half the total; and several who now live elsewhere, such as Mr. Child and Mr. Stears, originally came from Somersetshire.

**Dowsers in Somersetshire :—**

J. Blake, Hill End, Winscombe.

H. Chesterman, Anglo Terrace, Bath.

C. Cross, Hallatrow Heath, near Radstock.

Thomas Day, Shipham (miner).

Thomas Foord, Shipham (labourer).

L. A. Gataker, Weston-super-Mare.

J. J. Green, Cheddar.

Thomas Hawker, Somerton (farmer).

W. Hills, Wells.

C. Hole, Reward, Wells (carter).

William Kerslake, Wells (tailor).

W Mereweather (jun.), Bedminster, Bristol.

Rowland Pavey, Cheddar (miller).

F. H. Pavey, Cheddar (plumber).

C. Sims, Pilton.

Thomas Thomas, Worle, Weston-super-Mare.

H. Williams, Pilton.

W. R. Wyburn,[1] Woolavington, near Bridgwater (farmer).

**Dowsers in Gloucestershire :—**

D. Lacey, Yate.

---

[1] Since the above list was printed I have been informed that Mr. Wyburn (a member of the Society of Friends) takes no fee, therefore he can hardly be reckoned among professional dowsers. The list of Somerset dowsers might no doubt be easily extended by further inquiry, e.g., George Elson, labourer at North Perroth, p. 290

# The Credibility Of Dowsing

**Dowsers in Wiltshire:—**
H. A. Canning, Market Lavington (sanitary engineer).
H. W. Mullins, Colerne, Box.
B. Tompkins, Chippenham.

**Dowsers in Dorset and Cornwall:—**
W. J. Mitchell, Cerne Abbas (sanitary engineer).
G. A. Williams, Merrill Place, Falmouth.

**Dowsers in Wales :—**
T. Heighway, Llandrindod Wells.
W. Hoskins, Uplands, Swansea.
R. W. Robertson, Llanelly.
E. Rothwell, Cardiff.

**Dowsers in East Anglia :—**
R. Anthony, Yelling, Hunts (farmer).
H. Bacon, Newport, Essex.
J. Blanchard, Wisbech, Cambs.
S. T. Child, Capel Mills, Hadleigh, Suffolk.
W. Stone, Bolingbroke Hall, Spilsby, Lincolnshire.

**Dowsers in Yorkshire :—**
F. Rodwell, Wensley.
J. Stears, Hessle (near Hull).

It may not be out of place in this connection to give one or two practical hints to those who intend to employ a dowser, or " diviner," as they usually like to be called.

(1) Ascertain the geological conditions of the place where a water supply is wanted: in numerous cases where a water-finder is employed his advice is wholly unnecessary (see Appendix A. and also B.).

(2) If a large supply is wanted and a deep artesian well or boring to be made eschew all dowsers and consult a good hydro-geologist.[1]

(3) If only a moderate supply is required,—especially in certain formations where geology is of little help,—select a couple of dowsers of good repute, and let each give his opinion unknown to and independently of the other.[2]

(4) As the best dowsers I know have been more or less illiterate men, their loss of time would be amply repaid by offering them a moderate fee and travelling expenses.

---

[1] Mr. Westlake, F.G.S., in reference to this adds the following note:—"Even where deep wells are necessary, experience has shown it is sometimes advantageous to supplement geological advice by calling in a dowser, for, though a definite water level may exist, the quantity found at a given spot is often a matter of chance: such a case I saw recently near Newbury, where the dowser, Tompkins, had found, at a depth of over 100 ft. in the chalk, so large a supply that steam pumping-gear had to be used, whereas in two or three other wells in the neighbourhood, with water at about the same hydrostatic level, the quantity was much less. It is difficult, however, to say how far chance coincidence may account for such lucky hits."

[2] On the question of independent examination by different dowsers, see Part IV., and also the last sentence but one in Professor de Mortillet's letter, p. 323.

(5) If the water-finder is willing to sink or bore on the faith of his opinion, obtain his estimate, and if found to be reasonable, offer him so much per cent, extra on the condition of " no water no pay," taking care to have a written agreement as to the limit of expense involved.[1] What this extra percentage should be depends on the geological conditions. Taking the country indiscriminately, 15 per cent, would probably be reasonable, but if "fissure water" (see p. 341) predominates, and moreover, if geological advice has already been sought and on trial has proved a failure, an extra rate of 25 per cent, is not unreasonable, if a certain supply be stipulated for.

## § 2. Recent Cases of Complete or Partial Failure in Water-Finding by English Dowsers

Though nearly every professional dowser thinks he can be no more mistaken in trusting to the twisting of his rod for the indication of underground water, than a magnet can be mistaken in its selective attraction of iron, yet it is hardly necessary to say the dowser is by no means free from mistakes. He has his failures, sometimes costly failures to those who employ him. Several of his failures I detailed in the previous Report, and I will here cite a few more that I have since met with; others of course exist that I have not heard of. But whilst I have been obliged to omit numerous instances of the dowsers' success which were of no evidential value, I have not omitted any of their failures which were verified upon inquiry; meaning by failure, complete disappointment of the expectations raised by the water-finder.

As I have quoted an instance of Mr. Gataker's success at Aspley Heath, p. 185 [p 274 this volume - Ed], here is an instance of his failure in the same neighbourhood. It is contained in a letter to Mr. Myers from a friend of his —the daughter of a former Professor at Cambridge—who writes most indignantly, and states that Mr. Gataker's predictions were not in any way fulfilled. The place is at Woburn Sands, and it seems that before Gataker's visit a well had been dug about 70 ft. deep in the Oxford clay without finding water. When Mr. Gataker came, he fixed upon a spot where he said a large water supply would be obtained—at what depth is not stated. A well was dug and only a little water obtained, even when headings were driven radiating from the sides of the well.

The writer of the letter suggests that the investigation of every dowser should be confined to the question of whether "he ever made a mistake, for if water were not found in the place and at the depth predicted by the diviner, I should consider him an impostor." I am afraid this "short way" with dowsers would not carry the investigation very far. The writer concludes by expressing a wish to write to the Spectator "on the wickedness of diviners and the extraordinary folly and credulousness of educated persons in believing in them."

Other dowsers besides Mr. Gataker have their share of failures, in spite of all their attempts to explain them away. Here is a case of the discomfiture of another dowser, related in detail in the Daily Mail for December 28th, 1897. It seems that a member of the Legislative Council of Jamaica, whilst on a visit to England, engaged the services of a "diviner" to locate the site for wells in a district in Jamaica which had suffered greatly from the need of a water supply. Handsome terms were offered by five parochial boards in Jamaica to the waterfinder, who on his arrival in their neighbourhood was received with enthusiasm, and very soon, by means of his rod, pointed out several places where water would be found.

> At Mandeville, a charming village in the hills, he pegged out part of the course of a subterranean stream and retired to lunch at a neighbouring hotel. In his absence some wags removed his pegs and lined out a totally different course. On his return the diviner took up the new direction and continued it for over a hundred yards more, and did not discover his mistake until one of his admirers pointed out the deception. But no borings for water had yet been made, and the authoritative statements of the diviner were unchallenged. At length the necessary implements were obtained, and an attempt was made at several points to reach the water so confidently indicated. At one point where water was

---

[1] The reason for this will be seen in the next few pages. The dowser will usually make a rough estimate of the quantity of water likely to be found and the depth at which it exists; with some dowsers this estimate is often wonderfully close, with others it is as often wrong. It is desirable, therefore, to bear this in mind and also that the quantity of water yielded by all shallow wells varies largely with the season of the year.

## The Credibility Of Dowsing

predicted as at a depth of 40 ft., a boring of 150 ft. was made, with the only result that no water could be found, the machinery eventually broke down, and after going down about 200 ft., the borer could not be extracted. The same ridiculous result occurred in other places, and up to the present at none of the points indicated by the diviner has water been found.

Like all other newspaper reports, this needs confirmation, but it is no doubt fairly correct. In 1897, Mr. Stears informed me he had entered into a contract to dowse for water in Jamaica, and he no doubt was the unfortunate dowser employed. Nor is this the only costly failure he, as well as some other dowsers, have had.

In the previous Report [p. 141 this volume -Ed] I gave some details of a failure on the part of Mr. Stears which led the Parish Council of Bardney, Lincolnshire, to a very heavy and useless expenditure. At a spot indicated by the dowser they bored to a great depth and found no water. I have since heard from Mr. Hind, the Clerk to the District Council, who informs me they continued boring to a depth of 450 ft., at a cost of £300, and found no water. The bore-hole then caved in. Bardney is about ten miles east of Lincoln.

As I have pointed out again and again, whatever success attends the dowser is mainly due to his discovery of *a moderate water supply yielded by comparatively shallow borings or wells*, i.e., from 15 to 50 ft. deep. Hence it is a great pity that District and County Councils, when they want a large water supply, do not consult a good hydro-geologist. Mr. C. E. de Rance, F.G.S., one of the best authorities on water supply, published in 1891 an admirable paper on The Underground Waters of Lincolnshire, which I recommend to the Bardney District Council. They will find in it a record of deep borings not far from their own town.

Another case, more or less a failure, in which Mr. Stone was the dowser, has reached me from Messrs. Attenborough and Timms, of Northampton. They had originally sunk and bored to a depth of 70 ft. at Dassett Sidings, near Burton (between Fenny Compton and Kineton railway stations), and found no water. Mr. Stone was then engaged, and with his rod fixed on a place 125 yds. distant where he stated water would be found: "a sufficient supply, he thought, would be reached at 90 ft., but the exact depth he could not say." Here Messrs. Attenborough bored to a depth of over 100 ft.; near the surface, as Stone had said, a little water was met with, but on testing with an artesian pump at the greater depth, "the result was unsuccessful," and in a recent letter to me (June, 1900) Messrs. Attenborough state: "We spent a great deal more money than we were given to understand would be necessary, and, seeing no prospect of success, stopped the work after boring to over 100 ft."

Many of the professional dowsers undertake the work of sinking or boring for water at the spot they have selected, and, as in the above case, frequent disputes arise from this cause, the dowser wanting to go on boring, at his customer's expense, when he fails to obtain an adequate supply of water at or beyond the depth he estimated. It is necessary, therefore, to warn all those who intend employing a dowser as well-sinker to make a definite arrangement beforehand, such as I have suggested on p. 236.

Mr. Westlake, in the course of his investigations in the south-west of England, heard of some half-dozen cases of expensive failures on the part of the dowsers there employed; particulars of these cases and the names of the dowsers have not yet reached me. Mr. Gordon Harris, A.M. Inst. C.E., in a useful paper on "Water Supply to Country Mansions," read before the United Service Institution on December 4th, 1899, after referring to dowsing for water and my previous Report on this subject, mentions a case where a dowser predicted a water supply at 160 ft. depth on an estate in Hertfordshire. Mr. Harris, being consulted, showed that as the London clay had here to be pierced to reach the chalk, no water could be found under 200 ft.; a boring was made at the spot and geology triumphed.

Mr. T. V. Holmes, F.G.S., in his excellent paper on the Divining Rod published in the Journal of the Anthropological Institute for November, 1897, to which I have already referred, mentions three or four cases where dowsers had partially or completely failed; two of these I referred to in the previous Report (p. 236) [p132 this volume - Ed],—(1) one was when Mr. Tompkins was employed at Porthcawl in Glamorganshire; the geological formation at this place is, I find, some 15 to 20 ft. of red marl and shale, resting on a deep bed of Triassic Conglomerate: (2) the other case was at Ampthill in Bedfordshire, where 10 to 20 ft. of the lower Greensand rest on a bed of Jurassic clay over 500 ft. thick. In both these cases, as might be expected geologically, a small supply of water was found not far below the surface, and no increased supply after boring to a much greater depth.

These two partial failures are of considerable public interest, as the dowsers were in each case engaged by the respective District Councils, and the costs incurred were disallowed by the auditors to the Local Government Board. In reporting the case the local newspapers state that:—

> Mr. W. A. Casson, the Local Government Board auditor, in giving his decision, quoted Professor Barrett, who had written a monograph "On the So-called Divining Rod," which was published in the Proceedings of the Society for Psychical Research. Though apparently strongly biassed in favour of diviners, Professor Barrett admitted that their general ideas of water were absurd, as they imagined springs to exist like buried treasure, located to an area of a few square inches, or as underground rivers which they professed to trace within an inch on either side. He (Mr. Casson) regarded divination as a survival from times when magic and witchcraft were generally believed in.

Like many others, Mr. Casson was misled by the name divining rod; he should, however, be more careful in his official utterances; if he had read my report, he could hardly have made the foolish statement that I was "strongly biassed"; a judge or a jury are not said to be biassed when they arrive at a decision after patiently hearing the evidence on both sides that has been brought before them.

The reason assigned by the auditors for their decision was that the diviners made a pretence of claiming some supernatural power in finding underground water (this is a mistake; no dowsers claim such power; "abnormal" is meant), and it was stated the judges had laid down that

> "the pretence of a power, whether moral, physical, or supernatural, with intent to obtain money, was sufficient to constitute an offence within the meaning of the law."

The fees charged by the dowsers were therefore illegal, as they could not be recovered in a court of law. In addition, the Porthcawl auditor surcharged the District Council with the expenditure on the boring, amounting to over £500.[1] Throughout England and Wales the public interest excited in the matter was great. I received nearly 100 cuttings from various newspapers relating to the subject; the editors for the most part lamenting the benighted and superstitious practices of the Porthcawl and Ampthill councillors. "It is impossible," said the Leeds Mercury in reference to this case, "to plumb the depths of human credulity."[2] But the surcharged Councils appealed, and ultimately, in answer to a question in the House of Commons, on August 7th, 1899, the President of the Local Government Board, the Right Hon. J. Chaplin, upset many beliefs by stating that the appeals were allowed and the auditors' decisions reversed, "the Board having been advised by their own legal adviser that the reasons assigned by the auditors for making the disallowances did not support the action they took in point of law." Hence, after this, Urban and Rural District Councils are left free to employ any competent water-finder they choose to select, whatever method he may employ. This is surely a wise decision, founded, I expect, less upon legal views than upon the experience which Mr. Chaplin and other members of the Government have had of the usefulness of dowsers on their own estates.

---

[1] Subsequently, the auditor must have amended his decision in respect to this, for according to Mr. Chaplin's statement in the House of Commons, the only sums disallowed were the small amounts for the diviner's fees. The best accounts of the Porthcawl case will be found in the lengthy reports in the *Cardiff Western Mail* for July 20th, 1897. *et seq.* The Ampthill case will be found fully reported in the *Bedford Times* for June 5th, 1897, *et seq.*

[2] A few exceptions to this general outcry were to be found in some journals, notably *Truth*, the *Evening Standard*, and the *Local Government Journal.*

# The Credibility Of Dowsing

## § 3. Percentage of Failures

This leads on to the question of the percentage of failures of different dowsers. I have tried to obtain from some of the professional "waterfinders" a record of all the places they have visited in the course of say twelve months, so that by inquiry at each place I might ascertain the number of successes and of failures. But it is impossible to know if the record sent is a complete one. I have received from two dowsers a long list of persons and places, and have written to each person named with the result that all these cases were more or less successful, but the failures are just the ones that are not likely to be sent. Mr. Gataker frankly says in a letter to me that he has had occasional failures, which he cannot account for except by his state of health. The dowser very often explains away a failure by saying the depth is merely greater and the quantity of water less than he predicted, but all depends upon how much greater depth or how much less water. It would be much better if each dowser would keep a faithful record of all his engagements, and then take the public into his confidence, and give the results of his work and references to each of his employers. This, I suppose, we can hardly expect in the present state of human nature.

An estimate of the number of failures on the part of professional dowsers may perhaps be obtained from the extra charge some of them make when sinking wells on the " no water, no pay" system. That is to say, they agree to sink a well for a certain sum at the spot they have selected by the rod, and if water is not found at the place they predicted, and in about the quantity they estimated, then no charge is made; the loss falls on the dowser. If however, all turns out satisfactorily, a somewhat higher charge is made for sinking the well than an ordinary well-sinker would charge, or if no guarantee be given, by the dowser. This extra charge varies with different dowsers, and is of course their insurance against failure; it expresses, however, something more than the percentage of absolute failures, for water may be found, but the supply may be insufficient, or the depth may be greater than was allowed for in the contract.

I have inquired what this extra charge is, and, as might be expected, it varies. Mr. Gataker makes an additional charge of 25 per cent, on the "no water no pay" system; a similar additional rate is, I understand, charged by Mr. Chesterman;[1] Mr. Tompkins in reply to my inquiry, says: "25 to 30 per cent, extra would cover the risk"; Mr. Stone says he does not work on that system, but would be willing to undertake work on the terms of only charging out of pocket expenses, in addition to his fee, if water is not found.[2] The late John Mullins made no extra charge, and (as a rule) was willing to forego all payments if after sinking the well a sufficient supply of water was not found. His sons, who carry on the business, and one of whom is a dowser, inform me "we do not generally make any extra charge for giving a guarantee of finding water; on three occasions only we charged 15 per cent, extra on the contract for making the well." They enclose me copies of some of their contracts for large amounts; several of these, I notice, contain the clause "in the event of not obtaining a supply of 1,000 gallons per day of twenty-four hours, we will make no charge for the work done" But a thousand gallons per day is a very small supply for expensive operations, and contaminated surface water might easily yield this amount.

I am inclined to think we may take from 10 to 15 per cent, as the average percentage of failures which occur with most English dowsers of to-day, allowing a larger percentage for partial failures, meaning by this that the quantity of water estimated and the depth at which it is found have not realised the estimate formed by the dowser. This latter, however, though of great practical importance, is foreign to our inquiry, for what we want to know is whether, after making every allowance for shrewdness of eye, chance coincidence, and local or geological knowledge, the dowser has any instinctive or supernormal power of discovering the presence of underground water. The answer to this question is to be found by a study of the cases cited in this and the previous Report, and is discussed in a subsequent Part. Here I will only add that the reader who has followed me will have seen how absurd is the dowser's

---

[1] In a recent contract between the District Council at East Knoyle and the dowser, Chesterman, so many gallons per twenty-four hours were stipulated for, and a certain depth not to be exceeded. The contract was taken at ordinary rates, Chesterman to receive 25 per cent. extra if he succeeds and to pay all if he fails: as the District Council have, I understand, already lost £150 over a well sunk upon geological advice, they have made a good bargain.

[2] This is a most unsatisfactory arrangement, for the dowser, being the contractor, makes himself the judge of what is an adequate supply of water and what the depth of the boring should be. I have heard some complaints of Mr. Stone in this respect.

## Prof. W. F. Barrett

notion that the mere twisting of his forked twig is an infallible indication of underground water. As I have already shown (Vol. XIII., p. 253 [p. 205 this volume - Ed]), the movement of the twig is due to a sub-conscious suggestion, and this may arise from many causes besides the assumed influence of underground water on the dowser.

# PART IX

## Continental, Colonial, And Californian Cases Of The Use Of The Rod In The Search For Underground Water

### *§ 1. Continental Dowsers*

In the previous Report, on p. 23 [p. 15 this volume - Ed], I mentioned that a French writer had published in 1850 a little book called *Histoire de I'Hydroscopie et de la Baguette Divinatoire*, and I spoke of the author, who was in early life a successful and, I believe, professional dowser, as "a M. Mortillet." I was unaware at the time that the author was the same person as Professor Gabriel de Mortillet, who has a European reputation, and is one of the most distinguished anthropologists in France. I therefore owe an apology to Professor de Mortillet, and expressed this in sending him a copy of the Report. It is often remarked that it would be of great value if a competent scientific man were also a dowser, and could give us his personal experience. Here we have a case in point, and to this may be added the case of Mr. Enys, F.G.S., the President of the Royal Geological Society of Cornwall, a letter from whom is quoted on p. 219. Professor de Mortillet's little book is not now accessible; the author, in reply to my inquiries, writes to me as follows :—

St. Germain-en-Laye, près Paris, *18 Décembre*, 1897.

> Je regrette beaucoup de ne pas pouvoir vous envoyer in on *Histoire de Hydroscopie*. Je n'en possède pas même un exemplaire chez moi. Je vais m'informer s'il en existe encore. Elle à été publiée à Chambéry; si j'en retrouve, vous la recevrez.
>
> Permettez-moi de vous faire de sincères compliments sur votre *On the So-called Divining Rod*. Je n'ai fait que parcourir ce memoire, mais je compte bien l'étudier avec tout le soin qu'il mérite.
>
> Je mets à la poste, à votre adresse, en même temps que cette carte, un numéro de L'Intermédiaire de l'Afas,[1] contenant, page 23, le résumé de mon opinion sur la Baguette et le Pendule. Je vais announcer votre mémoire dans un prochain numéro de *L'Intermédiaire de l'Afas*.
>
> Agréez, cher Professeur, mes remerciments et l'assurance de mon haute considération.
>
> G. de Mortillet.

> [Translation - I deeply regret not being able to send you the History of Water Dowsing. I do not even have a copy at home. I will find out if any still exist. It was published at Chambéry. If I find a copy, I will send it to you.
>
> Let me give you sincere compliments on your 'On the So-Called Divining Rod'. I have only glanced at it, but I intend to study it with the care it deserves.
>
> I have put in the mail, to your address, along with this card, an issue of L'lntermédiaire de l'Afas, containing, on page 23, the summary of my opinion on the wand and the pendulum. I will be announcing your work in the next issue of L'lntermédiaire de l'Afas.
>
> Accept, my dear Professor, my thanks and the assurance of my highest consideration. – Ed]

---

[1] The word *Afas* is taken from the first letters of the Association Francaise pour l'Avancement des Sciences; this excellent journal is regularly issued as an organ of "Notes and Queries " to the members of the Association.—W. F. B.

## Prof. W. F. Barrett

As the summary Professor de Mortillet gives of his views on the baguette is of general interest, I append the following translation of the communication he refers to in *L'Afas*, February, 1896:—

> The name "hydroscope" has been given to those persons who experience certain special sensations on passing over subterranean watercourses. Sometimes, though very rarely, the sensation is sufficiently strong for the subject to be directly conscious of it. In most cases hydroscopes are compelled to use an instrument in order to recognise the fact. The instrument employed is either a pendulum (pendule) or a rod. The pendulum is carried in the hand, so that the least trembling of the arm sets it in motion. As to the rod, it is a twig slightly bent, which the operator rests upon the index fingers of each hand so as to balance it. The least motion of the fingers towards or away from each other is then sufficient to displace the centre of gravity, which, passing from the centre of the rod towards the ends, and from the ends towards the centre, naturally causes the rod to turn. But this is not the true divining rod. This last is a stem, dividing into two branches nearly of equal size, and forming as acute an angle as possible. The end of a branch is grasped in each hand, and it is bent back in such a manner as to be in tension (resisting the pressure of the hand). These recurved and bent branches endeavour to spring back to their original straight line, which causes their point of union to move. To use this rod, an equilibrium as unstable as possible is set up, so that it may be disturbed by the least nervous jar, which will cause the instrument to move. Such are the principles governing the pendulum and the rod. The nature of the wood is a matter of indifference. Hazel is preferred, because it forks more frequently, and the rods are more flexible than is the case with other trees.
>
> Pendulums and rods move over certain points in the hands of persons who are especially sensitive. These points are supposed to be over underground watercourses. As a matter of fact, this is generally, but not always, the case. I have seen important works undertaken merely upon indications furnished by hydroscopy, with full success. But, at other times, I have seen it fail.
>
> This much, however, is certain, which I can affirm as the result of experience, that the point chosen by one diviner will also be chosen by others brought from a distance, and completely ignorant of the preceding experiments. A real phenomenon to study does therefore exist.
>
> What has discredited this phenomenon is the attempt to employ it in moral matters, such as the search for robbers, assassins, etc.

I would call special attention to the penultimate paragraph, as expressing the opinion of a distinguished man of science who knows what he is talking about.

It will be noticed that Professor de Mortillet refers to the use of a pendule as well as a baguette.[1] The former is not, I believe, anywhere employed by dowsers in England, but it is in use in some parts of America, and is described in an article in an American journal, the *Democratic Review* for 1850. The writer calls himself "An Old Rodsman," and states that some diviners in searching for metals use a forked twig, or two pieces of whalebone, and others a "small metallic ball suspended by a horse-hair or silk thread. As the operator approaches the hidden mine, the ball deviates more or less from the perpendicular, and this points out the proximity of the object sought." A very similar *pendule* is referred to in the next case, as employed by some French *sourciers*, or water finders. These *sourciers*, I am informed

---

[1] I have referred to the so-called *pendule explorateur* in the previous Report, p. 10 [p. 7 this volume - Ed]. It consists simply of a ring or little ball, suspended by a thread which is held between the fingers, and, thus held, the involuntary motion of the hand sets it oscillating and appears to endow the *pendule* with a sort of intelligent activity. A considerable literature has arisen over the *pendule*, a toy which afresh excites the astonishment of succeeding generations. It is really a simple form of "autoscope," and can claim a remote antiquity, divination by an oscillating ring or *pendule* having been used by the ancients; it was employed by Hilarius in the 4th century to ascertain who would be the successor to Valens; Chevreul, in his *Baguette Divinatoire*, pp. 132 et seq., gives the whole passage.

## The Credibility Of Dowsing

by those in the South of France to whom I have written, are to be found in Dauphiné, Savoie, and Beaujolais, but in smaller numbers than formerly. A friend in France writes as follows :—

Lyons, *July 2nd*, 1898.

> M. Raoul de Cazenove (a relative of Dean Cazenove) lately built himself a chateau, and after all was finished, found he had everything heart could desire except water. He knew of an old farmer reputed as a "sourcier," and went to him. He consented to come, but as he expressed it, "for love, not for money, as I never intended doing it again; it exhausts me so terribly." He came, found, and was exhausted, so much so that they had much ado to fit him for returning home.

I wrote to M. de Cazenove, who kindly sent me the following particulars :—

Château du Solier, La Salle, Gard, *July 14th*, 1898.

> I am happy to send you the few particulars I possess on the subject. Answering your two questions, I may say, 1st, since thirty years or so, I have had on many occasions to ask the "sourciers'" services. I have asked their help fourteen times; their researches have been successful in nine cases. Our country is very irregular, abrupt and rocky; so no wells have been bored. Water is to be found in digging horizontal galleries; most of these go from twenty to one hundred metres [about 66 to 330 ft.]; many are bored in granite; some others in "calcaire" [limestone].
>
> 2nd. When I have observed the "sourcier" at work he feels a particular sensation, or malaise, which increases as he approaches the hidden water. Some use a rod; many of them a heavy watch, hanging by its chain; some of them don't use any instrument. We have a lot of "sourciers" in the country (mountains of the Cevennes); some of them are amateurs, many are professionals. Their estimation of the depth and volume of water is quite empirical; hence mistakes and frequent deceptions result. Sometimes their long experience furnishes them with sufficient indications, but they have no rules; only personal and nervous feeling.
>
> Many professional "sourciers" exist in France in various parts. I remain at your disposition for further inquiries.
>
> R. De Cazenove.

## Continental "Hydroscopes" in the Early Part of the Century

One of the most successful water-finders in the early part of the 19th century was the French Abbé Paramelle; he did not employ a rod, but trusted to his instinct, guided by a knowledge of hydro geology which he had gained through careful observation. I have devoted an Appendix to Paramelle (Appendix D), as his case forms an instructive contribution to our research.

The subject of Continental dowsers would be incomplete without reference to the writings of Thouvenel, Amoretti, Count Tristan and Baron Du Prel. Dr. Thouvenel I have already referred to, and his experiments with the dowser Bleton are given in the next Part. Thouvenel, towards the close of the 18th century, went to Italy and there experimented with another dowser, or "hydroscope," a lad named Pennet,[1] who professed to find buried metals and coal, as well as underground water. Some of the results were so surprising that the great naturalist, Spallanzani, was much impressed, but as Pennet was, according to a letter published by Biot,[2] subsequently found tricking at

---

[1] See an article by Dr. Thouvenel in *Mélanges d'histoire naturelle de physique*, etc.. Vol. III., Paris, 1807.

[2] Reprinted in 1858 in his *Mélanges scientifiques et littéraires*, tom. II., p. 80. In the Bibliography of the Divining Rod, which Mr. Westlake has with such immense industry prepared, numbers of papers in French, Italian, and German will be found between 1800 and 1810, arising out of Dr. Thouvenel's investigations.

Florence, Spallanzani concluded he also had been tricked and withdrew his former opinion. I do not know whether Biot had reliable evidence for his statement, for we all know that with many sceptics any evidence is thought good enough, if it serves to discredit phenomena new to science.

Amoretti, who was an Italian savant of some note, published various papers on his experiments with the Divining Rod, chiefly with two dowsers, one the lad Pennet, and the other, a boy, Anfossi.[1] In Vol. XIX. of the *Opuscoli Scelti*, Amoretti, in a letter to Fortis, dated December, 1796, states: (1) That an Augustinian friar had, by means of the rod, found an underground spring, which had since supplied the country house of Signor Dolbecchi; (2) that one Sanzio, a surgeon, found his pulse rose twelve to fifteen beats faster per minute when standing over subterranean water; (3) that an insensitive person holding a divining rod became sensitive and the rod moved, when his hands were held by a sensitive [i.e., a dowser]; (4) particulars are given of a sensitive (a boy) who could locate underground water by his feelings, without using a rod: Pennet and Anfossi (other sensitives) also said the same. Amoretti, like Professor Sementini, Ritter, and others, believed in the close connection of electricity with the movement of the rod. The Count de Tristan was likewise fully convinced of the electric origin of the dowsing faculty; his knowledge of physics was, however, very slight. In 1826 he published the result of numerous experiments with the divining rod in the valley of the Loire in a book called *Recherches sur quelques effluves terrestres*. An outline of these experiments is given by Dr. Mayo, F.R.S., in his excellent book, *Truths Contained in Popular Superstitions*, and by Chevreul in his *Baguette Divinatoire*, pp. 122 et seq.

The influence of "suggestion," whether conscious or unconscious, was not considered nor guarded against by any of these experimenters, nor was the effect of involuntary muscular action sufficiently recognised till later. Hence Amoretti, Ritter, Tristan, and very often Thouvenel, were led to attribute to animal electricity phenomena that were mainly due to suggestion. Thousands of experiments have been made and volumes written on the divining rod and the pendule (or magic pendulum), all of which are valueless owing to the non-recognition of this source of error; I will, however, return to this later on.

In the autobiography of that learned and singular man, Zschokke, an account is given on p. 143, of several dowsers (or Rhabdomantins, as Zschokke calls them) whom he had met in Switzerland; they are to be found, he states, in almost every canton. Dr. Ebel, of Zurich, a well-known geologist, sent Zschokke one of these dowsers to test; he adds that the Abbot of St. Urban, in Lucerne, was a successful dowser. Zschokke was at first very incredulous, but his incredulity disappeared after the numerous tests to which he subjected a young female dowser.

## *The German Dowser, Beraz*

Du Prel, who is best known by his suggestive work, *Die Philosophie der Mystik* (admirably translated into English by Mr. C. C. Massey), published a short essay on the Divining Rod (*Die Wünschelruthe*) in 1890. In this essay Du Prel gives an account of Beraz, a notable German dowser. The following is a translation of this part:—

> [In 1888] a friend in the South asked me to call upon Beraz, the springfinder (who is since dead, but who lived at that time in Munich), and to make arrangements with him. It was necessary to find springs in a newly laid out health resort, which was unprovided with a water supply. My friend gave me (the quite unnecessary) advice, not to consult any learned professors, etc., on the subject of Beraz. I visited Beraz, and while waiting for his appearance, noticed—amongst others—the portrait of a gentleman hanging in the room. This gentleman, Beraz informed me, was his maternal grandfather, Professor Ritter; I naturally asked whether he were the author of the *Siderismus*, and was answered in

---

[1] Amoretti's papers on the divining rod, in the British Museum, are mainly found in the *Soc. Ital. della Scienze* for 1813 and 1816. and earlier papers in the *Opuscoli Scelti sulle Scienze* from 1798 to 1801. The later papers were published separately under the title of *Della Rabdomanzia ossia Elettrometria animale*. Part I. of this book was translated into German, and a paper on the same subject by J. W. Ritter added, with plates showing various rods held both by hands and feet. Some of Amoretti's papers were also translated into French and published in Fortis' *Mémoires*.

## The Credibility Of Dowsing

the affirmative.[1] The testimonials that Beraz received are sufficient testimony to his powers. As the subject is one of great interest to the public generally, and to land-proprietors especially, I give a few dates of the finding of springs, with the places at which they were found, and addresses at which any one interested may obtain full proof for the asking :—The Capuchin Monastery on St. Nicholasberg in the Würzburg (1877); the Corporation of Gart, near Traunstein (1876); the Institute of Young Ladies at Altötting (1882); Narr's Brewery in Zirndorf, near Nürnberg (1875), the Community of Algund, near Meran (1882).

I have conversed with a person who witnessed one of Beraz's experiments on an occasion when he announced that there was a spring at a depth of 80 ft., and the spring was found at 83 ft. I do not doubt but that Beraz was sometimes unsuccessful, but, on the other hand, I am sure that many an enlightened corporation has lavished great sums on bringing water to their towns, which they might have obtained much more reasonably by employing a spring-finder.

In the London Times for February 11th, 1885, I find the following account of water-finding by Beraz in Bavaria :—

> The *Allgemeine Zeitung* gives some interesting particulars of remarkable success in indicating the presence of water springs on the part of a man named Beraz, who seems to be a recognised authority in such matters. The scene of his performances was in the Bavarian highlands, at a height of more than 1,300 ft. above the level of the sea. The commune of Rothenberg, near Hirschhorn, suffered greatly from want of water, and invited Beraz last autumn to endeavour to find some source of supply for them. He inspected the locality one afternoon in presence of the public authorities and a reporter of the *Allgeimeine Zeitung*, and announced that water was to be found in certain spots at depths which he stated. The first spot was in the lower village, and he gave the likely depth at between 62 ft. and 72 ft., adding that the volume of water which the spring would give would be of about the diameter of an inch and a quarter. After incessant labour for four weeks, consisting mainly of rock blasting, the workmen came on a copious spring of water at a depth of almost 67 ft. What he declared about a water source for the upper village was very singular. He pointed to a spot where he said three watercourses lay perpendicularly under one another, and running in parallel courses. The first would be found at a depth of between 22½ ft. and 26 ft. of about the size of a wheaten straw, and running in the direction from south-east to north-west. The second lay about 42 ft. deep, was of about the size of a thick quill, and ran in the same direction. The third, he said, lay at a depth of about 56ft., running in the same direction, and as large as a man's little finger. The actual results were as follows :—The first watercourse was struck at a depth of 27½ ft., running in the direction indicated, and having a diameter of one-fifth of an inch. The workmen came on the second at a depth of 42⅔ ft.; it had a diameter of 7/25ths of an inch. The third was found at 62½ ft. below the surface, and having a diameter of 3/5ths of an inch—all three running in the direction Beraz had indicated.

The statements made by the reporter, who says that he was an eyewitness, are so circumstantial that they have the appearance of being trustworthy, but it is to be regretted they were not the subject of careful inquiry and corroboration at the time; the more so as Rothenburg is in the very centre of German scientific culture. If any readers of this Report, who may be visiting Bavaria, can give me additional information on this case, I should be

---

[1] Ritter's *Siderismus*, Du Prel remarks in another place, had lain uncut in the Public Library of Munich from 1808 to 1887, apropos of which he adds very truly "the scepticism of many is merely ignorance." Ritter conducted some investigations on the divining rod in Munich in 1806, with an Italian named Campetti.—W. F. B.

grateful.[1] Assuming the facts to be as stated, they are of the greatest interest and theoretic importance, for this case must be classed along with the Waterford case and a few others of a similar type.

In Nasse's *Zeitschrift für Psychische Aertze* for 1821, Professor D'Outrepont, Ph.D., of Würzburg, gives some interesting facts concerning a dowser at Malmedy (a town on the Belgian frontier) with whom he was acquainted. Mr. E. T. Bennett has translated Dr D'Outrepont's paper, and published an abridgement of it in the S. P. R. Journal for June, 1899, p. 83. It is therefore accessible for those readers who wish for further information,

## 2. Californian Dowsers

Amid the mass of correspondence which has reached me, often from distant parts, I have had several letters from California, where it appears there are several professional ore-finders and water-finders, or "water witches," as they are often locally called.

One correspondent, Mr. B. F. Dixon, of Escondido, California, the head of a firm of orange growers, writes as follows :—

Escondido, California, *November 22nd*, 1897.

> Having read a review of your treatise on the Divining Rod in the papers here, the following facts may interest you.
>
> In the fall of 1865 an acquaintance in Kansas had engaged a person to locate a well on his place. The man held a forked peach twig, which moved strongly at a certain spot. Upon my laughing at such utter nonsense, the man asked me to try. Treating it as a joke, I did so, holding the forked twig as I saw it held by the water-finder. To my astonishment, at the spot where the water-finder had marked, I felt what seemed like a slight electric shock and immediately the forked twig turned violently in my hands. I held the stick as tight as I could to prevent it moving, but it twisted right round to the ground. I was dumbfounded and the joke was turned against me. A well was sunk at the spot and a good supply of running water obtained.
>
> When it became known that I was a "water-witch," my services were sought for and I have since located a large number of wells, without making any charge. I have been surprised to find how accurate the indications of the twig have turned out; even in the depth I have rarely been far out![2]

Mr. Dixon states he could give me many instances of his success when previous attempts to find water had failed. He quotes one case of his in considerable detail, which I will abridge. An acquaintance of his in Kansas had spent large sums in sinking several wells on his 40 acre farm, but had got no water, though some of the wells were 70 ft. deep. At last he begged Mr. Dixon to come over and try his hand. Mr. Dixon went and prospected with his peach twig; he was surprised to find the twig move strongly at one spot, indicating a plentiful water supply, which he estimated at only 18ft. deep. It suited the owner's purpose better to sink a well a few feet from this spot and at a depth of 22 ft. water was found streaming in from the direction indicated by Mr. Dixon. As the well caved in shortly after, the owner decided to sink a walled-in well at the very spot marked by the twig, and at less than 20 ft. from the surface came upon so abundant a supply of water that it has served the whole farm ever since. I have no reason to doubt the accuracy of Mr. Dixon's statements, but it is desirable to have them confirmed by independent observers, and therefore I should be grateful to any of our friends in California who may live near Escondido if they would kindly send me some further particulars.

---

[1] I have to thank the Editor of the *Times* for sending me the editorial address of the *Allgemeine Zeitung*, to which I wrote in the hope that the reporter referred to might still be on the staff of that paper and able to give me some additional confirmation of his statements. Unfortunately, however, I learnt in reply that this was not the case; nor could the Editor of the *Allegemeine Zeitung* ascertain who the reporter was; Beraz, he informs me, is dead (Du Prel had stated this).

[2] Mr. Dixon does not say *how* he ascertains the depth by the motion of the twig.

## The Credibility Of Dowsing

Concerning one Californian dowser, a Captain Godfrey, I have received an enormous mass of correspondence, forwarded to me by Dr. Hodgson and various other friends. Some of the evidence is remarkable, and I hope to find time to give an abridgement of it at a future time. Captain Godfrey declares he is so powerfully affected by the neighbourhood of underground veins of ore or running water that he is made quite ill. He attributes it all to electricity(!) and his wife writes voluminous letters, asking for scientific enquiry. This I have attempted to obtain, but Captain Godfrey declines to submit to any tests. Dr. Hodgson has taken much trouble over this case, and referred me to one of the members of the S. P. R. in California, Mr. Radcliffe-Whitehead, who had recently visited Captain Godfrey. I wrote to Mr. Whitehead, and had the following reply :—

P.O. Box 144, Santa Barbara, California, *March 6th*, 1898.

I called on Captain Godfrey in Pasadena, where he lives, two months ago. He is a fine old man, and from what I have seen and heard I should judge him to be above all suspicion of fraud. From the statements made to the Society and similar ones made to me, I have no doubt that he has some curious faculty, in fact, is a sensitive.

The difficulty of going further with this case lies thus. Captain Godfrey says :—

1. "I don't care a rap for the scientific aspect of my case."

2. "I suffer physically when I experience the sensations given me by underground streams of water or veins of metal."

3. "I don't care to make experiments, nor will I seek for water for a fee. I will only do so if I am to have a share in the 'development' (as we call it here) of said water."

Now I, as a developer of water on my own land,—I am making two water tunnels at this time, — should be willing enough to employ Captain Godfrey to "locate" water for me for a fee, but I am not disposed to agree to his terms, though I have complete faith in his honesty.

I will write to him shortly and try to induce him to change his mind, but as he has lately refused a neighbour of mine who made a similar proposal, I confess I have not much hope. However *nous verrons*. I will report.

Ralph Radcliffe-Whitehead.

In a subsequent letter Mr. Radcliffe-Whitehead informs me he has failed to induce Godfrey to change his mind, and mentions another Californian dowser he knows, and is about to employ. Another one of our Californian members, to whom I had written about Captain Godfrey, after undertaking to do what he could, writes as follows:—

2,727, Ellendale-place, Los Angelos, California, U.S.A.,

*February 17th*, 1898.

My own experiments have been with a man who is a little ashamed of his power, and does not attempt to explain it. He is honest beyond question, and has submitted to such complete tests—being tested when blindfolded; finding buried waterpipes; and by the actual discovery of water in places where it was least to be expected—that I am reluctantly forced to believe that some such power exists, especially as a complete test satisfied me that it was not a case of mind-reading.

I have no knowledge of divining for water without a rod, but one of my farmers, who is an honest and clear-headed fellow, tells me that in his Iowa home they found all their wells by aid of a man who almost had convulsions when passing over running water. He gives some curious cases of wells so found, after attempts to get water in the same farms without his aid had failed, and one case where the man had a fit at a house-warming, and declared that the trouble came from a spring under the house. On digging, a powerful and valuable spring was discovered near the surface. If you value such evidence, I shall be glad to get the exact facts and the man's name for you.

Walter Nordhoff

Various instances of the use of the rod for finding underground water in other parts of the United States and in Canada were given in the previous Report on pages 27, 44, 59, 62, and 215-220.

## 3. South African Dowsers

The use of the divining rod has even extended to Bulawayo. In an article in that able English journal, the *Surveyor*, which refers to the "cold scrutiny" and "careful dissecting" to which the diviner has been subjected in our previous Report, the following instance of the use of the rod in Bulawayo is quoted from a correspondent to a South African newspaper :—

> Having sunk on the spot located through the medium of the divining rod, I have, at a depth of 30 ft., struck the water; whereas my neighbour, at considerable expense, two years ago sank, on the same line and only 30 yards away, to a depth of 45 ft. without any result whatever. I am now convinced of the great expense which the rod may save in sinking for water.

This must be taken for what it is worth, as no names are given. In South African journals for August, 1897, particulars are given of a clerical water-finder.

> "It will be remembered," says the *Grahamstown Journal*", that some months ago the Rev. Father Marconnes, of St. Aidan's College, who is an adept in the use of the divining rod, made certain predictions as to the finding of water in certain spots, which he pointed out. The Government steam drill, under Mr. J. L. Caithness, has now found water just outside the Chronic Sick confines at Cape Corps Camp on the Commonage. The water was found at a spot pointed out by the diviner. It was first tapped at 21 ft. by an excavation Mr. Caithness was making to get his bore loose, and at 37 ft. a supply of quite 6,000 gallons per diem was tapped. The water is good and fresh. Again, at the St. Andrew's College, where Father Marconnes pointed out a spot, and said there was water at 40 ft., the precious fluid has been tapped exactly at 40 ft., and in good quantity."

Father Marconnes writes in a subsequent number of the *Grahamstown Journal* that he prefers to call his divining rod a water compass, or hydro-magnet, as it is a "scientific instrument," and clearly indicates that electricity is the true cause of its action; he does not, however, give any evidence in support of his belief. I do not quote this case as of any evidential value, for I have not been able to verify it, and moreover there is nothing to indicate that water would not have been found without Father Marconnes' aid, but I give it simply to indicate the widespread use of the rod.

As is well known, the divining rod was frequently used during the 17th century for tracking suspected persons, and for other purposes in the "moral world." Among the native races in South Africa the rod appears to be still in use for a like purpose. Though outside the range of the present Report, the following incident in connection with the siege of Mafeking has attracted so much attention that I will briefly refer to it here. A Press Association telegram appeared in the English newspapers of April 18th, 1900, to this effect:—

# The Credibility Of Dowsing

April 5th.

> Lieut. Frank Smitheman, the renowned Matabele scout, got through the Boer lines, and arrived here yesterday, carrying an Imperial Government despatch for Col. Baden-Powell. He had an adventurous journey, spending two nights in coming from Ramathlabama on foot.
>
> Lieut. Smitheman, who knows every inch of the country, was accompanied by a clever native runner, who uses a divining rod to ascertain the position of the enemy. This rod he handles after the fashion of the Wiltshire water-finder, thoroughly believing in its efficiency.
>
> Lieut. Smitheman's feat is one of the utmost importance. Only two whites have entered the town since the beginning of the investment.

Two centuries ago (in 1692) the famous dowser, Jacques Aymar, became notorious by his discovery (through following the indications of the rod) of the murderer of a poor wine-seller in Lyons, and in 1703 he was employed to identify the Camisards[1] by the same means. Since then (owing chiefly to the rod being condemned for any use in the "moral world,") its employment for criminal purposes has disappeared in Europe. Inquiry may prove that the South African report is not to be credited, or the "diviner" worthless, but the case of Jacques Aymar is as well attested as any fact in history.[2] I have in my possession a mass of original documents, published at the time, which place the really extraordinary character of Aymar's discovery of the murderer of the Lyons wine-seller beyond doubt. Nor is there any improbability in the circumstance, if we here regard the dowser as a bloodhound following a trail, which his sub-conscious self picks up and indicates through the involuntary motion of the rod he carries.

## § 4. Australian Dowsers

In the previous Report (Vol. XIII., pp. 45-47 [pp. 33-35 this volume -Ed]) I gave an account of four successful amateur dowsers in Queensland and New South Wales. Several other cases of Australian dowsers have since reached me. Two cases are of such interest that I will briefly refer to them, as in both these cases the dowsers were gentlemen of good standing and intelligence.

(1) The following account has been sent me by Mr. Vaughan Jenkins; it was published in the Sydney Stock Journal and in the Armidale Chronicle (a New South Wales paper) for April 14th, 1900. The report is too long to quote, and I give a summary of its essential parts.

> The President of the Armidale Cattle Show, Mr. F. J. White (a well-known man), was greatly in need of a water supply on his estate, Saumarez. For twenty-four years that his family have lived there they have had to cart water from a distance, as did their predecessor, Mr. Thomas, attempts to find water on the place having failed. Eventually Mr. White sunk a deep well, 120 ft. deep, through the solid rock, but no water was reached. A friend who was visiting the place happened to be an amateur dowser, and, seeing the useless well, offered to try his luck with the divining rod. He did so, and the rod turned vigorously at a certain spot. Here another well was sunk, and at 35 ft. water was struck, it rose to 20 ft. from the surface, and now supplies the place and the gardens. Mr. White then tried the rod himself and found to his surprise it turned in his hands: trusting solely to its guidance, he has since sunk six more wells, and found water in every spot so indicated. He is now so firmly convinced of the value of the rod that he has recently offered to pay the cost of digging any well if its indications turn out wrong. The writer of the article went as a sceptic to investigate and report, but his amused incredulity became astonishment when he found the twig turned in his hands also. He remarks: "I don't believe in that twig business, but the facts are against me. Will somebody explain?"

---

[1] [THE CAMISARDS were French Protestants of south-central France who rose in revolt against religious persecution in 1702. Ed.]
[2] The best modern account of this story is given in Figuier's *Histoire du Merveilleux*, Vol. II., Chap. 5.

## *Prof. W. F. Barrett*

The foregoing newspaper report must be taken for what it is worth, as I have not had time to verify it by independent inquiries.

(2) The other case I have received through the kindness of a West Australian friend, Mr. E. T. Scammell, 37, St. Mary Axe, London, E.C. The dowser in this case was his friend, the late Mr. E. H. Derrington, for many years an Australian journalist of high standing and unimpeachable integrity. At my request Mr. Scammell obtained a lengthy narrative, accompanied by the corroborative testimony of independent witnesses, from Mr. Derrington. This account is of interest from the fact that Mr. Derrington became a very successful dowser for mineral lodes, particulars of which will be given in that part of our work. Mr. Derrington writes :—

Coolgardie, W. Australia, *May 24th,* 1898.

Newspaper editorship during many years predisposed me to regard with strong scepticism all fads and faddists. I, with courtesy, declined even to witness experiments with the so-called "divining rod"—a name as absurd and untrue as any I have ever heard, since there is no divination in the whole process. Ignorance and credulity may still employ it, but no educated man would employ it. But, some fourteen years ago, there occurred in the colony I have made my home for now nearly half a century, one of the periodical droughts for which unfortunately South Australia has become noted. The misery and ruin in the out-lying agricultural districts were forced upon my attention, and then the pretensions of the waterfinders came to my mind, and I resolved upon an impartial investigation, remembering what a priceless boon would be conferred if hidden supplies of water could be discovered in the waterless districts. I applied to an old German of most respectable antecedents and strong common-sense, who was renowned as a successful exponent of the art. Without giving me any illustration, he at once placed in my hand a V-shaped eucalyptus twig, and whilst he remained at the entrance-gate, requested me to cross from one side to the other through his garden. I did so, and midway was astonished by the twig (held by the points in the forks of the thumbs, the fingers being closed over it in the palms of the hands) suddenly up-rising and standing perpendicularly, entirely without my volition, and falling back into its horizontal position when I had passed one particular spot. I repeated the experiment a number of times with the same result, only that I noticed a singular sensation as of an electric current through the spine whenever the twig moved as described. My friend watching then showed me that I had stood over a concealed water-channel fed by a spring from the upper part of his garden, and complimented me upon being the most sensitive waterfinder he had ever met. This was my first acquaintance with this unknown faculty. I laid aside scepticism and eagerly made use of this method to assist the distressed farmers with whom I came into contact.

I have since made very numerous experiments, with a view to an accurate estimate of the cause and effect; and I have submitted to a variety of crude tests, many of which were designed less for the discovery of a scientific basis than to throw ridicule upon an obscure phenomenon. Pseudo-scientists are prone to sneer at what they cannot understand, but I hold there is in ascertained results sufficient ground to justify the hope that, at some not far distant future, a possibility of effecting economic results of incalculable value in the discovery both of underground water and ore by means of the so-called divining rod.

As to the nature of the influence which moves the rod, I am inclined to believe that in certain sensitives there may possibly be set up a current or influence by the electrical currents in the underground water or metallic veins. For I discovered subsequently my "galvanometer," the rod, moved whenever I was over metallic veins or even metals on the surface of the ground.

E. H. Derrington.

## The Credibility Of Dowsing

In the foregoing narrative no evidence is detailed to show that Mr. Derrington's predictions were verified by digging or boring, nor that he succeeded when other means had failed; he adduces, however, some striking evidence of his success in the discovery of mineral lodes, but this part of his letter I will give in another place. His electrical theory sounds a plausible one; it is much the same as Dr. Thouvenel's a century ago, but is unsupported by any scientific evidence and will be referred to later on. I may add that in the recent obituary notices of Mr. Derrington in the South Australian newspapers, a high tribute is paid to him; he was not a man likely to be led astray by hasty inferences as to the value of the indications afforded by the divining rod.

I now propose to give a somewhat detailed account of that remarkable French peasant lad, Bleton, whose performances as a water-finder Dr. Thouvenel has made famous.

# PART X

## *Bleton, The Notable French Dowser Of The Last Century*

Barthélmy Bleton, to whom reference has already been made (on p. 20 et seq. of the previous Report [p. 13 this volume - Ed]) was born at Bouvantes in Dauphiny, somewhere between the years 1740 and 1750.[1] He was the son of a poor peasant, was brought up by charity in one of the Carthusian monasteries of Dauphiny, and became a herdsman. An accidental circumstance seems to have led to the discovery of Bleton's peculiar faculty. Here is the account which I find given by one of Dr. Thouvenel's correspondents, who writes from Dijon on April 14th, 1781, and who adds he has certain proofs of all that he has stated.[2] The following extract is translated from the original letter :—

> Bleton, when seven years of age, had carried dinner to some workmen; he sat down on a stone, when a fever or faintness seized him; the workmen having brought him to their side, the faintness ceased, but each time he returned to the stone, he suffered again. This was told to the Prior of the Chartreuse, who wished to see it for himself. Being thus convinced of the fact, he had the ground under the stone dug up; there they found a spring, which, I am told, is still in use to turn a mill.

A similar account is given by another contemporary quoted by Figuier, and by the writer in the *Monthly Review* for 1782, who quotes from a French pamphlet, the writer of which states the circumstance is "confirmed by many local witnesses." Some confirmation of the foregoing story is gained from a remark made by the Prior "de la Chartreuse de Lyon" in a document testifying to Bleton's extraordinary faculty (quoted by Thouvenel) that Bleton "was quite as well able to detect underground water when he was seven years old as he is now." (March 3rd, 1781.)

In any other part of the world except Dauphiny the coincidence of the boy's illness and the presence of an underground spring would probably soon have been forgotten. But, a century before, Jacques Aymar and his rod had made this province famous for its diviners, Aymar having been followed by many who claimed a similar "gift." As, however, the Inquisition had forbidden the use of the rod in the "moral world," that is, for tracing criminals, or determining boundaries, or settling lawsuits, etc. (its use for these purposes having become a most mischievous superstition and scandal), these diviners, or *tourneurs*, were chiefly water-finders, or sourciers. Bleton was therefore at once considered to be a new and sensitive *sourcier*. Some tests followed which confirmed this view. Doubtless, custom demanded that he should have a rod, and the subsequent use by Bleton of a nearly straight rod, resting on the forefingers of each hand, satisfied the sense of *sourcier* propriety. The rod was very slightly curved, and rotated more or less rapidly on its axis when Bleton came over an underground spring. Dr. Thouvenel states he counted from 30 to 80 revolutions per minute, and upwards.

The rotation of the rod was doubtless caused by involuntary muscular action on Bleton's part. There is no reason to suppose he moved it intentionally; in fact, it is a very difficult, if not impossible, feat to accomplish by volition, except to one long practised in sleight of hand, as any one can prove who supports a short slightly-curved stick on his forefingers, and attempts to cause it to rotate from "30 to 80 times a minute." On the other hand, there is no reason to assume any other motive power than muscular action, as the famous astronomer Lalande showed that Bleton's rod could be made to rotate by this means. To this I have already referred in my previous paper, and will quote Lalande's own words later on.

---

[1] The exact date of his birth is uncertain, nor is it of any consequence. The above date is deduced from an incidental observation in the evidence about to be cited. In 1773, as appears from another witness, Bleton's faculty was so well known that he was then in request as a water-finder or sourcier. Our principal knowledge of Bleton, as will be mentioned presently, is derived from the writings of Dr. Thouvenel, one of Louis XVI.'s physicians; he always spells the word Bleton, not Bléton.

[2] See Dr. Thouvenel's *Mémoire Physique et Médicinal*, 1781, p. 251; *Monthly Review*, 1782, Vol. LXVII., p. 554; Figuier's *La baguette divinatoire*, p. 365. Figuier quotes from a letter written by a contemporary of Bleton to the Editor of the *Journal des Spectacles*.

# The Credibility Of Dowsing

How Bleton came by this novel form of rod is not told us.¹ Possibly it was a survival in Dauphiny of an old type of the *virgula divina*. A straight rod, supported horizontally between the forefinger and thumb of each hand, is described and depicted on the title page of that interesting old book on the divining rod, *La Verge de Jacob*² (see D

FIG. 16.

on the woodcut, Fig. 16), which was published at Lyons in 1693. In the third chapter of this book the writer says that in order to ascertain if a person really has the faculty of finding a hidden spring, he must let a straight stick rest across his hands, in the manner shown in the lowest figure of the woodcuts on this and the next page; if he has the faculty the stick begins to rotate.³ Bleton was probably tested in this way, and subsequently used this rotating rod

---

¹ The only notice I can find of the peculiarity of Bleton's rod is in a letter "from a distinguished physician" cited by Thouvenel in support of Bleton's faculty. The writer says (p. 277 of Thouvenel's *Mémoire*) that although nearly all the *tourneurs*, i.e, dowsers, he has known, use a forked rod, yet some in Germany use a simple rod, very slightly curved, placed across the back of the hand, "ou comme Bleton, sur l'extrémité des deux doigts indicateurs." This reference to Germany is probably taken from De Vallemont's *Physique Occulte* (1693) where there is a picture of a man holding the rod in this way (see next woodcut). Still earlier, in 1640, the learned German Jesuit, A. Kircher, describes a straight-pivoted divining rod which rotates when held horizontally between the forefingers of each hand (see upper figure on the wood-cut, Fig. 17). This, he remarks, he has seen used by some German diviners: see Kircher's *Magnes sive de arte Magnetica*, p. 724 of the 1640 edition.

² It need hardly be said that this, like every other early work on the divining rod, is perfectly worthless from the point of view of modern science.

³ I am indebted to the kindness of the Editor of *Pearson's Magazine* for these two woodcuts; Fig. 17, he may be interested to know, was originally taken from Lebrun's *Lettres qui découvrent l'illusion des Philosophes sur la Baguette*, Paris, 1693; see also De Vallemont's *La Physique Occulte*, 1693. De Vallemont says the rod was sometimes held in the ways shown in Fig. 17.

as the outward and visible sign of the inward commotion he experienced. This is the more probable as the little book, *La Verge de Jacob*, was likely to be well known in Dauphiny, being published at the neighbouring town of Lyons, where also Bleton was frequently engaged. (See also the woodcut on p. 345.)

The singular physiological effect produced upon Bleton by underground springs seems to have been retained more or less throughout his life. A sort of convulsive spasm seized him, affecting the diaphragm and pulse. Abundant evidence of the genuineness of this "commotion" is given by a number of unimpeachable witnesses. But this aspect of our subject I will return to in a later section, when the medical report Dr. Thouvenel gives of the peculiar symptoms exhibited by his "patient" will be quoted. Here I will only add that Bleton's sensibility appeared to vary, being greater in dry weather and before meals. It entirely ceased during an illness he had, and did not return until

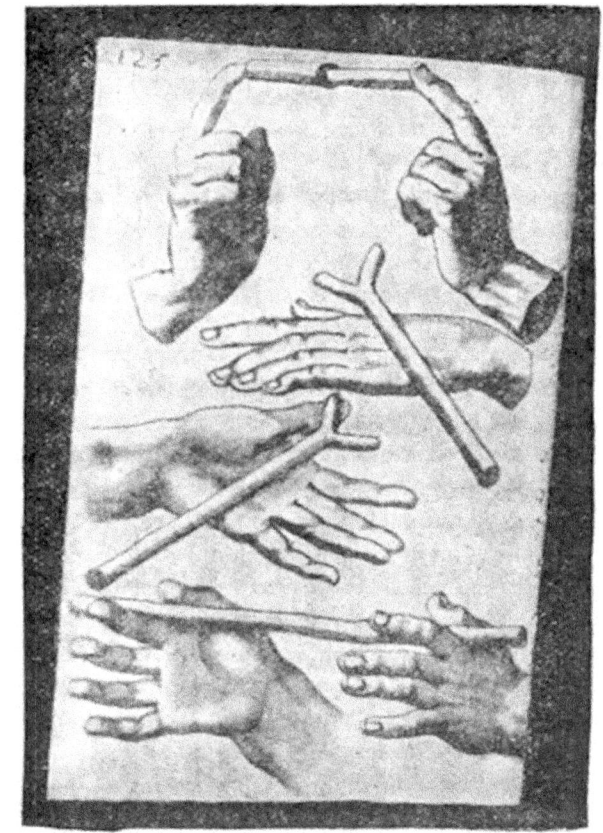

Fig. 17.

three months subsequent to his recovery. The rate of rotation of the baguette was observed closely to correspond with the physiological effect produced. When Bleton moved away from an underground spring, the symptoms disappeared as rapidly as they arose, and the pulse resumed its normal rate. Stagnant water appeared to make no impression on him, nor the water of exposed rivers, lakes, &c. This latter is indeed a singular, and at first sight appears a suspicious circumstance, difficult to reconcile with any physical theory of the phenomena. But equally singular is the fact that it is affirmed by all diviners from the time of Jacques Aymar in 1693 down to the present day,[1] and not in one country but wherever the divining rod is in use, not the least singular fact how this tradition

---

[1] In 1689 an interesting correspondence (to which I will return) took place between those acute intellects, Fathers Malebranche and Le Brun, on this very point. For a discussion of the sensations alleged to be experienced by dowsers, see Proceedings S.P.R.. Part XXXII., Appendix D., p. 272.

# The Credibility Of Dowsing

(if it be only such) has spread, for diviners, as a rule, are illiterate men, ignorant of any language but their own. Let us now examine what experimental evidence history has preserved on behalf of Bleton's alleged powers.

The principal source of information is found in two treatises entitled *Mémoire Physique et Medicinal*, by Dr. Thouvenel, who was a distinguished French physician.[1] The first treatise was published in 1781 and the second in 1784, and both are almost entirely devoted to a record of observations with Bleton and an exposition of Thouvenel's electrical theory of the phenomena.[2] The best English summary of these memoires is to be found in that old but well edited register of current literature, the *Monthly Review* for 1781, 1783, and 1784. There are, unfortunately, few details given by Thouvenel of his own experiments with Bleton.

No. 1.—Here, however, is one, which he says is a complicated test to which he submitted Bleton. I will give an abridged translation (pp. 69 and 70).

> Over a stone bridge, of one arch, pass four small wooden aqueducts, carrying water to Nancy. Only the engineer, who had never seen Bleton, knew the exact position of these four rows of pipes, their distance apart, depth underground, etc., the whole being well covered by earth and vegetation. He gave me secretly information on this, of which Bleton was entirely ignorant. The latter was then taken across this bridge, as though to return to the town, after various experiments had been made in the neighborhood, and without being told that fresh experiments were to be made. Just before reaching the bridge, he asserted water was flowing beneath him, and the sensation continued with slight gaps, while crossing and in front of the bridge to a distance of five or six feet. He retraced his steps several times before finding distinctly the four channels, and was much astonished to find them so near. He was then told that they were simply four hollow tree trunks made to serve as aqueducts.

Thouvenel then describes other tests as to the distance apart of these pipes, and remarks that as a small stream about 3 feet wide was flowing some 10 feet beneath the bridge, he endeavoured to ascertain what effect it had on Bleton; a careful experiment showed that the agitation of the diviner and the rotation of the baguette sensibly increased on crossing the stream. There is nothing, however, in these experiments to exclude the effect of telepathy or even involuntary *suggestion* upon Bleton's mind. It is, however, only within recent years that the powerful influence of suggestion, both on mind and body, has received the attention of physiologists, and therefore we need not be surprised that some of Thouvenel's experiments are capable of a different interpretation from that which he gave. For example, he found that when his sourcier was over a spring and the baguette turning strongly, the convulsive movements of the body and the rotation of the rod were almost arrested the moment he touched Bleton with various "magnetic compositions recently electrified"! Experiments were also made when Bleton was insulated, but these I will deal with in another part, as the belief that insulation stops the movement of the rod is almost as widespread as that of the different effects of running and stagnant water.

On pp. 77-80 of his first *mémoire* Thouvenel gives a summary of the tests he made with Bleton in Lorraine. The following is a translation of the passage[3] :—

> I took the precaution to repeat several times all the experiments just described in detail, after having carefully blindfolded Bleton; in addition his arms were sometimes fastened behind his back leaving his forearms only just sufficiently free to hold the baguette at the extremity of his fingers, sometimes

---

[1] The great French Biographical Dictionary gives an admirable account of Thouvenel's life, which deserves to be more widely known. Like Dr. Elliotson, in defence of mesmerism, Dr. Thouvenel had to face a storm of obloquy for his courage in defending Bleton. His long and patient investigations were treated with contempt. He left France for Italy at the time of the Revolution, and died in 1815.

[2] I have to thank M. Holland, of 2, Rue des Chantiers, Paris, for enabling me to obtain a copy of Thouvenel's earlier and more important *Mémoire*, together with other rare French, German and Italian books, pamphlets, and newspaper cuttings of the last century bearing upon the *baguette divinatoire*. To those engaged in any special literary research I can heartily commend M. Holland's courteous help and excellent agency.

[3] Already quoted in Part V. on " Blindfolding the Dowser."

even confining these, in order to hinder if possible all mechanical movement. These precautions were not taken for my own satisfaction, as I was already entirely convinced.

I conducted Bleton to places which he had never seen; I took him towards springs of which I knew, but which he could not know of, at other times over ground where neither of us knew what might be found. Whenever he experienced his peculiar sensations—and whenever the baguette repeatedly turned at the same spot,—I then led him far away, bringing him back by quite different roads, still with his eyes bandaged. . . When he had followed the course of an underground spring—sometimes for more than a quarter of a mile, across mountains, rock, or forests, and indicated on the way numerous sub divisions of the same spring—I made him return. He then re-conducted me himself, though still blindfolded, only supported by one arm, to the point from which we set out, without straying a single step from the line previously traced and marked by pegs, which were often hidden beneath the surface. He re-found all the subterranean rivulets already pointed out, and followed exactly the sinuosities of the underground stream. It frequently happened that we came across springs whose course was interrupted by walls, terraces, or wide ditches, so that in order to enable Bleton to overcover these obstacles, I had to procure ladders, or take long detours, or in some way get him conveyed across; nevertheless, although blindfolded, he soon regained the course without the aid of his eyes. Sometimes in order to try and deceive him, if his senses were concerned, I placed false marks as if to indicate a spring; sometimes after he had followed a spring across several fields, I moved the pegs some feet away without his knowledge. Nevertheless, he was never led astray and always rectified such errors. In fine, I tried all sorts of ways to deceive him, and I can testify that in more than six hundred trials, I did not succeed in doing so one single time.

M. Jadelot, the Professor of Medicine in Nancy, Thouvenel states, was a witness of, and co-operated in, all his experiments, which extended over a space of two months, and was no less struck than he was with the strength and importance of the evidence obtained. Another distinguished savant who was converted to a belief in the *baguette* was M. Sigaud de la Fond, whose published testimony Thouvenel quotes (p. 289 et seq.). But the most important evidence on behalf of Bleton is contained in the numerous letters and affidavits Thouvenel appends to his work. These are the replies he received from various well-known persons who had employed Bleton, and whose opinion he had asked. I will quote some of these directly. In addition to the foregoing, Bleton found one or more valuable springs (as testified by letters or *procès-verbaux*) for the Marquis de Torcy in Poiton, for the President of Lamoignon in Basville, for the Bishop of Laon in Annisy, for the Count dAdhémar in Thun, for the Duke d'Uzès, Count de la Blanche, Count du Bourg, President d'Ornacieux, M. de la Borde, and many other French personages of distinction. There are also brief statements from 20 other persons for whom Bleton found *plusieurs belles sources*, in addition to the 17 letters or affidavits quoted at length by Thouvenel. In these *pièces justificatives* Thouvenel as a rule gives only the initials of his correspondents; the documents, he tells us, are all signed and some legally attested, but some of the writers might object to their names being published; moreover, he adds that in physics names add nothing to the facts themselves.[1]

No. 2.— In one statement, however, this rule is departed from, and Thouvenel humorously prefixes the heading: "*Proces verbal sur Bleton . . . papier timbré, paraphé, collationné, etc., etc. (Bon pour ceux qui aiment ces petites formalités),*" ["Testimonies about Bleton…on stamped paper, initialed, collated, etc., etc., (Good for those who love these little formalities)" - Ed] and the testimony is certified by, and attested before, a list of signatories whose names and official titles are appended. In this case the evidence of the various municipal officers of the Commune of St. Jean-en-Royant in Dauphiny is given. Bleton was a native of, and resided in, this commune (Bouvantes being a parish therein), and the *procès-verbal* states that Bleton had possessed the gift of finding springs for about 30 years, and had practised it much to the advantage of the inhabitants of the commune. Specific instances are then cited of the more important springs Bleton had found in arid ground—springs which were still running, the witnesses affirm, and had largely

---

[1] This may account for the omission of his own name (initials only being given) as the author of these *Mémoires*.

# The Credibility Of Dowsing

increased the value of the property in the commune: owing to these discoveries, fertile and productive land had, in several places, now replaced the previously barren soil. The Chief Clerk of the neighbouring commune states that Bleton found for him an ample spring in a district where no water was previously known to exist, the result of which was that the ground, which formerly was of little or no value, now is a valuable property. The signatories of the *procès-verbal* further testify that Bleton had discovered during the preceding 20 years a quantity of springs in other neighbouring communes, some of these being of so great a volume that machinery was worked by them.

No. 3.—Another document also signed by M. A., an inhabitant of St. Jean de Royant, states that the value of his property had been increased tenfold by the springs discovered on it by Bleton.

No. 4.—*The Prior of the Chartreuse de Lyon* testifies (March 3rd, 1781) that Bleton had found several springs for him and had not once been mistaken, though his estimate of the depth and volume of the water he acknowledged to be conjectural. Bleton's discovery of his liability to err on this point being, he adds, the only progress he had made since he was seven years old, when "il etoit aussi savant qu'il l'est actuellement." [Trans. "When he was as learned then as he is now" - Ed] The Prior states that when he held Bleton's wrist, the change in Bleton's pulse was so perceptible upon arriving over an underground spring that the fact was as obvious to him as to the *sourcier*, a baguette being perfectly needless.

No. 5.—*The Chevalier de M------*, formerly Captain of the Piedmont regiment, testifies that he has been convinced of Bleton's powers in spite of the prejudices he previously entertained. Having put Bleton to all the proofs he could think of, he never once found him mistaken. "Whatever the power is," he remarks, "it is not the mere movement of the *baguette* that astonishes me—that might be a matter of skill—but the effect on Bleton's pulse and nervous system were unmistakeable, and these cannot be simulated. Moreover," he continues, "j'ai fait toutes les chicanes que mes doutes m'ont inspirées," [Translation – "I tried all the tricks my skepticism brought to mind." - Ed] until doubt became impossible. The Chevalier describes in detail one of several tests he made; he brought Bleton to his own house, arriving after dark; in passing through the village, which Bleton had not visited before, Bleton suddenly stopped and said water was there; he followed it in the darkness and arrived at a spot where he declared the spring existed; he was right; it was, in fact the source of the fountain of the castle. Other tests are also given: altogether a remarkable and weighty testimony.

No. 6.—M. de F., the receiver of taxes for Autun, states that a strong spring was discovered on his place by Bleton. In order to test the *sourcier*, M. de F. afterwards blindfolded him, and took him over the same ground; Bleton marked precisely the same spots he did previously when not blindfolded; this experiment he repeated several times.

No. 7.—*Dr. de C.* (a neighbour of M. de F.) took Bleton to his house, where Bleton accurately traced the course of the water pipes, a fact confirmed by the workmen who had laid them.

No. 8.—*M. le Comte de M.*, of Chagny, describes several careful tests he made of Bleton. In one, after Bleton had accurately indicated an underground spring (the existence of which was known to the Count, but unknown to Bleton) and traced its direction, which was noted, the Count then carefully bandaged Bleton's eyes with a thick handkerchief, and, in order to mislead him, turned him round several times; nevertheless Bleton correctly indicated the same course of the spring, in spite of frequent attempts made to divert him. Holding his wrist, the Count noticed that the change in the rate of Bleton's pulse was very marked when he came over the spring.

No. 9.—*The Bishop of M.* describes how his Archbishop tested Bleton's ability to discover running water: (1) Bleton correctly traced the buried water pipes in the Archbishop's grounds when water was flowing through them; (2) Unknown to Bleton the water was then turned off and he was asked to repeat the trial, and he completely failed to find the pipes; (3) Again the water was secretly turned on, and Bleton once more correctly indicated the direction taken by the pipes.

No. 10.—*The Chevalier de S.*, *commandeur de Mälte*, states that many years previously his grandfather had made several attempts to find water at his *Chateau pres de la Côte de Saint-André*, had even sunk a well to the depth of seventy feet, which had to be abandoned. The Chevalier de S., and his brother, the President d'O., in 1735 sent for a *sourcier* they knew of who traversed the estate, using an iron rod they had picked up as a *baguette*. Upon their expressing surprise at his ability to use so novel a divining rod, the *sourcier* replied, "the rod is of no consequence, it is the peculiar feeling I have when over an underground spring that guides me." In 1773 (thirty-eight years later) the Chevalier heard of Bleton and sent for him. On his arrival he was taken to the terrace, where the rod began to rotate, and the site of the well was correctly indicated. To estimate its depth Bleton went to a certain distance on each side, the rod rotating in an opposite direction as he moved away from the spring. By observing the distance and decreasing force of the rotation, Bleton estimated the depth of the well to be 64 feet: its actual depth was 66 feet.

Bleton was then taken to a hill behind the chateau, when he pointed out the existence of several springs in the spots marked; the following winter a well was sunk at one of these spots and water found at a depth of 18 feet, a narrow layer of sand being struck after piercing through the upper very hard rock. This spring has never run dry, even in times of great drought. Two years later (in 1775) Bleton was again tested on the same estate and he indicated another spring, the depth of which he estimated at 33 feet; a well was sunk at this spot and the prediction was verified. Some time after, the two springs were joined by underground conduits; these conduits Bleton accurately traced when he was again summoned to the chateau in 1779.

In 1781 a fourth visit to this estate was made by Bleton. This time he discovered another spring, which he estimated at 25 feet deep; a well was sunk and at 35 feet an abundant supply of water was obtained; this also issued from a layer of sand beneath the hard superincumbent rock.

Some experiments were then made by the President d'O. and his brother as to the movement of the baguette when Bleton was placed in various positions. The rod turned when he lay on his back, but not on his stomach, nor did it turn when it was placed on his loins when he was lying down. Bleton was then suspended upside down and the baguette placed on the soles of his feet; it did not rotate. Bleton, however, showed them that when the rod was placed nearly perpendicularly with one end resting on the palm of the left hand, and the other in the air, encircled by a ring formed of the finger and thumb of the right hand placed a little below the point, the baguette "pirouetted slowly," when over a spring.

This interesting document ends by suggesting the desirability of placing *le tourneur de baguette* on a sheet of resin or a glass-legged stool and noticing whether his peculiar sensations are still experienced, or whether they resemble the sensations one has when thus insulated and connected with an electric machine. If, remarks the Chevalier, running water gives off subtle emanations, they must be comparable to those of light, and possibly suffer refraction and reflection in their course. The document is signed by the President d'O., who states that he did not write it, but he approves; and that the facts narrated were all witnessed by him, his son, the Chevalier de S., and other persons, and he adds his conviction that Bleton employed no *charlatanerie* in any of his proceedings.

No. 11.—On the lands of the Abbe de Vervains there were certain springs, all trace of which had long been lost; they were, however, known to exist from the ancient title-deeds of the estate. A lawsuit hinged upon the question of their existence being actually proved. When search for the springs had been made in vain, Bleton was sent for. He came and indicated the place where these springs existed. Their actual existence was then discovered, and the lawsuit terminated.[1]

No. 12.—*Surgeon-Major N., of St. Geny Laval, near Lyons*, testifies that Bleton came to a part of his estate which was rocky and arid, and found one spot where the baguette indicated a considerable spring, which he estimated to be at a depth of some 55 feet. A well was sunk, but no water found at this depth. Bleton was, therefore, sent for again. He tested the ground once more, asserted confidently that a good spring would be found at a few feet lower, remarking that he was often mistaken as to the depth when it was over 30 feet.[2] The well was, therefore, deepened, and at 7 or 8 feet lower so powerful a spring gushed forth that it was impossible to sink deeper, as the water rapidly rose in the well, which was 5 feet in diameter. The witness adds, "A useless land has thus been converted into a meadow."

---

[1] Quoted from the *Monthly Review* for 1784, p. 572.
[2] There is evidently a misprint in the French text here, which reads "au-dessous de trente pieds"; from the context obviously au-dessus is meant. [The first reads 'Below thirty feet', the second would read 'Over thirty feet' – Ed]

# The Credibility Of Dowsing

No. 13.—*P. I. G., and Seigneur D., Conseiller du Parlement de B.*, affirm that they brought Bleton to Tanyot, in Bourgogne, where he was subjected to various tests, three of which are cited: (1) He was asked to find the course of some water pipes that had been laid some time previously and which were completely covered by earth and grass, so that no difference was apparent on the surface of the ground. Bleton immediately discovered the position of, and accurately traced, the course of these pipes. (2) He was asked to find the spring which supplied a neighbouring well, and to estimate its depth. This he did quite accurately, and stated it was a very feeble spring, which the owner of the well certified was also correct. (3) He was asked to find a supply of water for their chateau. For some time he searched in vain, but eventually in another direction he found six small springs: their position was marked by pegs. Upon digging at these spots, springs were found in each place at about the depth and volume he indicated. These springs were then connected by a deep trench, and furnished an abundant supply of water for both house and garden.

It is needless to translate and summarise the other documents, which contain similar evidence. Thouvenel's treatise, however, is not the only source of our information about Bleton. Accounts of this *sourcier* are to be found in many of the French journals of that period. I am indebted for much of the subsequent evidence to the excellent and impartial narrative of Bleton given by Louis Figuier in the seventh chapter of the second volume of his *Histoire du Merveilleux*, which contains some facts I have not met with elsewhere.

No. 14. —In the *Journal de Paris* of May 13th, 1782, an account was published of some careful experiments made to test Bleton's powers in the gardens of the Luxembourg under the direction of M. Guillaumot "intendant général des bâtiments du roi," who was accompanied by inspectors and officials of the gardens. The report states :—

> Sorti du Chateau d'Eau, Bleton a suivi dans la campagne l'aqueduc d'Arcueil avec une precision telle que, pour nous servir d'une de M. Guillaumot, si ce plan venait à se perdre, on le referait sur les traces de Bleton.
>
> [Translation – Leaving the Chateau, Bleton followed the aqueduct of the Arcueil in the countryside with such precision that M Gauillamot said that if we lost the plan (of the aqueduct) we could simply trace Bleton's footsteps. – Ed]

The report states that M. Guillaumot verified from the plans the angles and sinuosities made by the (I presume subterranean) aqueduct, and these the report adds: "nous dirons presque mathématiques désignés par Bleton." [Translation - We would say almost mathematically designated by Bleton - Ed] Two days later the experiments were repeated in the presence of the municipal authorities and a crowd of spectators. The report states :—

> Ici les expériences ont été telles qu'à l'exception de deux seuls témoins, qui avaient publiquement avancé qu'ils ne croiraient pas, même en voyant, qu' à cette exception près, sur cinq cents spectateurs, il n'en est pas un qui n'ait été convaincu de la faculté dont est doué Bleton de suivre les eaux souterraines avec la plus rigoureuse précision. Les yeux bandés, la baguette posée sur les doigts, il n'a pas quitté l'embranchement de l'aqueduc.
>
> [Translation – Here the experiments were such that, with the exception of two witnesses, who had publicly claimed they did not believe him, even after seeing him, that with those exceptions, of five hundred spectators there is not one who has not been convinced of the power of Bleton to follow underground water with the utmost accuracy. Blindfolded, with the wand on his fingers, he did not leave the line of the aqueduct. –Ed]

Other trials followed in the presence of ministers of state, ambassadors, magistrates, scientific men and the clergy, and the Journal de Paris, in summing up the experiments, records that Bleton followed

> Jusqu'à présent, de notre connaissance, plus de quinze milles torses des conduites, sans avoir jamais commis une seule erreur et sans avoir trouvé, dans le nombre de plus de six mille personnes, un seul

témoin compétent qui ait pu faire une objection fondée. Il a été soumis à toutes les épreuves les plus rigoureuses qu' ait pu suggérer l'incrédulité, même l'esprit de parti, et il n'en est résulté que plus de lumières, plus de convictions et plus d'étonnement.

[Translation – Until now, of more than fifteen thousand twists and turns, without ever committing one error, we have not found one competent witness able to make a valid objection out of 6,000 people. He was subjected to all the most rigorous tests that disbelief could suggest and it has resulted in greater astonishment, conviction and amazement. - Ed]

No. 15.—Some rigorous experiments were made by a committee of six savants, who drew up a report dated, "Paris, May 25th, 1782." This report, which was signed by all the members, states that Bleton, having been blindfolded with extreme care by a succession of black and then white linen bandages, with cotton wool stuffed up the sides of his nostrils, was taken to the garden of one of the members of the committee, wherein a water-pipe ran underground to a distant fountain. The jets of this fountain had been removed, so that the water ran into the basin, and off through an overflow pipe, quite noiselessly. Here Bleton indicated running water at certain spots which were marked; he was then made to retrace his steps 10 or 12 times, and it was found that the baguette turned nearly, but not quite, invariably when he crossed the same spots: at the places where the water entered the basin and where the overflow pipe discharged he was always right. This they verified at least a dozen times. The experiments lasted two hours, with a short interval for rest; during the whole time Bleton was blindfolded, and during part of that time M. Thouvenel was not present.

According to the writer of the article in the Monthly Review for 1782 :—

These successes led the Queen of France to employ Bleton, and the springs that have been found in consequence of his indications have fertilised and embellished several arid districts, among which Trianon is a striking example, as that delightful seat has acquired new charms by Bleton's discoveries.[1]

The Editor of the *Journal des Spectacles,* in a figure of speech, we must assume, states that Bleton, by his discovery of numerous springs, had changed Dauphiny from an arid soil, which produced nothing, to one of the richest in France. Dr. Ginetz, writing in the *Journal de Paris* for November, 1807, states that, "The efficacy of the baguette is nowhere contested in Dauphiny. I have myself," he says, "frequently observed the effects of the baguette, and can state from personal experience its success in seeking for springs and metallic veins."[2]

In Thouvenel's second *Mémoire*, published in 1784, a further account is given of his experiments with Bleton. This eminent physician was commissioned in 1783 by Louis XVI. to examine and report on the mineral and medicinal waters of France, and to aid him in the discovery of any fresh mineral springs, he obtained permission to engage the services of Bleton.[3] Most of this second *Mémoire* is therefore occupied with tracing hot springs and mineral waters, with conjectures as to the source of the former, and attempts to verify the electrical hypothesis which Thouvenel had formed, of the influence of subterranean springs on the diviner.

We need not concern ourselves with the latter, as the experiments cited are certainly open to criticism, and would only excite a smile in the wider scientific knowledge of the present day. It is, however, now known, as Thouvenel conjectured, that there are subterraneous electric currents, the strength of which fluctuates in various places and

---

[1] According to Figuier, however, Bleton had some failures at Trianon, mistaking averns and dry conduits for underground water. [Note: 'averns' here is probably a printer's error for 'caverns'. – Ed]

[2] It was in Provence (the adjoining province to Dauphiny) that Lady Milbanke, in 1772, first saw the use of the divining rod. In a dry, mountainous region north of the Durance, the Marquis d'Ansonis had found water by a *sourcier*, and the Marquis, whose faith in the divining rod was unbounded, converted Lady Milbanke to his views after witnessing experiments on his estate.

[3] Figuier states that, owing to Bleton having indicated the existence of some natural oil springs on this expedition, he was engaged on his return by the Government Department of Mines to search for similar springs in the neighbourhood of Paris. Figuier adds, the high sanction thus given to Bleton's peculiar faculty shows the esteem in which he was held, and distinguishes him from the common run of *tourneurs de baguette*.

from time to time. It is certainly a curious coincidence, if it be no more, that upwards of one hundred years ago this French physician, on the faith of Bleton's sensations, maintained that these electrical manifestations appeared in general to run east and west.[1] Current electricity itself was not discovered till ten years later, the existence of earth currents was not known till Barlow's experiments in 1849, and the general trend of these currents east and west was a still more recent observation.[2]

## Contemporary Opinion Adverse to Bleton

Among those who, after experimenting with Bleton, formed an unfavourable opinion of his reported powers was the Abbé Mongez, one of the principal contributors to the articles on Natural Philosophy in the Paris *Encyclopédie*; but, according to Dr. Thouvenel, these experiments were intended to be unfavourable, and the experimenters, by designing a number of ingenious tricks to deceive Bleton, in reality deceived themselves. Certainly the *parti pris* of most of the scientific investigators of Bleton was very evident, and to a large extent vitiated both the experiments made and the conclusions drawn from them.[3] These experiments were made for the most part in the church and garden of St. Geneviève in the presence of several *savants*. An account is given of them in the *Journal de Paris* for June 16th, 1782, and *procès verbaux* of the experiments are to be found in the *Journal de Physique* of that year.[4] It is needless to enter into the details; suffice it to say that the report concludes by stating that Bleton found water pipes, springs, etc. on all sides, whereas there were no water pipes and no springs beneath him. The attempt to explain away this failure, which Thouvenel made, shows that believers in the divining-rod can be no less blind and prejudiced than their opponents. Doubtless the experiments were wholly inconclusive in face of the abundant testimony in Bleton's favour, some of which we have cited. The writer in the *Monthly Review* seems to have given the true explanation of these experiments. Admitting that Bleton did fail, he remarks, "this will not appear surprising when we consider this poor timorous man led about blindfold, harassed, fatigued, and perplexed with cross questions," and he adds, "even the Abbé Mongez admits that Bleton was sometimes quite correct." In fact, as the Reviewer I have already quoted justly remarks :—

> "The public have no curiosity to know how far tricks and ingenious means of deception can go in disconcerting or suspending the exercise of Bleton's natural talent; they only desire to know whether he in reality possesses this talent, when left to himself and allowed the free use of his faculties."[5]

But, like all other dowsers, Bleton unquestionably failed at times. Figuier names four places, and also "dans quelques autres lieux," where wells were dug at the spots indicated by Bleton and no water found, even when the wells were sunk to a depth lower than had been estimated by the *sourcier*. In his able paper on the Divining Rod,

---

[1] Thouvenel thought that the electrical effects, east and west, were associated with all metals, except iron, which he affirms gives a north and south direction; as he associated the latter with terrestrial magnetism, this looks as if the results of his experiments were often vitiated by involuntary *suggestion* on Thouvenel's part.

[2] There are some other curious observations in this treatise which illustrate Thouvenel's scientific spirit. Thus, by the aid of Bleton, Thouvenel traced the source of the hot springs of Bourbon Lancy to a mountainous region abounding in coal; not only so, but a similar result appeared constantly to occur with other hot springs he examined, and he affirms that eventually their origin was to be found in or near masses of coal, to chemical changes in which he attributes their high temperature. Geologists would not, I imagine, endorse this view. Variations in the conductivity of rocks and the existence of past or present volcanic action,—in a word, the internal heat of the earth,—are, I believe, the sufficient causes now recognised: but we must remember our author wrote upwards of a century ago.

[3] As the able contemporary reviewer, to whom I have already referred, remarks (*Monthly Review*, 1782, Vol. LXVII, p. 554), "It is certainly possible that even an honest zeal for the discovery of imposture or enthusiasm may be exerted in a manner not perfectly adapted to the discovery of truth. . . . It is observed by all that Bleton is uncommonly timorous and easily disconcerted, even so far as to suspend his impressions. This we can well conceive, be his talent ever so real. The very talent seems to announce a sensibility of nerves that may render him peculiarly susceptible of perturbation. Who has not seen schoolboys of the most retentive memories lose the remembrance of the best learned lesson by being intimidated?"

[4] I have not seen these, and am indebted to Figuier for the references, who adds that Guyton de Morveau (a well-known *savant*) gave some interesting details about Bleton in the *Journal de Nancy*.

[5] Monthly Review, Vol. LXVII. p. 555.

read before the American Institute of Mining Engineers in 1883, Dr. Rossiter Raymond quotes,—without, however, naming his authority,— several instances where Bleton failed to find the same spot, after being blindfolded, that he had indicated previously. These experiments are probably those to which we have referred on the last page, and commented on by the *Monthly Review* for 1782.[1]

After the lapse of a century it is instructive to notice how frequently the adverse criticism of Bleton arose from his critics assuming a particular explanation of the lad's sensitiveness, or of the motion of his rod, and having demolished their theory, they roundly asserted the boy was a charlatan,—a mode of argument not unknown to scientific critics of the S.P.R. at the present day.

Thus, Bleton's sensitiveness being supposed to be due to some electric influence, he was mounted on an insulating stool and his rod at once ceased to move, but resumed its motion when he was on the ground. A famous physicist, Charles, who conducted this experiment a century ago, when Bleton was on the insulating stool, secretly connected the lad with a wire to the earth; still the rod remained passive although the insulation was destroyed. Whereupon Bleton was openly denounced as a charlatan by his scientific critic. All that this experiment proves is the influence of suggestion on the motion of the rod. As the lad knew nothing of electricity, he must have been told that the insulating stool would intercept the power, and so the rod ceased to move when he was mounted on the glass-legged stool, and it remained motionless when the insulation was destroyed, as care had been taken to avoid any suggestion of this reaching Bleton. I made a precisely similar experiment with a dowser at Waringstown, in Ireland, in 1896 (see previous Report, Vol. XIII., pp. 80 and 246), and the result was exactly the same; when the dowser believed he was not in electrical connection with the earth, his twig ceased to move; when he believed he was electrically connected, the forked twig instantly twisted round, though the electrical condition was the same in both cases. The object of my experiment was to dispose of the widely spread but mistaken idea that insulation prevents the motion of the rod. Even on his own hypothesis, the French experimenter with Bleton was mistaken; for the theory that some electrical *influence* from underground water affects the dowser, and so starts the motion of the rod, is not touched by insulating the dowser; as every tyro knows, standing on a glass-legged stool merely prevents electric *conduction* from the earth and does not impair electric induction. This latter, though a plausible hypothesis, has, however, no experimental evidence in its favour and need not be here discussed.

Again, the eminent astronomer, Lalande, believed he had conclusively demonstrated Bleton was a rogue because he established the fact that the peculiar rod Bleton employed could be rotated by sleight-of-hand. The fallacy of this line of argument, though persisted in at the present day, has already been pointed out (see p. 141, etc). As, however, Lalande is often quoted as having "exposed" Bleton, it is worth giving *in extenso* the communication which this famous *savant* made to the *Journal des Savants*, (or *Sçavans* as it was then spelt) for August, 1782, p. 558. Here is the quotation from the copy in the British Museum :—

> "Un nommé Bléton, né dans un village, près de Grenoble, a prétendu avoir un propriété extraordinaire de sentir les eaux souterainnes par un tremblement convulsif. Ce sourcier, ou hydropyrete, plaçait sur ses doits une baguette ou une verge de métal, courbeé en arc, et on la voyoit tourner rapidement. Ce stratagème était plus adroit que celui des sourciers qui courent les villages, et qui marquent des sources aux paysans, moyennant la plus mince rétribution. Ceux-ci serrent leur baguette dans leurs mains, et pour peu qu'on ait envie des regarder, on s'apperçoit facilement qu'il suffit de ferrer la baguette inégalement; sa courbure détermine nécessairement un mouvement de rotation ... il [Dr Thouvenel] n'était plus assez calme pour se rendre aux raisons de ses adversaires, ni même pour appercevoir la petite charlatannerie dont il avait été la dupe ... [il] a été parfaitement

---

[1] This is the case, I have since ascertained. Dr. Raymond has derived his information from Figuier's excellent essay on the *Baguette Divinatoire*, published a few years ago, but he does not give the facts quite correctly: moreover, following the example of many others who ignore what they cannot explain, he dismisses in a few words the abundant testimony that exists as to Bleton's successes, fairly enough given by Figuier, and emphasises (in fact, exaggerates) any failures that were reported. Chevreul did just the same;—see, e.g., p. 113 of his work on the *Baguette Divinatoire*, published in 1854.

# The Credibility Of Dowsing

séduit par l'addresse de Bléton, à faire tourner sur ses doigts une verge courbe de métal; il n'a pas apperçu que cela tenoit à uno cause mécanique.

En effet, si l'on place sur deux doigts une baguette de métal courbée en arc, de manière que le sommet de l'arc soit plus bas que les deux extrémités, mais que le tout soit presqu'en équilibre, le plus petit rapprochement des doigts, ne fût-il que d'une ligne, suffira pour que les extrémités l'emportent à leur tour, et que le sommet de l'arc vienne en haut. Si on les écarte, à l'instant le sommet de l'arc descendra, et avec une pareille alternative, le mouvement peut continuer aussi longtemps qu'on le jugera à propos. Un homme très-exercé n'a besoin pour cela que d'un léger tremblement qui est à peine sensible, quand on n'est pas prévenu.

Faute d'avoir apperçu ce petit mécanisme, M. Thouvenel a fait un livre sur la baguette, mais M. Demours, fils de l'Académicien très-connu, a fait tourner une baguette pareille dans une assemblée de l'Académie des sciences, de manière à lever toute espèce de doute à cet égarde.

. . . M. Needham . . . cite même quelques faits contre les prétentions de la baguette, qui sont renovellées de tems à autres par des fripons, ou par des dupes. Enfin, M. Paulet, dans la Gazette de Santé du 10 Juin, 1781, s'est moqué de la nouvelle physique, ainsi qu'on l'avait fait dans le dernier siècle.

FIG. 18.

[Translation – 'A person named Bleton claimed to have a special property of sensing underground water through convulsions. The dowser placed a stick or metal rod, slightly curved on his fingers and it was seen to rotate quickly. This was cleverer than those dowsers who find water sources for farmers without being discovered. They shake their wands in their hands making it easy to make it rotate…He (Dr Thouvenel) did not listen to his critics and was unable to see that he was being duped…He was completely taken in by Bleton, rotating the rod on his fingers, unable to see the purely mechanical cause.

If you place two fingers on a bent metal rod, so that the bow of the arc is underneath and everything is in balance, the smallest movement of the fingers will be sufficient to make the rod rotate upwards. Move the fingers when it is at the top of the arc and it will go back down and will continue to do so as long as appropriate. It is a very slight movement and is hardly noticeable if you are not forewarned.

Not having noticed this little mechanism, M Thouvenel wrote a book on the wand, but M Demours, well known son of an Acedemician, turned the wand in this fashion at a meeting of the Academy of Sciences in order to remove any remaining doubt.

M Needham…even cites some facts against the claims of the wand which are sometimes used by other charlatans. Finally, M Paulet in the Health Gazette, mocked modern physics as we did previously. –Ed]

But whilst M. de Lalande clearly demonstrates that slight muscular action can move the rod, somewhat as Bleton moved it, he does not trouble to make any enquiry on the only point of real value, viz., whether Bleton was more successful in finding underground water than chance or shrewd observation would account for. Nevertheless, the weight of Lalande's authority crushed Thouvenel and his *protégé* Bleton. It was taken as a matter of course that the latter was a clever trickster, who had duped the public. Conjuring books showed how to work the rod *a la Bleton*. A book by H. Decremps, called *La Magie dévoilée*, published in Paris in 1784, devotes a lengthy chapter to this, showing not only how to rotate a slightly curved rod (held as in Fig. 18) by the quivering of the index fingers, but also how a manikin can be made to imitate the search for water in this fashion. This chapter was copied into the *Encyclopédie Méthodique* for 1792, and an English translation of Decremps' book was published in 1785 under the title of *The Conjurer unmasked…with directions for the tricks of the Divining Rod*. But the whirligig of time brings its revenge; Decremps, whose book was all the vogue a century ago, is to-day forgotten, and Bleton is now the subject of scientific study.

The rotation of Bleton's nearly straight rod was no doubt due to the same cause as the twisting of the forked twig of the dowser at the present day, viz., an involuntary muscular movement arising from some sub-conscious suggestion; how he, in common with other dowsers, derived this usually correct suggestion of underground water, when no one else knew of its presence, is the problem that we must consider in the sequel to this paper (see Part XIII.).

Thouvenel gives no picture of Bleton nor of his manner of holding the rod. I have searched through many works in the hope of finding a picture given by some contemporary writer of the use of this curved rod, and at last discovered the accompanying drawing given in the reprint of Amoretti's papers entitled *Rhabdomanzia*, from the copy of the German translation of which, published in 1809 (in the Royal Society Library), Fig. 18 is reproduced. The picture shows the lad Pennet holding the rod as Bleton did, but the rod appears rather larger and more curved than Bleton's rod. Thouvenel, and afterwards Amoretti, experimented with Pennet.

Here I must conclude the report of this remarkable dowser, which has grown to a length much greater than I anticipated. My apology must be that it is the first time a full summary of the evidence has been presented to the English public.

# PART XI

## Involuntary Muscular Action And The Motion Of The Rod, Pendule, Or Other Autoscope. Motor Automatism

### § 1. Evidence as to the Involuntary and Uncontrollable Motion of the Rod

To an onlooker, who sees a dowser at work for the first time, one of the most startling things is the sudden and apparently spontaneous motion of the forked twig, a motion so vigorous that one of the limbs of the twig is frequently broken, whilst the dowser is apparently doing his utmost to restrain its motion. The common explanation of a sceptical public is that this is merely a trick on the dowser's part to mystify his dupes, but the evidence I have adduced, both in the previous and present Report, shows that this view is quite untenable.[1] The only other alternative recognised by scientific men is that the motion of the twig must be caused by some involuntary muscular action on the part of the dowser. It is true Melancthon and the rest of the learned world of the sixteenth century thought that the motion originated in the twig itself, and was a necessary consequence of the "law of sympathy[2]," but the learned Jesuit Father Kircher (one of the founders of experimental science) about the year 1650 showed that the twig itself was inert, and that in some way the motion was communicated from the dowser himself[3] to the forked twig. Malebranche and Lebrun, fifty years after this, urged with resistless logic that the explanation of the divining rod was to be found in the sport of good-natured or mischievous devils, "the badinage of demons "; but whether these philosophers thought the demons got hold of the end of the stick and twisted it, or gave supernormal strength and skill to the dowser, I do not know[4]. This spirit theory, apparently, is the view of some people at the present day. Spirits *may* swarm in the neighbourhood of mediums and dowsers, only it needs a good deal of evidence to prove it, and it will be some time before science will accept any evidence of that kind. Hence the only alternative before us is that some involuntary and more or less unconscious muscular action on the dowser's part causes the twig to turn and sometimes break.

In the previous Report I have discussed this question (see pp. 205 and 206) and shown that the curious muscular spasm, which probably causes the motion of the rod, is certainly involuntary, and,—when the rod is held as some dowsers hold it,—cannot be intentionally imitated by a conscious effort, without considerable skill in legerdemain. To this statement the only criticism I have received is from those who maintain that this is an inadequate explanation, and that the evidence points to some power beyond involuntary muscular action. Here is the view of that distinguished naturalist and acute observer, Dr. A. R. Wallace, F.R.S., who writes to me as follows :—

> If the rod does move wholly by muscular action, it does not at all affect the power of the dowser in finding water, —but the *fact* should be proved. To *me*, the evidence you adduce shows that it is *not* muscular action, and if *this* can be proved it, of course, places the dowser in the rank of a physical "medium," which I have always held him to be. If the two facts you state are *facts*: (1) That the motion of the rod cannot be intentionally produced (by any novice) without *visible* muscular action of an energetic kind; and (2) that in an outsider's hands, holding the rod for the first time, it will often move *if the dowser holds his wrists*, and with no conscious, and little visible, muscular action on the

---

[1] I am referring to honest dowsers; impostors may exist here as elsewhere.
[2] Every age has its fashionable fetishes, or *idola theatri*; this "law of sympathy" was a notable idol of the learned world in the 16th and 17th centuries. The movement of the rod to hidden veins of metal or water was supposed to be due to the "sympathy" between certain kinds of wood and metals, etc.
[3] See Kircher's *Magnes sive de Arte Magnetica* (1640), p. 724, and his later work, *Mundus Subterraneus*, Vol. II., p. 200.
[4] Malebranche refers Lebrun to both St. Augustine and Porphyry in support of his view that the devils cannot be always at work tempting mankind, but must have moments of relaxation like human beings! Hence come their little jokes in table rapping, opening doors, etc., so Porphyry thinks. (See *Lettres qui découvrent l'illusion det philosophes sur la baguette.* Paris, 1693, p. 230, et seq.)

experimenter's part,—then it follows that the motion is *not* produced by *muscular action* at all, but is a physical phenomenon analogous to hundreds of others occurring in the presence of "mediums."

I think you should have said: "The *obvious* explanation, of course, is that the rod is moved by the hands of the operator, acting consciously or unconsciously. There are, however, many difficulties in the way of this view, and many facts which seem directly opposed to it." After which your various statements would follow naturally. Now, they seem to me to be in the nature of a *non sequitur*! . . .

Of course, I am a confirmed lunatic in these matters, so excuse the ravings of a lunatic, but sincere, friend,

Alfred R. Wallace.

All that Mr. Wallace writes is worth attention; it would certainly have been wiser on my part, in the last Report, to have used the words he suggests rather than the more dogmatic phrase I employed. Other correspondents have also urged that muscular action, whether conscious or unconscious, is an insufficient explanation of the phenomena actually observed. In the Journal of the S. P. R. for December, 1897, Mr. E. T. Bennett cites some of the evidence I gave in the previous Report in support of this view. Mr. Bennett urges, with much cogency, that as Faraday's explanation of table-turning being due to involuntary muscular action is now recognised as inadequate to cover all the phenomena of this kind, so in like manner this explanation fails to cover all the cases of the twisting of the divining rod, and hence some other cause, external to the dowser, is probably at work. There is no doubt some force in Mr. Bennett's argument, to which I replied in the same number of the *Journal*.

The descriptions given by different observers are so similar that we may take them as correct, and certainly it would seem that no *conscious* muscular action could produce the effects described. Mr. Bennett (*Journal* S.P.R., December, 1897) therefore asks, "Have we any grounds which justify us in attributing to unconscious muscular action, physical effects which it is beyond the power of conscious muscular action to produce?" My reply is: in hypnosis, somnambulism, hysteria, etc., subjects can perform muscular feats impossible to them in their normal self-conscious state. Whatever tends to concentrate muscular action upon one single dominant idea enables the subject to accomplish what otherwise he could not do. Moreover known causes must be assumed as operative until they are *proved* to be inadequate. The two facts, (1) and (2), named by Mr. A. R. Wallace in his letter, are, however, sometimes disputed, and it is therefore desirable to cite some of the facts already given and add further information, from different witnesses, on these two points.

The violence of the motion of the rod is shown in numerous cases I quoted in the previous Report. Thus on p. 5, Mr. Enys, F.G.S., who is an amateur dowser, states "the rod broke short off in front of my hands, and did so a second time in the same place," i.e., where underground water existed. On p. 17, Miss Grantham (daughter of Judge Grantham), describing what occurred with the Rev. J. Blunt, another amateur dowser, states "so strong was the impulse, that we found unless Mr. B. relaxed his hold, the twig broke off near his fingers." Lady Milbanke, also an amateur dowser, had the same experience, p. 30. Mr. Percy Clive states, on p. 25, that when he held the rod and Mullins put his hands on his wrists, the rod "twisted round in my hands with such force that when I held it tight it broke." Mr. Cecil Woolley, of Lincoln, the agent to Trinity College, Cambridge, states, on p. 198, that the late J. Mullins having gone over the ground and indicated water in one spot, "I took the twig in my own hands and went over the same spot with no result. He (J. Mullins) then took hold of my wrists without touching the twig himself and when we together walked over the same place, the twig turned up in my hands. This was, I suppose, caused by muscular action on my part, but if so, it was certainly, as far as I was concerned, perfectly unconscious action. My mental attitude was one of neutrality!" Lord Burton makes a very similar statement, p. 80. Mr. Budd, a geologist, describes what occurred with Mullins when he came over underground water at Waterford. He writes, p. 87, "Mullins held the forked twig between his second and third fingers as if you were going to write, the point of the fork downwards. At No. 1 [i.e., over the spot where a large supply of underground water was found] the point lifted itself up, until it turned over backwards and twisted itself until it broke . . . The clerks then held [another forked

## The Credibility Of Dowsing

twig] with him, and held his hands; always the same effect." In another place, seeing the frantic motion of the twig when Mullins came over underground water, a gentleman tried to stop its motion by gripping the twig in two places with smiths' tongs, "one pair securing the tips and the other the fork, but the contortions still went on between the points held," p. 66, and so on.

In the present Report numerous independent witnesses of unimpeachable integrity and some with high scientific attainments testify to the same class of facts, viz. :—(1) the automatic and apparently irresistible motion of the twig in the hands often of a complete novice, and (2) that, when the forked twig does not move in a person's hands, if the dowser takes one limb of the twig, or even places his hand on the wrist of the insensitive person, the previously inert twig now turns vigorously and often breaks in two in the effort to resist its motion. As regards (1), see the letter from the President of the Royal Geologicaj Society of Cornwall on p. 303, who states that the clerk of his Parish Council, on finding the rod suddenly twist in his hands, called out, "It is alive, sir, it is alive!" Mr. Enys adds: "This exactly describes the sensation when the rod moves." Mr. Dixon, a large fruit-grower in California, on p. 327 states: "I held the stick as tight as I could to prevent its moving, but it twisted right round." Mr. Denison, of the Toronto Meteorological Observatory, on p. 292, gives a careful record of the violent twisting of a forked plum stick or bent wire used as a divining rod by an amateur dowser. Mr. Bennett, of Oxford, on p. 268, refers to the frantic motion and ultimate breaking of the twig "held firmly" in the dowser's hands. Other similar cases will have been noted by the careful reader. As regards (2), see Mr. Morton's letter to *The Engineer* given on p. 264; Mr. Morton found the rod would not move in his hands, but when the late John Mullins, the dowser, "laid his hands on my wrists and grasped them firmly, then the twig instantly began to turn and continued turning till he removed his hands. He never touched the twig while it was in my hands." Mr. Montague Price, in his letter on p. 272, states :—

> I held one side of the forked rod myself and the "diviner" the other, and when we came to water [alleged underground water] the strain was so great on my fingers I was obliged to ask him to stop. From the position of the rod it was absolutely impossible for him to produce the pressure, which increased with the strength of the stream.

Mr. Denison, of Toronto, states, on p. 292, that his friend "Mrs. Harris tried without any result; but when Mr. H. [who was an amateur dowser] grasped her wrists, as she approached the spring, the rod turned forcibly," and so on.

The usual practice, after watching a dowser at work, is for some of the onlookers to try if the forked twig will move in their hands. Generally speaking, one or more, out of perhaps ten or twelve persons, discover to their astonishment that the twig curls up in their hands at the same places at which it did with the dowser. Here is such an experience. Mrs. Hollands writes to me as follows :—

Dene Park, Tonbridge, *October 9th*, 1899.

> In answer to your note of inquiry about the divining rod, the whole thing is rather a long story, but the practical result of the water dowser's visit was to find water which now supplies the house. One of my daughters found she had the strange power which moves the divining rod, and it works for her now quickly over any spring. It is most interesting, as you can feel the rod if you take one side of it and take one of her hands, she holding the other end of the rod—it struggles up, and would break off altogether if you did not allow it to move. My daughter has since found several springs on the estate, where we have sunk wells. They have stood us in very good stead these last dry seasons.

Minnie Hollands.

A similar experience is given by Miss M. Craigie Halkett, who published some excellent photographs of a dowser at work in *Sketch* for August 23rd, 1899. Miss Halkett writes to me as follows :—

## Prof. W. F. Barrett

Lauriston, New Eltham, Kent, *September 8th,* 1899.

The man depicted in the photographs is not a water-finder by profession. He is a tenant farmer residing at Catcott, a village near Bridgwater, and merely exercises the art to oblige his neighbours. Several of the country people in this neighbourhood (Somerset) have the gift. It has never been known to fail.

Personally, I was rather sceptical on the subject, but was converted by the stick turning in my hands when standing over a spring. There were about six persons present at the time; all tried it, but it would turn for no one excepting the man in the picture and myself. I experienced a sort of tingling sensation in my arms and wrists, but otherwise was quite unaware when the forked stick began to turn, it seemed to go over so quickly.

Maude Craigie Halkett.

Miss Halkett does not say how she knew she was "standing over a spring" when the twig turned in her hands: this statement is very characteristic of many others that have reached me.

I received the following from a Civil Engineer, Mr. J. W. Parry, who also sent me an interesting article he had written on water-finding, which appeared in the *Pioneer* of India :—

19, Southmoor Road, Oxford, *November 2nd,* 1898.

I have read with much interest your work on "dowsing " in the Psychical Research Society. I was a sceptic, but after reading the 140 cases you mention, it is quite impossible to doubt any longer. I was lately at Padstow, Cornwall, where the following authenticated case occurred which you might like to verify.

It appears a dowser was lately sent for, as some waterworks were projected. The squire, Mr. Prideaux-Brune, and his two daughters came to see the operations of the divining rod. On a spot being indicated by the dowser, one of the young ladies said, "Oh! let me see if I can do it." Unfortunately, she had not the gift, nor had her sister. Squire Prideaux-Brune, then taking the twig, walked back a few paces. On passing the spot his arms shook violently, and would not be controlled. The young ladies were laughingly sceptical, and said, "Oh! papa, you are humbugging." He replied, "I am doing nothing of the kind, and can't help my arms shaking," or words to that effect.

You do not mention any cases as occurring in India, where there is a a good deal of so-called divining. I have seen diviners lying naked with their ears to the ground, pretending that they could hear the subterranean water. Don't you think that's somewhat beyond our ken, even though the Asiatic has marvellously sensitive organs of hearing on certain occasions?

J. W. Parry,<br>Late Executive Engineer, Indian State Railways.

I wrote to Mr. Prideaux-Brune, who is a Deputy-Lieutenant and J.P. for the county, and received the following reply:—

Prideaux Place, Padstow, Cornwall, *February 17th,* 1899.

Some months ago Messrs. Merryweather sent a diviner here, so I witnessed his extraordinary powers. I myself manifested a slight power, and when the diviner held my wrists it was intensified—one man,

# *The Credibility Of Dowsing*

a non-believer, was as successful as the diviner. Another man attempted, and was not in the slightest degree affected, even when the diviner held his wrists. A very strong man tried to wrest this rod from the diviner's hands without success, and, finally, in the struggle the rod broke. In my own case I felt the muscles in my arm between the hand and the elbow for a day or two affected in the same way as if I had a slight electric shock.

Charles G. Prideaux-Brune.

In this case, as in the former, there is no evidence to show that the involuntary motion of the "rod" had any connection with the nearness of underground water.

I will now cite some evidence that shows (1) how little visible muscular action there is when the twig moves in the hands of a dowser; e.g., Mr. A. Lang says (see below) he "could detect no muscular action;" and further (2) how the amateur in whose hands the twig turns believes he is exerting his will and muscular force to prevent its motion.

In *Longman's Magazine* (November, 1897) Mr. A. Lang writes:—

> I have thrice been with amateurs, in whose hands a twig twisted over subterranean water. One was a very learned professor of the Greek language, who, having seen the thing done by a water-finder, found that he had the same faculty. The second was a land bailiff, who had discovered his gift in the same way, and employed it for his own purposes on his employer's estate.
>
> ... The third was a lady, whose mother had the faculty, and found her own well by using it. I tried, in company with each of the three. With the two men I failed—my twig would not turn where theirs turned. It did twist where the lady's twisted, and the sensation was curious ["just as if the rod were alive," Mr. Lang adds in writing to me]; but I am inclined to fancy that the mere resistance and spring of the wood caused it to jerk itself upward at one spot, though I cannot say why it failed to do so at other spots. The bailiff tried holding my wrists while I held the twig, but without effect. I held his fingers, when the twig writhed in his hands, but could detect no muscular action on his part. In no case did we dig, or make any attempt to find water where the twigs twisted; all we were able to do was to examine the action of the twig; active at certain spots, passive at others. The forked twig is so held that you resist its natural spring. Of course, no twig at all is used by some water-finders, who rely on their sensations merely, and speak of the twig as a mere index or stage property.
>
> In Sir Herbert Maxwell's pleasant book of sport and natural history, *Memories of the Months*, is an account of experiments with Mullins, a professional, and not a man of education. Mullins had worked at Middleton, and Lord Jersey "had been not only gratified, but astonished at his success." Experiments were next made at Osterley, before scientific characters ... Mullins's rod, in this case, "twisted so violently that, when he held it tight, it broke in his hand." He said that he had a shivering along his spine on these occasions. When he stood on a plate of thick glass the rod did not twist, which he attributed to the non-conducting of electricity. An uneducated man always chatters about electricity. The glass acted, if at all, by way of negative "suggestion." Mullins was then blindfolded, but here Sir James Crichton-Browne objected that the blindfolding was inadequate. The researches of the Psychical Society have proved (in other experiments) that practically no blindfolding is adequate, or, at least, is beyond suspicion. Sir James wanted to introduce cotton wool. Mullins said, "Don't you believe my word?" Sir James replied, "I believe nothing but what I see" (not a very scientific posture, I fear), and Mullins would not play any longer. He was an uneducated man; he did not understand the position; he took Sir James's agnosticism as a personal affront, and so the matter ended. Nevertheless, Sir Herbert says, "were I in straits to find water, I should employ without hesitation a professional water-finder—rod and all—if there remains one as successful as Mullins was."

Practically the dowser finds water in a paying ratio of successes over failures. How he finds it he probably does not know himself. I do not doubt that the rod is wagged (where the finder is honest) by unconscious muscular action, as in "table-turning." So we are left at large in that cheerful and luminous field of inquiry, the Philosophy of the Unconscious, or Subconscious. Some indication, through the normal senses perhaps, or through some unexplored sense, reaches the successful finder, and, unconsciously obedient to this hint, he unconsciously uses his muscles and wags the stick. I conceive that to be the humour of it, but a large number of experiments is needed before one can even raise a good presumption in favour of the hypothesis.

The following letter which Dr. Hodgson has sent me is an illustration of the involuntary and apparently uncontrollable motion of the rod in the hands of a mining engineer, who tried it for the first time:—

350, East 69th Street, New York, *July 23rd*, 1892.

I see a paper on the divining rod in Vol. II. of your Proceedings, and would bring to your notice a curious experience of mine with regard to this which I published in the *Engineering and Mining Journal* of December 9th, 1876, which created quite a discussion in that journal.

"I was much interested in that part of a lecture on Mining by Professor W. Smyth, F.R.S., of the Royal School of Mines, London, relating to the use of the divining rod for finding mineral veins or subterranean springs of water, and published in your journal of September 9th. Because a reason cannot be given for an alleged phenomenon is no cause why it should not exist, or if existing, why it should not be inquired into. Most of the discoveries of science would not have been made, had inexplicable phenomena been set aside as being unworthy of attention because no reason could be given for them at the time when first observed.

"I have heard of the Cornish Witch-hazel from my childhood, but always thought it a fable till one day in the woods of Pennsylvania one of my men mentioned that springs could be found by means of a forked switch of any kind of fresh cut hard wood. I laughed at the idea, but he insisted, so I made a trial by standing astride a small brook, one branch of the fork in each hand, the stem standing out horizontally. What was my amazement to find that the latter bent slowly down with a force I was entirely unable to counteract. The experiment was quite sufficient to make me credit all that had been attested of the divining rod, though I have never tried it over mineral veins.

"Professor Smyth says that all persons are not able to produce the effect, which may very well be, just as Spiritualists pretend that some persons are naturally more adapted to act as mediums than others. And may not the power exerted by them on chairs and tables have some connection with the force manifested by means of the divining rod? Unless, indeed, the force which makes the twig bend be caused by the vital power of the person holding it. These, however, are the very questions to be solved, should a competent person take them up.

"I am glad to see that so distinguished a man as Professor Smyth has the courage to assert his belief in what it is the fashion to consider as an exploded fallacy by persons who have never tried it or made proper inquiries regarding it."

That some unknown force is at work I am confident. It seems melancholy that the very men who pooh-pooh such phenomena merely because they cannot explain them, are of the class generally called scientific.

D. Coghlan.

# The Credibility Of Dowsing

Dr. Hodgson wrote to Mr. Coghlan suggesting that unconscious muscular action was the probable cause of the motion of the rod; Mr. Coghlan replies as follows:—

350, East 69th Street, New York, *July 29th*, 1892.

> Your favour of yesterday received. In answer to your suggestion that my own unconscious muscular force caused the bending of the rod, I can answer decisively, No!
>
> When I said to my informant regarding the phenomenon that I could by my muscular exertion prevent the bending, he expressed the situation forcibly by saying the bark of the twig would be first twisted off. Of course in this he exaggerated, but still it expressed, rather forcibly to be sure, the tendency of the twig's point downwards. The switch is held with the palms of the hand turned upward and the branches of the fork grasped firmly, the main stem projecting horizontally. I cannot conceive how any unconscious muscular action could cause the horizontal stem to become vertical, which position is attained by a twisting of the fibres of the wood.
>
> I have lately tried the same experiment under what I considered similar circumstances, but failed completely, whether owing to the wood used not being of the proper kind, (for you may remember that in Cornwall they suppose the witch-hazel the proper thing to use in searching for mineral veins), or whether owing to decay of nervous power on my part through age, I cannot tell.
>
> D. Coghlan.

The opinion so emphatically expressed by Mr. Coghlan, that the motion of the rod was *not* due to any muscular action, conscious or unconscious, on his part is shared by nearly all who find the rod twist in their hands. Here, for example, is one of numerous instances I might cite. In a letter published in the *Standard* newspaper for January 2nd, 1889, Mr. W. Bell, of East-Lyss, Petersfield, states that after seeing a dowser at work, he tried the forked twig himself and to his utter amazement, when he came near the spot at which the twig moved with the dowser, he saw the point bend forward and then it suddenly turned down towards the ground as he crossed the spot. He adds:—

> Some force independent of my will, and acting contrary to my muscular resistance, drew the point of the twig towards the earth. Of this I am as firmly convinced as I am that the sun rose yesterday. It was not a matter in which I could have been self-deceived, and the same effects could not be produced by trickery [voluntary effort is no doubt meant].

In the same number of the *Standard* a professional dowser, J. Blanchard, of Wisbech, writes to say that he has "proved the rod is not moved by the involuntary action of mental expectancy on the muscles of the performer" (!), by putting on a pair of gloves, when the rod ceases to move. No doubt the rod would be more difficult to manipulate, whether voluntarily or otherwise, with gloves on. But all these results, however, like the standing on insulating supports, etc., are mainly due to what Mr. A. Lang, in the passage just quoted, calls "negative suggestion." That is to say, anything which gives rise to a sub-conscious suggestion determines the motion or arrest of the rod.

In connection with this I may cite the distinguished anthropologist, Dr. E. B. Tylor, F.R.S., who, in a lecture delivered at Oxford in 1883, relates his experience with the divining rod as follows:—

> "I happened to be staying at a friend's house in the Mendip district, where it [the divining-rod] is still used by well-sinkers and miners, and at my request a regular practitioner was sent for. ... It does not appear that he fraudulently moves the rod, but my sensations led me to agree with Chevreul that the slight movements of the hands are unconsciously guided to accumulate into impulses sufficient to cause the twig to dip or rise. I noticed that when I could allow my attention to stray, the rod would from time to time move in my hands in a way so lifelike that an uneducated person might well suppose the movement to be spontaneous. It is hardly necessary to say that the rod always moves

where the bearer's mind suggests an object." [Dr. Tylor then gives an amusing illustration on this point: the dowser having stated the rod always moved when he reached the main spring underground, the rod also moved over a watch, the dowser suggesting that it did so because it was over the mainspring of the watch; his mind, Dr. Tylor remarks, being controlled by the verbal association into a delusive analogy of effects] (*Nature*, May 17th, 1883, p. 58).

## § 2. Evidence that the Motion of the Rod is due to Unconscious Muscular Action

We will now pass on to evidence which shows that the motion of the rod is really due to the muscular action of the dowser, notwithstanding that there are certain positions in which the rod is held where it seems to be impossible for the dowser to move it. Such, for example, as that shown in the plate on page 134, in my previous Report [p. 109 this volume - Ed], where the dowser, Stone, is shown holding a thick forked rod depending from the forefinger, second finger, and thumb of each hand. Mr. Stone himself asserts that there is no movement of his fingers, and that he holds the rod in this way because it cannot be moved by the dowser; but a careful eye-witness, Mr. R. J. Charleton, writes to me as follows :—

> I must contradict the assertion that no movement of Mr. Stone's fingers could be detected whilst he is using the divining rod. I watched him most closely, and distinctly noticed that his forefingers, second fingers and thumbs, between which he held the ends of the forked stick, were strongly compressed upon the pliant wood. At the same time there was an inward twisting action of the fingers which had the effect of raising the apex of the rod. Tremendous muscular force was apparently being used, to such an extent, in fact, that the operator's hands became quite swollen and tremulous when he had completed his experiments. I have myself been able to verify this explanation in my own person repeatedly, though I could not move such thick twigs as Mr. Stone employs, but his muscular development is greater than mine and he is in constant practice.

I, too, watched Mr. Stone carefully in his use of the forked rod. In the Carrigoona experiments, the sudden *leaping up*, as it were, of the twig when Mr. Stone came to the position No. 1 in Fig. 3 was most remarkable, the more so considering the way the twig was held. There was evidently some muscular spasm, as Mr. Charleton says, but it was obviously involuntary, and neither I nor a friend who was with me could imitate the action by any conscious exertion on our part.

But perhaps the best testimony is afforded by the following letter I received from Mr. J. F. Young, of Llanelly, a most successful amateur dowser, animated by a truly scientific spirit. Mr. Young was at first inclined to think that the movement of the rod was entirely spontaneous and quite independent of the dowser, but after I had drawn his attention to the matter, he writes as follows: "I see that the motion of the rod, which is always held in tension by the water-finder, is really due to unconscious muscular action; this is specially noticeable with a watch-spring which I generally employ. In fact, I am so convinced in this matter, after endless experiments, that I defy any one to prove the contrary." A Somersetshire incumbent, writing in *Notes and Queries*,[1] gives corroborative testimony, and states that, when holding the rod in the same way as the professional dowser he employed, "the harder I grasped the stick to prevent it turning, the more it turned, till at last it broke in two, and hurt the hand that held it."

But this is no new explanation of the motion of the rod, for the fullest and best account of its motion,—based upon experimental evidence,—is given by the American writer to whom I have already referred, Mr. Emerson, in the pages of the *American Journal of Science (Silliman's Journal)* for 1826. The writer shows how startling and apparently miraculous is the sudden motion of the rod, in the hands of a good water-finder,—and remarks, if there be a fraud, the diviners are themselves the dupes. It is true, he goes on to say, that nearly every one can urge it to turn in a fashion, but only in the hands of a very few does it move, not only without urging, but contrary to their best efforts.

---

[1] Series 1, Vol. X. (1854), p. 155.

## *The Credibility Of Dowsing*

He himself tried again and again, but failed. At last, one day, watching a young and successful diviner, he noticed the peculiar spirit and air of determination with which he handled the rod.

> Hoping to catch his lively manner [Mr. Emerson says] I took the rod and tried my hand again. When I got to the bank of the rivulet the rod began to move, and I could not restrain it. He who for the first time in his life has received an electric shock will recognise the sensation which I experienced when I felt the limbs of the rod crawling round, and saw the point turning down in spite of every effort my clenched hands could make to restrain it. In this contest between myself and the rod the bark was stripped off the twig. The secret appeared to be to hold the rod in a spirited manner [by this he apparently means a determined and confident, not a weak and hesitating, manner], for since then the rod has never failed to move in my hands, nor in the hands of those I have instructed.

Mr. Emerson then gives directions how to hold the rod in order to exhibit its startling motion; if the diviner releases his firm grasp, he goes on to say :—

> The rod can no more turn than an unbent bow can throw an arrow. By grasping the forked rod smartly the bow is strained and then if the rod be pliant and the hands moist, it will creep round slowly and mysteriously. But if the rod be large, its motion when smartly bent may become ungovernable. The direction of the motion of the rod forwards or backwards depends on whether the wrists are allowed to turn to their natural position or are slightly more strained outwards.

Two large goose quills tied together at their tips, or two pieces of whalebone similarly fastened and held as a divining rod, Mr. Emerson found to work quite as well, or even better, than a forked twig. This part of Mr. Emerson's paper is excellent, but of course explains nothing more than the apparently spontaneous and vigorous motion of the rod.[1]

Professor Wadsworth, of Michigan University, has recently published a letter in *Nature*[2] giving a similar explanation of the motion of the twig to that given by Emerson seventy years previously. It is amusing to see how entirely ignorant of the whole subject are many scientific men who are ready to instruct us. Professor Wadsworth says, in concluding his letter :—

> The whole secret of the divining-rod seems to lie in its position in the hands of the operator, and in his voluntarily or involuntarily increasing the closeness of his grasp on the two ends of the branches forming the fork. If the foregoing conditions are fulfilled, the twig will always bend down— water or no water, mineral or no mineral. Any one can be an operator, and any material can be used for the instrument, provided the limbs forming the fork are sufficiently tough and flexible.

As I have said, any one can twist the rod if it is held in a particular manner, but I am afraid Professor Wadsworth's contribution can hardly be said to have solved "the whole secret of the divining rod."

Just as a pen or pencil registers *conscious acts* of the brain by small muscular motions of the fingers, so the divining rod indicates *sub-conscious* acts of the brain by small and usually involuntary and insensible muscular motions on the

---

[1] Mr. Thos. Blashill, F.R.I.B.A. (late superintendent architect of the London County Council) has sent me a lengthy and careful analysis of the illustrations given in my previous Report, showing the method of holding the rod, and he concludes that, "In every case in which the rod is shown in the hands of the water-finder, while he is actually searching for water, the two prongs of the fork are bent, sometimes slightly but often very considerably," and he infers that this bending accounts for the motion of the rod. No doubt a considerable strain is put on the forked rod by some professional dowsers, but not by all; the explanation of the motion of the rod is not quite so easy as Mr. Blashill and others who have not themselves seen it in use imagine. Even Mr. Emerson's and Mr. Young's statement that the rod is always held in a state of strain is not invariably true. Moreover the rod used by Bleton and others a century ago simply rested on the two forefingers: we shall deal with this in the sequel.

[2] "A Mechanical Theory of the Divining Rod," *Nature*, January 6th, 1858,

part of the so-called diviner. It is not necessary to call the man who writes or who reads a letter "a diviner," though he is so in a sense, and it is equally unnecessary to call a man "a diviner" who employs a forked stick to indicate the twitching of the muscles of his lower arm. Though the honest dowser himself declares he does not move the forked twig, this is simply a proof that the motion is to him both involuntary and unconscious. It is needless to labour this point, but it may be worth while to dispose of it once for all.

How, ask several correspondents, can a man move a stick, the motion of which he is consciously resisting ? The muscles, it is urged, cannot simultaneously be doing opposite things. It certainly looks mysterious, but it is not really so to the trained physiologist. Through the kindness of my friend, Dr. Purser, Professor of Physiology at Trinity College, Dublin, I have been able to have this question tested in the person of an amateur dowser, an Irish gentleman, to whom I have already referred, Mr. J. H. Jones, who was good enough to allow himself to be made the subject of experiment in the grounds of Trinity College, Dublin. Dr. Purser subsequently wrote to me as follows :—

T. C. D. , *December 19th*, 1897

> The interview with Mr. Jones was held under rather unfavourable circumstances, owing to the storm, but I think I was able to see the movement by which the turning of the stick is effected. .
>
> The movements by which the stick is turned are :—(1) A rotation of the forearms, or one of them; (2) a flexion of the inner fingers, by which the stick is made a lever of the first order with very short distance between the fulcrum and the power, or perhaps a lever of the third order. It was impossible to follow the movements when the stick was rapidly twirled, or when Mr. Jones walked rapidly and the rod suddenly turned and he said: "There is water here." But when he stood over the place where he said underground water existed, and professed to struggle against the motion of the stick, the movement was evident, and I had no difficulty in imitating the movements myself, although, of course, not so dexterously as Mr. Jones did. As to whether the movements are conscious or unconscious I cannot express any opinion,—but that the stick is moved by the muscles of the arm and not by any occult influence cannot be doubted, I think, by any reasonable being.
>
> F. Purser.

To the lay reader, no doubt, there is considerable difficulty in understanding how this explanation covers all the facts, if such cases as those I have quoted earlier are correctly described. The breaking of the forked twig can only be accomplished by a rigid grasp of one of the forks, and a rotation of the twig by the hand holding the other fork. This is probably what occurs;—the skill and strength required to do this, without much visible motion of the hand, being as much beyond the conscious effort of the dowser as the feats of a somnambulist or hypnotised person are beyond the power of the same person in his normal state; and the physiological explanation is probably much the same in the two cases, namely, an automatic concentration and discharge of most of the available nervous energy of the individual into one narrow channel. Only a trained anatomist is competent to give an opinion on this question, for he knows which muscles to observe, whilst the startling effects of autosuggestion are well known to physiologists.

In support of this view I will here quote an extract from the report of a small committee who, in 1894, critically examined a dowser at work. The committee of investigation consisted of the pathologist and the assistant physician of one of the Bristol hospitals, Mr. Mole, F.R.C.S., and Dr. F. H. Edgeworth,—the latter having made neurology a special study—and the Rev. R. A. Chudleigh, of West Parley Rectory, Wimborne, Dorset. Mr. Chudleigh, who acted as reporter, though not an M.D., has made a life-long study of both physiology and pathology.[1] The committee were therefore well qualified. They were fortunate in securing the co-operation of a skilful amateur dowser, who placed himself, as well as his estate (on the border of the Mendips), entirely at their service. In the course of a lengthy report, Mr. Chudleigh says: "If there be one thing which is perfectly clear, it is that the movement of the wand is

---

[1] I have since had a considerable correspondence with the Rev. Mr. Chudleigh, and have been much struck with his true scientific habit of mind and wide range of knowledge.

# The Credibility Of Dowsing

due to an unconscious muscular contraction, just like other muscular contractions, except that it is unconscious." Albeit, he goes on to say, "The violent tremor which convulsed the over-strained arm is itself enough to suggest witchcraft to an ordinary spectator, and yet I am sure that it is nothing more than what is known as *muscle-clonus*." Anatomical reasons are then given to account for the sudden violent motion of the rod, and the report continues: "A precisely analogous phenomenon is seen in those cases where a spinal wound or a spinal poison throws the whole body into universal spasm; but the flexors master the extensors and the back muscles overpower the front ones, the result being the frightful and well-known pose called *opisthotonus*." The writer then points out that the sudden spontaneous tension of the muscles of the arms which occur when the dowser believes himself to be over a spring is probably due to auto-suggestion; "this auto-suggestion makes a diviner positively tetanic when he knows or thinks that water is present."[1] The symptoms described in the foregoing were more strikingly exhibited by the late Mr. W. Scott Lawrence than by most other dowsers; a vivid description is given by an eye-witness on p. 69 of the previous Report [p. 53 this volume - Ed].[2]

Severe muscular spasm, as is well known, can be caused by suggestion in hypnotic subjects. In Hittell's *Somnambulism and Cramp*, New York, 1860, muscular contractions are described as caused by auto-suggestion—e.g., "If Miss A. ventured to eat with a silver spoon, the muscles of the mouth soon became rigid, etc." Every physician is acquainted with cases where often alarming muscular spasm, as of the glottis, is due to purely *ideomotor* action. "The idea of a particular motion," as the physiologist Müller long ago remarked, "determines the current of nervous action towards the necessary muscles, and gives rise to the motion independently of the will." Dr. Edgeworth sends me an instance of this under his care at the Bristol Infirmary. He writes:—

> A man who had an affection of the spinal cord was given mercury by injections into his arm. His legs (the part affected) got well, but he developed the idea that his arm had been poisoned, and as a result has a hysterical paralysis of the injected arm. These auto-suggestions are very difficult to remove. ... In my opinion they afford an explanation of the motion of the "divining rod."
>
> F. H. Edgeworth.

## § 3. Consideration of Bleton's Motor-Automatism

It may be argued by some readers that the foregoing explanation of the motion of the forked twig cannot apply to the singular and rapid rotation of the slightly curved rod used by Bleton. Certainly the facts, as carefully narrated by Dr. Thouvenel on pp. 53-76 of his first *Mémoire*, were very curious and are worth attention.

In the first place it is wholly improbable that the rotation of Bleton's *baguette*, any more than the twisting of the forked twig by the dowsers of to-day, was due to any *conscious* muscular effort on the part of the *sourcier* or water-finder. In fact, if the reader will try to rotate a slightly curved stick resting on his forefingers, as shown in Fig. 18, p. 344, he will realise how difficult it is to accomplish, keeping, withal, his hands and arms as far as possible motionless. But difficult as it is to imitate this motion, it is not *impossible*, as Lalande showed in the passage I have quoted on p. 343, though I have no doubt the attempt to imitate the rotation was a very clumsy one. For the effects of involuntary muscular action are surprisingly difficult to imitate by voluntary effort. That some muscular action really took place on Bleton's part is seen from Thouvenel's own admission, opposed as he was to this idea. On p. 114 of his first Mémoire, he says, in a passage I will translate :—

---

[1] See *Farm and Home*, May, 1894, p. 132.

[2] When Lawrence came over a place where he asserted an underground spring existed—and which proved true on sinking a well at the spot,—the writer states:— "I can only describe the antics of that twig as a pitched battle between itself and him! It twisted, it knocked about, it contracted and contorted the muscles of his hands and arms, it wriggled, and fought, and kicked, until it snapped in two—and then—what made it painful to watch until I got used to it, the old man reeled, and clutched hold of any one nearest to him for a few moments. It evidently exhausts him very much, though afterwards I asked him what effect it had on him, and he said it only made his heart beat most violently."— *Letter to Mr. W. Whitaker, F.R.S.*

> I have perceived several times that the approach of the arms and a certain *tour de main* on the part of the *sourier* [Bleton] contributed to give the baguette its first impulse of rotation over feeble springs.

It is true that he does not notice this at other times: but a careful observer (M. le Comte de M ) quoted by Thouvenel on p. 188 of his Mémoire, says :—

> I have reason to suspect that [the motion of] the baguette is a little aided by an almost insensible movement of the shoulder.

Albeit the Count himself tried without success to turn the baguette at a spot where it moved with Bleton. Thouvenel tells us Bleton judged with singular accuracy of the volume of the hidden spring by the rate of rotation of the baguette, as well as by the violence of the convulsive movements of his body which simultaneously occurred.[1]

Furthermore, he was able to judge of the *depth* of the spring in the following manner: on leaving the spot beneath which he alleged water was to be found, the baguette ceased to turn, but when he had gone a certain distance the baguette suddenly gave a single rotation in the *opposite* direction. The distance at which this occurred from the spot at which it stopped turning was, according to Bleton, the approximate depth of the spring. The results given in the depositions quoted by Thouvenel show that Bleton was usually fairly correct in his estimate of the depth when it did not exceed 30 ft.; beyond that he did not profess to be able to judge. One witness, however, states that even at small depths Bleton was often at fault.

The rate of rotation and the retrograde as well as the direct motion of the baguette were no doubt simply ideomotor phenomena, the result of an involuntary muscular effort prompted by some autosuggestion. The difficulty here, as elsewhere in our inquiry, is to trace the genesis of this probably subconscious suggestion.

## § 4. Apparent Transmission of Motor-Automatism from a Sensitive to an Insensitive Person

There is, however, another problem connected with the motion of the rod which we must not pass over, and that is, the remarkable fact so frequently noticed that when the dowser lays hold of the wrist or hand of a person with whom the rod will not turn, the twig instantly moves. I have quoted numerous instances of this from excellent witnesses on pp. 347 and 348. This apparent transmission of the power of involuntary muscular action was noticed by Thouvenel to occur with Bleton a hundred years ago. On p. 59 of his *Mémoire* Thouvenel says that, when Bleton placed his fingers on the hand of a person with whom the baguette would not turn, then the rod instantly rotated when they approached an underground spring. M. le Comte de M , whom I quoted just now, states that, whilst the baguette would not move in his hands, yet when Bleton held them the rod then began to turn, much to his astonishment. A few years later Amoretti independently discovered the same thing when Pennet touched his hands. He states the rod then turned against his (Amoretti's) will whenever he stood over veins of metal. I have referred to this on p. 363. Compare this with the similar experience (only with a forked rod) described by a mechanical engineer, Mr. Morton, given on p. 172 of the present Report [p.348 this volume - Ed], or with the precisely corresponding experience of an able lawyer (the land agent to Trinity College, Cambridge), Mr. Woolley, given on p. 347.

There can, therefore, be no doubt about this curious fact, which seems to occur most conspicuously only with notable dowsers, such as Bleton and the late J. Mullins. What is the explanation of it? I expect it will be found not in the transmission of any voluntary or involuntary motion from the sensitive to the insensitive person, but in the transmission of a suggestion to the latter. If so, any mode of impressing such a suggestion would do as well, if it be

---

[1] I have mentioned already (p. 331) that the motion of the rod with Bleton (as with some dowsers of to-day) was subsidiary to the convulsive spasm and malaise which he experienced, when, as he alleged, an underground spring existed beneath.

emphatic and indirect. The charming away of warts, of which we have such striking and well authenticated instances, is a case where any kind of indirect suggestion will do, if it be strongly impressed on the recipient.[1]

And by the word suggestion is meant, as Professor Pierre Janet defines it, *the influence which one person exercises upon another independently of the voluntary consent of the subject.*[2] That is to say, certain individuals will submit to a foreign influence and obey it, without having consented or intended to obey and without even knowing they were obeying. Now the influence of suggestion is most strikingly seen in these involuntary or automatic phenomena, and cases analogous to the apparent transmission of the motion of the *baguette* from one person to another occur with the *pendule* and in the so-called *willing game*. If one person, A, finds the *pendule* will not oscillate in his hands and another, B, finds it does oscillate freely with him, then when B clasps the free hand of A, the *pendule* now oscillates for A or the direction of the oscillation can be instantly changed by C clasping B's free hand, and again changed if D clasps C's other hand and so on through a large circle; B, C, and D desiring the change to occur. Again, in the "willing game," I found in 1879 that

> The intervention of a second person (who was ignorant of what had to be done) between the willer and the subject, the hands of each resting on the shoulders of the one in front, did not seriously interfere with the result attained.[3]

Furthermore, with a sensitive subject, if the operator or willer merely placed three fingers lightly on the back of the subject's head, the latter would write correctly words known only to the operator, even if Greek words and characters were used, though the subject knew nothing of Greek.[4] Professor Janet gives a simpler case where the operator holds the left hand of the subject and the latter with his right hand writes the words known only to the operator.[5]

If we admit telepathy, i.e., true thought-transference, as a *vera causa*, no doubt it plays an important part in many of these phenomena of suggestion, and my original object in 1879, when making the experiments I have described, was to show that the theory of the transmission of an idea by involuntary muscular action had to be pushed to such a grotesque extent that it became easier to believe in a purely mental, rather than in a muscular transmission of the suggestion made by the operator. Whichever view is taken, the important part played by suggestion in all these phenomena is unquestionable, and it was to this fact I drew the attention of psychologists, I believe for the first time, in a paper read before the British Association so long ago as 1876.[6]

## § 5. Historical Note

In concluding this part we should not forget that one of the first scientific men in this century who drew attention to the varied effects of involuntary muscular action was Chevreul. In his work on the divining rod (*La Baguette Divinatoire*, Paris, 1854), Chevreul shows how the rod may be moved in this way. The principle which Chevreul enunciates, and which he maintains accounts for many diverse phenomena, is one with which we are now of course perfectly familiar; he thus expresses it:—

---

[1] See Journal S.P.R., Vol. VIII. (1897-98), pp. 7, 40, 96, etc., also an admirable work by Miss Feilding on *Faith-Healing*, Chaps. I. and IV. (Duckworth and Co., 1899). In hypnosis a *direct* suggestion appears effective, whereas in the normal state an *indirect* suggestion seems most potent. e.g., touching or stroking the warts, tying a thread round the wrist, etc. But why is it that only *some* persons have this suggestive power? Is it the faith of the charmer in his remedy or the faith of the patient? And why is *faith*, with its necessary self-surrender, the nexus between the conscious and the sub-conscious life? the powers of the latter being so miraculous, because so foreign to the former.
[2] *L'Automatisme Psychologique*, by Professor Pierre Janet, p. 140; see also *Les Suggestions Hypnotiques*, by Professor Paul Janet.
[3] *Proceedings* S.P.R., 1882, Vol. I., p. 50.
[4] Ibid., p. 51.
[5] *L'Automatisme Psychologique*, p. 373. Paris, 1889.
[6] Printed in *Proceedings* S.P.R. for 1882, Vol. I., p. 240.

## *Prof. W. F. Barrett*

> Le développement on nous d'une action musculaire qui n'est pas le produit d'une volonté, mais le résultat d'une *pensée* qui se porte sur un phénomène du monde exterieur, sans préoccupation de l'action musculaire indispensable à la manifestation du phénomène, va servir de centre de railliement aux faits disseminés; je le désignerai par l'expression de *principe du pendule explorateur*.[1]
>
> [Translation – The development of a muscular action which is not caused by the will, but by the result of a thought or focus on something external, with no regard for the muscular action itself, will serve as a central concept which I will refer to as the principle of the researching pendulum. - Ed]

Twenty-one years before the publication of his work on the *Baguette*, Chevreul had addressed a letter to the famous Ampere, (published in the *Revue des Deux Mondes* for 1833) in which he clearly states that the movement of the *pendule*, which was exciting much attention at that time, was due to "un mouvement musculaire de mon bras, quoique insensible pour moi" [Trans. - "muscular movement of my arm, though insensible to me" - Ed] and he points out the intimate connection between the will or intention of the operator and the resultant movement of the little ring or ball suspended by a thread from his fingers. He thus clears away a mass of perplexing and misleading observations which had been published by numerous previous experimenters on the *pendule*, all of whom believed some intimate connection existed between the oscillation of the little ball and the electric state of the operator or of the object that was tested.[2] A German savant, Professor Gilbert, had before this shown in Gilbert's *Annalen der Physik*, Vols. 26 and 27, how worthless were the inferences drawn from these experiments by Ritter, Amoretti, Gerboin and others; Gilbert subsequently published his papers in 1808.[3]

In the numerous papers and books on the *baguette* and *pendule* published on the Continent between 1796 and 1816, the controversy, often violent in tone, does not turn upon the main question whether the so-called diviner or dowser could or could not discover underground water better than ordinary mortals,—for except in Thouvenel's original *Mémoire*, little or no evidence is adduced on this point—but whether "animal electricity" was or was not the cause of the twisting of the rod. The disputants, as usual, cared less to know the actual facts than to prove their particular theory to be true. Moreover the attention of the scientific world at the early part of the 19th century was directed to electricity by Volta and Galvani's discoveries, and it was natural that many investigators should see in the sudden and mysterious motion of the *baguette* and the *pendule* an effect analogous to the spasmodic contraction of the legs of a dead frog which Galvani had shown was due to an electric stimulus. In fact, Volta himself was consulted and took part in some of these experiments with the *baguette*, but his opinion is not stated.

From the *baguette* and the *pendule* public attention was afterwards directed to "table-turning," and the illustrious Faraday, in 1854, conclusively proved by experiment that it was quite possible for the sitters to make tables gyrate by involuntary muscular action on their part.[4] Chevreul refers to Faraday's experiments on p. 220 of his work on the *Baguette*, and groups all these cognate phenomena under one common explanation: the essential factors, according to both Faraday and Chevreul, being—(1) the intention of the operator that the movement should take place in a certain direction, and (2) that he should be unaware he is exerting any effort of will, or any muscular force, in carrying out his intention. Professor Ch. Richet has more recently discussed the subject with wider knowledge, but I have

---

[1] Chevreul, *La Baguette Divinatoire*, p. 187.
[2] See, for example, Professor Gerboin's *Recherches Experimentales sur un nouveau mode de l'action électrique*, Strasbourg, 1808; or Ritter's and Amoretti's writings from 1800 to 1807 on *Der animalische electrometrie, die baguette, und der pendel*, forming the subject of these papers.
[3] *Kritische Aufsätze Uber die in München wieder erneuten Versuche mit Schwefelkies-Pendeln und Wünschelruthen*, von L. W. Gilbert, Halle, 1808. I have to thank Miss E. Stokes for making an abstract for me at the British Museum of this and other old German and Italian works on the subject of the *baguette* and *pendule*.
[4] Faraday's explanation of table turning is undoubtedly a *vera causa* for a certain class of so-called spiritualistic phenomena, but it is only applicable within a limited range, as every investigator of spiritualism knows. It is of course not impossible that some of the phenomena of the divining rod may, in like manner, be found to transcend any explanation now recognised by science; for the varied manifestations of automatism insensibly pass from the normal to the supernormal. At present, however, we are not, in my opinion, justified in assuming the motion of the rod to be explicable by other than known causes.

## The Credibility Of Dowsing

not yet read his work.[1] Dr. Liébeault[2] takes much the same view as Chevreul, but believes that the dowser, from gazing at the point of his rod, becomes partially hynotised, a view that I have also suggested, but the hypnosis, if it exists, is certainly very slight in most dowsers.

In his masterly work, *L'Automatisme Psychologique*, Professor Pierre Janet devotes a section to the consideration of the motion of the divining rod. He confirms Chevreul's view as to the involuntary motion of the rod and *pendule*, but he goes further and shows that these automatic actions are "*1° sans le vouloir, et 2° sans le savoir.*" [ Translation – Primarily, unintentional, secondarily, without knowledge (on the part of the individual). –Ed] Chevreul admits the first, but asserts that the movements are due to a *conscious intention* on the part of the operator to make the rod or pendulum move in a certain direction; the knowledge and thought of the operator are, therefore, involved, though his *will* may not actively co-operate. Janet shows that this is a mistaken view; the movement, as he rightly insists, takes place *without* the conscious intention of the operator. He remarks :—

> M. Chevreul pousse aussi loin que possible l'explication des faits par la tendance au mouvement créée par les images conscientes, mais quand les faits dépassent cette théorie, il retombe dans les explications banales par la fourberie et la simulation. ... Il faut aller plus loin que M. Chevreul et, après avoir admis des actes sans volonté, il faut parler des pensées sans conscience [consciousness] ou en dehors de notre conscience.[3]

> [Translation – "Chevreul pushes as far as possible the idea of the movement being created by conscious images, but when the facts no longer fit this theory, it becomes simply an explanation of deceit… We must go beyond Chevreul and after having admitted acts without desire, we must speak of unconscious thoughts or those outside of our consciousness." Ed]

Chevreul, we see from the foregoing, was no exception to that familiar type of mind which fancies trickery or simulation afford the only explanation of facts that lie beyond the range of its experience or its theories. In one of his conversations with Eckermann, Goethe shows how every new scientific truth has to encounter the fierce opposition of this class (see the motto on p. 132).[4]

---

[1] *Des mouvements inconscientes*. Paris, 1886. This work is dedicated by M. Richet to Chevreul.
[2] *Le Sommeil provoqué*, p. 241. Paris, 1889.
[3] *L'Automatisme Psychologique*, p. 375. Paris, 1889.
[4] *Conversations of Goethe* (Bohn's Standard Library, p. 47).
[The quotation referred to here is actually in the first part of the Report; the presidential address. The quotation reads:
"I am the doubter and the doubt
And I the song the Brahman sings" -Ed]

## Prof. W. F. Barrett

Dr. Hodgson sends me, as this sheet was passing through the press, a case he has received from an American friend which illustrates the entire inadequacy of Chevreul's point of view.[1]

Professor Pierre Janet goes further and shows that in these and other phenomena of automatism,

> Il y a donc, dans certains cas, plus qu'un acte automatique, manifestation involontaire d'une image visuelle et auditive; il y a une véritable action sub-consciente, une véritable collaboration de la seconde personnalité avec la premiere.—(L'Automatisme Psychologique, p. 374.)

> [Translation "There is therefore, in some cases, something more than an automatic, involuntary visual and auditory image manifestation, there is a real sub-conscious action, a true collaboration of the second with the first personality." Ed]

*The class of persons* who exhibit one or more of the varied phenomena of automatism are those whom M. Janet calls *les individus suggestibles*; persons who are readily influenced by suggestion from within or without, whose mind is easily dominated by a single idea. This may explain why it happens, as was noticed 150 years ago, that the best dowsers are not educated people, but more or less ignorant persons, who—according to Pryce—(*Mineralogia Cornubiensis*, p. 118) "hold the rod without puzzling their minds with doubts or reasonings." Such persons best exhibit the "reflex" action to which the motion of the rod is due, the prompting of suggestion not being interfered with by volition. But where will and reason are supreme, such automatic actions are brought into subjection by the intelligence. In other words, when our conscious self, which speaks through voluntary muscular movements, is dominant, the subconscious self is submerged. Hence in order that any subconscious suggestion may take effect in some form of automatic action, the reason and will must be in abeyance.

*In fine, the controlling force of SUGGESTION is to the subconscious life and its expression in involuntary muscular action and tissue change what the WILL is to the conscious life and its expression in voluntary muscular action.*

## Summary

Summing up this lengthy discussion we see that the curious phenomena attending the motion of the so-called divining rod are capable of explanation by causes known to science. They are not isolated phenomena, but belong to the large group which exhibit in various ways the play of motor automatism, and illustrate in a striking manner the profound effect which suggestion has in determining, directing or modifying these phenomena.

When some instrumental means is used to exhibit these involuntary muscular movements, it is desirable to employ a generic term, such as the word *autoscope*, as suggested in the previous Report. The divining—or dowsing—rod is,

---

[1] "New Lebanon, N.Y., July 1st, 1900. I spent a whole day nearly with an old gentleman here—a farmer, rather above the average in intelligence—a man of much local influence. He says that ten years ago he laughed at the witch-hazel 'superstition,' thinking it nothing more. About that time he bought a farm, which he found—after buying—to be poorly watered. A neighbour, coming with a threshing machine, had difficulty in getting water for his engine. This neighbour said one of his neighbours had found water with the 'witch-hazel crotch.' My man sneered at the idea. Thresher man persisted; didn't know that it would work with him, but might with another. Got a stick; tried it; wouldn't work. Gave the stick to my man. The latter took it merely in complaisance; walked along a few rods; suddenly it went down. He couldn't stop it. Thought it was an involuntary muscular contraction; tried it again; held it as tightly as possible: passing over the same line, a few rods down the hill, it turned again, and so strongly that the bark 'peeled' in his hands. The thresher man declared there was water beneath. My man said he should want to see it before he believed it, the surface giving no indication of it. Thresher man wanted water for his boiler and dug. Only a few feet down struck a small stream, sufficient to feed his boiler. Since then my man has experimented a good deal. As a result of his work, he now has a small reservoir on the hillside back of his buildings, in a place where no water was known before, which supplies his barn the year round and affords a limited supply for use in case of fire. The reservoir is fed from two small springs discovered by the turning of the witch-hazel fork in his own hands. While with me he walked about over a good deal of territory. The fork turned down every time he passed over a trickle of visible water, without exception. It also turned several times where no water was visible or suggested. In two of these places I and a man with me dug down a few feet. In the one case we found a vein in the rock filled with iron pyrites crystals; in the other we struck a sheet of solid slate rock about 30 in. down, which we had neither tools nor time to drill into or through: there is an old tradition of lead veins—from which the Indians used to smelt out lead—in the very place where his fork turned over the slate rock."

therefore, a convenient out-of-door autoscope, and when held in a state of strain, as it often is, becomes, from its unstable or balanced equilibrium, very sensitive to almost imperceptible muscular action on the part of the dowser. (See, on this, Professor de Mortillet's own observations, given on p. 323.)

As I said in the previous Report: It is just because these automatic actions appear to be so novel, and detached from ourselves, that they are apt to be so misleading to some and so mischievous to others. Interpreted on the one hand as the play of a wonderful occult force, science has refused to have anything to do with phenomena which seem to obey no physical laws, but are capricious and self determined. Interpreted on the other, truly enough, as the exhibition of a free and intelligent agent, some infernal or discarnate spirit has been fixed upon as the cause, and a fictitious authority for which there is no warrant has been given to their indications. Whether in any case these intelligent automatic movements exhibit information outside the memory of the individual who uses the autoscope; or a knowledge beyond that which may have been unconsciously derived (a) from those present by sign-reading or thought-transference, or (b) from the surroundings of the automatist, by his hyperaesthetic discernment of faint indications, is a problem which can only be solved so as to gain general acceptance by long and patient enquiry, of which our Proceedings are an earnest, and to which this monograph may afford a small contribution.

# PART XII

## *The Malaise Of The Dowser And Its Origin*

Nearly all dowsers assert that when the rod moves in their hands, or when they believe that underground water is beneath them, they experience a peculiar sensation, which some describe as felt in the limbs like the tingling of an electric shock, others as a shivering or trembling, and others as an unpleasant sensation in the epigastric region. With all there is more or less of a convulsive spasm, sometimes of a violent character. This malaise is very marked in some cases, but not experienced in others. That these physiological disturbances have a purely psychological origin is obvious—(1) from the fact that they are not experienced when the dowser is off duty, that is, when he has no suspicion that he is in the neighbourhood of underground water, and (2) that like effects are not produced by the much greater masses of visible water in rivers, lakes, or the sea. The interesting point is that these psycho-physiological phenomena have a real existence; they exist among dowsers in all countries, and can be traced back, as historical investigation shows, for upwards of two centuries. In the preceding Report I devoted an Appendix to this subject, and to avoid repetition would beg those of my readers who are interested to refer to the cases I have there quoted.[1]

Let us briefly note the principal facts. In the first place it is not, as some imagine, only when the "diviner" is in the presence of underground water that this physiological disturbance occurs. In the *Journal des Sçavans* (Savants) for January, 1693, a copy of which I possess, a physician of some note, Dr. Chauvin, writes that, when the well-known Jacques Aymar was sent for to trace, by means of his rod, the murderer of a Lyons *Marchand de Vin*, Aymar was taken into the cellar where the murder was committed; suddenly his *baguette* moved violently, and he was seized with convulsive spasms. Dr. Chauvin, who was present, adds :—" Il ne fut pas plutôt entré qu'il se sentit tout ému, et que son poux s'éleva comme une grosse fièvre."[2] [Translation: "He had no sooner entered than he felt strong emotions, and his pulse rose as in a high fever" Ed.]

A century later another distinguished French physician, Dr. Thouvenel, independently notices much the same thing with the water-finder, Bleton. Dr. Thouvenel gives a detailed medical report of his own long-continued observations, and states that when Bleton believed he was over a subterranean spring he was seized with an extraordinary malaise, which affected his diaphragm and produced a sense of oppression in the chest; at the same time a shivering sets in and the pulse falls, his body trembles, and, in a word, he exhibits "all the characteristics of an attack of convulsive spasm."[3] Similar symptoms manifested themselves in the Prior of a convent at Autun, who was an amateur dowser and contemporary of Bleton. A few years later the Italian *savant*, Amoretti, noticed the same symptoms occur whenever the lad Pennet came over a vein of mineral ore or of coal. Amoretti states that a surgeon, Banzio, an amateur dowser, found his pulse accelerated twelve to fifteen beats per minute when the rod moved in his hands (see p. 363).

Dr. Mayo, F.R.S., who, as Professor of Anatomy and Physiology in King's College and in the College of Surgeons in London, was a most competent observer, describes corresponding symptoms which he observed in 1847 in a youth in Russia. The lad had never seen a "divining rod" before, but when Dr. Mayo instructed him how to use it, and made him walk over a spot where he had reason to believe an underground spring existed, the forked twig twisted round, much to the lad's astonishment, and at the same time Dr. Mayo states the lad declared that

---

[1] *Proceedings* S.P.R., Vol. XIII., p. 272, et seq. [Appendic D, p. 220 this volume - Ed]

[2] Aymar, as my readers probably know, set out on the track of the murderer, who had hitherto baffled all the attempts of the police to discover his whereabouts, and, guided by his *baguette*, tracked him "for 45 hours on land and 30 hours on the water," crossing and recrossing the Rhone, until at last he pointed out a man, found in a soldiers' camp, as the assassin. The man was arrested, taken to Lyons, tried, found guilty, and subsequently confessing his crime, was put to death by being broken at the wheel. There are numerous corroborative official depositions in this remarkable case; among others is the *procès verbal* of an eye-witness, M. de Vagny, the Procureur du Roi.

[3] *Mémoire Physique et Medicinal*, p. 53; Paris, 1781. The passage is quoted in full in the previous Report, Proceedings S.P.R., Vol. XIII., pp. 272 and 273.

> he felt an uneasy sensation which quickly increased to pain at the pit of the stomach, and he became alarmed, so that I bade him quit hold of the rod, when the pain ceased. Ten minutes later I induced him to make another trial; the results were the same.[1]

As Dr. Mayo was apparently unaware of Thouvenel's writings, he could hardly have anticipated or suggested the malaise experienced by his subject, but the effect observed was doubtless due to the same psychological cause as in the previous cases.

Abundant modern instances of a similar physiological disturbance and convulsive spasm occurring with various dowsers in different countries will be found in the cases cited in the previous and present Report. Mr. J. F. Young, whose experiences as an amateur dowser are given on p. 223, says :—

> I have noticed, when divining, unpleasant and peculiar symptoms always occur when I am over an underground spring; often a convulsive feeling and staggering comes on.

He goes on to describe how the sensation is chiefly felt at the epigastrium, and that his father, who was also an amateur dowser, used to stagger and vomit when the rod turned in his hands. An experiment was once made with old Mr. Young to test whether these symptoms were genuine; it is described in detail in my previous Report, p. 223. Mr. Young was carefully blindfolded and led about by a circuitous route, but directly he came over the spot where he had been seized with these symptoms before, and which had been purposely marked, "he reeled as before and would have fallen if I had not held him up. Directly he came off the place he was all right." The convulsions that seized the famous dowser, Mr. Lawrence, whenever he came to a place beneath which he asserted underground water to exist, have been described on a previous page (foot-note, p. 356).

There are some sceptical friends who would explain these phenomena by asserting that these different dowsers conspired to exhibit similar symptoms as a bit of stage business in order to impress the onlookers. It is, I think, unnecessary to waste time in disputing such a belief if any one cares to hold it.

How, then, are we to explain these curious pathological phenomena? The facts are certainly incontestable and, I venture to think, deserve more attention from physiologists than they have yet received. They are not, however, peculiar to the use of the so-called divining rod, but are found to exist more or less conspicuously in other cases of motor automatism. Professor Pierre Janet has drawn attention to very similar convulsive phenomena and physiological disturbances as associated with other phases of automatism.[2] Prior to this, however, in the first volume of the *Proceedings* of our Society, I pointed out that in trials with the "willing game,"—which is one phase of these varied automatic phenomena, — curious physiological disturbances were often produced, such as dizziness, hysteria, and incipient trance. [3] In fact, a *malaise*, manifesting itself in different ways, and with different degrees of intensity in different subjects, is a usual concomitant of motor automatism and its allied phenomena.

The singular connection of visceral sensation,—a visceral consciousness as it were,—with a particular psychical state is familiar to us all in emotion[4]. Emotion, in fact, is a feeling excited by an idea or train of ideas, and therefore the sensations experienced by the dowser are strictly *emotional disturbances*. Whether emotion is primarily a cerebral process, as some physiologists maintain, the visceral or vascular disturbance being secondary; or whether, as other eminent physiologists hold, the psychical process of emotion is secondary to the excitation of the visceral organs,—through certain stimuli causing the discharge of a nervous impulse into those organs,—is a matter that does not concern us here, albeit physiologists may find in the facts I have cited some fresh light thrown on this

---

[1] *Truths Contained in Popular Superstitions*, p. 18; London 1856.
[2] *L'Automatisme Psychologique*, p. 208, etc.; Paris, 1880.
[3] *Proceedings* S.P.R. for 1882. Vol. I., p. 57.
[4] Professor James holds that our feeling of the bodily changes as they occur *is* the emotion; he writes, "If I were to become corporeally anesthetic, I should be excluded from the life of the affections, harsh and tender alike." Physiologically, may we not really define emotion as certain visceral or vascular disturbances, set up by *suggestion*, the sensation of these disturbances being the feeling of emotion?

controversy. The point of interest to us is that (1) the *malaise* or other sensation felt by the dowser is probably an emotional effect, and (2) the fresh evidence afforded of the nexus existing between emotion and muscular action, whether this latter be conscious or, as with the dowser and his rod, unconscious. As Professor Sherrington, F.R.S., an able physiologist, in a recent paper on Emotion (*Nature*, Vol. 62, p. 331), has said :—" It would be consonant with what we know of reflex action if the spur that started the muscular expression should simultaneously and of itself initiate also the visceral adjunct reaction."

Furthermore, in many cases where subconscious acts are performed, as M. Janet points out, a state of *partial catalepsy* supervenes. Catalepsy, as Dr. Ochorowicz has shown, is a state of *mono-ideism*,[1] that is, a "mental condition which concentrates every action upon one single and dominant idea and is not counterbalanced by any other." Now this is precisely the condition of the dowser when he "sets" himself to dowse, and in some cases he passes into a state of complete catalepsy when the idea culminates. It is not, therefore, a question of underground water or mineral ore, but merely *the result of suggestion acting upon a state of mono-ideism*.

The *malaise*, or other sensation felt by the dowser, is, therefore, in all probability, *an emotional disturbance, the mind being dominated by a single idea and the subject being a person on whom suggestion is operative*: using the word "suggestion" in the sense which I have already defined as an impression or influence exercised without the knowledge or consent of the subject being concerned.

We have now narrowed the issue down to the problem of "*how* does this subconscious suggestion arise in the case of the successful dowser?" Here we enter upon the final stage of our inquiry.

---

[1] *La Suggestion Mentale*, p. 112; Paris, 1887.

# PART XIII

## Origin Of The Stimulus That Gives Rise To The Motor Automatism Of The Dowser

### § 1. Is it Derived through the Ordinary Channels of Sense?

It now remains for us to try and ascertain what gives rise to the suggestion or stimulus which causes the involuntary motion of the rod —in other words, what is it originates the motor automatism of the dowser? What is it "pulls the trigger"? Evidently this suggestion or stimulus cannot be purely accidental and worthless, for, as we have seen, the operations of a good dowser are attended with unquestionable success, a success far beyond that which mere chance coincidence can account for. This being conceded, we now turn to the possible explanations already stated at the beginning (p. 239).

(i.) *Is this success due merely to knowledge acquired by the dowser from experience and observation of the ground and perhaps occasional hints from bystanders?* In that case success would be arrived at by an exercise of judgment, or some would say cunning; shrewd observation and the piecing together of stray information would be the main business of the dowser. Under these circumstances sub-conscious suggestion and motor automatism are wholly out of the question—the motion of the rod must be a purely voluntary act; and if so the forked twig of the dowser, like the wand of the conjuror, becomes a piece of stage property, or of charlatanry, to mystify the public. This has hitherto been the usual scientific view, but it is, I maintain, now proved to be untenable; the motion of the rod is unquestionably, as Professor Janet has said, "*sans le vouloir et sans le savoir*" on the part of the dowser. It is quite possible the experience gained by the dowser, or any observations he has made on the spot, may be of service to him, but if so, it must lie at the background of his consciousness and not form part of a process of *reasoning*. We are thus driven to inquire :—

(ii.) *Is this information or suggestion derived from some sub-conscious process of observation on the part of the dowser, or hyperesthetic discernment of surface signs too faint or complex to be perceived by the ordinary observer?* There is much to be said on behalf of this view, for surface signs of underground water do exist and for shallow wells such signs are of great value independently of geological knowledge. On p. 248 of the previous Report [p. 202 this volume - Ed], I pointed out the nature of some of these signs, and since that Report was published, an excellent little Manual on the discovery of water-sources has been published in France, wherein the surface indications of underground water are very clearly set forth.[1] Much of this knowledge goes back to ancient times. Vitruvius, Augustus Caesar's famous engineer, gives a lengthy account of surface signs which were employed in his day to find underground water: some appear fanciful, but many are still in use. Pliny, in his *Natural History*, refers to the same thing. Moreover, the letters of Cassiodorus (the statesman and secretary of Theodoric, King of the Ostrogoths), written at the beginning of the sixth century, show that in his time there were certain people held in high repute, and called "Aquilegi," who appear to have been professional water-finders. Cassiodorus explains how this valuable art had arisen from careful observation of the surface of the ground, etc.[2] Now the modern dowser may more or less unconsciously note these indications and,—without being able to give any rational explanation of how it comes about,—the impressions made upon him by these surface signs may create the sub-conscious suggestion which causes the involuntary motion of the rod.

The extraordinary success of the Abbé Paramelle as a water-finder, or "hydroscope" as he was called, supports this view. Paramelle tells us he was guided entirely by the knowledge he had acquired from a careful study of the surface of the ground, and to defend himself from the attacks made upon him, he wrote a treatise to put on record the methods he employed. As this work appears almost wholly unknown in England, I have given an outline of it in Appendix D; to this I would refer my readers. But the rapidity and certainty with which Paramelle is stated, on trustworthy evidence, to have located the site, probable depth and volume of water in wells under 50 feet deep, can hardly be accounted for by an exercise of ordinary conscious observation and judgment. It is much more like an act of intuition, for between 1839 and 1854 he had located 10,000 sources of underground water and his failures

---

[1] I have given a brief notice of this little book by M. Auscher on p. 382 of the present Report. [P. 421 this volume - Ed]
[2] See Appendix F.

appear to have been only from 5 to 10 per cent, of the whole. Though Paramelle believed he could teach his system, his pupils did not achieve their master's success and the school he hoped to found died out. On the whole, there can, I think, be little doubt that the French Abbe arrived at his conclusions sub-consciously, though he employed no rod to give automatic expression to his instinctive opinion.

But it is not only in water-finding that the trained scientific observer, such as a field geologist, is often less successful in reading surface indications than those who appear possessed of some instinctive discernment of the signs sought for. Thus, in the discovery of china clay (the basis of our best English china), I am informed by a high authority, Mr. Fred. W. P. Jago, that:—

> The workmen in the china-clay district (near St. Austell, in Cornwall) will point out where a bed of china clay in its natural state of decomposed granite lies hidden under what they term the slad. [Mr. Jago goes on to say]: As my father and myself have been engaged in this kind of mining for nearly seventy years, I also could fairly point out where there was a bed of china clay below the surface, but I would defy the scientific geologist to do so from his inspection.
>
> Yet our workmen will even tell you the extent of such a bed—from their knowledge of the peculiar formation of the surface of the ground—before an atom of the clay has been seen or dug up from, say 8 or 10 feet below. The term slad expresses this, but it is as hard to describe as it would be for one to describe his own handwriting.
>
> I have always suspected that dowsers have a somewhat similar knowledge as to water and lodes.
>
> Fred. W. P. Jago.

Here then we have a case where success can hardly be due to any conscious process of reasoning; the judgment seems to be more or less instinctive, though doubtless it has been gained by experience. Much the same thing occurs in the location of metallic lodes. From very early times, the signs of underground ore have been noticed by miners, references to these indications are to be found in all the leading works on mining published in the 16th and 17th centuries.[1] A distinguished authority on mining, the late Professor Warington Smyth, F.R.S., remarked in a lecture delivered in 1869 :—

> There is some foundation for the idea that metallic lodes affect vegetation; the herbage is often brighter and better over certain lodes and worse over others. A certain class of plants will grow over the lode and not on adjacent parts. Veins containing decomposing iron pyrites are slightly warmer, so that there is rather a higher temperature over them; dew or hoar frost will not lie long on the lode, so that its presence can be traced early in the morning. A peculiar odour from the sulphurous gases pervades the direction of a lode, and sometimes at night a faintly luminous appearance is seen over certain metallic lodes.[2]

As we shall see in Book III., the dowser has gained remarkable success not only in finding underground water but mineral lodes, and hence the probability that he is guided by some surface indications is greatly increased from the fact that such indications are found in both these cases. It may, however, be urged that ordinary observation and judgment would be sufficient in each case to explain success without assuming any instinctive or subconscious process. But this view, as we have seen, is inconsistent with the phenomenon of motor automatism, and, moreover, common sense, aided by observation, knowledge and reasoning, would long ago have displaced the dowser had the latter not been found to be of greater practical value.

---

[1] See especially G. Agricola's *De Re Metallica*, Basle, 1546.
[2] Similar statements will also be found in the 9th Edition of the *Encyc. Brit.*, under the article "Mining." See also Pryce's *Mineralogia Cornubiensis*, etc.

It must, therefore, be admitted that if surface indications determine the suggestion that starts the automatic motion of the rod, these indications are not deliberately sought for, but that *a subconscious and hyperesthetic discernment of faint signs that escape the ordinary observer is quite possible on the part of the successful dowser.*

Many instances have been given in our Proceedings of definite motor reactions, sometimes of a remarkable character quite unaccompanied by consciousness,[1] and many illustrations have also been given of what at first sight appears an almost miraculous sense of perception, really due to a transitory hyperesthetic and subconscious condition on the part of the subject.[2] It is, therefore, I think, unnecessary for me to contend further that the foregoing explanation is really a *vera causa*, but I now proceed to show that it is not the whole cause and may really play a very unimportant part in the matter.

## § 2. Is the Suggestion Pure Chance or Derived from some Supernormal Source of Perception?

Whilst the explanation just given may cover some of the facts, it fails to explain those cases where surface indications of underground water do not exist, owing either to the surface being made ground or covered with buildings, or with a layer of 30 or 40 feet of "drift," or the water itself existing in fissures or cavities so far beneath the surface that it is inconceivable its presence could be indicated by any superficial signs. Now, an attentive study of the cases I have cited in the present and the previous Report shows that the dowser's success is not limited to localities where surface indications may be conjectured. Take, for example, the classical case of Waterford, so fully described and discussed in the previous Report, pp. 106-117 [pp. 83-93 this volume - Ed]. The able geologists who have examined that case clearly show that surface signs could have nothing to say to the dowser's success. Take again in the present Report the Errol case, p. 171 [p. 264 this volume - Ed], when the same dowser (the late John Mullins) was employed, or the Lytes-Cary case, p. 174 [p. 266 this volume - Ed], or the Carrigoona experiments, p. 144 [p. 241 this volume - Ed], or the Shanklin experiments, p. 164 [p. 258 this volume - Ed], or the case of Beraz, p. 248 [p. 325 this voume - Ed], or many of Bleton's cases, p. 264 [p. 336 this volume - Ed], or others I might quote. All these cases point to one of two conclusions — either they are the result of chance coincidence, lucky hits on the part of the dowser, or that the dowser possesses some faculty new to science.

Let us take the first alternative. What are the chances of success in, say the Waterford case? Here the geologists show that Mullins must have hit upon a line of fault in the Silurian rocks "80 ft. below the surface," or "a porous stratum concealed beneath the drift," —which is here over 40 ft. in thickness (see the Report by Mr. J. R. Kilroe of the Geological Survey of Ireland, given in my former Report, Proceedings S.P.R.,Vol. XIII., p. 116 [p. 90 this volume - Ed]). Now before the advent of Mullins three borings (in one case to the depth of 1,000 ft., in another to a depth of 392 ft.) had been made on scientific advice in places near the spot selected by Mullins; one of these borings had been made on the advice of Mr. Kinahan, F.G.S., of the Geological Survey, and yet in each case no water had been found. The chances of hitting a line of fault or porous stratum were, therefore, extremely small. I have talked over this with Mr. Kilroe, who has visited the spot and is one of the best geological authorities on that district, and he tells me that a "lucky fluke" on the part of the dowser, though conceivable, is almost incredible. This also was evidently the opinion of the local geologist, Mr. Budd, who was present at the borings, and of Mr. Kinahan himself. Moreover, Mullins predicted the exact depth of the fissure within a foot or two and was right in the volume of water that was found. These are contemporary statements made by those who were at first prejudiced against the dowser.

---

[1] Experiments in "normal motor automatism " form the subject of an interesting paper published in 1896 among the "*Studies from the Psychological Laboratory of Harvard University.*"
[2] See Professor Guebhard's experiences, *Proceedings* S.P.R., Vol. II., p. 411, and many similar illustrations cited by Mr. Myers in his papers on the "Subliminal Self" published in our *Proceedings*. I wonder the divining rod has never been used for *weather prognostication*. If a code could be arranged so as to interpret its indications, I have no doubt it would become as famous in foretelling the weather, say twelve hours ahead, as in finding underground water or mineral ores; *supposing* that a subconscious discernment of faint signs really occurs with the dowser. Leeches used to be employed as weather prophets: see on this subject of animal presentiments my last Report, *Proceedings* S.P.R., Vol XIII., p. 250 [p.203 this volume - Ed].

From the study of these and other cases I have therefore been driven to the conclusion that neither surface signs, nor hyperaesthetic discernment, nor chance coincidence, can account for all the successes of a good dowser like Bleton in the last century or the late J. Mullins and others in recent times. This is precisely the conclusion which Mr. Westlake, F.G.S., has independently arrived at from a careful geological examination on the spot of other cases selected from my previous Report, see Appendix A. (below). In his analysis, Mr. Westlake assumes the dowser knew all the local indications of the underground water, and he is disposed to read back into the dowser's mind the hydro-geological knowledge which was gained *after* the dowser's well had been sunk. Notwithstanding all this, Mr. Westlake concludes that a certain percentage of cases (10 to 15 per cent.) defy any explanation known to science except chance coincidence. Here then the issue is knit. Can it be shown that the outstanding cases are explicable as merely lucky hits due to pure chance on the part of the dowser? I think the *onus probandi* [the burden of proof - Ed] of this must be left to those who challenge our methods of inquiry, or deny the existence of any avenue of knowledge other than the recognised channels of sense.

## § 3. Is any Physical Cause at all Likely?

In seeking for an explanation of these outstanding cases, I do not think we need consider any *physical cause*. Recent scientific discoveries, such as the X-rays and wireless telegraphy, have made the public familiar with the fact that bodies like earth and bricks and flesh, which are opaque to light, may be transparent to electric waves. But though the penetration of opaque bodies by invisible radiation has long been known to scientific men, the unscientific mind naturally seizes the idea that just as electric waves have been shown to pass unimpeded through walls and mountains, so some electric influence from underground water is likely to pass through the superincumbent earth and affect the dowser. But then we must assume an electric influence also proceeds from mineral ores and that the dowser is a delicate electroscope, and this is pure assumption. It is true our knowledge of the world around is very limited, but 200 years ago the philosopher Malebranche showed, from the uniformity of nature, how untenable was any explanation based upon an imaginary physical influence produced by underground water or metals upon the dowser.[1] Whatever effect is produced by *underground* water or ore would be produced in a greater degree by the proximity of water or ore on the surface. Nevertheless, the dowser appears quite insensible to the mass of water in a river, lake, or the ocean, or to masses of metal or ore within his sight.

There is, however, another physical hypothesis which is more plausible, and which at one time suggested itself to me. We are insensible to certain physical forces which are ever streaming through us, such as the magnetism of the earth; we are likewise insensible to the motion of the earth in space, but we should become alarmingly sensible of the latter if it were interrupted or suddenly changed. It is conceivable the dowser may be a person gifted with a sense affected by any slight interruption in the continuity or modification of the lines of terrestrial, magnetic, or electric force. Underground fissures may be imagined to produce such a modification or want of continuity in the ambient field of force, and thus their presence might be detected by certain organisations. But I do not attach the least value to this conception as an explanation of the success of the dowser; for, inter alia, there is no evidence to show that the dowser is more affected than ordinary persons by any of the physical forces; and the interruption of a magnetic field of force enormously greater than that due to the earth is absolutely unfelt by the dowser. No, the key to the mystery that remains must, in my opinion, be sought in the psychical and not in the physical world.

## § 4. Probable Explanation of the Mare Remarkable Successes of the Dowser

There is abundant evidence in our *Proceedings* that the information subconsciously given by some automatists often transcends the ordinary sense perceptions. Cases of so-called clairvoyance resting upon excellent testimony are known, see e.g., the cases cited in Mrs. Sidgwick's paper on the " Evidence for Clairvoyance," or Dr. Alfred Backman's " Experiments on Clairvoyance," and the supplementary papers to both of these contained in Vol. IX. of the *Proceedings* S.P.R., also the evidence cited by Mr. Myers in Vol. XI., pp. 367-404. It is true the science of to-day does

---

[1] See " Réponse de l'auteur ' De la recherche de la Vérité ' " to Father Le Brun, published in the *Lettres qui découvrent l'illusion des philosophes sur la baguette*, p. 9 et seq. Paris, 1693.

## The Credibility Of Dowsing

not recognise any such super-sensory extension of knowledge, yet nothing is clearer to those who have made a careful and critical study of psychical phenomena, not only that telepathy is a fact, but that to the subconscious or subliminal self, the elements of time and space have not the same limitations as they have to our conscious self. Even Schopenhauer, in his *Versucht über Geistersehen*, long ago said, "He who doubts the fact of clairvoyance is not sceptical but ignorant." This is, perhaps, a stronger assertion than I should be disposed to make, but of the reality of this "far seeing" power, I, among others, have had indubitable proof after carefully conducted experiments with persons in the deep hypnotic state, and the same condition is often seen in the allied state of somnambulism. Those who on *a priori* grounds deny the possibility of any such transcendental perceptive power should read the conclusions unanimously arrived at by the nine distinguished members of the French Royal Academy of Medicine, who were appointed by the Academy to report on mesmeric phenomena. After five years' investigation this Committee presented their lengthy Report to the Academy in June, 1831. They state they began the inquiry with "inexperience, impatience and distrust," which at first militated against them. Ultimately, after the most rigorous tests, they "conclude with certainty" that the faculty which has been designated clairvoyance does really exist in certain subjects in the mesmeric state.[1]

The question arises, Is this condition ever found in persons who, like the dowser, are in their normal waking state, not in a hypnotic or somnambulic trance? I have tried to put this question to the test of experiment with an amateur dowser, and the result of the preliminary experiments (which are all that have so far been made), affords considerable support to the hypothesis of some kind of clairvoyant faculty in the particular dowser tested. I have given an account of these experiments, together with some additional evidence bearing on the same subject, in Appendix E., below.[2]

Professor Janet, in a passage I have quoted on p. 361, points out that evidence of a secondary personality is afforded in cases of motor automatism such as the dowser exhibits. Now. we know that in automatic writing the secondary self frequently exhibits transcendental sources of information; the Ego seems to pass beyond its usual narrow threshold of sensibility, the veil is lifted which hides scenes spatially distant.[3] Mr. Myers has cited cases of what he terms *cosmopathic impressibility* on the part of the automatist; that is, transcendental impressions which come to men from the surrounding world, impressions " borne like seed on the wind, rather than wittingly directed towards him by the voluntary or involuntary sympathy of any assignable intelligence."[4] The sensibility of the dowser may be of such a kind, but humbler, *geopathic* and not cosmopathic. I have no doubt, however, that in years to come we shall see in all these phenomena the manifestation of the transcendental Subject which lies in the background of our being, and remains unrevealed to our self-consciousness. Thus we have been led from the study of such a matter-of-fact and practical question as the discovery of underground water by the dowser to the very centre and mystery of our complex personality.

Here, however, we do well to remember that there is but a step from the sublime to the ridiculous. For the emergence of the subconscious self and its expression in some form of motor automatism involves the more or less complete surrender of our reason, of self-consciousness and the voluntary control over our actions; the reins of will are, as it were, thrown down and the automatist becomes the sport of every wayward impulse or passing

---

[1] See Colquhoun's translation of this Report published in 1833. In an Appendix the Editor gives several remarkable cases of clairvoyance, attested by some eminent Continental physicians as occurring in certain cataleptic patients, who—like the dowser—*appeared* to have the seat of this perceptive faculty in the epigastrium.

[2] A belief in the existence of clairvoyance among certain persons in the normal state is, I find, the foundation of the repute in which the so called Zahoris were once held. As the Zahoris are sometimes referred to in modern literature, and no one was able to give me any information about them, after some search I was able to obtain the historical information given in Appendix F..

[3] Upon this subject see Baron Du Prel's *Philosophy of Mysticism*, translated by Mr. C. C. Massey.

[4] *Proceedings* S.P.R., Vol. XL, p. 367.

suggestion.[1] Hence, the worthlessness of many of the indications and messages given through different forms of autoscope, whether forked rod, tilting table or scribbling pencil.

We may, therefore, expect any auto-suggestion to make itself apparent in the motion of the divining rod, and this is the case; when, however, the dowser "sets himself," as he expresses it, then the indications afforded by the movement of his rod are directed towards the object of his search, and the suggestion may now arise: (1) from various hints he has gathered or knowledge he possesses becoming unconsciously operative; or (2) from his subconscious and perhaps hyperaesthetic discernment of the surface signs of underground water or ore; or (3) from some kind of transcendental discernment possessed by his subconscious self. For my own part, I am disposed to think that this last cause, though less acceptable to science, will ultimately be found to be the truer explanation of the more striking successes of a good dowser.[2] My reasons for thinking so are: (i) the success which certain dowsers have achieved in discovering underground water, when surface indications were out of the question, and when previous borings, as deep or deeper, in the immediate vicinity failed to discover water; (ii) the success which has attended young or ignorant dowsers, such as Bleton, who cannot be supposed to have an intuitive knowledge of the surface indications of underground water; and (iii) the evidence afforded by carefully blindfolding the dowser.

The only alternative explanation in these cases appears to me to be that of *chance coincidence*, and to the majority of thoughtful persons this will doubtless seem the more probable alternative; but the probability of its being so will be recognised as extremely small by those who will take the trouble to apply, so far as can be done, the doctrine of chances to the facts I have cited. On the other hand, the probability that an explanation is to be found in some extension of our knowledge of human personality, something new to science, and something akin to what has been termed clairvoyance, gains considerable weight from a critical study of cognate phenomena described in our *Proceedings* and elsewhere. And surely, even if the majority of cases of the success of the dowser are explicable by known causes, yet, as Kant said of the attested story of Swedenborg's[3] clairvoyance, "the amazing inferences that would have to be drawn if only one such event could be proved" will, I hope, stimulate further inquiry, so that the conclusion I have reached may be confirmed or disproved.

I do not for one moment profess that the explanation I have suggested is anything more than a provisional and tentative one. A final solution is not likely to be reached until the subject has been critically examined and discussed by scientific men from different points of view. But if many years' experimental investigation gives me any right to express an opinion, I am convinced that the only method by which we can hope to bring these elusive and perplexing phenomena out of the "disorderly mystery of ignorance," in which they have lain neglected for so long, into the "orderly mystery of science," is by a careful collection of trustworthy evidence, supplemented by experimental investigation wherever it is possible, and then by the fearless suggestion of some working hypothesis which will enable future investigators to direct their inquiries to definite issue, and thus overthrow or establish the provisional explanation that has been suggested. This is obviously the method by which the whole edifice of modern science has been reared; it is nothing more than the application of the inductive philosophy to psychical research. And we may confidently expect much more rapid progress in this difficult region of inquiry when it becomes evident that there is not only something to investigate, but that some solid addition to our knowledge or some useful practical result will issue from the inquiry. A larger number of trained investigators will then be attracted, and though psychical research can never offer the commercial stimulus to which the recent development of electrical science is almost wholly due, yet it presents to us many problems of profound interest.

---

[1] It is obvious that such persons cannot be as fully responsible for their actions as the rest of mankind. Readily influenced by their environment and controlled by suggestion, such "suggestible persons" (among whom are all so-called "mediums") when met with suspicion and the suggestion of fraud, frequently exhibit the very characteristics their critics have imagined them to possess. The investigators, in fact, have unconsciously suggested the role that the subjects have played.

[2] If this be the case, the dowser ought to be able to indicate the position of *any* buried object, as well as underground water and mineral lodes, albeit surface indications in these latter may count for something. I have dealt with this wider question in Appendix E..

[3] [EMANUEL SWEDENBORG – 1688-1772, Swedish scientist, philosopher and theologian who later turned mystic and had several well-documented cases of psychic abilities. Ed].

## *The Credibility Of Dowsing*

For thirty years those of us who founded this Society have striven to ascertain whether the information derived through the recognised channels of sense embraced the whole of the accessible sources of knowledge; whether also the normal phenomena of Nature,—manifested to us as the accidents of time, space, and mass, in terms of which all natural phenomena may be expressed,—were really the bed-rock upon which the whole superstructure of human science must be raised; or whether the order of Nature can be proved to contain an even vaster procession of phenomena than is now embraced within the recognised limits of science: in fine, whether we could ever reach by scientific methods the profounder, more enduring, and transcendent realities that lie beneath the material surface, as thought lies behind its utterance in language.

There are some avenues of approach to this great quest which seem barred to many earnest searchers after truth; the limitation of our faculties may possibly render certain pathways to knowledge inaccessible under the conditions of our present existence. But we cannot, *a priori*, condemn any inquiry unless it has been conclusively proved to be phantasmal and worthless, issuing in a dreary and fatal waste of human effort, or beset with intellectual and moral confusion to those who engage in it. Such warnings can hardly be said to apply to the present investigation. And if the outcome of our inquiry only establishes the fact that what appeared supernormal and transcendental is, after all, explicable by an extension of known perceptive powers, even then our time will not have been wasted, for we shall have enlarged our knowledge of human faculty and human usefulness. For my own part, I have been driven to believe that some dowsers—

"Whose exterior semblance doth belie
The Soul's immensity"

nevertheless give us a glimpse of—

"The eternal deep
Haunted for ever by the eternal mind."

## Conclusion

(1) For some centuries past certain individuals locally known as dowsers have declared that they can discover the presence of underground water, mineral lodes, coal,[1] building stone,[2] or other buried objects which may be sought for by the apparently spontaneous motion of the so-called divining rod; when their pretensions have been tested, the result, though by no means uniformly in their favour, has been so remarkable that chance coincidence appears a wholly inadequate explanation.

(2) Any explanation based upon trickery or unconscious hints from bystanders, or the detection of faint surface indications of the concealed object, or other known cause is insufficient to cover all the facts.

(3) The *movement* of the rod or forked twig is only a special case of motor automatism exhibited by a large number of individuals,[3] and arises from a subconscious and involuntary "suggestion" impressed on the mind of the dowser.

(4) Accompanying the involuntary and usually unconscious muscular contraction which causes the motion of the forked twig or rod, many dowsers experience a peculiar *malaise* and some a violent convulsive spasm. This is a psycho-physiological effect, akin to emotion. Moreover, the state of mono-ideism of the dowser creates a condition of partial catalepsy when some suggestion causes the idea to culminate.

(5) This subconscious suggestion may arise from a variety of causes; sometimes it is merely an auto-suggestion, at others it is unconsciously derived through the senses from the environment, but in a certain number of those who exhibit motor automatism the suggestion appears to be due to some kind of transcendental perceptive power.

(6) Such persons appear only able to exercise this transcendental faculty when their normal self-consciousness is more or less in abeyance, or when it is completely submerged, as in profound hypnosis.

(7) This subconscious perceptive power, commonly called "clairvoyance," may provisionally be taken as the explanation of those successes of the dowser which are inexplicable on any grounds at present known to science.

I wish to add a word of hearty thanks to the Editor of our *Proceedings*, Miss Johnson, for the kind assistance she has rendered in the reading of the proofs of this paper and for many useful suggestions.

---

[1] Both Pennet and Bleton were tested for this a century ago, and several competent witnesses were convinced of the fact.
[2] See, for example, the full and excellent narrative of a Belgian dowser, given by Professor D' Outrepoint, translated by Mr. Bennett, Assistant-Secretary of the S.P.R., and published in the *Journal* of the S.P.R. for June, 1899.
[3] A century ago Professor Sementini estimated that 80 per cent. of Italians could "work" the rod, but Amoretti thinks this number excessive; he gives 20 per cent. My own impression is that Amoretti is not far wrong. In England, perhaps, one or two in every dozen persons would be found susceptible.

# APPENDIX A

## *REPORT ON SOME CASES OF WATER - FINDING BY THE DIVINING ROD*
By E. Westlake, F.G.S.

During the printing of Professor Barrett's paper published in July, 1897, I made an analysis of his cases, and selected forty in which it was stated that, prior to the dowser's success, a deeper but unsuccessful well or boring had been made in the immediate neighbourhood. These are cited, at the foot of page 252 of his paper [p.204 this volume - Ed], as offering presumptive evidence of something in dowsing beyond chance or experience. As it seemed desirable they should be looked into from a geological point of view, I have since undertaken, at Professor Barrett's request, an examination of twenty-one of them, i.e., of seventeen published in his paper (Nos. 9, 17, 24, 26, 27, 286, 42, 43, 47, 48, 57, 60, 77, 90, 99, 105, and 121),[1] and of four others subsequently received. Beyond aiding in their understanding, I soon found that geology had little to do with the matter; the dowser does not profess, and probably seldom has, a knowledge of it; his conclusions seem usually drawn from more obvious considerations.

In psychological experiments, essentially modifiable by suggestion, it is absolutely necessary to have the conditions, if not under control, at any rate precisely recorded; if they are not, it is impossible to arrive at certain results. An observer coming after the event must allow that the dowser may have seen, or heard of, the position of neighbouring water, and have drawn his conclusions accordingly.[2] This I have done throughout the paper, with the result, it may be, of minimising marvels that really exist: if so, it will only need experiments more precisely noted to lead to their establishment.

Of the twenty-one cases I examined, five were in the South and sixteen in the West of England; seventeen similar cases in the North and East I was unable to visit. Those in the Isle of Wight I saw in November, 1897; those in Surrey and Sussex in June, 1898, and those in the West of England in May, 1899. I have arranged them, according to evidential considerations, in the following groups, beginning with what appears the weakest evidence on behalf of the dowser.

(A) *Too old for evidence to be now obtainable.* Nos. 24, Sodbury; 26, Shepton Mallet gaol; 48, Bristol ...   Total 3

(B) *Where the old well was too deep.*[3] Yarlington House ...   Total 1

(C) *Where the old well was in the side of a hill.* (See Group (d), No. 28)...   Total 1

(D) *Where the dowsers well was the deeper.* Nos. 9, Evercreech; 17, Sturminster; 27, Shepton Mallet Brewery; 28, Locking; Ladyswood Park ... ...   Total 5

(E) *Where a heading was driven towards known water.* Nos. 42, Henbury; 60, Shepton Mallet Station ...   Total 2

(F) *Where the dowser's well was placed near known water, the old well being usually remote.* Nos. 43, Hedgecock's; 47, Park Farm; 57, Norton Hall; 77, Arnold's; 90, Wootton; [Arreton]; 121, Stroud; 99, Melksham ... ... ... ...   Total 7

(G) *Where there was little or no surface sign of water.* Lytes Cary; Wimblehurst Farm; 105, Toy Farm...   Total 3

21

---

[1] These numbers refer to the numbering of the cases given in Proceedings, Vol. XIII., Part XXXII. [Part one of this volume - Ed]

[2] As a matter of fact, dowsers do *not*, as a rule, seek for information about the local water supply; they believe so firmly in their " gift," that they trust implicitly to the twisting of the hazel twig to guide them. Merryweather is the only dowser of whom I have heard that looks for surface indications of underground water.— W.F.B.

[3] The term "old well" designates the deeper, but unsuccessful, well sunk prior to the dowser's.

## Group (A)—Too Old

Owing to remoteness of date, I have been unable to obtain sufficient information about these cases to include them in a critical examination, but append the following notes:—

*No. 24. Sodbury.*—The Rev. R. S. Nash, of Old Sodbury Vicarage, writes that in 1853, the date of the publication of Phippen's book, the Rev. Mr. Foster was rector of Dodington, about one mile S.W. of Sodbury. The Rev. J. A. James, the present rector, informs me that there are three wells on the premises, the deepest of which is about 60 feet. The water in it stands two or three feet from the surface, and has never been lowered to 20 feet even in two exceptionally dry summers, so that nothing is now known about the alleged tunnel. The strata are Lower Lias, as in the celebrated case at Shepton Mallet Station (Group (E), No. 60), to which this is, therefore, closely parallel.

*No. 26. Shepton Mallet Gaol.*—I am informed by a warder, Mr. J. G. Barnes, that all the wells at the prison are filled up; but the strata being Lower Lias, and only a quarter of a mile west of the well in No. 60, the geological conditions are doubtless similar.

*No. 48. Well at Mr. Samuel Lang's Kennels, Bristol.*—Inquiries in Bristol elicited that Mr. Lang had not been heard of for some years. Professor Lloyd Morgan, F.R.S., tells me that the kennels were at the further end of Cold Harbour Lane, Redland, on Lower Lias or Rhaetic, so that we have here another case of a tunnelled well in this formation. Seven out of the eighteen cases which follow were also in Lower Lias, which thus appears to present conditions, i.e., as to difficulty of finding water, which are adapted to the dowser's art.

## Group (B)—Old Well Too Deep

*Yarlington House* [Additional Case]. In a letter to Mr. Andrew Lang, Mr. T. E. Rogers, M.A., Deputy Chairman of the Somerset Quarter Sessions, Chancellor of the Diocese of Bath and Wells, etc., writes:—

Yarlington House, Wincanton, *December 4th,* 1897.

> Over fifty years ago a very respectable farmer at Ditcheat, Kingston by name, a tenant of Squire Dawes, was well known in this part of the country for his success in the discovery of underground springs.
>
> In my own case he was attended with extraordinary success. My grandfather, when building this house in 1782, sank 135 ft. for a well, and only then came to a very slight supply; so trifling, that after having for some few years drawn up water with the aid of a donkey, he closed the well altogether, and used to send nearly half a mile for spring water. Upon my sending for this man Kingston, in 1846, he found a spring not 20 yards from the old well, which has quite sufficiently supplied the house, and at a depth of about 32 ft.
>
> I should mention that Kingston used not a thorn but the main-spring of a watch. He had no idea how the action was produced, and was not conscious of any sensation passing through him. He assured me that the influence acted with equal force on the main-spring in his hand whether the spring [of water] was 10 or 50 yards deep. I have walked with him holding one end of the main-spring, which in my hand was perfectly stiff and immobile, while the end in his hand was twisting and turning so violently that, unless he let it go, it must inevitably have snapped; and on some occasions it did absolutely snap.
>
> T. E. Rogers

On visiting Yarlington, Mr. Rogers showed me the sites of the two wells, which are about 40 yds. apart. He informed me that the depth of the old well was 130 ft. or a little more, and that the water in the new well was found at a depth of 35 ft. in oolite.

# The Credibility Of Dowsing

At the entrance lodge, 300 yds. E.N.E. of the new well, and on the same level, is a well 40 ft. deep, containing 5 ft. of water: the lodgekeeper said it was a good supply, sinking only 3 ft. in the driest summers.

Mr. Rogers said that below the loose oolite (Inferior Oolite) which forms the top of the hill, is a little layer of marl, and below this a sandy loam (Midford Sands). The oolite and sands are seen in the sides of the road going down to Yarlington village, about 130 feet below the house.

From the water in the wells at the house and the lodge occurring at the same level in the same horizontal bed of limestone, I infer that it is held up by the marl and forms a continuous stratum, which in the old well was lost by penetrating into the permeable sands below.

Since writing the above, I see that sheet 18 of the Geological Survey, which was published July 5th, 1850, four years after the new well was sunk, shows a line of fault passing N. and S. exactly over it; but, as there is no reason to suppose that geological maps are drawn with this degree of accuracy, it is more likely, if a fault has anything to do with the matter, that the old well was on it, since its tendency would be to let out the water at the bottom—in which case the dowser may claim whatever credit there is for not putting his well on the same line. Mr. Rogers has revised the foregoing.

## Group (C)—Old Well On The Side Of A Hill

A well so situated is no evidence for any unusual faculty in a dowser who finds a better supply in the interior of the hill at a slightly higher level, especially where the escarpment is steep and the strata rather impermeable, as in the case of two wells (Nos. 2 and 3) on either side of Locking churchyard (see Group (d), No. 28).

## Group (D)—Dowser's Well The Deeper

*No. 9. Evercreech Junction.* — [An unsuccessful well was sunk to nearly the same depth as a second, which was located with the twig 6 yds. from it, and yielded 36,000 gallons a day. Date about 1892. *Proceedings* S.P.R., Vol. XIII., p. 33. [p.23 this volume - Ed] ]

The well at Messrs. Roles' milk factory is situated a few yards to the south of the railway station. The strata are the upper part of the Lower Lias. The proprietor called an old man answering to the name of Tommy, who had worked in the unsuccessful well. He said it was from 50 to 55 ft. deep in hard blue marl, and that about 40 to 50 ft. down they had tunnelled in three directions—in one direction for about 17 ft. This well is now filled up.

The new well is 12 to 15 ft. distant from the old one The proprietor said its depth was from 65 to 67 ft., and that it contained over 40 ft. of water. The top soil consisted of 10 to 12 ft. of yellow clay, blue at the bottom, and below this 55 ft. of very hard blue marl which had to be blasted, but which fell to pieces on exposure to the weather. At the bottom was a thin seam of "scale" or hard rock about half an inch thick, and on breaking through this the water rose quickly. About 3,000 gallons a day are used for the milk factory.

At Owley Farm, about 180 yds. S.W. of the wells and about 18 ft. lower, is an old well 49 ft. deep, containing 44½ft. of water. The bottom of this well is thus on a level with that of Roles' new well, and the water in it also stands apparently at the same level. From this we may infer that the strata are approximately horizontal, and that the same stratum of artesian water has been tapped in each case. I therefore quite agree with "Tommy," who said, referring to the unsuccessful well, "I believe if we had gone down deeper we should have found the spring." Mr. H. J. Roles, to whom I submitted the foregoing, writes:—" Your report re the well at this place appears to me to be correct."

The local opinion of the difficulty of finding potable water is shown by the circumstance that the supply for the Junction is brought by rail.

*No. 17. Sturminster Newton.*—[A well was sunk 50 ft. without a drop of water. Mr. J. F. Young and three of his family pointed out a spot a few yards away where a well was sunk, which at a less depth delivers a plentiful supply. *Proceedings* S.P.R., Vol. XIII., p. 40. [p. 29 this volume - Ed] ]

The wells referred to by Mr. Young are situated a few hundred feet from an escarpment of Corallian rock (Coral Rag on Calcareous Grit) about 50 ft. high, facing west and overlooking the river Stour. The "village doctor," Dr. J. Comyns Leach, The Lindens, Sturminster, informed me that the unsuccessful well, referred to by Mr. J. F. Young, was sunk by him (the doctor) at the house about 60 yds. to the N.E. of his own, now occupied by Dr. R. A. Beaver. It was first sunk to a depth of about 35 ft., when it held 16 ft. of water, but on sinking it 3 ft. lower the water was lost. In June, 1893, the well sinker lost his life in the well from bad air, in consequence of which it was abandoned, after going to a total depth of 41 feet.

The second or successful well is 30 yds. from the first, and was placed at a convenient spot in the stable yard without reference to any predictions by Mr. Young or his family, of which the doctor was unaware. It is 45 ft. deep and holds 6 or 7 ft. of water.

Eighty yards west of the second well, there is at the doctor's own house a third well (marked P. on the Ordnance map), which is only 38 ft. deep and holds from 7 to 14 ft. of water, according to the season. Hence, as these three wells are on level ground, and in a tolerably pervious rock, there is nothing remarkable in having found water in the stable well below the bottom of the unsuccessful one. Dr. Leach, who has revised this account, never had to pay for carting water; and this is confirmed by Mr. J. F. Young's father, Mr. Robert Young (the author of works in the Dorset dialect), to whom, as also to Mr. J. F. Young, I have submitted the foregoing. The latter writes that his report to Professor Barrett was first sent for local correction, but that probably part of the information sent him might have been based upon hearsay.

*No. 27. Shepton Mallet, Brewery.*—[A boring was carried to some 140 feet without success. Then the water-finder, Sims, indicated a spot on another part of the premises, where a well was sunk and a magnificent spring was discovered in a fault of the rock at a depth of 40 feet. *Proceedings* S.P.R., Vol. XIII., p. 49. [p. 36 this volume - Ed] ]

The diviner in this case was Mr. Charles Sims, a professional dowser, now living at Pilton, a village rather more than two miles from Shepton Mallet. The Anglo-Bavarian Brewery is situated on a submerged island of Carboniferous Limestone, and the unsuccessful well was sunk in the front yard, through Lower Lias and Limestone, to a depth, according to a foreman who had been present, of about 100 or 120 ft., the lower half of this being a 6 inch boring.

Mr. Sims' well is in the hamlet of Bowlish, 500 yds. distant from the unsuccessful well and 95 ft. below it. The land is at the extreme point of the Company's premises, and was acquired consequent on the successful sinking. The well is 22 ft. in diameter and 40 ft. deep. It is in the bottom of a narrow valley, and 65 ft. south of a small stream, the river Sheppey, which runs west from Shepton Mallet. Just above the well a quarry is being worked in littoral Lower Lias limestones without the usual clayey partings; on the other side of the valley, 200 yds. to the north, is a protrusion of Carboniferous limestone; but the well itself, according to Mr. Phillis, a geologist formerly at the brewery, is almost certainly in Lias.

He said they got no water at first even at 40 ft; but he went down the well, and, seeing a place that looked damp, told them he thought they would get it by driving there, which they did, and it was found to drain the wells in Coombe Lane to the south. The water came in from both sides of the valley, but he thought it too far from the stream to filter through, though possible. The supply was insufficient for the brewery, and is now discontinued in favour of that from an open spring at Darshill, a mile lower down the valley.

The case is not evidential on account of the wells being so remote the successful one being also the lower of the two, and placed at the most likely spot for water. This was also the opinion of the people at the brewery and of Mr. Phillis, who have both revised the above.

*No. 28. Locking.*—[Two wells, Nos. 3 and 4, sunk without a dowser, 33 ft. and 12 ft. deep respectively, are dry during summer. No. 1, a dowsed well, 150 yds. distant, is 20 ft. deep and has a constant supply. No. 2, a dowsed well on the Vicarage lawn 120 yds. distant, is 31 ft. deep with a plentiful and constant supply. *Proceedings* S.P.R., Vol. XIII., p. 50.[p. 37 this volume - Ed] ]

On visiting Locking, in company with our informant, Mr. W. G. Hellier, I found (referring to the sketch-map given on page 51 of Professor Barrett's paper [p. 38 this volume - Ed] ) that just north of well No. 4 an east and

## *The Credibility Of Dowsing*

west fault throws down horizontal Lias on the north against Red Marls on the south. The marl has been worked out by a stream, and the dowsed well (No. 1) is in the bottom of the valley not far from the same; whereas the non-dowsed wells (Nos. 3 and 4) are near the top and bottom respectively of the steep scarp of Lias, and are not less than 30 and 10 ft. respectively higher than No. 1. Hence, as No. 1 reaches a level 20 ft. or more deeper than either of them, the occurrence of a constant supply of water in it is no evidence for dowsing.

The church and vicarage on the top of the hill are on practically level ground, which, at the other dowsed well (No. 2), may be a few (say 5) feet above No. 3: No. 2 is also stated to be 2 ft. shallower, and to contain plenty of water. On the other hand, No. 3 is sunk on the steep side of the hill, which cannot be expected to hold water so well as at No. 2, some 50 yds. back from the edge.

Locking is the only place where I did not take measurements; going round with Mr. Hellier I could not at the time, and it did not seem worth while to return for the purpose. At the well on Sandford Green, which we next visited, I found the measurements had been correctly given by Mr. Hellier, so presume those he gives for Locking are correct. The well is in Red Marl of the Trias, and contained 19½ ft. of water. The site of the old well, now filled up, was about 20 ft. distant, but, as no record of its depth has been kept, no conclusion can be drawn.

Ladyswood Park [Additional Case].—The following paragraph appears in the *Bristol Times and Mirror* of March 7th, 1891, p. 16; and, with the words in brackets, in the *Medium* of March 13tb, p. 167 :—

> Ever since the erection of the new mansion at Ladyswood Park, Sherston Magna [Wiltshire], the question of its water supply has been one of trouble and serious consideration. A few years ago, Sir T. Dancer, Bart., had two wells sunk, but without success in finding water. The estate having recently been purchased by Mr. Francis Davis, he determined to requisition the services of Daniel Lacy [a local diviner]. Lacy went to work with his little twig, and discovered a spring about 15 yds. from the two existing useless wells. He at once set his men to work, and after sinking to a depth of 60 ft. found an abundant spring, the output being practically inexhaustible.

Ladyswood Park is the "Ladyswood Farm" of the old one-inch map; it is about a mile S.E. of Sherston, on a plain of Forest Marble. On visiting Ladyswood in May, 1899, Mr. Davis showed me the position of the three wells, and said he had just measured the depth of Lacy's, which was 74 ft., and that the water stood 53 ft. from the surface, higher than he had ever known it before. I then saw Sidney Lacy, of Sherston, who said he had helped his father sink the well, which was in thin bedded rock much the same all the way down. They struck the water at the bottom after putting in a blast. The new well is certainly lower than the old one, but they would not have got water by sinking the old one deeper, because his father, after trying the stick, said they would not, and he had never known his father wrong.

With regard to the old wells, Sidney Lacy said he went down the second (B) to remove the pump, and should think the depth was from 60 to 70 ft., but couldn't say exactly. The first (A) was also about 60 ft.: it was Lawrence, of Bristol, who dowsed it and sunk it. Mr. Davis said the B well was sunk by Mr. Simon Evans, of Sherston. Evans said that, as near as he remembered, its depth was 44 or 54 ft., with some water, and that on boring another 25 ft. with a three-inch bore they got plenty: the A well was, he said, 25 ft. deep, with no water.

As water in thin-bedded, horizontal limestones would probably lie in a uniform stratum, the failure of the old wells is sufficiently explained by, according to Lacy's figures, their not having been sunk deep enough, or, according to Evans', not deep enough to hold the water met with in his boring.

## Group (E)—Heading Driven Towards Known Water

*No 42. Henbury.*—[In this case Mr. Crisp, the architect, writing in 1883, says that when water was required at Mr. Butterworth's new house, a geologist predicted plenty at a depth of 150 ft., where he said the Mountain Limestone rested on a bed of clay. They sank 150 ft. and bored 10 ft., but found no water. Then the diviner, Lawrence, predicted water about 20 ft. from the well, and advised driving a heading about 100 ft. from the surface. They drove 30 ft., and got a good and regular supply. *Proceedings* S.P.R., Vols. II., p. 104, and XIII., p. 67.[p. 51 this volume - Ed] ]

Rockwell, which is the name of Mr. Butterworth's house, now occupied by Mr. Frank Jolly, is situated on the north side of the road, one mile S.W. of Henbury and five from Bristol. The well is in Mountain Limestone, and about 50 yds. from its escarpment, which runs parallel to the Severn and shows the rock much faulted and contorted, as it was in the well. This escarpment is a Triassic cliff flanked by a beach deposit of Dolomitic Conglomerate. On the lower slopes are Red Marls which help to hold up the water in the limestone; the ground at the foot of the hill at Lawrence Weston being 120 ft. or more below the ground at the well

The principal point omitted in previous reports of this case is the existence of an old well 123 yds. to the S.S.W. of Rockwell well and 123 ft. deep, with water standing 94 ft. from the surface. This old well belongs to a disused Friends' Meeting House: the place is now called Fern Hill and is occupied by Mr. H. Fedden. At Rockwell well the ground is about 19 ft. below the old well, and the water stands 81 ft. from the surface, or about 6 ft. below the water in the old well, which, allowing for the distance, shows both wells to be probably in the same stratum of water. And, as Rockwell well is 150 ft. deep, the bottom of it is 75 ft. below the level of the water in the old well. The heading at Rockwell runs from the well under the front of the house, which lies to the S.S.W. The length of the heading, Mr. Jolly told me, is about 75 ft.; but Mr. Crisp, the architect, in his report says it is about 30 ft.; and Mr. Mereweather, the contractor, gives it as 24 ft.; the important point is the direction, directly towards the old well.

Mr. Mereweather informed me that the Rockwell well was sunk without getting water beyond a soakage from the top layers after rain; he noticed, however, a damp place on one side about 100 ft. from the top; Mrs. Bengough then tried the ground with a divining rod, which turned at a point 16 ft. from the well. Mrs. Bengough in her own account (*Proceedings* S.P.R., Vol. II., p. 104) says the distance was about 6 ft., and that Lawrence came later the same afternoon, and in the presence of herself and of many persons who had witnessed her trials, pointed to the same place. [Crisp says the point Lawrence indicated was about 20 feet from the well.]

Mr. Mereweather told me that neither Mrs. Bengough nor Lawrence went down the well, and that he was not present when Lawrence came. But as we cannot now be sure that Mereweather's information about the damp place had not reached one or both of them indirectly, or that they had not heard of the old well—which indeed the old house itself was sufficient to suggest—it remains doubtful whether Lawrence's indication shows more than knowledge normally acquired. At any rate he proposed the obvious course of driving a heading in the direction of the old well, and 25 ft. below the level of the water in it.

*No. 60. Shepton Mallet Station.*—[The contractors write in 1882 that in 1874 they sank a well 103 (or 90) ft. through blue lias rock with no traces of water. Then John Mullins with a twig predicted an abundance at 15 (or 50) ft. from the well, and advised a heading, on driving which the water rushed in and the miners rushed out, and their tools and watches are there till this day. *Proceedings* S.P.R., Vols. II., p. 107, and XIII., p. 86 [p. 66 this volume - Ed] ].

The well in question supplies locomotives at Charlton Station, of the Somerset and Dorset Railway, on the eastern side of Shepton Mallet; it is placed between the rails and the building marked "Tank" on the 25-inch map. My principal informant here was Wm. Baiss, an old man at the station, who said that, though not present when Mullins found the water, he was working on the railway near by and heard all about it. He said they sank through several sorts of stone to a depth of 90 ft., without water. (Mr. Hickes, in the *Daily Graphic*, also gives the depth as 90 ft.; Mr. Whitaker, the locomotive superintendent at Highbridge, writes that it is now about 80 ft.) Then about 8 or 9 ft. from the bottom they drove a heading in an easterly direction through some blue marl, and struck a spring at from 15 to 20 ft. from the well. No red marl was met with, and he thinks the well is probably all in Lias. Mr. John Phillis, a local geologist (who has revised this account), agrees in this, and does not think they got down on the limestone (Carboniferous), the nearest outcrop of which is a mile distant. The engine-attendant stated that they pumped some 20,000 gallons a day, which has never failed even in the driest summers. Mr. Whitaker says that, when no pumping is done, the water stands below rail level about 37 ft. in winter and about 51 ft. in summer.

# The Credibility Of Dowsing

At a point 280 yds. north-east of the well, at the bottom of a valley in which runs a little stream—the river Sheppey—rises an open spring. It supplies Charlton brewery, and may have been long known, as the Roman Fosseway passes within a few feet of it. Its escaping level is 43 ft. below the ground at the station well, and hence within a foot of the average level of the water in it.

Close by the station well, and on the same side of the rails, a quarry shows 15 ft. of Lower Lias, dense, well-jointed blue and white limestones in beds of about one foot thick, alternating with from one to three inches of hard blue sandy clay. Notwithstanding the generally impermeable appearance of these beds, we must take it as possible, not to say probable, that, with a head of 50 ft. of water at a point variously given as from 15 to 50 ft. distant from the well, there would be at least a dampness on that side. In the account written by the contractors in 1882 (*Proceedings* S.P.R., Vol. II., p. 107), we read that "on his arrival he [Mullins] went down the well," so that his location of the water "after he came up" cannot now be taken as showing more than his conscious or unconscious observation, or inference from the position of the brewery spring, which he was probably told of, as I was.

Since writing this I have seen the quarry a few hours after heavy rain and found it hold the water, except in the N.E. corner, where a main joint, running exactly in the direction of the brewery spring, forms a swallow-hole. It was doubtless such a joint as this that Mullins' heading cut into.

## Group (F)—Dowser's Well Near Known Water; Old Well Usually Remote

*No. 43 (the same as No. 59) Hedgecocks.*—[The architect, who in 1878 (or 1879) was erecting a house for Mr. J. T. Renton, at Hedgecock's Farm, writes in 1883 that the contractors "proceeded to form a well close to the new building, and had bored a very considerable distance without coming to water." Then Lawrence predicted water a few yards from the boring, and they sank about 40 ft. (some 42 ft.) exactly on a good spring B, which, he believes, continues to supply the house. There was an old well A some 100yds. distant with little or no water. *Proceedings* S.P.R., Vols. II., pp. 103-104; and XIII., p. 68. [p. 52 this volume - Ed]

In 1897, W. Renton, son of J. T. R., writes that the two wells, about 27 ft. deep, were only land springs and apt to get dry. So he had John Mullins divine a place, C, within six inches of which he found a good supply at about 26 ft. He also employed Mullins on three other successful wells. *Proceedings* S.P.R., Vol. XIII., p. 86. [p. 66 this volume - Ed] ]

Hedgecock's Farm is on the border of Sussex about four miles N.W. of Horsham. On visiting it in June, 1898, I found it in the occupation of the Duchess di Santo Teodora, and the name changed to Oakwood House; and now (1899) to Oak Grange. Mr. Jupp, a well sinker, who had been employed on Mullins' wells, told me there were three wells on the premises, of which two had been found by Mullins about 1893. One C, at the back of the house, now built over, is, he said, in hard blue marl 25 ft. deep with only 2½ ft. of water, and can be pumped out in about twenty minutes, though Mullins said there was water sufficient for everything. Another well, D, marked by Mullins close to the road some 50 yds. west of the house, is 20 ft. deep in blue marl and has a good lot of water. Another, E, dug about 1893 is 15 (or 30) ft. deep and supplies the vineries.

I also saw a new well, F, that had just been sunk 100 yds. or so north of the house, 43 or 44 ft. deep in soft dark marl (Weald Clay). A slight spring had been met with at 25 ft.; and at 40 ft. in a dove-colored marl water was found, which rose 7 ft. in a night and stands about 21 ft. from the surface.

Thus against one unsuccessful boring we have at least six successful wells, of which A and F sunk without a dowser are 27 and 44 ft. deep; while the dowsed wells B, C, and D, are 42, 25, and 20 ft. As the ground is approximately level, I infer a main water-bearing bed at about 40 ft. and a minor one at from 20 to 25 ft.

This is supported by the occurrence of water at other points along the level ridge which extends from Hedgecocks over two miles westwards to Rudgwick (Ridgewick). Thus the entrance lodge has a draw-pump; the adjoining cottage, 15 ft. lower, has a well 25 ft. deep; Rudge Farm, 600yds. W., has a draw-pump; a cottage 1,600 yds. W. has a well 18ft. deep with 5 ft. of water; and a quarter mile further a spring rises about 13 ft. below the top of the ridge.

This ridge is the first high ground in the Weald south of Leith Hill, and represents the escarpment of a hard or porous bed; which, according to Topley (Geology of the Weald, p. 104) is the same, "No. 2, sand and sandstone," that forms the water-bearing bed at Warnham Lodge, 1½ miles E.S.E.—already described, *Proceedings* S.P.R., Vol. XIII., pp. 278-279 [pp. 225-226 this volume - Ed] . The elevation, about 280 ft. O.D., is also the same.

At Hedgecocks, though the bed is less permeable, water seems to have been found everywhere except in the contractors' boring, the actual depth of which I have been unable to ascertain; in their letter (Vol. II., p. 103) they do not refer to it at all. If as deep as the wells, it corresponds with the dry ground in the Warnham Lodge bed. The case is interesting from the successful employment of two leading English dowsers, though the necessity for their services may not be altogether demonstrated.

*No 47. Park Farm.*—[Lawrence marked two spots at each of which, after boring 10 ft., water was struck. As many persons said water might be found anywhere in the field, the tenant, as a test, bored to the same depth midway between the places, and found the subsoil to be perfectly dry. *Proceedings* S.P.R., Vol. XIII., p. 71. [p. 53 this volume - Ed] ]

This is the same place as the "Parks Farm" of the old one-inch map: it is on the Gloucester Road, S.E. of Frampton-on-Severn, and two miles north of Dursley Junction. The subsoil is stiff clay of the Lower Lias. Lawrence's well is just outside the garden gate, and is, Mrs. Prout said, 25 ft. deep; 10yds. south of it is a pond about 10 yds. in diameter and 2 ft. deep, the level of which is 4½ ft. below the ground at the well.

Sixty yards north of the well is another pond about 15 yds. in diameter. The unsuccessful boring was made midway between these ponds.

The other successful boring was made, I was informed, by a man on the farm, about 20 yds. to the north of the north pond; he said they got at the bottom a sort of marly stuff, not very hard, in which the water came.

Mrs. Prout said that the water in Lawrence's well is salt, and is not used, and that all the water to Stonehouse is salt. The ponds go dry in summer, but Lawrence came at the end of March, or beginning of April, when they were full.

I think the proximity of the successful borings to the ponds (10 and 20yds.) raises a presumption of their connection; and similarly the boring midway between the ponds may have been unsuccessful on account of its comparative remoteness.

I have not been able to communicate with Mr. Prout, but the steward, Mr. T. T. Vizard, of Dursley, writes in regard to the foregoing :—"Your particulars are, so far as 1 know, correct. I do not think the well can be supplied with water from the ponds near, because I believe the ponds become dry in the summer, but that the well always contains water."

Perhaps, however, as the well is not used, it would be safer to say that there is no evidence either way, as water would remain below ground after drying at the surface.

*No. 57. Norton Hall.*—[A neighbour had bored through over 1,200 ft. of Lias clay, then over 100 ft. more, and got no water he could utilise. At the lodge local well-sinkers got no water at 30 ft. J. Mullins predicted water in the stable yard at about 30 ft., which was found at about that, and rose 20 ft. He also predicted close to the house a very strong spring about 20 ft. down, and on sinking 17 ft. it came so fast they could sink no further. *Proceedings* S.P.R., Vol. XIII., p. 84. [p. 64 this volume - Ed] ]

This is the. same place as the "Lower Norton Farm" of the old one-inch map: it is three miles north of Campden. The Hall stands at the end of a ridge of Lower Lias. Mr. Bruce said that the "gravel" in the clay consists of pebbles, which is suggestive of Drift (?). He gave me every facility for examining the wells at the house, of which there are three, viz:—

(*a*) An old well in the house yard 25ft. deep, and 11 ft. 9 in. to the water; supply insufficient; this had been shown to Mullins.

## The Credibility Of Dowsing

(*b*) Mullins' well in the stable yard, 28 ft. 6 in. deep, and 8 ft. 9 in. to the water.

(*c*) Mullins' well, "close to the house," by the drawing-room window, 17 ft. deep, and 11 ft 8 in. to the water.

On levelling, I found *c* to be 6 in. above *a*, and *a* 2 ft. 5 in. above *b*. Hence the water in *b* and *c* is at the same level, and that in *a* 7 in. lower. But *a* had been pumped that morning. Hence the water in all three wells is on a level. Mr. Bruce said also that pumping *a* lowers *c*. Hence the water in all three wells is in the same stratum.

The unsuccessful well at the entrance lodge, though on the same ridge and nearly the same level as the Hall, is 600 yds. distant. It is probably in a different stratum, and at any rate is too remote to be any proof of the absence of water at other points in the neighbourhood of *a*, *b*, and *c*.

Mr. Bruce, who has revised the foregoing, writes :—"I have always thought that immediately round my house was 'Oolite' ('Brash' the country people call it) but only a little on the surface and a very limited area, 100 yds. or so." If stone occurs here it would tend to form a natural reservoir. He adds, "The deep boring is at Kift's Gate, 1½ miles to N.E. of this, and lies a good deal higher "—i.e., on or near Meon Hill (Marlstone, or top of the Lower Lias).

*No. 77. Arnold's.* — [The owner writes that the old well, about 60 ft. deep, had a quite inadequate supply, and was bored 100 ft. without getting more. He says, "I sent for W. H. Mullins, and he said there was water at about 60 ft. deep on the top of a hill 300 yds. from the old well. He dug a well on the site and found water at a depth of 90 ft., and now we have an abundant supply." *Proceedings* S.P.R., Vol. XIII., p. 99.[p. 76 this volume - Ed] ]

This place is in Surrey about three-quarters of a mile south of Holmwood Station, and is all on the upper part of the Weald Clay. Mr. Bayley said that the old well at the house was 60 ft deep in grey, soapy, shaley clay, and gave an inadequate supply of water; it was bored another 100 ft. without getting any more.

Mr. W. H. Mullins' well is about 650 yds. distant at the northern extremity of the property. It is close to the railway, on a little rising ground so as to be convenient for gravitation, and is 40 yds. from and 18 ft. above a stream of water which is fed by springs from Leith Hill and flows all the year round. Mr. Bayley's gardener informed me that the well was sunk 99 ft. deep in grey, soapy clay without stone (Weald Clay). There were little springs the size of a straw all the way down, but the supply was small —about 3 ft. in the twenty-four hours—and it became necessary to augment it.

Between the well and the stream is a narrow, flat piece of ground apparently alluvial in character, and about midway on this the rod indicated water. Here, 6½ ft. above the stream, a second well was sunk to a depth of 10 ft., and an abundant supply was found which rises to about the level of the stream. This supply is carried through by a drain into the first well, which, in Mr. Bayley's letter (*Proceedings* S.P.R., Vol. XIII., p. 99 [p. 76 this volume - Ed]). gets all the credit of it.

As, however, I see no reason to suppose that the water comes from anywhere but the adjoining stream, I cannot regard this case as showing more than ordinary observation.

*No. 90. Woodside, Wootton, Isle of Wight.*—[An old well, B, 12ft. deep had a small supply very scarce through the summer. Another well, A, was sunk 120 ft. and got no water. The diviner, W. Stone, then indicated an enormous spring at a point 200 ft. from and on the same level as B, and about 550 ft. from and 14 ft. above A. Here he sunk a well, C, 7 ft. deep, and got an abundant supply nearly always running. *Proceedings* S.P.R., Vol. XIII., pp. 130-133. [pp. 105-108 this volume - Ed]]

The unsuccessful well A is about 225 yds. (not 350, as Taylor said) to the north of Stone's well, and about 50 to 60 ft. lower (not 14 ft.). It is the lower part of the Bembridge Marls, and, as it is stated to be 120 ft. deep, must pass through the Bembridge Limestone into the Osborne Marls.

The other well B, according to Mr. Taylor, the gardener at Woodside, is 12 ft. deep, and afforded a small supply. According to Mr. W. H. Cole, a former tenant of Wootton Farm, it was dug when the Woodside house was built, about 1850, and the water was brought down in pipes. Mr. Stone's statements, that it is "30 ft. deep and no water," and that "the owners of the estate had never been able to obtain water," are incorrect. This well is in sands of the Hamstead series.

The first well sunk by Stone was, Mr. Taylor informed me, at a point about 20 yds. to the east of B, but he did not get enough water and the well was abandoned; if so, Stone's statement that he found an enormous spring in ten minutes is incorrect.

Stone then dug the well C 60 yds. to the S.E. of B, and thence carried a trench about 80 yds. to the south as far as the road, the ground at all these points being practically at the same level. This trench was about 10 ft. deep and cut through gravel (Pleistocene Plateau), sand (Hamstead Beds), and some clay (Bembridge Marls). The water is collected by a drain and carried into C; the principal flow was met with a few yards from C.

More recently, in order to supply another house, another collecting drain has been carried up on the south side of the road, and curved round into the field to the west of Stone's drain, so as to head off the further end of it, since when, Taylor said, there has been a noticeable falling off in the supply. Subsequently also to Stone's visit a sand pit has been opened about 130 yds. west of C, showing 3 ft. of gravel on sand, in which at a depth of 15 ft. a body of water was found. The outcrop of this sand coincides nearly with that of the plateau gravel; the two together forming a natural reservoir over a quarter of a mile wide capping the hill.

Along the eastern edge of the hill I saw some ponds, and rills of water running down to the creek: Mr. Cole said there were nine such "runs" of water within a mile, and that they run all the year round. I also discussed the matter with the agent for the Woodside estate, Mr. George Barton of Wootton Farm, with Mr. W. H. Cole, and with Mr. John Newbury of Wootton, all of whom agreed that there was water everywhere on the top of the hill, that it was known to every one, and that it did not want a divining rod to find it. These opinions expressed after the event must be taken for what they are worth; on the other hand, the occurrence of water at other points on the hill-top, and in particular at B, 60 yds. distant, from which the house had been formerly supplied, was a matter of common knowledge.

*Arreton, Isle of Wight.*[1]—[The diviner, W. Stone, writes that a dry well had been sunk to a depth of about 50 ft., within 20 yds. of which, he says, "I discovered in a few minutes a spot beneath which a good supply of water was flowing," and all the natives were astonished; "I however, guaranteed a spring at 10 ft. . . . and my men tapped water at 9 ft., which quickly rose to the top," and he laid it on to the rectory and village by gravitation. *Proceedings* S.P.R., Vol. XIII., pp. 130-131, 133. [pp. 105-106, 108 this volume - Ed]]

This is the only case inserted by Professor Barrett without local inquiry, which he asks for on p. 133 [p. 108 this volume - Ed] of his paper; as such it was not numbered or claimed as evidence; but, having been published, I give a more correct version as showing the humours of the subject. The village of Arreton lies at the foot, of the downs that form the central Cretaceous escarpment. Besides going over the ground, I obtained information from Mr. George Barton, of Wootton Farm, who had got the dowser to go to Arreton, from a resident at Arreton, and from Mr. Orchard, the parish clerk.

They say that the dowser's quoted statements are incorrect, and that where he placed his first reservoir he never got any water at all. He was so sure there was water that, before getting any, he began by making a large reservoir 9 ft. deep with pipes down to the cottages on the S.W. side of the church. There was rain and snow at the time (the *Daily Graphic* of April 18th, 1892, says: "the snow on the 16th was four inches deep in most parts of the Isle of Wight") which filled the reservoir 2 ft. deep, and with that and the water in the pipes he got, when the tap was turned on at the cottages, a powerful jet which was photographed; but after a few minutes it ran out and there has never been a drop since. The photograph appeared in the *Daily Graphic*, of April 23rd, under the heading "A Water Wizard in the Isle of Wight," together with a statement that the spring had proved more than sufficient to supply the wants of the village.

The dowser then tried, said Mr. Orchard, to find a spring higher up the hill by running back a trench from the top of his tank, but when he got 22 ft. deep he got into the freestone and then he stopped, because he knew that if

---

[1] This case was quoted from the report appearing in the *Morning Post*, and was given for what it was worth. It has nothing to do with the so-called evidential cases, and is only included in Mr. Westlake's report as he happened to be in the neighbourhood. It well illustrates, as already pointed out, the untrustworthiness, as a rule, of newspaper reports on any scientific question.—W. F. B.

## The Credibility Of Dowsing

he got any water it would run away. This point would be some 30 yds. north of the reservoir. Forty yards further up the hill Upper Greensand is seen dipping 40 deg. into the hill, and, if the "freestone" forms its base, then the dowser's reservoir and trench must be on the apex of a wedge of Gault Clay, the last place in the district where there could be any water. Or if they occupy (as according to the new six-inch geological map they do, though I doubt its accuracy) a similar position on the outcrop of the Carstone, a coarse, hard grit beneath the Gault, the apex of this mass of sand rock would be equally incapable of holding water. If, as the dowser states, an unsuccessful well was sunk within 20 yds. of his, to a depth of 50 ft., without finding a drop of water, it shows that the water-level in this Neocomian sandrock is still lower.

Failing to find water here, the dowser then made a second reservoir, 40 ft. below the first, on the east side of some marshy ground in a little valley above the churchyard, and thence carried a drain alongside the marsh some 30 yds. to the north. This reservoir is 7 to 8 ft. deep to the spring of the dome. Its bottom, which is 5 to 6 ft. below the level of the marsh, is a peaty "sog" (saturated bog) through which the water rises freely. The water contains iron and peat, and a new supply will have to be obtained.

This case is only quoted as an illustration of the untrustworthiness of statements made by interested parties and of newspaper reports.

*No. 121. Stroud.*—[A boring had been made to a depth of 70 ft. but no water found. At a point 300 yds. distant Mr. Gataker predicted water at 50 ft., and a good spring was actually found at 45ft. *Proceedings* S.P.R., Vol. XIII., p. 180. [p. 148 this volume - Ed]]

In this case the unsuccessful boring had been made at the bottom of an old well at Farm Hill House, in the terrace at the top of the lawn. The butler who showed it me said it was about 50 ft. deep, and contained plenty of water except one very dry summer. Before Mr. Gataker came, Messrs. Orchard and Peer, of Stroud, bored some 20 ft. at the bottom of it with the idea of getting more water, and did not. This firm, who are not professional well-sinkers, write that the well is 30 ft. deep, and that they bored 35 ft. deeper in clay, clay bats and marl clay. The well is about 240 yds. south of Gataker's, and at a level from 50 to 60 ft. lower. There is also a well under the house still in use. These wells are in the top of the Upper Lias.

Mr. Gataker's well is in the field above the house and is 45 ft. deep, with water 24 ft. from the surface. He (Gataker) said the water would be found 60 ft. down, but they got it at 40 ft. all round the sides of the well. The rock, according to Mr. Bastin, the gardener, consisted of 20 ft. of rock rubble and sandy freestone (Inferior Oolite remanié), with yellow clay at the base: below this was 10 ft. or so of slate-coloured clay, and several feet of loose reddish grit like sea sand, and gravelly rubble with water (Midford Sands).

At the house of Mr. Allen's gardener, 110 yds. west of Gataker's well and from 6 to 7 ft. above it, is a well which the gardener, Mr. Harwood, said contained plenty of water. Mr. Riley, a working plumber in Stroud, who had repaired it two years ago, said it was from 35 to 40 ft. deep, and contained more than 5 and less than 10 ft. of water, which would make the water about 30 ft. from the surface. Hence the water in Gataker's well stands at the same level.

There is also, 300 yds. E.S.E. of Gataker's well and from 60 to 70 ft. below it in the same field, a well 16 ft. deep, containing 8 ft. of water, affording a small but good supply for cattle. About 50 yds. short of this a spring rises in wet weather and forms a bog; this, according to the Survey map, marks the base of the Midford Sands.

Also along the ridge going to Whiteshill (called "The Plain"— see Geological Survey, sheet 34, N.W. corner), from quarter to half a mile north of Gataker's well and from 65 to 50 ft. above it, are five wells about 50 ft. deep, containing from 3 to 13 ft. of water at the base of the Inferior Oolite.

The occurrence of these wells to the south, west, east and north of Gataker's renders it probable that there is water everywhere in the field; especially as it is on the outcrop of the Midford Sands, which are the main water-bearing bed of the district.

Mr. G. P. Milnes, the water surveyor at Stroud, who had had charge of the job for Mrs. Holloway, agreed with me that the case did not need a dowser.

*No. 99. Melksham.*—[A well was sunk 21 ft. and bored a further 18 ft., but no water of any consequence was met with. In the extreme corner of the field Tompkins predicted water at not over 25 ft. At 30 (or 22) ft. a spring came up like a fountain, and has yielded a plentiful and unfailing supply. *Proceedings* S.P.R., Vol. XIII., pp. 146-148. [pp. 119-121 this volume - Ed]]

The town is situated just in the middle of an Oxford Clay vale. The unsuccessful well was sunk in the meadow at the back of the butter factory, and 33 yds. from the river Avon. It contained a little water which percolated from the river.

Mr. Tompkins' well is from 80 to 90 yds. to the W.S.W. of the first well, and 50 yds. from the river and from 10 to 12 ft. above it. The water is 11 ft. from the surface. The engineer said there was a good supply, and he did not think it had to do with the river. The soil, Mr. Maggs' son said, was stiff white clay and blue marl without any rock, and he thought was mostly made ground, as they found pipes and old chain. Since the feather factory had cut a drain 20 ft. deep, some 30 yds. to the south of the well, it had not had so much water; this a neighbour confirmed, and said that lots of water was met with in the drain at the point nearest to the well. There is also a well which supplies an old house some 40 yds. from Tompkins well on the side remote from the river.

Hence, as Tompkins' well is in what appears to be an alluvial flat, where water was known to exist within 50 yds. on either side, I cannot regard its occurrence at the point indicated by him as surprising. He did, however, find a much larger supply and at a greater distance from the river than in the first well.

Mr. J. Maggs, who has revised the foregoing, writes:—" In my opinion the general tendency of [your] report is to minimise the importance of Tompkins' well.

"But the facts are: The first well was absolutely useless as a water supply, whilst the present one rarely fails to supply 3,000 to 5,000 gallons daily. Further, Tompkins was unacquainted with the neighbouring well. Water was found at the precise depth named by Tompkins, and, when tapped, the men at work in the well had to hurry up or would have been overwhelmed with the sudden rush."

Two attempts I made to interview the well-sinker failed, so that I cannot say whether Tompkins hit on a permeable stratum in the Oxford Clay or on a permeable patch in the river alluvium.

## Group (G)—Little Or No Surface Sign Of Water

*Lytes Cary* [Additional Case].—Here water was found by a dowser at a depth of 25 ft., and only 40 ft. from a dry well 60 ft. deep. Further off were two or three other wells, one of which contained some potable water, which lessens the improbability of finding it, but the spot remains an unlikely one, nor could I discover any reason for its selection. I have described the case more fully on pp. 174-175 [p. 266 this volume - Ed].

*Wimblehurst, Horsham* [Additional Case].—On this estate, which is half a mile north of Horsham station, water has been found at two places by Mr. W. H. Mullins for the owner, Mr. E. Allcard. The well at the house is 76 ft. deep and supplies about 500 gallons a day. Fifty yards to the north of this, Mullins found water at 25 ft. only; the amount, however, that has been pumped daily is comparatively small, less than 100 gallons.

At the farm in North Heath Lane, about 350 yds. further north, is a well 67 ft. deep which always went dry in dry seasons, though bored to 83 ft. In October, 1897, at a point 50 yds. to the east, Mullins predicted a spring at 70 or 80 ft., and proceeded to sink on the terms of "no supply, no pay." Water was struck at 54ft., and the well, which is 60 ft. deep, holds 10 ft. of water and yields a large supply. The rock consisted of sand and sandstones of varying hardness with some lignite and ironstone; the water-bearing bed being a dove-colored marl. These beds are the Upper Tunbridge Wells Sand; and being of freshwater origin, and hence usually lenticular and patchy, may be expected to hold water in pockets. We have here a comparatively large body of water standing 17 ft. above the bottom of the old well and 33 ft. above the bottom of the boring; the surface of the ground being practically level, with no surface indication whatever to show that there should be water at one place rather than another.

Since writing this, I hear that at the two cottages by the road, 130 yds. S.W. of Mullins' well, there is a well (marked p. on the 25 inch map), only 11 ft. deep, which always supplies enough water for the two houses. Mullins did not put his well in the direction of this surface water; still its occurrence diminishes the argument from its absence in the deep well, and makes chance discovery a possible alternative.

Mr. Allcard, who has revised the foregoing, writes, November 16th, 1899:—"The well at the two cottages has been dry lately, whereas Mullins' well at the farm has given a good supply all the dry summer. What we should have done without it I do not know, and I recommend any one wanting water to employ him, and not waste money on chance on their own account."

*No. 105. Toy Farm.*—[The following abstract is from the accounts by the steward, Mr. T. W. Pickard, written in 1893 and 1896 (*Proccedings* S.P.R., Vol. XIII., p. 154 [p. 126 this volume - Ed]). It includes additions received from him dated November 6th and 25th, 1899, and the whole has had his revision :—

> About 30 years ago a well was sunk at the Farm for some distance, and then abandoned on account of bad air. After this another well was dug, 167 ft. deep, but no water was found. Some short time before 1893 I personally took the depth; it was then quite dry, and the old men living at the place never remembered water there.
>
> In 1893 Mr. Tompkins, of Chippenham, was engaged. I purposely met him at the station and drove him to the place. He had no idea to what part of the estate he had to go until he got there, and he had no private conversation with any of the men there. He went over the ground tracing all the springs to one point, 450 ft. from the old well and from 8 to 10 ft. above it, and said that water would be found at a depth of 70 ft. I have marked on the enclosed tracing from the 25 in. map, as near as I can recollect, the lines he traced (they form a star of six sinuous lines over 100 yds. long).
>
> After he had found the place for the new well I took him to the old well, which had been covered up with strong timber; to mark the site there was a small heap of mould on which cucumbers were growing. I sent him over this with his twig, which made no movement. I then told him he had been over an old well several times: I told him the depth, and asked him how he thought it possible to find water nearer the surface such a short distance away. He replied that the old well was out of the run of the springs.
>
> We dug at the spot selected, and the first 20 ft. of chalk was rubbly [probably decomposed]. Nearly 70 ft. down we came on a level bed of solid flint about 6 to 9 in. thick; and at 70 ft. on open fissures mostly vertical, which were wet as though water had recently passed through; there was a very slight dribble at the time.[1] At about 118 ft. we struck two springs on opposite sides of the well giving a strong supply, and sunk an additional 6 ft. before the water gained the upper hand. The well is 124 ft. deep, in ordinary white chalk with flints, which continued to the bottom. The well holds 12 ft. of water, the same as when first dug. The water at the bottom came through vertical fissures and horizontal veins, and principally from the west side from the directions Tompkins had named from either end of the plantation (an enclosure on the hillside to the W. and S.W.). We have since bored some 20 ft. to obtain a better supply, but I do not think it has improved it. The old well has been filled in with the chalk, etc., from the new one.]

This I regard as the best case I have yet met with in favour of the dowser. The farm is situated in a remote hollow of the Sussex downs, midway between Glynde and Newhaven. The valley of which it is a ramification falls into the sea at Bishopstone, three miles to the south: half way down the Newhaven Water Company are pumping a considerable supply from wells. The old well was close to the farm, and the level of the ground at the well is about 260 ft. above the sea.

---

[1] Through one of these, according to Mr. Sherlock, a young man at the Farm, a draught of air came with such force as to be heard at the surface, showing an open fissure of great extent. He said the well takes an hour to pump out, and refills in twelve or less.

The new well is 150 yds. further up the valley, and about 22 ft. above the old well. Hence the water standing 12 ft. deep in the new well has a level of no less than 77 ft. above the bottom of the old well. The new well is in chalk with flints. On the heap from it, shown in the photograph (p. 337), I found a spine of *Cidaris sceptrifera*, which is common in the zone of *Micraster cor-anguinum*, so that the thick flint-bed 70 ft. down is probably the strong and constant *M. cor-anguim*-tabular described by Dr. Rowe as occurring between Beachy and Seaford Heads about 62 ft. above the zone of M. *cortestudinarium* (*Proc. Geol. Assoc.*, 1900, Vol. XVI., pp. 322, 323, 329, 332, 336, Plate IX.). According to this reading the new well is sunk entirely in the *M. cor-anguinum* chalk and to within 8ft. of its base; which last may account for finding some other fossils, as two or three specimens of *Holaster placenta*, which are commoner in the lower zone. The bottom of the old well is similarly 57 ft. deep in the zone of *M. cor-testudinarium* and 52 ft. above its base—it being 109½ ft. thick on the coast (Ibid., p. 327).[1]

Water in the chalk usually lies at a gentle gradient[2] which is however, modified by the density of particular beds, and by the presence of fissures. In the lithology of the beds as seen on the coast there is nothing to explain the absence of water in the old well, or its preferential occurrence in the new well, which is doubtless due to fissures. Water in chalk usually flows in fissures, i.e., in the main planes of jointing, which in this district, as shown by the direction of the valleys, run N, and S., and E. and W.

The narrow valley, approximately N. and S., in which the farm lies, is slightly sickle-shaped. The house with the old well is about the middle of the handle, so to speak, and the new well at the ferrule end, the valley at this point being contracted by a slight bulge from the east, which may, and probably does, indicate the position of an underground fissure. With this may be taken the fact, noted by the steward, Mr. Pickard, that the water flowed into the well from the sides of the valley rather than from its upper end.

Whether Mr. Tompkins noticed a slight surface feature of this kind —I did not myself till I was leaving and saw it foreshortened—and, if he did, whether he drew the right inference from it, may be doubtful. I think a geologist at any rate would have taken no account of it, but would have advised deepening or tunnelling the old well.[3] We must remember, however, when we are dealing with automatism, that the mere existence of a difference in the valley unnoted, still less reasoned on, by the dowser, may have been felt by his subconsciousness, intensely alert for every indication, and so have determined his action—on which, unlike the geologist, he can, when his judgment fails, fall back. He can revert to that prehuman thinking of which Cowper says :— "Reasoning at every step he treads, man yet mistakes his way, whilst meaner things whom instinct leads, are rarely known to stray."

Hence, at Toy Farm, we have, I think, either a case of discovery by automatism, or else of accidental coincidence. In the latter connection we may note that where water has not been found at one end of a property it might be natural for a dowser, in the absence of anything to guide him, to try for it at the other end, where also the pump at (p) may have suggested it.

Since writing the foregoing I have heard from Mr. David Caplin, Messrs. Duke and Ockenden's foreman, who writes in reply to inquiries :-

New Road, Buxted, *November 27th*, 1899.

> By what I can remember about the well I sunk at Toy Farm, the chalk down to about 60 ft. was of a very hard yellow nature with a lot of black flints. Below this for about 10ft. there were places where I

---

[1] [THESE REFERENCES (M cor-anguinnum, Holaster placenta etc.) are to certain identifiable and typical small fossils associated with certain types of rock. Ed.]

[2] The gradient of water in chalk varies considerably, e.g., 13 ft. in a mile (Clutterbuck); 45 and 47 ft. in a mile (Bland); these are normal conditions. Exceptionally we have 93 and 102 ft. in less than a mile (Bland); 155 ft. in half a mile (Lucas); and 50 or 90 ft. in less than 100 yards (Anstead). This last, which Lucas says is greater than he had ever met with, is the only instance I have found at all parallel to that at Toy Farm. (See Prestwich's *Water-bearing Strata*, p. 62, and *Trans. Inst. Surveyors* for 1878, Vol. X., pp. 306-314.)

[3] Professor Barrett asks what a geologist would have done under the circumstances, He would hardly have sunk the old well another 50 ft. to the nodular beds in the *H. planus* zone, as they are here too doubtfully water-bearing; and, failing a damp place to drive on, the best plan would have been to drive from the bottom on the chance of cutting fissures. Water could so have been found, and the probable quantity and cost computed from similar work in the district, as at the Brighton Waterworks.

should think water had been passing through at one time. From 70 ft. to about 110 ft. the chalk was in more of a block, but not so hard. The remainder of the sinking was in a much whiter chalk with black veins in it, and we did not get any water till within about 2 ft. of the fissure, which I believe is about 6 ft. from the bottom of the well. There were two fissures coming into the well, not opposite one another, but one I should think about due west and the other north-west, and there was no water coming from the east side at all.

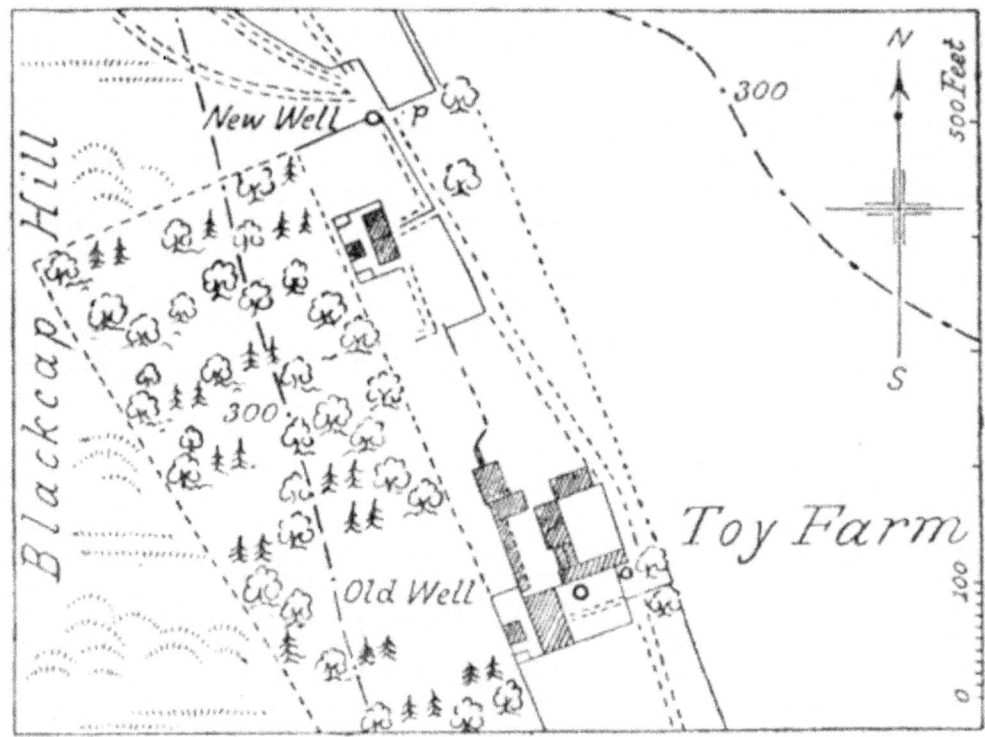

Fig. 19. Plan Of Toy Farm. From the 25 in. Ordnance Survey Map of Sussex. The strong dotted line is the 300 ft. contour. The well at the farm, to the east of the old well, is a storage tank: the pump at (p), connected with a storm-water tank, was removed after the sinking of the new well, dowsed by Tompkins.

This rather favours Tompkins' idea of springs meeting at a point than mine of a main east and west fissure; Mr. Pickard, however, mentions springs from opposite sides. The point could only be settled, if at all, by examining the well, which I was unable to do at the time of my visit owing to the obstacles of the pump and staging.

## CONCLUSION

Out of 21 cases of a water-supply obtained by means of a dowser, which I have now personally examined on the spot, there are, in my opinion, only three—the three last described—which may be called evidential of some supernormal faculty. To these may perhaps be added the partial evidence at Melksham (No. 99); and at Warnham Lodge (No. 58), where, though the bed was known to be water-bearing, the dowser had, I found, succeeded in predicting a dry place. I have thus met with from three to five cases, or from 15 to 25 per cent., in which his success could not have been due to information normally acquired.

Fig 20.
General view looking up the valley from Toy Farm; Tompkins' well is at corner
of road to left of shed

In the other cases, while the dowser may have known but a part of what I describe, I could seldom feel certain what he did or did not know. From what I have seen of Somersetshire dowsers at work, I agree with Professor Barrett that they do not seek for information— neither do they avoid it, and in the general conversation that ensues when the folks come out to see the water-finding it would be surprising if something was not said about existing water. Firmly believing in an external force moving the rod, the dowsers seek for water as one might seek for iron with a compass, and a group of them over a particular peg will confirm each other's indications with as much satisfaction as if "suggestion" had never been heard of. But as Professor Barrett has shown that the involuntary motion of the rod is due to unconscious suggestion, of normal or supernormal origin, —the subconsciousness standing ready to act on the slightest hint—. we must make sure that normal hints have been kept out of our experiments before we can use them as arguments for the supernormal. It seems to me, therefore, that most of the success in dowsing (say three-fourths) may be attributed to information reaching the dowser in a normal way, the subconscious synthesis of which determines the movement of the rod. The evidential fourth may be due to chance coincidence, or to some yet undiscovered faculty.

The popular vogue which dowsing has obtained in this country, and which appears to be increasing, is due to something more than mere success. The involuntary but visible movement of the twig inspires the dowser with a confidence in himself, and his employers with a confidence in him, that no amount of reasoning would. This confidence in subconscious pronouncements, which is as old as humanity, implies here a belief in some supernormal relation between the rod and water. If existing, and involving the dowser's mind, my own opinion is that it is likely to show itself in the same way as other subconscious faculty, i.e., fitfully and occasionally.

It is, I suppose, well within the mark to assume that three-fourths of most automatisms are subjective, i.e., revivals of memory, or dreamlike imagination, and that one-fourth is a liberal estimate for the supernormal. To suppose, then, that the supernormal element in dowsing, if such there be, will appear in any larger proportion, seems to me

# The Credibility Of Dowsing

highly improbable. We may expect it to form a residuum which will be discovered only when, as in stellar parallax, many concurrent causes have been eliminated. This is what I have attempted to do in this report.

## NOTE

[The foregoing able report by Mr. Westlake shows on the one hand the value of investigation on the spot by a competent geologist, and on the other how much easier it is to be wise *after* an event than before it. Moreover, with laudable anxiety to avoid any bias in favour of the dowser, Mr. Westlake has no doubt gone to the opposite extreme. For he assumes the dowser possessed minute local and stratigraphical knowledge, had inspected all existing wells, and had ability to draw inferences from all these data. These assumptions are not justified. The dowser, usually an ignorant man, is brought into a district he has probably never seen before, he asks no questions, but immediately sets to work perambulating the ground with his forked twig, and the whole business is over in a very short time. If under similar conditions, and before opening the ground, a field geologist would tell us whether the dowser's prediction is likely to be right or wrong, that would be a fairer test of whether the dowser's success is mainly due to "a sharp eye for the ground," and I hope this test will be made by any who may have the opportunity. I agree, however, with the general conclusion arrived at by Mr. Westlake, but think that probably a larger percentage of the dowser's success—especially of certain dowsers—is due to some cause at present unknown to science.—W. F. B.]

# APPENDIX B

## *NOTE ON THE GEOLOGY OF SOMERSET IN RELATION TO DOWSING*
By E. Westlake, F.G.S.

The mineralised ridge of the Mendip Hills just above the middle of the county has been the seat of mineral-dowsing since the time of Queen Elizabeth. The practice was probably introduced into Cornwall simultaneously, but has become practically extinct for this purpose in both localities. In Somersetshire, however, local conditions, favouring the later application of the rod to water-finding, have preserved its use to the present day. The Mendip itself consists of permeable Palaeozoic rocks—Mountain Limestone on a core of old Red Sandstone—in which the water for the most part sinks to too great a depth to be reached by wells. It is the Secondary rocks lying to the north and south—the Trias, Lias, and Oolite—forming what De Rance calls a "supra-pervious" series and yielding underground water, which have determined that Somersetshire and not Cornwall shall be the centre of water-dowsing.

The two last (Jurassic), which occupy about half the area of the county, may be described as alternations of clays and limestones, the sand beds being few and subordinate. The Oolites, especially in the upper part, consist of clays often of great thickness, alternating with massive limestones forming reservoirs in which it is comparatively easy for a geologist to predict water; although even here, the limestones being well consolidated, success where quantity is required may depend upon the accidental striking of a water-bearing fissure.

In the Lower Lias, which forms most of the low-lying arable land of the county, clays and limestones alternate every few feet or inches, and are alike impermeable, as De Rance indeed terms the whole formation. When uncovered in the quarries they are seen, however, to be traversed by cracks and occasional faults, like much-skated-upon ice, which allow of a slow percolation and the storage of small bodies of water.[1] There is no record of any copious supply, and the finding even of a domestic supply depends on a chance meeting with these water-bearing joints of which there is no sign at the surface. This, which is the geologist's extremity, is the dowser's opportunity; or, in other words, it is not surprising that where common-sense ends, the uncommon-sense attributed to the dowser should be in demand. The water, it is true, is sometimes impure, the fissured character of the formation being more favourable to pollution near farms or villages than to purification. Thus at the town of Somerton the well water was analysed by the Rivers Pollution Commission and found to be nearly all dangerously polluted.[2]

We may note, moreover, that dowsing is not carried on on the Somersetshire moorlands, which comprise the high-lying impermeable Devonian areas of Exmoor and the Quantocks drained by surface streams, and the low-lying alluvial levels debouching on the Bristol Channel where water lies near the surface. Cornwall also consists of palaeozoic clay-slate ("killas") with granite and other igneous rocks, all of which throw off the water, except the little that percolates in fissures.

---

[1] Water not only sinks through the Lias, but rises through it, as in the springs of Bath and Cheltenham.

[2] The local dowser, however, an old farmer, has proved equal to the occasion, and guarantees a pure supply by "andalyzing" the water, as he terms it, by means of two twigs held simultaneously.

## The Credibility Of Dowsing

There are two main types of underground water—what may be termed bed-water, or seepage, filtering through the pores of beds;[1] and fissure-water, or drainage, flowing through their joints.[2] The first type characterises permeable beds, the second the impermeable. To the latter condition the consolidation due to ages tends to bring all the aqueous rocks; all the igneous are so from the time of cooling: such rocks are seen in the Palaeozoic of Cornwall, Wales, the Lake district, etc.[3]

Bed-water is the more usual form, in the sense of being the one most met with in the populated lowlands. But as we pass from the looser rocks in the south-eastern counties to the more consolidated in the west, the proportion of fissure-water increases, till in the mountains there is nothing else. Tending to keep in compartments, it is difficult for a geologist to predict its level, and still more its exact place or quantity. In these Palaeozoic districts, however, surface water is usually abundant and good, and the dowser is superfluous; and so also in the Tertiary where the rocks hold only bed-water. His happy hunting ground lies therefore, as we have seen, in the intermediate conditions of the Secondary rocks, such as exist in Somersetshire.

E. W.

---

[1] There is no English term for this: "interstitial water," or "quarry-water," is properly the water *held* in the capillary pores of a rock and not expelled short of drying. The Scotch dialect word, *seepage*, is, however, used in the United States to designate the water that soaks through and oozes from the soil, and is so employed by Mr. King (see under). It has the sense of *oozage*, and contrasts with *drainage* (water flowing freely in non-capillary channels).

[2] The movement of underground water, or ground water as it is called (Germ. *Gründwasser*), has just been elaborately treated in two papers by Messrs. F. H. King and C. .S. Slichter, in the *19th Annual Report of the United States Geological Survey*, 1899, Part II., pp. 59-294, 295-384; *Washington*. The motion of water in the pores of beds, typically sands and sandstones, is very thoroughly discussed both from the experimental side and from the mathematical laws of capillarity. The authors allow, however, that their conclusions are radically modified by the occurrence of fissures, and that the actual motion of the water is very different from what it would be in homogeneous beds in which percolation proceeded through the pores alone. Thus, in the Dakota artesian basin, which consists of Cretaceous sands and sandstones particularly favourable for the storage and transmission of water, Mr. King shows that the largest theoretical seepage, or capillary flow, is only one-sixth of the observed flow (Ibid., p. 249), so that about 80 per cent. must take place through fissures. In less permeable beds this proportion is probably largely exceeded. Thus, in a flume of the West Los Angeles Water Company, the observed flow exceeded the largest capillary computed nearly tenfold (Ibid., p. 255). Mr. Slichter appends a list of 79 papers on the subject, chiefly in German.

[3] An illustration from Llanelly is furnished by Mr. J. F. Young, who says in a letter to Professor Barrett:—"In the Coal Measures exposed in a new dock near here numerous springs have been intersected, issuing with considerable force through fissures in the rock, some of which were horizontal whilst others were vertical. In a new coal pit they are sinking near my residence I noticed the same thing, showing beyond dispute that underground water in this and similar districts docs circulate through fissures, or follows the dip of the strata, and that intervening portions at some distance below the surface may be quite dry."

# APPENDIX C

## *Use Of The Rod In The Search For Mineral Lodes*

Owing to the length to which the present Report has grown, I have been compelled to postpone the publication of the mass of evidence I have collected regarding the use of the rod in the search for mineral veins. As already

Fig. 21.

*From G. Agricola's "De Re Metallica" (Basle, 1546)*

mentioned, this use goes back to a period long anterior to the first employment of the rod in the search for underground water. The introduction of the *virgula divina*, or, as it should be called, *virgula furcata*, into England took place, I have little doubt, in the reign of Queen Elizabeth, when German miners were brought over to develop the mineral wealth of Cornwall. They appear to have brought with them their *schlag-ruthe* (striking-rod)—our modern

# The Credibility Of Dowsing

forked divining-rod—and the phrase "striking" the vein, now extended to "striking" oil, etc., is probably a survival in modern English of the term used by these old German miners. The word "dowsing-rod " is, I venture to think,—with all deference to my philological friends,— the translation of *schlag-ruthe* into middle English.

On p. 393 is a picture (Fig. 21) of these German miners at work with their *virgula furcata*. It is taken from the edition published at Basle in 1546 of the great folio on mining, *De re Metallica*, by G. Agricola. Successive scenes are shown in one picture: at A the dowser is traversing the ground; at B he has struck ore, which on digging is subsequently found and pointed out by two overseers. The cutting of the rod from a willow is seen on the right. The serious, business-like air of the men holding the rod is evident; this is also apparent in another woodcut to be found in an edition of Sebastian Munster's *Cosmography*, published in 1550. These are the earliest authentic descriptions and representations of the modern forked divining rod that I have been able to discover.[1] Another early picture of dowsing for minerals (from a rare Italian work on mining) is given on opposite page; a photograph was taken by permission from the copy in the British Museum.

From Cornwall the use of the rod spread to the lead mines in the Mendips, and in the 17th century it was widely employed in the search for ore in that district of Somersetshire. Billingsley, in *his General View of Somerset*, published in 1797, gives a lengthy account of its use and of the esteem in which the rod was held in his time for the discovery of lead ore. But as the mines became exhausted the dowsers found employment in the search for underground water. A few Somerset dowsers still use the rod in the search for lead and zinc ore, and it was important to make a strict experimental test of such dowsers,—under the supervision of a competent geologist,—before they disappeared altogether. Mr. Westlake, F.G.S., kindly undertook to do this for me, and the authorities of the Friends' school at Sidcot generously placed their grounds at our disposal for this purpose. The following Report gives the result of Mr. Westlake's experiments with the different dowsers he employed. Some of these, however, were water, and not mineral dowsers. This should be borne in mind in reading the Report, for if the detection of surface indications affords an explanation of the dowser's success, as some maintain, then the results obtained with dowsers unaccustomed to search for mineral ore ought not to show greater success than chance coincidence would account for, whereas the report shows that they do.

---

[1] Chevreul and other writers attribute the earliest description of the rod to the alchemist who went by the name of Basil Valentine, quoting a passage from his *Letztes Testament*, in which the use of the rod (*schlag-ruthe*) in the search for ore is described, and erroneously giving a date in the 15th century for that work. The first edition of *Basilius Valentinus. . . His Last Will and Testament* was dated 1657, and translated from *Fratris B.V. . . Geheime Bucher oder letzes Testament* (1645). Mr. Westlake tells me that this is abridged from *Bergwerckschatz*, etc. (1618), edited in 1600 by Elias Montanus, a physician of Brieg, in Silesia. The authorship is attributed in a concluding poem to Nicolaus Soleas, but whether —as an MS. note on the title-page of the copy in the British Museum says— "genuinus Autor hj libri fuit," [Trans. – 'The real author of these books' - Ed.]is uncertain. This earlier work describes the *schlag-ruthe* and other rods at much greater length.

Fig. 22.
From M. A. Montalbano's "Pratica Minerale" (Bologna, 1673).

# The Credibility Of Dowsing

## EXPERIMENTS IN MINERAL-DOWSING AT SIDCOT
By E. Westlake, F.G.S.

Dowsing for mineral in the Mendips has been practised, as we know from various historical notices, for the past 250 years. On visiting, in the course of an inquiry into water-dowsing in 1899, the mining villages towards the western end of the hills, I found that mining operations had ceased some eighteen or twenty years back. I interviewed one or two of the old dowsers still living, who had used their art in former times, but found it was not now possible to obtain details or verification of the circumstances.

The only course open seemed therefore to be to make fresh trials with those dowsers who professed themselves able to find mineral. Several acres of land in the neighbourhood of Winscombe belonging to a Friends' school, which, while known to be mineralised, had not been mined, offered a favourable spot for experiment. I accordingly went over the ground with four dowsers independently, viz.:—

(1) Thomas Day, of Shipham, an old mining dowser, who professes to be able to find lodes, not necessarily mineralised.

(2) Rowland Pavey, a young miller of Cheddar, who professes to find underground objects by some secret art; (had not found mineral).

(3) Thomas Foord, a labourer of Shipham, an inexperienced dowser.

(4) William Kerslake, of Wells, a tailor and professional waterfinder; (had never searched for minerals before).

The localities tried were within a space of 300 yards east and west, and 100 yards north and south, and comprised :—

(a) An old cricket field west of the school, at a quarry in which ore had been found some twenty years since by Thomas Day.

(b) Some ground in and adjoining the girls' tennis court.

(c) A burial ground in which ore had been found in 1866, and a garden adjoining.

(d) A ploughed field a little to the north.

The soil at these places is mostly thin; the underlying rock is the Dolomitic Conglomerate at the base of the Trias, which consists of pebbles of various Palaeozoic rocks, the whole weathering reddish, and having a southerly dip of a few degrees. The rock is traversed by occasional lodes and veins, nearly vertical, running east and west, and carrying the ores of lead, zinc, iron, and manganese, but they are here too thin to have been worth mining.

The points indicated by each dowser separately I marked in such a way as to be imperceptible to those who came after, and I also so arranged that they did not have an opportunity of communicating with one another. I went round with each dowser, but except in a general way I did not know where the previous marks were, and therefore sources of error from conscious or unconscious collusion may be considered excluded. With each dowser the twig turned over a space of a yard or two, corresponding probably with their ideas of the width of the lodes, and I marked the central points. Pavey indicated 5 places, Day 28, Foord 2, and Kerslake 26. The marks are numbered consecutively 1 to 61 on the accompanying plan, and the dowsers who indicated them are distinguished for brevity by an initial, e.g., P3 = mark No. 3 indicated by Pavey (see plan on p. 399).

At seven places two of the dowsers approximately coincided within distances varying from 1¼ft. to 8 ft. Two of these, adjoining the tennis court, I found to be in made ground, and did not open up on account of the expense. Of the other five I opened, one in the field and one in the garden showed only solid rock; in the remaining three we found a well-defined vein of ore.

At three other single marks I opened up there was no sign of ore, though at one or two Mr. Clark thought there were signs of a lode.[1] In reckoning the dowsers' success their marks should be taken as extending a yard on either side the centre.

---

[1] I am indebted to Mr. George Clark, a Mendip and Kimberley miner living at Winscombe, for the interest he has taken in these experiments.

The results are given on the next page in tabular form.

At No. 4, though Kerslake's mark, K 56, was 4 ft. south of the vein, it was only 2 ft. from the south wall (foot wall) of the lode, and 1 ft. from the buff coloration due to the same, and was hence a practical success. Day's mark 3 ft. further south is neither a success nor altogether a failure; it may perhaps reckon as half successful. This No. 4 pair of marks I had thought before digging to be the most promising, on account of two others, D 33 and K 58, in the Friends' burial ground on the east side of the hedge, having also coincided within 6 ft.

Subsequently to the above dowsing I was told by Frank Knight that the grave of William Tanner, who died November 8th, 1866, had yielded lead ore; he was watching the meteors of that date from the school-house roof, and noticed that the grave-diggers stopped blasting, thinking the end of the world had come, and that graves were superfluous; they afterwards sold the ore in Bristol for 25s. The dowser Day was aware that ore had been found in one of the graves, and after he had made his marks I asked him to point it out, but he could not identify it. He might, of course, have retained some latent memory of its whereabouts; still as the gravestones are small, uniform in size, and flat on the ground, and hence neither legible nor distinctive 12 yds. away, I was interested to find on plotting the plan that his mark, D 33, was exactly on the straight line, 18 yds. long, joining the No. 4 vein with W. Tanner's grave.

At this point (No. 5) I opened the ground to verify the lode, and found it running just north of D 33 towards a point 2 or 3 yds. north of the grave aforesaid. Clark said it was "very promising lead-bearing ground," and, on sinking in it to a depth of 4 ft., we struck the vein. Day's mark was 1½ ft. south of the foot wall, and 3ft. south of the vein—another success. Kerslake's mark, K 58, was 6 ft. further south; so that, taking the two sides of the hedge, each dowser made one decided success and one doubtful one.

Taking the success of individual dowsers, Day, the miner, was right in 2½ places out of 5 ( = one half). As he had in former years seen the ore at the adjoining points, and knew the general run of the lodes, it may be said that his memory, conscious or subconscious, may have caused the twig to turn at the right places; and this view is favoured by the circumstance that in the garden, which was quite shut off by the hedge from any view of the burial ground, he was 5 ft. off the lode. Still, in making this criticism, we should bear in mind that one of the uses—according to Day, the chief use—of dowsing in practical mining, is to "pick up" the "lode" or "course" of mineral at no great distance from its working face, and that this he did at Nos. 9 and 33 with absolute accuracy, and of course without the ore being in the least visible anywhere. Mr. Knight told me that ore had also been found at the school at the S.W. corner of the inner court, near D 27, but I have not reckoned this anything for Day, not knowing how far he knew the circumstances.

Kerslake, the tailor from Wells, a comparative stranger to the place, was right in 1½ places out of 5 (= one-third nearly); I may have told him that ore had been found in the burial ground, but beyond this his success was not derived from local knowledge.

Pavey had a partial success at P 3 where he was 6 ft. off the vein, but in the two other holes dug on his sole indication there was nothing whatever, unless we reckon Clark's opinion about P 4. His proportion of success was thus one-sixth.

Among general objections which may be taken to these experiments, which I could only do quickly and extempore, are: (1) that the ground was known to be mineralised : (2) that the miner Day, having formerly dowsed over the property, refused to waste time by trying over the northern or southern portions (he made, however, one N. and S. traverse of the cricket field without result); (3) that to save the time of the other dowsers and with a view to getting coincidences I took them over the same ground; (4) that, by way of encouraging them, I mentioned to one or other that ore had been found in the quarry or burial ground, and must therefore assume it known to all. While such points make it difficult to calculate whether the success exceeds chance or local knowledge, I am inclined to think that it does.

The probable result of opening the ground at haphazard may be judged to some extent by the section exposed in the turnpike road, which lies in a cutting several feet deep for twice the distance shown on the plan, but shows

## The Credibility Of Dowsing

| | No.[1] | Place. | Nos. of marks. | Distance between marks. | Length, width and depth of hole in feet. | Nature of rock, etc. |
|---|---|---|---|---|---|---|
| Five coincidental places dug at | 1 | Old cricket field | D 9, P 3 | 8 ft. | 10 × 2 × ½ | Conglomerate with an inch vein of *calamine* (ZnCo₃) carrying lumps of *galena* (PbS). Vein 1 ft. north of D 9 and 6 ft. south of 3 P. |
| | 2 | ,, | D 11, K 44 | 1¼ ft. | 6½ × 2 × ½ | Solid conglomerate. |
| | 3 | Garden | D 28, K 55 | 2¼ ft. | 5 × 2 × 2 to 3 | Decomposed conglomerate on solid ditto. |
| | 4 | ,, | D 30, K 56 | 2¾ ft. | 16 × 2 × 2½ | Conglomerate with a *lode* 9 ft. wide having a high dip to N., and carrying a half inch vein of *galena*. Vein 4 ft. north of K 56 and 7 ft. north of D 30. |
| | 5 | Burial ground | D 33, K 58 | 6 ft. | 7 × 2 × 4 | Conglomerate with a *lode* carrying an inch vein of *galena*. Vein 3 ft. north of D 33, and 9 ft. north of K 58. |
| Two ditto not dug at | 6 | Tennis court | D 17, K 50 | 5 ft. | — | These points are on the strike of the No. 1 vein. |
| | 7 | ,, | D 20, K 54 | 1⅔ ft. | — | |
| Three single marks dug at | 8 | Old cricket field | K 36 | — | 6 × 2 × 1½ | Conglomerate with an E. and W. joint, which Clark thought might widen in depth and carry a lode. |
| | 9 | ,, | P 4 | — | 6 × 2 × 3 | 3 ft. rotten conglomerate on solid ditto. Clark said there was "every indication of a lode here," but there were no defined walls or sign of mineral. |
| | 10 | Ploughed field | P 5 | — | 6 × 2 × 4 to 5 | 4 ft. of reddish loam on conglomerate: no mineral. |

[1] The figures in this column correspond with the large black figures on the plan.

a lode only at one place opposite the quarry. It is also practically certain that the discovery of the mineral lodes did not depend on any surface indications, as both in the cricket field, garden, and burial ground, there was a layer of turf or vegetable soil over and completely concealing the lode.

These experiments in their practical success and in the difficulty of proving more, are in a line with ordinary water-dowsing. They are, I think, a further illustration of the power of the automatic mind to gather and utilise information from all sources. What these sources are can only be settled by more systematic trials, which should if possible take the form of tracing known objects, the chances of finding which can be calculated. Such are, e.g., water pipes, gas pipes, electric wires, and subways carrying water or mineral.[1] An old German mining-book describes the twig as used to find where to sink a shaft from the surface of the ground to some particular point in the mine. With known objects all the dowsers' predictions can be checked, which is impossible where, as in the above experiments, each point has to be opened up. Opening the ground to find unknown objects is not only expensive but inconclusive, as the dowser may always maintain that the object will be found at a greater depth.

E. W.

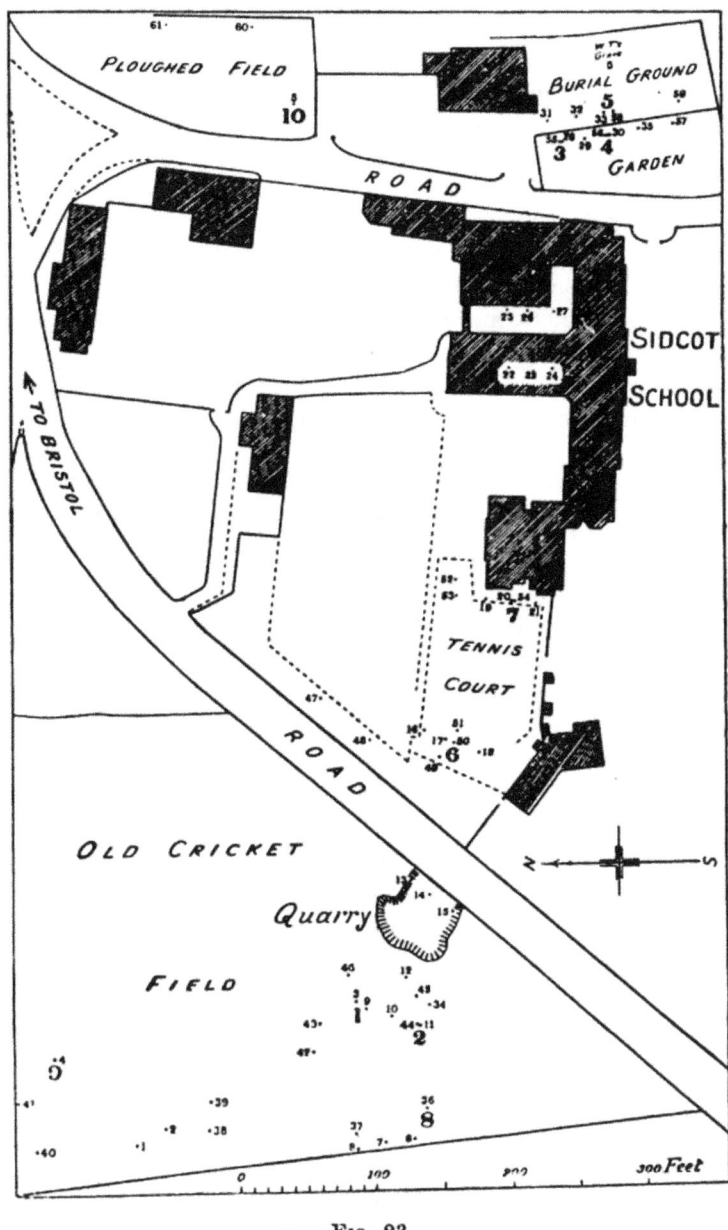

FIG. 23.

---

[1] Mr. Pavey is, I understand, prepared to trace underground objects of any kind; he has succeeded, I am told by Mr. M. P. Porch. Magdalen, Oxford, in finding human and mammalian fossils in the Cheddar Caves beyond the result of chance excavation.

# APPENDIX D

## *Paramelle*

The story of the Abbé Paramelle and his extraordinary success as a water-finder (or *hydroscope* as he was called) is so little known in England that it is worthy of more than a passing notice. Paramelle was born in 1790, and in 1818 was appointed curé and afterwards Abbé of St. Jean L'Espinasse, moving from there to St. Ceré in the Department of Lot in the south-west of France. A man of keen observation and scientific spirit, he was struck with the remarkable difference between the numerous springs, streams, and well-watered area of the eastern half of the Department and the difficulty with which water was obtained in the twenty-four arid cantons of the western half. Here the population were impoverished by having to expend a large part of their time in laboriously carrying water from distant wells to supply the wants of their families and their cattle. Prompted, he tells us, by charitable feelings, he spent two years in the fruitless search for springs, in the hope that he might be able to supply the poor folk of the arid region with the benediction of a bountiful water supply. In this he failed, and got the reputation of searching for the quantities of buried treasure which the English were supposed to have left behind when long ago they evacuated that district. He then set to work to compare the geological characteristics and rainfall in the two regions; the arid part was calcareous, but had the same rainfall. The springs, he rightly conjectured, were only due to the rainfall; where, then, did the rainfall go to in the arid region? It must penetrate the soil and accumulate, ultimately making its way underground to the river valleys. Guided by his own observations, Paramelle was gradually led to put his theories to the test, and found them verified. He then travelled further afield, and at last he tells us that after nine years of exploration and observation he felt sufficient confidence to go to what we should now call the County Council of the Department of Lot and ask them to place a certain sum at his disposal to test his theories by sinking wells in certain places where he predicted water would be found in the arid communes. The Council acceded, and in 1827 granted him a sum of 600 francs to make experiments, the communes that were benefited to contribute an equal sum. Eight places were selected by Paramelle in as many communes, but it was considered at that time so impossible to find water in these calcareous plateaux that three communes refused to incur the expense, though five who did were in each case rewarded by an abundant supply.

In the *procès verbal* of the Council of the Department of Lot for 1829 these remarkable successes are recorded. Paramelle,—now the learned savant, M. l'Abbé Paramelle,—is called in to explain his theories, and a further sum of two thousand francs placed at his disposal and a generous recognition paid to his learning and self-sacrificing devotion. Two years later the Council record that in sixteen out of seventeen localities the predictions of Paramelle had been verified, a perennial water supply being found at the place, depth, and of the volume he had indicated. His fame becoming known, applications to find water in waterless districts poured in to such an extent that with his Bishop's permission he relinquished his ecclesiastic duties and became what we should now call a hydro-geologist, what he called a "geognostic," and the public of that day a *hydroscope*. Disclaiming the infallibility which was thrust upon him, the local newspaper accounts of the period, some of which I have read, all speak of his modesty and marvellous success. Many explain his secret as a gift of God, others as the work of the devil. The poor people, however, answered very much in the words of the blind man cured by our Lord, "Whether he be a sorcerer or a messenger of God we know not; this we know, that whereas we were perishing for want of water, now by his help we have an abundance." By permission of the authorities, Paramelle hereafter made a fixed and modest charge of ten to forty-five francs for his services in each case, except to the poor, to whom no charge was made (I am afraid this would not satisfy our English water-finders, whether geologists or dowsers), and for twenty-one years he spent from sunrise to sunset every day, except Sundays, for nine months in every year at the work of water-finding.

In 1843 the *procès verbal* of the Council General of Lot records that in their department alone 338 wells had been dug at places indicated by Paramelle, and, of these, 305, or 90 per cent., yielded an abundant supply of potable water, in every case found at the depth he had predicted. In other parts he had also found 683 sources of water supply; and when in 1854, at the age of 64, he practically gave up his active work, the Abbé asserts that in 25 years he had located over *10,000 sources of underground water*, and he estimated that between 8 and 9,000 wells had been dug at the sites he had selected. He endeavoured to find out the percentage of failures he had had, but in spite of circulars he sent out, got very few replies; he believes, however, that his failures were under 5 per cent, of his total trials. Whether 5 per cent, or 10 percent., as the above official records indicate from his entire results, his astonishing success is, I venture to think, beyond anything I have heard modern expert geologists claim. A remarkable testimony to the value of his work I found in an old number of the *Journal d'Agriculture Pratique* for April 1845. The *Journal* quotes a letter the Prefect of Lot wrote to the Prefect of Versailles, stating that up to that time about 6,000 new sources of water supply in 30 departments had been discovered by the Abbé Paramelle, and the actual money value of the springs thus found was, he says, estimated at not less than four to five million francs.

In 1846 the *Académie* of Reims published a report in their Comptes Rendus from a committee of six of their members appointed to enquire into Paramelle's theory and work. In this lengthy and careful report the committee express their high opinion of Paramelle's character and the results of his work, and quote a number of letters and certificates from various officials in different parts of France, testifying to his success. His proportion of failures is estimated as rather less than 5 per cent. In almost every instance quoted, the depth at which water was found was under 50 feet. As to his theory, the committee report that, though true in a sense, it is imperfect and not always applicable, nor do they consider that a knowledge of it would enable another, not possessed of Paramelle's special talents, quick recognition of all surface indications and long practice, to be equally successful. Paramelle himself declared, however, that in a few months of study and three of field practice, he could teach anyone of ordinary intelligence all that he knew. That might be, but he could not communicate his almost unerring instinct.[1]

Paramelle, however, unlike most prophets, seems to have had more honour in his own country than elsewhere. His success was declared by outsiders to be impossible, doubt was thrown on the reality or permanence of the springs he had found, one savant asserts that his procedure was unscientific and valueless, whilst a writer in one of the French journals, for 1842, says whatever success he had was due to impressions, sensations, and convulsions, and, doubtless, diabolic visions that he experienced. This writer adds: "The only difference between Paramelle and other sorcerers is that he conceals the diabolic signs he receives, glossing over his magical proceedings with a lot of scientific jargon." [2]

To meet his critics Paramelle determined to publish the methods which had guided him. He states that in 1827 he had written a work "on the art of discovering springs." This he revised and published in 1856; three editions were quickly sold, a German translation was made by the Professor of Geology in Freiberg, a Spanish translation followed, and so highly was the work esteemed that the Spanish Ministry ordered every municipality to purchase a copy. A fourth enlarged French edition was published in 1896, after Paramelle's death. This I have read, and if the earlier ones resemble it, I do not hesitate to express my amazement at the neglect of this work in England. The wealth of geological and useful practical knowledge gained, through field observation, by this French Abbé two generations ago is astonishing. He must have been an odd mixture, for he includes in his work a number of laudatory press notices.[3] From these, however, we gain a description by eye-witnesses of his method of procedure; and these merit some attention. First, there is the unimpeachable evidence of one of the most distinguished French *savants*, M. Geoffrey St. Hilaire, who, in a memoir read before the Paris Academy of Sciences, in 1836, writes as

---

[1] M. Auscher, in his recent handbook of hydro-geology (*L'Art de découvrir les Sources*; Paris, 1899), states that the best known of Paramelle's pupils was M. Amy de Pannessières, who also wrote upon the discovery of underground water. But I do not know of his writings nor of any record of his success as a water-finder. M. Auscher refers repeatedly to Paramelle's work and successes, although his theory is said to have been found in part defective or erroneous. Some of Paramelle's occasional failures M. Auscher attribute's to his neglect of surface indications, such as the comparatively rapid melting of snow over underground water, local mists, the character of the vegetation, etc., but of some at least of these Paramelle was aware, and it is difficult to know to what extent he did neglect or rely on them in practice.

[2] *L'Eclaireur du Midi*, Juillet, 1842.

[3] It is possible that some of these laudatory notices were inserted alter Paramelle's death by the editor of the fourth and last edition, the only edition I have been able to consult. This contains the preface to the third edition, published in 1865; in this preface, which Paramelle himself wrote, he states that in spite of some hostile criticism, none of his statements have been controverted, and after exercising the greatest care in revision, he has found nothing essential to withdraw. Hence, he adds, the present (third) edition is merely a reproduction of the earlier ones with some additional facts and quotations which support the conclusions he had reached.

# The Credibility Of Dowsing

follows:—"The Abbé Paramelle's skill in discovering springs rests on the science of observation, and not on the instinctive movement of the divining rod. He has acquired by practice such acuteness of observation that, after a single and rapid inspection of the surface of the ground, he can indicate the place and the depth of any underground sources that may exist. His success has been so remarkable as to convince the most incredulous." Nearly every eye-witness says the same thing. A Journal at Aix says that, "Without any hesitation, and after a rapid glance, Paramelle at once indicates not only the very spot where to sink a well, but the depth it will have to be sunk and the volume of water that will be obtained. All this in so laconic and precise a fashion that scepticism vanishes." Another journal, *Le Rhutenois*, writes, on February 15th, 1837 :—"The Abbé Paramelle simply looks round, says, 'Here you will find the spring at such a depth and of such quantity; it comes in this direction, and the water will be of such and such a quality ' "; and so on, in upwards of a score of other Press notices which are included in the chapters XXX. and XXXI. of Paramelle's work. Similar testimony is borne in the Report of the Commission appointed by the Academy of Reims already referred to, and in a paper published in 1835 by the French *Société Centrale d'Agriculture*, LVII$^e$ Cahier, p. 326.[1]

The last chapter of Paramelle's book gives a very interesting summary of the various methods that had been adopted in ancient and in modern times (i.e., before the present century) for the purpose of discovering underground water; to this part of our subject we may return later.

What then was the secret of Paramelle's method? This he has disclosed, or professed to disclose, in his book, *L'Art de Découvrir Sources*. He did not use any form of divining-rod; he tells us the rod would never turn in his hands, though he had often tried it, and he regarded the users of the *baguette* with undisguised contempt,

The hypothesis upon which he worked, to state it in the most general form, was that underground water behaves precisely like water that is visible on the surface of the earth. Just as in the latter case waters that are precipitated upon the surface of the earth and fail to penetrate the superficial soil, gather into rivulets and join streams and rivers, following in their course certain suitable channels, so must underground waters behave. Thus the waters which percolate through the upper earth, on reaching a bed of impermeable rock or clay, will form into little filaments of water, these will unite into rivulets, which again will join larger subterranean water courses, and so on until they finally reach the surface or possibly emerge in the bed of a river or lake. Throughout their course they will follow hollows, depressions or folds in the impermeable stratum analogous to those in which surface waters flow. The position of these underground channels, our author asserts, can be determined by observation of the surface. This branch of his subject Paramelle explains with much detail, but it will be sufficient here to give a bare outline of his views.

Subject to certain exceptions, it may be said that he held the conformation of the surface to correspond in some important features with that of an impermeable stratum beneath it. A valley or longitudinal depression, whether large or small, marks, he says, the position of an underground stream. In broad valley bottoms the principal watercourse will usually be found on the line of intersection of the sides. Subsidiary gullies or hollows indicate the affluents. In a fairly level country, where the depressions can be only slightly marked, he describes how it is still possible with minute precautions and by close observation to detect them.

The existence of such outward signs of hidden streams of water Paramelle attributes to the natural tendency of the surface to conform to its supporting bed, and also to subsidence due to the constant carrying away of matter by the underground current.

The quantity of water likely to be found at a selected point he estimated from the area drained. The quality of the water he inferred from the nature of the soil through which it had filtered, and the depth at which it ran mainly from ordinary geologic data.

Paramelle did not claim that his method was applicable to the discovery of sheets of underground water or water-logged strata of wide area, or, one may suppose, to water at a great depth. The former case, however, he

---

[1] For these and other rare papers relating to Paramelle I am indebted to M. Holland, of 2, Rue des Chantiers, Paris, whose excellent book agency I have previously had to thank.

believed to be of very rare occurrence, and to others, for which his general plan. would be unsuitable, he refers candidly, and suggests several ingenious considerations.[1]

It may be inferred, from the foregoing brief sketch of Paramelle's views, as well as from the contemporary notices of his work, that his success lay in the discovery of shallow, or what are sometimes called surface, wells, that is, wells from 10 to 30 or 40 feet deep, and his observations are evidently based on the superficial beds which lie on the older rocks. As Mr. T. V. Holmes, F.G.S., has pointed out in the interesting letter I have already published,[2] "This perception of water-bearing surface beds is quite independent of a knowledge of geological structure. Indeed the rise of geology as a science tended to put this older knowledge of water-bearing surface beds into the background. The Geological Survey had been at work many years at the deep-seated geology of England and Wales, before any 'drift-maps,' or those showing these superficial beds, were even thought of. . . . But geologists seldom bestow much thought on these various drift-beds unless interested in flint implements." Perhaps I may here add parenthetically my earnest hope that good "drift-maps" of the whole of the British Isles will soon be published by the Geological Survey. The need for and practical value of such maps has been most strongly impressed upon me during these investigations. Both Mr. Kilroe and Mr. Holmes have pointed out to me how misleading the ordinary maps may be to a person who wishes to obtain a moderate water supply by sinking a well.

I am not in the least competent to give any opinion upon Paramelle's theories. They may excite a smile among geologists of the present day, or they may awaken interest or arouse criticism. In any case, his phenomenal success in the location of underground water needs explanation, even assuming that he did not discover the more abundant sources found in deep wells. For my own part, I believe that the experience he had gained by long observation in the field, and the instinct he had thus acquired, accounted for a good deal more than he could rationally explain. Hence, like the successful dowser of past and present times, it was his sub-conscious far more than his conscious life that was concerned in the process of water-finding. That no mere knowledge of the theories he sets forth in his book will enable any one to become a second Paramelle is obvious from the fact that, although his book has been widely read on the Continent during the last seventy years, no such renown has been subsequently gained by any Continental water-finder, nor, I believe, by hydro-geologists any where, as attached to this simple-minded French Abbé.

---

[1] Mr. B. St. G. Lefroy, to whom I am indebted for kindly making, at my request, the foregoing concise summary of Paramelle's working hypothesis, writes to me as follows:—"Paramelle's theory can hardly have been developed, *ex post facto*, to disarm the popular superstition which his abnormal success created, for in 1820 a local French journal (quoted on p. 382 of Paramelle's work) states that his success was based on geological theories he had arrived at, and the local newspaper reports emphasise the fact that he viewed the land, in some cases not going on it at all. "The impression which he makes on me is that, granting his premises, his conclusions are drawn with admirable common-sense and candour; and that even if he be a scientific heretic, twenty-five years of observation, a naturally good eye for ground and some modicum of truth in his conjectures, might well account for his successes without invoking any supernormal faculties." The gist of the difference between Paramelle and orthodox geologists, I venture (with the deference of conscious ignorance) to submit lies in the question :—Is a water-bearing stratum a sponge or a filter'! (I mean principally. Of course it must be both to some extent). If the latter, would not his view be correct—*ex necessitate rei*? (Water would percolate by gravity into depressions). Another way of contrasting Paramelle and hydro-geologists might be to say that the former fixed his mind on the impermeable stratum while the attention of the latter is mainly directed (I think) to the presence or absence of a water-soaked bed above it.

[2] *Proceedings* S.P.R., Vol. XIII., p. 222. [p.183 this volume - Ed]

# APPENDIX E

## *Evidence Of Clairvoyance In Dowsers*

It is obvious that if a good dowser has any power whatever of subconscious supersensory perception, surface indications of the object sought for will have very little to do with his success, and he ought to be able to tell the position of a hidden coin or any buried object as well as that of underground water and mineral lodes. Now it is well known that the majority of dowsers from the earliest times have always asserted that they could do this; in fact, the first use of the divining rod was for the purpose of discovering buried treasure.[1] It would take me too far aside from my present purpose if I entered into the history of this part of my subject and the evidence that exists on its behalf; this I propose to do in another paper. It is sufficient to say that I have collected a large amount of evidence which shows,—in spite of my strong previous belief to the contrary,— that the success of the dowser in finding concealed objects is greater than seems possible to account for by chance coincidence. Indications may in some cases have been unconsciously afforded by those present who knew where the object was hidden, but, allowing for this and other sources of error, there appears to be in these experiments a degree of success with certain good dowsers like the late John Mullins that points to the existence of some faculty analogous to clairvoyance. With several amateur dowsers there is similar evidence. Mr. Tosswill, of Budleigh Salterton (see p. 306), made in the presence of two witnesses a series of successful experiments in finding concealed coins, every care being taken to avoid unconscious indications being given by the witnesses. I have specially to thank Mr. Tosswill for his kindness in assisting this inquiry, and taking a railway journey of four hours solely for the purpose of enabling these tests to be made. Mr. Young, of Llanelly (see p. 304) has made similar experiments in the presence of a previously sceptical witness. Mr. Jerman, F.R.I.B.A., a well-known architect in Exeter, who is an amateur dowser, found he also was successful on making an attempt at finding a carefully concealed coin, though one such experiment is of little value. Enough evidence, however, exists to make it worth while for those who find they have the power of motor automatism to pursue somewhat similar experiments, and I hope this will be done.

I regret that I have not made more experiments of this kind myself with different dowsers. The fact is, I was for a long time entirely sceptical of the statements made, and my own experience confirmed this scepticism. For early in this inquiry I made some experiments with a dowser, Mr. Stears, on concealed masses of metal, which were unsuccessful; these are related in the previous Report, p. 176 [p. 144 this volume - Ed]. Again, Colonel Taylor made, at my request, a careful experiment at Cheltenham with the dowser, Mr. Tompkins, on concealed coins; these also were unsuccessful. And yet both these dowsers seem to have had singular success in this very direction on other occasions with different experimenters. It is natural to assume such success was due to careless experiment. Perhaps so. On the other hand, we do not require to assume—we know—how very fitful are the psychical conditions which ensure success in any experiments connected with the sub-conscious state, such, e.g., as telepathy. Hence it would be an error to attach as much importance to the failure of a particularly psychical test experiment as we should to the failure of a corresponding physical experiment the conditions of which are known.[2]

---

[1] There is an amusing account in the life of William Lilly, the astrologer, of how he accompanied Davy Ramsey, "his Majesty's clockmaker," in the year 1634, to search for buried treasure by means of the divining rod in the cloisters of Westminster Abbey, the Dean having given permission, and how the demons raised a storm and drove them away. One of the epigrams of Sheppard, published in 1651, satirises this use of the rod; but Continental and, to a less extent, English, literature of that and an earlier period, contains frequent reference to the use of the rod for finding buried treasure. Even so recently as September 28th, 1882, the Paris correspondent of the London *Times* relates how the Government Director of Fine Arts in Paris had that week ordered, in his official capacity, a search for treasure (supposed to have been buried a century previously), to be made by means of the divining rod. The search was, however, fruitless. A leading article on the subject appeared in the Times for October 6th, 1882.

[2] In his admirable address to Section A of the British Association last year, Professor Poynting, F.R.S., pointed out how essentially different are the results to be expected from experiments with living compared with non-living matter. He remarks: "Taking the psychical view, in the living being there is always some individuality, something different from any other living being, and full prediction in the physical sense, and by physical methods, is impossible."

## Prof. W. F. Barrett

Recently I have, however, had a certain amount of success in a more severe test to which I submitted this hypothesis of "clairvoyance." In my correspondence and interview with Mr. J. F. Young, of Llanelly, who is a member of our Society—and to whom I have frequently referred as a successful amateur dowser—I found that he had occasionally with success tried automatic writing. I therefore asked him to try if a pencil held in his hand would write certain words or numbers I would enclose in a sealed envelope: he agreed. Whereupon I printed some words of three letters, placed them between a fold of thick paper, and enclosed each in an opaque envelope which was sealed with my own seal as well as otherwise securely fastened. Three such envelopes I posted to Mr. Young at Llanelly, and asked him to try if by automatic writing or by the rod he could ascertain what words of three letters I had written. In reply he said :—

> On receiving your letter I gave the envelopes to my sister-in-law, who took charge of them till I was ready to make the experiment. When at leisure in the evening she gave me one of the envelopes marked (3), which I placed inside my cap, and put cap and envelope on the top of my bald head. I sat at a table, as usual, with a pencil in my hand, and made up my mind as blank as possible, patiently waiting till my hand appeared controlled to write without any volition on my part. After waiting for a little while my hand suddenly scribbled out, on an old postcard which was lying near, the enclosed, which looks like O N VV, or else the last letter is E, ONE. I send the postcard to you with the scribble on it. Will you please say what the word is? I return the envelope.
>
> I found the experiment very tiring, as if some vital force were exhausted, and will try the other envelopes another time.
>
> J. F. Young.
>
> P.S.—Before posting this letter, I made a second experiment with another of your envelopes, the one marked (2). First I tried with the rod in my hands, my sister slowly repeated the alphabet aloud; this she did three or four times. After the first repetition the rod moved at the letters A, B and C and no others. I then tried automatic writing with my eyes shut; the enclosed came, starting from the x —it looks like A. B. On a second attempt the same letters came somewhat clearer.

On receiving the envelopes from Mr. Young I examined them carefully; they had not been tampered with in any way. On opening No. 3, I found the word ONE, and in No. 2 the word CAB.

ORIGINAL.          REPRODUCTION.

Fig. 24.

Here is an exact reproduction of the writing Mr. Young sent me. Holding the writing of Fig. 24 sideways the last letter may be read as an E, and in Fig. 25 there seems to be an attempt at the letter C when the pencil began to write. I myself had no idea which of numerous words I had written was in any particular envelope.

## The Credibility Of Dowsing

The experiment, therefore, seems a fairly good one as a preliminary test, and encourages the hope that a more extended series of trials may yield results of no slight value.[1]

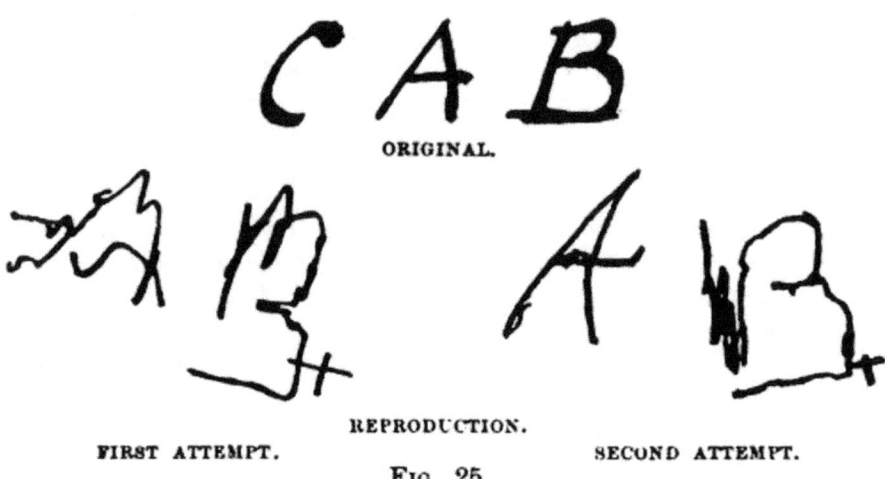

FIG. 25.

I begged Mr. Young to try the third envelope and let me know the result. He promised to do so, but unfortunately serious illness and death invaded his family, and after his own recovery he has not yet felt disposed to go on with the experiments. Prior to his experiment with my envelopes, he gave me the result of some experiments of a similar kind I had asked him to make in his own way. I have entire confidence in Mr. Young's integrity, but the results which I will give must be taken for what they are worth. Mr. Young writes on January 5th, 1900 :—

> I made a few trials this evening. I cut some squares of paper all alike, put a number of one figure on each, then turned the square upside down, shuffled them about in every way, and then picked up one of the squares with my eyes closed, put it on the top of my head and placed my cap on, it fitting close to the crown of my head. Then I made myself as passive as possible, and either slowly repeated the figures till a certain one seemed to be right, or the impression of a particular figure came as soon as I put the cap on my head; when it came thus quickly, it was invariably right. This is the result, and the order in which I took up the figures, of course one at a time, x denotes a wrong guess :—
>
> Figure on square ...   2|4|7|5|3|2|9|3|6|1|
>
> Figure guessed ...   x|4|7|6|x|2|9|x|6|1|
>
> The experiment was very exhausting, so that I could not go on any longer.

---

[1] I should be very glad if any of my readers, who find that a forked twig held between their hands automatically moves when they pass over certain spots, would make some, experiments to ascertain if they possess an incipient clairvoyant faculty. Let them, for example, take two packs of cards, spread out one pack (or one suit from the pack), on the table, faces up, draw from the other pack (or corresponding suit) a card, face down, and place it, unseen, say beneath the waistcoat; this humours the idea that the epigastrium is the most sensitive seat of this occult vision. Then walk slowly round the table on which the cards are disposed, note if the twig moves over any particular card, and compare the result with the concealed card. Or they might try the simpler card game which Mr. A. Lang has described in *Longman's Magazine*, Vol. XXXI., p. 279: viz., take up a card from the top of a shuffled pack and, without looking at it, try if some vision of a card floats into the mind; then compare the result with the actual card held. Mr. Lang finds he is generally successful in this game on the first two or three trials, but afterwards his guess becomes mixed or hopelessly wrong : this I have also noted in thought-transference experiments. I should be grateful for any record that may be sent to me (addressed Kingstown, co. Dublin) of such experiments, or of any similar ones that may suggest themselves to my readers.

## Prof. W. F. Barrett

It is curious that the figure 3 should both times be wrong. Mr. Young also tells me he was successful three times out of four with a similar experiment, only using a rod in his hands and repeating the figures to himself.

Previous to making these experiments, Mr. Young had written to me as follows:—

> In the year 1893 I had a remarkable experience when out water-finding with the rod. (It happened to be very dry weather at the time. Whether this had anything to say to it I don't know, but this peculiar experience ceased when rain set in.) I found that after "setting" myself to use the rod, i.e., getting into an abstracted mental condition, lost to all around, when, or just before, the rod turned, I could,—as it were clairvoyantly,—see the underground springs and actually appeared able to trace them out as I walked along. My friend Mr. Robertson, who, as you are aware, also uses the rod with success as an amateur water-finder, tells me he also had a similar experience,[1] and we have since read that a "diviner" named Adams, a Somerset man, frequently asserted the same thing.

All this may, of course, be a mere illusion, but that it is occasionally a veridical illusion seems to be indicated not only from the subsequent test experiments which I have narrated, but also from the fact that in the case of others who have had a similar experience, water has been found beneath the spot, though previously searched for in vain in the immediate neighbourhood.

Here, for example, is such a case. In the English edition of Reichenbach's researches on his so-called Od force, Dr. Ashburner devotes a lengthy note on pp. 90-106 to the divining rod, and gives a remarkable instance of a girl who when mesmerised appeared to be an excellent dowser; when entranced, if the hazel twig moved in her hands, she exclaimed she saw the water a few feet beneath the surface, and gave a vivid description of it. Dr. Ashburner quotes in full the letter he had received from a lady, a friend of his, giving a minute account of this experiment, which was made in a field adjoining the lady's house in Hertfordshire. At the spot where the rod turned and the girl declared she saw the water, a well was dug, and an abundant supply of good water was found a few feet below the surface, though previously the lady states that they had "very bad water and had long been unable to find a good spring."[2]

I hope that some tests may be made in England or in the Continental schools of hypnotism on the possible dowsing faculty of patients under hypnosis. Of the occasional "lucidity" or "clairvoyance" of subjects in the deeper hypnotic trance I have received some striking evidence, and have personally verified the fact in one very sensitive subject whom I had hypnotised.[3]

---

[1] Mr. Robertson is joint author with Mr. Young of a little book on the divining rod, in which they narrate their experience and give a good deal of miscellaneous information.—W. F. B,

[2] This took place more than 50 years ago, and it seemed hopeless to obtain any confirmation of this case, as no names were given by Dr. Ashburner; but, curiously enough, a letter was sent me from a lady living at Waterford, who, writing to a friend a propos of my previous Report, gave an account of a visit she paid in 1847 to her aunt in Hertfordshire, Miss B., and narrates the very circumstance described by Dr. Ashburner as happening in her aunt's field before her visit. The writer confirms several of Dr. Ashburner's statements, that the girl dowser was Miss B.'s lady's maid, and also that Miss B. (who narrated the facts to Dr. Ashburner) was an exceptionally clever and intelligent lady, not likely to be mistaken, and that there had previously been great difficulty in getting good drinking water, but the spring found by the blindfolded [this is probably a slip of memory] girl was still used in the house. Reference is made to Miss B.'s deep interest in mesmerism, but not to any mesmerising or clairvoyance of the girl. Miss B. probably would not speak of this to her young niece. My correspondent was unaware that Dr. Ashburner had written anything on the subject.

[3] On a future occasion I propose to publish the details of a remarkable case of this kind sent to me some years ago by a competent observer, the rector of a large parish in Cumberland, who was also Chairman of the local Bench of Magistrates. The subject in this case was a lady, a sufferer from chronic illness, who had greatly benefited by hypnotic treatment carried out by my informant under the direction of her medical attendant. In the course of time she developed what appeared to be a clairvoyant faculty, and the particular test experiment to which she was submitted,—and which I carefully investigated and verified (so far as it was possible) at the time,—convinced me, as it had already convinced my informant and others, that sooner or later science will have to admit the existence, in certain cases, of a supersensory perceptive power. In this instance any explanation based on fraud, or hyperaesthesia of vision, or chance coincidence, or thought-transference was more inconceivable than the admission of some faculty new to science.

# The Credibility Of Dowsing

Though of very slight evidential value, it may be worth referring to the curious old case of Parangue, narrated by Figuier in Chapter VIII. of his excellent treatise on the *Baguette Divinatoire*. Parangue was born near Marseilles in 1760, and when quite a child appeared able to discern clairvoyantly the presence of underground water, and was successfully employed at several places for this purpose. Figuier is naturally somewhat sceptical about this case, for the particulars of which he quotes the Abbé Sauri, who firmly believed in Parangue, and who states that the child was thrown into a paroxysm whenever it was brought over a hidden underground spring.[1]

Whatever value is to be attached to such narratives as the foregoing, there undoubtedly exists a body of testimony from many able and distinguished men, in different countries and in different professions, who have become convinced by personal investigation that certain persons can detect the presence of hidden objects in some transcendental manner. I have already referred on p. 325 to the opinion expressed by Zschokke. He was a man of great erudition and versatility, possessed of a wide knowledge of men and affairs, holding a high position as member of the Great Council of State, Lieut.-Governor of Basle, and historian of Switzerland. He is therefore an excellent witness. In his Autobiography, first published in 1842, he states :—.

> In almost every canton of Switzerland are found persons endowed with the mysterious natural gift of discovering, by a peculiar sensation, the existence of subterranean waters, metals, or fossils. I have known many of them, and often put their marvellous talent to the proof. One of them was the Abbot of the Convent of St. Urban, in the canton of Lucerne, a man of learning and science; and another a young woman, who excelled all I have ever known. I carried her and her companion with me through several districts entirely unknown to her, but with the geological formation of which and with the position of its salt and sweet waters I was quite familiar, and I never found her deceived. To detail circumstantially every experiment I made to satisfy myself on this point would take up too much space at present, but the results of the most careful observation have compelled me at length to renounce the obstinate suspicion and incredulity I at first felt on this subject, and have presented me with a new phase of nature, although one still involved in enigmatical obscurity.

The evidence on behalf of clairvoyance is really more extensive and of greater weight than is commonly known, and those who contest this evidence will find themselves impaled on the horns of a dilemma; they must either admit thought-transference and stretch that explanation to an absurd length, or they must admit the fact of clairvoyance, —meaning by this latter the transcendental perception by certain individuals of an object or writing which cannot be seen by, and is unknown to, those present. It is to be noted that cases of clairvoyance with persons not in the mesmeric sleep usually occur with sufferers from catalepsy or some allied disorder. The sense of vision in these cases (and also in some hypnotised subjects) appears to be transferred to the epigastrium; the subject pressing the card or writing to the pit of the stomach in order "to see it," as if the viscera were the seat of vision. Now it is worthy of note that this inquiry has led us to the conclusion that some dowsers also possess, in greater or less degree, a subconscious clairvoyant faculty, and that such persons exhibit symptoms of induced catalepsy and experience singular sensations in the epigastrium when the object sought for is transcendentally "perceived" by them. I have already pointed out in Part XII. that the visceral sensations of the dowser are probably emotional disturbances, arising from a psychical state, and it is likely enough that a similar explanation accounts for the cataleptic subject believing he sees with his stomach, the sensation being there. But this explanation merely accounts for the secondary effects observed; the induction of the psychical state still remains a mystery. And here it seems to me that a wholly independent and different investigation should ultimately lead to conclusions so similar to those arrived at by other investigators nearly a century ago can hardly be a mere accident. A cause common to both, to be found in some perceptive power new to science, appears *prima facie* to be indicated.

---

[1] In an article on *Modern Magic* by M. Shele de Vere, published in 1873, it is stated that "Catherine Beutler, of Thurgovia, Switzerland, and also Anna Maria Briegger, of the same place, were both so seriously affected by the presence of water that they fell into violent nervous excitement when they happened to cross places beneath which large quantities of water were concealed, and became perfectly exhausted." Long ago, a Portuguese lady, one Pedegacha, is also stated to have been similarly affected by underground springs.

# APPENDIX F

## *The Zahoris*

In a footnote on p. 5 of my previous paper on the Divining Rod (*Proceedings* S.P.R., Part XXXII.), I quoted a writer in the Quarterly Review for 1822, p. 373, who states that "the faculty of using the divining rod is evidently the same as that possessed by the Spanish Zahoris, though the latter do not employ a hazel twig." The *Spectator*, in an article on the Divining Rod on October 14th, 1882, also refers to the Zahoris in the same casual way, as if every one knew all about them. On inquiry I could find no one who could give me any information beyond a reference to the meaning of the word as given in Spanish dictionaries. Thus, in *Lopes' Spanish Dictionary* the word "Zahori" is explained as follows :— "A vulgar impostor pretending to see things, although hidden in the bowels of the earth, if not covered with blue cloth." Again, "Zahoria" is said to be "The art of seeing as above. The performer must be born on Good Friday." *Neuman and Barretti*, in their Spanish dictionary, use identically the same words, and the *Dictionary of the Royal Spanish Academy* has a similar description, ending, "Lynceus homo subterranea videns." [Lynceus was one of the Argonauts in Greek myth who was credited with being able to see through walls and underground. – Ed.]

The word "Zahori" is really from the Arabic, meaning "clear," "enlightened" ; it was, in fact, equivalent to the term a "clairvoyant," as that word is now used. The same root occurs in Hebrew, and is the origin of the title "Zohar," the famous bible of the Kabbalists.[1]

It seemed, therefore, to be a matter of historical interest to ascertain what was known concerning these Zahoris. The earliest account I have been able to find of the Zahoris comes to us from Mexico in the year 1557. It is contained in a folio volume in the British Museum, entitled *Phisica Speculatio, etc., Mexici*, 1557[2] written by one *Alphonsus (Gutierrez) a Vera Cruce*. This work was reprinted in Salamanca in 1559. In his discourse on the Soul,— *De Anima, lib. ii., speculatio ii.*, pp. 300-301 (or pp. 376-377 of the Salamanca edition), Alphonsus writes as follows :—

### *Speculation II. of Enchanters, Salutaturs,[3] and of the People vulgarly called Zahoris.*

> There is no one who denies that there may be such an arrangement in a man's eyes, that he may be enabled to see at a great distance to which another man's eyes cannot reach. In the same way there may be such an arrangement as to enable a man to see an object through some diaphanous medium, whilst other eyes are incapable of discerning the shape of the object through the same medium. But I cannot conceive that any one's sight can be so constructed that he can see an object behind a wall or any opaque substance; for sight is the effect either of outward transmission, [i.e. from the eyes] as some maintain, or of inward reception, as the majority declare. It is not clear how the shape of anything can reach the eye, when it is hidden in the earth, and behind something opaque and not diaphanous; for how would it pierce through the earth or penetrate the stone? For such shape would necessarily be absorbed on coming in contact with an opaque body, and could not find transit, because it is not a diaphanous body. Wherefore such shape could not reach the eye, neither could the object itself be seen. And I do not see how they [the Zahoris] can perceive (as they say) abscesses or humours in the internal organs of a man, (their sight not being impeded by the body or clothes); nevertheless they themselves assert that they can, and in the same way, on entering a temple where dead bodies lie, that they can clearly perceive the internal organs of the corpses, if they cast their eyes

---

[1] The Zohar is a mystical commentary on the Pentateuch, the title being suggested by the command in Gen. i , 4, "Let there be light," with the exposition of which the work begins; it was compiled between the 3rd and 13th centuries. The "Zoharites" were an ephemeral Jewish sect of theosophists, swearing by the Zohar; founded about 1750 they had, of course, nothing to do with the Zahoris of two centuries before.

[2] I have to thank Mr. E. Westlake, —who has devoted unwearied patience to the compilation of a complete bibliography of the divining rod,—for the discovery of this rare volume in the British Museum. It must have been one of the earliest books ever printed in Mexico. To Miss E. Stokes my best thanks are also due for the excellent translation of this and other passages in the British Museum.

[3] The word salutator means in low Latin a "pointer out." The index finger was called *digitus salutatorius*, not only from its being used for familiar salutation, but also for pointing out.—W. F. B.

## The Credibility Of Dowsing

down. Nevertheless I do not give full credence to their assertions. For these things may be illusions wrought of the devil. Nevertheless I do not condemn them; for I have known men otherwise upright, who have declared they see these things. I confess I do not know what cause can produce such natural power; for it is not the same as that alleged by enchanters and salutators; but is quite different, for the Zahoris say the object is made visible by natural means, by radiating its shape to the eye; if so, it is necessary that the medium through which it passes should be diaphanous; otherwise the shape does not become visible. All philosophers say that air and water are diaphanous mediums, and all things that partake of their nature; but the earth and opaque bodies are not of that kind.

A few years later a famous Jesuit of Louvain, Martin Delrio, published his great work *Disquisitionum Magicarum* in three folio volumes. I came across a copy of this work, published in 1599, in the famous library founded by Archbishop Marsh in Dublin.[1] In the first volume, ch. iii., pp. 11 and 12, of this work, Delrio refers to the Zahoris (he calls them *Zahuris*), and the following translation gives the principal statements he makes :—

A race of men in Spain are known who are called *Zahuris*; we may name them Lynxes; when I was staying at Madrid in the year 1575, such a boy was to be seen there. They relate that these people see things that are hidden in the inward bowels of the earth, veins of water and treasures of metals, and corpses placed within sarcophagi. This thing is most fully received and well known. Not only Pindar, Tzetzes, and other poets have thought this possible, but philosophers also (e.g., Coel. Rhodig., lib. 16), some of whom ascribe this power to a melancholy humour.[2] ... I think they know veins of water by the vapours exhaled from those places morning and evening. They know veins of metal from the grass, of whatever kind, that usually grows there. Treasures and corpses I would consider to be indicated by demons. ... They are accustomed to restrict this faculty of seeing to certain days, the third and sixth day of the week, which is a token of a secret pact. Besides, the redness of the eyes, which is particularly to be observed in Zahuris, would rather injure than assist clearness of sight.

It is interesting to note the prevalent idea of that period, and long afterwards, that demons have the principal hand in the discovery of hidden treasure, otherwise Delrio's conjectures indicate shrewd observation on his part. The "redness of the eyes" is a curious trait.

Another reference to the Zahoris is to be found in a work published in 1643 by Juan Eusebio Nieremberg, entitled *Curiosa y Oculta Filosophia*, 3rd edition; Madrid, 1643. (Reprinted in Barcelona, 1645, see pp. 81-82.) Chapter LXXVI. of this work is devoted to the power of the Zahoris, and the following is a translation of the chief portion (pp. 284-285) :—

Less is heard of the sight of the modern Zahoris, though it cannot be taken as certain. Celio Rodiginio favours their cause, judging that there may be a natural means of seeing through large, opaque bodies. Another attributes what they say they see to the effect of a melancholy humour. This would be a good explanation if facts did not follow their imagination or sight; but springs are found where they point them out, metal where they say they see it, and the dead with all their marks which they perceive, so that it must be attributed to some other cause than melancholy.

But knowledge of where water is to be found underground may be acquired without much difficulty, without its being necessary for the sight to pierce the earth. It was the ancient office of the Aquilegos,[3] whose art was the knowledge of where water was to be found, at what depth, and of

---

[1] Mr. Elworthy, in his treatise on "The Evil Eye," refers to Delrio's work as published in 1603. This must be a later edition. My own slight literary researches in connection with the history of the *Virgula Divina* have impressed me with the enormous labour and erudition displayed in Mr. Elworthy's classical work.

[2] Melancholy here means madness; as Milton says, "Moonstruck melancholy, moping madness."—W.F.B.

[3] *Aquilegus* (in Latin) was one skilled in seeking out water; see Facciolati's Latin Dictionary.—W. F. B.

what quality it was. Marcellus wrote of these things among the Romans, and is quoted by Cassiodorus. In the time of the king Theodoric a very celebrated Aquilegus came from Africa, whom Theodoric affectionately recommended to Apronianus that he might give him a suitable salary. The mode of discovering the water was by the presence of certain herbs, briars, reeds, and other green trees, by certain species of mosquitoes, and light vapours which arose from the spot, and by other means which they took, such as placing dry wool in certain parts at night, well covered, to see if it would be found damp. Sweet and salutary waters are qualified by the south and east wind, and the heavy and less salutary fall with the north and west wind. The same thing may be urged concerning the knowledge of mines of metal, for there may be in the same way natural signs of them, and certain herbs which signify their presence.

As to the assertion that the Zahoris can see the buried dead and certain particular marks upon them, Alphonso de Vera-cruz, in the second book of his *Anima*, and Father Delrio, on the *Medea of Seneca* and in the first book of his *Magia*, attribute this to evil arts; and I can see no grounds for opposing them, the more so that the power of the Zahoris is limited to certain days, such as Tuesdays and Fridays, which to me is a suspicious circumstance; also the redness and inflammation of the eyes usually found among these people seems to prove that they rather blind their sight than sharpen it.

The most interesting part in this quotation is Nieremberg's reference to an ancient cult of water-finders, or "aquilegos", as he calls them. In the State papers and letters of Cassiodorus, which form our chief knowledge of Theodoric, king of the Ostrogoths (circa A.D. 454-526), whose chief minister Cassiodorus was, the reference to the *aquilegus* will be found in Epist. LIII., lib. 3, p. 58. The famous Jesuit, Father Kircher, in his *Mund. Sub.* lib. 5, p. 266, also refers to the method employed by the *aquilex* (as he terms it) in waterfinding.

Another Spanish writer, Feyjoo, in his *Theatro Critico Universal*, Madrid, .1732, tome III., pp. 101-118, published a paper entitled *Vara Divinatoria, y Zahories*.[1] This paper is principally concerned with the discussion of the well known case of Jacques Aymar, whose story was then attracting universal attention. In section VII. the Zahories are referred to, and the author treats them with scepticism, remarking that the multitude is generally credulous, and among all people men of critical faculty and sound judgment are few. He continues:—

The name Zahoris is applied to a class of men of whom it is said that their vision penetrates opaque bodies, thus causing to appear whatsoever may be hidden away fathoms deep below the surface of the earth. Perhaps we have inherited them from the Moors, since the word Zahori seems Arabic.[2]

It cannot be advanced that this virtue is either natural or supernatural; consequently it must be condemned as either feigned or as superstitious. It is not natural, since light does not penetrate into the depth of opaque bodies. In consideration of this we have declared (in the 2nd Vol., Second Discourse) as fabulous what is pretended of the penetrating vision of the lynx, and at present we will include under the same rule that son of Aphareus, King of the Messenians, to whom many ancient

---

[1] My friend and colleague. Professor J. P. O'Reilly, Foreign Secretary to the Royal Irish Academy, most kindly translated the whole of this lengthy Spanish paper for me, and I wish here to express my great indebtedness to my learned friend for this and other laborious translations he has cheerfully made for the purpose of my inquiry.

[2] In the past century (says the Marquis de St. Aubin, tome 3. lib. 4, cap. 2) it was declared that there were in Spain certain men who saw what was under ground to a depth of 20 pike handles (picas). Many philosophers failed not to discover (as they thought) reasons for persuading people that this might happen quite naturally. He then states that the *Mercure français* of the year 1728, published an account of a Portuguese lady (named Pedegascha). She declared she saw what was in the earth to a depth of thirty to forty fathoms, but as regards the human body, she could not see into it if clothed, the clothing preventing her vision. But the body being uncovered, she was able to observe all the interior parts, even the abscesses or any other defect there might be, as well in the humours or soft parts as in the solid. It may be that this fable had its origin not in Portugal, but in France. But this author does not give credence to the existence of the Zahoris, justifying himself mainly for his refusal of assent to my testimony, since having cited my work, he terminates thus: "The testimony of this Benedictine, being that of a Spaniard, is of great weight to give assurance of the falsity of this opinion." [Feyjoo was a Spanish Benedictine.]

## The Credibility Of Dowsing

authors attribute the same excellence of sight as that ascribed to the lynx, giving him in consequence the title of "Lynx-eyed " (Linceo), because, said they, he could see through the trunks of trees and rocks, a falsehood which Apollonius, in his poem of the Argonauts, immensely exaggerates, pretending that he fathomed with his vision the depths of the earth, even to being able to see what was taking place in Hell. Nor do I think that more credit should be accorded to what Varro, Valerius Maximus, and other writers tell of that man called Strabo, who in the first Punic war saw from the promontory of Lilyboeum, in Sicily, and counted the vessels which were leaving the port of Carthage, the distance being 130 miles. Even were the atmosphere perfectly diaphanous, which it is not, there would still be the difficulty that the vessels situated at a distance of 130 miles would form in the centre of the retina an angle so extremely acute that the image would be insensible, as those know who are versed in optics.

As little can it be alleged that the talent or power of the Zahoris is supernatural. In the first place, it is not credible that it has God as its special author, since it is a virtue whose only use is to serve greed. It is not announced that the Zahoris disinter treasures to furnish assistance to the poor, or to make war on infidels. In the second place, because, neither in the sacred writings nor in ecclesiastical history do we read that God has granted this virtue as a permanent habit to any of His many illustrious servants. How then can it be believed that, while refusing it to all these His most intimate friends, He has reserved it for men in no way remarkable by their merits? In the third place, supernatural graces are not limited to any particular nation, and of Zahoris, they are said to exist only in Spain.

Among the vulgar there is the belief that God dispenses this grace only to those who are born on a Good Friday, without considering that there should be an infinity of Zahoris, since many there are who are born on that day. Others limit the power to the circumstance of being born at the particular moment at which the Passion is being chanted. Even with this restriction it would follow that there should be in the whole extent of Spain from 700 to 800 Zahoris, since this total, more or less, results from the supposition that about the same number of men are born every day and hour of the year, and that Spain (including Majorca and excluding Portugal) possesses seven and a-half millions of persons, which is the population determined by Señor Don Geronymo de Urtariz in his excellent work, *Theory and Practice of Commerce and of Sailing*. Consequently, on this computation there would not be a province of Spain which had not four or five dozens of Zahoris. Where are they, that we may see them? Nor can it be said that those who pretend to this grace hide it, since God does not concede virtues that they may be of no use.

There remains then but to say that this virtue is superstitious, and that those who exercise it have a compact, either expressed or implied, with the devil. In truth, the work of extracting gold from the depths of the earth is more of a nature to be attributed to diabolical influence than to the Divine assistance, since an abundance of that precious metal rather promotes vice than favours virtue. Such, indeed, appears to have been the thought of the ancients when they pretended that Pluto, the infernal divinity, was the first discoverer of mines of gold and silver.

The author then goes on to say that if the Zahoris really do exist, they are either wizards or rogues, and he prefers to think the latter, as the former would involve a diabolical compact, a far greater crime than being a mere rogue.

I have quoted this extract at some length, as it gives an interesting picture of the habits of thought of a learned Spaniard 120 years ago. It is evident the writer had no personal knowledge of the Zahoris, his information about them appears only to be derived from traditional stories coming from a preceding century. During the present century I have only come across casual references to the Zahoris, and this race of pretended seers, some of whom possibly may have had supernormal vision, has long died out, even the very meaning of the word being known to comparatively few.

## *Prof. W. F. Barrett*

In concluding this note I wish specially to acknowledge my indebtedness to the wide learning and scholarship of my friend the Rev. Maxwell Close M.A., for much kind assistance both here and elsewhere in this research.

# APPENDIX G

## Scientific And Literary Opinion

Before closing the present Report it may be instructive to refer to some of the scientific and literary reviews of the *previous* Report. Before doing so I will quote, by permission, the following interesting letters sent to me by two distinguished men of science.

I will first quote a letter from one of the highest authorities on geology, Sir Archibald Geikie, D.C.L., F.R.S., etc., to whom my hearty thanks are due for writing at such length :—

28, Jermyn Street, London, S.W., *November 8th*, 1897.

> On my return last week from a prolonged tour in Eastern Europe I found among the papers and books awaiting me your Monograph on the Divining Rod, and I spent most of yesterday in reading it. First let me thank you for sending me a copy and next congratulate you on the publication of so fair, temperate and interesting a statement of the whole case.
>
> As you may believe, my experience has chiefly been among the failures of the dowsers, and I have necessarily been led to form a rather low estimate of these men and their pretensions. But your narrative leads me to recognise that I have never seen the other side, and that I may have done them injustice. It seems to me that a large proportion of their successes are such as any intelligent man, giving himself up to the observation of water supply, might easily accomplish without anything more than mother wit to guide him. It is most difficult to get accurate information regarding their failures, and the true proportion these bear to their successes. The evidence of the men themselves in this matter is not wholly satisfactory, nor is that of their employers who have found water.
>
> In all such matters I try to keep my mind open. There are so many mysteries in nature that one learns every day how foolish is the attitude of those men of science who dogmatically assert that such and such phenomena are "bosh," "rot," "deception," "fraud," and all the other choice terms they have so freely at command. I have been accustomed to look at the dowsers as either self-deceived or consciously deceiving others. And even after perusing your most interesting volume I am not prepared at once to abandon this attitude. But you have brought forward such a body of evidence that I must hold my judgment in suspense for a time. If I can be satisfied that there is any instinct, faculty, or whatever you choose to call it, whereby a man can detect the presence of underground running water, I shall never say another word against dowsing, though I shall still think some of the dowsers little better than rogues.
>
> If there is such an instinct, why should it not show itself as unfailingly in a young and inexperienced hand as in an old and hardened sinner? You attribute some of the failures to the inexperience of the performers. But if the effects are due to some direct reaction of the water below upon the operator above, and not to any observation or reasoning on his part, it may be open to question whether the faculty or instinct requires experience for its development.
>
> Arch. Geikie.

Two criticisms are contained in the foregoing interesting letter: (1) Sir Archibald Geikie suggests that a large proportion of the successes of the dowser are such as mother wit would account for. The evidence adduced in the present Report enables us to judge whether this is so, and the question has been fully discussed. (2) The other criticism is that contained in the last paragraph of the letter. I do not for one moment believe there is any "direct reaction of the water below upon the operator above"; neither a direct nor an indirect action of a physical nature is at all probable. If, however, the dowser is able to detect the presence of underground water by any subconscious process, or even supernormal instinct, it is conceivable that experience and practice may consciously or subconsciously be of some assistance, and I am disposed to think they are. Sir Archibald Geikie refers to his experience of the failures of dowsers. I wish particulars of these had been sent to me, as sometimes they rest on hearsay. A great failure of Mullins was reported at Carlow and referred to by my geological friends. Here is the result of an investigation of it on the spot which I asked an able geologist to make:—

Geological Survey of Ireland, Dublin, *July 16th*, 1900.

I have made inquiries about Mullins at Clonmel, as promised, and found, to my disgust, that the people there made the poor man drunk and turned his performances into a laugh!

J. R. Kilroe.

I will here add the letter of another distinguished naturalist, Mr. A. R. Wallace, LL.D., F.R.S., who writes as follows :—

Parkstone, Dorset, *September 12th*, 1897.

I read your excellent and very thorough paper with the *greatest pleasure*, and noted a few points of slight disagreement on which I determined to write to you.

I have long been convinced of the reality of the power of the "dowsers." Your resume shows how impossible it is to convince men by any amount of evidence till the time is ripe for them to receive it. The large amount of the evidence is even a disadvantage. Few will read and weigh the mass of evidence you have collected, and I have no doubt many of the sceptics will accuse you of believing anything you are told.

Now for my criticism. At p. 239 you say there are two points adverse to the dowser—one being their "absurd" idea of the general distribution of underground water—either as springs on definite spots or as narrow underground rivers. But if they really and as a rule believed the former—of which I can find no evidence in your Report—it would, as it seems to me, not be adverse to their possession of some exceptional faculty, but in their favour.[1] For if they are totally ignorant of the real laws of water-distribution, the chief objection, that they work by acute observation and knowledge, falls to the ground. And as to the second "absurd" supposition—of water being often in narrow underground streams or veins—if your evidence proves anything, it proves that it is often a fact, and how can believing in a fact of nature be "absurd"? Again, the whole of the dowsers' business would be gone if the geologists' theory of saturated strata or surfaces was always or generally true. For then, as is the case over considerable areas, any one could get water by sinking to the necessary depths to reach the water-bearing stratum. Consequently, in such districts dowsers are never required. But where the reverse is the case—and your neighbour may have a good well at 30 ft. while you sink 60 ft. in vain—in such districts alone the dowser is employed; hence, to him, all the available evidence shows underground water to be strictly limited. If he professes to know that this is the universal mode of distribution, of course he would be "absurdly" ignorant, but I am not aware that he ever says so; whereas the geologists do say, or imply, that the reverse is so generally the case that the dowser can do nothing except by guess, etc., etc.! If either of the two is "absurd," it is not the dowser.

---

[1] I stated on the page referred to by Mr. Wallace that according to geological opinion "underground water usually exists in wide saturated areas" and this opinion was discussed more fully in Appendix B to the previous Report. At the same time I ventured to say that the evidence cited in that Report pointed to the frequent occurrence, underground, of permeable channels as well as permeable areas, and hence that geologists had not sufficiently recognised the truth of the dowser's point of view. As a matter of fact, the dowser's most successful achievements are just in those districts where geologists most often fail, viz., in regions where underground water *does exist* in narrow fissures or channels. This is shown in Mr. Westlake's useful Appendix B.—W.F. B.

# The Credibility Of Dowsing

> Some geologists are sublime in their inconsistency. One geologic critic says "any cottager could have given the same advice" as the dowser, —as if in a district where "every cottager" knew where to obtain water, any man would be fool enough to get either a dowser or a geologist to find it!

Mr. Wallace then discusses the question of unconscious muscular action as the cause of the motion of the rod, but this part of his letter I have quoted in Part XI. when dealing with that subject. As before remarked, whatever Mr. Wallace writes is worthy of most careful consideration, for his opinions generally prove to be right in the long run, his observation being keener, and his range of knowledge wider, than most of his critics.

In connection with the question of the influence of evidence on belief referred to in the second sentence of Dr. A. R. Wallace's letter, it may not be out of place to quote here the opinion of one of the earliest and best friends of the S.P.R., Mr. C. C. Massey, who writes to me as follows :—

> I am more than ever convinced that it is not so much *evidence* as a *disposition to credit* it that is wanted. Is there such a thing as a purely objective standpoint towards evidence? I doubt it, as also I doubt that any evidence whatever can avail to overcome an adverse subjective standpoint. I think the true function of evidence is quite misconceived when evidence is supposed to be that which *generates* belief.
>
> C. C. Massey

There is much truth in what Mr. Massey says; whether it be due to the inertia of our mental processes, which tends to preserve habits of thought in the straight line along which they have been started, or whatever be the cause, there is a real difficulty in believing in anything unfamiliar to us, and it requires a genuine, and often painful mental effort to overcome our tendency to keep on the old lines of thought. Hence it is that the flimsiest evidence, if it appeals to our preconceived ideas, is usually accepted without question; whilst, by the majority of people, the weightiest evidence is rejected, if it requires a dislocation of our familiar ideas. This is amusingly illustrated by a story recently told me of an old countrywoman, who firmly believed her sailor son, when he mentioned Pharaoh's chariot-wheels as lying on the shores of the Red Sea, but was insulted by his silly stories when he told her that he had seen *flying* fish!

On page 221 of my previous paper [p. 183 this volume - Ed] I refer to the then President of the Geologists' Association of London, Mr. T. V. Holmes, F.G.S., as having recently read a paper on the divining rod before the Anthropological Institute. That paper has since been published in the Journal of the Institute, and I have to thank Mr. Holmes not only for the kind reference to my work in his paper, but also for much valuable help which he has from time to time freely given to me, and for his suggestive criticisms from the point of view of a field geologist. And here let me say that in the practical examination of this question the co-operation of a geologist is necessary. With the exception of Mr. Westlake, F.G.S., whose valuable aid I have already acknowledged, the difficulty has been, just as in other departments of the work of this Society, to induce those to give us their help whose scientific training in a particular direction renders them specially qualified to conduct an investigation such as the present. If, however, I may judge from the letters that have reached me from some eminent geologists, the evidence given in my previous paper renders such co-operation less improbable in the future.

Turning now to the scientific Press, the leading organ of British science, *Nature*, had a lengthy review of the Report, a review which could hardly be described as written in a judicial spirit.[1] Nevertheless I am grateful to the reviewer for his kindly personal references, and for drawing my attention to a weak piece of evidence that was inserted in the Report, which I will deal with first.

On p. 130 of the Report {p. 105 this volume Ed] particulars are given of what appears to be a good case on behalf of the dowser at Wootton, in the Isle of Wight. The report in the Morning Post was confirmed by the dowser, and also by the owner of the estate, a clergyman, who, in reply to my inquiries, stated that "it is quite true that he

---

[1] *Nature*, October 14th, 1897.

[the dowser] discovered an abundant supply of water where efforts had previously been made in vain." The *Nature* reviewer, speaking from personal knowledge of the place, challenges this, and says that three useless wells were sunk by the dowser's advice, and that it did not need a diviner to discover water where it was eventually found. I asked Mr. Westlake, F.G.S., who has made a special study of hydro-geology, to visit the place and report to me: he kindly did so, and from his report, contained in Appendix A, there seems little doubt that this case affords no evidence for or against the dowser. It appears, however, that the Nature reviewer is inaccurate in one respect. After visiting the spot in November, 1897, and making careful inquiries from residents in the neighbourhood, Mr. Westlake writes to me as follows:—

> I found that local opinion did not coincide with that of the reviewer in *Nature*. My informants, Messrs. Cole, Turner, Newbury and Barton, said, after reading the review, they knew nothing about the three useless wells which, according to the reviewer, had been sunk at the diviner's instance in the waterless Oligocene clays. It was true that wells had been sunk in these clays near the railway station, and one at Woodside, without success, but they had not been located by diviners. It was the local people without the rod who made these mistakes, and as they were jealous of the diviner, a stranger "from the mainland," I think I should have heard of any mistake he made. What the diviner did was to find water where everybody—after the event—knew it was. The reviewer says it "did not need a diviner to discover" it—meaning, *should* not have needed—with which last I quite agree, and regard the Wootton experiments as no evidence one way or the other.

Curiously enough, not far from the place singled out by the geological reviewer in Nature is a case where the geologist failed to find water and the dowser succeeded. This has been given in detail in Part III.

To return, the "principal criticism," remarks the Nature reviewer, "we have to make on Professor Barrett's collection of facts is, that he does not give enough weight to the natural tendency of mankind to conceal their failures." I was well aware of the difficulty of arriving at a just estimate of the number of failures on the part of the dowser, but every effort was made to ascertain them, and this point is specially referred to at the outset of the previous Report. As I wish to emphasise this aspect, I will repeat what was then said:—

> It must be borne in mind that (especially among amateur dowsers) one is more likely to hear of success than failure, and therefore an extensive and searching inquiry is necessary before any safe induction can be drawn ... All that was possible in the present investigation was to make the range of evidence as wide and unbiassed as possible, and not exclude a single case of failure that was substantiated. This has been done.

It must not be forgotten that, even with skilled geologists, failures are by no means unknown in their predictions of water supply, though I am not aware of any treatise on hydro-geology that thinks it essential to arrive at and set forth the percentage of failures which different geologists have had. Because some people have had a costly experience of the vanity of human opinion, even of expert geological opinion, that is no reason for rejecting the indispensable help which expert geologists can give in selecting a suitable site for the boring of an artesian well. It is true they sometimes lead to an outlay of £19,600 to no very obvious purpose, but then what the town loses in water and rates, geology gains in stratigraphical knowledge. To some of these scientific gains, at the cost of the ratepayers, I have referred in the previous Report. In fact, one of the best English hydro-geologists, Mr. De Rance, F.G.S., states in a letter to me that the predictions (as regards water sources) of even leading geologists, who are not specialists, "rest upon chance," and he would not be surprised to hear their failures were as numerous as the dowsers'! If both rest upon chance, that certainly would be the case, but if either the dowsers' or the geologists' failures are notably fewer than chance would suggest, then the predictions of one or the other do not rest upon chance. Obviously, the question of the dowser's *success* is one thing; *how* he arrives at it quite another, and the latter is a matter of insignificance to any one who merely wants to sink a well. A scientific inquiry, such as I have attempted, necessarily embraces *both* these questions.

# The Credibility Of Dowsing

Following upon this review is a letter from Mr. Wadsworth, of the Michigan College of Mines,[1] a letter which was largely quoted by the English press as exploding the whole of the dowser's claims.[2] I have already referred to and quoted from this letter on a preceding page, so that I need only say that Mr. Wadsworth's theory is a little belated, apart from its failing altogether to account for the correspondence of the movement of the rod with the presence of underground water.

I will now briefly refer lo some of the comments on the Report that have appeared in the ordinary newspaper press. A large collection of press notices, reviews and articles based on that report have reached me[3]; but as might be expected, instructive criticism on any of the subjects which occupy the attention of our Society is rarely to be found in the columns of the ordinary daily or weekly newspaper press, with the honourable exception of one or two papers such as the *Spectator*, and from erudite critics such as Mr. A. Lang, to whom I am also indebted for the excellent outline of the Report given in *Longman's Magazine* for December, 1897.

A passing reference must also be made to an able and interesting review of the Report that occupied several columns of that influential French newspaper, the *Journal des Débats*. The review was signed, and was from the pen of a naturalist and critic, M. H. de Varigny, to whom my hearty thanks are due for his careful study and summary of my previous paper, and also for some useful information he has subsequently sent to me.

A well-known Cardiff newspaper devoted a leading article to a concise and fair outline of the Report, which led to a vigorous and protracted correspondence in its columns, between a worthy self-taught local geologist and our friend the Rev. A. T. Fryer, whose kind assistance I have already acknowledged, and to whom my thanks are due for his able and temperate letters in the *Western Mail*. I am also indebted to the editor of the *Richmond Times* for information he has kindly sent me, and for devoting so large a space in his journal to an outline of my Report and its discussion.

Several columns of a weekly journal, the *New Age*, were also devoted to a friendly discussion of the report and on the S.P.R. in general. The article is signed, and the writer, Mr. D. Balsillie, like so many others, assumes that a plausible explanation of any obscure phenomenon is probably the correct one, forgetting that any experimenter worthy of the name is sure to have exhausted all obvious explanations before he ventures upon the publication of any experiments which he believes point to some fresh addition to our knowledge. Mr. Balsillie takes it for granted, from Hansen and Lehmann's experiments, that nasal whispering "explains" thought transference, and says, almost in Dr. Scripture's[4] words:—

> Thus the mystery of thought-transference without contact has been cleared up in a way which any one can verify for himself who has access to a psychological laboratory.

This has been so conclusively answered by Professor Sidgwick and Professor James that I will not dwell upon it; but Mr. Balsillie draws from it the inference that, as the dowser only detects running, and not stagnant, water, he probably derives his information from some sub-conscious perception of sound, and hence he adds:—

> It might be worth Professor Barrett's while to give some heed to what we have said above about the psychological explanation of thought transference.

---

[1] *Nature*, January 6th, 1898.
[2] Mr. Wadsworth's theory was anticipated by his own countryman, Mr. Ralph Emerson, in 1826. As mentioned in my previous paper, this is not Ralph Waldo Emerson, but an able contemporary of his who entered the ministry a little earlier than his famous namesake; it was some time before I discovered there were two contemporary Ralph Emersons, probably fellow-students.
[3] It is only right that I should here acknowledge the care and skill with which Durrant's Press Cutting Agency have supplied me, not only with these press notices, but also with many hundreds of paragraphs and articles on the subject of the divining rod and the search for underground water in general. All of these have been read and a few have led to useful correspondence, but, as a rule, these newspaper extracts are wearisome and worthless.
[4] *The New Psychology*, p. 260.

## Prof. W. F. Barrett

The possible exaltation of sense perception on the part of the dowser has been dealt with in the previous and the present Report.

It only remains for me to thank the Editor of *Light* for the full and excellent summary of the Report that appeared in his journal.

A brief notice of two books on the divining rod, which have been recently published, may here be added. Neither of these books has any scientific or literary value. One is an extraordinary medley, written by an enthusiastic believer in the rod, and the other is simply a trade advertisement of a professional dowser. I should have passed them both over, but they formed the *points d'appui* [fulcrums – Ed.] for two interesting articles in the *Daily News*, and one was the subject of a lengthy review in *Nature*, usually considered a scientific journal.[1] The first-named book is by Mr. Beaven, and is called *Tales of the Divining Rod*. It is quite impossible to notice this book seriously, as it is a rhapsody in turgid English on the glorious "mysteries of rhabdomancy," compiled by a tenant farmer and fruit grower of Hereford, who has found the dowser of considerable use to his fruit farm. Mr. Beaven's experience of the rod I gave in the previous Report, but in his book, fiction is so intermingled with fact that the author tells us, when we come to Chapter XXI :—

> All that I have hitherto written concerning the divining rod has been mixed more or less with the imaginative . . . but now, to the end of the book, the truth, and the truth only, shall be stated. That at least is my intention.

This laudable intention he strives to carry out by transposing to the remaining half of his volume a large part of my previous paper; but, just as in the earlier half he allowed his readers to guess which was fact and which fiction, so in the latter half he leaves them, as a rule, to guess which are his own words and which are mine.

Mr. Beaven tells us on p. 201 his theory is that, owing to the beneficence of the Creator, every

> imprisoned spring sends up an urgent and unmistakeable message to the surface . . . for man's special benefit. . . . Were those electrical influences visible, we should probably see every hill and dale dotted over with electric waving mounds, each uprising coil containing a central column which whirls in an eccentric manner precisely over each fountain head; while connected with most of these magnetic mounds are electrical currents waving on the earth's surface over the exact track of every subterranean watercourse. (!)

These "waving electric currents" are perceived by certain "gifted individuals" who have a "secretive electric power," etc. But I need not proceed further, we shall all agree that somebody's brain certainly "whirls in an eccentric manner," and Mr. Beaven's book will at any rate afford entertainment to any scientific man who happens to read it.

The other book, as I have said, is an advertisement issued by the dowser, Mr. B. Tompkins, who writes after his name "W.F." (meaning water-finder). Mr. Tompkins' *Theory of Water-finding* (as his book is called), is even more amusing than the descriptive letters he has conferred upon himself; his theory is, of course, "Electricity." He and Mr. Beaven resemble the rustic who, describing to me a ghostly light he had seen at a certain spot, said (in answer to my inquiries as to what the light resembled), that "it was just like an electric light." When I asked him where he had seen the electric light, he replied "I never seen it, maister, but it were just like it." So Mr. Tompkins tells us all about electricity, what it really is, how it moves the rod, and how he has thus been able to "unfold the bewildering enigma of the divining rod "... and how he trusts ere long to receive the reward due to his efforts.

Of a very different character is an excellent little manual on the discovery of underground water by E. S. Auscher, entitled *L'Art de découvrir les Sources* (Paris, Balliere, 1899). This book is not meant for hydro-geologists, but to meet the needs of those who require a general knowledge of the method of finding underground water. It also includes a wide range of subject matter subsidiary to its main object, such as the analysis of water, the best methods of boring,

---

[1] *Nature*, November 2nd, 1899.

## The Credibility Of Dowsing

etc. A section is devoted to the *baguette divinatoire* (divining rod), but here the author, like so many other writers on this subject, falls into numerous errors, not only in the history of the *baguette*, but in its mode of use, etc. He states (p. 144) that

> the skill of the operator consists in moving the index fingers (les index) so slightly that the rod appears to turn automatically, as if it obeyed a supernatural impulse.

And yet, a few pages further on, the author states that the distinguished members of the commission appointed by the Paris Academy of Sciences to inquire into the *baguette*,[1] arrived at the conclusion that the motion of the rod was due to unconscious muscular action on the part of the operator. Moreover, M. Auscher appears to be unaware that one of the most eminent anthropologists in France, Professor Gabriel de Mortillet, was once a successful dowser with the *baguette*, and has written a little book on the subject, entitled *Histoire de l'hydroscopie et de la baguette divinatoire*, which was published in 1850. M. Auscher often refers to the work of L'Abbé Paramelle as a water finder, and speaks of him with a certain respect. So little is known of Paramelle in England that I have given an outline of his life-work and book in Appendix D, and have devoted some space to a discussion of his methods, in so far as they relate to the general subject of this paper.

As these sheets are passing through the press a statement has appeared in several English and foreign newspapers that a new French Commission had been appointed to inquire into the evidence on behalf of the *baguette divinatoire* (divining rod), and that a hydraulic engineer was appointed president of the Commission, giving his name and address. After several futile attempts to get further particulars, I received at last two badly printed circulars—one advertising the business of the engineer in question and soliciting the favour of a commission, and the other stating that the *Société Magnétique de France* (whatever that may be) had appointed a committee of five persons, chiefly members of that Society, to report on the "apparatus" employed by *sourciers* to seek for underground water. In answer to inquiries from an English amateur dowser, the business president of this so-called commission states that he is deputed "to make a precise inquiry into the mathematical laws (!) of the *baguette*," and he adds his opinion that money ought to be made out of the *sourciers'* business. From which the scope and scientific value of this commission may be inferred; very different from the 1853 Committee referred to in the foot-note below.

---

[1] Referred to in my previous Report. The facts are briefly these: in 1853 the French Academy nominated a Committee of three eminent men, MM. Chevreul, Boussingault, and Babinet, to report on a paper on the *Baguette Divinatoire* which had been presented by a M. Riondet. Chevreul was requested by his colleagues to draw up the report, which led to the publication of his work on the Divining Rod in 1854.

*Prof. W. F. Barrett*

## The Credibility Of Dowsing

*Prof. W. F. Barrett*

# Index

| | |
|---|---|
| AUTO-SUGGESTION | 356, 373 |
| AUTOSCOPE | 7, 8, 187, 200, 216, 219, 231, 293, 303, 306, 309, 323, 346, 361, 362, 371 |
| BLINDFOLDING | 18, 19, 22, 29, 35, 53, 73-75, 134, 143, 144, 153, 161, 168, 174, 186, 187, 201, 239, 288-297, 305, 312, 328, 338, 341, 350, 364, 371 |
| CLAIRVOYANCE (*inc.* Clairvoyant) | 22, 69, 239, 288, 369-371, 373, 404, 405, 406, 407-408, 409 |
| DIVINING Rod | 6, 9, 10, 208, 234, 308 |

DOWSING

| | |
|---|---|
| Physical effects | 5, 14, 16, 27, 35, 43, 45, 48, 52-53, 69, 71, 73, 100, 132, 134, 135, 138, 141, 145-146, 161, 165, 169, 172, 200, 220-222, 224, 233, 284, 292-294, 303-305, 307, 310, 312, 324, 327, 328, 331, 333, 335, 338, 339, 349-350, 356, 363, 364, 408 |
| Theories | 8-10, 14-15, 21, 31, 35, 44, 63, 75, 122, 153, 165, 174, 177, 182, 186, 198, 201, 205, 216, 222, 238, 288, 293, 301-303, 325, 328, 329, 331, 336, 346, 359, 369, 414, 419 |

DOWSING by Country (excluding the UK)

| | |
|---|---|
| America | 13, 32, 45, 177-181, 327 |
| Australia | 33-35, 330, 331 |
| Brazil | 134 |
| Canada | 18, 292 |
| France | 13, 141, 220, 221, 324, 333, 335-341 |
| Germany | 9, 325, 326 |
| India | 349 |
| Ireland | 58, 83-90, 143, 144, 241, 242, 244-246, 248, 250, 256, 281, 310 |
| Italy | 14, 181, 324 |
| Jamaica | 317, 318 |
| Jutland | 235 |
| Russia | 222 |
| South Africa | 130, 329, 330 |
| Switzerland | 181, 222, 325 |

## *The Credibility Of Dowsing*

DOWSING Faculty, The

    percentage of population with   36, 293, 373

DOWSING Success

    Due to chance     3, 12, 17, 40, 144, 273, 316, 368, 369, 371, 373, 389, 397, 399, 404, 417

DOWSING Tools

    various, *See* Tools used in dowsing

    theories for movement  5, 7, 16, 199, 420

    transfer of movement to non-dowser    25, 60, 61, 67, 80, 152, 165, 199

| | |
|---|---|
| GEOLOGICAL opinion | 51, 61, 74, 86, 90, 92, 93, 103, 182-185, 187-190, 225, 226, 247, 248, 251, 253-255, 258-268, 271, 272, 275, 278, 290, 313, 375-388, 390-392, 396 |
| HYDROSCOPE | 14, 213, 323, 324, 366, 400 |
| HYPERSENSITIVITY 371, | 7, 183, 186, 202, 203, 206, 223, 237, 239, 306, 349, 362, 366, 368, 369, 407, 418 |
| IDEOMOTOR effect | 357, 368, 373 |
|     Definition | 356 |
| INTENTION | 9, 200, 365, 371, 407 |
| INTUITION | 213, 216, 366, 371 |
| MINERALS (dowsing for) | 16, 37, 144, 166, 169, 171, 186, 198, 238, 304, 323, 331, 367, 393, 394, 396-399 |
| MINING | 9, 11, 12, 74, 367, 394 |
| MONEY | |
|     Locating hidden | 12, 20, 21, 35, 48, 60, 64, 65, 73, 121, 215, 304, 404 |
| MUSCLE movement | |
|     Involuntary | 5, 7, 9, 18, 30, 45, 88, 108, 112, 132, 134, 165, 198-199, 202, 205, 223, 238-239, 289, 294, 297, 298, 302, 303, 306, 308, 325, 333, 345-347, 350, 352-354, 356-359, 361-362, 373, 416, 420 |
| PHYSIOLOGICAL considerations | 16, 199, 206, 345-347, 352, 353, 355-357, 363-365 |
| PSYCHOLOGICAL considerations | 200, 201, 205, 216, 288, 302, 304, 343, 347, 351, 356, 358-361, 365, 369, 370, 403, 418 |
| RELIGIOUS attitude | 9, 410, 412 |

## Prof. W. F. Barrett

RHABDOMANCY, *See* Divining Rod

SCEPTICISM                              2, 4, 10, 16, 20, 27, 32, 34, 67, 71, 100, 154, 182, 190, 191, 195, 197, 203, 239, 264, 282, 288, 292, 295-297, 300, 302, 306, 307, 317, 331, 338, 340, 342, 343, 345, 350, 370, 404, 416

    on training dowsers      4, 154, 165, 186

SCIENCE

    scientific attitude       5, 6, 13, 194, 201, 202, 205, 224, 233, 239, 288, 293, 294, 301, 303-305, 323, 336, 337, 341, 351, 353, 355, 369, 371

    unscientific attitude     2, 5, 10-11, 14, 239, 288, 298, 342, 343, 354, 360, 362, 366, 414

SUB-CONSCIOUS                 6, 15, 187, 199-201, 205-206, 216, 239, 321, 330, 345, 352, 354, 358, 361, 366, 404

SUGGESTION                      15, 32, 45, 174, 205, 216, 222, 256, 289, 294, 303, 304, 306, 321, 325, 336, 342, 343, 345, 350, 352, 356-358, 361, 364-366, 368, 371, 373, 389

    Definition                358

TECHNIQUE                        4, 11, 12, 14, 17, 41, 56, 60, 83, 86, 89, 112, 139, 146, 166, 214-219, 233, 236, 277, 292, 306, 307, 323, 333, 339, 354

THOUGHT transference       7, 8, 12, 30, 141, 144, 198-200, 204, 206, 222, 290, 305, 358, 362, 418

TOOLS used in dowsing

| | | |
|---|---|---|
| | Aluminium | 13 |
| | Blackthorn | 17 |
| | Copper wire | 28, 31 |
| | Curved twig | 14 |
| | German sausage | 44 |
| | Hands | 5, 146, 150 |
| | Hawthorn | 138 |
| | Hazel | 17, 21, 24, 28, 30, 31, 36, 43, 44, 47, 50, 52, 65, 69, 77, 83, 87, 105, 112, 116, 124 |
| | Honeysuckle | 43 |
| | Iron | 31 |
| | Peach | 179 |
| | Pendulum | 7, 13 |

## *The Credibility Of Dowsing*

|  |  |  |
|---|---|---|
| | Quills (Goose) | 354 |
| | Snuffers | 44 |
| | Steel | 116 |
| | Steel spring | 55 |
| | Steel wire | 43, 44, 52 |
| | Thorn | 139 |
| | Tongs | 44 |
| | Watch spring | 5, 50, 56 |
| | Whalebone | 44 |
| | White thorn | 4, 122 |
| | Willow | 11, 44, 112 |
| | Wire | 5, 145 |
| | Witch hazel | 361 |
| UNDERGROUND Water | | 183-185, 188, 192, 193, 211, 212, 392 |
| | Theories | 2, 96, 135, 154, 179, 189, 196, 236, 268, 286, 287, 309, 314, 387, 392, 400, 402, 415 |
| | Visual clues | 202, 205, 237, 256, 258, 309, 310, 366, 401, 402, 411 |
| WATER Smeller | | 47 |
| WATER Witching | | 13, 47 |
| ZAHORIS | | 3, 203, 370, 409-412 |

www.ingramcontent.com/pod-product-compliance
Lightning Source LLC
Chambersburg PA
CBHW080418230426

43662CB00015B/2142